D1033946

THE
MARCH
OF
PATRIOTS

The Struggle for Modern Australia

PAUL KELLY

MELBOURNE
UNIVERSITY
PRESS

MELBOURNE UNIVERSITY PRESS
An imprint of Melbourne University Publishing Limited
187 Grattan Street, Carlton, Victoria 3053, Australia
mup-info@unimelb.edu.au
www.mup.com.au

First published 2009
Text © Paul Kelly, 2009
Design and typography © Melbourne University Publishing Limited, 2009

This book is copyright. Apart from any use permitted under the *Copyright Act 1968*
and subsequent amendments, no part may be reproduced, stored in a retrieval system or
transmitted by any means or process whatsoever without the prior written permission of
the publishers.

Every attempt has been made to locate the copyright holders for material quoted in this
book. Any person or organisation that may have been overlooked or misattributed may
contact the publisher.

Text design by Phil Campbell
Cover design by Phil Campbell
Typeset by Megan Ellis
Printed by Griffin Press, South Australia

National Library of Australia Cataloguing-in-Publication entry
Kelly, Paul, 1947–
    The march of patriots: the struggle for modern Australia / Paul Kelly.

9780522856194 (hbk.)

Includes index.
Bibliography.

Keating, Paul, 1944–
Howard, John, 1939–
Australia—Politics and government—1990–2001.
Australia—Politics and government—2001–

320.994

Praise for *The March of Patriots*

This is how political history should be written but seldom is. Paul Kelly's prose has the clarity of cut glass. His battleground is the world of ideas and his gift is for distillation. Few can compress so much into two sentences. Here is the antidote for the dross and alarums of the twenty-four-hour news cycle. Here is the same sure touch, the same sense of historical perspective, that Kelly brought to *The End of Certainty*, his book on the 1980s. Here, alive on the page, are the two dominant figures of the past twenty years: Paul Keating and John Howard, 'deep patriots' both, but men who see lights on different hills.

—Les Carlyon

The March of Patriots is brilliant—ambitious in scope and forensic in detail. In a tale of two governments and two remarkable leaders, Paul Keating and John Howard, Paul Kelly gets the key participants on the record about events that defined our nation. It is a fine work of analysis and storytelling.

—Laurie Oakes

For Joseph Lawrence Andrew Kelly
1907–70

CONTENTS

PREFACE

The March of Patriots is the story of the struggle for modern Australia. It is about two men, Paul Keating and John Howard, as leaders and patriots. It is an interpretation of their efforts to construct a new framework for Australia in economics, foreign policy and social policy. The book seeks to discern the meaning of their prime ministerships and their strategies for the nation.

I would like to thank Paul Keating and John Howard for co-operating over a long period and for their frankness in the interviews for this book. More than 100 people were interviewed, a number more than once. I am grateful for their assistance and their time. This has been a long project in its evolution and delivery.

I owe a special thanks to Chris Mitchell who, as Editor-in-Chief of the *Australian*, has supported this endeavour and tolerated my periods of leave to work on the book. I owe a debt to my publisher, Louise Adler, for her belief in this book and her untiring enthusiasm. At Melbourne University Publishing, Foong Ling Kong has been an astute manager of the project. I thank my wife, Margaret, for reading and editing the manuscript before its despatch.

The project deals with the Keating and Howard prime ministerships from 1991 to 2007, a total of sixteen years of Australian history. It is a two-book project. This book covers the 1991–2001 decade and finishes with Howard's third election victory. The next book covers 2001–07 and deals with the Iraq War, the national security agenda, the China boom, the emergence of climate change as a frontline issue, the Howard–Costello leadership struggle and Labor's revival with Kevin Rudd's 2007 victory terminating the Keating–Howard era.

INTRODUCTION
THE MARCH OF PATRIOTS

Paul Keating and John Howard were patriots at a time when patriotism had become unfashionable. The late-twentieth-century assault on national borders by technology and freer markets had bequeathed a strange and contradictory legacy—it made national leadership more important. Beyond their compulsion to win elections, Keating and Howard had a patriotic mission: to reshape Australia's political tradition for the transformed world they confronted.

The nation that Sir Robert Menzies had governed when they were young men was long gone. The task that befell Howard and Keating was to decide what to save from Australia's past and what to sacrifice.

Keating and Howard were old-fashioned brawlers and passionate believers, the last in a dying species defined by their authenticity in a business burdened by spin, manipulation and gesture. They saw public life as an honourable calling and they were political warriors ruthless in pursuit of party interest. They luxuriated in the exercise of power—the power of nation, state and markets.

Forged in the distant 1950s and 1960s they gave their best years to public life—Keating spent 27 years and Howard 33 years in the national parliament. They were pragmatists and believers—pragmatists ready to break rules to win office and believers in their causes. They governed Australia during the modern age of politics that began in 1983 with Bob Hawke's election and the challenge of globalisation. Keating and Howard saw that globalisation was making and breaking nations faster than at any stage in world history. As a stand-alone country of 20-million-plus people occupying a continent and without the option of political or economic union with comparable states, Australia was thrown upon its own resources for survival and success.

This meant that Keating and Howard were patriots in a new Australian project. This was the renovation of Australia for a more exacting chapter of global history beyond the beguiling comfort of the long Age of Empire into which Australia had been born and whose expiration had occurred during their own lifetimes. The Australia they ran had to accept responsibility for its own future—demanding a new economic philosophy, a confident cultural ethos and a national strategy to guide its role in the world.

The modern age of politics has seen three completed prime ministerships—Bob Hawke, Keating and Howard. Its unifying historical theme has been the final dismantling of the old Australian ideas based on Empire, race, protectionism, class warfare and state paternalism and the construction of a replacement model built upon new ideas for a different age.[1] The key to modern politics is to see Hawke, Keating and Howard giving effect to a new Australian project.

Building upon Hawke's foundations, Keating and Howard were pioneers and rivals in devising a model defined by free trade, competitiveness in world markets, a surplus budget, an independent central bank, an enterprise-based industrial culture, an immigrant ethos tied to an inclusive culture, retention of the egalitarian ethic, an Australian-made synthesis of a decent society and a strong economy, the search for reconciliation with the indigenous peoples, and entrenchment of a national interest strategy that reflected Australia's global interests and regional responsibilities.

They refined a new Australian model. It was not American; it was not British; it was not Asian. Under Keating and Howard there was a rise in national confidence along with an awareness of national failures, above all, the demoralisation and deprivation in many Aboriginal communities. While Keating and Howard fought over many issues, the 1991–2007 era saw the growth of a largely bipartisan Australian strategy for success in the globalised age.

The proof was Australia's superior position to the rest of the developed world at the outbreak of the 2008 global financial crisis. It was a stunning validation of the new Australian model. The legacy bequeathed to Kevin Rudd in November 2007 was a Keating–Howard product in its successes, flaws and unresolved conflicts.

The deepest fractures in Australian politics are based on generation not party, a universal truth long denied. The Labor Party has produced two great prime ministers, John Curtin and Bob Hawke, the founders of two historic eras. Curtin was the originator of the great nation-building age running from World War II, flowing into post-war reconstruction, mass immigration, rapid population growth, the 1960s mining boom and protectionism, state intervention and Keynesian economics over three decades that expired, finally, in the early 1980s recession that revealed the exhaustion of the old model.[2]

The continuity within this nation-building era was provided by RG Menzies who retained and enhanced the Curtin legacy. Menzies' genius was to establish the Liberal Party and yet, upon becoming Prime Minister a second time in 1949, perpetuate most of the Labor policy structure that he inherited. Menzies brought to its zenith the Labor goal of civilising capitalism while he became the oracle of Australian Liberalism, a duality that guaranteed him Labor's eternal hostility.

From 1983 Hawke's feat, with the help of Treasurer Keating, was to discern the exhaustion of the old era, redirect Australia towards sweeping new market-based policies and, critically, to win a series of elections that gave legitimacy to this direction.[3] Without Hawke's political gifts, Australia's 1980s transition would have been problematic.

The unique status of the Hawke government flows from its positioning of Australia to succeed in the modern age. This agenda was refined and expanded by Keating and Howard. These leaders were declared rivals yet undeclared collaborators. After Hawke's prior claims, they are co-architects of modern Australia. The fierce refusal of their polemicists to tolerate this idea does not gainsay its validity.

Politics is a story of conflict. In Australia, it is the Labor–Liberal conflict. For the media, conflict is the story that counts. For history, however, national progress is measured by the opposite test—where Labor and Liberal agree. Such agreement, rarely a story, is the foundation of all national progress.

Keating and Howard were divided by party, temperament and many values, yet they were united by events, pragmatism and many policies. They governed as intelligent improvisers often reaching the same conclusion, but also as conviction politicians forever divided by their faiths.

The Keating–Howard era was framed by two forces that marked its 1991 inception—the end of the Cold War and Australia's most severe economic downturn since the 1930s. The death of Communism saw the triumph of capitalism in its century-long contest with socialism. This demoralised the Left worldwide, enshrined the political triumph of economic liberalism, coincided with and encouraged the emergence of capitalist models in China and India, and gave legitimacy to the idea that market forces promoted the public interest. These tides crossed Australia's shores and were surfed by Keating and Howard.

Even more significantly, Australia rose phoenix-like from the ashes of the early 1990s recession to enter a low inflation growth cycle of such robust resilience that it became the longest economic expansion in the nation's history. While this upturn proved of limited political benefit to Keating, it defined Howard's eleven years in office. The expansion transformed Australian society—it more than doubled the size of Australia's GDP, delivering vast increases in household incomes and wealth, jobs, corporate profits and investment returns. In the fifteen years to 2007 real income per head rose more than 40 per cent and real wealth per head more than doubled.[4] This shifted the nation's political culture towards markets, aspiration and enterprise while it generated an anxiety that Australia was losing its egalitarianism and social conscience.

Keating and Howard assumed the wellbeing of people depended on the progress of their country. They knew the nation state was not being dismantled but that it demanded renovation for the globalised age. That meant a society that was balanced and functional. For example, OECD analysis found Australia in the Keating–Howard era had a highly redistributive tax/welfare system, delivering the most progressive redistribution of any developed country.[5] Another example was Australia's strategic decision for population growth, recognising that in the coming age rich nations will divide into two categories—those that renew via immigration and those that stagnate.

Upon Howard's 2007 defeat there were three areas where the new model was defective—Howard had failed to value sufficiently investment in education and in human capital; he had been too slow in responding to global warming and too reluctant to better coordinate infrastructure investment. These became Rudd government priorities because of Howard's failures.

Keating and Howard were party renovators. They came to renovate the crumbling ideologies of Labor and Liberal, plagued by ideological confusion and institutional apathy. That meant investing their parties with new faiths and new governing strategies. The Labor Party had fallen victim to the decline of the union movement, the fading of class as the basis of political loyalty and the rise of self-interested party apparatchiks. The Liberal Party has lost its ideological moorings, its claim on middle-class virtue and its appeal to voters as Australia become a more ethnic, diversified and fragmented society.

After arriving in the Lodge, Keating sought to nourish Labor's heart. The Labor Party needed a new Light on the Hill for a new century. Keating did not invent the 'True Believers' by accident but of necessity. He fashioned a new Labor ideology for the modern age that he called the Big Picture—redefining the market as the friend of the battler, reforming Australia's economic institutions to succeed in an internationalised age, reshaping Australian identity by abandoning the Crown for a republic, reaching reconciliation with indigenous Australians, embracing engagement with Asia as a national aspiration and entrenching the concept of a multicultural yet united nation.

Keating's Big Picture did not deliver success at the ballot box. For Keating, however, these ideas transcended the tyranny of the present. This is what made him such a political freak. He implanted his ideas on Labor's hill as a beacon to inspire future generations and to sustain Labor's soul. It was the ultimate hubris in the name of party. Keating was confident that as the years passed these beliefs, one by one, would become accepted Australian policy. His vision, he would say later, was for the future. Once he was rejected by the people in 1996, this argument became more attractive and most convenient.

Howard's redefinition of Australian Liberalism was the most important since Menzies founded the Liberal Party. Less dramatic than Keating's parallel effort, Howard waited for events with an intuition that leadership was most effective when reacting to opportunity: witness guns laws, the GST, Tampa, the East Timor intervention, the response to the 9/11 attack and *WorkChoices*.

Howard came to power aware that the 1960s social revolution that he opposed and 1980s economic revolution that he supported had detribalised Australian politics. Most forms of authority were under assault. Howard saw that rising libertarianism in personal, social and economic life had generated both opportunity and fear in the community—prosperity was matched by social dislocation as the consensus over values and standards disintegrated. His deepest insight was to discern the paradox of modernity—rapid change was coupled with a nostalgia for the stability once delivered by traditional moral and cultural values.

The new Liberal Party ideology devised by Howard was based in economic liberalism, social conservatism, cultural traditionalism and national security vigilance. No other Liberal would have built this design. It was a unique Howard creation and, for a long time, a success. These four ideas were laced together by a rising nationalism—a step beyond patriotism—that Howard cultivated. It misunderstands Howard to think he arrived with this gameplan, but this is manifestly where he finished.

This constituted the most contentious reinterpretation of Australian Liberalism in the party's history. Howard was a mix of conservative, liberal and populist, a conundrum that drove his critics to frenzy. The governing principle that guided Howard came directly from Menzies—the need to reach out and build a majority position for the Coalition since its loyalists were forever a minority.

While Keating shopped for ideas, Howard was weak at discussing ideas. In truth, Keating was intellectually curious and Howard was intellectually dogmatic. But both were governed by ideas. Keating's infatuation with ideas meant he talked about them too much; Howard's preference for the common man's vernacular meant he failed to discuss his ideas enough. In the end, however, Keating and Howard died at the ballot box for their convictions. They were the last warriors from an age of passionate intensity and their like will not be seen again.

Australian history from 1991 to 2007 is shaped by their absolute dominance of their governments. For better or worse, Labor was Keating and Liberal was Howard. They achieved the total capitulation of party identity to their will-to-power and plans to recraft the ideology of their parties.

In power for sixteen years, Keating and Howard built a new Australian model—a unique model that was a tribute to Australian Exceptionalism. It mirrored their grudging agreements and bitter conflicts. The Keating–Howard edifice was impressive, contradictory and incomplete, a commentary upon the Australia they served.

TWO MEN

They were rivals who came from the same nursery—Sydney's south-west suburbs, raised in homes of bedrock emotional security and instilled with the spirit of Australia's toughest city. Unknown to each other, Paul and John lived just a few kilometres apart, in families that were loving and disciplined. They were children of the 1950s Menzian age and for all their lives they carried the simplicity and optimism of these times within their hearts.

Paul and John were linked by city, generation and class. Each came from a small business family of four children with fathers as a role model and mothers of unbending dedication—the Keatings living at Bankstown and the Howards at Earlwood. Paul was the eldest and John the youngest. Separated only by a twenty-minute bus ride across the city's ugly brick and timber sprawl, they were inducted into Christianity, tribal loyalty and personal honesty. Their ethic was progress by diligence, the natural order of a society living close to the Great Depression and World War II.[1] Neither family belonged to the purple. Both men were self-made and they knew Sydney's rules—make your luck, seize your chance and punish your opponent.

The Keatings and Howards were integrated into the 'Australian way of life' with its parental authority, institutional respect and civic politeness. Religion had a place in the homes of Matt and Min Keating and of Lyall and Mona Howard but it was kept in its place. What mattered was not spiritual life but action in the temporal world. Paul and John prayed to God, obeyed their mothers and dreamt of power.

'My mother had views about how everyone should behave and if you didn't behave that way she'd give you a clip over the ear,' Keating said. 'The place ticked over.'[2] Paul always carried the expectations of his parents, feeling that 'the eldest children have a lot of investment in them from their parents'.[3]

Mona Howard had codes of conduct—'What you should do and what you shouldn't,' Howard's brother, Stan said. His other brother, Bob, said Mona 'provided good wholesome food, two chops and two veg and never experimented.'[4] Howard was sixteen when his father died.

'My mother and I were close,' he said. 'A lot of my personality and characteristics I owe to her. I was given as a child a very deep scorn of pretension and privilege.'[5] Family business was a way of life. Lyall Howard owned a service station at Dulwich Hill and then bought a second garage at Earlwood. As an adolescent John worked the petrol pump. Small business was bred into his bloodline as it was into Margaret Thatcher's. 'I liked serving petrol,' Howard recalled.[6]

Matt Keating graduated from boilermaker to part-owner in successful engineering and concrete enterprises. Paul was more entrepreneurial than John. If he had not entered politics he would probably have gone into the family business. 'I was always a bit of a frustrated entrepreneur,' Keating said.[7] Both fathers sold their businesses to consolidate the family position.

The schools the two boys attended were escalators of Australia's upward mobility—Paul went to De La Salle College, a local Catholic school, and John went to a selective government school, Canterbury Boys High. The Catholic system and New South Wales selective public schools were vehicles to propel children from working-class and middle-class families onto the path of material progress.

Neither excelled at school. Paul left, aged fifteen, after Intermediate level, later earning his Leaving Certificate at night. 'When I was a kid in an area like Bankstown there really was no tradition of going on to higher education,' Keating recalls. 'People today find it hard to believe. But (you) got what they called a secure job.' Paul went to the Sydney County Council as a clerk.[8] Meanwhile John won only a modest pass at the Leaving, which meant his mother had to help finance the initial year of his Sydney University law study. He did a straight law degree, no arts, losing the golden chance to broaden his vision, with the law school in Sydney's city centre isolated from the campus.

Both were raised in the certainty of Full Employment, the assurance of White Australia and the convenience of Male Dominance. They lived through the final gasp of a social order that seemed impregnable until just before its collapse. Neither Paul nor John could conceive of the political hurricane that would transform their city in its economic and social dimensions. Just forty years later the suburbs near their upbringing—Campsie, Belmore and Lakemba—had become the epicentre of the strongest concentration of Muslims in Australia.

Both Paul and John were conspicuous in their conformity. In adolescence they felt no impulse to rebellion; they were largely untouched by the 1960s counterculture. From an early age they joined the adult world and their energies took a serious path. They looked to the big stage.

Not only did they absorb the values of their homes but they lived at home. When in Sydney, Paul lived with his parents until he married at thirty while John, who married at thirty-one, had lived with his mother Mona.[9] 'My mother was a widow from the age of fifty-six,' Howard said. 'It was not uncommon in those days, living at home with widowed mothers.'[10] Paul and John grew to independence unencumbered by the impulse to reject their parents. The souls within such men were unburdened by self-doubt.

Paul and John belonged to Australia as a new world society—where a capable young man could leap from the Sydney suburbs to the prime ministership over twenty-five years. That both men accomplished this feat testified not just to their character but to the authenticity and mobility of Australia's remarkable democracy.

Their rivalry would become a fabulous story that conflated myth and reality. This rivalry, however, was never tectonic because they came from the same production line. Paul and John were more united by shared experience than virtually any other contestants in a Western democracy. This was Australia's social strength.

Paul and John grew into the politicians Keating and Howard. They were interested in ideas and driven by the will to power. The challenge they faced as leaders was to manage the disintegration of the 1950s world that had shaped their childhood and adolescent certainties. In devising their alternative worlds Keating and Howard would take different paths, yet it was a journey that forever bound them together.

The Tribes

Keating and Howard were drawn like magnets to their tribes. It was this lifelong initiation that would convert them into enemies. Sydney in the 1950s and 60s was littered with sacred symbols of tribal differentiation—Catholic versus Protestant, Irish versus English, public versus private school, trade unionism versus free enterprise.

The Keatings and the Howards were political families. While the Keating family ethos was working-class Irish Catholic, the Howard family ethos was free-enterprise middle-class Empire-based Protestantism. These faithful sons became warriors for the tribes they loved. Paul and John were tribalised early, a mark of Australian political civilisation.

Matt Keating had been a unionist, a local ALP official and a Catholic who fought communists in the unions but stayed loyal to Labor in the 1950s Split that saw the creation of the breakaway DLP. Paul's growth within the New South Wales right-wing Labor Party began at home. He joined the Bankstown branch of the ALP at about age fifteen and says that by the time he was in his later teens he 'was well and truly committed to the Labor Party intellectually, committed to it as an institution'. As an adolescent he knew the humdrum of the local branch when in those days business covered anything 'from traffic lights at the railway station to the state of Dr Evatt's mind'.[11]

Keating was tribalised yet distinctive. He was a natural fit in the Catholic-dominated New South Wales Labor Right, contemptuous of its federal leader, Arthur Calwell, hostile to the left-wing dominated Victorian ALP, alarmed that Labor may not recover from the 1960s malaise, sure that Gough Whitlam was the party's only prospect for survival. Unlike his colleagues, he was always well dressed. 'I can't resist a bit of good tweed,' he told former New South Wales Premier Bob Carr.[12] At just twenty Keating began a regular association with 89-year-old former New South Wales premier Jack Lang, who had been dismissed by the state governor during the Depression, a relentless opponent of Curtin and Chifley and detested by the Catholic right. They lunched over sandwiches once or twice a week for years as Keating soaked up anecdotes from Lang's fantastic, destructive and ignoble career. It was a much misunderstood relationship since Keating, in power, became the classic anti-Lang leader with his deregulatory agenda.

It showed that Keating preferred to *live* history, not read it – just as, when he was treasurer, he preferred oral advice to written advice. From Lang, he absorbed the ethos, history and stories of the Labor Party. From Lang, he absorbed the immortal phrases that dotted his speeches for thirty years—'always put your money on self-interest, son, it's the best horse in the race'.[13] From Lang, though a gigantic and expended volcano, he could feel the force of political leadership and its pitiless resolve. It was an omen that Keating would not be categorised.

From age twenty Keating began running for federal pre-selection for Banks and he and his close friend Laurie Brereton launched their campaign to take control of the Labor Youth Council, explaining that the purpose was 'to get skills and to get the feel of the state machine of the party'. Keating says 'from the time I was twenty, I worked flat out on the Labor Party, day and night'. For Brereton, it seemed Paul 'was basically born confident'. The Left hated him; Brereton they could tolerate but not Keating. By this stage he had been a delegate to state conference and 'could organise a speech with a start, middle and finish'. The young Bob Carr found him 'charming and he was a natural leader'. But the singular feature of Keating's activity was its long-range projection—a safe federal seat and the big time. He called it 'building the infrastructure'.[14] The boy was planned his adulthood.

Lyall Howard, a small businessman with a suspicion of trade unions, was a Menzies man. Young John, aged ten, listened with his father to Menzies' 1949 policy speech with the echo of emptying out the Chifley Socialists. 'I remember the 1949 election,' Howard said nearly six decades later. From his first year of high school, Howard confirms, he was thinking about a political career.[15] He joined the Young Liberals when he was nineteen and in 1958, the year Keating joined the ALP, Howard was campaigning for the Liberals at the general election. He was door knocking, involved in political debates and participating in Young Liberal weekend camps, therapy for a young man with a hearing problem and erratic social skills.

For Howard, the law was his path to politics—he had not the slightest desire to become the dreary solicitor depicted in Keating's caricature of him. Howard worked initially at the big end of town at Stephen Jacques and Stephen where brother Stan was a partner and later Clayton Utz before joining a smaller firm where he became a partner. By 1962 Howard was deputy chair of the Young Liberals with a place on the state executive. For Howard, the Liberal tribe was not just a career but a lifelong romance.

'I love the party,' he declared. 'I joined just after I left school. It's constituted a great bulk of my life. I care for it.'[16] His biographers argue convincingly that, more than any other leader, Howard was 'of the Liberal Party'. For fifteen years before entering parliament he was 'what might be described today as a political apparatchik'.[17]

Howard sought out his own mentor, who probably became more important for him than Lang had been for Keating. John Carrick, later Liberal Senate leader, was an indomitable figure, small, intelligent and meticulous, with a bizarre facial similarity to Kirk Douglas. Howard was a product of the New South Wales division and a protégé of Carrick as its general secretary. Taken prisoner of war in Timor, Carrick survived Changi and had worked on the Burma–Thailand railway at Hellfire Pass. He was a living embodiment of the Liberal Party postwar success—its grip on the hard-working ex-service generation. Carrick would return to Hellfire Pass, part of an Australian delegation led by Howard as prime minister.

As general secretary of the New South Wales division from 1948 to 1971, Carrick would escort Menzies about Sydney, collecting him from the Carlton Hotel, offering Menzies advice when asked. 'Menzies was very much my mentor,' he said.[18] Carrick was the political current that connected Howard to Menzies, the living force that united the two most influential Liberal prime ministers.[19]

Howard and Carrick had a shared view of the Liberal Party—it was not for the born–to-rule brigade but for people dedicated to self-improvement and national progress.[20] Howard absorbed from Carrick that the political endeavour, above all, was a contest of values and principles. The most important lesson he took was that the Liberal Party must forever be presented as a party of values, not expediency.[21]

The second lesson he took was how Menzies had won—that Liberal success lay in building a broad-based coalition of support that reflected practical outcomes. The party had to look beyond itself to the Australian community. This was the key to penetration of the Labor base; it became the Howard technique. When Howard lost office his relations with Carrick had spanned fifty years. 'For the first thirty years we spoke nearly daily,' Carrick says, either in the party or parliament.[22] In his May 2008 tribute dinner Howard hailed Carrick as my 'mentor who has taught me so much about politics'.[23] 'Howard was eager, he got actively involved in all aspects of the party,' Carrick says. It is fascinating, however, that not even Carrick saw Howard as a future leader. With his keen eye for talent, he described Howard as an able and valued recruit.[24]

United by the economic and social experiences of Sydney's south-west, Keating and Howard were divided forever along the tribal fault lines of religion, heritage and political culture that criss-crossed 1950s Australia with an invisible lethality that an outsider would hardly identify but a division that was compulsively felt by tribe members in workplaces, schools, clubs and churches. So Keating and Howard were willing conscripts, doomed to become enemies before they met.

Political tribalisation was a process that transcended their life experiences. In politics Keating wore snappy Zegna suits, obsessed about Sydney real estate, loved his clocks and antiques, drove a Mercedes and became the prime minister who owned a piggery. Howard was the dull, bespectacled sport-mad buff, unadventurous with his personal finances who, on becoming prime minister, refused for eleven years to rent his Sydney home and left it empty lest anyone accuse him of being a landlord prime minister. Herein lay the conundrum of their struggle. In their personal lives Keating and Howard reflected the de-tribalisation of Australia—yet their political lives were founded in tribal stereotypes.

Children of Menzies

The political schism between Paul and John originated with the 1950s Menzian age. Anybody who doubts the influence of Australia's longest serving prime minister, Sir Robert Menzies, should examine the story of Keating and Howard. The fracture between them over Menzies became a lifelong passion. Half a century later they were still arguing about Menzies and the 1950s.

As Menzies civilised capitalism and stole Labor's rationale, Australia's political class was divided more bitterly than usual by Liberal hegemony and Labor debacle. For Howard, it was the golden age; for Keating, it was an unrelieved nightmare. They were shaped by their Menzies legacy. Howard said his parents 'identified very strongly with Menzies wartime "forgotten people"—folk who were not wealthy enough for wealth to give them power'.[25] He recalled the 1949 campaign: 'the talk around the house was very anti-Labor, it had a particular bias because of petrol rationing'.

The pivotal election for the Howard family and the greatest for Australian conservatism was 1949. For Howard, it was the ultimate frame of reference. One of the glories of Labor's story is how John Curtin led Australia during World War II. But Labor declines to tell the next step—it lost the politics of the peace to Menzies; it lost the political capital of the war to the new Liberal Party. The scale of loss was stunning—34 out of 48 new Coalition MPs elected in 1949 had war service, as opposed to only one out of 19 new Labor MPs.[26] This is the single most vital statistic to explain the subjugation of Labor for the next generation. Menzies stole the postwar age from under Labor's nose. The vanguard of the World War II 'greatest generation' went Liberal.

Labor leader Ben Chifley was the architect of postwar reconstruction but he fatally misread the nation's mood. Menzies won the coming generation and the failure would debilitate Labor for many years. Menzies had a keen sense of Labor's weakness and Howard inherited that acumen. It was fitting, therefore, that when the ALP returned to power in 1972 it was led by an ex-serviceman, Gough Whitlam.

At the 1949 election Menzies carried the ex-service vote and the small-business vote and framed an ideological contest of private enterprise against socialism. On each measure he won the Howards, a triple loyalty.

Young John accepted his parents' view of the 1950s—a liberation after depression and war. Menzies' commitments to social stability, family life, economic progress and foreign policy vigilance were ingrained in Howard. He was branded for life; he would forever honour such values. As prime minister he would invoke Menzies even when departing from the Menzian way.

Keating, by contrast, loathed Menzies—his sonorous voice, his British honours, his colonial conservatism, his patronising arrogance. He loathed what he saw as Menzies' denial of Australia's full independence and, most of all, he loathed Menzies' command of politics and his effortless humiliation of Labor. The steel passed into Keating's soul—for him Labor's future was to purge the Menzian legacy, to obliterate the cultural shadow cast over Australia by the unconquered father of conservatism.

For Keating it was Labor's craven weakness that made Menzies. He hated Labor for making Menzies so great, so dominant, so defining. Keating loathed Evatt. He scoffed at Evatt's successor, Arthur Calwell—and, after the failure of Calwell's successor, Gough Whitlam, he was contemptuous of Whitlam too.

The instinct was implanted in Keating's brain cells—when the chance came he would dismantle the Menzian legacy, economic, cultural, strategic. He was driven by an intellectual and artistic rejection. It was Menzies who made Keating a radical. As he matured Keating concluded that the 1950s decade was the construct of mediocre old men, a Menzian museum tolerated by bankrupt Labor leaders. And he loathed Labor weakness even more than he loathed Menzies.

So Keating and Howard looked on the same suburbs but saw a different tribal vision. Howard radiated a deep satisfaction with the old Australian order. Virtually from the time he left school he was pledged to a 'Gallipoli, Bradman, Menzies' view of Australia's past.[27] This was the past that Keating disowned—he saw Gallipoli as an Empire-crafted catastrophe, dismissed Bradman as an arcane irrelevance and slated the Menzian edifice for detonation.

Their tribal journeys took Keating and Howard onto divergent paths. With each passing year they became warriors with competing visions of Australia's past and future.

Personality Rivals

Superimposed on the tribal chasm was another difference—Paul and John were temperamental and stylistic opposites. Their minds, emotions and imaginations operated in foreign constellations. This contrast, apparent early, only became more compelling. When magnified by executive power it culminated in an epic clash of personality.

As an adolescent with a quick mind, raw energy and few skills, Keating had ambitions that were almost frightening in intensity. He was a student of people before books. He matured as a born talker, cajoler and charmer, a master of the vernacular with a flair for style. He was also a genius at persuasion across the generations—young men or old women, it made no difference; it just depended on Keating's decision to engage, with his youthful looks, enticing grin and light voice with its distinctively Australian accent, all the while betraying beneath his enthusiasm a single-mindedness with a touch of menace waiting to be unleashed against enemies and, as his career advanced, a menace that was unleashed too often.

From the start there was about Keating an idiosyncratic edge. He would uphold the party's orthodoxies of behaviour and belief until he was ready to slay the orthodoxies and create his own. This is the mindset he carried as treasurer and prime minister, just a touch distant from egomania. Keating was of the New South Wales Right but never slave to it, a perception many of his colleagues were slow in grasping. 'I was never Ducker's candidate' he said of right-wing godfather John Ducker. Keating's cultivation of Lang was the first in the litany of his idiosyncrasies. He saw that politics was about fear and charm, so he mastered both arts. It was a young man's preparation for deposing Bob Hawke, charming Bill Clinton and negotiating with Soeharto. Lang told Keating that in politics he 'didn't have a moment to lose'. And Keating refused to serve his time.

Occasionally his close friends saw into Keating's private world—the restless, impatient spirit fed by a soaring imagination. Keating was a closet romantic who liked to dream and whose imagination led to dazzling horizons—he talked of Paris, played Mahler and trawled the globe for First Empire clocks. This was the antithesis of John Howard. Don Watson recalls how the young Keating returned home with a bust of Beethoven for his mother and told her, 'Here Mum, put some class in your life.' She put Beethoven on the mantelpiece.[28]

Beneath his hardness, there was a soft Keating. He wanted to make people happy and he wanted to be loved. His friends had long seen this warmth, humanity and deep generosity. Beneath the frenzy, he was a charmer. His prime ministership would be blighted by the bizarre combustion of anger and romance.

In 1968 Keating won a heavily disputed pre-selection for Blaxland that provoked a federal executive challenge.[29] 'I pursued it like a hungry dog, I never let it go,' he said.[30] From the moment he hit Canberra after the 1969 election, Keating had a youthful certainty. He deferred to nobody. His skills were persuasion—convincing older men to back him—and marshalling the numbers. Keating had his factional allies and was never afraid to make enemies.

In Canberra he lived with several dozen caucus members at the old Kurrajong, the guest house where Ben Chifley had died less than twenty years earlier, walking to and from Parliament House in those golden sunny mornings and brisk winter evenings, fitting comfortably but not too comfortably into its men's club atmosphere, a young man having tea and biscuits and ruminating on the course of politics with older men, occasionally wondering why he had grown up so fast but never losing sight of the goal and always sharpening his mind, passing judgement on the opinions of his colleagues, assessing them, his opponents and the press. He saw that his ability was as a generalist, 'meaning the structure of society and the economy'. His impatience drove him to find 'what made the place tick and how it could tick better'. Keating knew, like a jungle animal, that he would master the domain of politics.[31]

But too much passion is dangerous. In the early days Keating's passion sat easily with his sense of fun and ambition. He developed a refined sense of aesthetics, a passion for beauty in all the arts. Politics was his consuming business but it never stole his soul—his soul was pursuing perfection, another dangerous pursuit.

His most stunning 'acquisition' was Annita Van Iersal, a Dutch air hostess whom he met on a flight, a charming and cosmopolitan European whom he chased and married. In his most important personal decision, an eclectic Keating broke away. He transcended his past to enlarge his life— yet he stayed within the rigid rules of his upbringing. He expected Annita to live in Bankstown as a wife and mother to his political career—they lived in a house almost next door to Keating's parents. He saw working mothers as a disgrace, and told Parliament that the nation should feel 'ashamed' of the number of women forced to work.[32]

His future rival was a coat-and-tie Young Liberal, earnest, with a prematurely receding hairline, handicapped by a hearing defect that produced a dull monotone, methodical and emotionally steady to the point of humdrum. Equipped with a law degree and a natural flair in debate, Howard had an ambition that seemed beyond his ability. John presented as a solid man for the second eleven.

People usually formed an instant opinion of Howard and they were usually wrong. His best man, Alan Plumb, said of the young Howard that he was 'the sort of person everyone used to overlook or push around until he opened his mouth'.[33] The recurring pattern in Howard's life was proving that people had underestimated him. Over time his qualities emerged because over time his qualities grew—conviction, tenacity, judgement and a skill for sound advocacy.

No Australian leader was as firmly rooted as Howard. Where Keating had passion Howard had pride—pride in family, Liberal Party and nation. Howard's pride was reinforced at the foundations. He saw his family story as a template for the nation's story. Howard's certainty about Australia came from his certainty about his family.

The Depression and two world wars had branded the Howard family. He was named 'John Winston' after Churchill yet he was born two months before the war when Churchill's anti-appeasement stance was still unpopular and a full ten months before Churchill entered Downing Street. His parents had prescience. His father, Lyall, served on the Western front in World War I where, before the battle at Mont St Quentin, he met his own father, John's grandfather, who had backdated his age in order to serve. It was a story cherished by John and it ignited a burning pride in Australian achievement originating within his own family, a pride that would never be extinguished. More than eighty years later Howard as prime minister visited the former battlefield to locate the site of this meeting between his father and his grandfather.

In 1965 Howard spent a year in Britain and on 30 January he stood on Ludgate Hill watching the funeral procession of Winston Churchill. 'I was just one of the faces in the crowd,' Howard said. He was with his English girlfriend.[34] There was no jingoism at the death march; old and young, working class and middle class, enlisted in homage to a mystical figure, an age lost in time but an age that Howard loved and honoured forever.

With the 1960s cultural transformation underway in Britain, historian John Lukacs noted in the turnout the large numbers of 'long-haired, sad-faced young barbarians in search for something with their strange watery eyes'.[35] Churchill had saved them from Hitlerism but it was no longer known what he had saved them for.

But Howard knew. He was never a lost 1960s youth confused about values. His reaction was that of the common man, an omen of his success. Howard stood proud of Churchill, his father, his grandfather, his family, his British heritage, his nation; and proud of his leader, Menzies, whose famous words on that day were emblazoned on Howard's memory—'left the others for dead' he would say decades later. In his BBC peroration Menzies said:

> Some day, some year, there will be old men and women whose pride it will be to say—'I lived in Churchill's time.' Some will be able to say—'I saw him and I heard him—the unforgettable voice and the immortal words.' And some will be able to say—I knew him, and talked with him, and was his friend.' This I can, with a mixture of pride and humility, say for myself.[36]

And Howard knew he was right to be proud. He was steeped in the British cultural experience, not the American. In the 1960s his conservatism was orthodox without trace of the radical remaking of Australian conservatism that he would attempt as prime minister. His social values were entrenched, the product of family more than church, contrary to the claims of the critics who elevated Howard's Methodism as a weapon to beat him. 'I inherited Mum's values,' Howard said. 'The Protestant work ethic—that if you work hard and if you're honest in your dealings with people, you will get rewards.' This is how Howard lived his life in politics and these are the values he sought to implant in his social policy.[37]

He believed in civic politeness. This idea was enshrined in the boy Howard when his mother censured him for failing to show respect to a cleaning lady at the pictures and was told to apologise to her. It was an egalitarianism based on courtesy not social reform.

Howard's political strength was his mastery of convention. He did the basics well and as young activist he backed all the causes—Vietnam, the US alliance, the ALP 'soft on communism' credo. At each decisive moment of his life Howard has looked inwards to the tribal heartland.

It served him on St Valentine's Day 1970 when he found his wife from within the Young Liberals at a Liberal scrutineers' wake at Randwick. Perhaps it is more accurate to say that Janette Parker found him. Janette, wearing a short, white dress, had heard of John before, wanted to meet him, and said 'we picked each other out straight away'. Her account of their meeting reeks of happy calculation on her part. Howard's initial biographer, David Barnett, says 'he thought she was lovely and was instantly smitten'.[38]

Janette recollects Howard criticising Prime Minister John Gorton because 'he didn't understand the Liberal Party', a highly credible report.[39] Their partnership was dedicated to love and politics. 'For me it's just been a matter of time,' she said in 1987. 'I think it is our destiny. He told me he'd be prime minister the first time we met. He will be, wait and see.'[40] They were married in April 1971 at St Peters Church of England at Watson's Bay and honeymooned on the gold coast. For Howard, it was the perfect match—Janette became wife, mother and career partner. She knew the life John wanted and she signed up, reinforcing Howard's self-belief and making him a vastly more acceptable political commodity.

Within three years Howard was elected to Federal Parliament, but the trip was far from smooth. In 1968 he had won Liberal pre-selection for the state seat of Drummoyne but lost the election despite he and his mother shifting house to live in the electorate. He found defeat 'terrible at the time' and for nearly forty years had an indelible memory of every aspect of defeat. When asked, Howard shot back: 'I was beaten by Reginald Francis Xavier Cody who lived in Elswick Street, Leichhardt, a bachelor who lived with his widowed mother, he'd been stricken with polio when he was young and he was straight out of the casting set of the New South Wales Catholic Right.'[41] It was a character test—Howard learnt how to lose. In retrospect he found defeat to be a blessing: it taught him how to recover.

After marriage John and Janette relocated to the North Shore, chasing a federal seat. There was almost no limit to Howard's tribal dedication—during the 1972 campaign he took unpaid leave to assist the doomed Billy McMahon, one of Howard's tasks being to work McMahon's autocue. In December 1973 he won Bennelong pre-selection on the ninth ballot and his election campaign was launched at Hunter's Hill the following year by Andrew Peacock, a sublime irony.[42]

Howard's life, devoid of metaphysical crisis, is a study in balance. His physical stamina, emotional stability and personal tenacity grew over time. Unlike Keating, he was neither a hot nor a passionate politician. Howard rarely carried his emotion on his sleeve, almost never swore, was restrained in his political rhetoric and was a model of steadiness. His feet were planted firmly on the ground and he distrusted talk of dazzling horizons, beguiled neither by the grand designs nor sweeping ideas that eventually became the quest of Keating's life.

Howard was comfortable with the great Australian ordinariness and had no time for writers, intellectuals and artists who bemoaned its mediocrity. Howard knew in his bones that Australia was not mediocre—he loved its values, its mateship, its sporting successes and its down-to-earth equality. He forgave its past mistakes and predicted its future successes. His emotional world was closed by politics and family. He was satisfied with tribal life. While Keating loved to play with the idea of a life beyond the tribe—witness his so-called 'Paris option'—Howard never dreamt of Paris, let alone living in Paris, let alone re-designing Berlin, another of Keating's passing passions. Howard spent Sundays watching cricket or football while Keating nursed his soul with a collection of CDs.

The Politicians

Their maiden speeches were a contrast—the young Keating was searching for ideas while Howard was a model of Liberal Party stability. Keating's confusion was disguised by false certitude. He was, literally, all over the place—demanding that the Commonwealth 'fix prices for all goods and services used by the Australian people', that Parliament legislate for a strong minimum wage, that steps be taken 'to put the working wife back in her home' and that Australia look to Swedish defence planning. The education of Paul Keating would be a steep uphill run.

Howard had an easier target. He saw the Whitlam government's weakness and he nailed it. Menzies would have given him full marks. The Liberal Party, he said, believed in the dignity of the individual—the right to succeed, to accept responsibility, to work harder and be rewarded. Yet Whitlam was involved in a relentless transfer of resources to the public sector in violation of these principles. Howard attacked Whitlam within a Liberal philosophy. He was tracking Menzies and Carrick.

Keating was focussed on Commonwealth powers over taxation, prices and seabed boundaries. He was fascinated by the big men with grand ideas: Whitlam, Rex Connor and John McEwen. He was a power junkie—smashing his way into Whitlam's ministry on its death-knell, setting Bill Hayden against Whitlam in 1977 to become Labor's next leader and forming an alliance with Hawke, concluding that a fourteen-year age difference would allow him a run at the top job after Hawke's departure. His caucus colleagues were gobsmacked by his unfailing audacity.

Howard found his path early and he would be diverted neither by the media nor by intellectual fashion. It was the path of convention, family and individualism. On his feet in the chamber, Howard looked a natural. That astute judge of political horseflesh Malcolm Fraser picked him out early. Just three and a bit years after entering parliament, Howard was Fraser's treasurer—a meteoric rise. The man who lifted Howard from the ruck and backed him as a future star was Fraser.

Keating and Howard collectively laid claim to a generation since their prime ministerships ran from 1991 to 2007. This was the Keating–Howard era in its unity and divisions. Though they faced each other as leaders only once—at the 1996 election when the Coalition defeated Labor— this single contest misleads as a measure of their influence.

Before arriving at the Lodge, Howard and Keating had occupied the treasury portfolio for fourteen successive years from 1977 to 1991, Howard for the first five years and Keating for the next nine. It was their economic experience that provided the platform for their leaderships. Yet this mere listing of executive office fails to capture their impact.

Howard was the dominant political and intellectual force in the Liberal Party for most of the twenty-four years, from the time of Malcolm Fraser's 1983 defeat to his own 2007 election loss to Kevin Rudd. During this period Howard was, in turn, deputy to Andrew Peacock (1983–85), Liberal leader (1985–89), a backbencher briefly, senior shadow minister (1989–95) and Liberal leader (1995–2007), including eleven and a half years as Australia's second-longest serving prime minister.

During the first Peacock leadership Howard's intellectual drive as deputy was decisive. The only time his influence was in eclipse was the transition phase from May 1989 till January 1995 when Peacock, John Hewson and Alexander Downer became a trio of failed leaders eventually allowing for Howard's recall.

Throughout this period Howard's leadership hopes were enduring. They seemed dissipated, finally, after the Coalition's 1993 defeat when Howard challenged Hewson only to be rejected by the party. Yet within two years he was unanimously returned as leader. Despite his electoral failures and party rejection in the 1980s, Howard always aspired to guide the Liberal Party's outlook. The results were often mixed because of his own limitations and frequent lack of a systematic and articulated agenda. After his wilderness experience, post-1995 Howard became a more successful leader. His record stands as the most important Liberal leader since World War II after Menzies.

After 1983 Keating joined with Bob Hawke to create the longest period of Labor rule since Federation and the most successful ALP phase of government since the 1940s era of John Curtin and Ben Chifley. As treasurer Keating worked mostly with Hawke, though sometimes in competition with him. As early as 1985 Keating was consumed by the conviction that he was the government's primary source of ideas.

He laid claim to the prime ministership in 1988 and, when rebuffed, negotiated a deal with a reluctant Hawke in November that year at Kirribilli for Hawke to surrender the leadership after the next election. When Hawke reneged, Keating retired to the backbench, launched an open assault and, in a close-run event, deposed Labor's most successful prime minister six months later, in December 1991. Keating boasted there was an authenticity to his resort to political violence, a moment when he gambled his career for the ultimate prize.

While Keating's treasurership was far superior to Howard's and fundamental to Hawke's election wins, it was Howard who negotiated a more successful prime ministership, winning four elections to Keating's sole election success in 1993. The cycle of their careers was different. Howard served as treasurer during the Fraser era under the old regulated economy and then experienced a gap of thirteen years before becoming prime minister while Keating's treasurership and prime ministership ran virtually back-to-back over a thirteen-year period.

The tribes turned to Keating and Howard because they were the natural leaders—seasoned, dominant and ambitious.

The Economic Reformers

The unifying experience for Howard and Keating was the Treasury; here they took advice from the same Treasury officers, pondered the same mysteries within the national accounts, struggled to master the same policy connections that would make or break their careers, dined and dealt with the same journalists and businessmen—and became refugees from their families. They became recession treasurers and mocked each other for their recessionary failures.

At the Treasury Howard and Keating absorbed one great message: that a vulnerable Australia must improve its economic performance by deep structural changes. This idea framed their political brains. It invested them with conviction and a resolve to change the nation. It is the point when they became serious political figures.

For Howard, it was a difficult transition. He discovered that the Menzies–McEwen–Fraser–Carrick economic model, the only model known to the Liberal Party since its inception, was now broken. For Keating, it was easier, since his mind was geared to change and the early 1980s recession was the death-knell for the old system.

Under Treasury tuition Howard and Keating converted to market economics. As they pondered how to generate more growth, jobs and income, they saw that internal discipline was not enough and that Australia had to lock itself into global markets to succeed. Howard and Keating fought endlessly over the economy. They fought about the design of tax packages, the size of deficits and surpluses, the growth and employment forecasts—but the truth is they agreed on the fundamental direction of change.

Howard was a raw treasurer, working with cabinet's inner group, the battle-hardened veterans Fraser, Doug Anthony, Ian Sinclair and Peter Nixon, advancing slowly on a steep learning curve. He confronted the stagflation of the 1970s, the second oil price shock, the wages break-out of 1981 and the 1980s recession. He had no power base, no experience, no cabinet majority and few allies for a young man many felt had progressed too fast. Howard relied on Treasury yet looked with suspicion on its rigid advice and the intellectual dominance of John Stone whom he backed as Treasury Secretary in 1979. Howard always consulted his office where Dr John Hewson was senior adviser, with tension between his office and department mounting irresistibly.

The politics were hard but these were happy days. Howard was an improvement on his predecessor, Philip Lynch, and the entire party conceded this. His office worked long hours but had a reputation for good parties. Howard enjoyed late nights, the chat, the company, the journalists and lots of drinking in moderation. His home number was in the phone book and no treasurer took so many home calls from journalists. He was always ready with a quote and he was accessible—too accessible since it bred familiarity.

Under pressure Howard hardened on the great issues of the day. Treasury converted him on the need for a broad-based indirect tax. He took a submission to cabinet in early 1981 proposing such a tax reform, only to be humiliated by Fraser and the Country Party. In the party room he saw the rise of the Liberal Party free-market Drys in the early 1980s and followed them into the anti-tariff camp; it was part belief, part self-interest as they became as his power base.

His hostility towards the trade unions was firmed by intellectual conviction as Howard found, on issue after issue, that the unions played a spoiling role against him. As Business and Consumer Affairs minister he made the unions subject to the secondary boycott provisions of the *Trade Practices Act*. As treasurer he became a critic of the Arbitration Commission and centralised wages fixation and his belief in labour market deregulation sprang from the 1981 wages break-out that humiliated him and provoked the recession.

He became a champion of privatisation, an admirer of Margaret Thatcher and a believer in budget restraint. Howard had a showdown with Fraser over the 1982 Budget and the size of the fiscal stimulus when he pushed for a smaller deficit, another battle he lost. But Howard's most memorable failure came on financial deregulation when, after the report of the Campbell Committee, the Fraser government faltered in 1982 before the deregulatory sunlit uplands. It was paralysed by a prime minister who still believed in regulation and a treasurer unable to carry the cabinet.

Financial deregulation and the float became Howard's gift to Keating. This doomed the Fraser government before history and it made the Hawke government's reputation. It gave Hawke and Keating an early momentum that made them unstoppable.

Keating had picked in early 1983 the perfect time to become Treasurer. He rode the long economic upturn and mobilised the political capital of financial deregulation to batter Howard and the Liberal Party for years. Hawke and Keating had a brilliant model—they won union support through the ALP–ACTU Accord and they won business by financial deregulation. This policy announced in late 1983 was tantamount to four revolutions—the market would set domestic interest rates; the market would set the exchange rate; foreign bank entry was permitted; and exchange controls on capital flows that prevented Australian acquisition of foreign assets were lifted.

These decisions—the most important economic decisions since the war—transformed Keating's confidence and authority. From this moment he never looked back. Where Howard had faltered, Keating had delivered, a telling contrast.

As treasurer, Keating had little interest in the grimy task of cutting spending and he left that to John Dawkins and Peter Walsh. He became obsessed about reform and economic structure, soaking up ideas from Treasury, indulging the intellectual challenges and turning the job into a political powerhouse. He grasped how the pieces fitted together; he saw the link between his family's business and the nation's future.

The engineering company of which his father became a part owner, Marlak Engineering, won a contract in the early 1970s to supply dredges to the Malaysian Government. 'To cut a long story short,' Keating said. 'We needed capital to build the things banked against the contract from Malaysia.'

> We banked with the old ES&A bank. Well, they wouldn't give you any money. They would only give you 60 per cent of the land and buildings. That was it. There was virtually no way my father and partner could do it. And the bank didn't care. They just didn't care. The more I watched these banks, the more hopeless I realised

was Australia's plight. They were smug. They banked people whose creditworthiness minimised risk to them, people who had the wealth already.[43]

The more Keating analysed the Australian system, the more he disliked it. 'I saw it was a conspiracy against the common man,' he said. Keating is more radical than usually assumed. The reason lies in his grasp of how the old Australia worked. This made him an anti-establishment figure, not any underprivileged background.

During a 2008 interview he said:

You called the old model the Australian Settlement. I called it the Australian defence model. We had all the barriers up against the world but inside the system it was very structured, very privileged. You had to be part of the big companies, or in the directorship networks or in the banks and if you weren't then you were on the outside. And you were locked out. Menzies, you know, made the running of this economic system an art form. He looked after the banks. He put the tariff in the hands of McEwen and high terms of trade afforded a high tariff and that allowed high wages set by Arbitration. The merry-go-round lasted one hundred years. Many of the unions and their mates became de facto organisers for Menzies becoming commissioners and presidents within the wage system.[44]

This passage reveals the multiple forces driving Keating as reformer—the frustrated entrepreneur, the opponent of privilege, the disgust with Labor compliance. Above all, it reveals how Keating's mind worked—he began to realise his historic task as treasurer was not just to embark on a series of reforms but to change the economic system.

To a considerable extent this was his achievement. He operated with a popular and supporting prime minister, a strong Treasury and a weak Opposition. His drive and flair dazzled many of his colleagues and he established a political ascendancy over Howard. He moved the Budget back to surplus, eliminated the double tax on dividends, cut the top marginal rates and broadened the base with a capital gains tax, though he lost a bitter fight for a new indirect tax, sponsored industry-based superannuation, began a huge privatisation program and, with Hawke, began to dismantle the tariff wall.

For a short time in the early 1980s Keating and Howard were allies of convenience. The idea of their permanent hostility is false. In the early years of the Hawke government they had occasional joint Keating–Howard late-night parties, symbolic of their shared status as the main economic reformers within their tribes. They were the focus of media attention. In his first phase as treasurer, Keating looked for Howard's bipartisan support as shadow treasurer and won it on financial deregulation, the float and his thwarted 1985 indirect tax reform. In this period Keating and Howard were seen as fellow travellers fighting off internal attack from within their own tribes. It was inevitable that their mutual tolerance would fade.

In 1986 Keating, convinced that Howard had authorised a personal attack on him in relation to a breach-of-promise action before he married Annita, issued a melodramatic declaration that Howard would wear his leadership like a 'crown of thorns' and that Keating henceforth would do 'everything I can to crucify him'.[45] Howard shrugged his shoulders; the freeze never ended.

Infatuated by his success, Keating would discuss the economy like an artist chasing perfection, drawing the curves on his office whiteboard or with a marvellous pen on a fresh white pad at his desk. At first he delighted in excelling Howard's record as treasurer but that stage passed—it became, as Keating would say, a comparison not worth noting. But Keating, like Howard, discovered that the economy would humble its manager. In the early 1990s he succumbed to a recession that threatened his career, just as Howard had succumbed a decade earlier.

The framework they learned as treasurers they took to the Lodge. As the world became more globalised Keating and Howard became agents of change. The idea of Keating as economic reformer and Howard as economic conservative is not sustained by history. They were reformers, though with different priorities, aware that their parties had to adapt. They shared many solutions and they engaged in some epic disputes. Keating wanted a new and better capitalism in defiance of both Labor and Liberal traditions; Howard wanted to modernise the economy with least disruption to the community while forever reducing trade union power.

The Models

Keating became the architect of Labor modernism and Howard became a renovator of Liberal belief—this is the best way to discern their political models. Their contest was over which party, Labor or Liberal, offered the people the more convincing explanation about their future. Keating and Howard fought to shape the nation's mood and its intellectual direction.

For Keating, Australia's first century had been a disappointment: too derivative, too apprehensive and too insular. He felt that the meaning of the Hawke government (1983–91) had been to modernise Australia but that job was incomplete; he would finish it. His contempt for the past was visceral—he believed Australian racism had almost consigned the nation to a South African fate. He loathed the regulated economy, the ugly suburbs, the national neurosis of fear, the doctrine of assimilation, the business rent seekers, the cultural wasteland, fighting Britain's wars and bowing to a distant queen.

Keating became the advocate of a new Australian Settlement. He celebrated the demise of the Old Settlement ideas of white Australia, industry protection, wage arbitration, state paternalism and imperial benevolence. Keating and Howard were the first to govern in the generation after the collapse of the Australian Settlement ideas that had guided Australia in its first century.[46] Their response was to offer a new credo for their parties and the nation. The sheer power of the dying ideas left a mighty chasm in Australia's political psychology. Keating loved this chasm because he intended to fill it.

Keating championed new icons—the open, competitive economy that meant a better democracy, new instruments to maintain egalitarianism after the demise of protection and arbitration, reconciliation with the indigenous peoples and a repudiation of a racist past by seeking deeper engagement with Asia, termination of the last remnant of Empire by becoming a republic, the construction of a diverse society replenished by immigration and a foreign policy that saw Australia influence the shape of the regional and global order. He sought a resolution of all the forces Labor had embraced since the Whitlam era. This was the great Labor project. Keating wanted Australia's spirit and structure at its second century to be determined by the Labor Party in a new Settlement for the nation.

Keating did not pretend it was an ordered program. 'I don't think a political philosophy comes to anyone in an instant,' he said. 'Anyone who says that is either a fool or a liar. What you do is try and learn, you pick things up, you learn on the job, you carry certain ideas, some of them are good and some are not so good. But the ideas, in the end, mark you out. This is how you are judged.'[47]

He started to call it 'the enlargement business', saying 'you are either psychologically in the enlargement business or you are not. I am psychologically in the enlargement business.' It was a boast, made more urgent after the public rejected him in 1996.[48] In retirement he found

Howard's conservatism almost incomprehensible. 'One of the things I could never know is what it's like to be a conservative,' he said. 'I mean, the world's moving on, we've got challenges, things are changing, you can't be a conservative.'[49] For Labor, the Keating agenda was tantamount to a new Light on the Hill. Ben Chifley, the originator of the phrase, would not have recognised the new vision. Keating's reinterpretation of Labor belief stands for future Labor governments to borrow, embrace, reject or adapt. It cannot be ignored.

Howard saw the Liberal Party as custodian of the conservative and liberal traditions in Australia—he wanted to re-energise both arms. Howard was the first exponent of economic liberalism and its pro-market outlook to become Liberal prime minister. In keeping with Menzies' view that pragmatism triumphed over philosophy, Howard rarely invoked Adam Smith or Friedrich Hayek as his models. Howard was obsessed with the question 'What works?'

He felt economic liberalism would deliver greater Liberal Party gains. For him, a more flexible and competitive Australia liberated individual initiative and entrepreneurship and meant a less class-based society. After Hawke won in 1983, a total of 47 per cent of Australian workers were union members but when Howard left office it was only 19 per cent. There were more self-employed workers, more part-time non-unionised low-income earners, more people moving into the professions, knowledge-based industries and small or medium-sized business or acquiring income via shares and property. Howard's economic legacy would be his main achievement.

But Howard's equally abiding belief was in social and cultural conservatism. These ideas were given their earliest expression in his 1988 *Future Directions* document that became a landmark. With the sub-title 'It's time for plain thinking' and images of lifesavers, Menzies, sheep and diggers, it cast Howard as a leader for traditional Australians. The media rubbishing of Howard's manifesto as a museum piece launched the enduring schism of the Howard era—the rift between so-called elite and mainstream opinion. The truth is that *Future Directions* was well researched; it mirrored a deep strand of Australian opinion. The message was pivotal—Howard knew that successful economic management was not enough.

As a consequence in the 1990s Howard recruited to his cause the ideas of nationalism, family, social stability, individual responsibility and national security vigilance. This became a milestone in conservative politics and philosophy. Howard turned the Liberal Party into the party of ideological attack across a range of social and cultural issues, an event that left Labor in semi-permanent shock. As usual with Howard, the object was electoral gain. His technique as prime minister was to take established ideas and invest them with a populist, nationalist or radical twist.

His belief in social stability saw a firearm ban; his kindling of patriotic fervour saw a revival of the Anzac ethos; his re-definition of the relationship between individual and state produced the doctrine of 'mutual obligation', with emphasis on personal responsibility; his support for family values was verified by vast household payments; his belief in state power and national sovereignty won expression in denying the *Tampa* and protecting the borders from asylum seekers; his concern for moral values in an age of secularism was reflected in policy initiatives from drugs to school curriculum; his intersecting support for national security and Australia's military tradition saw the most wide-ranging overseas deployments since World War II; and his passion for 'One Australia' saw a campaign against ethnic tribalism in the cause of a united culture. In Howard's hands conservatism and traditionalism became potent weapons.

Far from being trapped in a Menzian mould, Howard recruited traditional ideas to combat contemporary challenges. The process was ad hoc, highly political and conceived in conviction. But it had a pervasive intellectual consistency—the idea that progressive social policies had failed. This gained its most dramatic manifestation with the 2007 Northern Territory intervention to address the crisis in Aboriginal communities. The overall success of Howard's social policies was mixed and the balance sheet will take time.

But there is no gainsaying Howard's mission—he offered an assertive reinterpretation of the Liberal Party credo in both its conservative and liberal traditions. The party will wrestle with his legacy for decades.

The prime ministerships of Paul Keating and John Howard had a unifying narrative: they knew the old methods of the Labor and Liberal tribes were finished. In the Lodge and reacting to pressure, they devised new governing strategies and positions for their parties. Keating was a Labor modernist who loved his Big Picture; Howard was a change agent who aspired to refashion Liberalism for a more turbulent age. Their efforts were filled with the imperfections of politics and men. This is the story of those efforts.

PART I

THE KEATING MIRACLE: BACK FROM THE DEAD

A NEW LEADERSHIP

There are two things in leadership: imagination and courage.
—Paul Keating, May 2008

It was the Lodge that disappointed him. Devoid of classical design, it was a comfortable provincial barn made for the bush capital. Hawke had wanted to remain in the Lodge until the New Year and he had agreed. But the house smelt of Hawke, his cigars and his complacency, the carpets stained from the Bob-and-Hazel television dinners. Paul Keating felt it belonged to a nation that had failed to unpack its past.

For his twenty-two years in parliament Keating had longed for the Lodge, yet his arrival came as a surprise. As late as November 1991, four weeks before he rolled Hawke, Keating was resigned to defeat. 'I felt we were unlikely to get the numbers and I was thinking about my life beyond politics.'[1] His numbers man, Graham Richardson, said it was virtually over. Loyalist supporter John Dawkins had seen Keating gearing for departure. Victory was almost a consolation surprise.

Keating won, but it was a scramble. On 18 January 1992 he was celebrating his forty-eighth birthday at the Lodge and was spinning new myths. The near-disastrous campaign against Hawke had become an act of precision. 'We had to knock him senseless without leaving any bruises,' Keating boasted.[2]

He was happy to have made it to the Lodge, yet he was also unhappy. When Don Watson was interviewed by Keating for the job of speechwriter, his impression of the new prime minister was sadness and melancholy.[3] There was an aura of disappointment. His political adviser, Stephen Smith, never forgot the look on Keating's face when he put the phone down having been told that Hawke would call a ballot, a ballot that would make him prime minister. 'What's the matter?' Smith asked.

Faltering at the precipice, Keating replied: 'Mate, I'm carrying such a crushing burden. You know, all this should have happened three years ago.'[4]

In Keating's mind he had arrived in the wrong summer; it should have been the summer of 1988 that brought him to power. In the intervening years no conversation with Keating was possible that did not include Hawke's infamy at clinging to office. It produced in Keating a cultivated anger, depression and self-pity. He raged about Hawke, blaming him for every mishap in his life—for denying his career, costing his health, sapping his energy. Above all, he blamed Hawke for denying him the prime ministership in 1988, when Keating believed he had reached the height of his powers and readiness. And he would not forgive.

This is because Keating brought a secret fear with him to the Lodge, a fear that he could never purge—that his best years were behind him. This was the demon of his Prime Ministership and it never left.

His loyal adviser Mark Ryan sensed he was not as sharp. 'As PM he didn't have the same laser-like focus and discipline that he had as treasurer,' Ryan said.[5] Treasury Secretary Tony Cole said that Keating as PM never found the discipline, efficient delegation and organisational control that had stamped Hawke's leadership. At their first meeting Keating told Watson he had 'wanted the job badly three years ago' but now he was tired.[6]

Keating's spirit fluctuated wildly. He was obsessed with the 'cycle' of politics—that Hawke had left him with the recession and a tired team. The 1992 winter provoked Keating's pessimism. His friend Bill Kelty, impatient at his black dog, said:

> I remember I went to see him and Paul was sniffling away with his cold. He was down and complaining, saying that Hawke 'didn't give me enough time and stayed too long, I've got the wrong end of the cycle and I got this bastard Hewson'. So I said, 'Well, give up mate. Just fuck off. If you don't think you can win, then leave. But you can beat him. He's an academic, people don't like him. You can actually beat him. But stop whingeing and complaining. Don't ever give me this speech again about Bob and the political cycle. I'm not fucking interested in the political cycle. Just remember this bloke wants a GST in the middle of a recession.'[7]

In office, he was disorganised and unpunctual. Cabinet ministers who knew him well were surprised. Sometimes he would arrive in cabinet not having read the cabinet submissions. Dismayed at Keating's style, his former treasurer, Dawkins, lamented: 'The essential discipline of the Hawke era was gone.'[8] And Dawkins was the politician who had demanded of Hawke that he resign in Keating's favour. Another supporter, John Button, said that Keating's 'best playing days were over, he kicked some brilliant goals and missed some easy ones—the team had declined in quality'.[9]

His biographer and adviser, John Edwards, wrote: 'Hawke's days had been filled with an orderly procession of appointments. Keating refused. He would not normally see delegations, ambassadors, public servants, backbenchers, members of the outer ministry, reporters, trade union officials or business people unless there was a particular and pressing piece of business to justify the appointment.'[10]

In his private domain Keating was devoid of any triumphalism. He knew his legacy was the fag end of an era. While liking most of his ministers, he didn't want ministers to bother him with tiresome detail. 'Paul didn't give his ministers enough attention,' Ryan said. 'He hated being constrained by a timetable and diary, and preferred to follow his instinct and mood.'[11]

The 24-hour media cycle was transforming politics—against Keating. He thrived on ideas and strategy but detested the view of modern politics coming from the ALP national secretariat. He distrusted Bob Hogg as national secretary and then loathed Gary Grey, his successor. Technology was privileging a new politics based on instant response and repeated media appearances geared to talkback radio, photo opportunities, extensive domestic travel and a relentless daily control of the news cycle. John Howard and then Kevin Rudd would master this process, but Keating loathed it. Often he just refused to participate. He mocked Hawke for being in 'shopping centres tripping over TV crews' cords'.[12] But Hawke was being a professional and feeding the media beast.

When Keating did engage, he was peerless, but this brand of 24-hour public relations politics fitted neither his temperament nor his physical capability. Before he became leader he promised to 'throw the switch to vaudeville' but Dawkins lamented years later that 'unfortunately he never did it'.[13]

There was a ripple of excitement in the caucus but morale was weak. Keating's staff were gloomy about the next election. Australia's economy was bouncing along the recessionary trough, with the jobless rate heading above 10 per cent. The public was despondent. Keating was neither loved by the party nor liked by the people. Once hailed as the world's greatest treasurer, he contemplated a landscape of economic desolation and personal political ruin. Within the Press Gallery there was a loud whisper: Keating was doomed. The smart money said he got the job too late.

Yet Keating, though wounded, was lethal still. A born political warrior, he was unmatched for vision, brains and persuasion. Keating moved effortlessly between the political violence of the street and the high ground of public policy. He had a capacity for political demolition rarely equalled since Federation and an ability to mobilise public support behind new policy such that Treasury officials of the 1980s were left agog as they saw him market a succession of economic reforms that recast much of the nation's political culture. Then he had persuaded the ALP caucus to execute the party's four-times-election-winning prime minister in favour of one of its most unpopular treasurers who had presided over a recession. Future historians would puzzle over how this could have possibly happened. But those who watched at close quarters knew: it was merely the latest demonstration of his remarkable persuasive powers, powers long familiar to the inhabitants of Parliament House and whose exposure to them from one year to the next never diminished the impact of the manipulative genius that Keating was able to summon up and deploy.

Keating injected the government with political electricity. Social Security Minister Neal Blewett found his tone in cabinet was usually quiet, unlike Hawke's hectoring. Occasionally he delivered a *tour d'horizon*. Blewett described one report to caucus as 'full of substance, frank, low-key, self-deprecatory, a far cry from the orotund, rhetorical mush provided by Hawke in the latter stages'. Above all, at a time of desperation, Keating had a sense of direction and purpose. Yet, summoned to meet Keating at 8.30 p.m. on 28 January 1992, Blewett was taken aback because he 'looked exhausted—has not the physical stamina of Hawke'.[14]

The heart of Keating's administration lay not in the cabinet but in his office. Within the inner sanctum Keating was respected; sometimes he was loved. It was a family affair. He was among friends who were chosen. He flattered them by saying it was the best PM's office in history. With his staff Keating was at his best—unpretentious, open, funny, creative and infuriating. 'Paul talked about being another staff member,' his office chief, Don Russell, would say. The fierce loyalty and affection 'for Paul' knew few bounds.[15]

Yet it was a protective arrangement: Keating used his office and the Lodge as a refuge. Ryan conceded that 'the office management was pretty hopeless, we were too isolated'.[16] Tony Cole felt Keating struggled with the bigger job, saying 'he was not a good delegator and he lost balance and perspective'.[17] Mike Keating (no relation), the head of the Department of Prime Minister and Cabinet, lamented that he 'did seem to drop the ball in engaging with key constituencies', revealed by the 'relatively few invitations he accepted' and 'even worse his failure to reply in a timely way'.[18]

The head of the Department of Foreign Affairs and Trade, Michael Costello, admired Keating's mind but saw the chink in his temperament. 'Paul himself is the first to admit that the other side of genius can be a certain craziness,' Costello said. 'You'd give Paul some advice. He'd consider it, turn it around, apply his highly original mind and send it back as a better proposal.'[19]

The Department of Prime Minister and Cabinet was filled with quality people but Keating rarely read its material. Edwards judged 'much less than a tenth' of its paperwork was read by Keating. Nor did Keating encourage his department to 'dictate' across the public service.[20] The message was manifest: Keating's energy and focus were geared to selective goals.

The most selective was winning the 1993 election. The validity of Keating's claim to the Lodge hinged on this victory. Keating deposed Hawke not on policy grounds; his sole claim was to revitalise the government. For some Hawke supporters this was fantastic nonsense. A bitter Hawke was sure Labor had signed its death warrant. With his legitimacy, reputation and prospect for a worthwhile prime ministership at stake, Keating would focus his entire political capital on a 1993 victory. Nothing would be allowed to impede this goal. As a professional, Keating gave himself a chance.

Keating carried into office one great conviction: the need to find a new political position for Labor. Long convinced that Hawke had been finished, Keating was equally convinced that his government must carry a different brand. Mike Keating said, 'Paul was absolutely determined that he would make a difference as prime minister. He was critical of Hawke. He felt Hawke had spread himself too thin, [that] he covered everything but made a difference to nothing.'[21]

The key to Keating's prime ministership was ideas. 'He was at his best when he had a rich menu of ideas,' Don Russell says. 'This was the role of the office and made it so special.' The staff felt Keating's ambition was for the nation, not for himself. His foreign policy adviser, Allen Gyngell, said: 'Paul was never the barrister in politics like a Peter Costello. He never saw the job as just mastering a brief. Paul was driven by ideas, and ideas are dangerous—you were never sure where he would take an idea.'[22] Keating's mind possessed a striking originality, freed from the stereotype of university tuition. 'Paul has the mind of an exceptional Queen's Counsel,' Russell told the staff tenth-anniversary bash but 'he was always the Catholic boy driven to do good'.

His obsession about ideas drove Keating to good policy—Mabo, competition policy, APEC diplomacy, enterprise bargaining. 'Keating understood issues very quickly and had a genuine preference for good policy outcomes,' says Mike Keating. 'I always had good access to him when I needed it and I got a good hearing.' But sometimes he became too focussed on the policy and lost the politics. Mike Keating praised his boss's economic reform agenda but identified a vital change from his days as treasurer. 'For whatever reason he let the politics slip,' Keating said. The master salesman from the Treasury went into retreat.[23]

Ideas are also indulgent. Keating rationalised his focus on big ideas to excuse more mundane failings. 'Paul had a thousand ways of avoiding things,' Russell said. 'You could nag but it was hard work and rarely stuck. The task was to find ideas to interest Paul that were consistent with his instincts.'[24]

The Paul Keating who entered the Lodge had learnt to step outside of himself. His softer, more reflective side was now evident. In the plane he could abandon any pretence and talk about how he was sick of meetings, functions, appearances. His mind would turn to music or architecture or what he might do when he 'had the place all set up' and could pursue his own passions. He would not be a long-run PM.

Keating had a refined grasp of power. He knew that power exists to be spent and to be saved. Power invested wisely returns multiple dividends but power spent unwisely is the road to ruin. It is leadership that shapes how power is used, and Keating arrived at the Lodge with a radical leadership philosophy—conceivably the most radical of any prime minister.

It was his conception of leadership that made and then broke Paul Keating. His leadership philosophy was forged in the white heat of nine years as treasurer. Its graphic outline came in Keating's 'Placido Domingo' speech delivered off the record to the Press Gallery on the night of 7 December 1990 in tragic circumstances: the previous evening a pivotal figure in economic policy making, the secretary of the Treasury, Chris Higgins, had died in a running race.

The mix of Keating's rivalry with Hawke and Higgins' death saw Keating arrive at the club in an emotional state. Sitting at the main table, over dinner he began writing furiously in his elegant longhand with its long flowing loops, looking up from time to time, exchanging the odd word with journalists, but in a focussed introspection. The speech was still under construction when he began talking. Usually seen as his manifesto to succeed Hawke, its significance lay in its leadership philosophy for government. It was a prophetic insight into how Keating would operate as prime minister.

This was the speech of a patriot. Its theme was Australia's ability to become a great nation. It is one of the most ambitious speeches for Australia ever delivered by a leading politician. For Keating, Australia was an incomplete project, poised between mediocrity and greatness. It was, he asserted, 'teetering on the brink' of greatness. A special moment had arrived—and the task of leadership was to seize this moment.

He said:

> We have this chance to pull Australia into one of the preferred countries of the nineties and beyond. We really do have this opportunity; it's not beyond us. The problems we have are not irreconcilable or incapable of being defeated. It just requires a national will and a national leadership to do it … Leadership is not about being popular; it's about being right and about being strong. It's about doing what you think the nation requires, making profound judgements about profound issues.[25]

The psychological message was clear: Keating would invest his prime ministership with a special meaning. It would be no ordinary event. If he had transformed the economy as treasurer then he would transform the nation as prime minister.

This conviction, formed before he entered the Lodge, never left him—it helped to explain his frustrations, his volatility and his search for crusades from Mabo to Asia. It was also a critique of Hawke, who led by consensus. The message was that sub-optimal consensus was not good enough. Australia needed a new leadership philosophy.

This was a romantic conception of the strong leader. His thesis was that Australia had the chance to build on its more competitive economy, its role within the Asia–Pacific, its multiculturalism and its independent mindset to redefine itself. Keating believed the true leader must be more ambitious, but his emphasis on willpower was exaggerated. He offered an evocative yet misleading leadership parable: America and its historical crises.

Keating said:

Our problem is we've never had one leader like they've had. The
United States has had three great leaders: Washington, Lincoln and
Roosevelt. At key times in their history that leadership pushed
them on to become the great country that it is. We've never had
one such person, not one. Now, Curtin was our wartime leader
and a trier but we've never had that kind of leadership. And it's
no good people saying, 'But there's 230 million people in the US.'
There weren't 230 million people when Thomas Jefferson was
sitting in a house he designed for himself in a paddock at the back
end of Virginia writing the words 'Life, liberty and the pursuit of
happiness.'

Curtin was unique in Labor's pantheon as a hero and martyr. But
Keating's analysis was valid since only a fool would hold Curtin equal to
the US presidents he nominated. His aim was not to denigrate Curtin
but to prove his thesis—if Curtin was inadequate compared with his US
counterparts then Australia's inferior culture was demonstrated. So was
his main proposition: what was required was a new brand of Australian
leadership.

There were several problems with this. America's crises over independence and Civil War were epic events that demanded great leaders while
Australia had been fortunate to avoid such a history. The culture of US
politics and its leadership ethic was far removed from Australia's 'one man
is as good as another' tradition. The speech betrayed Keating's alienation
from Australia's past, suggesting that a leader so equivocal about his own
nation's character might also be equivocal about the Australian people
themselves. When Hawke left office he told Keating to 'get close' to the
people.[26] But this advice was not heeded and by 1996 many Australians
had sensed Keating's equivocation about them.

The truth, though, is that reform cannot spring from complacency.
It was Keating's restless dissatisfaction with Australia that drove his quest
to improve the nation. As a politician he never lost the ability to get
outraged; he declined to be slave to the established order.

This speech reflected the contradictions that Keating took to the
Lodge; success had not bred contentment. His lifelong political vocation
ran parallel with the expansion of his soul into art, music and architecture.
There was a strange hybrid at the Lodge—a leader of unmatched
calculation and realism, yet a dreamer besotted by the search for the big

idea. As Keating grew more obsessed with ideas he was less interested in the tribulations of the people whose votes he needed.

At work, he fluctuated between passion and disinterest, a hot and cool chief executive, his bouts of self-delusion punctured by penetrating realism. Like his favourite politician, Winston Churchill, he would search for high policy and had no intention of being chained to a desk processing papers.

At the start he told Don Watson that, with the economy, 'most of the big changes had been made'; the rest was fine tuning.[27] And he wasn't happy about it. For years Keating's lament had been 'even if I become prime minister I'll never achieve what I've done as treasurer'.[28] His fear was that nothing would be left but the hangover from Hawke. Once he entered the Lodge this fear was ever-present. But it helped to produce a primal urge—the dream to do remarkable things.

In their contest Hawke had claimed that Keating understood only economics. In truth, Keating had cultivated passions that never troubled Hawke's landscape. Keating, as prime minister, would produce the new ideas. Nothing was more certain, even though in January 1991 he didn't know what such ideas might be.

One thing, though, was certain: he would not be dictated to by political advisers or party secretaries carrying the latest polling. 'As leader you've got a choice,' Keating said. 'You either read the polls and duck for cover or you say I will take a risk.'[29] Mark Ryan says: 'Paul was right about the things that mattered. Some Labor people thought leadership was a slogan, but Paul actually led. That's why fifteen years later we can say he changed Australia forever.'[30]

Aware that his powers were fading, Keating, in his press gallery speech, signalled that he would give the prime ministership a mighty whack:

> We've got to the stage where everyone thinks politicians are shits ... but politicians change the world and politics and politicians are about leadership ... I've been around for a long time and some of you think I'm a bit jaded and a bit faded and good on you. I probably am. And you say, 'He's up this week' and 'He's down next week'. Well, the fact is, my stocks might be down but the performances are never going to be down. I walk on that stage and some performances will be better than others; but they are all up there trying to stream the economics and politics together. Out there on the stage doing the Placido Domingo.

It was part delusion, part conviction. This was a leadership vision operatic in excitement and tragedy. The Placido Domingo brand of politics is not an established Australian method; it is a melodrama where the maestro sings and the audience swoons. Placido Domingo comes to perform, not listen. This was a metaphor for epic achievement and political self-deception. But it had got into Keating's blood and penetrated his being. Once implanted, it was fixed, surging back and forth, but ever-present. It would explain the polarising nature of his rule, the cheers of the True Believers and his rejection by the people.

Years later Keating was still spinning the same thrilling philosophy. 'There are two things in leadership: imagination and courage,' he said. For Keating 'leadership is meeting the challenge of the unknown'. 'It's about excitement, it's a determination to give the public a good break on good policy, not to play safe but to take the risk. I think there's another thing—the thrill of the ride. I've loved riding the tiger's back. In the end he might turn around and bite your head off, but God it's fun while it lasts.'[31] But such a leadership style has a limited shelf life.

Selective with his time and energy, Keating would be a prime minister for high policy; he would leave low policy for others. The Placido Domingo leadership philosophy was in his heart and in his head. Its existential meaning was that Keating would be prime minister on his own terms—a bravo performance … and then rejection.

2

BIG-BANG LIBERALISM

John Hewson would never agree on a policy that was
not the biggest bang he could produce.
—Liberal Party adviser Peter Hendy, 1997

The 1990s saw the most audacious experiment in Liberal Party history: a radical plan to remake Australia as a free-market libertarian nation. Its author was an economist and political novice, Dr John Hewson, whose star blazed across the political sky before a spectacular crash and burn. Hewson's failure had a double meaning—it saved Keating as prime minister and it triggered the resurrection of John Howard.

The Howard edifice was built on Hewson's collapse. After his defeat Hewson became the anti-model for the Liberal Party, a status he resented. His hostility towards Howard and his wife Janette was palpable. The story of Hewson's failure is pivotal because it set the template for Keating's prime ministership and for the Howard years.

Hewson, by default, created the Keating–Howard age and the direction that Australia would take over the next fifteen years. Over time Hewson forgave Keating but he would never forgive Howard.

The view developed later that Howard, as prime minister, implemented by stealth the Hewson 1993 election agenda. But this is a misleading interpretation of Australian history that cannot be sustained. The reality is that Howard absorbed the message from Hewson's defeat in the 'unlosable' election, changed the direction of the Liberal Party and revised how it should govern.

Elected to parliament only in 1987 Hewson's rate of progress exceeded that of Menzies and was virtually as fast as Hawke's. Unfortunately, Hewson had none of the skill of these masters. But Hewson had one redeeming quality: the courage and the consistency to develop a program on which he staked his fate, unlike another Opposition leader, Mark Latham, who in 2004 declined to back his beliefs.

Hewson was an unusual figure to lead a major party. From his installation he aspired to transform the Liberal Party by fiat. His aim was to destroy the stinking and hypocritical culture of old politics, riddled with intellectual corruption and policy weakness. This was fundamental to Hewson's thinking. Indeed, it was the reason he entered politics. He explained, 'I said in my pre-selection speech that I wasn't going to be a politician. I said I would be a policy person. You can say I was naïve but I told people at the start. I had worked for Lynch, Fraser and Howard in the 1970s and 1980s. I believed we had to change the quality of the policy debate in Australia.'[1]

It sounds incredible but Hewson refused to beat Keating off the broken hopes of a million unemployed. Hewson would not stoop that low—that was too cynical, that was old politics. He would attempt something else: he would ask the Australian people, battered by the recession, to remake their society. This plan came to be known as *Fightback!*

Fightback! was the most comprehensive and ideological agenda ever put to the people. It took courage into the domain of the foolhardy. Convinced that the Liberal Party, from Malcolm Fraser's 1970s leadership to Andrew Peacock's 1990 defeat, had been tainted by its refusal to be honest with the nation about problems and solutions, Hewson cast himself as a prophet: he would confront the people with the price of national progress. The man was guileless in his self-righteousness.

In one of the most extraordinary comments from any leader about his election agenda Hewson said:

> I did see *Fightback!* as a character test for the Australian people. I was putting the hard decisions before the community and I did that deliberately. I wanted to force them to choose. I believed it was time we raised politics to a different level. I wanted a better focus on policy solutions. Everyone used to tell me 'put your policy in the bottom drawer and pull it out after the election'. That meant playing the same old game and I wouldn't do it.[2]

Hewson was a crusader and theoretician unimpressed by Australia's political character. He got upset and agitated when thwarted. And Hewson had suffered a recent defeat—in 1989, as Peacock's shadow treasurer, he had been rebuffed by the leadership group when he pushed for a broadly based indirect tax. One of his advisers, Peter Hendy, said that, after this loss,

'Hewson was temporarily psychologically shattered' and that 'for the next three days he moped around his office railing against the pusillanimity of his colleagues'.[3]

Peacock's sponsorship had sanctioned the rise of Hewson. 'I liked the cut of his jib,' Peacock said of Hewson's performance at the 1990 election.[4] Hewson became Liberal leader after the March 1990 poll. Howard, deposed by Peacock in the disastrous May 1989 coup, had wanted to run again but he had little support. Peacock recruited Hewson as a 'new generation' solution to lock out Howard. It was that elemental and the Liberal Party was desperate.

Hewson defeated the tall, stoop-shouldered Peter Reith 62 to 13 in the main ballot and Reith became his deputy. Howard voted for Hewson as leader and Reith as deputy and shadow treasurer. Veteran Liberal Party Director Tony Eggleton declared that 'John Hewson is the luckiest politician I've encountered.'[5] Contrary to popular myth, Hewson and Reith were a united team.

The contest between Keating and Hewson that began in December 1991 would be vituperative, brief and decisive. It would last, in effect, only fourteen months and see Keating outmanoeuvre Hewson in political terms and outsmart him psychologically.

Howard had no doubt about what happened to the Liberal Party during the 1990–93 term. 'We didn't have a skilled politician as leader,' he said. 'A more skilled politician would have won with *Fightback!* though it would have been hard. But John Hewson's political weakness was a major factor, a very major factor.'[6]

More than fifteen years later, Hewson was unforgiving about his demise. Yet his venom was directed not at his conqueror, Keating, but at Howard. 'I like him very much,' Hewson said of Keating. Conversely, he felt sure that Keating respected him. But he charged Howard 'with trying to destabilise me from the day I became leader'. Hewson said: 'After I became leader Janette Howard said to Caroline [Hewson's wife at the time] that I should stand down for John. Of course, she'll deny that.' Reflecting on Howard's career, Hewson said: 'He ran on prejudice not policy. He would have spent his way out of any problem and taken any opportunity to play the race card.' For Hewson, 'Howard is a great hater and Janette is a bigger hater.'[7]

Hewson was suspicious of the young Peter Costello and their relations finished in protracted and unremitting animosity. At one point in 1993 Hewson raised with Costello the possibility of reintroducing the death penalty for certain offences. Costello was surprised. He later asked

Ian McLachlan:'Do you think we have an obligation to tell the Australian people our leader is a maniac?' McLachlan replied: 'No, the Australian people will figure it out for themselves.'[8]

Hewson believed the recession offered a unique chance—to win on a truly radical agenda that would transform Australia. But he made one fatal error: he was more obsessed about rectifying past Liberal Party failures than in devising a tactic to defeat Keating. This meant that Hewson made himself, not Keating, the 1993 election issue, a Herculean feat beyond the reach of an ordinary mortal.

Hewson became leader because he had the economic policy credibility that Peacock had lacked and which cost the latter the 1990 election. This was the trap: Hewson was obsessed with fighting the last election, not the next one. He was preoccupied with his own ideas and, for a political amateur, he was surprisingly resistant to taking advice. As leader Hewson operated with a smug intellectual superiority and a fatalistic moralism. He sought not just to reform but to purge. His startled colleagues only slowly realised that Hewson didn't just want to win—he wanted to win on his redemptive terms, otherwise he would be as bad as the old politics that he despised.

He said: 'My aim was to go to the 1993 election with a clear-cut position on every major issue. It was naïve because I left myself open to substantial attack and Keating was good at that. You know, we didn't lose by much.'[9]

Hewson's vision began with a Goods and Services Tax (GST). It was an old idea that should have been implemented long ago. The GST was radical politics and orthodox economics. It terrified the political advisers but was permanent advice from the Treasury. Access Economics principal Geoff Carmody, who was advising Hewson, said:'While *Fightback!* might have been seen—then—as a radical document in political terms, for most economists it was largely bread-and-butter solid economics.'[10]

The new Hewson–Reith team was united on the principle of the tax but had an initial difference over the size of the income tax cuts. Reith's preference was to avoid a shift in the tax burden from direct to indirect, creating scope for hefty income tax cuts as a 'sweetener'. Carmody opposed this method because it meant a GST at a high rate spilling into the CPI and demanding hefty compensation for low and fixed income earners. It threatened to turn indirect tax reform into an unwinnable contest over equity. Peter Hendy said:'This issue has been the single most important stumbling block for proposals to introduce a GST over the last 20 years.'[11]

But Hewson, like Whitlam, had come to crash through. He wanted a big tax cut and that meant a big GST. At a long night meeting in Sydney on 13 August 1990 Hewson and Reith decided the GST principle should be announced quickly. They took their proposal to a shadow cabinet meeting the next day. And Hewson got a terrible fright.

Hewson outlined his personal vision—an Australia with a massively reduced income tax, a competitive nation, a country that moved away from the 'gutlessness' of the Fraser era and brought 'wimp politics' to an end.[12] He had only contempt for his predecessors.

The shadow cabinet was shocked and lost its nerve. As each member spoke, it was apparent that a majority opposed Hewson. Embarrassment was mounting. A worried Hewson then asked each member to forget politics and assess whether the proposal was in the national economic interest. With a majority now saying 'yes' he argued this was tantamount to an endorsement, a statement that provoked anger around the table.

But Hewson had a saviour. Peacock intervened to declare that Hewson must be supported, that the party knew what he represented when it elected him as leader and said that 'if the guy thinks he can sell the policy then we should bloody well give him what he wants'. It was the turning point. After shadow cabinet approval, the party room stamped the decision. Hewson and Reith made a fateful joint announcement on the principle of tax reform on 15 August 1990. At this point Hewson took control of the Liberal Party, courtesy of Peacock.[13]

But the import of this meeting was unmistakable. Much of the Liberal frontbench had severe qualms about the Hewson strategy.

The idea for the tax was powerful because the Wholesale Sales Tax (WST) system was discriminatory and unfair and did not apply to services. It taxed business inputs and was biased against exports. Inquiry after inquiry had slammed its inefficiency and inequity. The reform was tied irresistibly to the idea of lower personal income tax rates, despite the efforts of Access Economics and Treasury to play this down.

Beyond this, the GST had an iconic symbolism. For reformers such as Hewson and Keating in his 1985 mode, the tax system was a pillar of the old order. It had to be remade in the cause of economic excellence. Hewson saw *Fightback!* as more than a tax reform—it would change Australia's political culture and deliver a more individualistic society.

As options were reviewed in coming months, Hewson drove the GST rate beyond 10 per cent towards 15 per cent. The main work was done in secret by a handful of Hewson's and Reith's staff with help from

Access Economics. The two leaders were 'hands on' and Hendy captured the mood:

> Many of the options were written up on a whiteboard in Reith's office and when the parliament sat we would often throw a blanket over it and march it through the corridors of the building to Hewson's office. We would have long meetings into the night deciding on the various combinations and permutations of policy. Hewson would argue the pros and cons of having a 'big bang' that would set the government and the press gallery on its heels. He would always order in the beer or the wine (which Reith invariably declined) and entrench himself for a long night of discussion.[14]

There was one constant in Hewson's head: the 'big bang'. He pushed the shadow finance minister, Jim Short, to extract more and more savings from the spending review process and he talked endlessly of vision and reform. At a Melbourne meeting on 3 October 1991 with the two leaders, their senior staff and Liberal Party Federal Director Andrew Robb, 'it became apparent that Hewson would never agree on a policy that was not the biggest bang he could produce'.[15]

In Reith, Hewson had a passionate collaborator. Reith revelled in the *Fightback!* process, its long hours, its policy thrill, its political audacity. He did much of the leg work and got the main accounting firms drafting its tax provisions. Like Hewson, Reith was mesmerised by the idea of the 'big bang'.

Fightback! was conceived as an act of astonishment and was a formidable achievement for an Opposition. Released at the National Press Club by Hewson on 21 November 1991, a full year before any election, there had never been anything like it before. Hewson's political testament was stretched out on the table for examination and Keating was invited to apply his demolition technique.

It is easily overlooked that *Fightback!* was an instant success. The first Newspoll after the launch showed a 53–35 per cent Coalition primary vote lead: its existential daring had outweighed its political traps. Hewson was euphoric but edgy. Don Watson confessed: 'I found myself admiring it—so did others who had never voted anything but Labor.'[16] Reith was taken aback at the reception. 'I'd never seen anything like it,' he said. 'I'd go to a breakfast and get a standing ovation before I spoke.'[17] Howard said: 'I supported *Fightback!* and I don't walk away from that. It was a very high risk political document. But the times suited that approach. When Hewson brought it out people lapped it up.'[18]

With a distant echo of John Kennedy, Hewson declared: 'We make an absolute commitment to generational change in leadership, a generational change in attitudes and a generational change in policies.' He warned that Australia's problems were the worst 'we have seen since the 1930s', with the nation entering the 'danger zone' of a crisis akin to the Great Depression.

The *Fightback!* philosophy was 'to start to move government out of the way so that people have a chance to get on with their lives'. Hewson slammed a dependence on government that is 'staggering' and the 'defeatist mentality' permeating business. Convinced that 'high taxes, big spending and government inefficiency' were strangling Australia, he pledged to roll back the size and cost of government. 'We are challenging average Australians,' Hewson said. 'We should settle for nothing less than the best, whether it is the best waterfront or the best education system.' He used the language of liberty from the United States and the classic liberalism of JS Mill, a new libertarian rhetoric for Australia.

But in pledging a small-government/low-tax future, Hewson misrepresented the Hawke government. The record shows that Whitlam expanded the size of government and that Hawke reduced it, a reality Hewson refused to address. In truth, there was little scope for the small-government neo-liberalism he offered.[19]

The media was enthusiastic about *Fightback!* Hawke seemed immobilised and Labor was stunned. Keating said later: 'The recession and the GST got Hawke.'[20]

Fightback! took several threshold steps, any one of which would normally have lost an election. Taken together, they delivered the 'big bang' beloved by Hewson. Yet sixteen years later, when John Howard left office, only a few of the *Fightback!* principles had been realised, even though the Coalition had enjoyed a Senate majority—mainly the GST, the Telstra sale, aspects of industrial relations reform and some outsourcing and privatisation. While Howard as PM moved in a pro-market direction, it is false to think he pulled *Fightback!* from the bottom drawer and sought to implement it by stealth. This is not what happened in the Howard era.

The package had a 15 per cent GST to finance a massive cut in business taxes, including abolition of payroll taxes and abolition of petroleum excise. More than 90 per cent of individuals would be on a 30 cents income tax rate, with a new top rate of 42 cents. Federal spending would be cut by $10 billion to largely finance the tax cuts. When Howard implemented his own GST in mid-2000 it was significantly different: the rate was 10 per cent, there was no abolition of payroll taxes or petroleum excise, the top tax rate was 47 cents, the tax incentives were not as large and he declined to make the Hewson spending cuts.

Hewson had tariffs being reduced to 'negligible levels' by 2000. This was his famous zero tariff pledge. Howard, in office, never gave this idea the slightest credence. He saw negligible or zero tariffs as a folly.

Hewson championed a new monetary policy with a statutory strengthening of Reserve Bank independence coupled with a severe inflation target of 0 to 2 per cent as the guide for interest rates. This was repudiated by Howard and Costello in office. They sought neither to amend the Reserve Bank statute nor to embrace Hewson's inflation target, which they viewed as a serious blunder.

Fightback! was a sharp retreat from Medicare. It attacked the idea of 'free' medical and hospital services, insisting that this policy was untenable, encouraged overuse and long waiting lists, and hurt the needy. Hewson believed that 'free' health care regardless of income defrauded the public. He wanted better price signals, patients meeting a higher share of the costs and abolition of ambitious levels of bulk billing. Bulk billing would be limited to pensioners and welfare recipients. Overall, this was a significant and partial dismantling of Medicare, though the universality principle was kept. Howard, by contrast, never contemplated any such radical surgery or compromises to Medicare in his eleven years as PM. Indeed, he moved in the opposite direction.

In higher education, Hewson backed a voucher system and partial fee deregulation to move power to students and dismantle central controls. Federal funds for universities would be channelled 'through the students' to allow individuals and institutions to choose their own future. Fee flexibility would see rigid control of university places, and courses removed, in the cause of autonomy and competition, allowing universities 'to offer places as they choose in any course'. Shadow Minister David Kemp said no university had a God-given right to survive and that the reforms were to tackle 'the Eastern European style' of Australia's university sector.[21] This type of market-based model was rejected explicitly by the Howard government when Brendan Nelson was minister for education.

Hewson's industrial relations policy was unveiled later by Howard as shadow minister and was far more radical than the 1996 reforms that Howard would pioneer as PM. Howard was in full reformist flight when he declared that this 1992 policy constituted 'a very important moment in the history of Australia'.[22] Howard's aim was more jobs, higher real wages and higher productivity. Industrial relations was 'by far the most important' Coalition reform, he said. Lest there were any doubters, Howard said: 'If I could do only one reform it would be industrial relations. Absolutely.'[23]

Judged against *WorkChoices* in 2005, the policy was both softer and harder. Howard's aim was to allow employees and their employers to make agreements with minimal interference from unions or tribunals. The pivotal provision was an automatic termination of all award agreements within a twelve-month period. For the award to be maintained the parties had to take a positive decision. This reversed the onus—rather than parties having to 'opt out' of awards into new agreements, awards were dissolved unless the parties decided to 'opt in'.[24]

'My prediction is that there will be a mass exodus out of the award stream,' an ebullient Howard said. In the transition no employee would lose any entitlements unless that was agreed. Workplace agreements had to comply with a set of minimum conditions and the most contentious of these had been announced by Hewson in a personal initiative to combat youth joblessness—a $3-an-hour rate for fifteen to seventeen year olds that was inconsistent with welfare benefits. It became a political gift for Keating and undermined the entire policy.

The Coalition position ended compulsory arbitration, industry-wide wage rises and national wage cases. Howard boasted that capital investment could be run 'twenty-four hours a day, seven days a week, 365 days a year'. He pledged to remove the 'stranglehold' of trade union power. It was an omen of *WorkChoices*.[25]

With unemployment above 10 per cent Howard and Hewson sought to wound fatally the regulated industrial system. The unions were horrified and business applauded. Keating said Howard wanted 'a return to the dark ages of the common law of master and servant last used in the 19th century'.[26] Peter Hendy said: 'The 1993 policy was far more radical than anything we did before the 2004 election.'[27]

The truth is that Hewson offered Keating a suite of scare campaigns. Keating chose the GST scare because it was the best. Andrew Robb confirmed that Liberal research showed public alarm about Hewson's Medicare policy and, to a lesser extent, the IR policy. If there had been no GST, Keating would have run a campaign on Medicare and industrial relations and it would have been a ferocious scare.

Incredibly, *Fightback!* was not designed primarily to combat the 1990s recession. It was a medium-term restructuring of economic and social polity. Its marketing demanded a leader of superlative communication skills. But Hewson was clueless on this front. The dilemma led to his refrain that 'if we can't win with the GST then we don't deserve to govern'. It remains his political epitaph.

Summing up *Fightback!* and its legacy Hewson said:

> I tried to force people to focus on choices. To accelerate the reduction of protection at a time of recession was difficult. I still think it was the right policy. There was a lot on self-reliance— we had vouchers in education. I think we set the future in many ways. But I also think there was a lot of *Fightback!* that Howard didn't want to take up. People point to the GST but, frankly, that was inevitable. The test is what did Howard do when he won control of the Senate years later? All he did was *WorkChoices*, a half-arsed variation of what we had at the 1993 election. You have to conclude there was a lot that he didn't take up.[28]

Among those senior Liberals who survived into the Howard era, Reith remained the most enthusiastic about *Fightback!* Years later, after he had left politics, Reith would ruminate over a drink about the 'might-have-beens', saying: 'Imagine if we had had a Menzies or a Howard spearheading the *Fightback!* campaign.' He offered a subtle appraisal:

> I think *Fightback!* was an education and a turning point for the parliamentary Liberal Party. Hewson's feat was to give coherence to many of the ideas on the Liberal side. He forced the party to think through what it believed and to confront issues—to argue for a GST and a zero tariff and other policies. That sharpened the mind and toughened up the party. While we lost the 1993 election a number of those policies would stick.[29]

In many ways *Fightback!* was a tribute to Keating's influence. It was hardly a secret that Hewson admired him. The more Keating won kudos as the architect of Australia's 1980s economic re-design, the more Hewson seemed almost crazed in his resentment. For Keating, *Fightback!* was an affirmation of Labor's governing strategy—forcing the Coalition to the Right and holding the middle. As Opposition leader Hewson hung behind his desk a large, unflattering portrait of Keating that startled when visiting the Hewson office.

Hewson's vision was clear—a neo-liberal society based on more individual incentive and reward for effort, greater personal responsibility, lower taxes and less government support. But he was operating at a time when people, battered from recession, were looking to the state for support.

His experiment was to cast the Menzian party in a radical mould. He built on, and extended, the direction in which Howard took the party during his 1985–89 leadership. Hewson's embrace of economic liberalism mocked the Liberal Party's more conservative traditions as they had been established under Menzies. Once the Liberals adopted the free market libertarian philosophy they became the radicals of Australian politics. But this created an immediate conflict between policy belief and party culture. The Liberal Party had never seen itself as a radical party.

Under Hewson the Liberal Party was locked in a contradiction: its ethos and culture as an institution remained as an upholder of the existing order, yet it had embraced a policy agenda that involved a systemic dismantling of this order. In truth, the Liberals failed to mobilise, campaign and organise as a party of radical change, a point that was confirmed at the 1993 poll.

Hewson aspired not just to change the Liberal Party but to transform Australia's political tradition. This was the obvious intent of *Fightback!* While Keating and Howard favoured a distinct move away from state power, Hewson sought to smash such reliance. The 1993 election would be a watershed—it would decide whether Australia became a nation of 'big bang' liberalism.

3

THE PRICE OF SURVIVAL

Keating wasn't interested in my advice.
He said that things will take care of themselves.
—Former treasurer John Dawkins,
December 2008, on the *One Nation* package

T he foundation of Keating's success as prime minister was his slaying of *Fightback!*—an improbable feat, given his ratings and the recession. The defeat of *Fightback!* required strategic insight, an outrageous scare and a will to power. Keating was capable of all three. The result was that he obtained a five-year prime ministership.

The mechanics for *Fightback!*'s defeat were devised over the first two months of Keating's rule. It was contained in his economic manifesto of 26 February 1992 called *One Nation*. The result of a profound tension within the new government, *One Nation* was the instrument that smashed Hewson, the weapon that backfired on Keating and a political gift that Howard would accept with gratitude. Its shadow would dominate the first half of the 1990s.

The *One Nation* statement was owned by Keating lock, stock and barrel. His treasurer, John Dawkins, said: 'The real story is that neither I nor the Treasury was genuinely consulted. This statement was about creating a prime minister out of a treasurer in less than tweve months. And I supported that.'[1] The head of the Department of the Prime Minister and Cabinet, Mike Keating, said: 'Paul wanted to turn around economic policy and to show, in comparison to Hawke, a new purpose. He wanted to prove that something big had happened with his arrival in the Lodge.'[2]

Keating thought not as a treasurer but as a prime minister who had once been treasurer. The package would be assembled through his own loyalists. Keating would not allow the Treasury to fool with his political survival. 'They always get it wrong,' Keating told Dawkins of Treasury forecasts.

One Nation was the work of a new prime minister luxuriating in absolute command but running an ageing and ailing government. This was the key to its strange chemistry.

It put Keating–Dawkins relations on a political fuse that would explode within two years.[3] 'Mate, you'll be treasurer,' Keating had said to Dawkins before the late 1991 challenge. But they made no deal. 'It's best if there's no arrangement,' Dawkins would tell him. The ministry Keating inherited from Hawke had Ralph Willis, the symbol of Labor decency, as treasurer. Keating dreaded the idea of executing Willis. Although ruthless towards his enemies, Keating hated punishing his friends. So he dithered. Anxious not to lose by default, Dawkins contacted Keating to tell him 'you should know that treasurer is the only job I want and if I'm not treasurer then I'm not anything'.[4] It was friendly intimidation. But Keating was always going to install him; their bond was too great.[5]

Keating came to the Lodge with two irresistible economic impulses. Convinced the recession was deeper than Hawke had realised, Keating would recast policy with a hefty fiscal stimulus and he would launch a brutal frontal assault on Hewson's *Fightback!*, depicting it as a fraud. Don Russell explains: 'Keating had to terminate the debate about blame for the recession. He made the question: What should we do? Everybody knew that Hewson had a plan. Keating's mission was to prove it was the wrong plan.'[6]

When Keating taunted Hewson with the line 'How many jobs does a GST make?' he had his story. Keating would offer a better plan to escape the recession than Hewson. Because Keating had been responsible for the recession this stance was brazen in the extreme. But Keating was a genius at selling a product assumed to be unmarketable. He operated in a psychological constellation where absolute boundaries had ceased to exist. Keating had destroyed Hawke to become PM, so who was to say he could not combat the recession as well? Keating led a government of desperation but this had been inevitable—Labor only moved from Hawke to Keating once the party became totally demoralised.

During his six months on the backbench Keating had campaigned for a stronger, old-fashioned Keynesian expansion. He knew that Treasury had underestimated the downturn. Free from Treasury and on the prowl, Keating, much to Hawke's rage, now became a champion of more spending and deeper interest rate cuts. When Keating, famous for his sublime ignorance of Australian Rules football, went to Collingwood Football

Club to propagate his agenda, Hawke was more incensed than usual. He took it as a double atrocity. Hawke accused Keating of populism, the ultimate insult among pro-market apostles.

For Keating, the strategy was obvious. Within the first forty-eight hours of his government his economic adviser, John Edwards, briefed senior officials on how to respond to *Fightback!* The first aim was to match Hewson's middle-income tax cut; the second to promote a recovery from recession more quickly than Hewson; the third to leave Hewson exposed with his GST, to isolate it and to destroy it.[7]

The *One Nation* statement was devised within Keating's office and the Prime Minister's department. Russell, affable, shrewd and elusive, told the department what was wanted: to match the Hewson tax cuts without a GST. Its elemental quality had a deceptive yet outrageous beauty. One of the most senior economic officials, Rod Sims, later said: 'We were instructed to match the tax cuts. And the moment Keating's office told us, we knew it was unaffordable.'[8]

Dawkins said: 'I agreed completely with Keating's view that we needed a strong fiscal stimulus.' But when it came to the forecasts Dawkins sang another tune. 'These were not Treasury forecasts as such,' he said. 'They were called scenarios. The Treasury believed they were far too optimistic and I told Keating about Treasury's alarm. But Keating wasn't interested in my advice. He said that things will take care of themselves.'[9] At this stage Dawkins realised it would be a wild ride.

From the 1980s Keating had learnt about the power of economic statements. Most years he had delivered two—in May and then the August Budget. They had made his reputation and enabled him to dictate the path of politics. Now he would employ this technique as prime minister. His purpose was to outsmart Hewson on the politics, beat him as economic manager and carry the election. That was all.

In Canberra the power edifices were tottering and burning. The comfortable stability of the Hawke court had evaporated. Desolation from the recession was spreading across the structure of government. The official family at Treasury and the Reserve Bank was in ruins, reeling from its recessionary blunders. Renowned for its intellectual arrogance and the peerless confidence of its secretaries, from Roland Wilson to John Stone, the Treasury had been humiliated. It was tormented by a guilty soul. Its incumbent secretary, Tony Cole, said:

The mood within the Treasury was one of profound depression. People felt guilty about the recession and about our role in the recession. In years gone by, when downturns had come, we had been able to say and believe it was because the politicians hadn't taken Treasury advice. This was not the cause of the early 1990s recession. With exceptions at the margin the Labor government had taken the advice of the Treasury and the Reserve Bank and it had been wrong. We had a sense of guilt and responsibility. That led, in turn, to a determination to get the nation out of recession. We became very focussed on this issue. We wanted a stimulus equivalent to 1 per cent of GDP and the other policy departments were shocked by this and told us that it was irresponsible. [10]

But power had shifted decisively away from Treasury. Keating had left the Treasury seven months before. The combination of recession and a new and wilful prime minister led to a massive concentration of power in Keating's office. There was, however, a problem: the office was dysfunctional.

But Keating did not mind. Perhaps he didn't even notice. There was one principle to his prime ministership: the hunt and destruction of Hewson. Despite the recession, Keating didn't have to perform miracles—he only had to outsmart Hewson. And he saw that Hewson wasn't actually fighting the recession. As Russell said to Keating: 'Australia has come to a sharp bend in the economic road but Hewson just goes straight ahead at great speed.'[11] *Fightback!* was about Hewson's dreams. Keating, by contrast, decided to fight Hewson with all the instruments available to an incumbent.

Keating's staff showed that Hewson's tax cuts were not financed by his GST but by his spending cuts and fiscal drag as taxpayers moved into higher income brackets. This generated the idea that Keating could also offer tax cuts without relying on any GST.

A special working group was established to produce the numbers, with its key figure being Ric Simes, an economic adviser to Keating, who had headed Treasury's forecasting unit during the 1980s. Beneath this complex task lay a simple arithmetic reality: the forecast revenue growth had to be sufficient to finance Keating's tax cuts in a responsible way. A 'responsible way' meant a return to budget surplus over the four-year period. *One Nation* was more a political document than an economic one—it was designed, first and foremost, to destroy *Fightback!* with the promotion of recovery a distant second.

'This was the Prime Minister's statement and the office was heavily involved in all decisions,' Simes said.[12] The forecasts would become the

subject of intense controversy because, in critical respects, they were seriously inaccurate.

This led to Hewson's charge: 'Keating ran a fraudulent campaign in
1993. He knew, and Treasury would have told him, that he couldn't deliver the tax cuts without a GST. It was that simple.'[13]

As Tony Cole said:

> Making accurate forecasts when the economy is turning is very
> hard. The Treasury told Ric Simes that we didn't agree with the
> forecasts. I spoke to our representatives on the committee to ensure
> that our views were put firmly. The Treasury forecasts were more
> modest and much more in line with the consensus among the
> forecasting community. But Ric Simes owned these forecasts and
> he argued that they were plausible and responsible. I was sceptical
> of the capacity of the economy to deliver the tax cuts because
> I was sceptical of the forecasts.[14]

Dawkins' office chief Tony Harris said:

> There was a big tussle between Keating's office and the Treasury
> over the forecasts. Dawkins' office had little to do with this because
> we didn't have the independent firepower. The Treasury was very
> opposed to these forecasts and relented only reluctantly. Both the
> Treasury and Dawkins' office pressed Keating's office to abandon
> the tax cuts because they were not affordable. The truth, however,
> is that Dawkins was not in a strong political position.[15]

An economic adviser in his own right, Mike Keating took the unusual
step of attending the final meeting of the forecasting group. He said: 'The
concern about the forecasts was real. My recollection is that while the
Treasury did not like it, they eventually had to acquiesce. I think the
forecasts were defendable in terms of Keating's package. But I was sceptical
at the time about the tax cuts and whether they could be delivered with
the reduction of the budget deficit that was foreshadowed.'[16]

Dawkins has said that 'in the end we had no choice but to embrace
the figures that were produced'. It was a time of agony and loyalty. 'I wasn't
going to pull the rug from Keating,' said Dawkins.

> I had made my own decision years before that we wanted Keating
> as prime minister. He had now devised this political/economic
> strategy to try to win the next election. We knew that *Fightback!*

was riddled with defects and my view was that if they are playing that game then so can we. Keating and I were at one on the political strategy to defeat *Fightback!* If that meant embracing some optimistic scenarios then that was okay with me.[17]

The Treasurer had political cover: these were not official Treasury forecasts. It was a neat rationalisation that allowed him, if necessary, to disown the numbers.[18] Tony Harris said that 'Dawkins was very loyal to Keating' but lacked any political leverage against him. 'Given Keating's experience he would automatically prevail over Dawkins.'[19]

One Nation is the bridge that took Keating's 1980s policies into the 1990s. It constituted three ideas fundamental for modern Labor: support for an open competitive economy in the teeth of recession; the revival of Labor's nation-building profile with new infrastructure pledges; and an assertion of Labor as the party of tax reform and relief. It would be a synthesis of the old and new Keating.

On 26 February 1992 at 7.30 p.m. Keating rose in the House and announced a four-year strategy 'to get Australia moving'. He sold the idea of an activist government tackling the recession: 'When I became prime minister a little over two months ago I pledged to fight the battle against unemployment and for economic recovery with all the energy I could muster.' He described travelling the nation for seventy days, meeting business people, union leaders, State governments and community organisations to determine spending programs.[20]

The public-sector stimulus centred on transport infrastructure—spearheaded by a standard Brisbane-to-Perth rail gauge, a new roads program and a series of initiatives to upgrade the national electricity grid. There was an array of targeted measures to assist families, vocational training and industries such as cars and tourism. Here was Keating the nation-builder in the tradition of Fisher, Chifley and Whitlam. In truth, the stimulus had little impact on the downturn. Mike Keating later said it was 'modest' and Cole said it was less than Treasury had wanted.[21] The stimulus was delivered too late, a mistake that future Treasury chief, Ken Henry, was determined to avoid in his advice to Kevin Rudd during the 2008 global crisis.

Keating's statement was more important for what it kept than what it abandoned. He made not a single concession on any policy that mattered to him—none—not deregulation, tariffs or privatisation. There was no retreat on any of the structural pro-market policies that he designed as treasurer and that the ALP hated. The polish sparkled but it was the same

Keating car. He fooled the Labor Party at every step. The real economic strategy was to return the Budget to surplus in five years and secure a low-inflation, high-productivity growth path.

Keating's message was that Labor would achieve recovery more quickly without Hewson's polarisation of the nation. This is the reason he branded his statement *One Nation*—an irony given that Keating would later be seen as an agent of division.

The key to the politics—call it the Houdini factor—was the tax cut. Keating's income tax cuts would trigger at two points—July 1994 and January 1996—which would see the 30 cents tax rate applying across the income range $20 700 to $40 000. This matched Hewson's pledge. Labor would entrench middle Australia on a lower 30 per cent marginal rate without any GST. The difference was that Keating had a 40 cent rate from $40 000 to $50 000. The tax cuts, like Hewson's, would not kick in for another two and a half years. Any suggestion that they were a recession-busting measure was a joke.

Political correspondent Laura Tingle wrote: 'A massive medium-term budget commitment was being made without the Treasurer, or anyone else in the cabinet, being told about it until it was a *fait accompli*.'[22]

With his neck on the line Keating trusted nobody but his loyalists. These would become the most contentious tax cuts ever put to an election. The numbers tell the story: the extra fiscal stimulus over the first two years at $1.9 billion was dwarfed by $8.64 billion for the first two years of tax cuts. The strategy was subtle: by matching Hewson on the income tax cut Keating was exposing the GST for the kill.

The government was fractured on the viability of Keating's election strategy. Tony Harris said: 'Whenever the issue came up, Dawkins' office was wholeheartedly with the Treasury that the income tax cuts were not affordable. We wanted them shelved. My view was that they should not have been announced.'[23]

The 1992 winter was Keating's darkest night. On 9 July unemployment rose above 11 per cent; full-time unemployment for fifteen to nineteen-year-olds reached 35.8 per cent. The media talked about a 'double dip' recession. Keating raged behind closed doors at the press gallery and what he would do to them. In public he took responsibility but still refused to apologise for the recession.

Within six months of its delivery the *One Nation* forecasts were a shambles—the revenue projections were not strong enough to finance Keating's tax cuts. The tax cuts, quite simply, were unaffordable. The

Treasury told Dawkins he needed new or higher taxes in the Budget. In the week starting 13 July, Keating and Dawkins brooded over Treasury forecasts for the next month's Budget. While *One Nation* had projected a return to surplus in 1995–96, Treasury was now showing an $8 billion deficit. The total turnaround was $10 billion. There was no escape—the problem was chronic revenue weakness.[24] It would contaminate and then terminate Dawkins' career.

'I would say to Keating,' he ruminated years later, 'that the difference between my situation now and yours as treasurer is low inflation. You didn't have low inflation, and low inflation means low revenue.'[25] So Dawkins decided to put new taxes into the Budget to make the income tax cuts over 1994 and 1996 look more feasible. Confronted with this, Keating vetoed the proposal.

'We had to contain the deficit yet pay the tax cuts,' Dawkins said. 'I wanted new tax measures. But Keating said, 'No, don't do that, just say in the Budget that if things don't turn out, then we will look to new revenue measures.' That was the formula we used.'[26] It appears on page 13 of Dawkins' August 1992 Budget speech.

The Budget was a badly received embarrassment. Dawkins had to abandon the *One Nation* 'return to surplus' deadline of 1995–96 and flag the prospect of several new tax measures. The 1992–93 deficit was forecast at $13.4 billion, whereas *One Nation*'s projection was $8 billion. For much of the media, the government was beyond the pale. It was dismissed on a weekly basis.

With his fiscal credibility torn apart, Keating, as usual, summoned up his imaginative powers. He took aim at Hewson's obsessive criticism of special interests—from business to welfare to greens. Enjoying himself immensely, Keating gave a devastating 2 September interview on the *7.30 Report*. With his eye for political psychology, Keating discerned the chink in Hewson: faced with a government he should have long since despatched, Hewson had developed a siege mentality. Keating told Kerry O'Brien: 'This week he attacked the nurses, he attacked the teachers, he said if you drive down an Australian street you can pick all the houses where the renters are, he is into renters. He is into BHP, Toyota and Ford, the Reserve Bank, the Tax Office, the Treasury, the Japanese … Almost everybody is out of step but him.'

Anxious to address his fiscal credibility problem, Keating next decided to legislate his *One Nation* tax cuts. What better way to purge the doubts that they could be paid in several years' time? It was a political stunt, pure and simple. Normally, tax cuts for 1994 and 1996 would be legislated after the election, closer to their start date. But on 16 September, Dawkins introduced the bill into the parliament, saying it would 'implement' the *One Nation* tax cut pledge 'without resort to the introduction of a broadly based consumption tax'. They were not just a promise, they were L-A-W. So they became the LAW tax cuts and were known, famously and infamously, by this title hereafter.

By early November, sensing his ascendancy, Keating wanted to tighten the noose. He decided before Question Time on 5 November to announce that Labor in Opposition would not oppose a GST in the Senate. Don Watson later recalled the staff reaction: 'No one spoke … we nodded. Greg Turnbull expressed the concern the rest of us, including the Prime Minister, doubtless felt—that it might be interpreted as capitulation.'[27] It sounded as though Keating was conceding election defeat.

Listening to their leader's declaration that afternoon, the Labor backbench was surprised and aghast. The Liberals were delirious, laughing, cheering and taunting Keating across the chamber. Reith rose to thank him for agreeing that Labor would vote for a GST. But by evening the mood had changed: the long-run impact began to settle. Keating knew that the essence of power is making decisions that close off options. That requires a judgement about when to commit and when to stay free. He was declaring that there was no escape: a vote for Hewson meant a GST.[28]

This was the *One Nation* strategy that Keating took to the 1993 election. Of course, as Don Russell said, 'Keating still had to win it.' But Hewson believed *One Nation* was political robbery. This claim gained authenticity after the election when Keating and Dawkins were forced to abandon the tax cut timetable despite its LAW status. The orthodoxy, for years, was that *One Nation* had been a fraud.

As usual, the truth is more complex. In an analysis for this book, Ric Simes, the key figure behind the projections, reached a different conclusion. This was independently supported by Mike Keating. The feature of the economic recovery was strong growth and weak revenue. Simes said:

> The key forecasts prepared by the *One Nation* working group—for economic growth from 1993–94 to 1995–96—proved to be very accurate. Indeed, as accurate as could be expected in any medium-term forecasts. This was the issue that generated most debate and led to the largest refinements of the model. I was of the view that

the initial forecasts for economic growth, for technical reasons, were unduly low. After working through these issues, the group accepted that position.[29]

It is a point Cole conceded. 'Ultimately, of course, the economy did grow that fast,' he said of the recovery where growth was about 4 per cent per annum.[30]

However, Simes concedes that some forecasts 'turned out to be inaccurate and created complications for economic policy in following years'. Where was the error? It was in the immediate years—in the forecast budget deficit for 1991–92 and 1992–93. Simes said both were determined within the bureaucracy. His working group agreed 'not to question' the official numbers for these two years, which came from Treasury and the Tax Office. There was 'no real debate' about these numbers. As a consequence 'any suggestion the Prime Minister's Office was responsible' for the inaccurate forecasts 'is quite wrong' and is 'either extremely disingenuous or the result of Chinese whispers'.

The problem was that the official forecasts 'expected the economic recovery to occur much earlier than it did and seriously underestimated how much the budget deficit had widened'. Because the starting point deficits in 1992 and 1993 were worse than realised, the Budget in coming years 'would take longer to return to surplus'.[31]

In his own analysis, which offered support for Simes' position, Mike Keating argued that there were two mistakes. First, the working group seriously overestimated inflation feeding into revenue overestimates, a mistake that nobody picked up. Second, the initial base year's figures from the Tax Office to the working group were too optimistic and underestimated the extent of the budget deficit. His conclusion was that if Simes had relied more on official or Treasury advice, then, in some respects, the *One Nation* forecasts 'would have been even worse'.[32] Tony Harris said: 'In the end, Keating's office did prove to be more accurate than Treasury.'[33] Paul Keating has rubbished any hint of deliberate deception, saying, 'The forecast represented the best collective judgement at the time.'[34]

The conclusions are fairly simple. The Working Group was a political device to give Keating maximum control and influence over the parameters for *One Nation*. The politics of the package penetrating to Keating's re-election were more important than the economics and they triumphed over the economics. But *One Nation* was not a fraud. The advisers made a collective misjudgement primarily because forecasting in the trough of a recession is notoriously difficult.

The statement, however, embodied a strategic mistake identified later by Treasury's tax expert, Greg Smith. The key to Keating's income tax cuts in the 1980s was their financing by bracket creep—but the recession, by killing inflation, had also killed this technique.[35] The 1990s was a new world with new rules. Put another way, Tony Cole said *One Nation* was the 'death knell' of using a fiscal stimulus to turn around the economy because 'it took too long to work and then it took too long to unwind'.[36] The *One Nation* tax cuts posed a threat to Australia's national savings by accentuating bigger budget deficits for longer. For Cole, this was basic to the story of the 1990s—'Keating was left with budget deficits that were too high for too long.'[37] They would become a gift for John Howard.

From the August Budget onwards it was obvious that the *One Nation* tax cuts were undeliverable as pledged. Economics editor Alan Wood declared that Keating and Hewson were perpetuating a 'big lie'—they both offered packages that could not survive post-election. Wood said: 'The really tough decisions will come when the new federal government, whether Labor or Coalition, has to face up to abandoning, as quickly as possible, the fiscal policy promises on which it was elected.'[38] This proved to be true.

The politics of Keating's re-election strategy was in conflict with the economics—that was the price he would pay after the election.

4

KEATING LAUNCHES THE CULTURE WAR

I pressed the starter's pistol on the history wars, no doubt about that.
—Paul Keating, May 2008

In his second month as prime minister, Paul Keating launched Australia's culture war as a frontline struggle over identity. The timing was exquisite—27 February 1992—the trigger being the official visit of Elizabeth II, the Queen of Australia. At this point Keating signalled that he would make culture and identity core issues of his prime ministership.[1]

This inaugurated the struggle over political culture between Paul Keating and John Howard that, in its symbols, would stretch until November 2007. Its essence lay in nationalism, identity and Australian history. Because this penetrated to the nation's wellsprings it would touch many aspects of Australian life—the ANZAC ethos, war history, the Constitution, the head of state, multiculturalism, Aboriginal reconciliation, school curriculum, relations with Asia, racial tolerance and egalitarianism.

Keating's motive, ultimately, transcends electoral politics. This was in his political character. He remains proud of what he did—demanding that Australians reconsider what it means to be Australian. 'I pressed the starter's pistol on the history wars,' he boasted when interviewed in 2008.[2] Keating thinks that history will vindicate his position and condemn Howard, even if vindication takes time.

It was the day after the launch of *One Nation*. Having travelled the short distance from the National Press Club where he spoke at lunch to Parliament House for Question Time, Keating could feel his prime ministership gaining traction. Equipped with a new economic policy, he unleashed his aggression—he would assault the Coalition in its heartland.

Keating was angry at Liberal Party criticism of his management of the Queen's visit. His behaviour had been impeccable but his formal speech three days earlier at the reception for the Queen and Duke of Edinburgh signalled his ambition to transform Australia.

Congratulating the Queen on the fortieth anniversary of her reign, Keating adopted the theme of how much 'we have all changed'. Australia was now shaped by a new generation taking the nation into Asia. 'Our outlook is necessarily independent,' he told the gathering. 'That independence in part was reflected in your becoming, in 1973, Queen of Australia. In 1992, it is reflected in our growing sense of national purpose.'[3] In the next breath he thanked the Queen for visiting and finished a speech of spartan politeness. With her ear for politics, the Queen of Australia would have got the message.

There was no ritualistic reference to the glories Australia had inherited from Britain, the ties of kin, language, war and culture. Keating declined to praise a British past. This was because he intended to dismantle the final constitutional link with Britain and enshrine an Australian republic. If public opinion permitted, he would also get a new flag. At the reception Keating was solicitous of the diminutive Queen's welfare, introducing her to MPs and senators of all parties, at one stage guiding her progress with his hand at her back. Whether his hand or fingers touched the Royal Person will remain unknown forever.

Keen to match Keating for aggression, John Hewson threw a punch when he saw an opening. At once he accused Keating of making a political speech and failing to show respect for the Queen. John Howard, with a premonition of Keating's plans, called the reception 'insultingly low key' and defended the golden age of the 1950s. He would not tolerate Keating's patronisation of Australia's past. Keating treated such remarks with scorn: here were the senior Liberals of the 1990s defending the Crown against Australian authenticity. He had a surprise for them.

The British tabloids provided a comic backdrop to this quasi farce. Their reporters, eyes straining for colonial misdemeanours, discerned that Keating, in his scrupulous attention to Her Majesty, extended an arm towards her back. They dubbed Keating 'Lizard of Oz' and screamed 'Hands orf Cobber!' Annita's failure to curtsy became a calculated insult in tabloid land. It was great fun. Keating, who had entertained the Queen with discussions of imperial architecture, was happy to be provoked. His target was the Rule Britannia crew on the other side of the chamber. [4]

During Question Time, amid his answers about tax and the economy, Keating took a Dorothy Dixer to parody his opponents, a parody that turned to fury. He said:

I should never have made that remark about independence to the Queen of this continent. I should have had more respect. How dare I even reflect modestly on the British bootstraps stuff? Of course we then had a flurry of comment by the honourable member for Bennelong [Howard] about the 1950s and what a very good period that was—he said it was a very, very good period, a golden age. That was the period when gross domestic product per head was half what it is now; when commodities occupied 85 per cent of our exports; when telephones were half what they are now; when there were half as many cars per thousand people of population; when pensions were half their real value of today and when 10 children per 1000 went to university instead of 30 per 1000. That was the golden age when Australia stagnated. That was the golden age when Australia was injected with a near-lethal dose of fogeyism by the conservative parties opposite, when they put the country into neutral and where we very gently ground to a halt in the nowhere land of the early 1980s …

It was a time of 'awful cultural cringe under Menzies which held us back for nearly a generation'. Warming to his theme Keating asked what 1950s icons might be installed in a museum of Australian cultural history:

The Morphy Richards toaster, the Qualcast mower, a pair of heavily protected slippers, the Astor TV, the AWA radiogram. And, of course, the honourable Member for Wentworth [Hewson] and the honourable Member for Bennelong could go there as well. When the kids come and look at them they will say, 'Gee, mum, is that what it was like then?' And the two Johns can say, 'No, kids. This is the future.' Back down the time tunnel to the future—there they are.

The House was roaring. Keating finished with the political knife. The chamber went quiet before its complete eruption:

I was told that I did not learn respect at school. I learned one thing: I learned about self-respect and self-regard for Australia—not about some cultural cringe to a country which decided not to defend the

Malayan peninsula, not to worry about Singapore and not to give us our troops back to keep ourselves free from Japanese domination. This was the country that you people wedded yourself to, and, even as it walked out on you and joined the Common Market, you were still looking for your MBEs and your knighthoods and all the rest of the regalia that comes with it.

At this point the Speaker asked Opposition MPs to cease interjections and gratuitously remarked that the Member for Bennelong 'is going to have a heart attack if his face goes any redder'. Keating said:

These are the same old fogies who doffed their lids and tugged their forelock to the British establishment ... We will not have a bar of it. You can go back to the fifties to your nostalgia, your Menzies, the Caseys and the whole lot. They were not aggressively Australian, they were not aggressively proud of our culture and we will have no bar of you or your sterile ideology.[5]

Keating was enjoying himself hugely. He was the warrior unleashed. Don Watson likened Keating to Ned Kelly with the Irishman's 'fanatic heart', a tempting insight. Yet Keating was more complex than Kelly—he manipulated his fanaticism according to his need. His denunciation was a release from the restraint that usually governs leaders yet a calculated tactic to break the pattern of politics, confuse his opponents and alter perceptions of the new prime minister. Keating, the agent of recession, now posed as agent of cultural liberation.

It was a double denunciation—the launch of a campaign to de-legitimise the Liberal Party for its betrayal of Australia's national interest and an attack on the long history of Australia's cultural provincialism. In this sense it was tacit recognition of conservative success in its long and successful hold on Australian identity. Keating wanted to break that hold.

While directed towards Hewson as Opposition leader, the real target was Howard. This was usual because Howard's star was in eclipse, with almost nobody contemplating his return to the leadership. But even in his demise, Keating sensed that Howard's values were the key to Liberal Party faith. Hewson was his opponent, but Howard was his philosophical enemy. It is as though Keating, with a sixth sense, had a premonition of Howard's ideological force and knew he must be buried, over and over again.

It was a declaration of cultural war against the Liberal Party, its founder Menzies, its faiths and its current leadership. No pollster would ever recommend such a crazy tactic. It came, literally, from nowhere. But

Keating's instinct constituted his own focus group. With the economy in recession Keating wanted a debate about identity. Hewson branded it a diversion, but Howard knew better. Howard knew what it meant. He saw that, with the Liberal Party ascendant, Keating, in his desperation, was striking at its heart.

Above all, this revealed the remarkable nature of Keating's nationalism and its equally remarkable evolution. There were two elements in Keating that drove his culture war: his faith as a radical nationalist in the anti-British Irish tradition and his modernist vision of a cosmopolitan Australia, a diverse, Asia-orientated republic.

The first nationalism was formed in his childhood: the Irish Labor tradition, the Jack Lang legacy and Ned Kelly romantic radicalism. The second arose from his political maturing and his patriotic conception of a modern and successful Australia in the globalised age. Both these sentiments were Keating's passion.

It is fair to say that Keating was the only Australian prime minister who belonged to the radical nationalist school. Indeed, he represented the last grasp of this romantic notion that ran from Henry Lawson to Manning Clark. As a radical nationalist, Keating rejected the legitimacy of the foundational idea of Australia—the concept of Australian Britons.

Australian nationalism originated in a duality of belief in nation and in Empire. Every important Australian prime minister, Labor and non-Labor, in the nation's first fifty years represented this fusion of nationalism and imperialism—Alfred Deakin, Andrew Fisher, Billy Hughes and John Curtin. They were Australian nationalists who put Australia first and they were British race patriots who championed the Empire. Deakin called himself an 'independent Australian Briton', a term now extinct. Hughes said: 'A man may be a very loyal and devoted adherent to and worshipper of the Empire and may still be a very loyal and patriotic Australian.' He included himself in this branding. At the start of the Great War, Fisher declared that Australia would fight to 'our last man and last shilling'. In the nation's darkest days of World War II Curtin pledged himself to save Australia as 'a citadel for the British-speaking race' and towards the end of the war he declared that Australia's future lay in family and racial ties of 'Empire cooperation'.[6] Such sentiments are striking in their intensity at times of crisis. During and after the war Curtin and Chifley wanted to intensify ties with Britain, not demolish them. They spoke as British race patriots whose view of Australian identity was close to that of Menzies. It is elementary, of course, that it made complete strategic sense for a small and isolated nation to bandwagon its influence via a great Empire.

Labor's cultivation of myths about Curtin has generated a false history In 1941 when Curtin made his 'look to America' statement in the Melbourne *Herald* he was confronting a security crisis, not trying to shift identity or seek independence from Britain. As for Keating's remarks about Britain and Singapore, military historian David Horner said: 'We [Australia] went along with the Singapore strategy and if we are to blame Britain we must equally blame ourselves.'[7]

Keating's idea that authentic Australian nationalism equated to anti-British sentiment for full independence misjudged the extent of national spirit and belittled the patriotism of the Australian people. The scholar of Australian nationalism, Neville Meaney, argues that Australians—unlike Americans—did not rebel against Britain and, as a result, 'they found it easy to accept their racial and cultural heritage as the basis for their idea of nationalism'. Meaney repudiated the radical nationalist story that generations of Australians were 'mindless products of cultural manipulation' in their attachment to Britishness and that Australian leaders had refused to pursue policies at odds with Britain.[8]

But Keating felt differently. He believed the 'whole flowering sense of nationalism was really finished in August 1914', destroyed by the Great War. The war was the occasion when 'conservative Australia essentially took it [nationalism] as their proprietary right and title'. As a consequence Keating saw Australian history in tribal terms—as the struggle between Labor's pro-independence disposition and the fawning lickspittles of conservatism perpetually genuflecting to Britain, then America, symbolised above all by a craven Menzies.[9]

This conviction, rooted in his Irishness, was reflected in his maiden speech filled with radical nationalist notions when he attacked Coalition MPs for being unable to 'think Australian', extending into his period as resources spokesman when he fashioned a nationalist resources policy in sympathy with supra-nationalist RFX Connor and, finally, it was affirmed by his success as treasurer in deregulating the economy when Keating interpreted the Liberal Party's prior failure to deregulate as proof of its lack of faith in Australia's ability and inventiveness.

Keating was drawing on a rich stream of Australian intellectual life. Many of Australia's cultural lions and its historians championed the radical nationalist school, with this polemic flowing into film, books and theatre. Peter Weir's film *Gallipoli*, with David Williamson as script writer, is a brilliant invocation of the radical nationalist myth. The school had a grip on Australian historiography, influenced by Marxism, romanticism and nationalism. Its most heroic work was Russel Ward's *The Australian Legend*, arguing the mythic version of a nation being defined by the values of its bushmen. No writer, however, did the legend greater service than Manning Clark, whose six-volume history of Australia degenerated towards the end into a radical nationalist fantasy. Seizing on Lawson's analogy, Clark subtitled his final volume 'The Old Dead Tree and the Young Tree Green' and insisted this was the choice facing Australia.

In Clark's fantasy, Menzies was the old dead tree, his life 'a tragedy writ large' because he stifled his conscience and talent in service to 'alien gods', becoming 'the darling of the British governing classes and the Royal Family', seeking ultimately the 'approval of the high and mighty' along with their British honours, a man who was seduced by baubles and dishonoured his country. Curtin, by contrast, was the young green tree, a leader 'greatly loved' and 'praised as the "best and fairest" man in Australian public life', charismatic with 'an abundance of wisdom' and inspired by 'a great dream' of Australia, a dream whose fulfilment was denied by his death so that Curtin never had 'the glory of teaching Australians how to cultivate "The Young Green Tree"'.[10]

Lawson and Clark said Australians had to choose between the old dead tree and the young green tree. But the Australian people, wisely, decided this was a false choice. They repudiated Lawson and Clark. For much of Australia's first century the people chose to be Australian *and* British. They elected Curtin and they elected Menzies. They were patriots and, mostly, they respected the Queen.

At the start of the 1988 bicentennial year Clark had declared that 'the coming of the British was the occasion for three great evils: the violence against the original inhabitants of the country, the Aboriginals; the violence against the first European Labor force in Australia, the convicts; and the violence done to the land itself.'[11] He captured perfectly the growing hostility of historians towards white male British originating authority.

Keating hardly knew Clark, who had died six months before Keating became prime minister. He loved Clark's interpretation of Australia as a struggle between the 'enlargers' of national life and the 'straighteners and punishers', quoting this in his tribute and raising it repeatedly over the years. He called Clark a 'very kindly person' and, in an affectionate touch, said Clark had embraced many of Labor's values just as Labor had 'adopted some of his values'.[12] Keating, long a convert to the radical nationalist cause, mobilised Clark as a useful ally.

In his history Clark wrote that 'accounts of the past became part of the struggle for power in Australia'—a precise summary of what the

culture war meant.[13] Don Watson said Keating wanted to 'reclaim' the
national story from the conservatives and the straighteners.[14] The arts
industries swooned. Weak on public policy but strong on fantasy, they
applauded Keating for this crusade.

In his view of Australia's past Keating broke from his Labor predecessors Gough Whitlam and Bob Hawke. Neither had such a tribal
perception of history nor such an obsession with cultural re-engineering.
Facing a desperate situation, Keating's launch of the culture war became
not only an assault on the conservatives—it began to rally the Labor
spirits. Watson now observed new recruits for Keating: sections of the
intelligentsia, radio jocks, artists, advertisers and designers. The political
landscape had been redrawn. Attitudes researcher, Hugh Mackay, suddenly found his focus groups were 'astonished by the turnaround in their
own feelings about Paul Keating'.[15]

But there was a trap. Australians don't loathe their past. The trouble
for the radical nationalist school and for Keating was that this interpretation of Australia's past was insulting. Its attitude towards the Australian
people was patronising. Its view of history was highly dubious. For
Keating, it was an ineffective method of pulling votes as opposed to staging a distraction.

Ultimately Keating redirected his campaign onto a firmer footing.
He focussed the contest on the different patriotic visions held by the
Labor and Liberal parties. Keating's conception of patriotism rested in the
daring notions of republic, Aboriginal reconciliation, engagement with
Asia and a modern internationalist economy—and he charged that the
Liberals were devoid of a modern patriotism. This was a debate about
the future, not the past. Keating's problem, however, was his refusal to
leave the past alone.

In March, Keating went to Adelaide Writers' Week to launch a
novel by Rodney Hall. He announced that Australia was 'healthier when
the arts flourish' and that the nation should not remain 'what Manning
Clark called Austral-Britons'. Watson reported that the audience clapped
and whistled. Unemployment headed towards 11 per cent.[16] Once the
cultural sector identified a leader as sympathetic to their causes, they
tended to forgive the bigger policy failures. For a leader under siege such
as Keating, this was both convenient and therapeutic.

Keating seemed to be shifting the nation's mood—or, at least, the
mood of some of the nation's people. On St Patrick's Day he said that
Australians should 'reclaim their history'. Context is everything in politics
and Keating was creating a new context; he was altering the way people

saw him. The once narrow-cast socially conservative Catholic MP who embodied the skullduggery of the New South Wales right wing and who graduated to become the pro-market treasurer scoffing at 'Balmain basket-weavers' was now attracting a constituency that once scorned him. This was not necessarily smart but it was therapeutic.

The risks were exposed when he attacked the flag. This was a reminder that Keating's culture crusade was a haphazard process of diversion and experimentation. In early February 1992 Keating told the media that he didn't think 'the Australian flag should have the flag of another country in the corner of it'. It was not widely known that Keating loathed the flag or, at least, its top left quarter. The flag, he said, left the impression 'that we're still in some kind of colonial relationship with Britain'. The conservatives were outraged and that made Keating even happier.[17] He wanted to get Australians talking about something new in their pubs, clubs and workplaces.

Visiting Indonesia in April 1992, Keating, buoyed by meeting with President Soeharto, said the Australian flag 'must change'. Hewson seemed incredulous when handed this gift—the Prime Minister had repudiated the flag when visiting a foreign country. How many leaders could match that? When parliament resumed in late April, Opposition MPs had miniature Australian flag on their benches. Hewson, Tim Fischer and Howard mounted an orchestrated provocation of Keating and he succumbed.

During a Question Time devoted to the flag, Keating lost his judgement and, towards the end, he seemed to become unhinged. Howard asked for a guarantee that he would not change the flag without a referendum. 'I do regard the flag as an ambiguous representation of our nation,' Keating replied, 'and I believe it ought to be changed.' His concession was not to make any change 'without clear evidence of public support'. In response to Hewson he said the government would not be rushed by 'lickspittles like you'.[18]

Hewson accused Keating of being a 'wrecker, in true Jack Lang style', ready to 'tear down' the flag for his short-term political needs. Mocking Keating's argument, he asked: 'Could honourable members imagine Lee Kuan Yew coming out to Australia and sitting down and saying, "I have a real problem at home—that flag has just destroyed our chance of being an independent nation"?'

In response Keating again targeted Howard as well as Hewson, insisting that the flag had to be changed 'to make our way in the world'. He defended Jack Lang because Lang knew the conservatives were 'snivellers to forces abroad, crawlers to forces abroad, lickspittlers to forces abroad' and they had not changed. 'Menzies, their founder, tried to separate and distinguish Britain's interests from those of Australia and, in the end, could not,' Keating charged. 'They do not understand Australian nationalism. Those opposite do not comprehend the notion of nationhood; they do not advance our nationhood; they have never understood it; they have always thought it subordinate and derivative.' But it was not, he said, and 'it never will be while ever the flag of Labor flies in this country'.[19] He was Lang, Lawson and Clark rolled together.

Howard listened throughout, convinced Keating's tactic was electoral poison. The iron had entered Howard's soul. Keating wanted a war over nationalism, history and culture. Well, Howard would give him that war.

Keating had to surrender on the flag. Indeed, the flag proved to be more popular than Keating, his government or the Labor Party. But he stuck by his campaigns to re-engineer the Constitution, break from Britain, reinterpret Australian history and reshape the ANZAC legend. Keating was serious about the culture war. It made him, eventually, a hero to the creative class and a deeply polarising agent in the country—loved and despised. And it revealed his fatalism—Keating was telling people they would have him on his own terms or not have him at all.

Interviewed sixteen years later, Keating displayed an undiminished contempt for Menzies. 'If he didn't want to be an Australian prime minister, why did he bother? Why didn't he pack it in, go to Britain and get himself a seat in the House of Commons or in the Lords?'[20] He ignored the alternative view—that Menzies' seven election wins confirmed that he represented a great body of Australian national sentiment running far beyond the Liberal Party.

The culture war initiated by Keating between February and April 1992 would enshrine a more intense debate about nationalism in Australian politics. This debate would run for the next fifteen years with a momentum that Labor could not envisage.

By 1992, Howard had sat in parliament for eighteen years. But Labor had misread him. Keating was blinded by his propaganda that Howard was a mini-Tory, a Menzies throwback and a groveler to London. It never occurred to Labor that Howard in office would seize the mantle of nationalism for the Liberal Party. It was an idea, literally, too fantastic for the Labor mind.

5

THE DEATH OF NEO-LIBERALISM

*The political home of neo-liberalism in
Australia is, of course, the Liberal Party itself.*
—Kevin Rudd, February 2009

The 1993 election extinguished more than John Hewson's dreams—it terminated the neo-liberal political experiment. This was the conclusion of both Paul Keating and John Howard and they operated on this assumption. 'Big bang' liberalism was finished as an ideology and a strategy for the Liberal Party.

Hewson's *Fightback!* program was the only package resembling neo-liberalism ever presented to the Australian people. Its defeat was a turning point. No future leader—not Keating, not Howard, not Treasurer Costello—would contemplate the model or its specifics as a package. This was the conclusion from the 1993 election despite occasional polemical claims that Howard as prime minister was actually a neo-liberal.

The claim won its greatest traction in early 2009 when Prime Minister Rudd, in a significant analysis, accused the Liberal Party of being 'the political home of neo-liberalism in Australia' and attacked the Howard government for being the local champion of the neo-liberal philosophy that had brought the world to the financial precipice.[1] Such claims generated a political bandwagon. But they cannot be sustained by the story of Australian public policy. It is tempting for Labor to depict the demise of Australian neo-liberalism in 2007 with Howard's fall but the only tenable location for such an event is the 1993 poll.

Hewson's defeat had an elemental impact within the Liberal Party: it drove the Liberals back towards the middle ground. The Liberal Party would have to decide on a new leader and a new strategy to replace the doomed *Fightback!* and its flawed crusader. Defeat left the Liberals devastated, confused and vulnerable.

The 1993 loss was strategic and tactical. John Hyde, the intellectual leader of the Liberal free market lobby—or 'Drys'—from the 1980s, said:

> The disappointment was particularly acute because Hewson had attempted two things that Drys had advocated. The first was to move on a broad front as had been done in New Zealand. The second had been to pre-announce a comprehensive reformist agenda, rather than just elements of it, and therefore to obtain a comprehensive mandate.[2]

Neither approach would be repeated.

The swing to Labor was 1.5 per cent in two-party-preferred terms and Keating increased Hawke's 1990 majority from nine to fifteen seats. Defeat represented an historic low for the Liberal Party. An unforgiving Malcolm Fraser declared: 'The Liberal Party has lost the most winnable election since 1949. It should have been just as winnable as 1975. The majority should have been at least 30 seats.'[3]

After the defeat, Liberal Party Director Andrew Robb said: 'Sadly, the bottom line was that the more information that people were given about the *Fightback!* plan, the more questions it raised, the more apprehensive they became and the more susceptible to Labor's scare campaign.'[4] Robb's message was that *Fightback!* could not sustain a long campaign. Reith's adviser and *Fightback!* advocate Peter Hendy concurred, saying 'the election was probably lost back in August 1990 when the Coalition adopted the GST as the centrepiece of its taxation policy'.[5]

Howard and Costello saw Hewson as the problem. Howard recognised that *Fightback!* and Hewson had been fused. The 'major flaw' had been Hewson's political weakness and 'once people doubted the author's grasp of a radical document they would inevitably begin to doubt the document'. For Howard, Hewson was finished and the party had to rethink.[6] Costello said:

> There was enormous anger when we lost. People turned on us. People walked up to me in the street and said things like 'I wanted to get rid of Keating but you made it impossible.' I thought we had lost because of Hewson's miscalculation. He did not have the experience to know which policy issues the public would stomach and which ones he should leave alone.[7]

Politicians hate to lose any election. The historical view, however, must be that defeat was a blessing for the Liberals. It is fanciful to think that Hewson would have been a successful prime minister. In 1993 the Liberal Party endured a humiliation in defeat but it escaped the catastrophe of victory. Even Hewson's new deputy, Michael Wooldridge, said: 'If he had won I think Hewson would have been a one-term prime minister.'[8]

Hewson's defeat terminated his effort to recast the Liberals as a party of economic liberal ideology. This was a bridge too far. Post-election Fraser charged that Hewson had overlooked the party's Menzian character, saying:

> The Liberal Party in its years of success believed in strong government acting in partnership with the private sector. It had a profound sense of obligation to all Australians. Above all, the party achieved a sense of balance of public policy. It is that sense of balance which has been so sorely lacking.[9]

But Fraser laid a direct charge against Hewson: 'It is extraordinary and tragic that people could have so little sense of history as to try to take the progressive and liberal party of Menzies back to 1776 and the doctrinaire, totalising synthesis of Adam Smith. It is even more remarkable that the majority of the Party were so silent during that process.'[10] As one of Hewson's targets, Fraser wanted to nail this story.

There is a difference between integrating policies that are economically liberal into the Liberal Party (the position of Howard and Costello) and seeking to impose economic liberalism as a universal philosophy— the real meaning of Hewson's *Fightback!* Classic political liberalism in the British tradition drew on Adam Smith and John Stuart Mill, with an enshrining emphasis on individual liberty, limits on state power and firm moral foundations. But this political movement did not survive as a major force in Britain.

The convulsions in British politics before the Great War brought the demise of liberalism. This story was captured in a 1935 epic of political writing, *The Strange Death of Liberal England*, by George Dangerfield, a book that has recently returned to fashion. Dangerfield wrote that pre-war liberalism and its belief in 'free trade, a majority in parliament, the ten commandments and the illusion of progress' can never return. 'It was killed or it killed itself in 1913.' Its glorious symbols endure in Mr Gladstone, the novels of Charles Dickens and the repeal of the corn laws, Britain's famous import tariffs.[11]

In Australia, classic liberalism was weak. Post-Federation, Alfred Deakin united the non-Labor parties in the 1909 fusion that established the Liberal Party on the principle outlined by historian WK Hancock: state power at the service of individual rights. Australian Liberalism championed the policies of protection, arbitration and state paternalism—an economic framework that delivered sub-optimal results for most of the twentieth century. Deakin had tied the tradition of progressive liberalism to strong and interventionist government. This became the Australian model.

It was built into the Menzies party of the 1940s. Menzies coined the notion 'forgotten people' as the backbone of his support. But these people were nourished and supported by the state. They believed in the Menzies concept of 'private enterprise' but they were neither entrepreneurs nor exponents of economic initiative and liberty. Authentic liberals in the classic tradition were virtually extinct in Australia.

Howard's 1985–89 leadership was the first effort to inject the philosophy of economic liberalism into the Liberal Party. This became a more ambitious project under Hewson, who was unaware of the full implications of his experiment.

With the 1989 fall of the Berlin Wall and rise of globalisation, Francis Fukuyama proclaimed in *The End of History and the Last Man* that liberal democracy may constitute 'the end point of mankind's ideological evolution'.[12] This book, coinciding with Hewson's leadership, was a hubristic high tide for economic liberals. Fukuyama did not write about economics but the triumph of 'free market' was integral to his thesis.

The truth, however, is that economic liberalism, while a powerful idea, is far from powerful in the political arena. It runs into conflict with contemporary political culture that looks to the state, not the individual, to solve problems from unfairness to obesity. In the Western world there are few, if any, political parties that embrace economic liberalism as their essential ideology, certainly not the Tories in Britain or the Republicans in America, the descendants of Thatcher and Reagan. The notion that the Liberal Party of Australia would cross this threshold was always unlikely.

The former chief of economics at the Organisation for Economic Co-operation and Development (OECD), David Henderson, an economic liberal, concluded: 'The fact is that economic liberalism as such has no solid basis of general support. In most, if not all, countries, majority opinion remains hostile to the idea of what is termed "leaving it to the market" and ready still to accept and endorse a much wider role for governments than economic liberals would wish to see.'[13]

When Hawke and Keating implemented pro-market policies from 1983 onwards they operated on a pragmatic basis, not an ideological one. They were searching for new policies that worked. Not surprisingly, they did not invoke Adam Smith, JS Mill or Friedrich Hayek. They sought re-election on performance, not as believers in economic liberalism as a philosophy. The Deakinite framework was demolished because of necessity, not because of any community or ideological demand for economic liberalism.

Analysing the post-1983 era, historian Gregory Melleuish said:

> In an inchoate fashion Australian society has moved slowly along a liberal road, though often with little understanding of what this involves and with a sentimental attachment to the illiberal values of protectionist nationalism. Part of the problem here has been that the Australian national identity has often been portrayed in protectionist terms. This has put liberals on the defensive.[14]

Hewson's epitaph is that he tried to win an election on economic liberalism, a blunder of great proportion. He confused necessary policy with overall political philosophy.

The year 1992 saw a visceral combat in which Keating gained the ascendancy over Hewson. Keating's personal attacks hurt Hewson—depicting him as a 'feral abacus' and a heartless econocrat. Yet Hewson kept playing into Keating's hands. He kept attacking interest groups, thereby confirming the Keating message. At various times Hewson seemed to deride people who rented their houses; he had a brawl with the tourism industry that wanted GST relief; he had an even more damaging brawl with the car companies, including Ford's Jack Nasser and Toyota's Robert Johnson.

Don Russell offered an insight into Labor's political strategy:

> Hawke and Keating had devised a model. They controlled the debate, set the pace of economic reform and pushed the Liberals out to the Right. The Liberals were repeatedly trapped into promising faster reforms that were too risky for the public. In this sense Keating created Hewson. When elections came, Hawke and Keating would package up all the hostility towards economic reform and direct it at the Coalition. This technique reached its zenith at the 1993 election.[15]

Hewson seemed unable to grasp the fact that hostility for the recession was being transferred to him.

The demise of *Fightback!* was a two-stage process. In December 1992 Hewson was forced into a poll-driven retreat by the Liberal Party, which resulted in *Fightback!* Mark II and then in March 1993 he was defeated by Keating at the election. He was vanquished first by the Liberal Party and then by Labor.

In April 1992 after the election of an independent, Phil Cleary, in the Wills by-election for Bob Hawke's old seat, the writing was on the wall. On 15 April, at a Sydney strategy meeting, Robb delivered the bad news—the skilled and semi-skilled workforce was moving back to Labor. Keating was disliked for his arrogance, yet people were prepared to give him a second chance, recognising his toughness and strength.

The pressure on Hewson to restructure his package was immense. It was spearheaded by the Victorian Liberal Party, talking with fresh authority after the election of Victorian Liberal Premier Jeff Kennett on 3 October. Research commissioned by Victorian Director Petro Georgiou showed that the GST was an electoral disaster and likely to cost the federal Liberals as many as nine seats in Victoria alone. The Victorian situation was compounded by the industrial reforms pushed by Kennett—laws to remove entitlements from awards—notably the 17.5 per cent annual leave loading and penalty rates—and to restrict the right to strike. With an industrial confrontation looming, the Federal Liberals felt that Kennett would be seen as an early dose of Hewson's agenda.

Two veterans whom Hewson trusted, Andrew Peacock and Fred Chaney, urged a major change in *Fightback!* Robb's research showed that the more people focussed on the GST—and the campaign would bring this to a new pitch—the more they left the Coalition. Robb was desperate for Hewson to redesign *Fightback!*

Peter Hendy captured the mood:

> A morbid game during this period among senior staff was to think up possible Labor television ads attacking the GST. Most revolved around the theme of a little old lady wandering around a supermarket to be confronted with a bill which was 15 per cent more because of the GST when she reached the cash register. The old dear would then have to turn around and take back some of those 'essential' items.[16]

Unemployment in late 1992 had reached beyond 950 000, yet Keating's position grew stronger. It was an event almost without precedent. Hewson's GST had injected Keating with near immunity from the record jobless that his policies had helped to create.

The churches were destroying Hewson. Their pitch was simple—
the GST was immoral. The Catholic Social Welfare Commission and
the Uniting Church had campaigned against the GST since before its
release. In late 1992 the Commission produced a paper purporting to
interpret Catholic doctrine and arguing that the taxation of food was
immoral. It was symptomatic of the hysteria the GST had generated
and the manipulation of the moral authority of the church for political
ends. The Coalition sought a meeting with the Commission's board,
attended by Reith, Chaney, Richard Alston and David Connolly, only
to find that the discussions were leaked. The *Catholic Weekly* campaigned
repeatedly against the GST. Hendy said: 'The straw that appeared to break
the camel's back was the campaign waged against the Coalition's policies
by the religious community.'[17]

The Newspoll survey taken over 4–6 November had Labor leaping
to a 45–41 per cent lead. As Labor firmed in the polls, the Liberals grew
alarmed that Keating would call a December 1992 election. Such fears
were justified. On 12 November Don Russell wrote a private memo to
Keating: 'If we survive the October unemployment numbers there is still
a good case for a 19 December election—perhaps even a strong one.'
Trend unemployment had risen over six months from 10.6 per cent to
11.1 per cent. 'The choice you have to make,' said Russell, 'is whether it
is better to wait until next year and have to deal with unemployment that
may be trending upwards or go now.'

> At the moment we have the electorate convinced that Hewson is
> inflexible and hell bent on nasty structural change. We have made
> Hewson the issue to such an extent that people have taken their
> eyes off the recession. This has been quiet a feat. Unfortunately, it
> would not be that difficult for Hewson to break this spell—all he
> has to do is prove that he is a bit flexible after all. On this score
> he could adjust the GST rate on food or match our tariff changes
> for instance. I have never seen the caucus more keen about our
> story nor more keen to campaign … We do have a good chance
> of winning although much will depend on the campaign. It is
> true that the electorate may continue to harden its views about
> Hewson which is a reason for waiting but it would be a mistake to
> think that the Coalition will not change its approach.[18]

This note embodied Labor's hopes and fears.

For Liberals strategists it was a race—to modify *Fightback!* before
Keating called an election. Hewson said: 'The pressure from the party was

just enormous. A lot of people had got very nervous. Would they have thrown me out as leader if I hadn't backed off? Maybe, maybe not. I think it was too late to change leaders.'[19] This was correct. But Hendy said that, among the party's key decision-makers, 'frustration was fast building up to a critical point'.[20]

Keating decided over the 15–16 November weekend not to call a 1992 election. Once this became apparent to the Liberals the drive to modify *Fightback!* intensified. It was debated at a series of meetings in November and early December involving Hewson, Reith, Robb and their senior advisers. The situation testified to the psychological dominance Keating had established over Hewson. During these internal debates Hewson was calm—he wanted to be persuaded why he should retreat.

The Newspoll published on 8 December was the final straw. It showed Labor further ahead 47–40 per cent, with unemployment heading towards one million. For any self-respecting political leader this was unbearable.

Hewson announced he would recast his package to prepare for the expected poll in early 2003. The next morning's headline in the *Australian* read: 'Hewson Loses His Nerve'. Two days later Buckingham Palace announced that Charles and Diana would separate.

At the same time the November unemployment figure reached 11.4 per cent and Keating said: 'Whatever problems we've got today with unemployment, what would we have if there was a 15 per cent tax on everything?'[21] But Keating was worried.

As usual Hewson had acted unilaterally. He announced his decision at a doorstop outside the Anglican Cathedral in Brisbane after a meeting with Archbishop Peter Hollingworth. Reith was not involved in the final decision. National Party Leader Tim Fischer was woken during the night at a London hotel with news of the decision. 'Poor Tim fell out of bed,' Reith said. The colleagues were scrambling.[22]

Hewson launched *Fightback!* Mark II at the National Press Club on 18 December 1992. 'We have heard the concerns expressed by the major church groups and by other organisations representing the less privileged and most vulnerable members of society,' he said. Yet Hewson was diffident, almost self-conscious; the visionary was in eclipse.

He had two objectives. The first was to build a 'recession-busting' front-end stimulus onto *Fightback!*, which would involve bringing forward $2.8 billion of tax cuts for low- and middle-income earners as well as a $3 billion 'nation building' fund, the sort of infrastructure initiative that

Hewson used to ridicule. The second, designed to address the fairness critique, proposed measures to help families, the unemployed and the needy by excluding food and childcare fees from the GST, abandoning the proposal to phase out the dole after nine months and deferring tax cuts for the better-off.

But *Fightback!*'s medium-term structural integrity was kept: there was no change to industrial relations, tariff, monetary and Medicare policy or the principle of the GST. Hewson was left trying to sell two messages—the incorruptible conviction leader now wanted to win votes from pledges made and benefits extended. Hewson told the media: 'I did believe, genuinely believe, that *Fightback!* Mark I was fair in economic terms.' But 'when the churches, in particular, came out and suggested it was immoral to tax food we were on a hiding to nothing'.[23]

Robb argued that the new policy was a net bonus and that the 1993 defeat would have been greater. But Hewson looked weak; he was a conviction politician who had compromised his convictions.

Interviewed in 2008, Hewson saw the retreat as a disastrous blunder. It had been imposed on him; his heart wasn't committed. 'I think it was a mistake,' he said. 'I was under huge pressure to, at least, exclude food. My view of these concessions is that we stood to lose a lot and gain very little.'[24] However, retreat was the only viable option at the time.

But the summer and a lazy Labor Party would help Hewson. When Keating called the election on 7 February for 13 March the Opposition was favourite to win and the Newspoll taken over 5–7 February had the Coalition leading 45–40 per cent, back in front.

Keating would win the campaign. Robb said later that the Opposition was treated as though it was the government and the government came under less scrutiny that its policies warranted. The lesson is that oppositions should not behave as though they are governments.

The campaign was not without impressive performances by Hewson. The first television debate on 14 February saw Newspoll point to a Hewson win. The Liberal Party launch at the Wesley Central Mission in Sydney a fortnight from the vote was an effective US-style communications package based on personal testimonies from five Australians on stage depicted as representing 'the forgotten people'—a small businessman, a single mother, a housewife, a pensioner and a farmer.

Hewson revealed his potential to mobilise the community's anger, saying: 'Every time I hear this [term] social justice uttered from the other side I start to choke. Because I can't find anything fair or just in a million unemployed. I can't find anything fair or just in those 700 000 kids who are living in families with neither parent in a job.'[25] But the social justice conscience of the churches, no doubt, remained pure.

After an unimpressive campaign start, a desperate Keating turned all his firepower on the GST and Hewson eventually wilted. His most embarrassing moment came in a Channel Nine interview with Mike Willesee on 3 March when he failed, famously, to answer a question about how the GST would apply to a birthday cake. By now Keating had the lethal reply:'I say this to people: if you don't understand the GST, don't vote for it. And if you do understand it, you'll never vote for it.'[26] Keating won by making the election a referendum on the GST—much to Hewson's disgust since in 1985 Keating had been ready to put his job as treasurer on the line in support of such a tax.

Hewson's defeat demanded a tactical and strategic reappraisal. The tactical reappraisal for opposition parties has been translated into firm rules: don't release comprehensive policies too early; don't pretend to be governments; don't give too much detail; and avoid decisions that allow incumbents to make you the issue. It is now part of our political practice, courtesy of Hewson and Keating.

The strategic options for the Liberal Party post-1993 were three-fold. The first was a retreat to traditionalism. It was advanced by Malcolm Fraser and the academics Robert Manne and John Carroll who edited the 1992 *Shutdown:The Failure of Economic Rationalism*. Speaking as a critic of the post-1983 embrace of market economics, Fraser said:

> The Liberal Party has come to be regarded as the ideological party … Laid bare, economic rationalists believe that the role of government should be minimised, that the marketplace should be the supreme arbiter of economic activity.There is no evidence in all of history that policies based on such views have ever maximised production or employment.[27]

Manne said the GST disaster 'must be viewed as symptom of a more general illness which has afflicted the Liberal Party since 1983'. This was the 'unequivocal embrace' of economic rationalism. He argued that Hewson, far from complaining that Labor's reduction of tariffs was too slow, should have opposed these policies, a position that would have struck 'powerful populist chords'. Echoing Fraser, Manne said the notion of free market economics was in conflict with Australian political values and the middle class from which the Liberals had drawn their historical support. He wrote: 'If the Liberal Party wishes to reconnect itself to its natural constituency—the vast urban and rural property-owning middle and lower middle class—it must reshape its programme and rhetoric. It must cease to be the party of radical reform. It must become again the party of middle Australia.'[28]

Carroll, as one of Fraser's champions, said in a press interview. 'This is the worst loss in Australian federal political history.' He continued:

> The Coalition lost because it frightened the electorate with a politically insane and economically dubious GST … The ALP did not win the election. The Coalition lost it … The Liberal Party must regain its soul … The 1980s is finished as of last Saturday. Hewson, Reith, McLachlan were 1980s figures.[29]

Despite such convictions, an embattled Liberal Party agreed on one issue: there would be no return to Fraserism with state paternalism and economic protectionism. Senior Liberals were united on this. Every potential leadership alternative to Hewson espoused free market policy to a greater or lesser extent—Costello, Downer, Howard and Reith—and these figures were the party's future. The notion that the Liberal future was a return to Fraserism was a sentimental delusion. The politicians knew that any return to the discredited Australian Settlement framework would constitute a mortal blow for the Liberal Party.

The second position, advanced by John Hyde, was a plea to retain the *Fightback!* ideology. Hyde wrote:

> There was nothing wrong with the broad thrust of Coalition policy. More than that, in general terms there are no alternatives to it … we are not competitive and we have no hope of becoming so until we deregulate labour markets, eliminate protection, privatise the inefficient public sector, deregulate product markets including those for rural produce, eliminate inflation, place health care and education on an efficient and affordable footing and reform the taxation system.
>
> The Liberal Party now stands for something. And that something is not in the least discredited by the loss of a federal election by about 1.5 per cent of the vote to a Labor Party that is singing a Liberal song … What Liberals must do is to explain those policies in moral terms: in terms of the liberty of workers, of a fair shake for unprotected industry, of justice for all and compassion for the needy. They should make it plain that they, and certainly not the Labor Party, are the party that is opposed to privilege

for big unions, big government or big companies. They must, in Chifley's words 'put a light on the hill'.[30]

It was a magnificent plea but too late. Neither Hyde nor anybody else had answers to the challenges he posed. Radical policy reform can only be won by a party imbued with a reformist culture and steeped in the arts of mobilisation, propaganda and recruitment. The problem was not just Hewson's inexperience. The Liberal Party was not made for this task. Middle-class suburbia of the 'Forgotten People' was scarcely the recruiting ground for political agitators backing the ideology of Smith and Hayek.

It is true that economic liberalism was founded in a moral philosophy expounded by Adam Smith and refined by John Stuart Mill's view of liberty. Morality was basic to its British nineteenth-century existence. But in the twentieth century morality had been hijacked to deployment of state power for virtuous causes—despite its repeated abuses. Economic liberals lacked the political strategy to confront and defeat the powerful traditions of Marxism and social democracy.

The failure of Hewson and the Liberal Party in the 1990s was the inability to wrap economic liberalism with a moral narrative. The ideas of liberty, free choice, policy governed by public interest, the integrity of the revenue, repudiation of privilege and special deals either for unions or the 'big end of town' were rarely marketed. It was difficult for Liberal politicians to translate this morality into contemporary terms and slogans.

Hewson failed to tell Australians what sort of society *Fightback!* implied because he had not applied himself to this question. He did not know in a way that he could explain to the people and this omission was inexcusable. This is not just about presentation but an issue of deep policy formulation that concerns the role of the state, Australian egalitarianism and the link between individual rights and responsibility. Utterly missing from *Fightback!* was any sketch of what Australian society would be like under this philosophy. The human dimension was lost. It was an omission Howard would reflect on.

The third position was the least articulated, yet the instinctive answer. It was the shared view across much of the Coalition frontbench and it took more shape as the 1993–96 term evolved. It was the position of Howard, Costello and Downer. Their sentiment was to avoid any over-reaction filled with recrimination, to recognise the policy integrity and energy within *Fightback!*, to review policies applying a sharper test of what the people would accept, to return to the political centre but stand by the pro-market economic reform agenda and to avoid any early detailed policy release.

No senior figure outlined such a blueprint. The party was too devastated for that. But this 'middle way' pragmatism would prevail and Howard would become its chief exponent.

Howard believed that *Fightback!* was a product of its time. Given the recession, there had been an opening for radical policy. 'It was a plan and all the research was telling us that people wanted a plan,' said Howard. 'A more skilful leader would have won. We only lost the campaign. I thought *Fightback!* was good. The *Jobsback* (industrial relations) policy that I wrote almost entirely was quite a radical plan and we all felt very comfortable about it.' But the election had been lost—Howard knew the party needed a new approach.[31]

Costello thought there were problems with the policy but that Hewson's ineptitude was the key:

> There was a lot about *Fightback!* that I admired and supported— the GST to replace wholesales sales tax, a vigorous deregulation of the labour market, a winding down of tariff protection. But the trouble was that in significant areas it went too far or lost its focus. For example, in the tariff area it was zero tariffs by 2000. Now we will get to 5 per cent by about 2005 to 2010. So, it wasn't done with a political feel … It's intrigued me that in 1993 the Commonwealth Budget was in deep deficit and *Fightback!* was a program that funded itself but would have made no inroads in balancing the Budget. It was almost as though it existed in a vaccum in terms of fiscal policy. In crucial ways it overreached itself or its ineptness blunted good policy.[32]

In truth, Keating and Hewson had conspired to kill neo-liberalism. Keating would not let it live and Hewson was unable to save it. The death of 'big bang' reformism opened a new Liberal Party era. It would be defined, as usual, by leadership. The Liberal Party would search for a new leader to unite the party around a fresh strategy.

PART II

THE BIG PICTURE

6

ECONOCRATS AND BLEEDING HEARTS

*We are the people who can dream the big dreams and do
the big things. There are no bigger dreamers than in our office.
It's a mixture of econocrats and bleeding hearts.*
—Paul Keating, 12 March 1993, address to his staff
on the eve of the federal election

The Prime Minister who claimed vindication in the 1993 election
was a fantastic hybrid—a demolitionist and a dreamer. Keating
posed as a statesman and he stooped to manipulate cheap fears.
He got into the gutter to fight Hewson and then proclaimed Labor 'as
the party of enlargers'. He was shameless, schizoid and idealistic—it was
impossible to feel neutral about him. Keating's 1993 victory gave his 'big
picture' the political take-off that would inspire his followers and deliver
electoral death three years later.

Keating would be suffocated, finally, by his political imagination. The
omen was his election-eve address, given to his staff at Sydney's Imperial
Peking restaurant adjacent to the harbour, in which Keating branded his
office a mixture of 'econocrats and bleeding hearts' and loved the idea.
It fitted with how he saw himself changing. His message was that only
Labor could get the chemistry right so that Australia succeeded in the
globalised economy yet had a society that valued compassion. 'Econocrats
and bleeding hearts' was an evocative slogan for his 'big picture'.[1]

This branding told so much. Treasurer Keating would never have
spoken in such terms but Prime Minister Keating seemed thrilled by
the 'econocrats and bleeding hearts' synthesis. It constituted a bizarre
amalgam of the two dominant identities in his office: Don Russell, the
econocrat, and Don Watson, the bleeding heart. It signalled the demise
of the Hawke era since Hawke never envisaged this sort of construct. It

heralded a new type of Labor government guided by Keating's leadership vision. The 1993 victory would embolden that vision.

Keating wanted to open a fresh chapter of Australian history. Every song he sang was consumed by this thirst—from the Republic to the Redfern speech to competition policy. On the night, he called it 'the sweetest victory of all'—but it was only the sweetest if people agreed that it flowed from Keating's vision and not Hewson's folly, and such agreement was unlikely.

Because Keating acted out the 'great man' theory of leadership he felt he was changing the country—and a changed country lives by different rules. In his policy speech he told the people they were 'bringing into being a new Australia', yet there was scant evidence that most people actually wanted a new Australia. It was Keating who wanted it. Though battered by recession he grasped the role of conviction in nourishing the life of political parties. Appeals to tribalism and self-interest were not enough. Keating sought to invoke new faiths, economic and cultural, for Labor's soul. For his critics, it was a case of self-obsession.

Keating was never presumptuous enough to call this a New Light on the Hill—but that is an accurate label. Russell said that 'Paul never succumbed to the fantasy that he embodied the destiny of the nation.'[2] True, but Keating offered the nation a new vision of itself. This is why he became a Labor hero. Bill Kelty understood this first and appreciated it longest. It is why Kelty was so drawn to Keating, declaring many years later that he 'was and is Australia's political prophet and soul'. Many would mock that label, yet for Labor followers it had a plausibility.[3]

Beneath the political thrill were the unpalatable realities. Keating became enthralled by his vision—a union of high policy and escalating narcissism—but it was never backed by a political strategy. The idea of 'enlargement' is inspiring, but it does not spell votes. There was no political strategy to sustain the vision, no gameplan devised by Keating and his advisers to win voters for his policy construct. For a prime minister, this was a fatal oversight.

Keating adviser Allan Gyngell saw the truism that most missed:

> The longer he went, the more tedious Paul found politics and the more focussed he became on policy—whether it was Mabo or APEC, Indonesia or 'super'. The political staffers would get furious because they wanted him at the Dubbo RSL, but Paul's fascination, more and more, became policy ideas. This is how he liked to spend his time.[4]

The policy vision became Keating's passion and his indulgence. Policy became akin to a gigantic toy, an obsession legitimated by the national interest. His 'big picture' was a mixture of economic, social and cultural reforms, mainly realist and courageous long-run projects. But the nexus Keating cherished from the 1980s—tying the policy and politics together—had collapsed. His 'big picture' was seen as an exercise in elitism. It stands as a monument to his policy audacity but as a symbol of electoral failure, an equivocal aftermath.

Russell described Keating's 1993–96 term politely, saying: 'The perception developed that Keating had moved too far to the Left.'[5] But this perception reflected a reality chosen by Keating. He had moved too far from the Hawke/Keating brand of 1980s pragmatic politics—occupying and owning the middle ground.

This failure reflected Keating's distaste for contemporary politics. The documented breakdown between Keating and the ALP National Secretary, Gary Grey, on the road to the 1996 poll was not just over tactics—it was over rival conceptions of politics. Integral to Keating's 'big picture' was an existential view of leadership driven by courage and imagination—witness his Placido Domingo template—yet this clashed with a research-orientated view of politics driven by party professionals based on avoiding mistakes, precise and disciplined messages, policy directed at targeted constituencies and a measured style of leadership. Keating loathed this technique and the party functionaries who managed it; he hated the way their minds functioned and he could not tolerate their advice. His adviser Mark Ryan summed up Keating's attitude: 'We could have humoured Head Office, but for what? Lowest common denominator politics, play-it-safe stuff. That was never going to do the job anyway and it was never, ever, what Paul was about.'[6]

Keating's 'big picture' originated in a rational and deliberate judgment. Keating knew his time as PM was limited. This drove him to err on the side of audacity because he knew most leaders retrospectively regretted their erring on the side of caution. Gyngell said: 'Keating said to me of Bill Clinton that he had never met a leader with political skills of such a high order. Yet Clinton was a disappointment to him. In the end, he felt Clinton's tragedy was that he failed to sort out the goals he wanted to achieve.'[7] Keating knew what goals he wanted and set out to achieve them. He was aware of the risks but his indulgence meant he failed to devise any matching political strategy.

In his 'econocrats and bleedings hearts' speech Keating's duality was on remarkable display. As the evening breeze came off the harbour his mode was prime ministerial confidential. Keating dissected the voters with an unsentimental precision in his cold, sharp eye.

> They [the voters] are contemplating taking us back, not with any relish whatsoever. It's Hobson's choice, but we want their votes, not their appreciation. We love their votes but we don't particularly need their love. I think they understand that, actually. They've worked that out … they'd like to dispense with us but they're just not sure … We've done especially well on the campaign. We have brought the GST up to a fever pitch. We've made it the election issue … So we have pulled off a very big trick. We've kept ourselves alive politically at the aftermath of a recession.[8]

This was hard, stripped of any self-delusion, and razor sharp. Yet within minutes Keating was spinning his story of Labor dreams as he moved into a parallel True Believer reality zone. 'The other bastards have never had any ideas,' he said. 'We are the entrepreneurs of political life and we are the people who can dream the big dreams and do the big things. There are no bigger dreamers than in our office.'

In seeking to put Australia on a new path, Keating had a model that became the emotional and intellectual bedrock of his prime ministership. He saw that the ideology of the old Labor Party was dying and he sought to install a new engine, road tested at the 1993 poll.

The 1980s phenomenon of internationalisation had seeded a change in Australia's political culture: a move towards individualism, away from state-based solutions, more emphasis on individual rights and responsibilities, an erosion of the old egalitarianism and a fragmentation of power with the rising influence of corporations, markets, voluntary organisations and private initiative, along with loyalty to interest groups—from greens to gays. The task for government was to respond with new solutions and policies. This is what Keating did best; he loved this challenge and he couldn't stop talking about it.

During 1992 and 1993 Keating was formulating tactics not just for re-election but for Labor's long-run position. On display throughout the campaign, it was the work of a political mind that was more creative than consistent. In effect, Keating's 'big picture' involved three stories.

The first was the closest to his heart, arising from his work as treasurer—that Australia must stay true to the pro-market economic revolution of the 1980s and repel the barbarians storming the deregulatory model. By claiming the 1980s economic policy revolution as his own,

Keating made its repudiation by his own government an impossibility. His 1993 policy speech involved a personal dedication to this journey:

> Today a whole generation of Australians know that the world does not owe us a living. We are the first generation of Australians to really understand what it means … Towards the end of the 1970s … I became convinced that Australia could be more than a quarry and a farm; that we could find a place in the front rank of trading nations … in the early 1980s it very rapidly became apparent that the idea was not an option but an absolute necessity. We no longer had any choice. The story since then has been a remarkable one.

He was merciless in repudiating the claims of phoney prophets that so-called economic rationalism had failed. Keating saw new economic vistas unfolding. Indeed, his conviction that the recession would be followed by an unprecedented prosperity would be vindicated. For Keating, the market-based economy, far from ruining Australia's values, was the means to a more dynamic nation and greater personal opportunity. He tried hard to stimulate the public's imagination during the recessionary gloom. Announcing the election on 7 February Keating said that Labor was prepared to 'make the big decisions—to engage the world, develop an export culture, seize the huge opportunities in Asia, revolutionise our industrial and business culture, rebuild our economic system and develop the big infrastructure projects'. Keating wanted to change the political culture.

His second story was that economic progress would not come by sacrificing Australian egalitarianism. At this point Keating posed as a traditionalist to fight Hewson and later Howard. He cast Hewson as the wrecker; Keating, by contrast, would conserve the best of Australia. The GST had become a symbol of the wrong choice. In his policy speech Keating declared: 'There rarely has ever been a clearer choice: between the Australian traditions of fairness and equity and the economic and social jungle of Reaganism and Thatcherism which other countries have just abandoned.'

Arguing that Hewson had no view of society and no commitment to fairness, Keating envisaged the 'economy and society in concert'. He warned that 'if the Coalition is elected, within six months there will be no Accord—instead discord—no universal health system, no safety net. And there will be a GST'. This was the old-fashioned compulsive Labor pitch—Hewson and then Howard would sacrifice the decent society.

His third story was the flight to romance as Keating urged his audience to become 'enlargers'—his invocation of a new ethos for the cadres and True Believers of a modern ALP. It was about ideas, ideology and dreams. This was the softer side of Keating, tied somehow to his artistic quest for perfection. In the plane one night, high over the Riverina, he told Watson that when he got the model right he would leave politics and enter the world of the senses. 'All he wanted,' Watson recalled, 'was pleasure, including music, and owning beautiful things ... the difference between me and Hewson, he said, is that Hewson wants to make life harder for people and I want to make it softer.' Melancholy was in the air—yet in the same discussion, he changed gears and talked about saying the GST would be the 'killing fields' of family life.[9]

In a dangerous step Keating would become a cultural icon in his own right. At Sydney's State Theatre on Sunday 28 February 1993 he spoke to what reporters called 'an adoring arts community' that was 'fiercely partisan, committed, socially aware'.[10] Prompting a frisson of excitement, Keating declared:

> The Labor Party is the party of the enlargers in Australia. We dream the big dreams. We have a sense of a compassionate, creative society ... How many countries have the chance to put together a new society? Here we are, on the oldest piece of crust on the earth's surface, with the oldest nation on the Earth, Aboriginal Australians. What a phenomenal opportunity we have to develop a new country, a multicultural country, a new society with new resonances. Labor is about creating that society ... I thought how great ... it will be when we are as one. When we say sorry and mean it.

They cheered and cheered again.

Once a narrow social conservative who rarely broke a conversation with a view about film, play or literature, Keating played his audience with a masterful touch and won three standing ovations. Yet there was an element of unreality and delusion in his comments. Keating was at once the manipulator of his audience and victim of his own polemic; the arch realist was starting to lose his grip. With Baz Luhrmann, Betty Churcher, Richard Neville, Garry McDonald, Sam Neill, Barry Otto and Bryan Brown as audience participants he announced that the Coalition were the punishers, the 'narrow hard people who never want people to lift their gaze, who preach there's no gain without pain'.

The scale of delusion was more apparent a few days later, in his 'Econocrats and Bleeding Hearts' speech, as Keating ruminated:

We have, if you like, put a new complexion on multicultural Australia. The ethnic people are all voting for us … [we're] getting that bigger view of the place, not just economics but social life, the country in a broader sense knowing about itself, and I'm more convinced than ever that we've got to make peace with the Aborigines to get the place right. That's got Australians interested. They think this is a bit different … It [a win] would be a great thing for Australian social democracy … a great thing for the region. Because we've made the break to Indonesia, to Japan and I think we're into the region in a way perhaps that other governments have never made it. If we lose, we'll lose that break. It will take years to re-establish it … the Chinese actually want me to go to over there … they want to thicken up our ties between Australia and China … Here's Bill Clinton still wondering whether he should let gays into the military, we've decided that some months ago … I was always on the gays' side … I reckon that we'll do more things here than any other Western government will do in the next three years if we get up … We've had great support from the arts … and we ought to give them a big bloody kick along as well … I think that seeing the economy back to growth—where we can start to really hit our straps in social and national policy—gives us the chance to do something that no other Commonwealth government has done before, and certainly no other Labor government has done before.[11]

It was a blend of idealism, ambition and megalomania laced with a thread of plausibility. This mindset would drive both strong policy reform and grand illusions. The leader who held these passions would never accept that the 1993 election victory was the result of a calculated destruction of Hewson and *Fightback!*

Keating would invest any win with a greater meaning: it would be a vindication for him and he would proceed on this basis, a fatal mistake. It is doubtful that Hawke could have won in 1993: witness his feeble response to *Fightback!* Keating's 1993 win created a Labor template for the rest of the decade and that was unfortunate because it was false. Labor blundered at the next three campaigns—1996, 1998 and 2001—by depicting the Liberals as the party of extreme change and seeking to win on negatives. In 1998 and 2001 Labor relied again on demonising the GST. Each of these efforts failed. The lesson is that 1993 was a one-off. It was never a template.

Amid the clamour and tears, however, Keating finished election night with a Labor model for the 1990s. It was his model, his vision, his hard work. It was not just a dream, because a prime minister's job is to translate dreams into policies, laws and institutions.

The model is known in general terms but its components are rarely evaluated. They constitute Keating's 'big picture' and the legacy of his prime ministership. After 1996 John Howard would be forced to make a decision on each aspect of Keating's 'big picture' inheritance.

7

THE OPEN ECONOMY

This is when we guaranteed the end of
Protection in the old Australian Settlement.
—Paul Keating, May 2005, on the early 1990s recession

The foundation of Paul Keating's economic policy as prime minister was his refusal to surrender on the path to free trade. Confronting an unemployment rate of more than 10 per cent, a frightened cabinet, a desperate caucus and a panicked union movement, Keating defied a century of political logic: he kept the tariff cuts in place. It was an act of practical fortitude. With the exception of Bob Hawke, no previous Australian leader, Liberal or Labor, would have done this.

Every economic achievement of Keating's prime ministership was built on this foundation. The unwritten law of politics, integral to Australian history, was that each downturn provoked higher protection in a doomed effort to save jobs. It was Keating who broke the mould. 'You have a choice,' he would reflect years later. 'You can either duck for cover or say, Come what may, these tariff changes will continue. That means taking the risk. I was prepared to take the risk. The hard part had been done—our task was to stick by the announced tariff reductions.'[1]

Keating's decision was an insight into the most extraordinary political consequence of the early 1990s recession—there was no wholesale policy panic and no trashing of the market-based reforms of the 1980s. This position defied history and populist instinct; it defied sabre rattling from the academy and cries about the death of so-called economic rationalism.[2] On the enduring structural issues, Keating held firm.

This is why Australia, finally, emerged stronger, not weaker, from the recession. It is Keating's main achievement as prime minister. At this point the foundations were enhanced for the Keating–Howard prosperity era until 2007.

The first critical condition was holding the line on free trade. The 1991 protection reductions were the most important decision of Hawke's final term. In effect, this demolished the tariff protection edifice that had dominated Australia's first hundred years. Its policy ownership was contested between Hawke and Keating but there was no gainsaying its historic import. The general level of tariff assistance would be reduced from 10 and 15 per cent in 1992 to 5 per cent by 1996; tariffs on cars would be reduced from 35 per cent in 1992 to 15 per cent in 2000; and tariff cuts on footwear clothing and textiles would be accelerated so that quotas would be eliminated in 1993 and the maximum tariff by 2000 would be 25 per cent. This would reduce the average nominal rate of industry assistance to 3 per cent overall.

Cabinet took the decision before the recession's depth was known. This was the key to the politics. The tariff cuts were imposed on an economy where unemployment was rising steeply. From the time Keating entered the Lodge the resistance became fierce. 'These tariff reductions were very hard for the unions,' Bill Kelty said. 'The unions were never comfortable with it. I had accepted it, sometimes reluctantly. At the time I thought we had to get it.'[3]

In the politics of recession Keating had two supreme achievements: he held his Labor government together and he did so without compromising the tariff reductions. The 1990s recession, unlike past recessions, did not provoke the disintegration of a Labor government. In fact, the broader movement rallied behind Keating despite its misgivings. Keating's ability via rhetoric, policy, union ties and sheer spirit to keep Labor together in the worst recession for half a century was an astonishing achievement almost entirely overlooked in commentary.

But the mechanics of this consensus were vital—Keating switched dramatically on fiscal and monetary policy while holding the line on longer-run structural policy, notably the tariff cuts. He was a champion of Keynesian fiscal stimulus via the *One Nation* package and pushed the cause of lower interest rates. Yet his language in *One Nation* was a striking defence of his pro-market economics as treasurer. 'I want to keep up the pace of change,' Keating said. 'I want Australia to be fiercely competitive in the world so that we can deliver opportunity and care at home.' The Prime Minister was not for turning.[4]

Mike Keating felt that people exaggerated Keating's economic policy shifts as PM. 'I don't believe there was a huge difference between Paul

Keating as treasurer and prime minister,' he said. 'The evidence shows a strong line of continuity. As prime minister he upheld the model of a deregulated competitive economy and then took it into new areas.'[5]

But the pressure for turning reached intense levels during the April 1992 Wills by-election in Melbourne for Hawke's old seat. With its strong manufacturing base, the seat was won by a populist, leftist football hero, Phil Cleary, running as an independent on a true-Labor, pro-tariffs, pro-jobs platform. The ACTU backed Cleary, not the ALP candidate. Cleary secured a 19 per cent swing to decimate both government and Opposition. It was a vote for old Labor values. The base was in revolt and Keating was put on notice.

In March, before the by-election, Keating changed his formula: he ruled out further tariff cuts beyond the current timetable. After outlining the current reductions he declared with emphasis 'and that is enough'.[6] In policy terms it had scant import but Keating was telling the unions he had heard their protests and he was gunning for Hewson's zero tariff stance. 'Going to zero is thoughtless and useless,' Keating warned. He cast Hewson as a heartless technician.

From this moment the folly of Hewson's position became monumental. It was conscripted by Keating during 1992 and 1993 to buy himself political immunity from internal attack over the tariff. Hewson was indispensable to solving Keating's dilemma.

The unions and left took heart from the Wills result. The ACTU made its push in May at a meeting of the Australian Labor Advisory Council (ALAC) in the cabinet room.[7] They had a lot of support.

Nervous nellies were thick on the ground as winter loomed. Cabinet ministers had begun to discuss a retreat, initially in whispers, then in hope. Keating's political adviser Stephen Smith had suggested a two-year moratorium. The National Secretariat had made sympathetic noises for concessions. Victoria's manufacturing base was being decimated. Labor state governments in Victoria and South Australia had called for a slowdown in tariff cuts. From the ACTU there was now a concerted economic argument and political campaign for policy change.

At the ALAC meeting the federal secretary of the Metal Workers Union, George Campbell, led the charge, followed by the joint national secretary of the Textile, Clothing and Footwear Union, Anna Booth. Campbell warned that more independents such as Cleary would steal ALP seats. Kelty spoke for his constituents and then for the country. Great harm was being done, he said. Why should tariff policy be inflexible? Wages policy was not inflexible. Superannuation policy wasn't inflexible.

Kelty always framed his critique as Keating's friend. This occasion was no different. 'You have to be very careful,' he said to Keating, adding:

We have marched a long time behind this banner, a long time, but the banner is slipping down the flagpole … The March 1991 statement was based on the false premise of growth. We lower tariffs when there is growth. They said then it would be all right. That was not our view then and it is not our view now. If you lose the next election it will be because of the March 1991 [tariff] statement. Then you'll have Hewson for a decade.[8]

Martin Ferguson backed Kelty.

Years later, explaining the view he put that evening, Kelty said:

In 1992 there were three arguments available about the tariff. The first was stop them, just stop them, a view held by a lot of unions. There was the 'Let's go ahead with them anyway view'—Paul's view. The view I put was that the tariff reductions will occur but you don't make the reductions until the economy starts to recover. That was my view. I felt this was how you brought the debate to an end and got the best outcome.[9]

This was the voice of union moderation. It reflected not just union sentiment—most of the Labor Party would have seized the Kelty position for a tariff pause.

In his response Keating was practical. He was pushing uphill and he knew it. He knew that only a handful of ministers, a few MPs and some advisers still believed in his economic model. And many believers had joined the compromise camp.

But Keating wasn't persuaded. He said a pause would not be sufficient to engender new investment if the end point reduction remained. And if there was a pause 'we might never get started again'. He worried about what a pause might mean for the government's stocks. 'We would write ourselves off,' he ventured. The universal response from commentators, economists and markets would be that the government was finished, Keating thought.[10] So the pause was stillborn.

In truth, Keating had been gentle:

Tariffs were a bit like breaking the back of inflation. You either do it or you don't. I mean, when does a country ever get out of this stuff? You have to ask yourself where is the political momentum to actually make the break? We had announced tariff cuts in 1988. We had announced the new ones in 1991 and they had barely started. But we had taken the decisions. People thought I was too dogmatic—or, shall we say, rigid. They felt that, with a million people out of work I was throwing the switch to imports. That's how they saw it, you know. But I didn't. My view was that we had more chance of losing by being unsure and uncertain and seemingly standing for nothing. You have to ask yourself: what hope does the country have if we can't find the political momentum to make the break?[11]

George Bernard Shaw once wrote: 'The reasonable man adapts himself to the world; the unreasonable one persists in trying to adapt the world to himself. Therefore all progress depends on the unreasonable man.' In 1992 Keating was the unreasonable man. Ever susceptible to Canberra's cold, Keating headed into his worst winter, his first in the Lodge.

His refusal to budge on tariffs was a classic in the difference between old and new politics. For Keating, the 1980s were transforming. It was absurd to think the old economic model was better politics. 'How does stopping tariff cuts help us?' he would ask. The answer lay in spin and cosmetics: Labor and Keating would look more caring. The decision would not create new jobs. It was the sort of thinking Keating loathed and the mindset he sought to destroy.

Keating's contempt for the old model was unrelenting: 'What was Labor, really, in economic terms, before 1983? It believed in regulation of the banking system. It believed in regulation of the exchange rate. It believed in tariffs. We had low profits, therefore low investment. We had high unemployment. I mean, what did we abandon? It's like losing an eczema.'[12]

The old system, he argued, meant that the three vital prices were 'uncompetitive and wrong—the price of foreign exchange, the price of capital and the price of labour'.[13] But Keating had to convert Labor's heart, not just its head. The party was a well of sentimentality that serviced a collection of special interests.

The two 1980s reform pillars were the float and the shift towards free trade. Keating knew they did not stand alone—they drove reform through the rest of the economy. It was these decisions that remade Australia and tied the economy to global financial and trade markets for the coming generation. Because Keating assumed ownership of such historic changes, retreat became an insurmountable step.

But the pressure was trapped in cabinet's engine room. Industry Minister John Button was a Victorian, a friend of the unions, a supporter of industry, neither a populist nor a backslider. But Button wanted a policy change. Not a minister for cabinet surprises, he liked to prepare the ground. The showdown came on the eve of the August 1992 Budget and played out for several days.

'Button came to see me,' Dawkins said. 'He was worried about manufacturing and wanted to soften the tariff cuts. I was happy to talk about it, so we had a meeting with Keating.'[14] Dawkins had encouraged Button. They met with Keating and a handful of ministerial advisers. When they met with Keating one of his advisers, John Edwards, noted that Button was nervous. Button said the debate was about politics; he wanted a minimum market share for Australian cars and a softening of the end-point tariff reduction.

Dawkins' office chief, Tony Harris, said:

> When Button spoke I was dumbfounded because it ran counter to what the government stood for. It wasn't a vituperative discussion. It didn't last long and it was calm. I think Button felt that, because we had high unemployment, any such decision would be well received. Towards the end Keating asked me what I thought and I said 'I don't think people would understand if we did this.' I remember that Dawkins was agnostic.[15]

Keating had no animosity for Button. He and Button had collaborated closely on the 1991 package, with Keating saying this agreement was to Button's 'eternal credit'. Now Keating told them: 'Having fought for this for years I hate giving up on any of it.' The budget deficit was blowing out, he said. Aware that he had a shocking problem on fiscal policy about to become public, Keating feared that markets might think the entire economic model was being abandoned.[16] This was Don Russell's concern. He told Keating that the situation was filled with danger. 'Macroeconomic policy is being transformed,' Russell said, 'and in this climate it is vital we keep our discipline on tariffs.'[17]

Before the meeting Keating had been warned that Dawkins would favour some concessions. This was significant because Dawkins' reputation was that of a crazy, brave reformer. Dawkins said: 'My position was that if Keating wanted to support Button then I would go along with a more extended phase-down period.' In the end, they decided against any change. Dawkins was happy with that outcome. It meant that Keating was unpersuaded, again.[18]

Summing up the internal tariff debate, Russell said: 'There were a number of discussions. Keating listened to it all. In the end it was a practical decision. Paul felt there was very little if any political gain from a policy change.'[19] Keating had an ally that kept him strong—Hewson. He could maintain the tariff status quo and still have a very different policy to Hewson's zero tariff. It was a perfect outcome.

The power dynamics were obvious—Button wanted the change; Dawkins was neutral; and the decision lay with Keating. It was his choice.

For Keating, it was bigger than just tariffs. His touchstone was Labor's claim as architect of the modern Australian economy. Sometimes this claim boiled down to a single policy decision on a single day—such as keeping your nerve on free trade. Explaining his decision he invoked Max Walsh, the former gallery chief for the *Australian Financial Review*, the journalist who most influenced Keating in his early days as an MP. Walsh had been a de facto tutor. He occupied a special place in Keating's firmament, even as a latter-day critic of his economic policy—a critic whose approval Keating sought.

In early August 1992, with the *One Nation* forecasts about to be demolished in the 18 August Budget, Keating sensed he was on the precipice. 'I don't know that we stood for much by that stage,' he said in retrospect, adding:

> If we had broken on a big thing like the tariff changes I think the intelligent comment in Australia would just write us off. You need to remember at that time many commentators were dead opposed to the Budget even going into deficit at all. Many people I regarded as friendly, like Max Walsh, were already arguing that the Prime Minister has lost his economic credentials.[20]

So Keating finessed his way through the pressures. 'Paul rarely did anything he didn't want to do,' Russell later observed. 'You could see the big picture evolve before your eyes.'[21]

Keating and Hawke's former adviser, Ross Garnaut, had many differences. But they were united on this issue. Keating would have agreed with Garnaut's earlier warning about the risk 'that Australians will think too soon that they have changed enough, that it is enough to weaken the pillars of our protectionist minds and policies without bringing the great monuments to past mistakes crashing to the ground'.[22]

As a realist Keating knew the traps. The history was dismal—in the Great Depression, Australia took flight to protection; in the early

1970s recession, the Whitlam government went protectionist; and in the late 1990s the Howard government would pause the tariff reductions. But Keating was counter-intuitive—he figured a leader legitimises his convictions by paying a price for them.

As usual, when things looked blackest, the Hewson Opposition saved the day. On 27 August, Russell sat down at his desk and unfurled the newspapers to find that the *Australian*'s main story had Ian McLachlan telling the car industry to 'revamp or perish'. In case anybody had doubts, McLachlan said the Coalition had resolved to achieve zero tariffs. It was the virility politics that Hewson loved. 'We are saying we are not in the business of picking which industry is going to survive,' McLachlan said. 'We simply cannot say to all the industries that walk through the door in Canberra by the hundred claiming special consideration that they are special. Who is going to pay for it?'[23]

As soon as he read the story, Russell saw sunlight. Though he was an old Treasury hand and a market economist, Russell thought to himself 'How mad are these Liberals, talking about the car industry perishing?' With an unusual urgency, Russell told Keating: 'This means the end of the car industry. That's the difference between you and Hewson on tariffs.' Russell reminded Keating of his talk with Ford Chief Executive Jac Nasser at the time of the 1991 tariff statement when they confronted this question. Keating had told Nasser that 'at the end of this process we do want a car industry'. It was what Nasser came to hear; it was what Keating pledged. It is the reason Keating branded Hewson 'Captain Zero'.[24]

So Keating hit the warpath. He raged against Hewson, warned that the car industry would be finished, the jobs gone, the industry wrapped up—all for Hewson's blind ideology. He kept up the attack and sometimes even sounded like arch-protectionist John McEwen whose collective works Keating was dismantling. He said it 'should send the shivers through' Adelaide, Geelong and Melbourne, the homes of car making. The Liberals branded him a terrible hypocrite; the media criticised him; and some of the policy advisers grew alarmed. Russell was sure it was a turning point. 'The start of our political recovery was our response to the McLachlan article,' he insisted.[25]

Hewson said: 'Keating is the person who now claims credit for the tariff cuts. But he campaigned against me flat out. I was the one who wanted to eliminate tariffs. This policy, by the way, was in the context of a huge package of benefits for the corporate sector.'[26]

The idea that Keating lost his integrity by attacking Hewson's policy is unsustainable. Hewson could have avoided the attack by accepting Labor's tariff reduction timetable. Instead, he thought it was smart to run on zero tariffs in a recession, and he paid the price.

The August–September 1992 furore over car tariffs drew the political line. It helped Keating defuse the tariff issue inside the ALP, where Keating's policy looked moderate compared with Hewson's. It was a gift. This became the basis on which Keating united the Labor Party.

'The Liberals called me arrogant,' Keating said. 'But I gave the public its due. That's what we did on tariffs. John Button, John Dawkins, the ACTU, George Campbell, Bill Kelty, they all wanted me to abandon the policy. My view was that if you blink once, you will be lost. This is when we guaranteed the end of protection in the old Australian Settlement.'[27]

Australia spent the next fifteen years as a beneficiary of integration into the global marketplace—enjoying its capital, technology, low inflation and trade. In 1993, in the recession's shadow, Keating was re-elected on a platform promising the move to freer trade. Everything was built on this platform.

8

EMPOWERING THE BANK

Paul Keating loved this institution.
—Former Reserve Bank Governor Ian Macfarlane, February 2006

From the ashes of the 1990s recession emerged a new giant. The Reserve Bank of Australia, located at Martin Place in Sydney, surrounded in mystique and foreign to most Australians, would now move to centre stage. It was a gigantic irony—the Bank had provoked the recession but would emerge empowered from its trough. Its governors would become household names as the Bank took command of interest rate policy.

The RBA's rise was sanctioned by Paul Keating and implemented by its dour, soft-spoken governor, Bernie Fraser, during his 1989–96 term. This would transform economic governance in Australia and lay the foundations for the longest expansion and greatest prosperity in the nation's history.

The Reserve Bank story was pivotal to the success of the Keating–Howard era. The politics of the Bank's rise were an 'inner sanctum' event—but its narrative is decisive in Australia's economic and political history. It hinged on an idea that drew on half a century of economic history: that the guiding star for monetary policy should be an inflation target. Once inflation was broken and locked in its cage, the prospects for growth were optimised. This was the lesson of the 1990s recession. Underwritten by the central bank, this idea would create a new era for Australian households and businesses.

The orthodoxy that central banking was a dull business was mocked in this period. Along the way were many flashpoints—tension between Fraser and Keating, a public brawl between Fraser and Hewson and, in

2007, Prime Minister Howard being reduced to a rage when Governor Glenn Stevens lifted interest rates in an election campaign.

Fraser knew that the RBA's rise depended on a political consensus and felt his task was to build that consensus. 'We needed to be a bit political to achieve independence and to keep it,' Fraser said. 'But we got to the point where everybody—the markets, the treasurer, the government, the ACTU and even the Treasury—accepted the Bank was best placed to make these decisions.'[1]

In Keating's December 1990 'Placido Domingo' speech he implied that the Reserve Bank was 'in his pocket'. But like many Keating remarks, the language concealed a more complex reality. It was Keating who conceded the Bank a conditional independence during his prime ministership, a prelude to the formal independence of the Howard–Costello period. For Keating, this transition was based on trust.

'Paul Keating loved this institution,' Ian Macfarlane said. 'It was under Paul Keating that this institution evolved towards a far better system.' But trust is personal and the trust was anchored in the relationship between Keating and former Treasury Secretary Bernie Fraser whom he appointed as governor in 1989. At the time the appointment was misunderstood—Keating appointed Fraser to strengthen, not to weaken, the RBA.

'They were so close,' said Macfarlane, who observed their bond from his vantage point as Fraser's deputy. 'Paul Keating was the only outside invitee at Bernie's wedding.'[2]

'I chastised Paul about it,' Fraser said of Keating's line that the Bank did his bidding.

> I was very disappointed when I heard about it. It caused enormous problems. Paul acknowledged that to me and said he wished he hadn't said it. The comment provided an endless round of ammunition for the Opposition to attack me and to attack the Bank. It made life much more difficult and made it harder to establish the Bank's credibility. Paul said he would correct it publicly when he got an opportunity but it never really was withdrawn.[3]

Keating knew his man. Aware that the culture and judgements in the Bank's Martin Place headquarters had the potential to break the economy and smash governments, Keating wanted a governor with wide experience. While Keating fancied himself as a monetary policy artist, he disliked the notion of actually setting interest rates. He wanted a governor on his wavelength. But for Keating, trust wasn't about academic brilliance or smart suits; it was about character and judgement.

His regard for Fraser was immense. The son of an unskilled labourer and a railway worker from Junee who wrote school essays on the kitchen table and made money shooting rabbits, Fraser had not forgotten his roots. His background and the rise to Treasury secretary made a farce of academic theorising about Treasury's neo-liberalism and unconcern for working people. A hard man with a soft heart, Fraser had contempt for greedy businessmen and weak politicians. 'I get very pissed off with people who just take,' he said.[4] He believed in a disciplined growth economy with jobs and equity—that's why he loathed the Whitlam government.

As a senior Treasury official, Bernie had been won over by Paul. He had never encountered a treasurer like Keating and he knew the 1980s would not come again—a treasurer with a glint of crazy brave and an economy close enough to crisis to ignite the torch of reform. 'I'm happy to be a mate of Keating's,' Fraser said. 'I put a good deal of credence and value in my mates. No, I don't see much of him, never have.'[5] So Fraser went to Martin Place to be his own man and to help Keating.

He came as an outsider and a monetary policy dove. Given Treasury's rivalry with the Bank, the appointment was met with sentiments ranging from apprehension to alarm. Fraser says that Deputy Governor John Phillips was 'more hawkish' than him and that the future deputy, Ian Macfarlane, was inclined to a hawkish stand.[6] 'It was a culture clash at first,' Macfarlane said.[7] Fraser agrees—he was repelled at any rigid exclusive anti-inflation stance. 'The culture of central banks was that you fight inflation first, second and third,' Fraser said. 'That was true generally of the Reserve Bank. It meant I was on constant alert. I kept reminding people we had two objectives—inflation and employment growth—with their inevitable trade-offs.'[8] In truth, the process was a cross-fertilisation. The Bank changed Fraser and Fraser changed the Bank.

There was one bonus from the recession: it had broken inflation. And the aim was to keep it broken. For Keating, this was his lonely prize from the recession; he knew the prize must not be lost. Macfarlane said: 'By about 1989 the Bank had worked out that you had to have a monetary policy that would basically focus on inflation. And we were convinced that we could handle this task better than Canberra. Of course, we had to keep our mouths shut publicly.'[9] Winning acceptance of this view was Fraser's achievement.

The late-twentieth-century evolution in central banking represented a global change in economic governance. The 1970s stagflation, with its erosion of living standards, had initiated the generation-long quest for a new star to guide central banks around the world. There were many false trails along this road but it led in one direction: towards a formal separation between the central banks and the politicians.

Outsourcing of interest rate policy is an epic experiment whose longevity remains uncertain. Politicians do not usually surrender power. This surrender was based on two ideas: a recognition that central bank management might lead to a longer growth cycle; and a calculation that letting the Bank, not governments, determine interest rates might work in the long-run favour of politicians.

In the 1970s, under Malcolm Fraser, a cabinet committee on monetary policy saw politicians setting interest rates. After the 1983 float of the currency, interest rate instructions flowed to the Reserve Bank after consultation between Keating and Hawke. At the official level the deregulated economy had triggered a shift in monetary policy from Treasury to the Bank, where such power was nominally supposed to reside, with the Bank using open market operations to set the cash rate. Post-1983 the empathy between treasurer and governor became critical. Keating enjoyed a special relationship with Bob Johnston, Fraser's predecessor.[10]

While Keating and the Bank had been in broad agreement on the monetary policy tightening of the late 1980s, Keating was convinced the Bank had let the boom get out of control, thereby begetting the bust. The Bank's mistakes were central to the recession, with cash rates reaching 18 per cent in an effort to contain the boom.

Post-recession the Bank had a choice: it could either reform itself or have reform imposed on it—there was no alternative. Driven by healthy intellectual egotists and leaders of genuine quality, the Bank decided to become master of its own destiny.

The early 1990s constituted the most serious potential crisis in the Reserve Bank's history, brought to a peak by the Opposition leader, John Hewson. Its future as an institution became an issue of partisan political rivalry. The Opposition pledged to amend the *Reserve Bank Act* and impose an inflation band of 0–2 per cent as the rule for interest rate policy. This was driven by Hewson, a former employee, now deeply suspicious of the Bank. It mirrored a conviction among economists that the Bank had failed to prosecute the case against inflation and that it was not sufficiently independent.

It is unsurprising that people believed the Bank was under Keating's thumb. Keating had made this boast too often. He had upset Governor Bob Johnston in 1989 by making such comments and Johnston didn't know whether to correct Keating or to resign, though in the end he did neither. Keating's remarks drove Macfarlane to declare of the recession-induced interest rate tightening that, 'if you think it is a terrible mess, blame us, blame Martin Place'.[11] It was a plea for the Bank's integrity and growing autonomy to be recognised. In a famous Craig McGregor interview, Bernie Fraser was even more direct. 'I'm my own man,' he said. 'I do my own thing. I don't feel a member of any group. I formulate what is in the interests of the public as a public servant.'[12]

In effect, Hewson's proposal would have limited the Bank's traditional commitment to full employment. The RBA's charter, engraved in the entrance to its Sydney headquarters, required the Bank to direct itself to 'the greatest advantage of the people of Australia' and do so by means that will 'best contribute to the stability of the currency, the maintenance of full employment and the economic prosperity and welfare of the people of Australia'. This philosophy originated with the postwar Keynesian age. The charter was initiated by Labor governments after World War II and upheld by Menzies. These were splendid words—but they obscured the tension between price stability and full employment.

During the 1990s Fraser presided over four years of interest rate cuts to combat the recession. The early absence of a defined policy goal meant these initial interest rate cuts were met with the accusation that they were made for political reasons. The first cut came in January 1990. Fraser said: 'It would have been December but Paul was away and he wanted to be around.'[13] The second cut was in February—and Hawke called the election immediately afterwards. Hewson led the assault. His target was the Keating–Fraser relationship and his message was simple: political influence was corrupting monetary policy. Macfarlane said, 'There was clearly great distrust of monetary policy, the government and the Reserve Bank—or, in modern parlance, a lack of credibility.'[14]

There was a hefty intellectual and political momentum behind Hewson's push. The Reserve Bank of New Zealand and the central bank in Canada had recently adopted the 0–2 per cent inflation target to guide policy. But the Reserve Bank's leaders, Fraser and Macfarlane, were appalled by Hewson's position. They felt the Bank's mission was under threat. It was a watershed moment.

Fraser's instincts as guardian of the Australian economy were on alert. He would not tolerate what he saw as Hewson's undermining of one of the nation's vital institutions. He believed Hewson's target was in conflict with the Bank's statutory charter, sound economic policy and Australia's postwar polity. Fraser decided to take a stand against Hewson's position.

I was very anti such a tight target. It was instinctively abhorrent to me. But it was the fashion at the time. The New Zealanders were making a lot of play with their rigid target and the markets liked it. But this didn't gel with me. It was too much emphasis on inflation and that would be detrimental to growth and jobs.[15]

Macfarlane felt the same way. 'I thought Hewson's 0–2 per cent was out of the question,' he said. 'It would be just disastrous for our economy.' The Bank risked being trapped—it was under popular attack for causing the recession yet was under attack by Hewson and the *Fightback!* brigade as a bunch of pathetic 'wishy washy wets', to use Macfarlane's phrase.[16] Inside the Bank the distaste for Hewson was palpable, the feeling intense, the policy dilemma acute. The Bank's future was on the line.

In reality Fraser and Macfarlane held the middle ground. Macfarlane said: 'This was probably the most unpleasant part of my career. People were shooting at us, saying, you are hopeless, look, the Americans have got inflation under control, the New Zealanders, the Canadians, the Brits— they are all doing something and you are doing nothing.'[17] Hewson had the wind behind him.

The Bank was alarmed at the ideological fix led by Hewson. The existing objectives of full employment and price stability gave the Bank a discretion that would be curtailed if Hewson's extreme inflation target became its exclusive guiding star. By this stage the Bank's intellectual transition was advanced. It was devising its own solution, a long way from Hewson's.

'We believed we could achieve what our critics wanted—a return to a low inflation environment,' Macfarlane said. But that involved a different mechanism. It meant no rewriting of the act. The Bank felt that would be a blunder. It rejected the extreme 'independence model' of New Zealand and Canada. It shunned the 0–2 per cent inflation target as prejudicing the commitment to employment.[18]

Fraser and Macfarlane eventually settled on a preferred model with a 2–3 per cent inflation target over the cycle, a position significantly different from Hewson's. This was an economic and political judgement. Fraser and Macfarlane wanted to prevent an inflationary resurgence but retain the flexibility to promote employment. They were convinced the statute was fine: it provided for the Bank's independence—an independence not previously realised, but now a realistic concept.[19]

These judgements came from within the Reserve Bank, not from Keating. The Bank did not seek Keating's specific approval. The position evolved informally during a period of interest rate reductions, not increases, and that helped to defuse any political resistance. But it was consistent with Keating's vision. 'I saw my job as being to create a new institution,' Keating said. 'I wanted a Reserve Bank able to stand on its reputation and to assist in the fight against inflation.'[20]

In its mid-1992 Annual Report the Bank identified a turning point for Australia. Low inflation had been achieved in the second half of the 1980s but the Bank now believed that 'a critical threshold' had been breached and that 'Australia [could] sustain a low inflation environment'.[21] History would vindicate this assessment—but only after the reprieve of the 1993 election.

In the prelude to the election, relations between Hewson and Fraser were acrimonious. There had been a series of mishaps, the most amusing being Fraser's 1991 interview when he attacked *Fightback!* as a 'very divisive, very diverting proposal' that was unnecessary and ill-timed. Fraser said he didn't want an ignorant Hewson, supported by Reith, mucking things up. Reacting to the suggestion that Hewson would want to force him out, Fraser's immortal reply was: 'I won't go just to appease some dickhead minister who wants to put Attila the Hun in change of monetary policy.' Bernie didn't talk much but it was obvious why Keating liked him.[22] Such a conflict between the Bank and an alternative prime minister had not happened before.

In fact, the nation was on the brink of an unprecedented institutional crisis. This has since been confirmed by Fraser, who said in a 2008 interview that as governor he would have resisted any Hewson government attempt to introduce its policy. Given Fraser's character, there should be no doubting his seriousness.

Under the disputes provision of the *Reserve Bank Act* the Australian Government has an ultimate authority over the Reserve Bank but in a disagreement both must provide relevant statements to the Commonwealth Parliament. This provision has never been triggered, for an obvious reason—it would be a risk to both sides but particularly to a government defying the Bank's best advice. Its purpose is to encourage co-operation. This provision has been referred to as 'the nuclear button of monetary policy destined never to be pushed because its implications are just too awful to contemplate'.[23]

Asked what would have happened if Hewson had won the election and implemented his policy, Fraser said:

> We would have had a rare occasion [on which] the government
> would have had to perform, as required by the *Reserve Bank Act*,

and table documents in the parliament and that would have meant tabling my response as governor to them. And we would have seen how that worked out. It's no accident, really, this situation has never developed. I think that's basically because it is likely that more validity would be seen in the central bank independent viewpoint than the alternative view the government would have had to mount.[24]

This statement makes crystal clear Fraser's willingness to confront a Hewson–Reith government and his belief that the Bank would have prevailed against them in such an historic showdown. Yet the notion that Hewson and Reith would back off, having won an election mandate, was unlikely. Nor was there much chance that Fraser, given his own views and sentiment within the Bank, would crumble without triggering the statutory provisions. The showdown was averted due to Keating's election victory.

There was a visceral nature to this conflict. Fraser later said:

The background to my Attila the Hun comment was a constant tirade from the Opposition against the fifteen interest rate reductions from 1990 trying to revive the economy and prevent the slowdown. Every time interest rates were reduced Reith and Hewson and others would say 'This is just doing Keating's work.' The implication was that they would have kept interest rates much higher when we were winding them back. It was fifteen reductions in a fairly short period of time but, in retrospect, we should have been winding them back a bit faster.[25]

This reveals Fraser's contempt for Hewson's interest rate judgements and his repudiation of attacks on his integrity.

On election night the Reserve Bank held its breath. Its future was on the line in the Keating–Hewson contest. 'There was no doubt the champagne corks were popping in this institution,' Macfarlane said of Keating's victory.[26] Hewson's defeat gave life to the Bank's model. It had played high stakes and it had won.

Within days of the election, Fraser, for the first time, publicised the Bank's position and dismissed that of the defeated Opposition leader. 'Our role as guardians of low inflation is important in part because there is no strong natural lobby for it in Australia,' Fraser said. 'My own view is that if the rate of inflation in underlying terms could be held to an average of 2–3 per cent over a period of years, that would be a very good outcome.' Fraser had nominated the range but, significantly, he did not call this as an inflation target.

Taking aim at Hewson, Fraser attacked the Coalition's 0–2 per cent target as doing 'more harm than good' and claimed that much of the debate had been rendered 'sterile by gladiatorial notions of independence' that did not ring true.

Fraser then delivered a homily:

> I have said many times that the Reserve Bank does, in fact, have a high degree of independence. We can and do pursue our statutory responsibilities without political interference. But we seek to do this in close consultation with the government—to exercise independence with consultation … The Reserve Bank cannot (and does not) expect to have independence without accountability. In simple terms, the *Reserve Bank Act* entrusts the Bank with certain responsibilities and the Bank should be held accountable to the parliament and the public at large for its actions in pursuit of those responsibilities. The Bank should be required to explain what it is doing and why: such accountability is part and parcel of good governance.[27]

But this speech revealed the differences between Fraser and Macfarlane: while Macfarlane believed in an inflation target, Fraser believed merely in inflation guidelines. While Macfarlane believed in working towards a formal declaration of independence, Fraser felt this was unnecessary. These were subtle yet critical differences, and they meant that only Macfarlane could work with the Howard government's new policy after the 1996 election.

Fraser had a powerful argument against an exclusive inflation target: such a system, he said, would have delayed the Bank's 1990s rate cuts, four percentage points of which were made before there was a clear sign that inflation was falling.

However, by his words and actions, Fraser set out to make Australia a low-inflation nation with a central bank that was largely independent but accountable. Over time, Fraser toughened his own formula so that by October 1993 he was moved to say: 'We believe the underlying rate will be held around 2–3 per cent. This belief reflects several factors, not least being the determination of the Reserve Bank and the government to see that Australia stays in the low inflation league.'[28] It was an unfolding narrative.

Australia, in the view of Fraser and Macfarlane, had devised its own central bank model consistent with its act and its political tradition. 'We had to persuade people,' Fraser said. In 2008 he argued that results showed Australia's model had delivered better results in containing inflation and allowing jobs growth.[29] But the test came, inevitably, when inflation went on the prowl. It is easy to be an anti-inflation hawk when the demon is subdued. Fraser proved true to his word: he put slaying inflation before Keating's political interest.

The showdown came in 1994. In the fourth year of recovery spending was too strong, the current account deficit was too high and Fraser judged that growth at 5.5 per cent was untenable. He unleashed his sword. In a preemptive strike the Bank lifted interest rates three times between August and December 1994—a total of 2.75 percentage points. It was a cruel blow to Keating but a message to markets: Australia would not tolerate an inflation break-out. Fraser kept repeating the word *preemptive* to explain the Bank's resolution and notify all financial players of its intentions. Keating would pay a high price.

'There was a loss of confidence,' Macfarlane said. 'It looked as though all the good work of getting inflation down in 1990 and 1991 might be lost again in 1994. And Bernie agreed with this view.'[30] Putting aside his soft heart, Fraser went on the warpath.

The first increase in the cycle is the hardest. Political resistance is greatest because it constitutes a turn in the cycle. Keating summoned Fraser and Treasury Secretary Ted Evans to the Lodge. Fraser's recommendation was for a full 1 percentage point increase. The meeting was on Keating's turf. 'The Prime Minister had concerns,' Ted Evans said in a masterly understatement.[31]

These men knew each other intimately. Bernie and Ted were the officials most loved by Keating, men whom he trusted completely, the advisers with whom he had fought through the economic trench warfare of the protracted 1980s reforms. Bernie and Ted had working-class Australia engraved on their faces—they looked just as comfortable in the front bar at Ipswich as they did sitting in the Treasury secretary's seat. Their lives mocked the academic stereotype of sleek-tailored, smooth-talking mandarins. And there was no doubt they loved Keating.

The Prime Minister wanted a concession. He argued that the increase was too much, too sharp. In the end, they knocked 0.25 per cent off Fraser's proposal. 'The Prime Minister didn't alter it as such,' Fraser said in a defensive explanation. 'We reached an agreement to scale it back.'[32] Macfarlane said: 'I was told they brokered it down to three-quarters of the point.'[33] In monetary terms it was essentially a token, but Keating got a concession.

How should this meeting be described? Clearly, it was neither an example of the Bank being in Keating's pocket nor of the Bank being fully independent. It was an institution in transition—it had reached a position of partial independence. The Bank, in effect, was setting policy but that policy was subject to the Prime Minister's prior approval. It illustrates Fraser's statement that to become independent the Bank had to play some politics. Yet the incident shows that Keating's control over the Bank was fading.

For Keating, the dilemma was acute. The governor he appointed was now raising interest rates against him. Keating said, 'When rates went up I thought that was the end of us. The fact is I had a choice of either running with it or having a first rate argument with Bernie Fraser. My call on inflation turned out to be correct. But my prize would have been to wreck a decade of progress in building the Bank's independence.' Keating knew the consequences if he seriously challenged the magnitude of the tightening. 'Bernie would have had to resign and a decade of institution building would have gone out the door,' Keating said.[34]

The political winner was John Howard. These interest rate increases provoked his famous 'five minutes of economic sunshine' line of early 1995. A bitter Keating noted that 'by then we'd had five years of growth'.

Fraser and Macfarlane were convinced they had made the correct call. 'I think it was a very good piece of monetary policy,' Macfarlane would later say of the overall 2.75 point increase. 'Yes, there's no doubt that we wanted it. I think Keating exaggerates the damage this did to his election prospects in 1996.' For Macfarlane, the moral was that the Bank had reached a stage of 'conditional independence'—the Bank was in charge but 'we had to get Keating's approval before action was taken'.[35]

Fraser said:

> We had a classic soft landing. The fact that we acted preemptively helped a great deal. Acting decisively meant we avoided a longer period of interest rate increases. I think Paul realised the political implications if inflation had got out of control because that would have made things more uncomfortable for him closer to the election.[36]

The 2.75 points was the most abrupt switch in contemporary interest rate settings until the 2008 financial crisis.

On reflection, Evans said: 'The Prime Minister had concerns at the time and his judgement was probably correct. We tightened too much. The lesson from this experience for me is that monetary policy had become a sharper instrument—you could get the same effect as before without moving rates so far.'[37]

Fraser rejects this view. He also rejects the view that it killed Keating's 1996 election hopes—an interpretation sometimes advanced by Keating.

> The notion that it betrayed Keating is one that I found hurtful. Paul has had no more staunch defender than me over the last twenty years. Paul says now he was terribly upset about this tightening. But Ralph Willis, who was treasurer at the time, said that those three interest rate increases were initiated by the Bank and they were all supported by the government. All this stuff about those interest rates hitting the economy for six and causing Paul all these problems doesn't fit with the facts.[38]

Once he began the interest rate increases, Fraser was unforgiving. Like any decent central banker he used the trail of financial blood to impose a low-inflation culture. In April 1995 Fraser said the Bank was prepared to lift interest rates 'irrespective of any overlapping election or budget timetables' and observed that 'this should be more widely appreciated than it appears to be at present'. Fraser was telling the markets he could be a bastard. Explaining the 1994 tightening, he told a London audience that the purpose was 'to put policies in place before inflation actually picked up'. He noted that the underlying inflation rate had been kept to 2 per cent and that economic growth was being sustained.[39]

This 1994 tightening was the prelude to a new age. Its moral was manifest: the Bank's informal inflation target would make the recovery of the 1990s far more enduring than that of the 1980s. Fraser was building a monument. It would be enjoyed by Howard and Costello for the next decade.

Ken Henry, Treasury secretary under Howard and Rudd, told colleagues that the 1994–95 period was decisive because it saw two new transitions in place: inflation targeting and enterprise bargaining. 'For Treasury, the issue was would this work?' Henry said. His point was obvious: a new economic model was being put in place with significant changes to both monetary policy and industrial relations. This model preceded the election of the Howard government; it was initiated by Keating.

The Keating government formalised its endorsement of the Bank's inflation target and in mid-1995, in the Accord Mark VIII, the ACTU agreed to wage rises consistent with an inflation outcome of 2–3 per cent.[40] It was an extraordinary pledge by the trade union movement. The policy was becoming institutionalised and the political culture was changing to entrench low inflation. It is exactly what Fraser had envisaged. The significance of this agreement was lost because Keating fell the next year. In fact, it harmonised the Reserve Bank's inflation target with the trade union movement's wages policy—a formal harmony not available to the Rudd government when it came to power in 2007 because the Accord had passed into history.

A more independent Reserve Bank was an idea whose time had come. Once seen as heresy, it had become the consensus, championed even in Treasury. Former Treasury secretary Tony Cole said: 'In Treasury we felt the most important monetary policy reform was to allow the Bank to operate in an independent way. We were applauding Bernie.'[41]

Speaking from a 2008 perspective, Fraser reflected: 'In Glenn Stevens' time you might ask why do central bankers have all this power? Well, it's because of the initial care that went into pursuing these two objectives— inflation and employment—and the trade-offs between them and getting general support for this position.'[42]

Cole studied this narrative. 'It was Bernie Fraser who created an independent central bank,' he said. 'He was the person who really did it. I think Keating's absolute trust in Bernie was what made it possible. It is difficult to imagine that anybody else as governor during the Keating period would have been able to achieve what Bernie did.'[43] Ted Evans agreed, saying 'the bulk of the progress was made by Fraser'.[44]

The irony is that the Labor Party disowned the legacy. It went into Opposition and didn't want to know the story of the Bank's evolution. The real beneficiaries were Howard and Costello. They arrived in 1996 to expand on the Keating–Fraser project—to take the Bank from conditional to full independence.

9

TOWARDS A COMPETITIVE AUSTRALIA

I say that competition is a Labor word.
—Paul Keating, May 2008

National competition policy sprang from Australia's new demands as a market economy and an historic leap in Labor's political ideology. The idea was a violation of Australia's political tradition, with its domination by producer interests, public sector monopolies and a protectionist mindset. It came into existence only because the transition to free trade had transformed Australia's politics.

'My task was to make competition into a Labor ideal,' said Paul Keating, looking back more than a decade later.[1] For Labor, it would be a road to Damascus journey. To brand this journey a conversion would be presumptuous, but the logic was irresistible—an open economy meant Australia had to become a comprehensive national market.

The policy was imposed by Keating on the Labor Party, negotiated with the state governments and introduced into a community that had little grasp of its consequences. It was pervasive yet elusive. The scale of the 1995 federal–state agreement finalised between Keating and the six premiers was immense. The first president of the National Competition Council, Graeme Samuel, described it as 'the greatest bipartisan multi-jurisdictional agreement we have managed to achieve since Federation'.[2]

Keating dodged frank exposition of what competition policy meant and such disguise was wise. It was radical because it equated the public interest with effective markets, not government controls. It rang with the ideological overtones loved by big business and market economists. It was an attack on state government monopolies in power and energy. For Labor traditionalists, it was heresy. It guaranteed a fierce backlash spearheaded at various stages by a bizarre conga line that featured the oil companies, Pauline Hanson, the local chemist, Telstra, the ALP left and talkback chief Alan Jones. Anything that produced such opponents had to be worthwhile.

Five years after the policy began, the executive director of the National Competition Council, Ed Willett, said:

> Whether you are a doctor or a lawyer, whether you own shares in a power company, own a bottle shop, work on a wheat farm, ever catch a taxi, like to shop at weekends, have gas heating in your home, have sugar in your tea, have milk on your cereal, take public transport, own a mobile phone, post letters, have a flutter at the casino, water your front lawn or drive a car, you are benefiting from competition policy reforms.[3]

This comment hinted at the political conundrum: the gains were spread thin. Many consumers were unaware that they were winners, while the losers were specific, aware and angry. Competition policy spelt trouble because it attacked vested interests.

'Getting this policy approved was Keating at his best,' says Fred Hilmer, who headed the inquiry into competition policy.

> Competition was a big thing for Keating but it wasn't for Howard. I think the most distinctive thing Australia did in terms of economic reform was competition policy. If you take an OECD perspective then competition policy was more important than, say, the GST or labour market reform, two of Howard's better changes. In terms of importance I rate competition policy in the top three after fiscal and monetary policy.[4]

The idea was to enshrine the notion of choice, a classic Liberal Party idea. The theory was that competition would promote economic efficiency and productivity gains. Its theory laid siege to monopolies, price fixing by big business, anti-competitive laws by governments and producer arrangements that compromised consumer interests. This meant confrontation with interests ranging from power utilities and the legal profession to agricultural marketing boards. Because many were firmly entrenched, competition policy was riddled with holes and dashed hopes.

However, Australia became a pioneer and launched a new breed of regulatory crusaders—witness successive chairs of the Australian Competition and Consumer Commission (ACCC), Allan Fels and Graeme Samuel. It was Fels who created this innovation in public administration. The acceptance of competition policy in Australia cannot be grasped separate from the Fels persona.

A rare public official who was a populist, academic and tactician, Fels, rather than any minister, became the voice of competition policy. He depicted the policy as a path to justice for the powerless—not the application of a cold market ideology. As a result he frequently made competition into a popular cause, an astonishing feat. This technique was the key to his genius, yet it came at a price—Fels was seen as a grandstander, and that irked Coalition politicians. His opponents schemed repeatedly to bring him down and Fels survived only by becoming an astute politician himself—under Labor his ties with Bill Kelty purchased him a degree of political protection and under Howard he used the GST to salvage his position.[5]

'I believe before 1991 Australia was riddled with anti-competitive behaviour,' Fels said.

> I arrived with the firm view that public opinion must be mobilised for the cause. That could only be done by challenging big business and recognising that justice is a public process. Competition policy was a new concept for the 1990s. From the time the Berlin Wall fell the challenge facing countries became how to make their market economies work better. I am sure that, when Australia's politicians embarked on national competition policy, they did not realise the difficulty it involved. It meant, in effect, a twenty- to thirty-year implementation process by law, agreements, test cases, decisions and appeals.[6]

The policy was both an economic idea and a revolution in governance. It was designed to replace two previous ideas now deemed to be obsolete: industry policy via tariffs; and industry policy by 'picking winners'. Competition policy reached into the non-traded sector and areas previously untouched—government enterprise, service delivery, statutory authorities, energy utilities and professional bodies—and imposed new operating rules. For old-style managers its penetration was offensive and obscene. It purported to shift the balance in Australia's political culture from producer to consumer interests. This struck at the patronage and vote-gathering that had long defined Australian politics and administration. In the 1990s globalised age, such 'producer power' had become unsustainable, given the need for the entire economy to meet international benchmarks.

Competition policy was introduced by Keating and tolerated by Howard. With the notable exception of the GST phase-in, Howard was rarely an enthusiast for the idea and his sympathy for small business reinforced his suspicions. At the twentieth-anniversary dinner of the Business Council, Samuel, as ACCC chair, listened to Howard's speech about Australia's main economic reforms over the past twenty years. After Howard failed to mention competition policy, an irritated Samuel approached the Prime Minister's chief of staff, Arthur Sinodinos, who told him: 'Graeme, he hates the word. He'll never use it.'[7] But Howard kept the policy in place.

Competition was a departure in Australia's political philosophy but its nature was rarely grasped. This is best explained by Fels:

> Competition policy is different to just cutting tariffs. It is about government intervention to get free markets, an idea that confounds many people. The high priests of libertarianism, Milton Friedman and Hayek were sceptics about intervention even for this virtuous cause. At the same time the traditional left-wing was sceptical about intervention to win more competition because of fears this would depress wages and squeeze worker benefits. This meant we started with significant resistance from both the libertarian right and traditional left. Competition was never a simple left-right issue and it wasn't just a government versus markets issue.[8]

The libertarian principle being compromised by the policy was the sanctity of property rights. For libertarians, it was unethical for government to intervene thereby diminishing the rights to property justly acquired. The reply from Samuel was that corporate rights are not absolute but demand interpretation in terms of community interest.[9]

In the 1990s, as Australia approached the centenary of Federation, it was not a genuine national economy. A common market for the nation had yet to be created across huge tracts of the economy. Competition policy aspired to do this. Keating's intention was to create for the first time a consistent national regulatory framework for Australia spanning areas such as transport, road, rail, energy, agriculture, product standards, occupational licensing and government business enterprises. It was part of making Australia into a genuine nation; in its essence it was a nation-building project.

The origins of national competition policy lay in the Hawke government's microeconomic reform agenda. Pursued over many years by ministers such as John Dawkins, John Button, Peter Walsh and John Kerin, microeconomic reform was seen in Bob Hawke's March 1991 statement 'Building a Competitive Australia' under the over-arching heading of competition. Hawke announced a more national approach to competition policy and a plan to widen the scope of the *Trade Practices Act*. In November 1991, on the eve of Keating's ascension, the premiers agreed to assess a national competition policy.

Senior public service advisers were enthusiasts for the idea. The push for a more sweeping approach came from within the public service, notably the Prime Minister's department, and discussions involving Deputy Secretary Rod Sims and two senior economists, Mike Waller and Peter Harris. 'We should have a national competition inquiry,' Waller and Harris argued. Sims cleared the idea with Keating's office. He began talks with the states using the head of the New South Wales Premier's Department, Roger Wilkins, as point man.[10] And Sims picked Hilmer to head the inquiry and got Keating's approval.

Hilmer was a professor at the Australian Graduate School of Management at the University of New South Wales and had an MBA from the Wharton School of Finance in the United States. Sims knew Hilmer well. 'Fred was a great ideas person who could bring clarity to complex issues,' Sims said. At Hilmer's instigation the terms of reference were deliberately broad. Sims and Hilmer agreed on a sweeping provision: 'to develop an open integrated domestic market for goods and services by removing unnecessary barriers to trade and competition'. It was radical in scale and purpose. 'This was an inquiry where we knew the result we wanted,' Sims said. 'Paul Keating was happy with the initial process but he didn't drive it.'[11]

After Hilmer had been appointed he had a brief talk with Keating. Hilmer said: 'Keating's message was "I want this." The only other politician I spoke to was New South Wales Liberal Premier Nick Greiner and his response was "Go for it." So it was bipartisan from the start.'[12] This was decisive—a partisan brawl over the new policy would have been fatal. Victoria's premier, Jeff Kennett, was a strong advocate.

Reporting to the national and state governments in August 1993, Hilmer sought to entrench competition as a new economic and social value for Australia. His report rested on the idea of the 'public interest' as opposed to the 'special interest'—the rock upon which the entire post-1983 reform agenda was built. 'The essence of the report is that competition is a very powerful force in shaping an economy and society,' Hilmer said, 'and that Australia had restrained this force for much of its history. But it wasn't competition *über alles*. It's not about having no rules. There's no competition policy that has no rules. I used the cricket analogy—all competition is within a rules framework. And it's up to the politicians to set the limits.'[13]

The philosophical justification for competition begins with Adam Smith and the idea that markets are a good way to allocate resources. But Keating's vision was that government must keep its political control. 'Competition policy meant that government signed up markets as force multipliers,' Keating said. 'It wasn't about unfettered market power. It was about recasting the role of the state to meet the demands of a more individualistic society.'[14]

The Hilmer principle was no restriction on competition unless it was shown to be in the public interest. But Hilmer did accept that governments may privilege a monopoly or a special interest for equity or social reasons. His aim, therefore, was to 'leave much of competition policy squarely in the political domain'. He said: 'We took the view that the most significant trade-offs should be made by elected representatives, not administrators or judges.' Hilmer said competition cannot be an end in itself. It is about trade-offs to achieve efficiency and 'not fundamentally about right or wrong, good or bad'.[15]

The Hilmer Report identified six areas of competition policy: a toughening and widening of the *Trade Practices Act* so that it applied to public agencies, statutory marketing authorities and the private professions; a new uniform test that anti-competitive measures could only be justified if found to be in the public interest; a dismantling of public monopolies on electricity, gas and telecommunications; provision to allow third parties access to essential facilities such as gas pipelines, telecommunication networks, airports and railways where this met the public interest; oversight to check the impact of monopoly pricing; and ensuring that government businesses competing with private sector rivals were not gifted advantages due to their ownership.[16]

From the start Keating had two obstacles: selling it to the Labor Party and selling it to the state premiers. Sections of the caucus and the ACTU feared for public sector employees, the spread of privatisation and the sanctity of ALP social justice policies. At one point the caucus Economics Committee narrowly voted 5 to 4 in support of competition policy. ACTU President Martin Ferguson insisted that negotiations be within the Accord process. The labour market was excluded from the policy's scope.[17]

The critical political factor was Keating's authority within the party, his fidelity to the Accord and his status as a reinterpreter of Labor tradition. This preempted any internal revolt. It is difficult to believe that another Labor figure could have carried the policy.

At the end Wayne Swan advised Hilmer on how to brief the caucus. 'Just tell them what it means for lawyers,' Swan said—a reference to the busting of legal monopolies on conveyancing, with home buyers paying cheaper fees. 'That will get them on side.' Swan was right—and Hilmer learnt that the key to competition policy politics was its litany of individual stories, a lesson Fels had long absorbed.[18]

For Keating, management of the premiers was far tougher. State statutes were littered with anti-competitive practices, monuments to the patronage system of state politics over decades. As usual, the debate was reduced to funds. The premiers were suspicious of Keating for his October 1991 backbench assault on the Hawke–Greiner New Federalism with its pledge to consider giving the States more tax discretion. For Keating, this was heresy. It is noteworthy that Keating and Howard were revenue centralists.

Keating's speech, given two months before he became prime minister, had radiated fear across state borders. Warning that any such tax plan meant 'the dismembering of the national government', Keating said he had not entered public life to surrender tax powers to the states. Deploying Churchillian rhetoric, he said Federation had created one nation and redistributing revenue powers back to the states was a line 'we should not cross'. Rattling his sabre, he said Australia's success 'depends upon the national government having the power of the purse and not the states'. He repudiated any notion of fiscal 'imbalance' and said efforts to address this non-problem would become a 'macro disaster'.[19] On becoming prime minister, Keating removed the head of the Department of the Prime Minister and Cabinet, Mike Codd, who had pushed the co-operative federalism agenda.

Given this background, the premiers feared that competition policy by improving economic performance would further enhance Canberra's fiscal dominance. They demanded a share of the revenue gains from the new policy. The deadlock was broken by the commissioning of an Industry Commission report that predicted a $23 billion boost in GDP from competition reforms. This laid the basis for the deal. Samuel said that once the states signalled they could be purchased, 'Keating had leverage over them to get his own way.'[20] The principle endorsed by the Council of Australian Governments (COAG) was that all governments would share the economic dividends from the policy.

At the final meeting, when breakdown threatened, Mike Keating negotiated with the premiers. 'I took it upon myself to talk to Jeff Kennett and Wayne Goss,' he said. 'I pressed upon them the importance of reaching a favourable conclusion and I asked what compensation figure would seal the deal.'[21] The principle was established—the states would get payments earmarked for the competition policy reforms and these payments ran for a decade.

Treasury Secretary Ted Evans said: 'The Treasury opposed these payments at the time, but we got that wrong.'[22] Mike Keating drew the line, saying 'the premiers got a very good deal'.

> My attitude was that the States should not be 'compensated' for taking actions that were in their own best interests. In other words, competition policy was bound to lead to faster economic growth—as it did—and the states would gain from this without any extra compensation from the Commonwealth.

But, he conceded, 'the threat of withholding some of the compensation payments was useful in keeping the States up to the mark'.[23]

In a sense the entire saga constituted a win for Keating's view of federalism—in 1991 he smashed the fiscal reforms that might have threatened the national government's dominance and in 1995 he extended that dominance by bribing the states to embrace National Competition Policy.

Victoria's former pemier, Jeff Kennett, said years later: 'I did my first deal with Paul Keating on a handshake. It was the start of a good relationship between our governments. Keating and I hit it off as reformers and coming from different parties meant there was never any internal rivalry. The payments to the states were helpful but for Victoria they weren't the key factor.'[24]

Competition policy was prescient because Australia's economic progress would become increasingly dependent on state performance. Reflecting in 2008, Keating said: 'The days when the Commonwealth cabinet made the big changes, those days are over. It's what the states now do that will lift national productivity. After we had completed the big macro reforms, the operative things were being done in the states— management of transport, energy, health, education and rivers.'[25]

The key to competition policy lay in its dual structure. On the one side, the 1995 decisions created a more powerful regulator, the Australian

Consumer and Competition Commission (ACCC), from a merger of the Trade Practices Commission (TPC) and Prices Surveillance Authority. As TPC chair, Fels became more powerful with his appointment to head the ACCC. It was on his advice that the word *Consumer* was added to the title. On the other side an independent National Competition Council was created to oversee the reforms and arbitrate on the competition payments to the states. Its initial president was Graeme Samuel, who later replaced Fels at the ACCC. This structure was completed on the eve of Howard's 1996 victory.

'The timing of my appointment was pivotal,' says Fels. 'It came in November 1995, just before Keating lost office. Howard would not have appointed me but he inherited me as ACCC chair for five years.'[26] The Commission had sole responsibility for enforcement of the *Trade Practices Act*.

Before the ACCC was established Fels had persuaded the Keating government to toughen the merger test and increase the maximum fines under the law, and he had busted a series of cartels. He was convinced that Australian industry was too concentrated and that a number of unjustified mergers had previously been tolerated, notably Coles/Myer, News Ltd/ Herald and Weekly Times, and Ansett/East–West. The Fels technique was aggressive use of the law through test cases to change Australia's business culture.

'We greatly stepped up the rate of litigation,' Fels said.

> The aim was to shift the centre of political gravity on competition. The paradox is that people like the general idea of competition but not when it is applied to themselves. Everybody tries to pretend they deserve special exemptions—farmers, manufacturers, utilities, media, pharmacists. The philosophy of our system is that the independent regulator acts as a police force to investigate and then prosecute. The final decision rests with the courts. A court case means a confrontation, a winner and a loser, and lots of media publicity. In my view it is the heat across the economy on a daily basis that makes the difference. My strategy was to use a limited number of cases to generate an economy wide change in business behaviour and culture.[27]

In a deregulated economy competition policy is essential. As the alternative to tariffs and 'winning picking', it is a means to keep the marketplace honest and geared to consumer benefit. Competition policy was never conducted by Keating and Howard direct—only by the independent regulators.

Tension between Fels and political leaders was institutionalised. His feat, in retrospect, was to survive for so long. At the start his support base was narrow, mainly the Keating economic ministers and sections of the ACTU. In this situation Fels judged that popular support was indispensable. He said:

> The politics is hard. There is massive pressure from business not to act. It comes in a million different ways—from threats not to invest to getting politicians to lean on you. I know that Keating called me a publicity nymphomaniac. But the more active the ACCC became, the greater the resistance to us. Look around the world and you see many examples of competition bodies that succumbed to these pressures.[28]

Fels believed that, under Labor, his personal and family ties with Bill Kelty offered a degree of protection. 'It was important since Keating and Kelty virtually ran the country,' he said. Kelty's support had a long history. From 1991, as TPC chair, Fels showed a willingness to confront major corporations which enhanced his standing with the ACTU leaders and made the Coalition highly suspicious.[29]

At the 1996 change of government Fels was a potential target. He said: 'Ted Evans called me to a meeting and said "I feel it is my responsibility to let you know the new government is very hostile towards you and you may want to be cautious." I was also told Howard was looking into the option of removing statutory officials such as myself.'[30]

The reality is that the Howard government didn't like Fels's grandstanding style. Fels says that he 'felt uneasy in Howard's early years', yet removing him was hardly a viable option for the government. 'Things changed with the GST when I was given a free rein and the ACCC's resources were expanded,' he notes. 'From 2001 onwards relations were on a case-by-case basis.'[31]

Meanwhile, from 1995 onwards, the Hilmer-based National Competition Policy reforms were implemented across the states with a mixture of enthusiasm, apprehension and confrontation. Hilmer said: 'The big competition issues are around infrastructure. We made a lot of progress in rail, ports, coal loaders and electricity. But there were always political pressures. Take New South Wales, where the electricity issue got caught up with trade union power. The problem is when you have state governments who think as owners of assets not as regulators in the public interest.'

The governance implications were raised by academics Andrew Parkin and Geoff Anderson in a review of Tasmania's situation:

In 2001 the Tasmanian State government reported that, as a direct consequence of National Competition Policy (NCP) compliance requirements, it had amended or repealed 124 of its Acts. It had been forced to review and reform, in conformity with the principles of competitive neutrality, a host of its key services and authorities, including taxi licensing, car safety, retail trading hours, regulation of the legal profession, electricity competition, mineral exploration regulation, liquor licensing, motor accident insurance, water supply arrangements, ports management, public transport, dairy regulation, student housing, ambulance services and public swimming pools.

Parkin and Anderson highlight the transfer of political power. Competition policy made local decisions 'subordinate to a regulatory regime beyond the reach of state politics'. When Western Australian voters rejected retail shopping hours reform, the state was still penalised by losing competition payments. The conclusion is that independent political action by states has been reduced.[32]

The reality, however, is that the states, left to their own devices, would have made very few of these reforms. The New South Wales crisis over electricity privatisation in 2008 proved the point. Samuel said: 'Keating's initial motive was that too many sections of Australia's economy did not have competitive disciplines.'[33] His entire purpose was to force reforms on the states by agreement on competition policy.

From a 2008 perspective, Samuel said:

The political barriers to competition have been serious. We have had major battles with state governments, problems with the taxi industry, dairy farmers and pharmacists. The continuing dominance of Telstra over virtually all aspects of the telecommunications industry continues to retard effective competition. But the results overall are in and the policy has gone like a bomb. I think competition is crucial to the well-being of this nation and the quality of life for all Australians.[34]

In 2005 the Productivity Commission finalised its balance sheet on the policy. The Commission found that in the five years to 1998–99 productivity growth had been the highest for forty years. This boosted the average Australian household's annual income by $7000. While many factors drove productivity, competition policy was a 'major contributor'.

Commission modelling found that productivity and price changes had lifted Australia's GDP by 2.5 per cent, or by $20 billion, and it stressed that these were conservative estimates. It found that the benefits of competition policy were widespread, even reaching into rural and regional Australia. While the regions had suffered from falling export prices and population drift to cities, competition policy had helped by putting downward pressure on prices.[35]

The Commission found that competition payments to the states had totalled $5.6 billion over the previous seven years. Reform would have been 'far slower' without this incentive. The Treasury strongly supported the payments. After the initial decade they were abandoned by the Howard government. Howard said he would not pay the states to do 'what they should be doing anyway'. Costello had never liked them. Rod Sims, the bureaucrat who drove the Hilmer process, said: 'It was a great mistake for Howard and Costello to turn off these competition policy payments.'[36]

But the Commission warned that significant anti-competitive areas remained in electricity, water and telecommunications. It said competition policy gains via lower prices cannot be delivered on a recurring basis and that many are one-offs. Fels felt 'the gains have been exaggerated'—there had been too much hype and the ACCC had delivered the most progress. The failure to deliver more and faster competition in telecommunications had been conspicuous.[37] Howard's greatest competition policy blunder was his decision to privatise Telstra as a monopoly, thereby maximising the revenue but keeping an anti-competitive industry structure. He should have separated Telstra into two companies, one owning the network and the other offering telecommunications services. Hilmer said that, while Howard had protected newsagents and pharmacists, where political pressure was intense, the gains here were only small anyway.[38]

The competition policy 'balance sheet' is more hopeful than the history of Australian federalism would have predicted. But Keating, thirteen years later, charged the Howard government with lack of conviction. He said:

> I was never about killing the states. I was about saying if we're giving the states money I want some value from it. That was what

drove competition policy—getting value. It was obvious to us that the big productivity gains from cutting tariffs and from enterprise bargaining would dry up. At that point we would have to look to the states—this was the job we left to Howard and Costello. Because they refused, the Rudd government had to tackle it.[39]

This leads directly to another broader conclusion—within both the Coalition and Labor the lobby against competition policy remained unbowed and relentlessly active.

ENTERPRISE AND SAVINGS

It was my Labor principles that drove me to introduce
universal superannuation, a system similar to Medicare.
—Paul Keating, 2005

The 1990s recession gave life to two ideas formulated by Paul Keating and Bill Kelty that would touch the lives of most working Australians: enterprise bargaining and industry-based superannuation. These were the death knell of the old unionism and the old Labor Party. They dictated a reinterpretation of Laborism by harnessing enterprise culture and the share market to employee advancement.

The recession saw Australia's century-old egalitarian experiment mired in compulsory arbitration. The death warrant was signed jointly by Keating and Kelty and, for them, it was a happy funeral. They signed on behalf of the system's two greatest allies, the Labor Party and the trade unions. The reality, though, was that many of their supporters were unconvinced and dreamt of a better day when another Labor government might offer a reprieve.

Conceived in the 1890s depression, enshrined in federal Labor's 1901 first platform, lauded as the judicial embodiment of the fair go, compulsory arbitration was abandoned by Keating and Kelty as a decaying fortress. The fact that it endured for nearly a century was astonishing. Few Australian institutions have brought such ruin in the cause of justice. It was part of a wider system that helped to destroy the Whitlam and Fraser governments, perpetuated a legal framework of class conflict and left its dead weight on Australia's productivity.

Keating and Kelty despatched compulsory arbitration and its centralised wage machinery only when they had a new faith to embrace: enterprise bargaining. The transition to enterprise bargaining was a cautious affair but one imposed on a surly union movement. It was realised by Keating and Kelty in the most remarkable partnership between a Labor leader and a union chief.

The enforcement mechanism was the ALP–ACTU Accord, a vehicle of remarkable versatility. The 1990s system of enterprise bargaining was a potential turning point in the twentieth century workplace saga that began in 1904 when Liberal Prime Minister Alfred Deakin introduced the *Conciliation and Arbitration Act* in a quest to civilise capitalism. The enterprise model passed into law by the Keating government in 1993 was inherited by John Howard in 1996.

Howard built on the Keating–Kelty enterprise model. The history of these events is obscured because Howard's 1996 victory is seen as the trigger for contentious workplace reform. While true, this conceals another reality: an equally important shift came under Labor. Kelty said: 'The decision we took was that the unions couldn't live forever off the tit of the Arbitration Commission and we couldn't have judges deciding the wage increase in every industry. This was a judgement made by trade unions.'[1] But it was a judgement made under economic duress and political seduction by Keating.

In the early 1990s enterprise bargaining became the position of Keating, the Treasury, most employers and the ACTU brains trust. The enthusiasm varied but the principle was constant. It was this consensus that made the transition achievable. It was delivered by three events: the 1991 National Wage Case that saw the ACTU's final rejection of the centralised system, the 1993 re-election of the Keating government and the 1993 *Industrial Relations Reform Act* introduced by Keating's minister Laurie Brereton.

The old system originating with Deakin, best called compulsory arbitration, testified to a noble ideal that became a bureaucratic burden. Its philosophy was that fairness was unobtainable in direct bargaining between bosses and workers but needed tribunals and judges to arbitrate between recognised bodies of employers and trade unions. Individuals were banished as bargaining units. Unionism was promoted, and complex awards became the method by which tribunals protected employee and union gains. As its greatest champion, Henry Bourne Higgins said 'Reason is to displace force; the might of the State is to enhance peace between industrial combatants'.[2] The system was defined by uniform wage flows across the economy, with little regard for the distinctive features of individual workplaces. It bred low productivity, apathetic enterprise management and inferior international performance.

Australia waited almost too long before building an enterprise culture into its workplace laws. The delay revealed a blind fidelity to the folly of wage equality, judicial intervention and economic protection—a lethal troika. The toll extracted from the Australian people by the manipulation of the idea of equality is legion but none exceeds the utopianism of compulsory arbitration.

The dam wall broke with Keating's 1980s reforms. The Hawke government was based on deregulated finance and regulated labour—Hawke and Keating, via the Accord, used the centralised system to deliver wage restraint and more jobs. Its success was stunning but its shelf life was limited. By the early 1990s Kelty and Keating knew that the model was finished and a new debate began: what workplace model would Australia adopt for the next century?

Once Australia began to dismantle tariffs, the unions faced a choice: to endure even deeper real wage cuts imposed by a more competitive economy or to devise a wages model that saw progress through productivity. For several years ACTU Secretary Kelty, the strategic general of the union movement, thrashed about to find a model. Having arrived, in true Kelty fashion he campaigned as a believer. 'By 1991 Australia was going into an open economy,' Kelty later said. 'The productivity growth of some industries was going to be 6 per cent and of others minus 2 per cent. You can't sustain a centralised system in an open economy like that, even with all the goodwill in the world. We knew we had to change the system.'[3]

For the unions, it was a grudging transition. The Arbitration Commission had been their wage guarantor of last resort. But Kelty ruminated that the centralised system had been 'partly responsible for the destruction of the Whitlam and Fraser governments' in the wage explosions of the 1970s and 1980s—and 'a nation cannot shoot itself three times'.[4]

The prelude to Kelty's conversion was a sustained campaign by the free-market lobby long detested by the Left. Loose and disorganised, it spanned a coalition of Liberal Party Drys; senior Labor ministers such as Hawke, Keating, Dawkins and Walsh; prominent public servants, activist business leaders, columnists and academics; and a range of institutions, including the Treasury, the Industries Assistance Commission (later the Productivity Commission), the National Farmers Federation, the Business Council of Australia, publications such as the *Australian* and the *Australian Financial Review* and think tanks like the Centre for Independent Studies. One of its enduring goals was labour market deregulation. As Kelty knew, this idea was a threat to the future of trade unions.

The Hawke government was re-elected in 1990 on the basis of Accord Mark VI. This was a Keating–Kelty deal for a hybrid wage system that included for the first-time over-award enterprise payments. After the election the Commission heard the case for the new Accord as the 1990s recession began to bite. In a judgement in April 1991 the Commission, worried about the downturn, rejected the Accord partners—it offered a low pay rise and dismissed the enterprise bargaining proposal as phoney.

In words that engendered an unforgiving hostility from Kelty, the Commission said Australia needed a 'whole new management and workplace culture' to make enterprise bargaining viable. There was much wisdom in its conclusion, but this ignored the politics. The Commission said the system had yet 'to develop the maturity necessary' to justify the Commission authorising serious enterprise bargaining. At this point Keating and Kelty turned their venom on the Commission—both its decision and its institutional authority. They were used to getting their way. Infuriated, they would kick it close to death.

In parliament Keating said: 'I disagree most strongly with the conservatism of the Commission', arguing that it should have backed enterprise bargaining when the labour market was weak. For Kelty 'this was the most significant dispute with the Commission in our history as a union movement'.[5] But shadow Industrial Relations spokesman John Howard praised the Commission for exposing 'this sort of phoney, Clayton's enterprise bargaining that you reckon you can have inside a centralised system'.[6]

The moment of truth had arrived. That same week, on the night of 18 April 1991, Hawke, Keating and senior ministers met with ACTU leaders Kelty, Martin Ferguson, Laurie Carmichael, George Campbell and Iain Ross, with Kelty still breathing fire. 'Do you want us to abolish the Commission?' Keating asked quietly across the table. He forced the issue. The question hung in the air. Kelty said: 'No. The Commission is a worthy institution … [but] it should look after the safety net, not try to control outcomes.' Kelty refused to kill the Commission but he wanted its role permanently downgraded and he insisted that the ACTU, for the first time, would reject a National Wage Case decision.[7]

Keating's economic adviser, John Edwards, wrote: 'Thereafter we were in a new world. The Commission would not again be asked to make single decisions for the entire workforce.'[8] Meanwhile the unions struggled in the field, with meagre success, to win the pay rise that Kelty had rejected. Before year's end the Commission, in a revised judgement, conceded reality and paved the way for limited enterprise bargaining.

These events seeded a redesign sought by Keating and Kelty—the Commission's main role henceforth was responsibility for the safety net, not giving pay rises to most workers. This meant that, during the 1990s, negotiated enterprise agreements through collective bargaining would replace tribunal sanctioned awards as the main instrument for determining wages and conditions of Australian workers.

The transformation was rapid. By the end of 1999 enterprise agreements applied to more than 3.5 million workers, or 48 per cent of all employees, while those reliant on awards amounted to just 23 per cent. Melbourne University specialist Mark Wooden has shown that the overwhelming change to enterprise agreements came between March 1992 and June 1995—it happened before the advent of the Howard government.[9] Years later, Keating said: 'Kelty and I decided we had to break the system and get into a new structure where the Arbitration Commission was no longer setting wages and union leaders weren't just sitting in their offices waiting for the Commission's once-in-a-year decision.'[10]

Enterprise bargaining was a Keating–Kelty revolution. It downgraded, without abolishing, the Australian Industrial Relations Commission. It transferred power to the enterprise and it put the onus on collective bargaining. They had two motives. The economic motive was to improve productivity and the political motive was to salvage trade union power as Australia became an internationalised economy. But, for Kelty, there was another motive: to get muscle into individual unions for certain combat against a new Liberal government likely to abolish awards and shut down the Commission in a 'no prisoners' assault. Kelty was getting ready for a war with Hewson or Howard.

The new wages system helped to entrench Australia as a low-inflation nation. In February 1991 Keating declared: 'I want to snap the inflation stick ... I don't want to just bend inflation a little and then see it spring back.' Low inflation would run from 1991 to 2007, the entire Keating–Howard era.

The recession had two consequences for wages: it destroyed the market power of the unions and it provided a 'safety zone' to create enterprise bargaining. The increase in unemployment to 10 per cent entrenched low wage increases. Basic to this result was the responsible behaviour of the Commission—in 1991 it had offered only a modest pay rise; in 1992 it refused a pay rise because of record unemployment; and in 1993 the Keating government legislated to enshrine enterprise bargaining as the wage model.

Reviewing this period as Keating's economic adviser, John Edwards concluded:

> If there was one set of decisions which is most clearly linked to the prolonged upswing which followed, it was the decision of the Commission [the AIRC] to refuse further increases from April 1991 to the end of 1993 and the concurrent policy of the Keating government from 1992 through to 1994 to turn awards into safety nets and encourage much of the workforce into enterprise bargaining.[11]

Emerging from recession, Australia had a workplace model geared to low inflation and high productivity. Keating's 1993 election victory purchased a further three years to see the model established. This meant that Labor and the trade unions, not Hewson and Howard, would initially shape the post-recession workplace settlement.

As usual, Keating and Kelty cut a strategic deal before the 1993 election. Keating said: 'If we win I want to give unions more bargaining power. We'll legislate to entrench enterprise bargaining. But I want you to assure me it won't get out of hand.' Kelty replied: 'At a certain stage you have to test it. The parties must be given more responsibility. We must own the outcomes. To be honest, Paul, some of our unions are incapable of bargaining anything, let alone a 4 per cent wage increase, so I wouldn't worry about it.'[12]

The truth is that many unions, riven by weakness, were resistant. Greg Combet, who would replace Kelty as the most influential ACTU official, said: 'In that climate, because of the Accord, the ACTU and the Keating government had the ability to just go, bang. And that's what happened. It was the Accord that made enterprise bargaining possible. Kelty said the unions had to get much more into the workplace and argue their case. I can assure you this was not an easy argument to prosecute with unions but he won.'[13] Reflecting on this theme Kelty said:

> You can understand why some unions were very resistant. I had virtually negotiated everybody's personal wage increase for the best part of eight to 12 years, what was going to be acceptable for nurses, for teachers and so on. When we did the Accord I promised the unions one thing—I said we would borrow the power but we would give it back. So now we said 'We're devolving power back to unions.'[14]

Keating's 1993 victory changed the internal power balance in that it strengthened Labor in relation to the ACTU. After his election, Keating had a shock for Kelty: he appointed his friend Laurie Brereton as Industrial Relations Minister. 'I gave the job to the hard man of cabinet,' Keating said. He had no intention of letting the ACTU steamroll his government.[15]

In April 1993, Keating flew to Melbourne to deliver a post-election speech to the Institute of Directors. It stands as one of the benchmark speeches of his career. The points were agreed in drafting between Edwards and ACTU Assistant Secretary Iain Ross. The re-elected Prime Minister said:

> Let me describe the model of industrial relations we are working towards. It is a model which places primary emphasis on bargaining at the workplace level within a framework of minimum standards provided by arbitral tribunals. It is a model under which com-pulsorily arbitrated awards and arbitrated wage increases would be there only as a safety net. Over time the safety net would in-evitably become simpler. We would have fewer awards with fewer clauses. For most employees and most businesses, wages and condi-tions of work would be determined by agreements worked out by the employer, the employees and their union. These agreements would predominately be based on improving the productivity performance of enterprises.

Howard would have gone further—but he would have endorsed virtually every word. It was a revolution from the Accord of the early 1980s. The aim was more jobs, higher real wages and better productivity. Keating and Kelty wanted to establish their version of enterprise bargaining ahead of the next Coalition government.

At this point Keating passed the issue to Brereton. The unions, bitter about the recession, were hostile. 'Brereton would become their whipping boy,' Keating later said. 'They really wanted to whip me but they couldn't because I had delivered them so much. But they thought they'd kill Brereton on the way through and, you know, they gave him a terrible time.'[16]

The government wanted to abolish the union monopoly over enterprise agreements by creating a non-union negotiating stream. 'The situation I inherited was that the trade unions had a monopoly on enterprise agreements,' Brereton would say a decade and a half later. 'The ACTU was determined to keep this monopoly power. I felt this situation was unsustainable and so did Keating. We wanted to create fresh opportunities in the non-union sector. There was lots of animosity. On one occasion I was booed by the ACTU congress in the Sydney Convention Centre.'[17]

Kelty resented Brereton's criticism of the unions. 'Brereton was being brave with his bill,' he later reflected. 'He didn't need to attack the unions. But he kept talking about non-union agreements and it was destructive.'[18]

The unions had over-played their hand. 'Union leaders assumed they were going to win,' Brereton said. 'It took some time before they realised the jig was up. It would have been untenable for the cabinet to surrender.'[19] Brereton said that Kelty was frustrated because 'he didn't have the same access to Paul as before'.[20] In the end Kelty conceded: 'we had to get this bill through'.[21] Howard was waiting on the other side.

Brereton's bill reflected a complex political deal. Enterprise bargaining was defined by a 'no disadvantage' test so employees would not be worse off in totality while allowing variations to award conditions. The award system was strengthened as a safety net. This constituted a 'no losers' guarantee overall. It enabled Brereton to contrast Labor's system against the Coalition's offering of 'spartan minimum standards'. Enterprise bargaining was extended to non-union workplaces but the safeguards hardly made this an open door.

The unions had multiple wins—covering equal pay; weakening of secondary boycotts by moving them into industrial law; and a previously agreed measure to legislate for unfair dismissals destined to become an iconic issue in the Howard era.

Equipped with his bill, Brereton operated as a Labor warrior and made Hewson and Howard his targets. He defined the politics of industrial relations for the next fifteen years, running to the 2007 election. Brereton enshrined Labor's new law as the embodiment of Australia's fair go in the open economy—as opposed to the market ruthlessness of the Hewson–Howard Liberal Party.

How did he do this? By claiming to stand in Deakin's political tradition and arguing that the Liberal Party had abandoned Deakinite compassion. In his first sentence Brereton quoted from Deakin's 1904 speech introducing the *Conciliation and Arbitration Act* and hailing it as 'the very basis of civilised society'. The opponents of his bill, Deakin had said, were those 'whose God is greed, whose devil is need and whose paradise lies in the cheapest market'.[22] Such people, Brereton charged, were now Hewson and Howard.

The quote symbolically positions Deakin as a formidable opponent of *WorkChoices*. Brereton accused the modern Liberals of betraying Deakin. He sought to stigmatise the Liberal Party for its more purist view of deregulation and for trashing the 'fair go' faith that Deakin had championed. It was a neat inversion. Labor's future strategy is captured at this point. Each Labor leader would run the workplace fairness line against the Liberals—Keating, Beazley, Crean, Latham and Rudd in his assault on *WorkChoices*.

The intellectual reality was far different. Modern Australia (Labor and Liberal) was repudiating Deakin and the closed economy that he wrought. As Brereton said: 'In its previous incarnation our economy could live comfortably with a system of centralised arbitration and high tariff barriers. In the modern era it cannot. The legislation marks the culmination of the government's break with the past.'

For Keating and Kelty, the mission was to find a viable position for the labour movement in Australia's open economy. 'Don't forget the wood for the trees,' Keating said during a 2005 interview.

> This reform delivered our progress in the 1990s: rising real wages and falling unit labour costs—that means higher productivity. We delivered high profits to companies by making the workplace smarter. That's what happened and it was impossible under the old system. Kelty's achievement was to deliver his constituency. In terms of the Australian Settlement this is when I as prime minister knocked out its last leg.[23]

From the vantage point of 2008 Kelty went for hyperbole:

> This is the most important industrial relations bill in the history of the country. What you've got to understand about Howard—what he did in 1996 and with *WorkChoices*—is that he didn't destroy the model. We got the model in place—fair minimum rates of pay, enterprise bargaining with union rights to bargain. It's not like the United States, lower paid people are protected. We knew we had to get to 1996 with the system working. Paul wanted a model that would be sustained, that would outlive a Liberal government.[24]

'Enterprise bargaining was the most significant reform affecting workplace relations in at least the last fifty years,' said Mike Keating. 'It put the main responsibility for workplace reform in each enterprise where it belonged with the people who worked in that enterprise. This opened the way for significant increases in productivity.'[25] Former Australian Democrats workplace spokesman Andrew Murray said: 'I think the real fracture between early and late industrial Australia is the 1993 Keating–Brereton law. This brought modern flexibility into a more complex world.'[26]

Many of Labor's opponents agree, among them the 'brains trust' behind the deregulatory Australian Chamber of Industry and Commerce (ACCI), Peter Hendy and Peter Anderson, advisers who also worked for Reith. Anderson said: 'I think the 1993 reforms were a real turning point. The trade unions decided they had to embrace enterprise bargaining and that was their decision.'[27] Hendy has said: 'Its significance is that the labour movement as a whole—the Labor party and the trade unions—signed onto enterprise bargaining at this point. It was a very important step.'[28] 'Ultimately, politics cannot sustain the model,' Kelty said. 'It must be sustained by low inflation and high productivity.'[29]

The politicians were engineers who directed bigger forces. The dismantling of compulsory arbitration was driven by the open economy, the individualisation of society and the rapid decline in union membership. From 1990 to 2000 union membership fell from 41 to 25 per cent of the workforce. Beneath the Keating–Kelty deals Australian values were changing in an environment of 'indifference to unions and industrial tribunals'.[30]

But the habits of a century are hard to extinguish. After Rudd's 2007 victory there was a rallying cry among some unions and ministers for a return to compulsory arbitration. How far the Rudd government re-regulates the labour market remains unclear—but the forces aligned against such a revival will probably prove too great.

The story of the early 1990s is that Keating and Howard were marching in the same direction but with different models. Keating's was governed by trade union agreement while Howard's challenged trade union interests. This struggle over models ran unabated from 1991 to the 2007 election and beyond.

Before the 1996 election Kelty had a meeting with Reith during which he urged Reith to appreciate the model.

> He didn't have much of an argument with us. He said to me, 'You're more persuasive in person than you are in public.' I told him, 'Forget persuasion; this is reality.' After the election we saw Howard and I said to him, 'The economy's in the groove. This is our future, don't ruin it.'[31]

At the same time a parallel transformation was occurring with the drive to universal superannuation, initially via the industrial system and then by law. One of the Keating government's earliest decisions was to authorise this political revolution building on Hawke government policy. It became a unique Australian model that involved mandatory contributions to private superannuation funds.

The system owed much to Keating as a frustrated entrepreneur in politics. 'I have always thought that owning the home was fine,' he said. 'But being able to share in the nation's wealth in the stockmarket was a way of having the mums and dads getting a share in the bounty.'[32] Keating wanted universal superannuation to match home ownership in Australia's culture.

For the Labor Party this involved an intellectual transition from retirement welfarism to a compulsory self-provision through the share-market. By the end of the Howard era the system had created the fourth-largest funds management industry in the world, though its returns were savaged by the 2008 global crisis. Under Howard, industry-based superannuation funds became the orthodoxy, although Howard was not an enthusiast.

The reform originated in the early 1980s when Kelty, influenced by trade union chief Charlie Fitzgibbon, crossed the Rubicon to make superannuation an industrial entitlement. He later said: 'Charlie Fitzgibbon said to me, "Whatever happens, Bill, if Labor only governs for two months, we've got to get super." In my judgement Fitzgibbon was the greatest union leader, in intellectual terms, this country has had—and I agreed with him. We had to get super.'[33]

This was delivered in the Hawke–Keating–Kelty negotiations, which had their sublime moments. Kelty reflects:

> At one point we were having a heated argument at the Lodge, a real set-to. So Hazel [Hawke] came in and said we needed a break and a cup of tea. Then Paul disappeared. 'Where has he gone?' Bob asked. But Keating came back with a video tape. So we put it on, though Hazel had to get the machine working. Anyway, it's Ginger Rogers and Fred Astaire dancing. Bob said, 'What the fuck is this all about?' And Paul says 'That's got to be us, perfect steps, getting the symmetry right.' We all piped down. This story, by the way, is true.[34]

Accord Mark II in September 1985 saw the ACTU agree to a 2 per cent real wage cut and the government agree to support the union claim before the Arbitration Commission for a 3 per cent employer superannuation contribution to be paid into industry funds. Historians will be shocked to realise that universal superannuation had its origins in centralised wage fixation. By the time Keating became prime minister six years later, superannuation coverage of the workforce had risen from below 40 per cent to above 80 per cent.

'Keating was our champion,' Kelty said. 'We accepted real wage cuts and he delivered on super. The day he agreed, our relationship changed forever. I became Keating's greatest supporter. I realised Keating was a very rare person.'[35]

For Keating, the aged pension would not suffice as the main pillar of retirement provision. But award-based superannuation had two problems: the contribution level was inadequate and nearly a third of private sector employees were uncovered.

This led to the second Keating–Kelty deal embodied in the Accord Mark VI on the eve of the recession and the 1991 Hawke–Keating leadership meltdown. The deal was done at an Indian restaurant near the ACTU in Melbourne. The proposal was to lift the superannuation contribution from 3 per cent to 6 per cent as part of the next National Wage Case. But there was an historic change in the mechanism: if necessary, the government would legislate. This would transform the scheme. Progress would no longer depend on industrial negotiation but be delivered by law. This pivotal addendum had another element: if legislation was needed then the contribution rate would be set at 9 per cent. It meant the locomotive was gathering pace.[36]

In April 1991 the Australian Industrial Relations Commission (AIRC) rejected the further 3 per cent in the Accord Mark VI and a furious Kelty invoked the pledge to legislate. He said: 'I rang Paul first and asked him "Are you still prepared to legislate on super?" When he said "Yes" I told him "Good, then we'll reject this decision."'[37] But the next month Keating resigned as treasurer, challenged Hawke and went to the backbench.

With his champion gone, Kelty was alarmed. Fearing that the new treasurer, John Kerin, might renege, Kelty told Hawke that the entire union movement expected the deal to be honoured. 'I told Hawke we needed this deal. I said, "If we don't get this it will hurt the labour movement forever." Hawke agreed to talk. Then I asked Keating to make a speech supporting super.'[38]

From the backbench Keating turned up the pressure with his 25 July 1991 speech calling for a comprehensive superannuation scheme—he said the aim by 2000 should be to have contributions at 12 per cent of wage levels. Keating predicted that for most people this would double their retirement income from the pension.

On the eve of finalising the 1991 Budget Hawke agreed to the superannuation initiative. It was an historic shift in public policy—Labor would introduce a mandatory superannuation scheme by legislating a Superannuation Guarantee. Employers would be required to make contributions on behalf of their employees, making the system near universal. It was a political fix. There was no policy analysis, no Treasury White Paper that might be expected of such a sweeping compulsory measure. Hawke had honoured the Keating–Kelty deal.

In the August 1991 Budget Kerin announced that by 2000 the prescribed level of employer support would be 9 per cent of earnings. But he went further: consideration would be given to lifting this another 3 per cent by employee support and tax cuts.[39]

In 1992 Keating as prime minister oversaw the passage of legislation for the 9 per cent contribution target. When incoming Treasurer Dawkins asked Treasury Secretary Tony Cole about the target, he was told: 'We don't know anything about this policy and Treasury has done no work on it.' A grinning Dawkins said later: 'We had to do the policy work after the event.'[40] His aide, Tony Harris, said that 'it was a real scramble'.[41]

But Keating was ebullient. 'Under my model you preserved national savings by taking them off the Budget where they would otherwise be spent by ministers,' he said. 'You put them into privately managed super where they are preserved until age sixty. The real wealth in the world is made in stockmarkets and the average person never got into them. We created a new model. Super was the flag carrier of the new turbo-charged capital markets.'[42]

This gave Australia a three-pillar retirement strategy: the aged pension, mandatory superannuation, plus voluntary private superannuation. But Keating wanted more. Superannuation was in his brain. After the 1993 election, when his LAW tax cuts could not be afforded, Keating proposed, finally, that the second leg of the tax cuts be paid as superannuation into employee accounts.

The idea gripped him with a passion. It was a pre-election strategy to lift superannuation savings to 15 per cent from the legislated 9 per cent. It was Keating's last gasp for glory as an economic reformer—to be achieved through a combination of contributions from government, employers and employees. Keating sold this as a virtue that would boost savings and buttress retirement provisions. But the public mood of 1995 had no interest in Labor virtues. The idea disappeared like a puff of smoke with the election defeat.

Before the election, Howard and Costello said, quietly, that they would honour existing arrangements as distinct from future arrangements. The Howard government stuck by the 9 per cent contribution for its entire life. Years later Keating lamented that he did not legislate the full 15 per cent, an option Kelty had raised with him at the time.[43]

Keating never forgave Howard for abandoning Labor's 15 per cent commitment. But this was absurd since it would have been unusual for Howard to display fidelity to Labor's pledges. In a more philosophical assessment Kelty said:

> Howard should have gone to 15 per cent. But he didn't destroy our model. It was still in place in 2007 when he left, just like enterprise bargaining was in place. The nation had decided this is a sensible policy for retirement incomes and even in the Liberal Party it had gained acceptance. You see, our ideas survived Howard.[44]

11

THE PATRIOTISM PUZZLE

Australia must have a new idea of itself.
—Paul Keating, 8 May 2001, at ALP Centenary Dinner

Throughout his four-and-a-half years as prime minister, Paul Keating aspired to bring forth a more independent Australian national identity. Its essence was a new patriotism and it was probably his most elusive quest, fluctuating between politics and metaphysics. It was perceived variously as either foolhardy or heroic.

It was a project in which Keating delighted. He rarely seemed as happy as when engaged in this activity that became the heart of his declared 'big picture'. It fitted his leadership concept that privileged 'imagination' as a quality. His preoccupation with national identity was an effort to provoke the imaginative daring of the people, many of whom remained mystified by his project.

In his January 1992 Australia Day message Keating said that 'we must re-make Australia'. This was the language that usually thrilled the True Believers and unsettled conservative Australians. Invoking the 1890s decade as the cradle of the old Australia, he declared, with his eye on the 2001 centenary of Federation, that 'the new Australia, I firmly believe, can be born' in the 1990s. He was impatient to move. His intention, as the writer on Australian nationalism James Curran argued, was to 'redefine the nation'.[1] It suggested the mind of an artist in the body of a politician. It came from Keating's heart as much as his head and it was hubris-filled. The metaphor of a 'big picture' suggested a creation beyond the mechanics of finance and administration. The man was chasing a new Australian spirit.

Keating wanted to liberate Australians from what Manning Clark called the Kingdom of Nothingness. Although Keating did not invoke such comparison, it may be accurate to say that what he really sought to combat was the great Australian indifference identified by DH Lawrence during his New South Wales sojourn. For Lawrence, Australia was a 'really weird show' with its mixture of fascination and indifference, as though it came from a place 'before souls, spirits and minds were grown at all'.[2]

The identity issue fitted Keating's temperament and his wandering moods. 'In no small measure the future of Australia is a cultural issue,' Keating declared in mid-1992. 'The economic imperative and the cultural one can't be separated—they have the same conclusion.'[3]

What, exactly, was that conclusion? The essence of Keating's conclusion lay in faith and it is likely that his Catholic childhood drove his vision. In 1994, at Notre Dame University, he committed the heresy of suggesting that faith was more important than education: 'As an old De La Salle boy and a Labor Party man, let me tell you that while education is essential to your lives, and always will be, there is no substitute for faith. That's my lesson: believe in yourselves, believe in your generation, believe in your ideals, believe in your country. Keep the faith.'[4] This transmission came direct from the 1950s Catholic school system, reinforced by Labor tribalism and Australian patriotism. Only the script was different—this was faith in temporal world institutions and, ultimately, in Australia.

Faith was important because it would drive the Australian reinvention that Keating craved. This became the pervasive purpose of his prime ministership. He could have presented his agenda just as a series of public policies. He did this, but he did far more. He presented such ideas—the market economy, republic, Aboriginal reconciliation and Asian engagement—as articles of faith. Once treated as new faiths, they demanded acts of national redemption.

Keating wanted atonement for past sins. He was interested in the nation's soul. In office he provided, in speech after speech drafted by Don Watson, an extended dialogue about the 'sacred things which no generation should be allowed to forget'. He said, 'In truth, politicians who believe in their cause are always conscious that they have a story to tell. When a government cannot convey a story, a consistent story, the people lose faith in the government.'[5]

Like all good stories, Keating's had a start, a middle and an end. The start was Australia's decision to liberate itself from the racism, insularity and xenophobia of its past. He would ruminate on this theme for hours. 'We came close to being marginalised,' he would say, 'we escaped White Australia in the nick of time.'[6] The middle of the story was the contemporary struggle to deregulate the economy, terminating a century of insularity. In reflecting on the 1980s economic reforms, Keating decided that their cultural essence lay in greater national maturity. The Age of Empire, with its rules of loyalty and obedience, had died. This conclusion led directly to the story's mythic end: the emergence of a new Australian spirit founded in independence.

Keating could frame this story as a parable of economic progress or as foreign policy realism or as a social justice narrative. Its power lay in its universality. He spoke with great eloquence and undisciplined passion. Much of Australia's educated class could not decide whether he was a madman or a genius; yet he captured, substantially, Australia's intellectual class.

Donald Horne, a critic, saw the defects in Keating's journey: 'The romantic idea of a great voyage is useful because when Mr Keating set out from Bankstown the basic knowledge he carried with him was a bundle of myths. He is highly intelligent (although not necessarily very wise) but his knowledge is mainly bits and pieces, held together by mythic conviction. When one of his myths is working well, this can provide the charm and confidence of a Pied Piper.'[7]

Historian and former New South Wales Labor Minister Rodney Cavalier believed that Keating's history agenda was a fatal diversion. Cavalier said:

> Paul was sounding like the National Library and the great institutions of public life had become his own property. The only legitimate sense of Australian identity was the one Paul defined. His ideas agenda based on the republic, native title, engagement with Asia and multiculturalism cut no ice with the electorate at large, especially core Labor voters. In various ways these items were seen as being away with the fairies or antipathetic to everything a generation of Australians believed were the reasons that made Australia into the country they loved.[8]

Keating's mind ran in another direction. He felt that, in the globalised age, Australia must be strong in both economic and cultural domains. Nations with poor self-esteem would be broken. He warned that 'in the 1990s we need to be confident in ways that we have never been, independent in ways that we've never been'. This was because all the old supports were gone—the Empire, White Australia, the regulated economy.[9] Australia was in new psychological territory and, accordingly, it needed a deeper patriotism. 'We need that certainty, the inner confidence about who we are and what we've become,' he said.[10]

He dreamt of a better Australia but his identity project was liable to many interpretations. It was offensive to those who disagreed with him and risky given the Australian public's suspicion of the motives of politicians. Keating's identity improvisation was pursued too often with reckless disregard for his electoral health. This was Keating as national therapist. He hoped that his vision—a cultural renewal amid a more dynamic economy—would carry the people across the psychological impasse that lay between themselves and their future.

For Keating, the elements of his vision were in wonderful harmony—a pro-market economy tied Australia to Asia; strong ties with Asia fitted Australia as a multicultural society; such a society would be more disposed to republicanism and Aboriginal reconciliation. It was very neat—a renovated Labor ideology. Mark Ryan said: 'Paul wanted to give the Labor Party a new set of ideals. He was appealing to a whole new generation of voters.'[11]

The nation was in a recession-induced despondency. In his impatience, Keating wanted to change the music and re-energise the place. His starting point was Australia's holy grail: he decided to offer a reinterpretation of Gallipoli and the nationalist tradition.

In a sense the timing was right. Keating became prime minister the month that saw the fiftieth anniversary of Japan's attack at Pearl Harbor launching the Pacific War. He had to preside over a series of anniversary events that commemorated World War II. His *One Nation* economic statement was delivered a few days after the fiftieth anniversary of the fall of Singapore. Keating's time as prime minister would be surrounded by war memory. Running parallel to such memories was Keating's task of preparing the nation for the 2001 centenary of Federation and a chance for self-realisation in the decade leading to the centenary.

For Keating, it was time to quit the past. 'I want to see us leave home,' he said in 1992 of the ties to Britain.

> Of course, we do not remain there in any substantial material way—but we are there emblematically and to a degree psychologically and it would be much better for us in the real world that we now inhabit if we removed the emblems and excised the doubts. We need very badly that spirit of independence and faith in ourselves which will enable us to shape a role for ourselves in the region and the world.

Compressed into one single line his view was: 'We will go into the world independent or we will not succeed.'[12]

Few people grasped the emotional depth of Keating's belief. Years later, at a splendid 2001 Melbourne function to celebrate the centenary of the Labor Party coinciding with Howard's fifth year in the Lodge, Keating, as last speaker—following Beazley, Whitlam and Hawke—unfurled his true beliefs about Australia's first century. 'I think the lesson of the Federation should be that the lesson is over,' he told the legions of Labor faithful. 'Australia must have a new idea of itself. We have to strike out in a new direction ... I conclude my remarks by saying that I wish Kim well and the party well. I hope it bodes well for another century. But a century of our own and not someone else's.'[13]

The audience was thrilled but it missed the point. The last Labor prime minister of Australia's first century, in effect, had repudiated the century's legitimacy. Our first century had belonged to others. He called for the next hundred years to be an Australian century. The nation needed to be liberated. 'I hoped, as we approached the new century, we would have an Australian model of what we are, not a British model or an American model,' he said.[14] This is what he attempted in office.

Keating was obsessed with the notion of Australia as a derivative society needing liberation. In his 1990 'Placido Domingo' speech he said:

> We never laid it all down in a constitution. Well, we did at the turn of the century, but it had the signature of the British Parliament on it. We never said, 'This place is ours and we're going to run it ourselves; and we're going to sit down, we're going to write a constitution which a couple of hundred years later could be as fresh as the day it was written.' These are the things we never had. It might have been our convict past. God knows what it was. Maybe it was all the rip-off merchants that came with free settlement or what-have-you.[15]

There is, however, a danger for a leader so ambivalent about the origins of his own nation. For Keating, there was a shadow across Australia—the shadow of its failure to achieve independence in heart and mind. The idea had lodged in his brain.

On Keating's first Anzac Day as prime minister, he went to Kokoda. It was a trip conceived in reinvention, making him the first national leader to launch a critique of the origins of nationhood. This revealed Keating's ambivalence about the Gallipoli legend and his conviction that it had distorted Australian history.

The dawn service was at Port Moresby's Ela Beach and Keating arrived late. He called Gallipoli an 'indissoluble' memory, upheld the

Anzac legend and said that Australia 'must move with it' as the world moved on. While acknowledging that 'legends bind nations together' Keating declared that such legends 'should not stifle us' or 'restrict us when we have to change'. Conservative alarm began to rise.

Invoking one of the imperishable historical events, Keating reminded his audience of Curtin's stoic defiance of Churchill in returning Australian forces from the Middle East to fight the Japanese. Curtin, said Keating, 'took the Anzac legend to mean that Australia came first'. The Australians who fought in Papua New Guinea died in defence not 'of the old world but the new world—their world'. 'That is why it might be said that, for Australians, the battles in Papua New Guinea were the most important ever fought.' He quoted Sir William Slim, saying it was the Australians 'who first broke the spell of invincibility of the Japanese Army'.[16]

Keating had waited a lifetime to deliver this speech, the most contentious Anzac Day speech ever given by an Australian prime minister. In seeking to relocate the Anzac legend he was attempting to tell Australians that Gallipoli was not the most important battle in their history, that when it came to Australia's national interest and survival, the most important battle was Kokoda. And Kokoda could only have been fought successfully because of Curtin's will to defy Britain and the old world. It was a Labor achievement as well as an Australian achievement. While Gallipoli looked back to Britain, Kokoda looked forward to independence. The Coalition's anger was incandescent.

On his trip Keating was accompanied by Professor David Horner, Australia's distinguished military historian. Horner offered the intellectual foundation for Keating's comments. In Horner's view, if Port Moresby had been taken by the Japanese advancing over the Kokoda Track, 'the whole strategic situation would have been transformed'—and 'in that sense Kokoda was the most important battle fought by Australians in the Second World War'.

This did not deny, however, that Australia's position in World War II had been secured by the naval battles of Coral Sea and Midway; it would be a falsification of history to diminish the centrality of these battles. Such American actions forced Japan to change its tactics and to try to take Port Moresby by land, leading to the debilitating battles along the Kokoda Track. Japan's strategy at this stage was isolation, not invasion, of Australia—a point rarely grasped and sometimes deliberately distorted to cultivate the myth of a 'Battle for Australia'.

As Keating approached the Kokoda memorial he suddenly fell to his knees and kissed the ground. It was an unexpected gesture that shocked everyone. Kissing sacred ground has never been a ritual for Australia's political leaders. It is impossible to imagine Menzies or Curtin or Howard doing anything like this, just as it was inconceivable to think of Keating kissing the ground until it actually happened.

For Keating, it was an act of homage to focus attention on his re-interpretation of Australia's history. Don Watson betrayed the extent of delusion, suggesting it was an act to 'mark Kokoda in Australia's collective memory, as perhaps Gettysburg was marked in the American mind by Lincoln'.[17] Many veterans were uneasy. This was too different, too political.

Keating's effort to elevate Kokoda was overdue. In Australia there was little awareness of the New Guinea campaigns and such history was being undermined in the school curriculum. His mistake was of a different order: trying to re-engineer the national legend.

At the precise time when Keating was worrying that the Gallipoli story might 'restrict' or 'stifle' the nation, its people had launched an act of spontaneous homage. The return to Gallipoli had begun. Starting with the seventy-fifth anniversary in 1990, young people, relatives of those who had fought, backpackers and others drawn by nationalism, family ties, adventure and discovery began visiting Gallipoli in large numbers each Anzac Day. Despite official patronage it was a grass-roots movement integral to a bigger event: the resurgence of Anzac as a day of united commemoration with the spirit of Gallipoli at its heart.

Those Australians visiting Turkey explored a stony beach below a daunting cliff where the atmosphere was different from that of any other beach they had walked and where a shallow amphitheatre constituted a killing ground on which the Australian spirit was first thought to have been realised and where these Australians felt touched with an elusive yet sharp sense of the sacred. No Australian who visited Gallipoli remained untouched.

The truth about Gallipoli and Anzac was its universality. The legend belonged neither to conservatives nor to Empire loyalists. This is where Keating misconceived his project. The commemoration, from its 1915 origins, belonged to the entire nation. Its universality was built on its reality. For Howard, the return to Gallipoli movement was a vindication of the Australian tradition that Keating distrusted.

The power of Gallipoli lay in its authenticity. War correspondent Charles Bean said the force that drove the troops had been 'their idea of Australian manhood'. On the first Anzac Day anniversary 100 000 people gathered at Sydney's Domain in a mass commemoration. Ken Inglis, in his book *Sacred Places*, quoted his age-mate, Peter Shrubb, a child of the culture of the Great War, writing that 'Anzac Day was the only day of the year that had any kind of holiness in it.' Bean's prophecy that 'Gallipoli never dies' was being vindicated. The moral was that Gallipoli could be added to but not detracted from—it was impervious to political reconstruction. The fused Australia–British nationalism that it embodied was authentic, not an inferior ethos, another point that Keating did not comprehend.

Launching Graham Freudenberg's book *Churchill and Australia* in 2008, Keating was even more unforgiving. He now argued: 'I have never been to Gallipoli and I never will [go]', suggesting a dogmatism that defied balance. Dismissing Gallipoli as an 'ill-conceived and poorly executed campaign' conducted by imperial interests, he repeated the radical nationalist refrain of 'none of it in the defence of Australia'— overlooking that, in a world run from Europe, Australia's strategic fate at the time was determined almost solely by European events. The reason Australia's leaders were united in their commitment to the Great War was its strategic centrality for Australia's future.[18]

The Kokoda–Gallipoli tension was an unnecessary Keating contrivance. It revealed the flaw in Keating's identity politics—his obsession with deliverance from a British past—and his vision required acts of national contrition. But this is not how most Australians thought. Keating was not just taking Australia into the future; he wanted to repudiate a conservative past, issue by issue.

'I always had this point of difference with the Coalition about Gallipoli,' he said. 'It has been a matter of dogma for the Coalition parties once they lured [Billy] Hughes to their side and fought the First World War that, upon the Armistice, they took over the grieving as though it was theirs to take over.' Keating's charge is that, after the Labor Party split of 1916, the conservatives 'believed the war was theirs to be prosecuted and to be won'. For Keating, the conservatives seized the political capital and national ownership from the Great War. They appropriated Gallipoli and the Anzac legend and 'wilfully pursued it for years'. He was open about his motive at Kokoda—to break the conservative hold on Australian nationalism; it was elemental to his prime ministership.

Referring to the New Guinea campaigns, Keating said: 'I had a chance to make the case about the sacrifice of those that went out in the defence of Australia, not in the service of the King or Empire.'[19] This is astonishing nonsense. Curtin, who underwrote the New Guinea campaigns, was a British race patriot and an upholder of the Empire ideal who appointed a Briton as Governor-General. The Labor Party had been a dedicated advocate of the British Empire whenever it governed. The World War II battles in the Middle East and New Guinea were different in strategic terms, but there was no difference in terms of the outlook or nationalism of the troops. The claim that one group was fighting for Empire and another for Australia was absurd—a construct unsubstantiated by history, unpersuasive to the Australian people, and a despicable violation of the motives of the troops.

But Keating's quest for redemption was unyielding. The republic was to purge past attachment to Crown; Aboriginal reconciliation was a repudiation of past violence and injustice to indigenous peoples; engagement with Asia was the purification for the long age of race-driven insularity. These policies were presented not just as a vision for the future but as a critique of Australia's past—and this was their defect.

Keating wanted to reinterpret history to fit into his new patriotism. He wanted to shift the balance in the national myth—from Gallipoli to Kokoda, from Britain to Asia. He developed the idea that Australia's engagement with Asia had begun with the fall of Singapore. This was the point where the failure of the old patriotism gave birth to a new patriotism. Kokoda was 'the place where I believe the depth and soul of the Australian nation was confirmed', he said. It was created at Gallipoli but enhanced at Kokoda. As Curran said, 'His [Keating's] view was that if Australian engagement with Asia began in the crucible of war a more powerful moral authority could be lent to Australia–Asia relations.'[20]

It would be misleading, though, to think Keating was an unrelieved critic of the past. When his personal memories of suburban Australia were triggered, a very different ethos was recalled—a picture of decency, tolerance and national pride among ordinary and newly arrived Australians. Keating said:

> I lived in Bankstown where it had gone from Anglo–Irish to Greeks and Italians and then to Lebanese and Vietnamese and I lived there until I became treasurer in 1983 and I'd never seen one nasty ethnic inspired event. I'm not saying there hadn't been some … I thought the thread that held the place together, in the minds of the public, the tolerance of different cultures, religions and ethnic groups, was the fact that they would and should commit first and foremost to the new adopted country, to its principles and standards, to Australia. And that this was not too much to expect.[21]

The point is that Keating saw multiculturalism strictly within a unifying patriotic vision. This was Howard's view. It was a reminder of the shared Keating–Howard perception of how Sydney had changed, with each of their electorates being a study in such multicultural diversity. They drew the same conclusion—the need for a singular identity as the foundation for successful diversity. Contrary to mythology, Keating and Howard were not far apart on multiculturalism. On occasions Keating warned that multiculturalism might contribute to 'circumvent the emergence of a singular Australian identity'.[22]

It was a reminder that Keating wanted a new patriotism, not any fuzzy weak multi-ethnic internationalism often championed by the Left. As prime ministers, Keating and Howard operated within a national interest framework. This often alienated them from the intellectual class with its distaste for patriotic sentiment and suspicion of national interest concepts.

There was, however, no gainsaying the challenge posed by Keating's new patriotism. He was treading on people's fears, lifestyles and conventional wisdoms. No market researcher would have advised this tactic.

In April 1992 Keating, having outlined his vision, spoke to those generations 'who I know regret the passing of the old Australia'. He offered sympathy but no concessions. 'My point is that we can no longer be Australian in the way Bob Menzies was Australian. These echoes of Menzies cannot be allowed to get in the way,' he said. 'We are not about treason here but nationhood.'

Recognising that Australia had been dealing with Asia for a long time, Keating wanted a deeper process. 'I mean cultural reform, the reform of our outlook,' he said. 'In truth, we've not done badly. But we'll do best when we've removed all signs of our being a branch office.' By this he meant a president, a new flag and a multicultural diversity that brought cross-cultural skills. He meant a nation 'sure of who we are and what we stand for'.[23]

His vision was heroic because he mocked the timidity of leadership in the poll-driven age. History is likely to offer a favourable judgement on his vision. Australia, sooner or later, will become a republic; engagement with Asia offers an enduring template for dealing with the region; Aboriginal reconciliation is an eternal project subject to reinterpretation; and a diverse nation is a reality that demands national cultivation.

But Keating's vision was of no use at the 1996 election. It did not save him and it helped to damn him. It typecast him as 'out of touch' when there were more tangible issues. Ultimately, he lectured too much and listened too little.

His leadership vision was only accentuated in his retirement. 'What is this game about?' Keating asked years later. 'Is it all about the maintenance of Labor governments? No. The game is about the resetting of Australia's fortunes. I don't much care whether Kevin Rudd or a Coalition leader changes the Australian flag. But I sure as hell want [to see the change].'[24]

In a sense Keating's new faiths were too abstract and distant from the people. They lacked the tenacity of the old faiths—White Australia, a British–Australian nationalism and Imperial loyalty. His vision was too beloved by writers and artists, a sure sign of a sceptical public reaction. The deeper issue is that patriotic myths are embedded in a nation's history, the story of the United States being the supreme example. The real trick is to integrate the nation's future direction with the historic myth rather than seek, as Keating did, to repudiate the narrative from the past.

Despite such problems Keating's claims on an emerging national ethos are unmistakeable. His vision, for better or worse, was deployed to inspire Labor followers and to assault the Howard-orientated Liberals. In the process Keating had shown that, in the 1990s, patriotism and culture were staple ideas for political leaders. Howard understood the lesson—he was planning his own patriotic onslaught.[25]

12

ASIA AND AMERICA:
THE GRAND STRATEGY

*It's clear to me having watched from the White House that this
was a special relationship. It is not an exaggeration to say
that Paul Keating inspired President Clinton.*
—Stanley Roth, former US Assistant Secretary of State
for Asian and Pacific Affairs, June 2008

Paul Keating came to foreign policy as a frustrated architect—he
looked for grand structure and clever design. With Asia, he sought
to impose an orderly political blueprint and with America he hoped
to open new windows. Arriving in office in the 1991 year of destiny,
Keating felt the end of the Cold War created a new opportunity for
Australia. He pursued a grand strategy based on two ideas—to entrench
Australia in the rising economic dominance of the Asia–Pacific and to
integrate the US alliance into Australia's Asian future. He pursued them
with passion and with remarkable consequences.

This was not an original strategy—it had belonged to the Hawke
government, where Keating had participated in trade and security
decisions—but Keating refined this strategy, giving it fresh energy.

He approached foreign policy as a national interest realist who
rejected the notion that shared values were essential for close ties, the
Howard position. His foreign policy adviser, Allan Gyngell, said:

> Keating saw the world in terms of realpolitik. As an adviser you
> get to know what angles interest a PM. Keating was interested in
> the big picture, the size of GDP and the source of national power
> and influence. He saw the world in power terms. The central
> strategic vision Keating pursued in foreign policy was to entrench

for Australia a place in the emerging Asia–Pacific region. This was the organising principle of his policy.[1]

But this does not fully capture Keating. The leader with a passion for French antiques saw foreign policy in a nineteenth-century, 'from the Palace' style of personal brokerage that recalled the pre-democratic age when the fate of nations was decided over dinner. 'Politicians shape the world,' he loved to say. For Keating, this wasn't a cliché but a principle for action. Whether sitting with Clinton or Soeharto, he enjoyed high diplomacy and put a premium on his ability to persuade.

'When I became prime minister all of Australia's vital interests coalesced in Asia—trade, security, cultural,' Keating said.[2] It was typical of his hyperbole. He represented the zenith of an intellectual revolution among Australian elites mesmerised by the Asian economic miracle that had run for four decades with Japan at its epicentre. During the 1980s Hawke and Keating had become fixated on the opportunities for Australia flowing from the economic rise of East Asia.

Keating embraced two faiths that defined modern Labor's approach: that Asia was the key to Australia's future and that a system of Asia–Pacific regionalism was the means of harmonising Australia's diverse national interests.

This vision originated with Hawke, beginning with his insight into China's vast growth potential after the 1978 launch of its economic reforms under Deng Xiaoping. Hawke had sensed the huge potential of China–Australia trade and was able to establish the closest personal ties between an Australian prime minister and China's leaders, notably Premier Zhao Ziyang and Party Secretary Hu Yaobang. Hawke was influenced by his adviser, Ross Garnaut, whom he appointed as ambassador to China, and Garnaut's report, 'Australia and the Northeast Asian Ascendancy' offered a strategic blueprint for Australia's path. Hawke talked about 'enmeshing' Australia with Asia. Keating, as an enthusiast, aspired to institutionalise 'engagement with Asia' as a foreign policy and, in a more risky manoeuvre, he sought to popularise the idea.[3]

Integral to Keating's framework was to persuade the United States to shift its focus from the Atlantic to the Pacific. He ran diplomatic campaigns to this effect with President George Herbert Bush and President Bill Clinton and he used the Asia–Pacific Economic Cooperation (APEC) forum, a Hawke government initiative, as his regional focus.

Having become prime minister in the year that saw the death of Soviet communism, Keating hoped a more fluid international climate would encourage the United States to rekindle a Pacific strategy based on economic opportunity and the evolving Asian balance of power. The irony, as Bush's National Security Adviser Brent Scowcroft told Keating at Kirribilli House on New Year's Day 1992 (with the President having a bathroom break), was that: 'You are anticipating, Prime Minister, a modus operandi for the United States in Asia that we have not yet articulated for ourselves.'[4]

The origins of the modern Australian–American relationship lie, like so much else, within the Hawke government. Often reluctant to admit it, Keating and Howard stood on Hawke's shoulders. It was Hawke who had invited George Bush to Australia—the first visit by a serving US president in twenty-five years. This visit became the threshold to a remarkable flourishing of closer Australia–America ties over the next generation. The extent of the transformation is underestimated and popular depictions that it was just a Howard–Bush 'love affair' miss the point.

The alliance had matured under Hawke's management, his government's dealings with the Reagan administration, and the diligence of Kim Beazley as Defence minister in winning US support for the philosophy of defence self-reliance. Hawke and Bush had a personal relationship that saw Bush seek Hawke's political advice during 1988 in his White House contest against Democrat Michael Dukakis. Hawke's private views were firm: he was backing Bush and found Dukakis, like many Democrats, uninterested in Australia.[5] The new era would see a premium on personal ties: Hawke with Bush, Keating with Clinton and Howard with George W Bush. But these ties would translate into deeper institutional links. That no serving US president had visited in the previous quarter century mocked any idea of Australia as a US priority and suggested that Australia's leaders had been deluding themselves.

When President Bush planned his visit he expected Hawke to be his host, but Hawke had been deposed. For Keating, the timing was perfect. 'I was determined that this would be the moment when Australia re-pointed itself in the new post-Cold War world,' he said.[6] Keating threw away the 140-page official brief and convened meetings with advisers to formulate a proactive stance.

On New Year's Day, ahead of the formal Canberra talks, the two leaders met at Kirribilli, each with a single adviser—Bush with Scowcroft and Keating with Ashton Calvert, a future head of the Department of Foreign Affairs and Trade. Keating, unfortunately, did most of the talking. He offered Bush and Scowcroft a regional analysis with a focus on America's leadership role. The Americans were unaccustomed to flying halfway round the world to sit beside a dazzling harbour and be lectured about how the world worked and what Australia expected from them.

Keating was shameless and compelling.[7] He wanted the United States in the post-Cold War world to fashion an integrated Asia–Pacific strategy. Like a good social democrat, Keating focussed not on bilateral but on multilateral economic mechanisms. This was the Labor way.

'We have to avoid the risk of the world fracturing into three separate trading blocs in Europe, Asia and the Americas,' he told Bush. 'You have the scope to put in place institutions as influential as the postwar Bretton Woods arrangements.' Keating argued that there was no political architecture in the Asia–Pacific, just unresolved rivalries—Japan and China, the Taiwan issue and Korean peninsula. It wasn't enough to allow the US Navy to run America's Pacific policy. Keating argued that a bigger US trade and commercial role would create a better basis for strategic involvement. His main proposal to Bush was that APEC become the region's major political architecture by being reconstituted at head of government level.[8]

Keating's APEC concept revealed Labor's attachment to a regionalism founded in mutual economic interest as a device to entice China's participation and broker new arrangements as a substitute for dangerous national rivalries. This culture of 'middle power' Australian diplomacy was embedded in Labor's thinking. As usual, Keating put the emphasis on leadership—his dream was that APEC leaders meeting together, away from their advisers, would produce a new political chemistry.

But American leaders do not see Asia the way Australian leaders do, and it is a lesson Australians are notoriously reluctant to learn. After the meeting the story circulated that Bush had been 'mostly mute with perplexity' while Scowcroft had listened in 'polite wonder'.[9] Keating felt pleased but this encounter was not a meeting of minds.

The meeting of minds had occurred earlier that day over a lunch cruise when Nick Greiner hosted the Bushes at a table that included Scowcroft, Australian businessman Phil Scanlan and Scanlan's American wife, Julie. The President invited their thoughts and Scanlan suggested that Australia presumed the permanence of the alliance at its peril. 'I don't want to wake up one morning and find the US has unilaterally declared independence from Australia,' he said. That got Bush interested. He told Scanlan he believed the alliance was in America's interest. 'Well, Mr President, please say that today,' Scanlan replied. Scowcroft said he had served two presidents but this was his first visit to Australia—he felt Scanlan had a point.[10]

They discussed the shift in alliance dynamics with the inevitable passing of the World War II generation as represented by the President. Scanlan said fresh ties were needed and suggested the formation of a new group of Australian and American leaders. Bush liked the idea. 'Why don't you arrange something?' he suggested. But Scanlan replied: 'I don't think there's much point in me arranging something until you take a prior decision—it needs your imprimatur, it must have the White House and the Lodge behind it.'

Two nights later, at a black tie Canberra function, Scowcroft told Scanlan: 'We've spoken to people. We've checked you out. The President wants you to go ahead.' Scanlan had Bush's sanction. In anticipation he had held a prior discussion with Greiner and Beazley and they had agreed to his request to become standard bearers for Liberal and Labor in the new group. Scanlan then imposed another condition: he wanted Scowcroft to become chief recruiter on the Republican side, and Scowcroft agreed. Hence the Australian American Leadership Dialogue was conceived.[11]

A unique group, privately organised, with meetings alternating between the two countries, the Dialogue would become an institution of influence over the next generation. Many issues were informally processed through the Dialogue. One of the initial attendees invited by Scanlan was a young official, Kevin Rudd, who was unfamiliar with the United States but became educated in American ways and built his US networks virtually entirely from the Dialogue.

In April 1992 Keating formally launched his initiative. He wrote to the leaders of the United States, Japan and Indonesia to propose the upgrading of APEC. It was a tactical move to get the 'big three' committed. Keating felt that, if he could win Bush, Japan's Miyazawa and Indonesia's Soeharto, he had a real chance.

In his 3 April letter to Bush, he wrote:

> I believe the absence of head-of-government meetings is an important gap in Asia–Pacific regional relations. It set the region apart from most other areas of the world. … And yet the region, which will enter the next century as the most dynamic in the world, and which is already acquiring increasing weight in global terms, stands out as having no such forum.

He suggested that APEC leaders met 'perhaps every two or three years', that 'this would be a useful way for the United States Government to consolidate its engagement in an increasingly important regional economic process'.

The problem was subtle yet acute—there was no sense of the Asia–Pacific as a community. Keating needed to foster a political consciousness that did not yet exist. Critical to his vision, as he wrote to Bush, was that APEC 'seems to me to offer the best foundation for such meetings'. In order to win acceptance Keating proposed 'an exclusively economic agenda' given the problems arising from the 'three Chinas'—Beijing, Taiwan and Hong Kong.[12]

In his 29 April reply Bush offered a glimmer of hope, but no more. He said: 'I believe the most effective means of moving your suggestion forward at the proper time would be for Australia to take the lead. Too prominent a US role would be counterproductive.'[13] This reflected Bush's previous remark to Keating that if the United States pushed the idea then 'China and Indonesia will run away from it'. In truth, Bush was unenthusiastic; Keating's initiative was not a US priority. Bush had a crowded Asian agenda dominated by US trade tensions with Japan that assumed a sharp edge in the Bush–Clinton 1992 election contest.

In September 1992 in Detroit, Bush announced that if re-elected he would pioneer 'a strategic network of free-trade agreements across the Atlantic and the Pacific and in our own hemisphere'. Australia was one of the nations mentioned. The bilateral agreements idea came from an influential Republican, Bob Zoellick, a future architect of the Australia–America Free Trade Agreement who felt his proposal would benefit Australia. Howard would later draw on these ideas for his bilateral trade deal with the United States.

But Keating was dismayed. 'The more we thought about the Detroit speech, the more we worried,' he said. It followed messages from the Bush administration to the Australian embassy in Washington about the need to 'encircle' Japan with a network of free trade agreements. For Keating, this violated Australia's interest since Japan was our main trade partner. He feared the United States would split the Pacific into a dollar-and-yen bloc. Keating saw Bush's speech as a threat to Australia's region-wide trade liberalisation stance embodied in its APEC vision. He feared rising US scepticism about the sort of multilateral solutions that constituted Australia's core strategy.[14]

So Keating turned critical. This was not the US leadership he wanted. That same month Keating made his first visit as prime minister to Japan, his old stamping ground from his time as shadow Resources minister. He became the first Australian leader to repudiate the United States from Tokyo.

Keating said that Australia wanted an open global trading system; it saw 'no overall gain' from entering any trade pact with the United States that discriminated against Japan; Australia disliked Bush's 'hub-and-spokes model' of trade and security deals across the Pacific. Keating said his own vision was for a regional trade area involving Japan, America, Australia and others that reduced trade barriers internally and did not impose new barriers on those without. It was a patronising rejection of Bush's idea.

The message that echoed down the Tokyo corridors was that Australia would not enter a trade agreement that 'discriminates against Japan, or which in one way or another is directed against Japan'.[15] Australia would not do Washington's bidding at the cost of its best friend in Asia. Keating's rejection of bilateral trade deals amounted to a repudiation of Howard's strategy nine years later in his quest for a bilateral Free Trade Agreement.

The earth began to move in Washington. Zoellick complained to Australia's Washington ambassador, Michael Cook, that Keating was 'going after the US'.[16] Keating's office chief, Don Russell, recalls:

> Zoellick was saying, in effect, 'Good luck with your new friends, but I doubt they will deliver you anything'. Zoellick's advice was that Keating should follow the behaviour of the UK and Canadian prime ministers who knew how to deal with an ally. Zoellick also said he was a young man with a long memory.[17]

Russell applied the velvet gloves. He said: 'I replied to the effect that Keating was a loyal supporter of the US and that he wanted to cement the place of the US in the Asia–Pacific region. I said I too was a young man with a long memory.'[18]

Fortunately for Keating, Clinton defeated Bush at the election. His winning slogan 'It's the economy, stupid' seemed made for Keating's style. At the same time Keating had launched his 'engagement' crusade at home, a campaign that would become fundamental to Keating–Howard foreign policy disputes. It was based on his view that Australia would succeed in Asia only if it changed itself. Keating was sure that cultural transformation was essential for Australia's success in Asia, a position Howard rejected with contempt.

The persuasive case for engagement was put years later by one of Australia's most prominent Asia scholars, Whitlam's ambassador to China, Dr Stephen FitzGerald, who wrote: 'It is difficult to think of any other country, perhaps any country in history, in which a nation's elites have knowingly committed themselves ... possibly to becoming part of a region or "world" whose dominant histories or cultures and ethical and value system they do not understand.' For FitzGerald, Australia's commitment to Asia 'was not of the mind'. He said the intellectual and cultural divide was the outstanding issue in engagement—a view that Keating endorsed and Howard rejected.

FitzGerald saw Australians as struggling outsiders in Asia. For this reason he wanted the debate to run to cultural, moral and ethical norms and argued that Australian elites had to be equipped with the history, cultures and languages of the region. This was a 'national necessity' since Australia had to 'get inside the Asia ingroup'. For FitzGerald, failure would leave Australia without a 'strategy for survival in a world in which we have no protector'.[19]

Keating didn't necessarily agree with all of FitzGerald's cultural arguments.[20] He did, however, seek to popularise engagement with Asia, launching this process with an April 1992 speech to FitzGerald's Asia–Australia Institute. The core argument was well known. More than 60 per cent of merchandise exports went to Asia; as Asia's market broadened, 'the opportunities for Australia cannot be over-stated'; the key question 'is how to position ourselves to take maximum advantage of the changes'. Stressing that Australia's GNP was the third-highest in the Western Pacific and equal to all ASEAN countries combined, Keating said Asia was where 'our national interest truly lie'. His vision was for more Australians to speak Asian languages, for Australian business people to become an integral part of the region's commerce and for full use to be made of those Australians of Asian origin. He saw a future where 'our national culture is shaped by, and helps to shape, the cultures around us'.[21]

Yet Keating remained forever an Australian nationalist. 'We go as we are,' he said of Australia's engagement. 'We are neither Asian nor American nor European. We go to the region as Australians—the only way we can go. What else can there be?'[22] Keating never fell for the absurd line that Australia was an Asian country.

He was launching a crusade. Engagement was an emotional term—it implied a relationship, a meeting of hearts and minds. Keating wanted the Australian people in his project. It would become a test for the public—a test of its ability to adapt and change its ways. Turning his foreign policy into a project of national reinvention was high risk. He could not predict the future but his successor as Labor prime minister, Kevin Rudd, a Mandarin-speaking Asianist, must constitute some vindication of his engagement project.

The strategic foundations of Keating's policy reflected a Labor reappraisal of Australia's foreign and security policy in the late 1980s and early 1990s. This reflected several deep-seated ideas.

First, economics were paramount—Asia was a success story and its economic progress was assumed to be the basis for deeper Australia–Asia ties. Ashton Calvert remarked: 'The impact of Asia's economic success upon our elites was immense and political leaders embraced the position of maximum economic integration with the region.'[23]

Second, modern Labor saw culture and strategy in harmony. Keating felt that true acceptance in Asia meant liberating Australia from its 'great and powerful friends' mindset and the inferiority complex engendered by its historical dependence on Britain and America.

This idea was backed by Kim Beazley who said such constraints were not imposed by Britain and America but 'had been self-imposed psychologically'. That is, Australia had to discover a cultural confidence to embark on a successful Asian strategy. In his explanation of what Hawke and Keating were doing, Beazley said: 'It was their belief that a new nationalism was possible: it would take pride in Australia's capacity to be an effective middle power.'[24] The sheer addiction with which Labor governments from Whitlam onwards pursued regional initiatives betrayed a deep anxiety—at a psychological level they were seeking Asian forgiveness for the White Australia Policy and acceptance of their place in the region.

Third, Keating saw the US relationship not in narrow bilateral security terms but in the Asia–Pacific context—he wanted to influence US strategy in the region. When Keating and Howard confronted the question 'What should Australia do with the US alliance?' they had different answers. Howard wanted to deepen bilateral ties, thereby adding layers of value. Keating wanted to influence US policy towards East Asia. He concluded that the main benefit of ANZUS was the standing it accorded Australia 'to have our voice heard in Washington'.[25]

After the Cold War, Labor took an elemental decision. Fearing the US might be tempted to retreat from the region, Labor supported a forward strategic position for the United States in Asia. Far from concluding that the alliance was less relevant with the communism's demise, Keating said Asia's future security depended on the United States playing a balance of power role. This was the gospel within Australia's strategic establishment; it was incorporated into Labor's 1994 Defence White Paper under the guidance of Defence Minister, Robert Ray.

But this was combined with another idea—that Australia must aspire to defence self-reliance. The White Paper reflected the philosophy

Beazley had developed in the 1980s—namely, that Australia must possess the capability to defend itself and that the US alliance, by offering Australia access to intelligence, weapons systems and technology, was a vital instrument in achieving self-reliance.[26] This was a conceptual transformation in thinking about the alliance. It is Beazley's greatest contribution as a politician and defence minister.

The 1994 White Paper bluntly said: 'We do not rely for our defence upon combat assistance from the US', yet Australia also expected that, because of its obligations under ANZUS, the US would offer 'invaluable help' in any crisis. It was a new way of seeing the US alliance, yet it was too sophisticated for the public to comprehend. Beazley would often ruminate about how to convince the public that Australia could defend itself—a very recent idea in our history—and how to explain our changed relationship with the United States.

Defence self-reliance was a step towards national maturity. The problem was that it required a level of defence spending that Labor refused to make. The policy meant that the main role of the Australian Defence Force was to defend Australia—as opposed to 'expeditionary' commitments, whereby Australia projected power and fought with its allies in the region or the world. This risked a split, therefore, between a 'defensive' ADF anchored to the continent and an Australian statecraft obsessed with projecting Australia's influence abroad.[27]

Defence self-reliance was tied to the matching philosophy, championed by Keating, that Australia must find its security 'in Asia', not 'from Asia'. This was dangerously in advance of public opinion. It meant a deeper strategic partnership with the region and, in Keating's view, a closer partnership with Indonesia. He was determined to confront this unpopular notion.

Keating saw that much of Australia's success in Asia would depend on Indonesia. As the dominant power in South-East Asia its support was pivotal to virtually every Australian initiative and objective—APEC, the APEC leaders' meeting, regional free trade and regional stability. 'He wanted to break from Hawke's position,' Gyngell said. 'He felt that Indonesia had been ignored, that Australia's priorities had been misplaced, and that we were too defensive about Indonesia.'[28]

In fact, Keating privately attacked Hawke of failing with Indonesia—he had not tried enough. Keating believed that public opinion prejudice against Jakarta had compromised the national interest. It had intimidated Hawke from getting close to Indonesia. It would not intimidate him.

In April 1992 Keating initiated his most pivotal relationship with another head of government when he met President Soeharto at Jakarta's presidential palace. For those with a Machiavellian bent it was an encounter between an ageing king and a young prince. Once again, he was accompanied by Calvert. Remembering the mistake with Bush, Calvert told Keating: 'Pay your respect to him and let him talk.' This is what happened; Keating offered deference to Soeharto as a prelude to building a concord.

Keating came with the conviction conceived in realpolitik that Soeharto was the key to many Australian policy ambitions. After the meeting he offered Calvert a cool summary: 'Soeharto can handle any domestic opponent but he can't govern his own nation well any more.'[29]

There had been a long history to this encounter. From the 1960s Keating had been imbued with the security ethos of the New South Wales ALP right wing that had seen the fall of Indonesia's Sukarno as a decisive event in Australia's future. As a Sydney lad he had absorbed the Jakarta news reports from 'The Year of Living Dangerously' and the New South Wales Right had cheered the rise of Soeharto as an anti-communist military chief putting down the communist push.

Keating was sure that Soeharto's legacy had been far more positive than negative. From his 1992 perspective Keating saw a leader who had destroyed the pro-communist Left, imposed order, made economic development the national priority, abandoned regional adventurism for responsibility, opposed any arms race or nuclear option for South-East Asia, run a benign policy towards the United States, sought friendly ties with Australia and championed a constructive South-East Asian regionalism—this was the alternative story to the internal corruption, repression and denial of democracy in Soeharto's Indonesia.

An imagination as powerful as Keating's appreciated the alternative fates that might have befallen Indonesia—and Australia. He concluded that 'the coming to power of the New Order government was arguably the event of single greatest strategic benefit to Australia after the Second World War'. He said this for dramatic effect, but he also meant it.[30]

Keating came to Jakarta with a radical idea: he wanted to bandwagon with Soeharto. The two nations were divided by religion, language, culture and wealth. No other Australian relationship was subject to such volatility or hypocrisy. The opinion-making class and much of the media genuflected to the idea of engagement yet patronised Indonesia as exotic, backward, repressed and burdened with a murdering dictator. The public was suspicious of Indonesia and antagonistic to its incorporation of East Timor. Nearly a decade had passed since Hawke's last visit to Indonesia.

The pattern established under Fraser and Hawke was apparent—seek a sound relationship with Indonesia but don't visit the country very often, stay away from Soeharto and be ready for the next culture-laden bilateral fracture. But Keating was coming for business.

Soeharto was the first foreign leader whom Keating met abroad. His aim was to 'weave of web' of relationships with Indonesia so strong that it would withstand the stresses. He made six visits as prime minister and later boasted that it was more than the total number of visits made 'by all my predecessors since the Second World War'.[31]

Keating accepted Indonesia's incorporation of East Timor and he assumed it would not be undone. He refused to make the relationship with 120 million Indonesians hostage to 800 000 East Timorese. He knew the real history—that Soeharto had not the slightest interest in any 1975 Indonesian takeover of East Timor but had been reluctantly driven to incorporation by strategic issues, its civil war and the prospect of a pro-leftist government. For those who said Australian governments should have pushed harder on behalf of East Timor the answer was obvious. As Gyngell said, 'nothing would have happened with Timor and nothing would have happened with Indonesia'.[32]

But Keating's mission was to recruit Soeharto for his expanded APEC vision. Singapore's Lee Kuan Yew had told Keating that if Soeharto was persuaded then the initiative might succeed. Beyond his Javanese evasions he found Soeharto 'completely strategic in his thinking'.[33]

Soeharto had dealt with seven Australian prime ministers, but only Whitlam and now Keating strove for a genuine connection. Calvert thought Keating had done well—his skill with older men was again at work. Keating used a touch of flattery to get onto the wavelength of Javanese deference. Keating operated on the principle that he would soon enunciate—that for Australia there was no more important country than Indonesia given its size and proximity to Australia's northern and western approaches. This remark, unsurprisingly, was misinterpreted to mean that Indonesia was our most important relationship, a point Keating was not making. For Howard, all such phrases were dangerous.

Keating wrote to Clinton in the early days of his presidency proposing the launch of an APEC leaders' meeting. Being the political entrepreneur he was lucky—Clinton thought the same way and the United States was APEC chair for 1993. During the autumn and winter Keating raised the concept with South Korea's president, Kim Young Sam, China's premier, Li Peng, and vice-premier, Qian Qichen, and Japan's prime minister, Miyazawa. Critically, Japan was a strong supporter.

By this stage Keating's concept had deepened. He wanted to galvanise the region by seeking an integrated market—Australia, North America, North-East and South-East Asia. The plan was to use APEC as the instrument for trade liberalisation and economic integration and this was embodied later in the Bogor free trade commitment.

Australia's nemesis was Malaysia's prime minister, Dr Mahathir Mohamad, an anti-Australian leader consumed by postcolonial resentment. Mahathir was pursuing a culture-bound 'Asia for the Asians' regionalism that would include only East Asian nations, thereby excluding North America and Australia.

In June 1993 Keating won his breakthrough: Clinton decided to back an APEC leaders' meeting in Seattle, providing Keating could summon sufficient support from other leaders to attend. Keating then asked Soeharto to host the following year's meeting in Indonesia. His tactic was to inaugurate the meetings with Clinton and Soeharto as the successive hosts—and it succeeded. Soeharto's prestige was essential for the South-East Asians to defy Mahathir.

Keating saw Mahathir as a threat to Asia's strategic future. He said that Mahathir's vision was 'a racially based concept' that sought a dangerous separation of the United States from East Asia. It struck directly at Australia's national interest. Australia's media usually treated Mahathir better than Keating and was reluctant in the extreme to state the obvious and brand his stance as racist.

In September, Keating made his only visit to Washington as prime minister. This time it was a meeting of minds. Clinton promised Keating that he would attend any leaders' meeting hosted by Soeharto. Clinton said he could live with an APEC arrangement 'based on trade but not on security'. By this stage Keating's most trusted adviser and office chief, Don Russell, was ambassador in Washington, working closely with the White House.[34]

The US official most closely associated with East Asia was Stan Roth, who operated at the National Security Council in the White House and then as assistant secretary of state for Asian and Pacific Affairs. Roth said:

> What Paul Keating did was to offer a vision to President Clinton of what APEC could be. Not just a meeting—though no-one's diminishing the value of meeting once a year—but rather that it could be more substantive, namely, trying to forge an Asia-Pacific Community with the US in it. Clinton came to office more interested in economic issues than foreign policy and as a free

trader. Keating seized his imagination by offering him a vision for APEC with the opportunity to do something different including big things like the Bogor vision of trade liberalisation. Paul Keating was thinking big picture. He didn't just say, we'll never get there because it's too hard. Instead he found an ally in Bill Clinton and got him motivated. It is not an exaggeration to say that Keating inspired Clinton. It's very clear to me having watched this from the White House that this was a special relationship.[35]

Keating liked to call the United States 'the biggest dog on the block'. 'Paul was pro-US but he did not share the fascination for American culture of the Beazley-Carr-Loosley wing of the Labor Party,' said Gyngell.[36] In private Keating could be strongly critical of the United States in ways inconceivable to Howard. His dealings with Clinton were warm but tightly geared to Australia's objectives. He loved talking politics with Clinton and in one phone call spent a long time advising him how to sell free trade to the American people.

In November 1993 Clinton hosted the first meeting of APEC leaders on Blake Island, near Seattle. There were no officials in the room. Keating was unsure whether it would degenerate into an 'enjoyable picnic' or make history. Before the meeting he introduced Clinton to China's President, Jiang Zemin. Clinton was a brilliant chair. The dialogue was frank and Keating said 'it was a beginning'.

That meeting endorsed the Keating-driven initiative of APEC support for free and open trade in the region by 2010 for developed nations and by 2020 for developing nations. Known as the Bogor Declaration, it was a close-run decision achieved after ferocious personal lobbying by Keating. The goal was regional free trade on a non-discriminatory basis. On his return Keating told parliament that 'Australians can say for the first time that the region around us is truly "our region".'

The reality was different. The Bogor goals slipped over the years and APEC was expanded and weakened with the injection of new members, a process that infuriated Keating. Howard, initially wary of APEC, became its sustained champion. The leaders' meetings remained and they served Australia's interest under both Keating and Howard, most of all in 1999 during the East Timor crisis.[37]

The template from Keating's diplomacy was an Australian prime minister shaping policy across the America–Asia divide off the back of personal contacts with Clinton and Soeharto. Reflecting on this, Stan Roth said: 'As president of the United States, Clinton had the stature to make this happen. But it would not have happened if Keating had not inspired him. This is how head of government relationships can work. And you have to give Keating much of the credit.'[38]

For Keating, Australia's advantages lay in a 'diverse, technologically mature, scientifically and culturally creative society, with strong legal and administrative structures and open to the world'. He asked: 'Is it possible for us to squander these advantages? Easily. Our passage is entirely in our own hands.' It was up to leadership.[39]

The most audacious example he provided was a formal security pact with Indonesia, turning a nation that most Australians viewed with suspicion into a security partner. The pact was delivered only by Keating–Soeharto personal ties. 'The idea came from Keating himself,' said Gyngell. 'In my entire career it was the purest example of a major foreign policy idea coming direct from a prime minister.'[40] It was the big idea that Keating craved.

The pact was negotiated in secret, a fact that would enrage its critics. This testified to its nineteenth-century, pre-democratic brand of realpolitik. As one of Australia's negotiators, former Chief of the Defence Force General Peter Gration said: 'If Keating had floated the idea publicly it wouldn't have had a hope—it would have been shot down.'[41] This was a security treaty that did not have public support in Australia, a reality that did not dissuade Keating for a minute but that fingered its defect.

It was a remarkable exercise in solo leadership. Ministers shook their heads, Indonesia specialists warned Keating off and the Defence Department was horrified. Defence's most influential strategist, Deputy Secretary Hugh White, recalls: 'I argued at the time that the agreement would be a liability, not an asset. The essential view in Defence was against it.'[42] Gyngell says: 'My immediate reaction was to think it's a bridge too far. I felt "Excellent aspiration but you don't know Indonesia." I think both Gareth Evans and Robert Ray felt the same. In the Defence Department there was alarm.'[43]

Only a prime minister of vaulting ambition would embark on this path. On bad days Keating longed for more excitement and on good days he assumed his political genius. Even before he met Soeharto, he felt he understood him as a strategic leader who would buy a good deal. Keating saw that institutions such as ASEAN and APEC could not have developed without Soeharto's commitment.

Gareth Evans had been working with Indonesia's Foreign Minister, Ali Alatas, on an umbrella agreement that would cover the basic principles of the relationship. But Keating didn't like this—he didn't want a new roof on relations but better foundations. Given the strong military-to-military ties, he developed the idea of a new security treaty. Australia had ANZUS, the Five Power Defence Arrangements involving Singapore and Malaysia, and a Joint Declaration with PNG, so Keating felt there was logic in seeking a formal agreement with Indonesia. He wanted to change the mindset.

Keating favoured an agreement that set the stage for action together based on common interests. This was an imaginative departure, typical of the way his mind worked. His senior ministers agreed to explore the idea but Keating said 'I didn't detect much enthusiasm.' His advisers warned that Indonesia's non-aligned status would create a difficulty. His department began to work the project under direction from Michael Thawley and it was canvassed by a senior officers' strategic policy committee.[44]

At this committee Hugh White said: 'This is an absurd idea. The Indonesians will never agree and it offends their non-aligned stance.' As time advanced, White assumed it had been abandoned. Official scepticism was widespread but Keating would confound the advisers. He was not prepared to give up.

During his June 1994 visit he raised the issue with Soeharto. When Soeharto volunteered that closer defence ties were possible Keating said: 'We are willing to put our cards on the table, face up, and make a clear declaration that such trust exists.' Australia would support a formal security arrangement. When Soeharto agreed to explore the concept, Keating authorised two emissaries, General Peter Gration, a brilliant choice, and Gyngell. In an 'up and down' process over more than a year, they negotiated with the Indonesians until in November 1995 the two leaders approved the final text. On 14 December the cabinet endorsed the agreement and it was announced by Keating.[45] Howard and Downer made it bipartisan support.

Titled 'Agreement on Maintaining Security', it contained three simple provisions: promotion of security co-operation; consultation in the context of 'adverse challenges to either party'; and consideration of individual or joint action. Drafted by Australia, its language reflected Australia's security culture and its treaty 'canon'. It borrowed from ANZUS. Such a text from the Indonesian side would have been inconceivable.

This document was an intellectual expression of Australia's deepest geographical dilemma—its location as a continent south of the sprawling Indonesian archipelago which meant that any serious strike on Australia had to come from, through or over Indonesia. Keating said the decision for Australia and Indonesia to become security collaborators was 'a highly important step forward'. He was telling Australians that Indonesia was our friend and ally. Soeharto said it should 'wipe out' any doubts harboured in Australia about Jakarta's intentions.

'In the ADF there was a lingering view that Indonesia was still the enemy,' Gration said. 'It was time that was tackled and the ambiguities removed. The agreement was a very big ask for Indonesia. It was the first security agreement they had signed with another nation and they worried about how to explain this to their own people.'[46] Gyngell argued that it was not a defensive non-aggression pact but about positives. 'It saw strategic relations in a new way,' he said.[47]

Only Soeharto could have delivered this deal to Keating. Only Keating could have persuaded Soeharto to make the offer. It was imposed on the Indonesian system by its president and was Soeharto's reward for Keating's commitment. It showed Soeharto's favourable outlook towards Australia. Keating's plan was to seize the deal before Soeharto left the stage.

'I reject the critique the agreement was premature,' Gyngell said. 'It wasn't that Keating thought we'd have another fifty years of Soeharto; it was just the reverse.'[48] The claim that Keating was tying himself to Soeharto was ludicrous—he was using Soeharto to set up the future.

Keating stressed that it was not a defence pact that triggered automatic action. It was in the genre of the Five Power Defence Arrangement. Significantly, he said the agreement related only to external challenges—a reply to critics who feared closer security ties were a risk when Indonesia had unresolved conflicts in East Timor, Irian Jaya and Aceh.[49] His long-range strategic goal was to anchor Australia and Indonesia as permanent partners—an idea pursued by both the Howard and Rudd governments. Keating knew periodic tensions would erupt with Indonesia; his aim was to contain those eruptions.

When White first read the agreement he could hardly believe it. His inclination was to dismiss it as 'rubbish'. 'I don't know what you guys think this means,' he said to Labor's advisers. 'But our interpretation will be different to Jakarta's.'

White said:

The agreement did not reflect the reality of the two countries. In Australia, the public was simply not ready to see Indonesia as an ally with all that that entailed. In Indonesia, the idea of a traditional security treaty was anathema to very deeply held concepts of independence and non-alignment. The agreement lacked strong roots in Indonesia's security culture. For Australia, this was serious security language and it reflected our treaty culture. But when I would talk to Indonesians they would say, 'Oh, it doesn't really mean anything', and I would have to explain that the language was similar to the Five Power Defence Arrangement. I don't think the Indonesian system understood how much of an alliance they had entered into.[50]

There would be two postscripts to the agreement. In 1999, after the Australian-led East Timor intervention, Indonesia's President Habibie ripped up the agreement; it had lasted only four years. This was interpreted to mean that its ambition exceeded political reality: when a crisis erupted the agreement buckled.

But in 2005 another leader, Indonesia's President Yudhoyono, called for a new security treaty. The upshot was that, in November 2006 in Lombok, the foreign ministers signed a new Framework for Security Cooperation, different from the Keating–Soeharto compact. It is more defensive and traditional, embodies a non-aggression pact and lays the foundation for expanded bilateral co-operation. It is now enshrined by both sides as the framework for relations. Gyngell said: 'In a sense the Keating legacy endured. It gave the Howard treaty a smoother passage.'[51]

Keating's grand strategy did not deliver its full potential. APEC is a vital instrument but will never become a central mechanism for America's role in Asia. The priority he gave Indonesia was initially rejected by Howard—yet with Yudhoyono's election, Howard became an enthusiast for the strategic relationship with Jakarta.

Keating's vision was often egocentric. Yet he got results and created new Asia–Pacific mechanisms that served Australia's interest. He led from the front by refusing to tolerate second-best results. He envisaged the region not only as it existed but as it should exist. Above all, he popularised the idea of a grand Australian strategy—seeking to integrate ties with the United States and East Asia. His 'engagement with Asia' is a national project that will have no end.

13

EMBRACING THE REPUBLIC

Governments can wait for opinion to force their hand or they can lead.
—Paul Keating, June 1995, announcing his plan for a republic

Paul Keating was a republican by instinct, upbringing and conviction. Once he became prime minister his republican faith erupted early, shocking many and delighting others. It was Keating who paved the way for Howard's 1999 referendum that left Australia in a political twilight zone—the republic was the future but it seemed unobtainable.

Keating had not addressed the issue before 1992. 'The republic was an after-dinner-mints and coffee conversation for forty years,' he said. It was the Queen's February 1992 visit that convinced him to act. The moral he drew was that the Queen could no longer represent the nation that Australia had become.[1]

In the process, Keating ruined his image as a narrow, right-wing operative fixated on markets and ignorant of the wider world. As an issue the republic was controlled by Keating's office, with senior ministers shut out. It was over an Indian restaurant lunch in Canberra on 1 July 1992 that Keating told his senior staff—Don Russell, Don Watson, Ashton Calvert and Mark Ryan—that he intended to propose a republic.[2] For the first term the issue was strictly a debate in the office family.

It was a natural step from the February 1992 unfurling of his anti-British nationalism to his attendance at Kokoda for his first Anzac Day as prime minister. There was a tolerable argument that the republic suited Keating's political needs. But his primary motive went to his vision of Australia. The afternoon of the lunch an ebullient Watson recalled that Keating was light-hearted, talking about the Queen's lack of interest in Australia and was 'quite unaffected by the momentous decision'.[3]

The republic was a cause for True Believers; for most Australians it was not a priority. This created the danger for Keating—the risk of false priorities that pandered to Labor's dreams while the economy rotted in recession. His closest advisers were divided, with the enthusiasts being Watson and Ryan.

From its inception the republic was linked in Keating's mind with his drive to change the flag. Despite their fusion in Keating's heart, these were separate issues. There were many republicans who upheld the existing flag. Yet Keating made the flag an issue before the republic, declaring in April 1992 that it 'must change' and prompting Neal Blewett to warn of the blunder: 'We need to disentangle republicanism from anti-British jibes.' It was obvious, yet Keating was his own worst enemy. It meant that, before he mounted his campaign, the venture was seen as 'Keating's republic' and was cast in an anti-British light. It was an unpromising start.[4]

Howard never forgot it. Even on the expiry of his prime ministership fifteen years later, Howard was saying of Keating that 'instead of arguing [the republic] is the next natural thing to do, not because we're unhappy with our British past … he couldn't bring himself to do that … Keating had a sort of chip on his shoulder.'[5]

In September 1992, six months before the election, Russell launched a rearguard action to force his boss to re-assess the republic push. In a memo to Keating headed 'The Republic, The Flag and The Oath', Russell wrote:

> If we continue on our present course there does seem some prospect that we will be able to dull the electorate's natural inclination to punish us and we may be able to force them to look at Hewson critically and actually make a choice between us and them. This is a tall order and will require all of our ingenuity and discipline. In this context there is a real risk that we will derail what we have just achieved if you push the national symbols back onto the national agenda again.
>
> In the circumstances I think it is best if you make it clear that while you are not backing off one inch in your personal view that the symbols should change, such changes are not key issues at the moment and you are not investing the Keating energy or the energy of your government on bringing about such a change.

Russell then gave Keating a form of words to use on the Republic:

> I have always believed that Australia should be a republic and I am sure that one day we will make the change … Obviously

there has to be much more discussion with the community and with the States in particular. I am pleased that my comments have encouraged this process. But it still has a long way to go. I suspect that it will take the better part of a decade to resolve how a republic would actually work and build the community understanding and acceptance to bring it to pass. I will be pleased to participate in the generation of ideas and the building of a consensus for change but I won't be busting my gut dragging the nation along on this issue. There are much more important things I need to do at present with my energies and time.[6]

Russell felt Keating should focus on the economy and GST where he had a glimmer of hope. The republic, Russell feared, was seen by the public as proof of a distracted leader. These views had much support in the ALP National Secretariat and the party. It was one thing to talk up the republic but another to embark on a program of constitutional change. The republic was not an easy issue; it was difficult and Russell wanted to force Keating to confront this.

Economic adviser John Edwards said there was 'no urgency' to achieving a republic and recalled:

Within the Labor Party counsels, however, there were those who properly warned that more votes might be lost than won by giving high priority to an essentially symbolic issue. For all these reasons it made sense for Keating to declare himself in favour of a republic, to deliver a speech on the subject every now and then, but to move only very slowly towards the goal. In some ways it was more useful to be in favour of a republic than to have a republic.[7]

At first Keating neither took Russell's advice nor rejected it. The question was resolved, finally, in the office debate over the 1993 election policy speech.

Watson and Ryan made a joint pledge to get the republic into the policy speech. At the penultimate moment, Watson recalled, there was a crisis of confidence. Russell got nervous and Keating almost faltered. 'No one wants it more than me, mate,' Keating told Watson, but there were political problems. Fearing it would slip away, Watson and Ryan put the best argument possible: if Keating believed in the republic but not enough to do anything, how was he an improvement on Hawke?[8]

'It was a pretty difficult decision,' Keating said. 'I knew what it would do in xenophobia land. I knew it. The problem was that the government had been through many turns since 1983. By the time I got into the cultural issues—you know, native title, the flag, the republic, etcetera, we were cutting against a very old grain.'[9] But he could not resist it. Mark Ryan said: 'He had to listen to all sides of the argument, but I never countenanced that he wouldn't do it.'[10]

Keating's 1993 policy speech won an exultant response when he promised to advance a republican referendum in the next term. The True Believers were enthralled. Watson claimed they had seen a leader without the mask. In the speech Keating conceded that the republic was 'far from the most pressing matter' yet said it should be advanced in the 'decade leading to the centenary of Federation'. He pledged to create a committee to prepare options for a Federal Republic of Australia. There was an element of fatalism, along with emotion, in the approach. 'Once the political shell is broken, the political inhibitions are broken, then it becomes much easier to do things later,' Keating said of his decision. 'You know, if somebody will take the burden on his back, it will become much easier later.'[11]

Mingling with Labor luminaries after the speech, Keating found that 'a number came up to me and said "Oh, mate, you've lost it for us, you've just lost the election for us."'[12] He was standing just below the stage, smiling and unswayed. Next morning the *Sydney Morning Herald* headlined the policy speech story 'Pork Barrel Republic'—but Keating, having smashed the mould, was happy. He enjoyed the thrill of irrevocable commitment.[13]

Keating's surprise election victory in 1993 gave the kiss of life to the republic for the first time in Australia's history as a nation. A Keating defeat would have buried the republic for unknown decades, whereas the win launched what would become a six-year process that taught Australia what being a republic meant and how hard it would be to carry a referendum.

In April, delivering the HV Evatt Memorial Lecture at Sydney's Wentworth Hotel, Keating announced the Republican Advisory Committee headed by Malcolm Turnbull and comprising Nick Greiner, Mary Kostakidis, Lois O'Donoghue, Susan Ryan, John Hirst and George Winterton. The state representatives were Glyn Davis and Namoi Dougall. Keating said the task was to try to establish a consensus for a republic. Winterton had previously drafted a republican constitution. Turnbull's appointment enshrined his role at the centre of the debate. In effect, it established a nexus between the Keating government and the Australian Republican Movement (ARM), a body that had become active in July 1991 to pursue the cause. It was heavy with famous names, Sydney-centric figures, and became the source of the 'chardonnay' drinking socialist image used to mock the republican cause. Turnbull was the ARM's driving force, ready to apply his unmatched combination of brains, energy and money.

As a realist Keating wanted bipartisan support. 'I gave Turnbull the job because he was always a sort of pocket Tory,' he said. 'I wanted a model that the Liberal Party could accept; otherwise it wouldn't succeed at referendum.'[14] But this was only half the story.

Keating picked a committee to deliver the model he wanted. He felt sure that Turnbull and his team, with its practical feel for politics, would deliver. Keating's aim was a republic, not a fundamental change to Australia's political and constitutional system. The link with the Crown would be broken. The new Australian head of state would duplicate the office of Governor-General. No new seat of power would be created; the prime minister and president would not become rivals. This meant an impartial non-executive presidency, acting on advice, without any mandate arising from direct election by the people.

A popularly elected president would be created only over Keating's dead body. The system of prime ministerial government beloved by Hawke, Keating and Howard would remain untouched. Australia would not be remade along French or American designs. This fitted with ARM policy for a presidency elected by a two-thirds majority of the federal parliament to guarantee impartiality.

In late 1993 Keating visited Great Britain where, among other tasks, he met with and briefed the Queen on his plans. It was the first occasion on which an Australian prime minister informed a British monarch of the intention to terminate Australia's position as a constitutional monarchy. 'I think she thought there was an inevitability about it,' Keating said later.[15]

The Keatings spent the weekend at Balmoral in Scotland and had a convivial experience. Annita was much taken by some of the events—notably, when they were treated to a barbecue, with the Queen personally driving them to the location in her version of a four-wheel drive. Informality was the tone. Before the barbecue Keating met alone with the Queen. The room in which they met had been Queen Victoria's favourite, she told him. Elizabeth II and Paul Keating were professionals; they knew their business and it was conducted with deft courtesy.[16]

Over tea Keating gave Her Majesty a homily on why Australia had to pilot a new destiny. 'I said that Australia would have a better and more modern relationship with Britain if these constitutional arrangements were changed,' Keating said. 'While Britain had become an integral part of the European Union, so Australia had to go with its geography and its history in the Asia–Pacific. I believed it was no longer appropriate for our Head of State not to be an Australian.' Keating advised the Queen that she should break with the convention of confidentiality and allow Keating after their meeting to make public the essence of what he had said. He explained that, with the coming debate in Australia, this would 'remove you from the point of focus' and he promised to do 'all that I can to keep you, in a personal sense, or the monarchy in Britain, away from the issue in Australia'.[17]

The Queen told the Prime Minister: 'I'll always do what the Australian people think best and take the advice of my ministers.' She said her family had always tried to do the right thing by Australia. And she agreed to let Keating make the public statement he desired. Watson hoped the meeting would procure 'a more grown-up environment for the debate at home'.[18] Keating then flew to Dublin.

Meanwhile the debate was turning sour in Australia. In May 1993 Liberal Leader John Hewson had declined Keating's invitation for the Opposition to appoint a representative to the Republican Advisory Committee. It was the death knell for hopes that the Liberals would keep an open mind. Recognising that his rank and file were monarchists Hewson said a convincing case for change had not been made. By July the Liberal Federal Executive took a hard line against the republic. The lobby group Australians for a constitutional monarchy had appointed the energetic and media savvy Tony Abbott, a future Liberal MP, as their executive director, pitting him against Turnbull, a contest of Rhodes scholars.

In August 1993 Turnbull had tried to salvage the furniture. 'Those in the Liberal Party who take the view that a republic is inevitable, or even desirable, but nonetheless believe it should be opposed because to support it would give Mr Keating a win should think very carefully about the choice,' he told a Liberal rally. '"Not invented here" is the worst possible reason to oppose a good political idea. By wrongly characterising the republic as a Labor cause you help Mr Keating.'[19]

The Liberal Party was divided, particularly in New South Wales. A long line of state Liberal leaders were republicans: Greiner, John Fahey, Peter Collins and John Brogden. But New South Wales was home to monarchists such as Howard, Bronwyn Bishop and Abbott. Sensing the republic was coming, Turnbull felt Howard's hard pro-monarchist stance 'may imperil not merely the success but the very survival of the Liberal Party in Australia's largest state'.[20] It was the onset of Turnbull's long winter of frustration with Howard.

In October 1993 the Turnbull committee gave Keating a two-volume report, the most comprehensive study on an Australian republic. Its central theme was reassurance: that a republic was more a symbolic than a substantive change to the principles of Australian governance. It showed the republic could be achieved without detracting 'from the fundamental constitutional principles on which our system is based'—federalism, Westminster responsible government, the separation of powers and judicial review. While canvassing options, its preference was for parliamentary election of the president.[21] For Keating, it was a sound basis for action.

The report, however, revealed the conundrum of the republic: the split among republicans between those who merely wanted an Australian head of state and those who believed the republic must deliver something greater by revitalising Australia's political system through giving the people a greater direct power. This unresolved dilemma among republicans would eventually ruin their cause. It meant that divisions between republicans would become as significant as divisions between monarchists and republicans.

In early 1994 the Prince of Wales made an official visit to deliver a message: the Crown laid no claim to Australia. In an Australia Day speech cleared beforehand with Buckingham Palace and Keating, and in selective media interviews, Prince Charles spoke for the monarchy but with a personal sympathy for the country where he had spent some of his school days. The Prince said the republic was an issue for Australians to decide and the debate was 'a sign of national maturity'. He encouraged the process, saying it was 'perfectly sensible'. The Royal Family, he said, was 'merely doing what we consider to be, as a family, our duty' by Australia and he added 'we don't own this country'.

The Prince offered not the slightest support to the monarchist cause. Just the contrary: he ruined monarchist hopes that the Crown would be recruited to their campaign. While neutral on the substance, the Prince said he had 'the greatest possible affection for Australia' and felt that if Australia became a republic then he would have more freedom as a visitor and might 'find out a damn sight more about Australia'. He revealed that nearly twenty years earlier he had been approached about the possibility of becoming Governor-General at the 1988 Bicentenary but the idea had withered due to lack of support in Australia. In a long interview with the author about the republic, the Prince, by his body language, showed that he was happily reconciled to the loss of his Australian kingdom.[22]

The Liberal Party of Australia displayed little of the Prince's magnanimity. It was divided over the republic and Alexander Downer, in one of his few enduring policies as leader, had persuaded the Coalition to the idea of a People's Convention as a means of responding to Keating while saving its internal unity. For the Coalition, it was a self-protection device lest Keating deploy his mesmeric skill to drive a political stake through its heart on the republic.

Despite periodic doubts Keating finally crossed the Rubicon on 7 June 1995. In a televised speech from the floor of the House of Representatives he delivered one of the great speeches of his prime ministership. It was what he did best—statecraft without pugilism—and what he did too rarely.

Declaring his government's conviction that Australia should become a republic by 2001 Keating pledged a referendum in 1998 or 1999—the delay being a recognition that support was still inadequate. 'Governments can wait for opinion to force their hand or they can lead,' Keating said, making his weakness into a virtue. At this point he buried his anti-British instincts. 'The creation of an Australian republic is not an act of rejection,' he said. 'It is one of recognition: in making the change we will recognise that our deepest respect is for our Australian heritage.' So the republic was a natural step. It contained 'as much commonsense as patriotism' and it was accompanied neither by 'the beat of drums [n]or chests'. The involvement of the Queen with Australia was now 'very limited' and she was Queen not only of the United Kingdom but of fourteen other countries. It was time for an Australian head of state and for every Australian to be able to aspire to that office.[23]

Support for the republic in mid-1999 ran at only 50 per cent. Newspoll surveys over the previous three years showed support in the 39–50 per cent range. This offered no hope of a successful referendum short of a transformation in public sentiment. Republicans were periodically optimistic about their cause but devoid of any practical strategy to lift their community stocks.

The preferred republican model had been selected by Keating and he opposed any Constitutional Conventions to alter the model. Branding it the 'minimalist' option reached after study of the Turnbull Report, the 'Commonwealth of Australia' name would be retained, with the president having the same role and functions as the Governor-General. His constitutional duties would be exercised on advice from the government.

Confronting the core issue—whether the president would be elected by the parliament or by the people—Keating supported election by two-thirds of the national parliament in a joint sitting, the favoured position of the Labor Party and the ARM. The intent was that a presidential appointee would require bipartisan support from the major parties.

Keating demolished the popular election option with clinical precision. 'Popular election guarantees that the head of state will be a politician,' he said. The president would be the 'only person in the political system so elected', thereby ensuring the accumulation of real power in the office. Keating quoted former Governor-General, Sir Zelman Cowen, as saying that direct election 'would ensure political outcomes'. The government wanted the office to remain 'above politics' and Keating felt that this was what Australians wanted. As a consequence, popular election was unsustainable with a neutral president.

The president would retain the unwritten Reserve Powers of the Crown that lived within the Westminster system and that were exercisable by the Governor-General. In a wise move, Keating had decided against their definition and codification. Codification risked dragging the High Court into adjudication of such powers, thereby exposing the bench to greater political involvement. But Keating's deeper reason was that codification meant addressing the issues raised by the 1975 crisis—whether Sir John Kerr's resort to the dismissal power on the Senate's denial of supply was to be validated or delegitimised. Because this issue was unresolved in constitutional and political terms its re-ignition would be the political kiss of death to the republic, a truism that seemed to escape many people. Keating believed that codification was unnecessary given his model.

However, the argument did not apply for any directly elected president. This was an entirely different situation. Keating was convinced that Australia's political and constitutional system could not risk a popularly elected president without the safeguard of full codification of the Reserve Powers, including the dismissal power.[24] This view was soundly based and widely shared.

Despite its cogency, Keating's position had a fatal flaw: the public wanted direct election. It seemed disengaged from, and uninterested in, the powerful logic against popular election. The extent of this sentiment was huge. In March 1995, Newspoll found that support for direct, as against parliamentary, election ran at an incredible 74–16 per cent. In 1993 it had split 79–10 per cent. These figures guaranteed that, at a referendum, Keating's model would face resistance not just from monarchists but from republicans.

The significance of Keating's project was to reveal the lion in the path to the republic—the inability of republicans to agree on a model. Keating embraced the 'minimalist' position because of his beliefs but it mirrored the hope that a 'small target' republic had the best prospect of success at a referendum. This view was highly contested by opinion polls that offered evidence against Keating's model, the choice of the political establishment.

As the new Opposition leader, John Howard gave a response that was dictated by caution. It was Keating who chose this battleground, not Howard. In response Howard had a two-pronged objective: to ensure that the republic did not divert his 1996 campaign and did not splinter his Coalition. Struggling to find the right balance, Howard supported the existing Constitution, conceded there was a mood 'to perhaps embrace change' and insisted, like Keating, that Australia's Westminster parliamentary system be retained.[25]

His significant promise was to establish a People's Convention to review the republic and other constitutional issues if the Coalition won the election. This was designed to buy time and keep Coalition unity. But Howard pledged to hold a referendum based on the outcome of the People's Convention, a substantial concession that ran against the grain of Howard's own beliefs. It was a pledge that Howard would honour. The proviso that made this pledge possible was that a future Howard government reserved the right to oppose the referendum.[26]

Howard's commitments, made in June 1995, had an historic import. They proved that Keating had shifted the political system. As a monarchist Coalition leader, Howard had been forced into conceding a pathway for the republic. It was done grudgingly but from self-interest. It meant that Howard as prime minister, sooner or later, would have to confront the Federal Republic of Australia.

14

PROTECTING THE BORDERS

Do not let any people … think that all they've got to do is break the rules, jump the queue, lob here and Bob's your uncle. Bob is not your uncle on this issue. We're not going to allow people just to jump that queue.
—Prime Minister Bob Hawke, 1990

The Keating government imposed a regime of border protection based on mandatory detention for unauthorised boat arrivals—a strategic and constitutional declaration of national sovereignty in the globalised age. This was a response to the 'second wave' of boat arrivals from Cambodia and China that began in 1989, following the 'first wave' of Indochinese refugees in the late 1970s. The decision was the latest manifestation of an instinct deep within Australia's political culture—that the state should control the arrival of migrants and refugees.

The principle of Labor's 1990s border protection regime was bipartisan. It was the Keating government that established the system and the Howard government that would intensify its scale, abuses and punitive impact. But this reflected a bigger story. Refugee policy was not just a humanitarian exercise; it was about power and authority.

There were two ideas shared by the Keating and Howard governments: that control of people movements was a legitimate exercise of state sovereignty and that, within Australia's constitutional system, it was an issue of executive government prerogative.

The arrival of asylum seekers from the late 1980s would trigger a struggle between executive and judicial power remarkable in Australia's constitutional history. The Keating and Howard governments were united in seeking to restrain judicial power while the refugee lobby, legal establishment and human rights groups saw judicial power as the instrument to free asylum seekers and civilise policy. This became a consuming tussle that involved the government, the parliament, the judiciary and the Australian Defence Force.

The climax came in 2001 when John Howard denied landing rights to the Norwegian freighter *Tampa*. The conventional wisdom is that Howard's border protection stance, as exemplified by the Tampa, was an aberrant electoral stunt. The evidence, however, is firmly against this interpretation. Howard's position, while extreme, was a manifestation of an entrenched and bipartisan Australian policy tradition. The challenge is to locate Howard in this tradition.

Bob Hawke once argued that the most important decision in Australia's first hundred years was to become, from the late 1940s, a nation of mass immigration. Since the program's inception Australia has accepted about seven million migrants, the highest per capita in the world outside of Israel. At the end of the Howard years, one in four Australians had been born overseas compared with a much lower figure of 10 per cent for the United States, testimony to Australia's remarkable acceptance of people from around the world.

The immigration program was conceived not in humanitarian sentiment but in national strategic interest. This remains its prime motivation and the only basis for public support. It is dominated by a philosophy of management control reflected in a universal visa system. The ethos of control arises from Australia's geography and it is bipartisan. The number of illegal people in Australia is very low—about 50 000, compared with 12 million in the United States.

In 1945 the program's ministerial architect, Arthur Calwell, said: 'If Australians have learnt one lesson from the Pacific War now moving to a successful conclusion, it is surely that we cannot continue to hold our island continent for ourselves and our descendents unless we greatly increase our numbers ... We may have only the next 25 years in which to make the best possible use of our second chance to survive.'

The politics of people movement in Australia originate in this enduring 1945 compact between the Chifley government and the nation. It is conceivably the most powerful political compact in Australia's history. Mass migration was presented to people, business, unions and churches on the condition that government would control who came to Australia in the interests of the people. This is the platform on which the program was created. It is the platform on which the program has been sustained by every prime minister from Chifley to Rudd. The government administers the program as trustee for the public. The reason boat arrivals excite antagonism—as they do regardless of race, religion or origin—is because they violate this compact.

Australia, unlike the United States, is unique in being able to control its borders. That is the gift of being the world's only continental island state. In short, politics, culture and geography drive Australia to a sanctioned process for people entry. Since World War II, Australia has accepted about 700 000 refugees from many cultures and countries. Their entry has aroused little dispute, with one exception—boat arrivals, whether they are Afghan Muslims or Vietnamese Christians.

The view of the Australian community is entrenched—people are granted entry into Australia; they do not self-select Australia. The difference is fundamental and is readily perceived by the public. As professional politicians, Keating and Howard were steeped in this tradition.

The control philosophy also applies to refugee policy. Australia accepts refugees offshore through the UNHCR system. This permits the Australian government considerable control over the type of refugee and their source country. It is a bipartisan Australian practice.

The detention policy was launched at the onset of the age of globalisation, with its threat of greater uncontrolled people movements. It was a deliberate declaration of constitutional authority from the Australian state. It verified the principle on which postwar migration was founded— that the Australian government would decide who joined the Australian nation. This idea, buttressed by popular support, is as strong as any in the history of Australian public policy.

The boat people, most of them authentic refugees, broke these rules and they were met with a visceral response from the Labor Party, the Coalition and the public. Australian prime ministers will alter the administrative mechanisms such as detention—but no prime minister is going to abandon the idea of control.

There are two issues at stake: the principle of detention, and how detention is practised. Over the years detention centres became sites of desperation, self-harm, poor management and human rights violations. Because of a complex policy failure some people were left in detention for years. Children were subject to inhumane and unforgiving conditions that constituted a serious moral failure on Australia's part. Some children born in detention knew a life only of confinement. The trade-off was brutal: border protection through sacrificing the human rights of boat people.

The Hawke government's attitude highlights this point. Hawke had wept for the Chinese persecuted in Tiananmen Square and allowed thousands of Chinese students already in Australia to stay. But Hawke shed no tears over the boat people. Indeed, he was their resolute opponent. From 1989 Hawke's government resisted the arrival of Cambodians. Because Foreign Minister Gareth Evans was architect of the peace process the government was anxious not to alienate the Cambodian government and it refused to recognise the bona fides of fleeing Cambodians. By branding them 'economic refugees', a meaningless term in international law, it said they were not entitled to protection. This stance was basic to Evans' negotiation for a peace settlement.

In 1990 Hawke gave vent to Labor's feelings towards the Cambodian boat people:

> We're not here with an open door policy saying anyone who wants to come to Australia can come. These people are not political refugees. There is not a regime now in Cambodia which is exercising terror, political terror, upon its population … People [are] saying they don't like a particular regime or they don't like their economic circumstances, therefore they're going to up, pull up stumps, get in a boat and lob in Australia. Well, that's not on. We have an orderly migration program. We're not going to allow people just to jump that queue by saying we'll jump into a boat, here we are … do not let any people, or any group of people, in the world think that because Australia has that proud record, that all they've got to do is break the rules, jump the queue, lob here and Bob's your uncle. Bob is not your uncle on this issue. We're not going to allow people just to jump that queue.[1]

When pressed by television presenter Jana Wendt about whether he had any qualms about such a ruthless policy, Hawke replied: 'Not only no qualms about it, but I will be forceful in ensuring that that is what's followed.'[2]

A decade later, John Howard would use almost the same language with the same sentiments and the same arguments. This was not an accident. It reflected enduring Australian attitudes towards boat people held by a succession of Australian leaders. This was driven, above all, by the need to protect public support for an orderly immigration program. The major difference between Hawke and Howard is that Howard confronted many more boat people. The threat of more boats was a permanent factor in calculations. In 1989 and 1990 the Hawke government was warned by Australia's embassies in Vietnam and Thailand that more boats would leave unless strong disincentives were imposed.[3]

Hawke's attitude, however, was not nearly as hostile as that of Gough Whitlam's in the 1970s towards the Vietnamese boat people. Few issues so provoked an incandescent rage in Whitlam, who declared that 'I'm not having hundreds of fucking Vietnamese Balts coming into this country with their political and religious hatreds.' Indeed, there is evidence that the final straw in turning Whitlam against his former deputy, Lance Barnard, was Barnard's commissioning of measures to help Vietnamese refugees.[4]

During the 1990s the Immigration Department's practice had been to hold border arrivals in custody until its officers made a quick determination on whether they should be allowed entry or deported. Up to 1991 most asylum seekers were located in old migrant hostels in major cities with very loose controls. The decision whether an asylum seeker was found to be a refugee and granted residence was made by departmental officials. But in the late 1980s and early 1990s pressure on the system came from two sources: the courts and more boats. It was the arrivals of Cambodians in the early 1990s that led to mandatory detention.

In 1989 the High Court, in a decision about a Chinese stowaway, Chan Yee Kin, who entered the country illegally but claimed to be a refugee, found the decision of the departmental official to be 'so unreasonable as to amount to an improper exercise of the power to determine refugee status'. It was an invitation to lawyers to bring more applications.[5] The struggle over Cambodian and Chinese boat people had seen, in the analysis of refugee law specialist Mary Crock, 'the emergence of an extensive network of refugee advocates in Australia'. This had quickly polarised the debate. She said: 'It is difficult to underestimate the resentment that the courts appear to have engendered first in the bureaucracy and then in the parliament.'[6]

In 1992 the Keating government took policy to a new level. It decided to make detention mandatory for unlawful arrivals, to create a Refugee Review Tribunal to make the determination process fairer, and to restrict judicial intervention. The government was alarmed that the Federal Court was about to order the release from detention of a number of detainees.

These 1992 decisions constitute the origin of the tougher system. They were implemented by Immigration Minister, Gerry Hand, a Victorian left-winger addicted to the control philosophy, hostile to the refugee lawyers and proud of Labor's record on immigration. His second reading speech for the 1992 Migration Reform Bill is an unrestrained denunciation of refugee lawyers.

Keating's detention system was based on the distinction between authorised and unauthorised arrivals. An authorised arrival might fly to Australia on a valid visa and subsequently seek refugee status; an unauthorised arrival would come by boat. The first principle of the new policy was, in Hand's words, 'that all persons who come to Australia without authorisation not be released into the community'.[7] Boat people were the targets. The policy was a uniform regime for detention and removal of persons illegally in Australia. Hand enunciated the core principle: 'Non-citizens who are in Australia without a valid visa will be unlawful and will have to be held in detention.'[8]

It was brutal and sweeping. Mandatory detention was being made the law of the land—the provision for administrative discretion was abolished. Australia was passing a new threshold. When the refugee status of boat people was determined they would either be free as residents or deported. Mandatory detention and deportation became the pillars of Keating's border protection.

Responding to Hand, Opposition spokesman Philip Ruddock said Australia faced a 'crisis' in asylum-seeker applications due to the acceptance of onshore Chinese student applications. Despite Australia's advantage of 'water boundaries' and a visa system, processing was under enormous strain. Ruddock had no complaint about the 'quality' of detention. But its length was 'having a very disastrous effect' on some people. Overall, he wanted the government to 'get control of the process'.[9] Ruddock seemed to favour a greater emphasis on control.

This was the punitive reality beneath Keating's speeches about an Australia that was multicultural, creative and renewed by non-discriminatory immigration. It is a paradox of Australia's political culture: a society of remarkable tolerance existed side by side with incarceration of boat people. Such arrivals were supposed to be protected by the 1951 Refugee Convention to which Australia was a party. Because boat people numbers were smaller under Keating the issue was low key. But the Keating policy, if arrival numbers increased, was a political time bomb.

Keating justified his policy on functional grounds. 'We wanted to hold people long enough to ascertain where and what they were from,' he said. 'We wanted to get a good measure of their credentials rather than see them do one interview and then disappear into the community.'[10] The point is manifest: if refugee claims fail then people in detention are available for deportation.

The critical event for the government was the High Court's 1992 finding that detention was valid. This relied on the distinction between aliens and citizens. Such laws would not be tolerated if applied to Australians but they were found to be valid to the extent they were necessary to enable the refugee determination process to be conducted and, if necessary, deportation effected. It was a critical point—the court was saying detention was justified on functional grounds—but not as a policy of deterrence. On this basis the court concluded that detention did not infringe on the 'judicial' power.[11] But the court found that detention before the passage of the new law had been illegal, prompting the government to pass another law saying that any compensation for people previously detained would be paid at 'one dollar a day'.

The High Court decision secured the detention system from the time of the Keating government onwards.

Keating says his detention system was less punitive than Howard's. 'I would not have seen this system become a penal type structure the way it did under Howard,' he said.[12] There is no reason to doubt Keating's argument. Nor is there any doubt that his government made detention mandatory for men, women and children, expanded the system and defended its policy in the High Court. Hand expanded the Villawood centre in Sydney to handle boat people. But his major decision was to establish a detention centre at Port Hedland, in remote Western Australia.

The head of the Immigration Department under Labor, Chris Conybeare, says there was a 'distinct difference' between the Keating and Howard policies:

> When I ran the department, oversight of the conditions in detention to ensure they were sensitive to the situation of asylum seekers as individuals, with adequate health care and provision for families and children, was a priority. Trying to make sure that the detention arrangements were humane, while also being effective as holding facilities, took about 20 per cent of my time.[13]

Conybeare was deeply involved in establishing Port Hedland. Its main requirements were that 'it was close to the boat arrivals, the facility could be made quickly available and it was far distant from urban Australia'.[14]

But the government's 1992 reforms had a more important objective: to halt the march of judicial power. Conybeare says the chief motive was 'to strengthen the hand of the executive government against the courts'.[15] Hand's argument was that the courts were being used to keep boat people in Australia against government policy. 'This must stop,' he said, explaining that the Labor government believed it was 'essential' that all provisions under the act be interpreted 'in the national interest'. Words to this effect were inserted in the law for administrators and courts. The intent was to remove much of migration policy from judicial review.

In an emotional assault Hand attacked human rights activists for waging political campaigns rather than 'assisting in a speedy resolution' of cases. Suggesting that asylum seekers had become 'fodder for a noble crusade', he said: 'Some lawyers employed by the Refugee Council of Australia cared about their clients so much that they put up a sign on the door of their interview room which said "Suicide is just two steps away—you might as well jump."' Hand savaged the irresponsibility of the human rights lobby whose tactics, he said, were to exhaust every avenue of appeal.[16] His 1992 speech offers an insight into the magnitude of the cultural clash between the executive and the refugee/legal lobby.

The numbers of Cambodian and Chinese arrivals were small but for the Australian Government the combination of arrivals and the refugee lawyers posed an urgent problem. 'There are people who are intent on bypassing the established categories of entry into this country,' Hand said. 'The boat people are a good example. Many manage to stay here, even though they do not fall within the specific visa categories which is the only lawful way to enter and stay in Australia.'[17] The strategy was clear: to dissuade people from coming by boat and to reduce the role of lawyers who found techniques to keep people in Australia.

Ruddock was less emotional but more lethal. Replying for the Coalition, Ruddock attacked the High Court for the 'creative way' it had 'got into the business of determining refugee claims when it was always intended that these should be administrative matters dealt with by the government of the day'. He warned that 'the role of the courts collectively in this area has brought about a significant problem for the government of the day'. Ruddock's alarm at judicial usurpation and his determination to fight this trend were unmistakable—it was the prelude to constitutional hostilities.[18]

Hand's stance inaugurated the battle over the migration jurisdiction that Ruddock would intensify and that would run with unabated intensity for more than a decade. In essence, the conflict is simple: it is over whether government or judges should decide who comes to Australia. It is a clash between domestic and international law, between executive and parliament on the one hand and judiciary on the other. As Crock said: 'Put in crude terms, the courts were seen to be letting in people that the government, acting through its bureaucracy, wanted to keep out.'[19] This struggle is fundamental to the debate about a Bill of Rights.

Why was the executive so alarmed? The question was rarely asked or answered. But the history provided an answer. There was a landmark decision—the High Court's 1985 ruling in *Kioa v West*—establishing a new rule, namely, that the validity of a deportation decision would hinge on whether natural justice had been preserved.

The courts would determine what this meant from case to case. This decision and others, in the assessment of Mary Crock, provoked 'an explosion of migration cases in the Federal Court' such that 'in the space of five years the Federal Court [turned] the notion of administrative discretion on its head'. It declared unlawful decisions where the court decided applicants had not got an adequate hearing.[20] The problem, as explained by Commonwealth Ombudsman John McMillan, was the absence of any procedural definition of natural justice, leaving 'a legal obligation of inexact and uncertain dimension' on decision-makers, opening the door to more judicial intervention.[21]

Hand's law spelt out a procedural code to be followed by the department and tribunals to achieve natural justice—but this was quickly rejected by the courts. The system was locked in a downward spiral: the refugee lobby adopted a litigation strategy; the courts responded by being more interventionist; and the executive retaliated with fresh laws to curb the bench. The battle lines were drawn.

The tension within Australia is intense between the international obligations of the 1951 Refugee Convention often seen as an 'outside' imposition to protect asylum seekers and Australia's sovereign right exercised by government to decide which non-citizens can settle in this country. The quest for a system of 'perfect control' is embedded in the political culture of an island continent that enjoys the protection of three great oceans.

Responding to his critics, Hand sought to improve independent merit-based review of refugee claims. The first decision is taken by an official on behalf of the Immigration Minister. The government created a two-tier review—the Migration Review Tribunal and the Refugee Review Tribunal—to buttress independent assessment. The point, however, is that the Keating government's effort to restrain the judges was repelled. There were two consequences: policy deterioration and court gridlock. It was a special Australian failure of stunning dimensions.

By May 2002 more than 54 per cent of all cases decided by the full Federal Court were immigration cases, an unacceptable situation. By 2002–03 a total of 99 per cent of applications to the High Court for constitutional writs under its entrenched judicial review jurisdiction involved migration matters. Towards the end of the Howard government 72 per cent of all appeals in the Federal Court related to migration. Australia's higher courts had been wilfully hijacked by non-citizens and lawyers seeking means for them to stay in Australia, an event that was never envisaged and a result that was untenable.[22]

The defect was identified by McMillan: 'The principle that must stay supreme is that of democracy—if you don't like the government then you vote in another. The judiciary's role is to restrain government, but it should not become the forum for an alternative public policy without democratic legitimacy.'[23] This was precisely what was happening.

McMillan's point highlights the absence in the media debate during the Keating and Howard periods of the foundation of administrative law: under the separation of powers doctrine embodied in the Constitution, judges cannot make decisions on the merits of a case since that responsibility rests with the executive and parliament. The task of judicial review is not to make policy, it is to ensure the law has been upheld and proper process followed by the decision-makers. Yet the aim of much of the human rights lobby was to change Australia's constitutional system and have judges make decisions on the merits. That some judges have strayed beyond this boundary is unquestioned—a point criticised by the High Court, by the Commonwealth Ombudsman as well as by the Keating and Howard governments.

From its inception the refugee issue was tied to the question of power in one of its most vital dimensions: who determines who comes to Australia. For a genuine democracy it is a defining question. The Keating government's 1992 law answered this question: it is the executive who decides on behalf of the people. This has been the answer of every Australian government and there is no sign that it will change.

However, when the executive's solution involves incarceration of asylum seekers, often for long periods amounting to significant denial of human rights, it is inevitable in a democracy such as Australia that relief will be sought in the courts. Ultimately, however, the correction must come via public opinion and public policy. This happened when the Rudd government modified the more punitive aspects of Howard's policies after Howard's own concessions in his final term.

Writing after the *Tampa* crisis, refugee analyst Mary Crock said: 'The Labor government's response to the Cambodian and Chinese boat people of the early 1990s set the course for the policies and institutional hostilities that continue to this day.'[24] This is the inheritance Keating left Howard.

Keating, naturally, does not accept any responsibility for Howard's decisions. Asked what he would have done with the *Tampa*'s boat people, Keating was emphatic: 'I would have allowed them to land.' However, his policy would have sent them into detention.[25]

15

A FRACTURED RECONCILIATION

*I had this impending sense of doom about Keating's
association with us and with Mabo.*
—Noel Pearson, November 2008

In 1993 Paul Keating presided over a revolution in Australian governance. For the first time a prime minister made indigenous justice his main priority in time and politics. This had never happened before, and it will not happen again. Keating produced the 1993 *Native Title Act* enshrining a system to process native title claims, passed in the teeth of fierce Coalition resistance, with Opposition Leader John Hewson branding it 'a day of shame for Australia'.

This agenda was imposed on Keating by the High Court's 1992 Mabo judgment when it corrected an historical injustice and created a crisis for Australia's political system. After his election victory Keating decided to make Mabo his 'personal priority'. In fact, he became consumed by Mabo to the frustration of his ministers—and, in a sense, his government never recovered. 'Mabo was the hand history dealt me and I was never going to walk away from it,' Keating said years later.[1] But his deputy secretary, Sandy Hollway, saw the damage at close quarters. 'He paid a high price,' Hollway said. 'During 1993 Keating sat in endless native title meetings. I saw this sapping his time and corroding his energy. His government's vigour and momentum were sacrificed.'[2]

This was Keating's choice. There was no electoral dividend for him—only a favourable historical judgement based on social justice. 'I think the politics was a negative,' Keating said later. 'People feared I was changing the way Australia functions.'[3] Yet he misread the intensity of the voter backlash against Labor revealed at the 1996 election in regional, rural, pastoral and mining areas.

In truth, Keating was conscripted by the High Court. No other prime minister would have sacrificed as much political capital. The Mabo judgment was a strike at the integrity of the political class and the conscience of the nation. Claims that it was legally orthodox miss the point—its judgment that the colonisation of Australia by England did not extinguish Aboriginal rights in land was a frontal challenge to the way Australians had seen themselves.

This decision altered power relations between black and white; it compelled the Keating government to legislate for a system of native title; and it invested the idea of an official apology with fresh momentum. It seeded a bitter divide between the Labor Party and the Coalition for the entire Keating–Howard period until the election of Kevin Rudd. It brought the issue of race into recurring prominence in the most contentious of all the Keating–Howard disagreements.

The *Native Title Act* shattered any bipartisan hopes for Aboriginal reconciliation. From its passage, the Coalition was pledged to significant amendments when it returned to power. This is the real origin of Howard's subsequent Ten Point Plan unveiled in 1997. The politics of native title disorientated much of conservative Australia. Its self-interest and its beliefs were under attack by a High Court that offered a new interpretation of property rights, saying that native title rights existed within the common law.

A Keating office briefing note said:

> The most powerful player in the Mabo debate is the High Court. It is an undisguised move by the Court to right a perceived wrong in Australian society … the High Court is the most powerful player in this game because the strong majority of the Court unfettered by checks and balances other than public opinion has the potential to keep making up the law until it gets its way … the key to keeping the High Court from deepening the political crisis is to go along with the Court's clear wish for government to assume responsibility for delivering justice to Aborigines.[4]

The High Court's decision upheld a position that Australia's politicians, state and federal, Labor and Liberal, had declined—recognition of a national system of Aboriginal land rights. By rejecting the doctrine of *terra nullius*—that the land had previously belonged to nobody—the court's decision was an opportunity and a curse for Australia's political leaders.

From the start, Keating accepted its validity. 'It rejected a lie and acknowledged a truth,' he said. The hallmark of the Mabo decision was its convincing 6–1 majority. Chief Justice Mason later declared: 'Our previous approach to the position of the indigenous inhabitants of this country was based on a fiction—namely, they did not own the land … Now in this day and age, it was vitally important to ensure that these inaccuracies, these legends, these myths, were dispelled.'[5]

There was a moral fervour in the language. Justice Brennan said the law must not be 'frozen in an age of racial discrimination'. Justices Deane and Gaudron described the consequences of European settlement as a 'conflagration of oppression and conflict which was, over the following century to spread across the continent to dispossess, degrade and devastate the Aboriginal peoples and leave a legacy of unutterable shame' such that the Aboriginals were cast as 'intruders in their own land'.

The decisive judgment came from Brennan, supported by Mason and Justice McHugh. Brennan said:

> The common law of this country would perpetuate injustice if it were to continue to embrace the enlarged notion of *terra nullius* and to persist in characterising the indigenous inhabitants of the Australian colonies as people too low in the scale of social organisation to be acknowledged as possessing rights and interests in land.[6]

The High Court was responding to the failure of the politicians. This helps to explain the intensity of the reaction and hostility from the non-Labor side. McHugh said that one of the strengths of the judiciary was the ability 'to alter the common law to reflect contemporary values and assumptions'.[7] The High Court, in effect, drove the executive by creating a crisis of uncertainty over land management.

It applied what it believed to be the values of the age, just as former Chief Justice, Sir Owen Dixon, when serving as special minister in Washington during World War II, had said in a Memphis address: 'The analogy in this country is the Red Indian but the Australian Aboriginal is of a much lower state of development. He belongs to the Stone Age and no success has attended efforts to incorporate him in a civilised society.'[8]

Keating accepted that Labor's conscience was stained. 'I knew that Labor had a moral void for its capitulation to Brian Burke,' he said.[9] This referred to Bob Hawke's first-term abandonment of a national land rights law after its veto by Labor's Western Australian premier. After this event nobody—not Hawke, not Keating—banged the Labor cabinet table for Aboriginal land rights. The Whitlam–Fraser 1976 land rights bill for the Northern Territory remained a lonely beacon.[10]

Only the High Court could have broken the impasse that the politicians had failed to break. No prime minister would have confronted *terra nullius* and its consequences. With its constitutional *fait accompli* the High Court pushed the nation towards a more just future. It was lucky that Keating responded with diligence and skill.

Explaining the Mabo decision, Jesuit priest and lawyer Frank Brennan said:

> Native title is a weak form of title. It can be extinguished at whim by the Crown and this happened until 1975. The sting in the tail was the 1975 *Racial Discrimination Act* (RDA) that said, in effect, that from that time wherever native title had survived, it could not be extinguished in a discriminatory way. This gave blacks real political leverage for the first time. They got something to trade and they had an option—they could say to the miners 'We'll see you in court.'[11]

The High Court said while native title survived the assertion of sovereignty it was extinguished when government granted land for freehold and other purposes. Native title extinguished before 1975 was lost forever. It existed only where it had not been extinguished and where an Aboriginal group had maintained its connection with the land.

The senior official from the Department of Prime Minister and Cabinet who headed the Mabo process, Sandy Hollway, said: 'The Keating government set out to deal with Mabo at two levels. One was as a land management issue and the other was more abstract but vital— how to use native title as an instrument of reconciliation.'[12] The real business was postponed until after the 1993 election. 'If we win we do native title and if we lose we leave the Liberals a timebomb,' Keating told his advisers.

It was the Mabo decision that created the context for Keating's historic December 1992 Redfern speech of atonement, penned by Don Watson. Keating wanted to make an act of recognition. Watson chanced his arm but he knew his master. He called it a 'Hath not a Jew eyes?' speech. It was not cleared in the office—Watson gave it to Keating who read it over breakfast and changed not a word.[13] The themes were historical truth and democratic responsibility.

Given to a black audience, it was an appeal to white Australia. It began with an echo of Whitlam—that Australia would be judged in the world according to its treatment of Aboriginal people. Keating said the problem started 'with us non-Aboriginal Australians'. He was greeted with catcalls but the audience fell silent when he talked about an 'act of recognition':

> Recognition that it was we who did the dispossessing. We took the traditional lands and smashed the traditional way of life. We brought the diseases. The alcohol. We committed the murders. We took the children from their mothers. We practised discrimination and exclusion. It was our ignorance and prejudice. And our failure to imagine these things being done to us ... We failed to ask, how would I feel if this were done to me? As a consequence, we failed to see that what we were doing degraded all of us.

Moving on to Mabo, Keating said there was 'everything to gain' from recognising the truth. His belief was that Mabo could provide 'the basis of a new relationship between indigenous and non-indigenous Australians'.[14]

Patrick Dodson, chair of the Council for Aboriginal Reconciliation, said the speech envisaged a time when 'we would be able to walk as friends or mates, as Gough Whitlam and Vincent Lingiari had done'.[15] Aboriginal leader Noel Pearson said:

> I thought his Redfern speech was courageous and extraordinary. My view was that this guy is gonna have the confidence of Aboriginal Australia to make real changes. What I didn't realise at the time was that the language had timebombs in it. The speech says it's not about guilt, it's about opening our hearts. But the timebomb was the guilt. I think the conservatives were unfair to put this interpretation on it, but the speech left itself open to that interpretation.[16]

An Australian prime minister, sooner or later, had to make this speech. It is untenable to criticise Keating for making it too early. The High Court had created the context; Keating was addressing the void at the centre of Australian nationhood. In time, it will probably be seen as a great speech.

Keating was exaggerating his hopes for symbolic impact. The more subtle problem with the speech was its impossible idealism. Its compassion was moving as Keating said: 'We are beginning to see how much we owe the indigenous Australians and how much we have lost by living so far apart.' Keating told Aboriginals that they could have 'justice' for past wrongs when the entire history of Australia testified that this was unobtainable. There could never be full restitution for the previous 200 years and Australia could not indulge in an endless process of unfinished business for past sins. There were strict limits to justice and compensation. These limits were inherent in the court's Mabo decision. They would be inherent in Keating's *Native Title Act*. They would be obvious in decisions by future national governments. This was the chasm between words and reality.

This sharpened the politics of reconciliation. Labor and the Coalition would divide over both native title and the apology.

Keating said: 'I know native title confirmed in the minds of some, notably in the outlying states, that I was taking the social contract too far, you know, changing the society too much underneath. The truth is we couldn't avoid this. In my view we got out of the native title issue very expeditiously and in a fair way.'[17] It remains a sound assessment.

Pearson, one of the negotiators, said:

> I'd had a scarifying experience first hand with the Goss government when Kevin Rudd was involved. I knew how Labor can run for cover when it comes to black fellas. Keating won me when I was told that, before the 1993 election, his private message was 'We have to make peace with the black fellas'. There were a lot of doubts whether he'd stick with us when things got rough. But he did. Once Keating had a loyalty it was hard to shake. In my view he stayed with us when it would have been far easier for him to quit.[18]

'The Mabo settlement has three parts,' said Keating as a political realist. 'It's got the black bit, the white bit and the grey bit.'[19]

The 'black bit' was refusing to extinguish all native title in defiance of the *Racial Discrimination Act*. 'If we had just let this alone, the States would have extinguished native title wholesale,' Keating said. The formula adopted was that Crown grants of land since 1975 would be validated under a 'special measure' provision of the act, thereby keeping the integrity of the law, a core Aboriginal demand. Keating described his position as an 'ungrudging' recognition of native title. It meant a system that allowed registration and approval of native title claims and standards that would make the States more accountable in their land decisions. Keating said he wanted to protect native title 'to the maximum extent practicable'.[20]

The 'white bit' was the delivery of certainty by providing that all Crown grants since 1975 were deemed to be valid so 'nobody holding land tenure need fear on this score'. The demands of public opinion and economic development made this essential. Without this guarantee, Mabo crashed before mainstream Australia and the ritualistic 'threat to the backyard'.[21]

Keating's preference had been to win Senate passage with the negotiated support of the Coalition parties. 'Let there be no re-writing of history,' said Aboriginal Affairs Minister Robert Tickner. 'Indisputably, it was cabinet's priority to reach an accommodation with the states and territories.' Tickner and other ministers were dismayed at cabinet's early October 1993 decision to authorise Keating to conclude such a deal by winding back further the application of the *Racial Discrimination Act*. Tickner felt 'defeated and demoralised' at this, so upset he could barely speak. On the morning of 8 October, driving to Jervis Bay to meet a local indigenous community, he decided to resign from the ministry rather than tolerate such a compromise.[22]

But this day witnessed the indigenous counterattack, with ATSIC chair Lowitja O'Donoghue, Mick Dodson and Noel Pearson leading the charge. 'On the major issues we cannot and will not concede any further,' O'Donoghue told Keating by letter. 'The *Racial Discrimination Act* must not be suspended simply to satisfy the States and the mining industry.' Keating's Redfern speech was raised against his actions. On 'Black Friday' 8 October the Aboriginal leaders rejected the cabinet strategy.[23]

'The Labor Party has always been ambivalent about indigenous issues,' former shadow minister Daryl Melham said. 'This was the decisive stage in Mabo. But Keating took advice and backtracked to a more conciliatory *RDA* formula that upheld the principle of what he wanted.'[24]

The political reality was that the Coalition parties had entered a 'Mabo crisis' that rendered them divided and unavailable as Senate partners. They would take years to recover. The Coalition, in the end, opposed Keating's bill outright and declined to consider any amendments. The Mabo decision was an assault on Coalition attitudes and interests. Keating had no choice but to look to pass the bill via the minor parties.

'You have sold out the miners,' Hewson said. 'You have sold out the farmers, you have sold out the state leaders and you have sold out all other Australians who are going to be significantly worse off.'[25] Hewson insisted the land issues be separated from reconciliation—a stance, according to Hollway, that 'poisoned the well'.[26] The Opposition Leader accused Keating of a 'power grab' by moving beyond the terms of the

High Court decision and usurping the prerogatives of the states. Across the nation conservative intellectuals warned that Australian unity was at risk. The Liberal premier of Western Australia, Richard Court, led the resistance by legislating a sweeping extinguishment of native title, only to have his law's validity knocked down by the High Court in 1995.

The critical players, courtesy of the Coalition, became the two Greens senators Dee Margetts and Christabel Chamarette. 'They're just a pair of trots who've blown into the place and think they run the show,' Keating snorted. Having initially declared they would not vote for the bill, the Greens were carried over the line by intense pressure and government concessions.

This where Keating's 'grey bit' became decisive. It was about competing claims—the conflict between native title on one hand and pastoralists and miners on the other. The miners were isolated from the negotiations and helped to shape the Coalition's hostility to the bill. In the end, the act gave Aboriginals a right to negotiate with miners with an easy threshold test for the registration of indigenous claim.

Frank Brennan said:

> There was a sense of euphoria when the bill was passed but we knew in our heart of hearts that the registration test was unworkable. The miners felt excluded by government and snubbed by the Senate. The Greens had a political commitment to maximise Aboriginal gains and they succeeded. But these were short-term gains purchased at the cost of workability of the act. They constituted a political imperative for John Howard to promise to amend the law—and this was long before the Wik decision.[27]

But the most famous 'grey bit' concerned native title and pastoral leases. Such leases dominate much of Australia's land mass where farmers and Aboriginals interact on the same lease. Hollway said: 'Keating would not stomach the idea of writing into the bill that pastoral leases extinguished native title utterly and for all time. This was what the farmers wanted and what he rejected.'[28] It was a door for Aboriginal Australia that Keating left open, slightly.

Acting on Keating's behalf, Hollway, on 13 October 1993, asked National Farmers Federation chief Rick Farley to accept a bill where a pastoral lease did not extinguish native title. The next day Farley wrote back saying: 'The proposal is totally unacceptable … this would create enormous uncertainty about land tenure.' Farley said it would be 'a gross and unforgivable breach of political faith' if Labor retreated from its pledge that pastoral leases would extinguish native title.[29] But Keating was determined.

'I had my own intuition on this,' Keating said.'I resisted the Attorney-General's and the Solicitor-General's advice. I felt from individual judgments in the Mabo case that the court in future might hold in favour of co-existence (of native title and pastoral leases).'[30]

This was not the legal orthodoxy. The advice to government was the reverse—that pastoral leases extinguished native title. Frank Brennan had no doubt that the High Court that took the Mabo decision did not endorse such co-existence and, put to the test, would have voted 4–3 against the proposition.[31] But what would a future bench decide? Nobody could be sure.

Keating secured a deceptive compromise—the deal was that the bill would not extinguish native title on pastoral leases. The presumption that this was the position would, however, be stated in the preamble, without the force of law. Keating said: 'We put the advice from the Solicitor-General in the front of the bill, in the preamble. The National Party wanted me to decide the issue then and there but I refused. In the actual bill I left the issue open.'[32] In the parliament Keating hinted at his support for the idea, saying:'(This) is not co-ownership, as some people have tried to express it. It is a co-existence of rights'.[33]

By keeping open the co-existence option, Keating wanted the courts, not the parliament, to settle this question. In short, he was holding out the hope of a more radical outcome in favour of native title down the track. Keating thought there might be another win yet for Aboriginal Australia, and he was right—it came in the Wik decision. In the interim he had offered Farley other concessions to secure his agreement.

The Native Title Bill was passed after the longest debate in the Senate's history to that point. It was near midnight and four days before Christmas 1993. The galleries were filled. Senators were conscious of the historic nature of the event. Gareth Evans, who carried the bill for the government in a masterful feat of drafting and negotiation, declared that Australia owed the indigenous peoples 'a huge debt for the destruction and dispossession … I hope that by the passage of this legislation tonight we have repaid just a little of that debt'.[34]

The process highlighted the emergence of a diverse Aboriginal leadership and negotiating team that had largely risen through indigenous institutions, many of whom sat in the Senate gallery that night and were acknowledged individually by Evans—O'Donoghue, Pearson, Marcia Langton, David Ross, Darryl Pearce, Peter Yu and David Cronin. Their relations with government had been a roller-coaster ride. But Labor encouraged such leaders and had a vested interest in their credibility.

The lesson from the negotiation was that Aboriginal Australia would not get its way: it had to negotiate the best compromise available. When negotiations had broken down between Keating and the Aboriginal team on the so-called 'Black Friday', Keating questioned their psychological ability to close an agreement and take responsibility for it. 'My initial reaction was to think, what a racist comment,' Pearson said of Keating's critique. 'But then I realised he'd pinpointed our weakness. Our problem was a psychological reluctance to make the deal.'[35]

Ultimately, the deal was done. Keating said his aim had been to bring Aboriginal leaders for the first time 'to the central seats of power with a place as a full stakeholder'.[36] He called this a 'turning point for all Australians' and, contrary to his previous comment, congratulated indigenous leaders for having the courage 'to seize the moment'. Afterwards the Aboriginal leaders felt Keating had engaged with them with integrity—a standard many felt that Howard did not uphold.

The moral Keating drew overall was the triumph of politics—the doomsayers predicting that the conflicting interests could not be reconciled had been disproved. It was a victory for the people and the institutions, he said. But the Coalition was not part of that victory and, in that sense, the nation was profoundly divided. 'The Opposition presumes ill will among Australians,' Keating told the House. 'We presume goodwill … We will hear the Leader of the Opposition [Hewson] say that he supported the High Court decision; but he immediately wanted to wipe it out.'[37]

In his Senate summary Evans paid tribute to Keating—he saw the opportunity and got involved in the detail 'to a greater extent than any prime minister has ever done on any single issue of which I am aware'. Daryl Melham, who opposed Keating in the leadership struggle, said: 'No other Labor leader would have done this. It was Keating's finest hour and this was his greatest achievement as party leader.'[38]

The Mabo legacy tied Aboriginal gains to Labor and alienated the indigenous leadership from the Coalition. This happened before Howard returned to the leadership in early 1995. The consequences for the indigenous peoples were disastrous after the Coalition was elected. Keating had been enshrined a hero while Howard would become a demon.

Keating said the agreement 'will warm the soul of the Labor Party for two generations', proof that he saw native title as integral to modern Labor's new credo.

The politics of Mabo and the *Native Title Act* changed Australia and its institutions decisively. Native title was a practical and symbolic advance for Aboriginal Australia due to the High Court and Keating Labor. Such gains were built on the fracture of bipartisanship and a Labor–Coalition rift over native title and reconciliation. The consequence was a highly equivocal public opinion about Mabo and native title, and in Western Australia, Queensland and the regions, a distinct hostility. The High Court's audacity had been rewarded by Keating and the parliament. But the High Court had contracted a dose of hubris.

While public opinion would turn against Keating, he had mined the terrain of Aboriginal policy with a series of shocks for the Coalition— growing expectations about an official apology, greater ambitions for reconciliation and a long fuse leading to the Wik detonation. Beneath the passage of the *Native Title Act* the country was more polarised over indigenous issues and competing interests. Howard would return to the Liberal leadership convinced that Keating had transgressed too far, determined to rebalance the *Native Title Act*, worried that the nation had become too fractured, and pledged to speak up for mainstream Australia.

PART III

THE SHOWDOWN: KEATING VERSUS HOWARD

16

THE BETRAYAL

I made the decision to resign about a week before the Budget.
—John Dawkins, December 2008

After his 1993 election victory Paul Keating was neither humble nor magnanimous. His government's death warrant can be dated precisely—it was signed on 17 August 1993 at its post-election Budget. This document betrayed Labor's election promises on taxation and saw relations between Keating and John Dawkins collapse. Dawkins decided to resign during preparations for the Budget, one of the worst received in recent history.

The irony was rich. It was Treasury's demand for its own mini-*Fightback!* to regain fiscal rectitude that finished the Keating government. Keating, as master strategist, went missing-in-action in 1993. He conspicuously failed to resolve the conflict between the Treasury-driven Dawkins' economic agenda and Labor's political agenda. The origin of Keating's 1996 loss lay in the misconceptions he drew from his 1993 victory.

Keating became fixated by the idea that he had won on his 'enlargement' agenda and not the GST. This was the view he put at his 'victory' media conference on the Monday after the poll when Keating seemed more angry than happy. He said the election was 'not a referendum on the GST, it was a referendum on the way Australians lived'. The media blinked. Not a referendum on the GST? What had the past month been about? It was vintage Keating, but he had gone too far.[1]

'I wasn't surprised Paul said that,' his adviser, Mark Ryan, said. 'This was Keating laying personal claim to the victory. That's Paul's style and there was some basis to it. No election is won single-handedly, but if ever one was, it was Keating's in 1993.'[2]

It is a privilege of every winner to capitalise on victory and another to succumb to the polemic. Rejecting suggestions that Labor had run a negative campaign, Keating asked: 'If the huns are storming the battlements how negative is it to drive them back? If the Liberal Party wanted to jettison Australian values, how negative is it to stop them?'[3] He said the republic had been endorsed at the poll. His aim would be to achieve the republic 'at least' by 2001. Asked about the flag, he had no doubt that it would be fixed as well since once the republic was created 'all the other things would [fall] into place including the flag'.[4] It started to sound easy.

Keating was angry at predictions that he would lose. He attacked the journalists for predicting the wrong result. After the poll he said that he 'never had any doubt' of victory.[5] Yet many ALP figures had famous stories to the contrary. Ryan said: 'We were crossing the bridge on the afternoon of the election returning to Kirribilli. Paul was quiet, a bit despondent and not at all confident—just the opposite. Not surprising really.'[6]

Now he couldn't let it die. 'The next time any of you are absolutely certain of something,' he said to the journalists, 'ask yourself, "Can I be as confident of these views as I was about the election result of 1993?"' He then added: 'If any politician had done as badly as the commentators have performed in the last three to four weeks the media would be baying for his or her blood.'[7]

It seemed Keating had fought too many wars—against Hawke, Kerry Packer, Hewson, the GST, the recession and a legion of real and alleged enemies. Not content with the win, he wanted something more—he wanted others to admit that they were wrong.

Since nearly everybody, at one time or another, had believed he would lose, including himself, the circle of distrust was hopelessly wide. Never has an election winner complained so much. Don Watson captured his outlook:

> Only the *Telegraph-Mirror* editorialised for Labor … The [press] gallery, and, even more, the newspapers … had turned on Labor. They were supporting a half-baked conservative tyro against the man who had given the country a modern economy … In the last week of the campaign the press put the poison in Keating's soul. It never left. He would never be able to forgive them.[8]

Interviewed for this book, Don Russell said:

No politician had given the gallery as much attention as Keating. He had developed relationships and he saw them as allies and friends in his design to improve Australia. But the gallery had marched to a different drum. Paul felt that he hadn't changed but the gallery had abandoned him in favour of Hewson, of all people. He felt a sense of betrayal.[9]

Once, Keating would have sworn at the media and scolded them before charming and cajoling them with policy vistas for his new term. But he couldn't do that any more. The music had died. He talked as though the media had insulted him for giving them his time over the years, the thrilling talks and the engaging meals. It was less than ten years since the *Sydney Morning Herald*'s veteran correspondent Peter Bowers, standing in his press gallery office, had declared of Keating: 'I won't go near him. Once he gets you in that room, you're gone, the will to resist disappears, you know he's going to persuade you.'

But Keating was now losing the will to persuade. A vague plausibility disguised his reality denial at the election result. Ryan spoke for most observers when he said: 'There is a simple equation to the 1993 election. We couldn't have won without Hewson and the GST.'[10] Former New South Wales minister Rodney Cavalier was tougher. 'Paul did not win a victory in 1993; he gained a reprieve. Nothing more.'[11] But Keating accepted neither view.

Labor's campaign director, Bob Hogg, said in 1993: 'Our major strategy was to make the GST and all that related to it the main issue and, at the same time, negate the wishful thinking that the GST would create one new job.'[12] The truth is that Keating had won as a supreme demolitionist. In the campaign he had followed, eventually, the edict from Labor's most ruthless adviser, Peter Barron—run on the GST, not compassion, Asia or Aboriginals.

One of the turning points was when Keating turned a mid-February prime time debate with Mike Willesee on the Nine Network into a ferocious GST assault. The *Australian*'s Kate Legge said: 'He demolished Hewson by sheer jawpower ... butting in, even intruding into the second of silence when his opponent paused for breath ... he put Alfred Hitchcock to shame with his horror stories about Hewson's "monster tax".'[13] Keating called it the 'biggest lifestyle tax in the nation's history', hitting every aspect of life—restaurants, dry cleaners, ferries, ballet, taxis, electricity bills. He was outrageous, out-muscling Hewson, appalling, un-prime ministerial but effective. It was compelling television because it shattered the normal rules. Keating had violated Hewson on television.

That night the Liberals watched him in cold fury. Howard conceded Keating was 'undignified' but 'he got the issue up'. For Costello, it was the turning point. 'Keating's turned it round,' he said. 'It'll be GST every day from now on.'[14]

Whenever the subject arose after the victory, Keating's message was the same. In mid-1995 he said: 'I've never accepted the popular analysis of the 1993 election that the government won because of the GST. It's just not true ... the government won the election because it was offering something larger and bigger: belief in Australia and belief in Australia's enlargement.'[15] This view justified Keating's 1993–96 pursuit of his 'big picture' agenda, a project the ALP National Secretariat saw as a voter train wreck.

'Keating was determined to tell everyone that we had won the election,' Dawkins said. 'This became an issue in the caucus. Most of the caucus felt that Hewson had lost the election. When anyone said that, Paul would get upset and shout at them.'[16]

Keating in victory did not seem to be a happy man. 'Paul craves love,' Leo Schofield said many years later. After the election he felt his feats were not recognised. Bob Carr reflected that Keating would argue 'that only he had the hunger to haul Labor over the line in the GST election'.[17] But the sweetest victory had not bequeathed tranquillity.

Keating's biographer and adviser John Edwards wrote about this phenomenon with acumen:

> He began to interpret the outcome of the March election not as a rejection of *Fightback!* but as an endorsement of a philosophy of growth with equity and of engagement with Asia. He also believed that women, people interested in the arts, and Aborigines had been important in his election victory, although the weight of evidence was that Paul had recovered the traditional Labor vote diminished in the last two elections. 'Pig's arse, pig's arse' he would tell Victorian backbencher Peter Cleeland during a fierce caucus debate in September 1993, after Cleeland said that Labor had not so much won the election as the Liberals had lost it ... as the months went by Paul actually seemed to convince himself of his story, despite the clear evidence of studies of the poll result ...[18]

The lightness that was once Paul faded as he succumbed to an introspective intensity. Somehow he had been damaged in the struggles of politics. As a realist Keating knew the truth: the people didn't love him and didn't trust him. The tragedy is that he abandoned that golden chance to reach out with generosity, show humility and fulfil the promise of his 1993 victory. Any sports fan could have written the script for an Australian champion in triumph, but Keating did not follow sport. 'He polarises people emotionally as well as intellectually,' his friend Phillip Adams said.[19]

In politics, as in life, there comes a time for accounting. It happens far from the cheers at election night. The messengers are the bureaucrats who count numbers and draft estimates. The politicians, familiar with the ritual, ponder over how to exculpate themselves. The messengers in Keating's moment of truth were the head of the Prime Minister's Department, Mike Keating, and stony-faced senior Treasury officers. Keating's government never recovered from their message.

Dawkins said: 'What made the 1993 election so difficult was not just the promised LAW tax cuts but a whole series of spending decisions not taken by cabinet but by the Prime Minister and his office. After the election we knew these pledges were unsustainable.'[20]

A fortnight before the vote the Treasury had briefed the *Australian*'s Alan Wood, who wrote:

> The Federal Treasury has advised the Keating government that its future budget deficits are too big and risk major instability later in the 1990s … The advice was given before Labor added several billion dollars to the deficit outlook in election promises, additions which made the need for tough action post-election even more urgent. The Reserve Bank shares the Treasury's concern. A clear implication of the Treasury's advice is that Labor should drop its promised income tax cuts but these are already in legislation and the Prime Minister, Mr Keating, is determined they will go ahead.

Wood said Treasury would tell any Hewson government that its budget priorities 'are no more tenable than Labor's'.[21]

'We will need to find an extra $10 billion,' Mike Keating told his prime minister at Kirribilli. Maybe it was this advice that stuck in Keating's craw.[22] At Treasury, it was a time for steel. 'Our priority recommendation was for the government to introduce a GST,' Ted Evans said deadpan when interviewed for this book. 'But that was not an appealing option and our next position was to increase a range of indirect taxes.'[23]

Treasury Secretary Tony Cole, who left in mid-1993 to be replaced by Evans, said: 'The principal economic objective of the 1993 Budget had to be to set in place a medium-term strategy to wind back the deficit by a combination of spending cuts and revenue increases.'[24]

Dawkins knew his moment had come. It was only five years since that surreal day in August 1988 when Dawkins had walked into the Prime Minister's office and told an astonished Bob Hawke that he should resign in favour of Keating—a flirtation with pyrotechnics that made Dawkins a man to watch. Yet Dawkins and Keating had never got their personal chemistry together as prime minister and treasurer.

Dawkins, a poor man's Keating, stepped into the final phase of his tumultuous career—accounting for the 1993 victory. He would become its first victim. The morning after the election win, Dawkins came to see Keating to offer congratulations. 'I'll be more assertive this term,' he said. 'There are things to do.' Dawkins felt that Keating had dominated fiscal policy far too much—witness the LAW tax cuts. Keating understood the message.[25]

The problem was the same, regardless of the angle from which it was examined. Keating had bid too high for victory. He had run the political strategy for re-election and Dawkins was left with the ruins.

Dawkins sat at his desk staring at Treasury's gloomy revenue forecasts. Such forecasts made it impossible to deliver the tax cuts yet keep a credible trajectory to return to fiscal responsibility. This was the inexorable wheel that would break the Keating–Dawkins partnership.

Keating was taken aback by the scale of Dawkins' demands. The Treasurer wanted to cancel the LAW tax cut. 'I don't think we can do that, John,' Keating told him. As a former treasurer, Keating understood Dawkins' psychology. But Keating had a government to save. When interviewed, Dawkins qualified this somewhat, saying: 'My initial position was that the tax cuts were unaffordable and had to be substantially reduced.' Keating's impression was that Dawkins wanted the entire LAW tax cut abandoned, the lot.

Dawkins had entered his crazy brave zone. 'I'll give you a choice,' he said at one point to Keating. 'You can either support me or I'll resign.' Keating saw that Dawkins, fearing he would be branded a weak treasurer, was on steroids. He had become the Treasury's hit man. The government's stability was under threat.[26]

'When we put all the promises together along with the promised tax cuts it didn't add up,' Dawkins said. There were agonising talks between the two men. 'Keating came to the same conclusion,' Dawkins said. 'It wasn't going to work.'[27] But Keating had a different solution. He offered Dawkins a compromise—bring forward the first round of the tax cuts but push back the second round. It would be a humiliation, the media would raise a thunder but some honour would be preserved.

They reached tentative agreement on this and the betrayal announcement was unveiled by Keating in his July National Press Club speech. The LAW tax cuts would not be paid on the timetable. As Keating was driven from Capitol Hill to the media lunch he told Don Watson his speech was 'too good for the bastards' and then said that if Dawkins didn't calm down he would have to knock his block off.[28]

Sorting out the compromise had been an agonising affair. Dawkins obsessed about the 'bottom line' and the impact of bringing forward the first round of tax cuts. Their respective versions of these discussions do not exactly coincide. At one stage Dawkins said to Keating: 'If you insist on paying the tax cuts then I'll raise the revenue by indirect tax increases.' Dawkins accused Keating of creating the problem—of getting Ric Simes to fudge the *One Nation* forecasts.

'Don't be crazy, John,' Keating said. 'This is absurd.' But Dawkins was agitated—he felt Keating's election victory had been purchased by sacrificing his standing as treasurer. The point, of course, as Dawkins admitted, was that he went along with Keating's strategy.[29]

'John, this game is about staying on your feet,' Keating told him. 'You don't have to prove anything to anybody. You don't have to prove anything to the Treasury. Otherwise, we all fall over.'[30] When he dealt with agitated complainants face-to-face, Keating could be very calm, very quiet.

The problem was that Treasury needed more revenue. 'The hardest Budget is the one after an election,' Dawkins reflects.

> It was difficult because the old expenditure review committee of ministers had broken up and discipline had weakened. I chaired the Expenditure Review Committee in 1993. Paul was not as attentive as he should have been. Peter Walsh was gone. I told Paul that if he didn't want a serious savings round then we had to raise more taxes. I wanted to cut Defence but Paul wouldn't take on Robert Ray. There was no way other senior ministers were going to accept serious cuts. The essential discipline of the Hawke era had gone.[31]

Dawkins was sinking. Left isolated, he felt his prime obligation as treasurer was to bring down a tough Budget. But he knew the politics. Dawkins was marching to his doom. 'I made the decision to resign about a week before the Budget.'[32]

The Dawkins Budget of 17 August 1993 was an act of economic courage and a political death sentence. He operated within the parameters he was given and his Budget extracted the toll for Keating's pre-election promises. It is best seen as a combined Dawkins–Treasury strike to recast the fiscal trajectory. Access Economics principal Geoff Carmody called it 'a poor man's *Fightback*'.

The budget deficit for 1993–94 was $16 billion, or 3.8 per cent of GDP, a slight deterioration. The essence of the Budget, however, was measures to save an extra $9 billion such that the projected deficit for 1996–97 would be cut from nearly $15 billion to under $6 billion— meaning that the deficit in three years' time would be reduced to the 1 per cent of GDP target.[33] In his Budget speech Dawkins said a four-year framework had been established.

The LAW income tax cuts would no longer be law. The first round of the tax cut was to be brought forward from 1 July 1994 to 1 November 1993. But this eight-month carry-forward meant the Dawkins Budget had to absorb the cost, thereby creating even more dire immediate pressures. The second round, due from 1 January 1996, was postponed 'until a time when fiscal conditions permit, probably in 1998'. The government refused to commit to a delivery date. It left open the possibility—which most analysts saw as a probability—that the second round (the bulk of the tax cut) would never be paid.

The idea of betrayal took hold. Keating's election pledge of tax cuts without a GST was shown to be unsustainable. The howls were raised; the public had been played for mugs. Dawkins drew the irresistible conclusion: 'The 1993 Budget was the necessary child of *One Nation*,' he said. 'After the election I had to clean up the consequences.'[34] Dawkins had said it: he was victim to Keating's unsustainable election policy.

But it got worse. Having opposed a GST the government now increased the wholesale sales tax (WST) across the board by two percentage points. In addition there were excise increases on petrol and tobacco, an additional increase for leaded petrol, an increase in the tax on wine and a tightening up of benefits under Medicare. Three years out these indirect tax rises would reap an extra $3 billion.

The reaction was predictable—the government was accused of a double betrayal. Not only had it fought against reform of the indirect tax system through a GST but it was now increasing the indirect taxes that would have been abolished by the GST reform. Dawkins had proposed an even wider range of tax increases, but Keating had vetoed them.[35] In the end, however, they failed to find a politically viable position.

Michael Keating said: 'Paul didn't agree with what Dawkins was doing. But he had been a former treasurer and he understood how Dawkins felt. I think he allowed Dawkins to run his own race.'[36] It was Keating's gift to Dawkins. In a perfect summary Don Russell said: 'I guess one has to say that the election strategy was Keating's and the budget strategy was Dawkins' and that it didn't work overall.'[37]

For Dawkins, the Budget was a second-best path. He would have preferred to extend the wholesale sales tax base instead of increasing the tax rates. This was Treasury's advice to him. 'I told them in an ideal world that's what I'd like to do, but we don't control the Senate.' Dawkins said. It would have been more difficult to get a broadening of the indirect tax base through the parliament after an election during which Keating had depicted a GST as the embodiment of evil.

The Dawkins Budget was battered by the caucus and then by the Senate, with a number of changes being made. The caucus was more angry about the tax rises than deferral of the LAW tax cuts. The open rifts within the government compounded the high policy betrayal. But the Treasury was satisfied.

Ted Evans and Tony Cole felt that fiscal responsibility had been regained. And they praised Dawkins' effort. 'John Dawkins had a short fuse but I think he did a good job as treasurer,' Evans said.[38] On Budget night Evans told Dawkins that he done a good job, a comment Dawkins valued. 'This Budget was about Dawkins taking back his authority as treasurer,' Cole said. 'It was the right Budget and it was courageous.'[39]

From his perspective as Keating's gatekeeper and a former Treasury officer, Russell reached the opposite view:

> The Treasury wanted to win back the tax base and they persuaded Dawkins that he had to increase taxes. This did immense harm for little fiscal gain. The recovery when it eventually got underway was always going to deliver a large and probably unexpected revenue surge and the need for immediate revenue replacement was peripheral. These Budget decisions were very important for Dawkins but very damaging for the government.[40]

The responsibility lay with Keating as prime minister. These events were proof of a distracted government. In Keating's defence, Russell had said: 'Given the Treasury forecasts, Keating was caught in a bind. What could he do? Change the forecasts? Hardly.'[41] But the consequences were disastrous.

A puzzled Watson suggested a government in dysfunction, claiming the Budget 'bore no semblance' to anything Keating's office had expected. 'It was a mystery of how it came to be,' he lamented. Watson asked later: 'How had the politics been so abysmal, so stupid, so unconsidered? The awful haunting truth about the Budget was that not once in the Prime Minister's office did the advisers meet with the Prime Minister to discuss the politics of taxing unleaded petrol or breaking promises on Medicare.'[42] The point is that Keating didn't want such talks. In truth, the Budget had no political strategy.

It was partly procured by the Dawkins resignation threat. John Edwards said Dawkins had threatened to resign on three occasions before the Budget was finalised.[43] Interviewed for this book, Dawkins confirmed that resignation was a live option. 'We had to reduce the deficit,' he said. 'For me, this was non-negotiable. As treasurer, I was not prepared to bring down an irresponsible Budget that did not involve a reduction in the deficit. I told the cabinet as much.'[44]

Keating's economic adviser, Ric Simes, backs Russell's view that Treasury had exaggerated the fiscal problem. 'The tax cuts proved to be unsustainable primarily for political reasons,' he says.

> That is, the Budget would be in deficit for longer. From an economic perspective, a lower deficit would have been better but it was not a serious economic problem given the size of the deficit and the pace with which it was moving into balance (about 1 per cent of GDP a year) and the fact that unemployment was still high.[45]

In an analysis he did for the Chifley Research Centre, Simes concluded that 'the depth and length of the recession was significantly reduced by fiscal policy'.[46]

Meanwhile, Bill Kelty watched with a cold rage from Melbourne as the Budget unfolded. He said:

> After the Dawkins Budget, I thought we were fucked. I said to Paul, 'We're fucked, you couldn't have done anything to upset people more.' Paul had said, 'Don't vote for a GST, vote for me', and then we increase all these taxes. The ACTU never wanted Dawkins. I said to Paul at the start, 'Don't have him, we don't want Dawkins, his whole family is Liberal Party, he'll fuck you over.' The Budget was a catastrophe.[47]

The media, the Opposition and the minor parties savaged the government. The Newspoll taken the weekend after the Budget showed the worst ALP vote in Newspoll's history, with a Coalition lead on the primary vote 54–31 per cent. When Keating was defeated three years later, Labor MPs still blamed this Budget.

The Budget furore only confirmed Dawkins' departure decision. 'I had a gameplan in mind,' he said. 'I would produce the necessary unpopular Budget, take responsibility for it and then retire from politics.' There was something else playing on his mind—he was loyal to Keating but uneasy about him.

'The truth is that Hawke gave Keating as treasurer more support in cabinet than Paul as prime minister gave me,' Dawkins said. Fortified by Treasury's view, Dawkins believed 'the Budget was the right thing'. 'Frankly, it was a hard and solitary exercise. I believed it would create new opportunities for Keating and the government.'[48]

In mid-December, at the fag end of a shocking year, Dawkins pulled the plug. A week before Christmas he went to see Keating in his office where he was preparing his valedictory speech for the end-of-year session. 'When we're doing the valedictories I intend to get up and "valedict" myself,' Dawkins said. 'I'm going to retire.' He gave Keating no notice.

'That's a pity John, what are you doing that for?' Keating replied. Dawkins said he'd had enough; there was a range of reasons. 'Mate, you should rethink this,' Keating said. But the die was cast. Dawkins said it was too late: he'd made up his mind a while ago. They expressed their affection for each other. Keating was nice to him.[49]

Keating reappointed Ralph Willis as treasurer. Later he told his staff: 'The worst was over. Dawkins only had to wait and ride the economic upturn.' Sometimes he would speculate whether he was wrong to have made Dawkins treasurer. Perhaps Dawkins had been too volatile. As Keating knew, the authentic political warrior cannot lose his nerve in the snows of winter.

But Dawkins had sensed that the government was decaying. He believed it lacked the quality and discipline of the Hawke years. He had served twenty years in parliament and had reached his limit. Dawkins knew that, when Keating went, the next leader would be Beazley. Laura Tingle reported that during his farewell drinks Dawkins said he had been a 1980s reformer when you acted first and explained yourself later; he didn't like the inhibitions of the 1990s.[50]

The 1993 Budget crisis materially weakened the government. As Tony Cole remembers, 'The political backlash was terrific. It unnerved the government and I think it ruled out any further tough reformist policies that term.'[51] Evans, always a Keating fan, says: 'I think overall 1993–96 was a disappointing period for economic reform. Keating didn't pay too much attention to the economy. Maybe that was a sensible outlook since he had other priorities.'[52]

Keating had lost more than his treasurer; he had lost the grand opportunity offered by the election victory. For Kelty, it was the death knell.

'The 1993 Budget shot Keating in the heart. People said this is a breach of faith. It wasn't just deferring the LAW tax cuts. It was all the indirect tax increases. The government never recovered.'[53] The 1993 fiasco had a profound impact on John Howard. 'In my opinion the 1993 Budget was the final nail in the coffin for Keating,' he said.[54]

As he struggled through the gloom, Keating knew no future was pre-ordained. The folly of the Liberals always gave him heart—but the Liberals were about to play their last option.

17

HOWARD: THE FINAL OPTION

I thought two terms would be enough.
—John Howard reflecting on the events of 1995

John Howard's return as Liberal leader delivered a new order that would last a dozen years and transform the party's fortunes. The compact of January 1995 was an agreed division of power—Howard as leader and future prime minister, Peter Costello as deputy, future treasurer and successor, Alexander Downer as future foreign minister.

The reality of Liberal power over 1995–2007 is often misconceived—this was a Howard–Costello–Downer compact to win office and stay in office. It delivered the most prolonged Liberal stability since the Menzian age, it brought together New South Wales and Victoria, it united the parliamentary and organisational wings and it was based on a consensus of conservative and moderate opinion. Events and personalities had brought the party to this settlement. The pact was endorsed by Howard, Costello and Downer.

Neither Howard nor the most optimistic Liberal MP imagined the scale of its eventual success, and the notion of a four-term prime ministership never crossed Howard's mind. The terms of the compact would later be disputed between Howard and Costello. The pact worked best for Howard and Downer and least for Costello, who never succeeded to the leadership in office.

Howard had wanted to be drafted, he wanted the Liberal Party to come to him, he wanted his former enemies to declare a truce. And he won on all counts. Howard often said that he secured the leadership in 1985 by surprise and lost it in 1989 by ambush. But there was neither surprise nor ambush about his 1995 recall—it was by design.

It would be fashionable to say that Howard never doubted he would return but that would be wrong. 'I honestly thought that it was over,' he said of the leadership. 'I had to have a knee reconstruction by Merv Cross's partner and I spent a lot of time at home recovering. The anesthetist at the operation had chatted to me about our new political team [Downer and Costello] and I said that I'd stay around to help them.'[1] But Grahame Morris said: 'I think while it was Howard's desire to have another go, it was Janette's conviction.'[2]

It was Liberal desperation that drove the party to Howard after the triple failures of Peacock, Hewson and Downer. Instead of being seen as yesterday's man, Howard became the last best hope.

Howard's second leadership would not be contested in the party room from its 1995 start to its 2007 end. His recall ended fifteen years of leadership instability ever since Fraser's third election victory in 1980, a period that had seen six distinct leadership phases under Fraser, Peacock, Howard, Peacock again, Hewson and Downer, during which the party lost five successive elections. The scale of Howard's recovery was more impressive than Menzies' in World War II. Howard's exile from 1989 to 1995 spanned six years while Menzies had resigned the leadership in 1941 only to return in 1943.

Blighted by poor timing in the past, Howard saw the stars coming into alignment. He was utterly convinced that Keating was finished. 'My view was that once the Liberal Party got its act together people would vote Keating out,' he said. 'As soon as I returned and the party folded behind me and we started to attack Keating there was a huge—you could almost feel it—sense of relief in the community.'[3]

Even in his wilderness years Howard had remained a force among Liberal loyalists. Victorian moderate Michael Wooldridge, who became Hewson's deputy, said: 'One night in 1993 I bumped into Howard in Collins Street. I was on my way to a Women's Section Liberal dinner and at my invitation Howard joined me. I was the guest of honour but I was ignored. They couldn't get enough of Howard, who was IR spokesman at the time. And this was Melbourne. It was very revealing of the party's true sentiments.'[4]

The key to Howard's return lay in his character. Defeat can break politicians but Howard had not been destroyed by rejection. He had learnt from his mistakes and had become a more formidable politician. As Howard walked the lobbies on his return he looked and sounded the same (just a bit thinner on top), yet Howard had matured.

Howard's return exposed a psychological flaw in Keating—he resented having to fight Howard yet again. As treasurer, Keating had been instrumental in Howard's defeat at the 1987 poll. This should have given Keating a psychological edge. Yet from the time of Howard's recall Keating was consumed by frustration and upset by favourable media coverage of Howard's return. Don Watson described his mindset:

> The Prime Minister was angry … All year long it riled Keating that the press refused to recognize that Howard's past spoke for his real beliefs … It was easy to understand the PM's frustration and why he found the prospect of dealing with Howard exhausting. He had dealt with him before. He had buried him. And the media who had seen it happen and declared Howard politically dead were now pronouncing him resurrected and giving him the leniency they had never given Keating.[5]

Keating tried to pretend that nothing had changed, that Howard was the same, that the media should rewrite the cuts from the 1980s. But everything had changed—there had been a recession, broken election promises, disillusionment with Keating and a new Liberal unity. No wonder Keating wanted the media to pretend it was still yesterday.

After the 1993 defeat the Liberal Party was governed by two sentiments: it didn't want Hewson and it didn't want Howard. Howard felt it was 'probably' the worst defeat in the party's history. He was determined to contest the leadership despite his slim prospects.[6] Howard knew Hewson was ruined.

Hewson was re-elected—not in his own right but because the party refused to accept Howard. 'My instinct was to go to the backbench,' Hewson said. 'But I changed my mind. If I didn't run then Howard would become leader and I couldn't let that happen.'[7] Peacock, still obsessed with denying Howard, spearheaded Hewson's campaign to a 47–30 defeat of Howard. In the deputy's contest, Wooldridge defeated Costello 45–33 on the final round. Downer became the shadow treasurer.

Reith lost as deputy and went to the backbench, fall guy for the election defeat. Finished with Hewson, Reith told Costello: 'This will not last.' Costello and Hewson had no time for each other. During one of their disagreements Hewson had told Costello: 'You will never be a minister in a Hewson government', a joke Costello would retell for years. Hewson had three formidable enemies: Howard, Reith and Costello. His execution was only a matter of timing.

The significance of this ballot was that power was moving towards Costello and Downer. They were the future—young, modern, professional. But Costello and Downer were pro-Howard, a cardinal point. They had voted for Howard in the leadership ballot and they had good relations with Howard. So did Reith, who was aligned with Downer and friendly with Howard.

When Hewson called a snap party meeting in May 1994 to renew his leadership the Costello–Downer momentum was revealed. Once Hewson called the ballot, Costello was ruthless—he moved to finish Hewson. Aware that Howard would not win a ballot, Costello rang Downer and, in a famous phone conversation, he said: 'I am going to make you the offer of your life. Do you want to be leader?' It was the origin of the so-called dream team.[8]

Howard wanted to run but was vetoed by Peacock—again. When Victorian powerbroker Michael Kroger asked Peacock if he would back Howard, he replied: 'Never.'[9] A resolute Howard told Hewson he could not win an election and that he would vote for Downer. Downer defeated Hewson 43–36 and Costello was elected unopposed as deputy. After his defeat Hewson announced that the Liberals could never return to Howard, a premonition of his deepest fear.

This vote represented a historic realignment within the party. The Hewson–Peacock axis was broken; both men would rapidly fade. Downer and Costello, in effect, were the instruments to dismantle the anti-Howard nexus. Those people, later to become a veritable army, who said the Liberals blundered by electing Downer, missed the entire meaning of the event. It was the Downer leadership that enabled Howard to convert from a minority to a majority position within the party. Howard could not succeed Hewson—but he could succeed Downer. Downer's leadership failed for Downer; but it was the bridge that delivered a united Liberal Party to Howard.

From the day of Downer's election on 23 May 1994 the three key Liberals became Downer, Costello and Howard. The Liberal Party had been transformed. They would remain the three key figures for the next twelve years but in reverse order.

The Downer–Costello elevation had been spectacular but this dream was too cute to last. Downer was out of his depth. The scion of a political dynasty, Downer had a touch of self-parody and no sign of authority. He confessed to his wife, Nicky, that he doubted he was ready for the leadership. Costello had been adroit and had entrenched himself, aged thirty-seven, as deputy.[10]

Downer's self-destruction was fast enough to allow the party time to orchestrate a replacement well before the election. Liberal Party Director Andrew Robb knew it was a 'no brainer'—the party must recall Howard. This door began to open in September 1994 when Peacock announced that he would leave politics. Howard could barely conceal his delight. 'I'll never forget him ringing with excitement in his voice to tell me Peacock was going,' says Costello. 'He said to me, "You know what this means."'[11] The Peacock veto was lifted.

Robb says:

People knew what had to happen. We had to go back to experience. We knew Downer couldn't win. By September/October 1994 there was a virtual acceptance that Howard was the only candidate. In late 1994 I was getting ready for the changeover. In the end we had the benefit of nearly three months of getting ready for Howard.[12]

The Liberal Party's future now revolved about the judgements of Downer as leader, Costello as deputy and Howard as successor. Howard was remorseless and hungry; he needed Downer to sacrifice his leadership and Costello to postpone his ambition. Costello's intimate, Michael Kroger, told Howard to avert a ballot at all costs—a ballot would re-ignite his stereotype as a divisive figure. Howard said: 'I took the view that after I'd been rebuffed in 1993 that the only way I could credibly return would be through a draft.'[13]

Costello told Howard to back off and give Downer time to consider. Repelled by Howard's pressure tactics, Costello warned Howard off against any pre-Christmas push. His threat to keep Howard in line was to run against him—Costello knew Howard was desperate to avoid a ballot.[14]

This was the backdrop to the 5 December 1994 meeting in Costello's office that became famous. It was attended by Howard, Costello and frontbencher Ian McLachlan. Costello says: 'Howard asked me not to nominate for the Liberal Party leadership because he did not want a vote. He told me he intended to do one and a half terms as prime minister and would then hand over. I did not seek that undertaking. He volunteered it.'[15]

Howard accepts the accuracy of this account. Seen in context, the discussion makes complete sense. Howard was pushing hard and Costello's consent was the final step he required. 'It wasn't a deal and nothing was resolved there,' Howard said.[16]

McLachlan disagrees. 'I saw this absolutely as a deal,' he said. 'Given the election was more than a year away, it meant Howard would stand down as PM in about six years' time.'[17]

Costello said:

I saw it as an undertaking, that's the word that was used. I'm not going to get into semantics as to what constitutes a deal. McLachlan was there on Howard's behalf trying to convince me not to run … The proposition was put to me [by Howard]—'Don't run, this is my last chance, I only want to serve one term and stand down in the next term and give you a go, this will be good for the party, there won't be a ballot, I'm such and such an age, nobody would expect me to go beyond a second term.' And Ian is saying 'I think this is the right thing to do.' Ian is urging this on me.[18]

A few days later McLachlan pointed out to Costello that it had been a 'significant meeting' so Costello suggested he make a note of it. McLachlan did and carried it in his wallet for more than a decade. It referred to Howard's 'undertaking' on a one-and-a-half-term timetable.

The issue, however, was unresolved. Howard agonised over Costello's position. 'Why won't Peter move?' Howard repeatedly asked Kroger, who was working for Howard's return. Kroger told him to be patient. He advised Howard that Costello would not run and that he would help the transition. It was a matter of time. This was the perfect counsel. 'Kroger was a good friend and he was very helpful,' Howard said.[19]

Costello's position was complex: he wanted to be a loyal deputy; he wanted Downer to take the decision; and he was prepared to facilitate a transition to Howard. The pivotal issue has been misread. Costello did not have the numbers to defeat Howard as leader—but Costello's support was vital for a successful Howard leadership.

Years later Howard said: 'When Downer got into trouble a lot of people thought Peter was too right-wing … look, if you've got the support as leader, then you run.'[20] Costello didn't run. Subsequent claims he had the numbers but stood aside for Howard are nonsense.

But Costello did Howard a different favour: he gave him a united party. This was an immense gift, basic to Howard's future success. A Howard–Costello ballot in January 1995 (when Costello would have got a respectable vote) would have changed the atmospherics of the Liberal Party and the future Howard government. It would have meant that a fractured party based on Howard–Costello tensions would have taken office in 1996.

Despite his concerns, Howard always doubted that Costello would contest the leadership.[21] The point is that Howard's ambition suited Costello perfectly. Costello felt that he needed more experience—this is why he had backed Downer for leader a few months earlier. As his biographer, Shaun Carney, says: 'Howard had given Costello one of the things he craved most: time.'[22] But Costello's opinion about time would change in the future.

With the shadow cabinet meeting in Adelaide on 13 December, Downer, Costello and Howard met at the Adelaide Club. Costello says:

> The three of us agreed that Downer should be given one last chance to see if he could pick himself up in the polls but that, if his position had not improved by Australia Day, he should stand down. If he did that I would not run against Howard but would continue as Deputy Leader so that Howard could be anointed unopposed.[23]

During the same day Howard had spent time with Adelaide businessman and Liberal backer, Bob Day, and that evening he attended a party dinner at the Hilton hotel. At the pre-dinner drinks Day, who lived in Downer's seat, was anxious to assure Howard there was local support for him to take over the leadership from Downer.

Day said:

> At that point John Howard took me by the arm and led me away from the main drinks area and said to me, 'This is how it will go. I will take over the leadership and if we win the next election, then midway through our second term I will step aside and hand over to Peter Costello.' We had spent time together during the day and Howard was being almost fatherly with me, telling me it was all fixed up.[24]

Day said that Howard 'left me with the impression it was an agreement'. Within twenty-four hours he made a note of his discussion with Howard.

Despite these remarks, Howard doubted whether the commitments were that firm. He took nothing for granted—he worried that Costello might run and he worried that Downer might not resign. In early January, Howard flew to Melbourne and lunched with Costello. Howard wanted a firmer commitment from Costello before the deputy's upcoming overseas trip. 'He was still holding out for the possibility that he [Costello] would run,' Howard said. In London the Liberal Party federal president,

Tony Staley, asked Costello if he would run and the answer was non-committal.[25] The intensity of the lobbying weakens claims of any firm and agreed Howard–Costello deal. 'Any suggestion that we'd wrapped up some deal early in December 1994 is absolutely untrue,' Howard says.[26]

Just before Australia Day, Howard told Downer over dinner at Melbourne's Athenaeum Club that his leadership was untenable: if Downer refused to resign then Howard would have no choice but to challenge—but this wasn't the best option for either of them or the Liberal Party. It was a pressure tactic.

Within twenty-four hours the deal was done—Costello would stay as deputy and shadow treasurer, Downer would take foreign affairs. Howard said that Downer 'to his credit wasn't going to take the party down with him'.[27] Downer would resign on Australia Day. Despite the tensions between them, the trio had negotiated the optimal result. They would serve as prime minister, treasurer and foreign minister for the entire government and become the keys to its longevity.

Howard's appreciation of Downer was palpable. The Howard–Downer partnership, vital in the coming years, was sealed. Downer would become, eventually, the minister closest to Howard. 'Downer is a good friend of mine,' Howard said years later. 'I think he has done the honourable thing by the Liberal Party … he is one of those people the party owes a great amount to over the past twenty years.'[28] When Howard–Costello leadership tension emerged in office, Downer was a resolute Howard supporter: he argued with passion that Howard was a greater prime minister than Menzies.[29]

Costello believed he had done Howard a favour by standing aside. Howard recognised this but the emotional bond, so strong with Downer, was non-existent with Costello. A wedge was driven between them in these manoeuverings represented by the McLachlan-witnessed meeting. Costello said: 'Howard's constant message was for an orderly transition. His mantra was "I'll only be there a couple of terms and you're 38 and the party will do the same for you."'[30]

This was Howard's intention; it was not a deal. It was an expectation that was very seldom expressed. One of the rare occasions when it did surface was the August 1995 Australian American Leadership Dialogue held in Canberra, chaired by its founder, the Australian businessman Phil Scanlan. The US delegates had a meeting with Keating and also saw the Opposition team, Howard, Costello and Downer. It was a senior US group that included future cabinet member Bob Zoellick and many Americans who would form close ties with their Australian counterparts. Speaking to an American audience in Parliament House, keen to inform them about political realities and aware that expectations were for a change of government, Howard was frank.

At one point he explained that, if he won the coming election, 'my intention would be to seek re-election and then retire during the second term'. There was no visible reaction from Costello or Downer but the comments were noted in such a politically aware gathering. Howard would not have made this remark to an Australian audience. He assumed confidentiality. There was no embarrassing leak. But the event was deeply revelatory.[31]

'Look, we'd been in Opposition for nearly thirteen years,' Howard would explain. 'Of course in those days I thought two terms would be enough. Nobody was talking about four terms.'[32] For the kid from Earlwood, a couple of terms in the Lodge would make his life. Costello had every reason to think the timing would be perfect for his own transition. The episode reveals Howard's passion to become prime minister yet the modesty of his aspirations in office. He was still in his modest phase—it never occurred to him he might become Australia's second-longest serving prime minister.

However, Howard returned to leadership with an abiding conviction—to repudiate the blunders of his 1980s leadership. Having reflected for years on these tribulations he had a sharply revised approach. Howard didn't discuss his previous blunders; he acted on them. He recognised that his worst mistake from the 1980s was his failure to unite the Liberal Party. Unity had driven the way he returned to leadership; unity would now drive the way he conducted his leadership.

He operated on the principle of the Liberals as a 'broad church'. As prime minister, he repeated this phrase endlessly. It meant Howard had to become less of a factional player, a discipline he accepted. Former Finance minister Nick Minchin said: 'It was obvious he'd learnt so much from being leader before and being rejected. The first time round he wasn't collegiate, not a consensus guy, sometimes dictatorial. Now he was different. Something had changed.'[33]

Howard had a different leadership philosophy. This was the key to his progression from failure to success. It was captured by Wooldridge when he said: 'When Howard was leader in the 1980s he led the largest faction in the party. When he was leader in the 1990s he led the entire party.'[34]

This was what Howard set out to achieve—to ensure that conservatives and moderates alike were represented in the cabinet. In a 2005 interview he explained:

I had fallen before into the error of not including the moderates enough. I had been too concerned to make sure the ideological balance in the party was reflected in the shadow cabinet. One of the big differences was when I learnt that lesson. I have been very conscious the entire time I've been leader [since 1995] of ensuring there's a broad representation of both conservative and moderate sections of the party. If you look at my present cabinet and nominal allegiances there are just as many wets and moderates as so-called conservatives.[35]

When Howard returned, the focus of this strategy was Robert Hill. Howard explains: 'I set out at the very start to get close to Hill because he was the leading moderate. I believed this was the best way of burying for all time the factional thing.'[36] Wooldridge says: 'I think Howard gave Robert Hill as Environment Minister a lot of political protection in cabinet.'[37]

Robert Hill said:

When Howard returned he treated internal management as a priority. I had a good day-to-day relationship with him. In sitting weeks I saw him each morning at 8.30 and he was always available if I needed him. I found that he usually accepted my arguments.[38]

Howard's aim was to repair the old 1980s wet–dry division, a schism that he understood as a prominent dry. Howard listed some of the ministers he recruited from the moderate wing—Hill, Philip Ruddock, Brendan Nelson, Amanda Vanstone, Michael Wooldridge, Kay Patterson and later Joe Hockey and Malcolm Turnbull. Making peace with a departing Andrew Peacock and posting him to Washington was a stunning symbol the old divisions were dying.

Over time a new group of moderates took on the post-2001 issues of asylum seekers and anti-terror laws. But this does not gainsay the bigger point: from 1995 Howard procured a new internal settlement that delivered unity. There was some angst that moderates had become Howard's supporters—most prominent among them Ruddock on refugees. This was the purpose of Howard's strategy: to move the Liberals beyond the divisions of the 1980s.

The best explanation of the party's evolution came from Wooldridge:

What happened was that the Liberal Party had changed. It was no longer the party of the 1980s obsessed with the issues of that time. Howard became leader in 1995 with the support of the moderate or wet faction. If Howard as leader took the party to the Right—and I believe he did—the equally important point is that the party itself was moving to the Right. In my view 98 per cent of what Howard did was as leader of the entire party and 2 per cent was factional.[39]

Howard put a philosophic framework on his unity strategy. He said the Liberal Party embodied two great traditions: conservatism and liberalism. 'We are the custodians of both traditions in the Australian polity,' he said. This view saw the Liberals as being a broader party than Britain's Conservatives or Germany's Christian Democrats.[40] Howard was championing, on the one hand, the ideal of liberty in the market economics of Adam Smith and, on the other hand, the pragmatic conservatism of Edmund Burke. It was a pointer to the stars he would follow: economic liberalism and social conservatism.

The resurrected Howard was a political networker who guarded his heart. While accessible, few people knew him. The Howards often went out to political functions but John and Janette held very few dinner parties. Howard had built networks in the political, business, finance, media and sporting worlds, yet almost nobody had penetrated his inner sanctum. He had a good memory for people, their spouses, their children and their careers and he thrived in conversation over dinner, at receptions and at the cricket—friendly conversation, rarely about policy. Howard kept his guard up.

The confidence factor was at the heart of Howard's new leadership. 'The second time around he handled people, MPs, ministers, much better,' said Arthur Sinodinos. 'He displayed a much better capacity to understand people.'[41]

Now he felt his moment had come. It was as though all his bad luck from the 1980s had expired and his good luck had arrived. His new political style was tough, down-to-earth pragmatism with a streak of ruthlessness. His bent was for practical solutions, not big ideas or grand designs. But Howard's Liberal Party unity strategy rested on two assumptions: that he could match Keating and that he had the confidence of the Australian people.

Keating came at Howard hard and early. He savaged Howard as the Liberal Party's third preference, a 'part-time thinker who has no original political ideas', and who left behind 'an inward-looking industrial graveyard, a low-growth, low-investment, low-profit, high-inflation, high interest rate, high-unemployment, high-tariff country'.[42]

Howard showed that Keating would neither intimidate nor rattle him. He said:

> The more you talk about the past, the more you proclaim your embarrassment about the present and the fact that you have nothing to say about the future … You can talk about John Howard and Malcolm Fraser, you can talk about Sir Henry Parkes and the prophet Moses, but nothing will relieve you of the responsibility you carry for what you are doing to Australian families …[43]

Howard claimed that Australians had 'a bare five minutes of economic sunshine'—a brilliant line, untrue, but effective.

Howard brought a ruthlessness to Liberal policy. The pivotal judgement he made was that because the Australian people knew him there was no need for any early policy release. Peter Reith told him: 'John, you're a walking policy. People have got a fix on you now. They don't need more.'[44] Howard now applied only one test: what delivers election success. Smart policy and old faiths didn't count—Keating's defeat was the only measure.

So Howard pledged no GST, no new taxes, no tax increases. The GST pledge was a tactic, not a change of faith. Howard still felt a GST was right for Australia but he put it in cold storage. At first Howard had tried to leave a crack of light for the GST option. As a result he was asked by the media in May 1995 to rule it out. He did. In response to the follow-up question 'Never ever?' Howard said: 'Never ever. It's dead.' It was the only responsible answer. To have left open this option would have guaranteed the GST as an election issue, at great damage to his party, when he had no intention of introducing a GST in the next term. Asking leaders to rule policies 'in' or 'out' for the rest of their political lives is a media gimmick that sensible politicians should not entertain. Howard slammed the door knowing that each future election generated its own mandate.

But his attitude on Medicare was different. Unlike the GST, Howard had changed his mind. He calls Medicare the 'one thing where I worked out we had to change', not as a tactic but as a belief.[45] The twenty-year campaign to dismantle Medicare was abandoned. Howard's Medicare conversion was a consequence of the defeat of *Fightback!* It previewed one of Howard's electoral successes as PM—turning Medicare into a bipartisan position.

His third retreat came on industrial relations in early 1996. Howard offered 'a rock solid guarantee' that 'our policy will not cause a cut in the take-home pay of Australian workers'. He would not allow the IR debate to become 'a scare campaign'.[46] Drafted by Reith, it was a retreat from Howard's own 1993 *Jobsback* election policy. Reith had designed a broad 'no disadvantage' test to protect workers moving from awards to workplace agreements. Social analyst Hugh Mackay said it showed Howard was 'deadly serious' about becoming prime minister. In effect, he was saying 'the gap between us and the government now is narrow, you can jump it without hesitation'.[47] Keating said Howard 'will ditch anything he believes in'. But Labor's campaign on overtime and penalty rates was ruined. Howard would stick by his 'no losers' IR stance until his fourth term.[48]

On Telstra, Howard went for another tactical retreat. He pledged to sell only one-third of Telstra—the upshot being it would be stranded as a part-private and part state-owned hybrid for years. There was a political fix—the sale proceeds would fund a $1 billion Heritage Trust creating a nexus between Telstra privatisation and environmental protection.

The principles on which a re-elected Howard operated were Liberal Party stability, unity and tactical denial of Labor's main attack. Howard saw that, once the default option went, Labor would be caught on its record. At that point he would destroy Keating's government.

18

HOWARD'S BATTLERS: THE CRISIS
OF MODERN LABOR

Sitting in the Georgian-style red-brick Liberal Party headquarters in Canberra, Andrew Robb saw an electoral earthquake shaking the Labor Party. It was only six months since Keating's 1993 victory, a defeat that still hurt Robb as federal director. Now Robb identified a new political force of epic consequence: the collapse of the Whitlam model that had sustained modern Labor. This was Labor's alliance of working-class and middle-class voters fashioned by Whitlam in his 1970s reinvention of the party that had underwritten a generation of Labor success.

The 1996 election marked an electoral and philosophic watershed. It terminated the 25-year-old Labor election-winning social model originated by Whitlam that had seen Labor win seven of the ten elections between 1972 and 1993. Under Whitlam's progressive model, Labor had broadened its social base, renovated its ideology and assumed new causes embracing the environment, Aboriginal reconciliation, working women and multiculturalism. But Keating had pushed the model to breaking point and it had shattered.

This was a double defeat—a rejection of Keating's performance as prime minister and a rejection of the 'big picture' modern Labor vision by which he wanted to be judged.

Robb says:

> The results I saw when we surveyed after the 1993 Budget were profound. The problem seemed to be everything about Keating—the policies, the tone, the body language. He was so self-congratulatory. There was just a lot of hubris and people saw it. Suddenly the situation clicked for working people—they felt that they were being betrayed. This wasn't their government at all.[1]

The public was hostile to Keating's arrogance, his tax betrayal and his priorities. Yet the dilemma transcended any of these specifics. Its essence, in Robb's words, was that 'not long after the 1993 Budget I became very clear in my own mind that the Labor Party no longer represented its base'.[2] A variation of this phenomenon occurred in America during the 1980s when Republican President Ronald Reagan had stolen a constituency from the Democrats, known as Reagan's Democrats.

The 1996 result meant a re-alignment was underway. At this point the Liberal Party got lucky—it had, in Howard, the perfect leader for this event. Howard took the alienated Labor voters and the disillusioned undecided and made them his own. He gave them a home—and that was how the 'Howard battlers' were born. It would have been inconceivable to think there could have been Hewson battlers or Peacock battlers.

The concept was real yet mythical. This became its political magic—there was no doubt that Howard penetrated the Labor base but the idea of the Howard battlers would generate its own momentum. It would become a self-fulfilling prophecy; the battlers would look to Howard and Howard would govern for his battlers.

Howard drew a mighty lesson from the 1996 election: that Labor's values were in conflict with mainstream values. This conviction would guide him for four terms and permeate his economic, social and foreign policy.

Labor's National Secretary and 1996 campaign director, Gary Grey, said:

> Howard didn't steal the Labor base vote. Paul Keating drove people away because of his style, outlook and language. Keating was sending people to the Liberals. The things that defined Keating as a stylish, admired and unique leader became the hallmarks of his self-indulgence, arrogance and disengagement from the Australian community.[3]

Who was a Howard battler? His adviser, Grahame Morris, said:

> Most of them had mortgages and families. They were family people. Many had been hurt in the Keating hard economic times. Most were sick and tired of being told what they should think and say. They were hard workers who felt politicians weren't listening to them. They were looking for somebody down to earth, a safe uncle, somebody who understood their needs, maybe because he was a battler himself, somebody who was committed to family, somebody who wasn't into French clocks.[4]

The notion was anchored in values. The Howard battlers were created over 1993–96. They would not have existed had Keating lost the 1993 election on the perfect excuse of the recession. They are a reminder, as Grey said, that 'the 1996 defeat didn't need to be so bad'.[5] The voter re-alignment was complex—it was founded in class, culture and geography. Because Labor lost the election it suffered across-the-board setbacks. But some mattered more than others because they became incorporated into Howard's political persona and his governing model.

Howard and Robb saw the 1996 election as a special event because Labor lost working-class and lower middle-class voters; it lost the votes of cultural conservatives and Catholics who distrusted Keating's values; and it lost voters in the bush, the regions and 'development' states typified by Queensland because Labor was seen as dominated by south-east city interests.

This leads to the true meaning of the 1996 election. It was a change-of-government election but it was something greater—it changed the Liberal Party and it created Howard's governing model. The result provided Howard with an interpretation of Australia that guided his eleven years in office.

This was a comprehensive Labor failure and did not occur overnight. The long-run trend was concealed by Keating's 1993 victory that became a mirage of false hopes. Labor's campaign report after the defeat said: 'In the five years from mid-1991 the ALP trailed the Coalition's primary vote for all but a few weeks.' In fact, Labor's primary vote headed the Coalition in less than 30 out of 250 weeks.[6] Grey said: 'The Labor Party had been out of touch with its core constituency for most of the 1990s. Our primary vote was very low, apart from periods in 1993 and 1994. The problem was deep-seated and structural.'[7]

There was a breakdown in the Keating years between executive government and political strategy. This was epitomised by the rupture in relations between Keating's office and the National Secretariat.

Mark Ryan said: 'In political management terms we did almost everything wrong after the 1993 election. The issues were the right ones—Mabo, Asia, republic, *Working Nation*—political management of them was the problem.'[8]

Howard's majority was forty-plus seats in the new House, with a 5 per cent two-party-preferred swing to the Coalition. He won a larger majority than either Hawke or Keating did at any of their five election victories. There had been two previous Coalition victories over ALP governments since World War II: Menzies in 1949 and Fraser in 1975. Howard's win fell between them—greater than Menzies' but less than Fraser's.[9] Yet there was less enthusiasm for Howard than for leaders in other post World War II change-of-government elections. The nation was impatient to dispose of Keating yet it remained uninspired by Howard.

It did, however, believe in Howard's reliability. This quality fitted into the national psychology. At the 1996 election Australia was still living in the recession's shadow. The public seemed tired of economic reform and the big ideas so beloved by Keating. Neither Keating nor Howard ran a bold economic reform agenda. The brave days of 1980s reformism, embodied by these two leaders, seemed consigned to history.

The historical evidence suggested that Howard's margin had purchased a certain two terms. This was also Labor's view. But the key to unlocking this election result was to separate the strategic and tactical factors.

The tactical explanation of Howard's win was compelling. The 1996 election was 'the general election of March 1993 delayed by three years'. The public had waited three years to punish Keating for the recession. When the Liberals abandoned their GST the public did not miss. The blow against Labor was hard as expected.[10] Without its GST scare, Labor was exposed.

Keating's 'miracle' victory in 1993 engendered a false notion of invincibility in Labor, a feeling the public would baulk at the brink about voting Liberal. It created a 'keep our nerve' mentality within Keating's government that saw mistakes perpetuated rather than corrected. The government failed to respond to the Canberra byelection debacle of early 1995 that recorded an anti-Labor swing of more than 16 per cent, one of the highest ever against a government. Finally, Keating failed to devise a response to Howard's 1995 arrival as leader.

The ALP campaign report said: 'The whole party underestimated our opponent. The new John Howard was a ruthless pragmatist, an experienced manipulator and effective campaigner. As one party member put it: 'it was as if we were still fighting Alexander Downer when Howard had taken over'.[11]

The anti-Keating factor was deep—he was unpopular with a wide section of the community. The most lethal comment came from Keating minister and ALP veteran, Robert Ray: 'People everywhere woke up to the fact that Keating didn't like them and they didn't like it.' Ray said the PM's staff was 'an impenetrable barrier' that made it impossible to reach Keating.[12]

In his defence of Keating, Ryan revealed the extent of dysfunction: 'It's true he [Keating] could have been more disciplined and conventional and actually taken notice of Gary Grey's research. But the research wasn't telling him anything he didn't already know. We needed constructive advice, not hand-wringing. We'd all have been happy with a hollow victory but the polling was telling us to cadge our way towards a hollow defeat. Where was the merit in that?'[13]

The biggest element in Keating's defeat was the 'time for a change' factor compounded by unpopularity. Once the Liberals looked plausible, the entire Labor position collapsed. One lesson from Keating's defeat is that the campaign could not redeem mistakes made over the life of the government.

This leads to the strategic dimension—it is a striking point that by 1996 Keating had abandoned the political strategy that delivered every Hawke–Keating election win since 1983. This was recognised by the two competing advisers in his office, Russell and Watson, suggesting it is right. The Coalition's 1996 slogan was 'For all of us'—but it would never have worked against the Hawke government.

The foundation of Hawke government politics was occupying the middle ground via consensus and forcing the Coalition to the Right. This had been Keating's gospel as treasurer. It was the technique he used in each campaign, but it was abandoned after the 1993 victory.

Russell said: 'The perception developed that Keating had moved too far to the Left. This was necessary to win the 1993 election but it was not corrected after the election. This gave Howard the chance to occupy the middle ground.'[14]

The magnitude of the confusion was captured by ANOP's Rod Cameron: 'The Labor agenda in the last 12 months (before the election) was about Mabo, Carmen Lawrence, an obscure bridge in South Australia, Asian migration and also a republic. It wasn't about anything of interest to the middle ground. The politics was totally lost. They were off on a totally undisciplined tangential set of issues and Keating was not able to, or chose not to, embrace it (the middle ground).'[15]

In 1995 Watson, realising that Labor's reform story was being lost, rang Russell who was Ambassador in Washington, asking him to come home. Alarmed about Keating's condition, Watson thought that Russell 'might inspire discipline'.[16] But Russell, on his return, discovered the situation was worse than he had imagined.

He found 'Keating hemmed in and isolated. He was absorbed in the issues close to his own heart—the republic, Mabo, the arts and foreign affairs. The government got little credit for growth in the economy or for its array of social welfare programs.' Most of all Russell was 'alarmed to find' that the politician who had 'once been the public face of Labor's economic successes ... was now identified almost exclusively with the concerns of special interest groups'.[17]

In Russell's view, Keating had dressed as a Labor traditionalist to beat Hewson in 1993 and forgot to reposition after the victory. 'One problem with the 1993 victory was that it reignited the old Whitlam coalition,' Russell said, referring to the pro-Labor interest groups. 'This was always a trap for the Labor Party.'[18] Russell was adamant—Keating 'should have come back to the Right but he didn't'.[19] In terms of the 'econocrats and bleeding hearts' model it was too much 'bleeding hearts'. This was no way to beat John Howard.

Influenced by Bill Clinton's post-1994 new position that ditched leftist orthodoxy in favour of surplus budgets, welfare reform and personal responsibility, Russell and Watson urged a similar path on Keating. The irony, of course, is that this was Keating's 1980s mantra. They talked to Keating about a Clintonesque move to the Right.

Post-election, Russell described to journalist, Pamela Williams, the ideas he had proposed:

> We talked about re-launching Keating's image to come back to the mainstream concerns of middle Australia and to highlight a few issues that had been lost. They all had to do with responsibility: it was about changing Keating's image to re-emphasise what he had stood for, mainly over his years as treasurer ... Personal responsibility was not about what Australia gave to every little group, but about what everybody gave to Australia.[20]

Operating separately from Cape York, Noel Pearson had reached the same conclusion. He said:

> I had an impending sense of doom about Keating's association with us and Mabo. I knew we were a liability for him, an albatross around his neck. For this reason I tried to get him to run the responsibility agenda, to change the message, to balance rights with responsibility. It made policy and political sense.

> But it was too late and there was too little time.[21]

Cracking down on dole cheats and pushing welfare-to-work transitions were proper Labor positions. Russell reminded Keating that in May 1987 he had abolished the dole for young people and replaced it with a means-tested job search allowance, an audacious policy.[22]

This debate highlighted the Keating strategic tragedy. On the eve of his defeat Russell was ruminating with Keating about how to recapture the policy direction and political profile that had made him so successful. Keating had fallen victim to his True Believers rhetoric.

At his 1993 re-election Keating had declared it 'a victory for the true believers', but the True Believers had not re-elected the Keating government. They no more saved Keating than they had elected Hawke four times. This statement mocked the exhaustive effort of both parties to persuade sceptical Australians in a compulsory voting democracy to support them. From the instant of its delivery this message was transmitted like a provocative electrical impulse, implying Labor was a party of insiders who looked after each other. The Howard battlers felt they didn't belong in Labor's exclusive club.

In the end, the Russell–Watson repositioning was a bridge too far. Keating feared 'it would look phoney if he launched a new conservative image months before the election' taking up positions for which he had attacked Howard. So the authentic Keating was not recreated.

'If Keating had been harder and tougher then Howard would have had nowhere else to go,' Russell lamented.[23] Watson said in his memoirs that while not foolproof, this was 'the only political idea' left for Labor.[24] Keating, as Treasury knew, had gone too soft. This decision would not have saved the election, but it would have left Labor a better legacy.

Howard and Robb were the beneficiaries of this post-1993 failure. Keating did not just lose an election—he gifted Howard a new position.

The first sighting of Howard battlers came in the 1993 post-Budget research commissioned by Robb from Mark Textor, a young statistician who had recently worked as pollster for the Northern Territory's Country Liberal Party. During the Howard years Textor would become integral to the Liberal Party's strategy. 'Textor is different because he can articulate the strategic significance of his results,' Robb said.[25]

Describing the research, Robb said: 'In the results there was a deep sense of Keating's alienation from Labor voters who felt their concerns and interests were being ignored. This was about minorities. People felt that minorities were being listened to and were the winners. Ordinary people were paying their taxes. But people at the bottom gained through welfare and people at the top gained though lurks and perks.'[26]

Robb represented a phenomenon of the Howard years—Labor families who converted to Liberal via the Democratic Labor Party. Coming from a rural working-class Catholic family of nine children, Robb's parents were ALP voters who had defected to the DLP in the

1950s. When the Split ended in the 1970s they prepared to return to Labor, but faltered before Whitlam's social libertarianism. The Robbs hated it; they were lost to Labor forever.

Robb knew that old Labor had been a conservative party—it believed in White Australia, fair wages, a proud nationalism, working-class responsibility, the importance of marriage and core family values. He felt this began to change with Whitlam. 'In my view Whitlam sowed the seeds for long-term Labor troubles,' Robb said.[27] He believed, sooner or later, the contradiction over values would emerge between Labor's working-class base and its Whitlam-inspired middle-class interests.

Whitlam constructed the modern Labor Party by grafting a series of expanding social constituencies onto Labor's working-class base. They involved public-sector professionals (teachers, public servants, nurses), academics and students, migrants, Aboriginals, the arts, media and entertainment industries, the welfare and NGO sector, feminists, gays and greens. As Labor won these political allegiances to a greater or less degree, its values shifted to hold such constituencies. Many Labor strategists believed the party's ties to these groups was basic to its success as a modern political force—and there was evidence to sustain this view.

The Whitlam technique was a brilliant success for a generation. It worked best under Hawke when the primary emphasis was placed on economic and social progress for middle Australia. But Textor's research over 1993–95 told Robb that Keating had pushed Whitlam's model into unsustainable terrain—he was giving the special interests too much.

Keating's dilemma can be precisely stated—he wanted his prime ministership to be defined by a transformed national identity but this quest lacked grass-roots electoral backing. He was unable to resolve this conundrum. He neither abandoned his crusade nor carried the people behind it. The ALP post-election report said the government's style appeared to be 'all or nothing'. The community had a false choice mindset: republic or drought relief, Mabo or lower unemployment.

The reason issues such as native title, Mabo, Asian engagement, the republic and multiculturalism figured so prominently is because Keating wanted his leadership to be branded by these ideas—along with a successful economy and society. The failure of political strategy was to determine how Keating's priority agenda could be successfully presented to the people or, more accurately, integrated into a broader agenda of modernisation.

As Keating's term advanced, Robb was baffled. 'I could never under-stand why Labor didn't self-correct,' Robb said. 'They did nothing about this problem that was obvious in the research.'[28]

John Edwards reported Keating telling a staff meeting on 5 April 1993 he would be 'lofty' in the coming term. That meant keeping his focus on foreign policy, the republic, Aboriginal issues and parliamentary reform. Keating said he would become more 'Menzian', a phrase Howard would never use.[29] It was delusional. It was neither possible for Keating to be Menzian in this sense nor for any PM to operate successfully along these lines. The notion completely misconstrued the demands of leadership in contemporary politics. It revealed Keating's distaste for political combat dictated by the 24-hour media cycle.

For Robb, the proof of Keating's electoral failure was his 1995 statement on the republican model he would take to the election. This was Keating striking out from the front. Watching Keating's speech from his office Robb, as a republican, was moved and impressed.

'You couldn't help but be affected by it,' Robb said. 'It was very powerful. It blew a lot of people away. The media coverage was favourable. There was a sense around the traps that it could be a turning point for him. We were careful never to write off Keating. Now he was leading from the front and leaving the impression he was back in the race.'[30]

On the following Sunday night Robb got the Liberal research when Textor rang him at home. 'The results are unbelievable,' Textor began. They showed the biggest single lift in measures of being arrogant and out-of-touch. The republic was a major potential negative for Labor not for what it represented but for what it told about Keating. Labor's hope that people would move towards Keating as a strong leader was doomed. It would bring only the converted; it would anger many others. The republic was not critical to peoples' lives. Robb concluded that 'the republic was just playing to Keating's Achilles heel'.[31]

Grey made a similar point with a different example. He had tried to warn Keating about Mabo but had been dismissed. Grey said: 'Mabo came through in the research as an obsession of Keating's. It was something that meant nothing to the daily lives of most people. They decided that Keating wasn't with them.'[32]

Keating should have made more of his economic strengths. The economy was growing strongly going into the campaign. A more aggressive economic reform agenda would have put the Coalition and Howard under pressure—as it had during the 1980s. The irony in 1996, as Russell saw, is that Keating had surrendered what he did best. Years later Keating said: 'The two things that crippled us in the 1996 election were that first Dawkins Budget [after the 1983 election] and Bernie Fraser's interest rate increases over 1994.'[33] These remarks imply that what really mattered was the economy.

The economic reality—as Howard's first term would show—was the need for a 1996 economic reform agenda based on fiscal consolidation, welfare reform, improved education and health delivery. The shadow of *Fightback!* intimidated Keating and Howard from offering such reforms. Given that Keating faced defeat, it was in his interests to revert to a bold agenda to confound Howard. In the end, as Cameron said, Keating went meekly to defeat. 'I couldn't believe,' Cameron said, 'how soft and un-Keating like he was'.[34]

For Howard, the anti-model was Hewson. Howard showed his psychological toughness when he refused to release his policies during 1995. He would not be dictated to by Keating or the media. There would be zero tolerance on any opportunity for Labor's scare campaign. For Robb, this decision was 'critical'—it kept the focus on the government and it showed Howard's ruthlessness. So desperate was Howard to avoid releasing the policies that they did not exist. It was only in early January 1996 that senior Coalition figures met in Sydney over several days to finalise policy documents.

The campaign was Howard's moment of truth. The fight against Keating had a gladiatorial element. Despite his weakness, Keating was still feared. Morris said: 'Until the very end of the campaign John Howard and I still expected Keating to pull things together or spring some surprise.'[35] But it never materialised. Howard and Robb stuck by their winning psychological insight—they believed Keating could not beat them; they could only beat themselves. Their entire campaign was based on this 'safety-first' assumption. Howard offered Keating nothing—no GST, no wage cuts, no Medicare abolition. Keating was reduced to fighting an opponent who wasn't there.

Keating said he knew Howard so well he could shut his eyes and hear his beliefs 'playing like a broken record in my head—and it is the voice of the most conservative politician in the last quarter of a century'.[36] Keating's frustration was that the Howard in his head and the Howard on the trail were different politicians.

The contrasting psychology of these leaders was a paramount factor. Keating was at the end of his career—his monuments were behind him; his place in history was assured; if he won the election he would retire anyway. Howard, on the other hand, had to win to make his career—the election would stamp him either a hero or an abject failure. Howard had far more at stake than Keating and it showed. Kelty said: 'Paul was trying hard. I think he felt it was the end. There were issues with his family and with Annita that worried him.'[37]

A fortnight after the vote Robb told the National Press Club that for the first time in history more working-class and Catholic voters had backed the Coalition parties than Labor. Howard's new base lay in battlers and families.[38]

Robb reported Liberal exit polls showed that the Coalition won the blue-collar vote by 47.5 per cent to 39 per cent, a nine-point lead for Howard over Keating. They showed that among Catholics, once a solid ALP constituency, the Coalition beat Labor 47 per cent to 37 per cent. Robb's polling also showed a gender gap opening among middle-aged men with the Coalition holding a 13-point lead over Labor among 35 to 49-year-old men.

'This shift is not an overnight development,' Robb said. 'It owes much to Labor's attempts over 15 years or more to chase the votes of the socially progressive, often highly educated, affluent end of middle-class Australia. Along the way Paul Keating and his colleagues came to reflect far more closely the values and priorities of this narrow, affluent, middle-class group. Labor ended up governing for a few and not for all of us. There are now deep contradictions within the Labor Party in regard to what they stand for and who they represent.'[39]

The Labor Party disputed Robb's exit poll figures and was resistant to this message. But Grey said: 'Labor saw an erosion in its base first because of economic factors and then because of Keating's cultural agenda. These factors were reinforcing because the same people tended to be affected.'[40]

The trend was most obvious in Western Sydney. Howard penetrated into ALP seats he never expected to win with an unknown Jackie Kelly winning Lindsay with an 11.8 per cent swing to become a symbol of the power of Howard's battlers. The big swings for Labor came in New South Wales and Queensland.

Labor's campaign review reported a 'spectacular drop' in support among people whose household income was less than $20 000. It found working-class families were 'increasingly alienated by the approach of our government' and identified talkback radio as a force feeding blue-collar alienation.[41] In a report to Grey, Labor pollster John Utting said: 'In terms of addressing the blue-collar alienation, that is not something you can do in a campaign. Keating had left it too late.'[42] Morris said of Howard's campaigning: 'We'd go to a workplace canteen. People weren't throwing punches at us. They seemed happy to see us.'[43]

Robb said: 'We have a situation where all 10 of the poorest electorates and 35 out of the 40 poorest electorates are held by the Coalition. Considering the fact that the ALP is forever mouthing notions of equity and social justice, these statistics raise questions about whether Labor's rhetoric fits with its actions and real priorities.'[44] The truth is that the Coalition's traditional strength in the regions, typically poorer than the cities, meant this was an old trend, not a new one. But it played to the battler narrative.

Subsequent analysis suggested the white/blue-collar distinction was less important than self-employment and public employment as pointers to voting decisions.[45]

The third dimension of the re-alignment was regional. In Queensland, Western Australia, South Australia and the Northern Territory Labor won seven out of 51 seats or 13 per cent. In south-eastern Australia comprising New South Wales, Victoria, Tasmania and the ACT, Labor won 42 of 97 seats or 44 per cent. The Keating government did not govern for the entire country. The Liberal slogan 'For All of Us' was perfect. Robb said that 16 of Labor's 32 wins were in regional Australia. Bill Kelty said: 'We lost because too many regions didn't share in the recovery.'[46]

Howard won 60.2 per cent of the two-party preferred vote in Queensland where Labor recorded its worst vote since Federation and was left with two seats. It was appropriate, therefore, that Labor's recovery when it arrived in 2007 saw a Queenslander lead the party back to office. In the interim the Coalition 'owned' Queensland.

Grey said: 'After the 1996 election we faced a very serious threat to our party's future.'[47] Howard took the Coalition to power by offering safety and sound management. But Howard invested the result with a deeper meaning—as a shift in values from Keating to himself. This was the literal and mythic meaning of the Howard battlers. The election gave Howard a governing formula.

PART IV
THE HOWARD SYSTEM

19

A NEW POLITICAL MANAGER

Howard understood the Liberal Party better than any leader since Menzies.
—David Kemp, February 2008

The Howard Liberals were exiles returning to office after a thirteen-year absence, their longest since Federation. It was a new world. During their exile Australia had changed—it had a new Parliament House, expansive ministerial offices, a 24-hour media cycle, a floating currency, a disappearing tariff and departmental heads on contract not tenure. John Howard's team was untested and suspicious of Labor's governing system. His victory demanded a new model of Liberal Party governance.

Given such uncertainty, Howard returned with a firm idea. 'He wanted to assert his authority at the start,' Arthur Sinodinos said. 'This was Howard's government,' David Kemp said. 'He put his own stamp on it. Howard was determined to be a strong prime minister.'[1] This fixation shocked many people. It was not a Howard–Costello government; it was not a Howard–Fischer government; and it was never a return to Menzian nostalgia. This government belonged to Howard from the first day to the last.

Howard built a structure that gave him more power than Menzies or Fraser. He wanted a transfer of power from the public service to ministers. In his 1997 Garran Oration, while upholding the principle of an impartial public service, Howard said ministers would assume greater control of policy in its 'planning, detail and implementation'. This was one of the most significant statements about government by a prime minister since World War II.

He arrived as an outsider, naked but for his credentials—Howard had no mentors, no guiding philosophers, no blueprint for action. He felt such plans were a bad omen. 'We used to have blueprints for office but we forgot to win the elections,' he complained of the 1980s and 1990s.[2] There was no 'best and brightest' team for Howard; he shunned any such notion. The media rightly branded him as 'boring' but Mr Boring knew what he wanted—he created a structure of political management without precedent.

In this task Howard was not a conservative—the 'people' became the justification of his prime ministership. He assumed this on a daily basis, unlike Keating. As a consequence Howard changed the method of governing. He became prime minister, chairman of cabinet, de facto head of state, a talkback radio personality, economic manager, war leader, cultural commentator and sporting ambassador. He climbed over everything, every waking hour. It is hardly a surprise that Australians, finally, got sick of Howard.

In constructing his model Howard was plagued by crisis, confusion and mishaps. He learnt on the job and his learning curve was steep. Howard's transition to power was far more traumatic than either Hawke's in 1983 or Rudd's in 2007–08.

Like an opening batsman under pressure, Howard experienced a first term that was a mixture of ambition and blunder. His government nearly bled to death, losing five ministers and three parliamentary secretaries. Its administration was defective and its performance error-prone. Howard suffered multiple problems at work and a near tragedy at home—his wife Janette had a serious cancer scare. He struggled to establish his authority in the nation. The issues of race and class warfare engulfed him. Often he was stubborn rather than strong; too many of his ministers were inept.

Indeed, Howard's first term was dominated by an existential struggle: to fathom the essential purpose of his prime ministership. His opponent, ALP leader, Kim Beazley, likened Howard after his first year to the ineffectual Harold Holt.[3] At mid-term, Labor optimists hoped that Howard would be a 'oncer'—both Grahame Morris and Andrew Robb admitted this was a real fear.[4] Keating delivered the insight that Howard had won 'a large majority on a small mandate'. Howard's win was based on expediency not conviction. The real Howard was still in disguise.

This was his difficulty—reconciling his cautious mandate with his political convictions. It culminated in the 1997 crisis when Howard, aware that he looked irresolute, resurrected the GST-led tax reform as the platform for his 1998 re-election. It became his most important decision and it unlocked the tide of success. This crisis is the dramatic metaphor for Howard's first term—its unifying theme was John Howard learning how to be prime minister. 'He grew into the job,' Robb said. 'We were all relieved.' Michael Wooldridge saw that 'over time a court developed around him'. David Kemp, who ran Fraser's office, said 'Howard understood the Liberal Party better than any leader since Menzies.'[5]

Howard came to office with two contradictory instincts: to be a force for stability after Keating but to impose fundamental cultural and economic change on the nation. These are his two strategic cores and he cannot be comprehended without reference to both. 'We have not been elected to be a pale imitation of the government we have replaced,' he said. This tension between his quest for order and his belief in change was embedded in Howard's character. It explains the confusing views of his government.

The key to Howard, therefore, is identify where he was a manager of change. Because Howard was satisfied with Australia's character and identity, his change agenda was often downplayed. Yet it was ambitious. At retirement, Howard's record is more conspicuous for the changes he made than for the changes he refused to make.

His leadership philosophy was to be ordinary. 'There's one thing the Australian population will never stomach and that is arrogance, hubris and being taken for granted by their political leaders,' he told the Liberal Party room on 6 March 1996. 'Australians don't like triumphalism' he said on another occasion. 'The sportsmen they like most are those like Pat Rafter, or to give a rugby example, John Eales, who are very understated.'[6] Howard believed there was no natural party of government; his career was a repudiation of the old born-to-rule mentality.

'Howard turned the Liberals, more than before, into the party of initiative in Australian politics,' Liberal adviser Michael L'Estrange said to his colleagues. Howard saw his government as the most robust example of Liberals being the source of initiative and Labor being the source of resistance—witness his support for fiscal reform, labour market deregulation, privatisation, mutual obligation, tax reform, stronger border protection, funding private choice in health and education, strong anti-terror laws and a closer alignment with the US. As Labor rejected much of his agenda, Howard was able to define Labor by its opposition.

His profile as a conservative is exaggerated, owing too much to his status as constitutional monarchist. As he grew more confident Howard quoted Edmund Burke, saying that 'a state without the means of some change is without the means of its conservation'.[7] It was a reinterpretation of himself.

Despite his 1996 victory there was almost no expectation that Howard would become a significant prime minister. Howard, like Hawke, had the tastes of the common man, without Hawke's personal persuasion, flair, sex appeal, sporting prowess, emotional range or larrikin streak. Hawke met Walter Bagehot's description of a statesman—'a man of common opinions and uncommon abilities'—while Howard appeared to be a man of common opinions and common abilities.

How did he rise above this?

The first part of the answer is that Howard built an effective model of prime ministerial political management. The source of Howard's strength was not administration but politics. Howard understood that the Canberra model, with Parliament House as its epicentre and location of executive, parliamentary and media authority, was unique among democracies and gifted a clever incumbent with multiple instruments of power.

His guiding stars were public sentiment and Australia character. Howard was interested in results, not abstract principles about ministerial responsibility or freedom of information beloved by media. He was utilitarian, shunning utopian visions and grand schemes. He had a practical and populist view of the office and aspired to represent an 'Australian way of life' to the people. As Sinodinos put it, 'He held up a mirror to the Australian people and they liked what they saw.'[8]

The beating heart of such power was Howard's office, located on Capitol Hill, in a building far grander than either the White House or Downing Street—though, in truth, Howard always preferred the 'living history' of old Parliament House. Howard would arrive and leave by car from his executive courtyard located close to the parliamentary chambers, ministerial offices, hundreds of staff advisers, 300 press gallery journalists and, at the foot of the Hill, the great policy departments whose chiefs would trek up the Hill to advise and listen to Howard.

As a veteran out of power for thirteen years Howard had an insight into the gift of incumbency. He knew that political parties were weak and getting weaker, that their voter loyalty and ideological appeal were collapsing. The role of Labor and Liberal was no longer as flag-carriers for permanent class interests—their function as parties was to find a leader to deliver executive power. In office, weakness was turned into strength; leaders like Howard could become giant-killers overnight. In opposition, the parties were exposed as non-viable, unhappy and demoralised. Better than anybody else, Howard understood this as he would ruminate over dinner at the Lodge on 'the terrible days' of Opposition and how he would 'never go back'.

Fascinated by national consciousness, Howard projected the office as a symbol of nationalism. The flag was everywhere: on the car, in his office, at media conferences. Howard was convinced that Australians were becoming more nationalistic, a trend he encouraged. At Rugby League State of Origin matches he refused to barrack for New South Wales as he wanted to represent the whole nation, not separate states. 'He felt the states were in decline as political entities,' David Kemp says.[9]

Howard was a 24/7 leader who ran a permanent political campaign—another critical innovation. Mocked as old-fashioned, Howard adapted to the technological revolution that created the 24-hour media cycle. Howard's commitment to political management was pervasive. It circulated like a gas through the air-conditioning system, invisible yet intoxicating. It became the hallmark of his era. In Howard's energy and outlook nothing could have been more removed from the distant administration of his hero, RG Menzies, of whom it could be said the people knew he was there but rarely saw him.

The first decision the Howards took was to live at Kirribilli, not the Lodge. 'Janette didn't want to destabilise the family,' Morris said.[10] This broke a long tradition; Howard would be only part-time at The Lodge. It reflected one of Howard's strengths—his ability, with Janette, to integrate family and politics.

Morris said:

> Janette was the unpaid sounding board. He bounced things off her and her judgement wasn't bad. The idea that she had the final say on policy or deciding who was Governor-General is ridiculous; she didn't. But Janette liked politics and liked being involved in what her husband was doing. Over the kitchen table or dinner they'd talk politics. It didn't matter whether we were in Bourke or Cairns or Beijing, he would ring home at least once every day.[11]

'I think Janette helped him to stay in politics after 1989,' Sinodinos said.

> She would say to him 'You must do what you're happy with', knowing he was a professional politician. Janette was not interested in power for herself. Her objective was the political advancement of John Howard. In my view her instincts were good—I used to argue you got two for the price of one.[12]

The worst event of Howard's first term was Janette's cervical cancer, discovered within months of the election. Howard didn't talk about it. 'He'd come to work but he wasn't there,' Sinodinos said. 'He'd be walking around the office glassy-eyed. He found it hard to function. She was indispensable to him and it took a big toll.' But, Sinodinos recalls, when she was cleared Howard wanted to tackle the job 'with renewed vigour'.[13]

Kirribilli became a symbol. While Howard used the power of Canberra he was not a Canberra person. Like his departmental head Max Moore-Wilton, Howard would travel to Canberra for parliament and Cabinet; then he would return to Sydney and the nation. By living in Sydney he was in touch with Australia's main city, its largest collection of marginal seats and its commercial heartland.

Howard, like Hawke and Fraser, was a cabinet traditionalist. In Australia, an effective cabinet cannot create good government but there can be no good government without it. 'I was determined to run a proper cabinet system,' Howard said years later.[14] By contrast there was no functioning cabinet system in Washington; under Tony Blair cabinet government in Westminster would be abandoned.[15]

His cabinet was tight and secretive. It became the tightest cabinet since Menzies and an instrument of Howard's power resting on the principle of cabinet responsibility. There is no report of Howard not getting his way. He insisted, whether ministers won or lost, that they defend the decision. Howard sent the message: he would not tolerate ministers leaking for individual gain and his intimidatory discipline was effective. 'He used cabinet as an instrument to keep the government united,' Kemp says.[16]

Howard said he 'set out to do things differently to Fraser'.[17] He had been dismayed at Fraser's cabinet method—long meetings often at short notice with protracted decision-making. 'He reacted against the Fraser legacy and he didn't want his government bogged down in process', Sinodinos said.[18] 'I start meetings on time,' Howard said. 'I try to finish them in reasonable time. And I try to give everybody a go.'[19] There was no Whitlam petulance and little Fraser-type agonising. The truth is that Howard had remodelled the Liberal Party in his image—with wide acceptance of his framework of economic liberalism and social conservatism.

The keys to unity were Howard's proper relations with Fischer and Costello, neither of whom was a personal friend. Like Fraser and Menzies, Howard was a dedicated coalitionist, offering nominal respect to Fischer and real respect to his successor, John Anderson. 'He wouldn't have a bar of those Liberal elements saying wipe out the Nats now,' Fischer said.[20]

While Howard and Costello were not close they were mostly policy allies. 'I don't think their relations were ever warm but from what I saw, and I attended cabinet, they worked pretty well together,' Moore-Wilton said.[21] Costello had entered politics to the right of Howard, a cardinal point. It meant that in cabinet they agreed on the big issues: the GST, border protection, debt reduction, the US alliance, anti-terrorism and the Iraq war. But it was always delicate. 'Whenever I was in the room with Howard and Costello I felt an underlying tension,' Sinodinos remembers.[22]

Not long after the swearing-in, Howard, Downer and Reith were at the Lodge together one evening, rumbling around. 'We were looking about, just checking it out,' Reith said. 'And reminiscing about the struggle to get there.'[23] This was the heart of the engine. In this group, Costello was an outsider. Howard didn't run a 'mates' cabinet, but his 'mates' were Reith and Downer.

After his victory Howard created a new Cabinet Policy Unit adjacent to his own office. It was headed by his adviser, Michael L'Estrange, later to become secretary of the Department of Foreign Affairs. Management of cabinet business and priorities was shifted, in effect, from the Department of Prime Minister and Cabinet to Howard's office. The engine room would be run not by public servants but by Howard's strategists. 'He wanted to ensure the cabinet reflected his political priorities and not those of the public service,' an insider said. The Cabinet Policy Unit evolved under L'Estrange and later Paul McClintock into a whole-of-government management instrument.

This prompted Kemp to say that Howard 'co-ordinated the whole government in a way that Malcolm Fraser, for instance, never did'.[24] Decoded, this meant Howard was accumulating more power. In the end, Costello was appalled—he saw ministers getting weaker, Howard getting stronger and the government in decline. Costello said:

> A practice had grown up the longer the government went on, ministers used to get their instructions from the Prime Minister's staff. At the end, there were only two ministers who had been there for the whole period, me and Downer. By that stage, he [Howard] was running most of his policy through his staff. My suspicion is that sometimes the staff would think up the policy without checking it with Howard.[25]

It was dysfunction by dominance.

The Cabinet Policy Unit formalised two streams of advice to Howard—departmental policy submissions and a short political/policy brief from the Cabinet office on every substantive issue. Howard saw cabinet as an intensely political process; it was about policy and politics. The organising principle, however, was not 'due process' but Howard's authority. Whenever a big issue arose Howard was 'all over it', according to Morris. He was an activist who sorted things out. Because Howard was unchallenged as leader his authority did not depend on cabinet. This meant that the big decisions, in fact, were taken informally outside cabinet but legitimised by it. The two classic examples are the GST and the Iraq war, virtually the most important domestic and external decisions of Howard's era.

Howard and Downer decided on the commitment to Iraq; Howard and Costello settled on the GST—cabinet approval came when needed. The most famous solo decision by Howard was his post 9/11 pledge to stand with America—a war pledge. For most of his government the budget revenue decisions (tax policies) were decided separately by Howard and Costello acting together and not taken to cabinet for debate. 'On these decisions we would talk one-on-one,' Costello recalls. 'When we cut taxes, they were my tax cuts though he did moderate a few times.'[26] As Sinodinos says, 'The big revenue decisions were taken outside cabinet.'[27] One example was the much criticised final term 2006 decision to abolish tax on superannuation payouts. 'I rang Howard about it a couple of days before the Budget and said I am going to announce this,' Costello says. 'I think he was a bit shocked. He asked me to explain it. I said it was a pretty good policy, a dramatic move on superannuation, and that it was affordable.'[28]

In January 2007, with his political future on the line Howard announced his $10 billion Murray–Darling water plan without cabinet approval. When questioned, an irritated Howard said: 'The only reason it didn't go to bloody cabinet was that it was New Year. I wanted to get the announcement out on Australia Day.'[29] Once again, the test was Howard's political needs.

Howard's view on ministerial responsibility was transformed under pressure. In the end, Howard formulated a new convention—ministers were responsible to the prime minister, not to the parliament or anybody else. Howard never put it this bluntly, but this is what he meant. Its virtue was its authenticity.

On his first day in parliament as prime minister, Howard unveiled a ministerial code, prepared by his department, to underwrite higher ministerial standards. It contributed to him losing five ministers in his first term because of personal failings over pecuniary interests and travelling allowances.[30] An additional victim was his trusted adviser Morris, whose 1997 farewell saw both men in tears. These casualties reduced the government to a near shambles; the loss of National MP John Sharp, a future leader, was far-reaching.

Eventually the government decided that the code was a terrific blunder. Howard went into reverse: he would defend his ministers, not sacrifice them. 'One of the conclusions I drew was that you don't let people go, except on issues of substance,' he said.[31] 'The code produced some shocking events,' Nick Minchin said. 'There was a feeling that Howard's manic commitment to the code was putting nearly everybody at risk for the most mundane transgressions.'[32] Years later Morris said: 'The code was written by public servants and Mother Teresa couldn't have lived with it. A lot of good people got sacrificed.'[33]

Howard's new rules became that ministers should resign only 'if they are directly responsible for significant failings or mistakes or if their continued presence in the government is damaging'.[34] Who would make such a judgement? Howard would, of course. During the 2005 crisis over the Immigration Department's performance, Howard retained Amanda Vanstone as minister but removed the departmental head. It was a neat reversal of the classic doctrine of ministerial responsibility. Public service veteran Roger Beale warned of the risk that 'as the minister takes more power, the departmental head assumes more responsibility'.[35]

The process was classic Howard—ignore abstract principle and find a political solution. As prime minister he felt 'you get rid' of the minister only if the 'continuing damage' was too great. In short, ministers were responsible to the prime minister.[36]

Howard began with a brutal sacking of six departmental heads, a third of the secretaries, without explanation. Sinodinos said Howard felt the public service 'had grown very close to Labor and that, in many ways, it was pro-Labor'. As a result 'he wanted to send the message that a new crew was in town'.[37] Defending his decision, Howard said: 'After thirteen years of Labor government I felt significant change was justified.'[38] Howard acted within his rights. But it was a blunder.

Public service veteran Tony Ayers said later: 'I have no argument if they got the sack for non-performance. My worry at the moment is that people get sacked because someone doesn't like the colour of their hair.'[39] The service was traumatised. It was the greatest blood-letting upon a change of government. Another departmental head at the time,

Sandy Hollway, said: 'In my view all of the six departmental heads would have worked loyally for the Howard government. Its mistake was to act preemptively rather than giving everybody six or eight months and then make judgements.'[40]

Moore-Wilton said he felt both Costello and Reith believed 'the public service had been heavily politicised under Labor'.[41] In Howard's early years Canberra was a town in a state of high tension partly caused by Moore-Wilton. He was Howard's 'enforcer', an appointee from Sydney's business community and a former public servant, ruthless and charming. Howard and Moore-Wilton wanted a change in the culture or, as Moore-Wilton put it, a public service that was 'behind the government's agenda', not bogged down in process.[42]

Morris recalls: 'Some of the big departments took a long time to wake up that dishing up what they had given Gareth Evans or Paul Keating wouldn't work for John Howard.'[43] The adversarial edge to relations lingered for a long time. Howard was suspicious of public service orthodoxy, from foreign affairs to Aboriginal policy. In its early years the cabinet fretted over statutory appointments, desperate to eliminate the so-called Labor institutional culture.

Howard's approach, in fact, extended the trend begun under Hawke and Keating. It was Keating who abolished tenure for departmental heads and introduced a contract system. This was the fundamental change. It terminated that mythical age of 'frank and fearless' advice much romanticised by the media.

Howard was explicit. He wanted the public service to deliver his policies, not try to rewrite them. He succeeded, but success came at a cost—the service was reluctant to advise Howard in conflict with his policy outlook, from the labour market to *Tampa*. Howard's second appointment as head of the prime minister's department, Peter Shergold, said: 'I would not offer advice to the PM to re-regulate the labour market because I know that is contrary to his deepest objectives. For the same reason I would not have advised the former Labor government to embrace assimilationist policies in indigenous affairs.'[44]

Iraq is the revealing study into the nature of Howard's power and the culture that he wanted. This war, one of the most contentious conflicts in the past half-century, saw an astonishing and complete unity of opinion in Canberra. This is an insight into both strategy and governance. Ministers made clear they did not want contesting advice and the public service offered no advice on the merits of the war or Australia's commitment.

DFAT head, Ashton Calvert, the head of Defence, Ric Smith and Shergold confirmed this. So did the Foreign and Defence ministers.

Downer said:

> Did people inside the government come to Howard and me saying don't do this? No, I cannot recall any. DFAT didn't express any reservations about our strategy. The leadership of the department agreed with our policy on Iraq. I don't think Ashton Calvert had any reservations about it. He didn't say so.[45]

Asked about his advice on Iraq, Calvert said:

> My approach was for the department to prepare for Australia's Iraq role and to try to make it work. DFAT did not argue against that war role. In my view there was a strong and shared sense of policy direction on Iraq from Howard and Downer. I was personally satisfied with their strategic judgement on Australia's commitment. In my view they didn't need advice on what they should do because they had, in effect, made up their minds. I think John Howard had concerns about Iraq and was uneasy, but he was committed.[46]

Former Defence minister Robert Hill confirmed that this situation was replicated at Defence. 'I don't think there were too many formal cabinet decisions [on Iraq],' Hill said. 'Howard was doing a lot of it bilaterally. He'd speak to me, he'd speak to Downer, he'd speak to Costello.' Asked if anybody argued against Australia's involvement, Hill said: 'No, not that I can recall. Nobody argued not to do it.' Questioned further about his department, Hill said: 'I think the department did seek to reflect the view of the government of the day.'[47]

Smith did not become head of Defence until November 2002, by which time war-planning was advanced. He said:

> The message from ministers by that time [November] was that they did not want strategic advice from the Defence department. This reflected a conviction that ministers knew the issues and would take the decisions for or against the war. By that time, the department's role was thus limited to advising on the type and nature of our deployment and the risks to our forces from Iraq's assumed WMD capability. Ministers were not seeking advice from the department on whether we should go to war as distinct from how we should go to war.

The role of Cabinet's National Security Committee (NSC) as a decision-making powerhouse receives much attention. But Smith puts this into perspective:

> The NSC was meeting frequently and it was always busy. But it did not, in my time at least, address the big issue because by then the Prime Minister and ministers seemed to have a firm view about where they were going and why.

Like Calvert, Smith confirms the pro-war sentiment of senior officials. He said:

> I think key officials involved felt an Australian commitment was right. I was not aware of any senior official advising against it in my time. We accepted the advice on WMD and understood the alliance's interests that were involved although there was continuing concern about the state of planning for 'phase four'.[48]

The experience at the Department of Prime Minister and Cabinet was the same. Shergold said:

> It was made clear to me that the Howard Government wanted to review the intelligence before and during the war. But ministers felt it was their responsibility to decide whether or not Australia entered the war. It would be wrong to think they were not interested in advice but the advice they wanted from the policy departments and intelligence agencies was about the conduct of the war and capabilities, not the decision to go to war.[49]

Howard's foreign policy adviser, Michael Thawley, said: 'Howard is always keen on advice. But his views on the big issues are clear and he really wants advice on how to best achieve his goals.'[50]

As a general proposition, former Public Service Commissioner Andrew Podger said senior officials were 'too concerned to please' and that the system was too geared to protect ministers at cost to the public interest.[51] The iconic symbol of this malaise became the 2001 'children overboard' saga when the military and public service chiefs failed to robustly give ministers the true and accurate advice—no children had been thrown overboard.

However, Shergold was right in his further claim that a fabricated history of a glorious past had been constructed to damn the present. There is an endless list of examples but two will suffice: no senior officials advised Menzies against the Vietnam War (a far more serious commitment than Iraq that cost 500 lives) and during the 1966–67 VIP affair (with shades of 'children overboard') senior officials, such as head of Prime Ministers, Sir John Bunting, were responsible for Holt's lies to parliament.[52] So much for 'frank and fearless' advice from the past; it is often forgotten that the main task of the public service is to assist ministers to deliver their agenda.

The ultimate source of Howard's authority was the people, and over a decade he conducted a continuous dialogue with the public. No previous incumbent—including Hawke—gave such time or priority to this task. Howard had no interest in media background briefings; he used the media to speak directly to the people and he spent more time on the media than he did in either cabinet or parliament. Howard was a media addict—morning, noon and night. Talkback radio was his super-highway to the people and he formed links with the main shock jocks in each capital.

Howard became a prime minister of routine who would rise at 6 a.m., glance over the papers and take a thirty- or forty-minute brisk walk. 'I am quite religious about it,' he said. It made him mentally and physically sharp.[53] Often he was on radio by 7.15 a.m. It was not unusual for him to do several radio interviews before mid-morning. He developed a close relationship with Sydney's most popular radio broadcaster, Alan Jones, an interviewer and a supporter. But Howard evolved as a commentator on the nation, from its curriculum to cricket. By his third term he was the omnipresent uncle transmitting into almost every household unless switched off. The main reason given by returning ALP leader Kim Beazley in early 2005 for establishing a home base in Sydney was to combat Howard's grip on talkback.[54]

No previous prime minister had done as much domestic travelling. Howard loved Australia, its cities, towns and bush and its regional differences. He was a good traveller, a natural speech-maker and, over the years, he became adept at the 'meeting and greeting' phase of the job that had driven Keating to distraction. As he travelled, Howard listened; he would return to his desk keen to fix problems by putting more funds into rural roads or flood mitigation in northern New South Wales or some other project. He was an 'eyes open' PM who believed in empirical observation, not just being advised by a Canberra public servant.

Howard had a practical mind fixated on political advantage. He had little focus on government accountability, for good reason—his taxpayer-funded advertising campaigns cost more than $1 billion over eleven years. These campaigns blurred the distinction between public information and partisan politics—witness the GST and *WorkChoices* television campaigns. Throughout Howard's time, proper auditor-general scrutiny was rejected by the government, the process was manipulated for political gain, and such campaigns constituted a blatant abuse of executive power and public funds by Howard. The system became a priority reform for the Rudd Labor government.

Howard's life was a seamless immersion in politics; this was his job and his hobby. Whenever possible, Howard watched the evening television news bulletins to see how the daily political contest was being judged. He retired between 11 p.m. and midnight, sometimes catching cable TV, CNN, *Lateline* or *Fox News*. During the summer break he read political biographies and watched cricket. He needed no diversions such as Fraser's farm or Keating's artistic passions. His emotional foundation was unbreakable and his narrow upbringing tightened his focus. He had no time for cant or academic theorising. He always saw himself as the people's Prime Minister.

In August 1996 Howard went to Bowral to open the Bradman Museum and to declare that Sir Donald was 'the greatest living Australian', a judgement that would have been endorsed by the people but not by the opinion-makers.[55] He reflected Australia as it existed in its conformity and suburban conservatism, not the idealised construct of Keating's new identity. Howard never suffered a 'great man' complex because, like Curtin and Chifley, he never saw himself as a great man. He was too Australian in his tastes. He rarely had to imagine what ordinary Australians thought. He only to ask 'What do I think?', the answer usually being the same.

He didn't see himself competing in Hawke's 'love affair' with Australians. Any such notion was too narcissistic, as well as being plain wrong. Howard knew he was not loved by the people and he didn't expect to be loved. He sought, instead, their respect and, to use a famous word—trust. Howard had a precise grasp of what trust meant—winning the votes of people who disliked him or disliked many of his policies. That was trust, and it was measured by results.

With his clerk's countenance, balding head and repetitious rhetoric, Howard could at best hope to be positioned as a reliable uncle. It worked for a long time because Howard, as a professional, built an effective system of political management whose flaws were embedded in its design. The risk was that his cabinet dominance would become counterproductive, that the public service would not function as a source of ideas, and that Howard would become too infatuated by his relationship with the public. Each of these risks was realised but it took a long time.

20

THE ECONOMIC MODEL: A STORY OF AUSTRALIAN EXCEPTIONALISM

Driving the Budget back into surplus—the symbolic value of that is enormous.
—John Howard, 1996

J ohn Howard's pivotal year as prime minister was 1996 because this is when he refined the economic model that would last eleven years and deliver the longest expansion in Australia's history. Presiding over this expansion was Howard's greatest achievement. It defines forever his era and it was the key to his re-elections. It helped to transform Australian lives, values and prosperity. And it was reached in collaboration with Peter Costello, despite their later fractured relations.

There are two popular, opposing views of Howard's economic success—that it was all his own work and that it was all Keating's legacy—and both are false. What happened is that Howard accepted the Hawke–Keating structure and superimposed on it Liberal Party values. The result was a unique Labor–Liberal synthesis.

The proof came in Kevin Rudd's 2007 campaign when, climate change and *WorkChoices* apart, he won on an agenda of economic policy continuity with Howard, presenting himself as fiscal conservative. It is why such a tribal Labor loyalist as Bill Kelty said: 'If you want a Howard legacy, it's unemployment low, a good surplus, inflation low most of the time, economy in reasonable shape—it's not something you should dismiss. It's not like the comedy figure of George Bush.'[1]

The model that guided Howard and Costello was launched in 1996 with a conviction unusual in a new government. It had three planks: a fiscal consolidation and government debt reduction based on a commitment to surplus budgets; a formal agreement on central bank independence to entrench a low inflation culture; and a deregulated labour market in the cause of individual freedom, more jobs and higher productivity.

These three ideas ran for the entire Howard era. Critics who branded Howard a vote-buying cynic devoid of belief missed the main story. Years later, when the success was apparent, Costello would lean back in his chair and boom: 'We had a model. It was obvious. People didn't seem to realise this.'[2]

Howard–Costello history reveals a fidelity to the model. This was essential to the government's character, its success and, finally, its defeat. The trio of ideas was conspicuous for the economic benefits it delivered and the political pain it could inflict. The electoral backlash came from spending cuts in Howard's first budget that alienated permanently many interest groups, the punitive interest rates levied by an independent bank that finally crippled Howard's credibility in the 2007 campaign and the devotion to labour market reform that produced *WorkChoices*, an instrument of his destruction. Following one's model to political death is serious fidelity.

In retirement Howard said his government kept winning elections because 'it governed in a predictable and consistent fashion'.[3] This predictability came from the model. Howard's initial achievement, after the debacle of Fraser, was to prove the Coalition could govern successfully in the post-1983 globalised age.

The Howard era provoked disputes as to how much credit government deserves for economic success as opposed to forces beyond its control. As Treasury veteran, Greg Smith, said: 'No one really controls a market economy. Australia's economic cause is charted mainly by the business sector [but] public policy remains important … the task is to facilitate, not to create or control.'[4]

The origins of the economic model that defined Australia's long expansion from 1991 to 2008 belong with Hawke and Keating. John Howard did not create the model; he adapted the model. Its creation lay with Hawke and Keating in the post-1983 reform era and this creation is one of Labor's epic monuments. The Labor foundations were the float, financial deregulation and tariff reductions. Upon this, Labor built a central bank that started to target inflation, competition policy and privatisation, enterprise bargaining and a long-run fiscal trajectory to return to surplus.

Taking this inheritance Howard adjusted and refreshed the model for his needs. His political aim, above all, was to put the Liberal Party stamp on Australia's economic success. Howard and Costello were fixated by this idea and Labor in opposition after 1996, in an act of high folly, conceded the territory.

Surveying Australia's economy in 2001 at the start of a new century, Treasury Secretary Ted Evans said:

> Just how good was the economic performance of the 1990s? About as good as it gets: a prolonged period of strong growth and low inflation, with unusually high productivity growth the source of both outcomes … It is certainly the case that several [policies] made critical contributions—among those were tariff reform and competition policy more generally; reform of the fiscal policy framework; improvements in the conduct of monetary policy; and, perhaps most importantly, reform of the labour market arrangements.[5]

This was a Labor–Liberal shared achievement, as Evans' comments implied. As early as his second term Howard puffed out his chest and boasted: 'If you look at the last twenty years, you've really got five pillars—financial reform, tariff reform, industrial relations reform, fiscal consolidation and, finally and importantly, taxation reform.'[6] It was a self-interested list. Howard gave Labor credit for two (financial and tariff), while he claimed the other three for the Liberals (industrial, fiscal and tax).

Keating would have choked. In fact, Labor's policy contribution over 1983–96 was distinctly more dynamic and substantial but the Liberal contribution over 1996–2007 was important and path-breaking in changing conservative ideology. Howard saw himself as completing (with key refinements) the reform agenda launched by Labor, as distinct from tearing down the Labor edifice. That Howard openly admitted this continuity is an unusual concession in a politician.

During the 1990s every industrial nation had to come to grips with the new world order—but Australia's transition was one of the most impressive. It sprang from Hawke, Keating, Howard and Costello and drew on a quality public service team that still reflected the nation's postwar public policy tradition.

The new model justifies the label of Australian Exceptionalism—it testified to a transformation from the pre-1983 protected economy of the old Australian settlement. The new model was faithful to Australian values of economic pragmatism, social egalitarianism and practical utility. It avoided the *laissez-faire* laxity of the American system and the stifling controls of the European system. Despite their differences Keating and Howard both sought to empower market forces, retain government regulatory authority, guarantee a strong social safety net and promote a more entrepreneurial and competitive capitalism. The results were imperfect but conspicuous for more success than failures.

Theories that they were swayed by US economic fashion or some abstract neo-liberal ideology are nonsense. The new economic model was conceived in practical self-improvement driven by Australia's public policy tradition.

The 1983–2007 generational creation was running out of puff towards the end. In its last term the Howard government was tired, short on ideas and beguiled into soft options by the post-2003 China boom and the income surge it delivered Australia. No government could have saved Australia from the overseas hurricane of the 2008 global financial crisis. Australia's economic model, however, meant that it entered the crisis in better shape than virtually any Western nation. The global recession offered a decisive judgement on the Keating–Howard economic era.

In 2008, Prime Minister Rudd and his senior ministers, Julia Gillard and Wayne Swan, asserted that, among OECD nations, Australia was in a position of unique strength to withstand this test. Reserve Bank Governor Glenn Stevens offered a contrast: while the global crisis was the most significant recession of the postwar period it was unlikely to be 'the biggest recession of the postwar period in Australia'.[7] That title would remain with the early 1990s recession. Stevens said the 2008–09 downturn was 'essentially an international episode and not really an Australian-specific one'.[8]

For Australia, the crisis was different from most downturns—it was not home grown but external in its origins. It did not constitute a domestic policy failure. Former Westpac chief executive and Treasury official, David Morgan, said: 'The global financial crisis is an external event imposed upon Australia. It is not caused by any public or private policy failure in this country.'[9] Former HSBC chief economist John Edwards said: 'Australia's financial system has survived intact and is in reasonable health while the US financial system broke down.'[10] Dramatising its external origins, former Governor Ian Macfarlane asked what could Australia have done if it had foreseen the hurricane? The answer was very little. 'We could have made some tougher speeches,' he said. 'But I don't think they would have had any effect.'[11]

The trigger for the crisis was the climate in the US where investors took high risks to increase returns, creating a situation of excessive financial leverage. This was manifest in the extent of unsound loans made by US banks with such loans being securitised by the original lenders and onsold to other investors. The turning point was the failure of the US investment bank, Lehman Brothers, in September 2008, sparking a loss of global confidence and a fall in world equity markets of about 50 per cent. The deeper causes of the crises lay in global financial imbalances and misjudgements by central banks in offering cheap interest rates for too long.

In Australia, unlike other nations, the government was not required to provide capital injections to banks, nationalise lenders or buy toxic assets to prevent financial institution insolvency. This meant Australia avoided the huge debts incurred from bank rescues. Macfarlane said that while the crisis had 'invalidated' the international deregulation financial model this was not the case with the Australian model. Indeed, a few months into the crisis Macfarlane pointed to the upheaval in bank ratings, where 'nearly a quarter of the world's highly rated banks are Australian'.[12]

However, these judgements were questioned or, at best confused, by Rudd in his February 2009 essay in *The Monthly* when he declared an ideological war on the policies of the previous generation saying 'the great neo-liberal experiment of the past 30 years has failed'. Rudd's charge was that the global financial crisis was also an intellectual and ideological crisis that signalled the demise of the ideas and regulatory frameworks that had failed so spectacularly. Arguing that the crisis was a 'turning point between one epoch and the next' Rudd said neo-liberalism had failed and that the role of the state must become more important to economic life. He said social democrats were called upon to save capitalism from itself and speculated that the title for the new epoch might be 'social capitalism' or 'social democratic capitalism', with the state playing a greater role.[13]

While much of Rudd's analysis was international, he invested it with a domestic focus, charging the Liberal Party with being 'the political home of neo-liberalism in Australia'. Rudd put the Howard government in the dock for Australia's economic woes, a stance inconsistent with claims, including his own, that Australia was the best placed of any OECD economy at the onset of the crisis. Rudd highlighted the 'competing political traditions within Australia' between Labor and Liberal over the role of government and markets and attacked Howard for his pro-market beliefs.[14]

The truth, however, is that much of Rudd's analysis was equivocal. Indeed, it may have been written to deceive. At the same time Rudd warned against reversion to 'an all-providing state'. He supported, in effect, a middle way, saying the wisdom of social democrats would be judged by their ability to 'harness the power of the market'. While launching an ideological war against neo-liberalism, Rudd cast himself in the Hawke–Keating pro-market tradition. The specific roles he identified for the state in the crisis seemed limited and sensible—to save financial systems from collapse, to provide fiscal stimulus to ameliorate the downturn and to devise better financial regulations. Such functions do not necessarily constitute a new epoch.

The test for Australia is to draw the correct intellectual conclusions from the crisis. Three propositions are central from the contemporary history of the Keating and Howard governments.

First, the Australian economic and financial model was a Labor–Liberal joint project constructed over the 1983–2007 era and not even unremitting party propaganda can disguise this truth. Indeed, on balance, deregulation in Australia (apart from the labour market) was pursued more aggressively in the Hawke–Keating period than in the Howard–Costello period.

Second, the international crisis arose within the financial system. While it is a comprehensive failure in relation to both financial institutions and regulatory regimes, there is no comparable argument that market-based policies failed in relation to goods, services, labour or international trade. The case for a generic re-regulation of OECD economies does not arise. The moral is beware of false prophets carrying ideological banners attempting to hijack the politics of the crisis for their own causes.

Third, the crisis highlights the exceptionalism of the Australian model, drawing on Australia's political and policy traditions. The historic folly for Australia, in response to the crisis, would be to import overseas solutions to problems that Australia does not have. The post-1983 reforms implemented by the Hawke, Keating and Howard governments can be listed precisely. They are the float, financial de-regulation, cutting the tariff, an independent central bank targeting inflation, enterprise bargaining and labour market deregulation, competition policy, privatisation of government enterprises, tax reform, award-based superannuation, a budget surplus, elimination of government debt and, in relation to the financial system, bank supervision through the Australian Prudential Regulation Authority (APRA) and the four pillars policy that prevents bank mergers and, in effect, regulates bank competition.

Did these policies cause the crisis? The answer is obvious. It means that Australia's embrace of economic liberalism post-1983 is not the cause of the domestic downturn and, indeed, is the reason (along with our economic ties to Asia and, in particular, to China) that Australia is strongly positioned to weather the crisis. There has never been a neo-liberal model in Australia. Neither Keating nor Howard were neo-liberals. The key to grasping Australian policy is to realise that while Australia absorbed global intellectual currents it implemented its own solutions according to its own values. This is the essence of patriotism.

Morgan said:

> The quality of public policy since 1983 is one reason why Australia will emerge from the crisis better than virtually any other OECD nation. It is incontrovertible that the economic reforms of the last 25 years have been fundamental to Australia's strong economic position and its ability to manage the crisis. Arguments to the contrary have no intellectual or empirical standing.[15]

As Ted Evans, a former Treasury Secretary who was Westpac chair during the crisis, said:

> I don't believe responsibility for the crisis or blame for its magnitude can be sheeted home to the Howard government. In relation to financial regulation, from my perspective at Westpac, I think the regulator APRA did the job properly, certainly better than in other nations. This is basic to the healthy position of Australia's major banks at the onset of the crisis.

Evans argued that a global downturn was not needed to identify Howard's economic mistakes—in the latter years he should have done more to tackle the tax/welfare interaction that inhibited employment and better planned for infrastructure projects. But such flaws played no role in the crisis.[16]

In a penetrating analysis Edwards said that Australia's large current account deficit and large net external liabilities were the characteristics that 'posed a threat to any country' once the crisis arose. The question is why these potential vulnerabilities did not undermine or ruin Australia. Answering his question, Edwards said:

> I have no doubt that if we had not shifted from compulsory arbitration to wage bargaining, from high tariffs to low tariffs, from persistent budget deficits to a balance over the cycle, from high inflation to low inflation—and taken the opportunity provided by the long upswing to eliminate federal debt, then global confidence in Australia during the crisis would have faltered and we would have faced an intractable current account problem … I think it is quite wrong to suggest the global financial crisis exposed the flaws of economic policy in the Howard period … the suggestion

that it [the crisis] exposes the Howard period or indeed the whole eighteen-year expansion as some kind of illusion is just ridiculous.[17]

This analysis emphasised the delicacy of Australia's economic existence—reliance on overseas savings and an accumulated foreign debt imposed a premium upon Australia to operate as a sound economy. The lesson Treasury Secretary, Ken Henry, drew from the crisis was Australia's ability to survive better than 'most other developed nations' provided governments pursued reforms 'rigorously, persuasively and tirelessly'. It was a significant proviso—it demanded a renewed commitment from Rudd to the reform agenda, not false conclusions that the post-1983 reforms had been misguided.

Macfarlane rejected the thrust of Rudd's neo-liberal critique:

Our economy is in a stronger position because of the reforms, the float, the labour market changes, getting rid of protection and the rest. The bulk of the reforms were done by Hawke and Keating. I find it very hard to think of any grounds in which Howard is to blame for the crisis. The criticisms he [Rudd] makes apply only to the financial sector although not in Australia. It blew up and people like Alan Greenspan who had faith that it would be stabilised were wrong. So I think it is legitimate for him [Rudd] to say that that did not work and that it brought great discredit on the US and other countries. That part is certainly true. But it is not true to say that market-based policies generally have not worked in other parts of the economy or to argue that because they have failed we have to go back. I think he is quite wrong there.[18]

Costello, who spent eleven years as Treasurer in the prelude to the crisis, argued Australia's banks were in a sound position for three reasons. First, APRA's regulation was thorough and involved 'stress testing' of banks, a process Costello said was 'critical' to keeping high credit standards. Second, as Treasurer he kept the pressure on bank chief executives and the regulator 'to ensure we didn't have any fall in credit standards' – he said this was a deliberate effort to avoid the US sub-prime eruption of bad loans. And third, the Reserve Bank kept lifting interest rates to ensure the steam was removed from the housing bubble.[19]

Morgan said: 'In Westpac, we took a conscious and explicit decision to avoid the high risk financial products. It didn't happen by accident and it wasn't because we couldn't access liquidity to finance such investments. We dipped our toes into the riskier products and, as a result, we decided that this was an unwise strategy.'[20]

Macfarlane said the two banking systems 'that held up' were Australia and Canada and he attributed this to controls over bank competition. In Australia, this was the 'four pillars' policy, in effect, a position shared by Keating, Howard and Costello that allowed competition for customers but not for corporate takeovers among the majors (Commonwealth, Westpac, ANZ and NAB). Keating said he had stopped the banks 'from cannibalising each other'. Macfarlane said: 'Because banks don't live in fear they'll be taken over tomorrow, they haven't been pushed into such risky behaviour.' However, this view was rejected by Morgan. A critic of the policy, Morgan argued that if it had been lifted, the most that would have happened was that the number of majors would have been reduced from four to three and even this was 'very unlikely'.[21]

In April 1997 Costello announced the 'four pillars' policy in response to the Wallis Report into the Financial System. He was unpersuaded by the report's preference for keeping the door open to such mergers. The bottom line was Costello's resistance to bank mergers, lighter financial regulation and any 'let-it-rip' liberalism, a position apparent from the start of the Howard government.[22] There was no shred of neo-liberalism in Costello's regulatory outlook.

'I was lobbied for over a decade by the banks to withdraw the policy and allow such mergers,' Costello said. 'The banks wanted to merge and the "super" funds wanted this as well to gain more value. The pressure to relent on the 'four pillars' never stopped.' Costello said the most intense lobbying came from the NAB chairman, Don Argus. 'He said to me that Australia didn't have a bank in the top 50 in the world in terms of market capitalisation', a situation that was dramatically altered in 2008 by overseas bank failures.[23]

This reveals the policy character of Howard and Costello. On financial regulation they were the liberal traditionalists—they believed in a freer financial system with more play to market forces but recognised that a sound regulatory regime was essential. Unlike many governments, they took such responsibility seriously and were ably assisted by the Reserve Bank and APRA.

There was no denying, however, that Australia's 2009 downturn, accentuated by steep falls in global commodity prices, would become a turning point. History tells that each recession begets its own political and intellectual legacy. Rudd is correct in his argument that a resurgence in state power has been the necessary global response to the crisis. The scale of intervention suggests this is unlikely to be a brief affair. As Rudd discerned, there is a strong intellectual momentum for revived state power, though its scope and duration defy prediction. The question for Australia is the extent to which Rudd presages a new economic era in which he redefines the balance between markets and the state after the Keating–Howard period.

The brand of Australian Exceptionalism from 1991 to 2007 saw average annual economic growth of 3.7 per cent, a sharp lift in incomes and wealth, a fairly wide redistribution of the income benefits, a market-based economy with firm regulation, a greater sense of national self-confidence, a superior Australian performance compared with most other developed nations and, despite a ferocious domestic political contest, a tolerable agreement between Labor and Liberal on the policy direction such that politics did not derail the expansion. The real story was an ability to manage Australia's vulnerabilities; yet the worst mistake would be for Australia to succumb to complacency.

Howard enjoyed good luck. The 1996 poll in the fifth year of recovery was the golden moment to ascend. It coincided with a period of global disinflation and a buoyant domestic economy. As Keating foresaw, the 1996 election was the perfect victory. 'The reason I want to win,' Keating confided mid-campaign, 'is because this place is set up for a long growth phase. And the Labor Party, not Howard, deserves to be the beneficiary.'[24]

At Howard's end it became fashionable to assert Australia's success was mainly luck—but sustained success in any project is never just luck. It is misleading to interpret Howard's economic success purely as a gift from the China boom, a frequent claim made by Labor in 2007. This is easily dismissed. The take-off in commodity prices and the terms of trade began in 2002–03, after Howard had won three elections. Howard faced two elections after the China boom—2004 and 2007—for one victory and one defeat, an equivocal gift from the Heavenly Kingdom. The evidence suggests he did better before the China boom than after. The boom's benefits were equivocal—higher national income created policy problems that Howard struggled with.

While Howard governed during a favourable global era, the hazards of the period are too easily overlooked given the 2008 convulsion. At the end of Howard's third term, Treasury Secretary Ken Henry said:

If, at the start of the 1990s we had predicted that our largest trading partner [Japan] would experience average growth of just one per cent and suffer four recessions over the coming decade, that a large part of emerging East Asia would experience a financial crisis and severe recession (1997 and 1998), that US bond markets would effectively grind to a halt for a period (late 1998), that US equity markets would experience the emergence and bursting of a major bubble (2000), that the US economy would experience a not insubstantial recession (2001), that significant acts of terror would occur in New York and elsewhere, that Asia would experience health scares like SARS and avian flu and that oil prices would rise sharply to levels not seen since 1985, most of us would have thought that the next 15 years would be pretty miserable ones for Australia. Yet this has been a period of historic economic prosperity for us.[25]

Macfarlane made a similar point in his 2006 Boyer Lectures: 'Luck no doubt plays a role in economic development just as in other areas of human activity, but a lot more than luck has been involved in the long expansion.'[26]

Political leadership has been basic to the new economic model. Australia's post-1983 political leadership has been of a higher quality— Hawke, Keating and Howard as prime ministers and Keating and Costello as the main treasurers. Ted Evans, reflecting on his entire career, said: 'The Hawke government was the best government I worked with in my thirty years and the driving force in that government was Paul Keating as treasurer. I would rate the Howard government as better than the Keating government. Before that Malcolm Fraser was just bloody hopeless.'[27] In 2006 Macfarlane said: 'On the macroeconomic side the improvement has just been enormous compared with the 1970s, absolutely enormous.'[28]

The age of globalisation assisted Australia—developing-nation de- mand spearheaded by China saw our export prices rise and import prices fall; new technology assisted the services sector; because Australia never got into IT manufacturing it avoided the dot.com meltdown and 2001 recession; the float meant that Australia absorbed via the exchange rate a series of international shocks that once would have meant a recession; its strong immigration program and attractive location were further assets. The reality is that Australia adjusted extremely well to the globalisation phenomenon.

Over time Howard's budget surplus was driven by the economy. From 2002 huge revenues fuelled the surpluses, giving Howard licence for his incessant 'buying' of votes off the budget. This began seriously in 2001 and reached dizzy levels from 2004 onwards. It became the paradox of Howard's latter years. He was a champion of budget surpluses but became a big spender, a dual identity courtesy of the commodity boom scaling stratospheric peaks. During 2004–07 it triggered Howard's most serious economic failure—his refusal to maximise the boom year revenues in the cause of long-run reform and productivity gains.

This weakness, however, reveals Howard's true identity: he was a politician of the 1980s. His ideas, his missions, his reformism all originate within 1980s politics. The 1980s were when he broke into prominence and made his name. Howard loved the 1980s economic debates and he never left them. In many ways, he did not make the transition to the new century. All the economic ideas of his prime ministership arose in the uncompleted 1980s agenda—the fiscal surplus, labour market deregulation, privatisation and a GST. This was when he won prestige as an economic reformer attacking Hawke and Keating for their alleged timidity.

'Howard was completing an economic agenda he had devised in the 1970s and 1980s,' Arthur Sinodinos said.[29] It is the critical insight. His government was shaped not by new ideas but old ideas. When he won the Senate in 2005 and saw the economic reform vista unfold before him what did Howard do? He reached back to IR reform with *WorkChoices*; he was faithful to his 1980s model. The public knew where Howard stood on the economy; he had been standing there for twenty-five years.

Howard's policy mission as PM was apparent from the start—it was for the Liberal Party to complete Australia's economic transition. It was to bring the 1980s to finality; this was the meaning of Howard's economics. He never created a new economic agenda for the early twenty-first century boom.

This leads in to another basic misconception about Howard: that he was a neo-liberal ideologue pledged to smaller government and lower tax shares. The persistence of this fiction is extraordinary. In fact, Howard shunned this guise. Having not promised this agenda, it is unsurprising that he did not achieve it.

Treasury papers show that, at the end of the Howard years, tax as a portion of GDP was 24.6 per cent (including the GST) compared with 22.8 per cent in his first year. He finished with tax at a higher level than it was under Whitlam, Fraser, Hawke and Keating. Former Treasury Secretary John Stone lamented that Howard ran the 'highest ratio of taxation to GDP in Australia's peacetime history' and left 'a largely unreformed personal income tax system'.[30]

On tax and spending Howard said: 'We had no quantitative commitments. No, we did not.'[31] Costello was far keener than Howard on low tax/spend results.

In Howard's first term income tax rates were not cut. In Howard's last term the government declined a more radical tax reform when the revenue was available, a deliberate choice. For nearly a decade Howard and Costello refused to cut the top marginal rate from Keating's 47 per cent until, finally, they slashed it to an heroic 45 per cent. On Howard's departure, Australia's top marginal tax rate and its threshold were about the OECD average. The company tax rate was above that average.[32]

On the spending side, total federal spending as a proportion of GDP fell in the Howard era but reduced interest payments on public debt was a principal factor. Spending finished at 24.2 per cent of GDP compared with 25.6 per cent in the first year. Howard described his government as being 'lean but not mean'. He dismisses much of this debate as an accounting furphy.

> It's a phoney argument. For example, our family tax payments appear on the spending side of the budget and so does the cost of the private health insurance rebate. I discovered this one day in the ERC. When people talk about middle-class welfare what there're really talking about are family tax payments. But if these were shown on the tax side of the budget [as concessions] then the right-wing would be lighting candles in the cathedrals for me.[33]

The reality is that by OECD standards Australia has been a small government and relatively low tax nation for some time. The Treasury concluded that Australia was a 'low tax country'—the eighth-lowest by OECD standards. Australia is also 'a low expenditure country—the third-lowest in the OECD'.[34] The scope for a quantum shift towards small government beloved by neo-liberals was limited.[35]

Howard was proud of his economic liberalism but it was tempered by pragmatism. While admiring Margaret Thatcher and New Zealand's Roger Douglas as the global champions of economic liberalism, Howard's position was different and less purist. 'I am not flint dry—I'm just on the dry side,' he said.[36]

His emphasis was on results—jobs, low interest rates, profits, income growth and appreciation of assets. For Howard, the aim was not ideology but a growth economy with improved prosperity for households. Howard invoked the need for 'balance' in public policy. While he believed in markets and privatisation, he was not a crusader for deregulation. 'Ours is a party which rejects extremes,' was his mantra. He saw lower taxes and less government as useful incentives, not as ideologies. His record affords no other view.

The first and last priority was the budget surplus and debt reduction. This was Howard's foundation economic principle. It is where Howard's political strategy as prime minister began. Surplus politics would become his economic pride and his political magic. It is where he destroyed the Labor Party. The tactic worked for nearly four terms until Kevin Rudd's arrival as Labor leader. It was a model for stable government. In economic terms, fiscal policy was recast as a medium-term instrument to build public savings and reduce government debt. The task of adjusting economic growth, faster or slower, fell to monetary policy.

In March 1996 Howard and Costello wanted to convince Australians that something dramatic had happened. Their sales pitch was the budget surplus. It would badge their government. 'The surplus was a sign of policy strength,' Arthur Sinodinos said. 'We were running the place and turning away from debt and deficits. We were laying down firm rules by which we would govern.'[37] The surplus would instil confidence and generate a circle of virtue.

It was a sharp break from Australia's past. The previous generation had been dominated by budget deficits despite Keating's 1980s efforts. Howard and Costello came to make Keynesian deficit financing look like a museum piece. Their policy would break not just from Australia's past but, more conspicuously, from the global practice led by the United States that, for much of Howard's era, was in heavy deficit. It was about refining an Australian model. Any notion that George W Bush would have made the sacrifices to replicate Howard's surplus strategy was a fantasy.

On the morning after his 1996 victory, Howard, who stayed the night at Sydney's Intercontinental Hotel, strolled up the road to the Commonwealth offices to meet Mike Keating and his senior officers. They were professional yet funereal. But they bore Howard a golden gift.

Keating produced the blue book and told Howard the underlying budget deficit for the current year had blown out to $9 billion. Howard was 'not the least bit surprised'.[38] But he must have felt déjà vu. Howard had been humiliated as outgoing treasurer in 1983 when he passed a $9.6 billion deficit to Paul Keating. In proportionate terms Howard's 1983 deficit was worse than Labor's 1996 deficit. It had taken Howard years to recover. Now he would claim his revenge. He knew the politics of fiscal 'black holes' and he would nail Beazley Labor.

Peter Costello's new life began on Monday 4 March when he went to the same building in Sydney to begin his relations with a slow-talking thickset man of working-class origins with a Queenslander's ruddy face, Treasury Secretary Ted Evans. Flanked by his senior officials, Evans gave Costello the same numbers—but the reaction was different.

'I was shocked,' Costello said. 'I had no idea it would be this bad.'[39] Costello's mind flashed to the fiscal blood he would expend over coming months. His first term would be about fixing Labor's 'black hole'. But the tyro treasurer had the psychological edge. 'I thought Ted looked physically sick about the figures.' Costello said. He sensed a vulnerable Treasury and Costello picked it—from this moment Treasury acted with zeal to restore fiscal prudence.

Talented and arrogant but only thirty-eight years old, Costello needed a wise adviser. Once a Stone protégé and later mesmerised by Keating, Evans had grown pragmatic with age. Hawke had once offered him the Prime Minister's Department, only to be knocked back. Costello was suspicious of Treasury. 'When Costello arrived there were certain senior Treasury officers he didn't want to deal with,' Evans said. 'Three in particular, but to his credit he learnt to respect their ability.'[40] They were Ken Henry, Greg Smith and Martin Parkinson, three of Treasury's best.

Like Howard, Costello knew the deficit was a catastrophe for the Labor Party. His script was written and Labor was doomed. On 12 March, the day after the swearing-in, Costello conducted the ritual slaughter. The damage lay in estimates for the coming year: the projected deficit for 1996–97 was now $4.9 billion; compared with Labor's prediction of a strong surplus in its previous budget. The deterioration was not because of Labor's election bribes but due to parameter changes, mainly lower revenue.

Labor's problem was not fiscal irresponsibility but conducting, and then losing, an election on a false view of the budget trajectory. Six weeks earlier Kim Beazley, as Finance minister, had declared: 'We're operating in surplus and our projections are for surpluses in the future.'[41]

Understand what happened at the 1996 election—Labor lost a decade. Its worst mistake was to conceal the budget position in the hope of winning. Once it lost the election, the revelation of this deception not only discredited Labor but invested Howard's debt reduction agenda with a sense of vindication and moral authority.

Costello said the Coalition would change the budget methodology. It would use the concept of underlying deficit (extracting asset sales), an overdue reform. And this made Labor's accounts look far worse. Treasury estimated the underlying deficit for 1995–96 to be $9.04 billion and for 1996–97 to be $7.64 billion; this compared with $590 million at the time of the previous budget. The deteriorations gave Costello his polemical $8 billion or $9 billion 'black hole'. 'The crime of the Leader of the Opposition,' Costello said, 'was not that the parameters changed but that he [Beazley] refused to come clean about it. We were in deficit.'[42]

Costello argued that, after seventeen quarters of growth, Labor's budget should have been closer to surplus. He stigmatised Labor as the party of debt and deficits. The 'guilty' sign Costello tied to Labor's neck would last for three terms. Not bad for his first day's work as treasurer.

When parliament resumed, Howard went for the jugular. Highlighting an $8 billion hole he said, 'I cannot believe my luck.' And he meant it. Looking at Beazley across the despatch box, Howard said: 'You chose to close your eyes.'[43] Nine years later, in January 2005 when Beazley returned as Opposition Leader, this attack still had credence.

Labor was delegitimised far beyond the extent of its fiscal crime. Keating's former economic adviser, Ric Simes, said the budget was moving towards balance at around 1 per cent of GDP a year. This may have been a political problem but 'it was not a serious economic problem'.[44] But Howard seized his chance—he invested the surplus goal with prominence, urgency and symbolism.

Howard chaired the Expenditure Review Committee (ERC) and Costello said 'the days of sloth and waste are over'. It was melodrama with a short shelf life. But Treasury quickly saw it had a capable treasurer and Costello established himself as methodical, with an eye for detail. Reviewing Costello's career, Ted Evans said: 'Costello was very good, intellectually strong, capable in the ERC. On the negative side, he didn't work hard enough and let things run on.'[45]

Whenever Howard was asked to nominate his government's best budget he gave one answer—it was the first, always the first. Howard said:

I think the first budget was our best because it set a very good pattern. It had a number of difficult decisions but it was seen as fair. It sent a strong signal to the public that we were good managers. Driving the budget back into surplus—the symbolic value of that is enormous—the public derives great reassurance and confidence from the knowledge that the government is putting the budget in the black.[46]

His judgement was correct. Costello's first budget, on 20 August 1996, was his best of twelve. Its centrepiece was a surplus projected for the third year. Savings totalled $9.8 billion over two years. The Treasury was lyrical. In the budget papers Treasury said the budget position 'has been generally unsatisfactory for the past twenty years or so'. As a result fiscal consolidation had become 'a matter of urgency'.[47] Treasury seemed back in charge, hoping Costello would revive its authority.

The burden fell on interest groups and Labor voting blocs—the public service, universities, welfare recipients and the ethnic lobby. The unemployed took the main cuts as labour market training surrendered to job placement. 'I don't want to touch school education,' Howard said when ERC looked at education, but universities were punished and students penalised via HECS changes—launching the long conflict between the Howard government and the tertiary sector. In the ERC, the universities were friendless. The head of the Education Department, Sandy Hollway, said: 'Senior ministers felt the universities were sloppy with money, poorly run, inefficient and should be more commercial. The vice-chancellors were ineffective in dealing with the new government.'[48] Funding for Aboriginals was reduced, the ABC was cut sharply, running costs for the public service were cut by 2 per cent, the immigration intake was cut by 9000 and migrant welfare benefits curtailed, and there was a cut in child care for middle and high-income earners. A 15 per cent superannuation surcharge hit high-income earners, enabling Costello to boast that he was 'soaking the rich'. The Commonwealth Dental Program was terminated and the aged care system reformed to allow up-front fees and bonds, a decision subsequently altered.

As Howard walked away from his election promises, his blunder was to categorise them as 'core and non-core', a phrase used against him for a decade. Howard rated himself 'between seven and eight' out of ten on keeping promises, betraying a 'break rate' of 20 per cent plus.[49] The *Sydney Morning Herald*'s Economics editor, Ross Gittins, called it 'the most mildly received horror budget in history'. But there would be no repeat of this budget. For Howard and Costello, it was a once-in-a-career hit. When economic writers attacked the duo in subsequent years for not delivering tougher budgets, Costello privately dismissed them as 'crazy'. Ken Henry said 'spending constraint stopped after the first budget'.

On the other hand, this budget launched the political strategies that defined Howard's social vision and kept him in office. With egregious fanfare, it targeted the rich and undeserving poor—to exploit envy of the 'top end of town' and resentment towards lazy dole recipients. The purpose was to win the Howard battlers. The 'super' surcharge applied at the $85 000 income level was opposed by Treasury as pure tokenism.

There was a far-reaching reform: the Commonwealth Employment Service in its fiftieth year was privatised—marking the origin of the Job Network and the quest for a competitive job employment market. The reform originated with the public service. The future head of the Prime Minister's Department, Peter Shergold, said: 'I believe the Job Network was the most important administrative innovation during the Howard years. They took a fifty-year-old monopoly and replaced it overnight with a competitive system for job providers. The reform was more far reaching than either John Howard or Amanda Vanstone expected.'[50]

Hollway said:

It was an extension of our initial thinking in Working Nation under Keating. It rested in two ideas—to provide a competitive market for job placement to get more people into work and to provide performance pay incentives for the companies involved. The thinking of the department and Howard ministers came together around a new reform.[51]

The budget polarised the nation in favour of a big Howard majority and a small, bitter, noisy minority that would grow over the years. The pro-Labor interest groups campaigned with moral outrage, unable to accept Howard's legitimacy. On budget eve, a mob broke security lines and rampaged through Parliament House. 'The choice was a tough government or mob rule,' Costello said.[52] In Newspoll's history this budget, at 59 per cent approval, had the third-highest rating over a generation.

The political delegitimisation of Labor was stark. Keating, in fact, had bequeathed no fiscal crisis to Howard. Australia's public debt was, by OECD standards, neither exceptional nor critical. Evans said that among significant OECD nations only Japan had a lower net debt that Australia's at 20 per cent of GDP.[53] Yet the debt had escalated to $96 billion and Treasury was worried about the trend. This meant rich pickings for Costello.

The real aim of the Howard–Costello model was a solvent, debt-free government—rather than smaller government or a lower tax burden. The Howard–Costello ideology was the elimination of public debt. This is why 21 April 2006 became so important for Costello. He named it 'Debt-Free Day', the day Labor's debt was finally discharged and the government was no longer a net borrower. Borrowing for development was seen as a private sector activity. Debt-Free Day became an objective in its own right.

In late 1996 the first sledgehammer fell on Commonwealth debt. The Senate approved Howard's election pledge to sell one third of Telstra. On the opening page of his second budget in May 1997 Costello boasted that net debt to GDP was being halved. Telstra's protracted sale would become basic to debt eradication.[54]

At this point the nature of Howard's policy became apparent. Its priority was not bold economic reform but fidelity to its model—the fiscal surplus, central bank independence and labour market deregulation. It was more a commitment to stability than reform. The Treasury and the Reserve Bank recommended this medium-term model and it delivered for the long haul.

In a prophetic declaration Costello said: 'We should be aiming for a very long run of sustainable economic growth in this country, the kind that we have not seen for a couple of decades'[55] Asked how long the growth cycle might last, Costello said: 'I'm looking for economic cycles that can run for a decade, yes.'[56]

The government unveiled a new rule—to achieve a budget balance 'over the cycle'. In effect, it was a long-run pledge of budget surpluses. From 2003–04 Costello's goal was a surplus of 1 per cent of GDP. It meant budgets would be geared to public savings, with no new calls on Commonwealth net debt. This maximised election options for the government.[57]

The Howard–Costello abolition of debt became their great gift to the Rudd government. When the 2008 global crisis saw a collapse in financial confidence the IMF authorised governments to launch the greatest fiscal stimulus in 80 years. The Rudd government, with its debt-free inheritance from Howard, had far more scope than virtually any other nation for an aggressive stimulus to ameliorate the downturn. Rudd stood on Howard's shoulders.

Costello introduced a Charter of Budget Honesty in response to 'the persistence of budget deficits over the past twenty-five years'. By law this required a pre-election fiscal outlook to ensure that election campaigns were conducted on an updated view of the economy. The re-quirement transformed the tactics of elections, spooked the Labor Party and meant Howard was able to dictate policy at each election, with Labor intimidated into delaying its costed promises until election eve. Evans found the Charter was a 'good thing' that helped public accountability.[58] But it would not halt a profligate government.

As early as 1997 the difference between Costello and Keating as treasurers was apparent. Costello was the 'barrister in politics', savvy, intelligent and conventional, the opposite of Keating's passion, intensity and insights. Where Keating was impatient, Costello was patient; where Keating was bold, Costello was careful; where Keating would crash or crash through Costello shunned confrontation. They had no time for each other.

Such animosity became deeply personal with Costello's second budget. The main savings came from a painless stroke of Costello's pen—the repudiation of Keating's LAW tax cuts sitting across the forward estimates as proposed superannuation contributions. Costello wrote them out of existence. He sank Labor's policy and got a windfall budget saving. Keating never forgave him.

Costello's second budget was soft, but it didn't matter. The model had kicked in and was unfolding like a political dream. With growth running at 3.75 per cent, Howard saw a projected budget surplus stretching before him. He would recruit these surpluses to totally dictate the course of politics, starting with a mega-tax reform for the 1998 election.

Howard and Costello had decided in their first week to run a surplus government. It was driven by strategy, values and identity and they took this decision long before the great commodity surge. They rejected the deficit policies that would prevail in America and much of Europe. This strategy endured over four terms. Converting Australia into a surplus nation proved to be prudent economics and brilliant politics.

21

THE MAINSTREAM MOB:
HOWARD AS SOCIAL CONSERVATIVE

I am fairly mainstream. I can't be, in any way,
typecast as an Establishment figure.
—John Howard, February 1996[1]

John Howard came to office to resurrect conservative social values, convinced that this campaign would entrench his political position in the nation. For Howard, social conservatism was an aggressive ideology that permeated his words, policies and budget agenda. Its relentless pursuit for eleven years meant that his social legacy is second only to his economic legacy. The centre of Howard's social conservatism lay in the family, just as the centre of his cultural traditionalism lay in the nation.

Howard knew that economics was not enough—he felt his differences with Labor were as great on social issues as economic issues.[2] The month before his victory he said, 'I give you this pledge: I want to do everything in my power to preserve the social fabric of this nation.'[3] Howard enraged his progressive opponents by rehabilitating social conservatism—an idea they assumed to be moribund—and converting it into a vote-winning instrument.

His family attitudes were influenced by the most important women in his life—his mother Mona, his wife Janette and his daughter Melanie. His critics were blind when dismissing Howard as a Margaret Thatcher 'there is no such thing as society' caricature. He was passionate about society.

Howard's social conservatism was a heart-beating ideology radiating from the centre of power that stamped his Liberal Party. It possessed a varied appeal being tied to family aspirations, Christian values, mateship, a stable society and working and middle-class self-improvement. As usual, Howard never offered a rhetorical blueprint. But his social conservatism was on permanent display, seen in family tax benefits, tight gun laws, the Work for the Dole scheme, 'mutual obligation', welfare reforms, backing the baby bonus over paternity leave, rejection of a Bill of Rights, anxiety about welfare dependency, repudiation of gay marriage, anti-drug campaigns, his Northern Territory intervention and his conviction that the 'fair go' was integral to a stable social order.

He transformed Liberal political theory. Howard's conservatism shifted Liberal philosophy away from individual freedom or rights towards individual obligation to achieve a decent social order. Howard made the Liberals the party of social attack, a reality that Labor, for a long time, seemed unable to comprehend.

If there is one single concept that unlocks Howard's philosophy it is his insight into the Australian character. This was symbolised by his creation of the 'mainstream'—the device that gave political lift-off to social conservatism. Howard began using the word *mainstream* in 1995. It was a deliberate decision, the most important 'brand' label of his prime ministership. Howard says the decision 'may' have been taken in talks with Janette.[4]

He detested words such as 'middle ground', which he saw as vacuous. 'Mainstream' was never a compromise between two competing positions. It was about strength. Howard liked 'mainstream', he said, because 'on some issues the mob had very firm views'. It was a populist concept. 'It was my sense of where the public sat,' he said. Mainstream became a code, an impulse that connected Howard to the people.[5]

Labor MP Mark Latham, an acute analyst, saw what was happening. 'The political spectrum is best understood as a struggle between insiders and outsiders,' Latham said. He was one of the few ALP figures to grasp that Howard would crusade on social values. Howard was taking command of the 'outsider' culture, turning it against Labor.[6]

The month after his victory, Howard said: 'We won because the mainstream of the Australian community identified with us.' By contrast, he asserted, Labor 'drowned in the elitism'.[7] Howard invoked 'mainstream Australians' as the backbone of the nation who, like Menzies' 'Forgotten People', had felt sidelined. In his 1996 campaign he pledged to govern for the mainstream and enshrine Australian families 'at the centre of policy making'.[8] Howard was faithful to this pledge.

Howard talked in values, not class, because his mainstream was open-ended: it included working class, middle class, city or bush. Most

Australians, if inclined, could join Howard's mainstream. He saw the mainstream or 'the mob' as virtuous; the values that Howard attributed to it included hard work, parental sacrifice, faith in country.

The idea showed his debt to Menzies and John Carrick. He was stretching out to construct a broad social, economic and moral coalition. It was a weapon to disenfranchise Labor. In a lunge at Keating, Howard said the mainstream had been treated with contempt by 'the noisy self-interested clamour of powerful vested interests'. He said the mainstream was denied by selfish Labor insiders caring only for themselves and that it 'feels utterly powerless to compete with such groups'. Howard would become its leader and saviour.[9]

Social conservatism was Howard's lifelong identity. It was coded into his brain cells. Howard's feat was to turn this idea into an effective political instrument two generations after the 1960s revolution on behalf of social libertarianism. It led to two conflicts: a major political war with the Left and a smaller political battle with the Right.

'I think I am fairly mainstream,' Howard said in 1996. 'I can't be, in any way, typecast as an Establishment figure.'[10] This comment told so much—Howard saw himself as belonging to the mainstream, a conservative Australian whose values, he believed, had been under attack by the Left Establishment in universities, educational institutions, media, the ABC, welfare bodies, social institutions, NGOs, and arts and cultural organisations.

Howard was fixated on mobilising community values against Labor's special interests. He demonised Labor as the party defined by greens, feminists, ethnics, artists, Aboriginals, gays and others, a distortion to assist his cultivation of a pro-Liberal mainstream consciousness.[11] Howard had his own constituencies: small business, traditional families, over-55 year olds. He bribed them with huge financial support but he never gave them a group identity—they remained forever mainstream Australians.

Howard recruited the 'mainstream' mob against the pro-Labor Establishment. He cast himself as an anti-Establishment figure, a master stroke. His social conservatism was invested with an ideological edge that would attract cadres, columnists and polemicists.

Yet it deeply offended the pro-market Right. The Right was aghast to realise that Howard was serious; he used the Budget to finance his social conservatism to the tune of hundreds of billions of dollars. Greg Lindsay's Centre for Independent Studies (CIS) was dismayed at his middle-class welfare and appalled at his 'big budget' paternalism but was unable to dissuade him.[12]

Howard's most important social insight was to realise that progressive visions and ideas were failing, the prime examples being dysfunction in Aboriginal communities and welfare dependency within single-parent households. From this insight he acquired another: the pressures of modernity only made conservative values more important.

Howard intuitively grasped the organising idea in Francis Fukuyama's 1999 book *The Great Disruption*. Summarising his thesis, Fukuyama said:

> The breakdown of the social order is not a matter of nostalgia, poor memory or ignorance about the hypocrisies of earlier ages. The decline is readily measurable in statistics on crime, fatherless children, reduced educational outcomes and opportunities, broken trust and the like ... the culture of intense individualism which in the marketplace and laboratory leads to innovation and growth, spilled over into the realm of social norms where it corroded virtually all forms of authority and weakened the bonds holding families, neighborhoods, and nations together.[13]

Acting on this insight was one of Howard's achievements. It was the crisis of modernity that fuelled his social conservatism. The progressives who loathed Howard had missed what was happening in front of their eyes. It was one of the epic events of modern history—the revival of the individual responsibility ethic in order to save the family and social order.

Once again, it was Latham who saw Labor's vulnerability. Howard seized the 'responsibility' position in Australian politics because it was left wide open. In Britain, Tony Blair was champion of the 'Third Way'—a device to engage and win the values debate. In Australia, the ALP was mainly clueless.

For Howard, 1960s individual libertarianism had been socially destructive. With 40 per cent of marriages ending in divorce, problems of drug dependence, the rise of inter-generational welfare and single parents struggling on the poverty line, Howard's argument was credible. He said the erosion of the 'fair go' was caused by the 1960s social revolution authorised by the Left. He argued: 'The thing that has produced poverty in Australia, more than perhaps anything else, has been the greater degree of marriage failure. Look at the profile of single-parent families—they are overwhelmingly not the product of teenage pregnancy but of relationship and marriage breakdown ... they're a product in part of the social revolution of the 1960s rather than the economic globalisation of the 1980s.'[14]

Launching the publication *The Conservative* in 2005, Howard offered a homily on his mainstream values. They originated with 'the greatest institution in our society', the family, a commitment to 'an ordered society' as the basis for community, a faith in individual liberty tied to a 'strong belief in personal responsibility', remembering that 'the average Australian believes in a classless society' where individual worth was determined by 'a person's character and hard work', not religion, social roots or class.[15] This was a conservatism of great political utility.

Howard's conservatism was a furnace of ideology. It is best seen in four ideas: redefining the bond between the individual and society according to 'mutual obligation'; supporting families as the bedrock of the social order; enshrining the idea of 'private choice' by individuals in meeting their family needs; and upholding the 'fair go' as integral to the social order. For the Liberal Party, it was a unique Howard fusion and it was riddled with contradictions.

Each of these ideas became his crusade. Howard said if social stability was lost then 'everything else becomes unattainable'.[16] In many speeches he put society first, economy second. Before his 1996 victory Howard said he had 'never seen economic rationalism' as a 'stand-alone political credo'.[17] Before his last election Howard said he strove 'to temper the raw outcomes of market capitalism' for the cause of social order.[18]

In office Howard sought to marry economic liberalism and social conservatism. This was his high strategy—the unique intellectual contribution he made to the party founded by Menzies. Howard was the first Liberal prime minister to embrace economic liberalism, the first since the 1960s to champion social conservatism, the first to seek a synthesis of economic liberalism and social conservatism. This is Howard's legacy. It can be endorsed, rejected or modified; it just cannot be ignored.

In fact, Howard's 'mainstream' legacy is deeply equivocal, it is a mixture of prescience, reaction and old-fashioned vote-bribery. Some of his views were sound, for example, the need for more individual responsibility. Some were futile resistance to necessary change, witness his refusal to tolerate maternity leave and better integrate work/family policy. Some loaded the Budget with family support that pushed the limits of fiscal tolerance.

Howard argued that, in the 'maelstrom' of the globalised age, Australians wanted 'reassurance'. In the best statement of his outlook, he said: 'The more change and ferment that economic globalisation and economic liberalism unleash, the more meaning there is for social stability and social constancy. Otherwise all is change, all is ferment, all is unease. In a sense you need the one to act as stabiliser against the other.'[19]

For years Labor attacked him for stripping compassion from the economic machine—reducing industrial protections, imposing a GST, selling Telstra and cracking down on welfare—an agenda, Labor said, that mocked his pretensions to family values. In 2006 Rudd accused Howard of being a philosophical fraud. Rudd said that '"traditional conservative values" are being demolished by an unrestrained market capitalism that sweeps all before it'. Declaring the Howard project a failure, Rudd argued that 'no such accommodation is possible' between Howard's conservative social values and the 'rampant individualism' his economics had unleashed.[20]

The results, however, over a decade pointed to Howard's success in combining liberal economics with conservative values. Listening to the people, Howard was convinced he was correct: economic reform would survive only with a conservative social ethos. The real lesson is that economic and social policy must be better integrated, given the rise in two-income households, deeper work/family pressures and longer work hours.

Howard's first social policy test came over gun controls, provoked by the April 1996 Port Arthur massacre that saw 35 people slaughtered. It is noteworthy that ten months earlier, before coming to office, Howard had said 'it would be a cardinal tragedy if Australia did not learn the bitter lesson of the United States regarding guns'. He declared that 'every effort should be made to limit the carrying of guns in Australia'.[21] Once the massacre occurred, he had to act.

While an admirer of the United States, Howard was an opponent of many aspects of American society—the gun culture, the US Charter of Rights, its election of judges, its televising of court proceedings (he said the OJ Simpson trial coverage was 'high farce'), the lack of an adequate social safety net and the extremes of income and wealth. Howard, unlike Bush, never invoked God. 'Even religious people [in Australia] are secular in their political tradition in the way that Americans aren't,' Howard said. 'Australians are more sceptical of politicians who frequently invoke religious beliefs to justify policy.'[22] It is hard to find a single policy idea that a patriotic Howard took from the United States.

Howard's anti-gun policy to ban automatic and semi-automatic weapons, establish a gun buy-back scheme and set new standards for sale and storage won the support of the states. The internal politics were more difficult than implied by national opinion polls showing strong support. Howard was indebted to National Party leader Tim Fischer, a Vietnam veteran who put Coalition loyalty before his own base. In response to

Howard's question, Fischer said he owned a bolt action .22 calibre gun and an old 303 rifle. Howard put the same query to Fischer's deputy, John Anderson. 'I've got anything between one and 20 guns lying around,' Anderson said.[23]

Keating said later 'the best thing Howard did was guns'.[24] But it provoked one of Howard's humiliations: his June 1996 speech at an anti-gun rally in Sale, Victoria, when his office was warned by police that his security could not be guaranteed. On advice, he wore a protective vest that was apparent in the TV footage. It was an ignominious occasion, a leader who appeared frightened. Howard was enraged, angry with his staff, but even more with himself. It would never reoccur.

The issue provoked Fischer's worst experience in politics: an angry meeting with the firearms lobby at Gympie, where Fischer's effigy hung from a bloody noose on a tree and police were everywhere. 'It was awful, just awful,' he said. But Fischer never lost his humanity or professionalism. Federal police had to monitor the threats against him. 'It's a chance to break away from the National Rifle Association agenda, so let's do it,' Fischer told Howard. Thus Howard became a hero and Fischer bore the backlash.[25]

The guns issue pointed to Howard's philosophy. Facing his first crisis, Howard rejected the principle of individual rights in favour of social order. For the next eleven years Howard usually accorded social protection a higher priority than expansion of individual rights—witness his support for detention, national security laws, opposition to same-sex marriage.

Liberal Senator George Brandis argues that Howard compromised the sacred Menzian philosophy that the party ultimately represents 'the primacy of the rights of the individual'. Brandis argued that the historic triumphs of liberalism came from putting individual rights first, as in the abolition of slavery and elimination of racial discrimination. He highlighted Menzies' statement that the Liberal Party should be judged by its treatment of minorities.[26]

While Howard would fail this test, so, in practice, would Menzies. It was Menzies who banned the Communist Party during World War II, tried to ban the party during the Cold War, interned enemy aliens, denied basic rights to Aboriginals and refused to amend the White Australia policy. His justification, at each point, was a stable social order. If Menzies had faced the 1990s problems of welfare dependency, marriage breakdown and decline of educational standards, it is highly likely that he would have responded in ways similar to Howard.

Even the truth that Howard cared more about social order than individual rights needs some qualification. Howard opposed capital punishment; as prime minister he stopped Tony Abbott from trying to restrict abortion rights; and he said he would have voted against Menzies' 1951 effort to ban the Communist Party.[27] Howard's rejection of the Bill of Rights arose not just from political philosophy but from his social philosophy. He believed the premium on individual rights had reached a tipping point—more rights without responsibility had become a social disaster.

In championing the idea of 'mutual obligation' Howard said welfare payments should be conditional. This was first implemented via the Work for the Dole scheme, reflecting Howard's view that welfare recipients had obligations to the society whose taxpayers funded their welfare. The mid-2000 report by Patrick McClure, head of Mission Australia, found that nearly 900 000 children lived in jobless households—triggering a debate about the welfare-to-work transition and mutual obligation. Aware of the risky politics, Howard moved only with caution. But the 2005 Budget, the first of Howard's final term, saw a sharper test applied to benefits for single parents and the disability support pension (which had become a welfare alternative to the dole).

While Howard's welfare policy reform was modest, there is no gain-saying the impact he left. Asked about Howard's legacy for indigenous policy, Noel Pearson had not the slightest doubt. 'It is the idea of responsibility,' Pearson said. 'Howard's legacy lies in asking people to take greater responsibility for their lives.'[28] The idea had universal application.

This is the single most important legacy of Howard's social conservatism. It was a political, intellectual and moral attack on the failure of progressive policies and it recognised the limits of the centralised and passive welfare state. It will be unwound by the Rudd government only at its peril. As Latham realised, this was an old-fashioned Labor position. It is why the idea appealed to working people. 'We should reclaim the responsibility agenda,' Latham bemoaned before becoming ALP leader. Howard was sounding like Curtin and Chifley, Labor leaders who, in Latham's words, believed 'that people are responsible for their own behaviour'.[29]

The financial fortress of Howard's social conservatism, however, was located elsewhere: in his support for families. Howard made the family support pledge in the 1996 election policy; it was implemented in the first Budget and it was extended in the 2000 GST package under Family Tax Benefits A and B. When Howard discusses these achievements his voice rings, his arms wave in the air and his body language radiates pride.

Family support embodied two of Howard's core values. The first was his unyielding support to assist families with dependent children. Family Tax Benefit A, subject to a means test, was designed to target poverty, cushion the escalating costs of raising children and operate as a low-income supplement. It was a child tax credit. At the end of the Howard era, Peter Davidson, a senior analyst from community services agency ACOSS, said this system offered 'a higher level of in-work support for low-paid working families than in any other OECD country'.[30]

The second value was Howard's conviction that single-income families were disadvantaged by the tax system compared with two-income families and deserved special assistance. He held this belief throughout his political career but struggled to find a delivery mechanism before settling on Family Tax Benefit B. Howard argued that this assisted choice by helping one parent to care for children at home—in effect, giving a tax break to such families. This benefit had no means test on the primary earner. It reflected a social value that transcended means testing.[31]

By Howard's final Budget the scale of family support was huge, worth $29.7 billion in 2007–08, more than the Defence budget. It testified to Howard's priorities. It rose with the strong surpluses from 2003 onwards. By 2007 a single-income couple on an average wage with two dependent children paid no net tax until a threshold of $50 813, while a dual-income couple with two dependent children, one partner on an average wage and the other on two-thirds of the average wage, paid no net tax until a threshold of $54 820.[32] Research conducted by the National Centre for Social and Economic Modelling (NATSEM) showing the huge financial burden represented by children offered strong support for Howard's commitment.

This monument to Howard's social vision provoked an assault from the Left and Right, the social progressives and pro-market economists. The progressives led by feminists damned his bias towards stay-at-home mothers. Keating's former adviser, Anne Summers, said the effect of Howard's policies was to 'entice or coerce women from employment' with the consequence of 'increasing their vulnerability and reducing their future options'.[33] The economic liberals, led by the Centre for Independent Studies (CIS), attacked Howard for preferring family cash payments to lower income tax rates. Peter Saunders from the CIS painted Howard as a welfare state czar—where nine out of ten families with children received family payments and one in six Australians of working age was relying almost totally on welfare benefits. 'In the last 40 years real incomes have doubled,' Saunders said. 'The expansion of the welfare state has therefore occurred at precisely the time when the need for government support has been falling away.'[34] Howard was unmoved. His social ideology was not for turning. The longer he stayed, the greater the family support became.

In 2006 Howard launched an aggressive defence of his social ideology. 'Menzies knew the Liberal Party would never survive as a sectional party, an elitist party or a party of privilege,' he said.

> A healthy set of books is a necessary condition of good government. It is not, however, a sufficient condition for a good society. And a taxation system that fails to recognise the costs of raising children—that adopts an antiseptic, economically neutral view of the responsibility carried by Australian parents—is a taxation system without a social vision. My government places the low- and middle-income families of Australia squarely in the foreground of our policy lens. That is how we said we would govern. That is how we have governed. That is how we will continue to govern.[35]

He was just warming up. Over the years Howard had accepted invitations from CIS chief Greg Lindsay to attend the think tank's annual retreat at Coolum, where he would enjoy the sunshine and mix with the nation's free market purists. Now he attacked such friends, slamming the claim by the pro-market Right that such payments were 'middle-class welfare'. 'They are nothing of the kind,' Howard lectured. 'They are tax relief for a universal reality—that it costs money to raise children.' Howard said: 'Australians have always believed in something more than Adam Smith's night-watchman state.' Was Australia a nanny state? 'Definitely not,' he boomed in answer to his own question. It was a caring and prudent state.

Howard boasted that Treasury analysis showed almost 40 per cent of all families now received more in cash benefits than they paid in tax.[36] This surely prompts the question: how did Howard ever lose office? The answer is that most families did not think or live according to such analysis.

At this point in his Menzies lecture Howard turned to savage the Left. The Labor Party, he declared, was 'vicious' in opposing his support for single-income families. Howard argued that Labor's pledge to means test Family Tax Benefit B was because Labor hated stay-at-home mothers and deployed equity arguments to pursue a social ideology. He said: 'In government Labor would have a much tighter income test which would affect tens of thousands of single-income Australian families who could by no stretch of the imagination be described as rich.' Labor was agog at Howard's fixation when he attacked its proposed income test at a $250 000 threshold. For Howard, it was the thin end of a wedge to destroy this benefit.[37]

For Max Moore-Wilton, the benefits were too much. 'A number of us felt the locking-in of the middle class went too far,' he said. 'The Prime Minister was very conscious of the stress on families. This was a matter of judgement. What were the policy objectives you were trying to achieve? A number of us couldn't see the policy objectives.'[38]

Occasionally there were divisions within the Left over its hostility towards Howard's social conservatism. Academic David McKnight, in his book *Beyond Left and Right*, argued that 'protecting the family from the inroads of the market should now be seen as a vital progressive cause'. Criticising feminists and the Left for damning the phrase 'family values', McKnight said their historic folly was to cede this political territory to Howard, allowing conservatives to speak for the millions of people worried about the market undermining the family.[39]

For Howard, family support and good economics went together. 'The family is the greatest social welfare system mankind has ever devised,' he said. While rejecting the notion that good government made happy families, Howard argued that bad government policy did weaken families. Interviewed in 2009 for this book, Howard insisted: 'Let me tell you, it is not middle-class welfare to help people to bring up children.'[40]

Howard's biographer, Sex Discrimination Commissioner Pru Goward, reports that, when she was pregnant, 'I never heard him say to me "You should be home with the kids."' She insists Howard was never prescriptive with women: 'For God's sake, half his staff were women.'[41]

Yet Howard's rejection of paid maternity leave stands as a monument to his refusal to adapt his social conservatism to women at work. The irony is that Howard was handed an opportunity by Goward, who used her office to launch a campaign for taxpayer-funded paid maternity leave. Goward argued that maternity leave was 'mainstream', a proposition Howard could buy:

> I was a nice middle-class girl who had no idea that women were going back to work with two- and three-week-old babies. The demographics are that 90 per cent of women earn less than $50 000 and that 60 per cent of women got no paid maternity leave and the ones that did are the better-off. This was an argument for his battlers.

But she misjudged the Howard cabinet and was nearly broken by the battle. Her maternity leave blueprint report was seen as overt pressure, not how Howard's loyalists should behave:

> When I informed Tony Abbott's office the report was coming their reply suggested it would be dead within the day. When the report was released I was heartbroken. There was a campaign run against me. Abbott said 'Not over my dead body.' I did not have a supporter within the cabinet. I think Howard started off believing it was a good idea but was persuaded it was a political dog.[42]

The initial resistance was cost. Then Goward was told 'It's not fair because it doesn't apply to women who don't work.' This was the real obstacle. 'They saw it as an extra benefit for women who worked,' Goward said. 'That was the problem. When I left as commissioner there was no exchange with John Howard. The relationship had finished at that point. Since then he has been very polite with me.'[43]

The cabinet embraced instead a maternity allowance, known as the baby bonus, a generous lump sum worth $3000 in 2004 and rising to $5000 from 2008, paid to all mothers without discrimination between mothers at work or at home. It was a declaration of Howard government ideology—no special arrangement for working women. Howard said:

> I accept total responsibility for this decision. I looked at this carefully—and Peter Costello had the same view. We both felt the solution was to have a large non-means tested baby bonus, roughly equivalent to 12 or 14 weeks' paid maternity leave. We weren't going to discriminate between women. Once you talk about paid maternity leave as the principal vehicle for helping women how do you accommodate different situations, for example, the situation of a woman who, when she has her first child, decides to drop out of the workforce? How do you accommodate that? Our decision had strong support around the cabinet table.[44]

The baby bonus was decoupled from employment. By contrast, paid maternity leave integrated employment with provision for children. It allowed women to retain their jobs while recognising their need to care for babies and signalled that this was a normal expectation of community and government. In 2008 the Productivity Commission released a report supporting the type of program advanced by Goward.[45]

For Goward, the decision was a 'huge political mistake'. She said: 'It explains a lot about why Maxine McKew won in Bennelong. In the eyes of working families Mr Howard did not reflect their values. Women took this very personally. The sentiment was that "we want to be recognised as respectable families".' As for Costello, Goward said he had a golden opportunity to highlight the generation shift but she found him 'missing in action'.[46]

The ideology of 'choice' was the third arm of Howard's conservatism. He loved the word, its appeal and its illusions. Long a Liberal Party concept, choice was resurrected by Howard and implemented with a spending surge for private schools and private health insurance, ideas close to his heart. The concept of choice arose from a seminal event in his own life that long predated his conversion to economic liberalism.

In the early 1960s, a dozen years before he entered parliament, a young Howard first spoke out on his party's future—making the historic call for state aid to private schools. Howard chaired the New South Wales Education Policy Committee when it advocated direct assistance to private schools. The Protestant resistance was strong; even Howard's mother was unsympathetic.

This leap became Menzies' masterstroke at the 1963 election and Howard, unlike many others, took the leap with him. He said that John Carrick, 'more than anybody in the Liberal Party I have met, understood the significance of unlocking the upwardly mobile Catholic vote'.[47]

For Howard, it was a turning point in Liberal history. At this stage there were very few Catholics as Liberal MPs. Carrick had initiated a dialogue with the New South Wales Catholic bishop, Eris O'Brien, who told him the Christian denominations were 'too remote from each other', a message Carrick never forgot. As he pushed the issue, Carrick realised that 'we had no idea of the plight of the Catholic schools'.[48] Howard saw there were 'half a million middle-class Catholics voting Labor and shunning the Liberal Party when it was their natural home'.[49]

For Menzies, this decision secured a voter realignment that lasted half a century. Few events are more important in shaping Howard's view of politics. The Liberal Party, once manifestly anti-Catholic, eventually became a refuge for Catholics fleeing Labor. When Howard sat in cabinet as prime minister, he was surrounded by Catholics—including Abbott, Andrews, Alston, Vaile, Turnbull, Nelson, Hockey, Coonan and McGauran (at one stage eight out of eighteen cabinet ministers), living proof of a social and political revolution.[50]

Howard saw choice as a basic conservative value and an electoral weapon. He grasped that Labor, with its collectivist mentality, distrusted the concept. 'Choice has an intrinsic value in a free society,' Howard said. 'It is the golden thread that connects all our party's policies—from private health insurance rebate, to funding for schools, to workplace relations, to giving families choice about the work and family arrangements they desire.'[51] On Sydney's North Shore, Howard's spiritual home, this was a way of life.

The icons of Howard's 'choice' were private schools and private health insurance and he smashed Labor on both fronts by sheer financial weight. The ALP detested his private health insurance rebate but decided to submit and to bury its principles. The 30 per cent rebate was part of a broader set of policies that saw the proportion of people with private insurance rise from 30 to 44 per cent.[52] By the time Howard lost office, more than 9.3 million Australians had private insurance and the cost of the rebate was about $3.5 billion annually. The ideology of choice had been recruited to the needs of private health. Prominent economist Ian Harper justified the policy, arguing that without the rebate total health spending would be higher, given extra demands on public hospitals.[53]

On schools policy, by contrast, an emotional ALP was compelled to war. At the 2004 election, in one of the purer ideological contests of the Howard era, Latham invoked equity to demand a redistribution from private to public schools. Not only did Latham lose but his policy was interpreted as a failure of ideas—Latham's appeal to class resentment succumbed to Howard's pitch to aspirational choice. Behind such labels the vested interests were huge.

While Howard lifted funding to public schools he backed private schools more generously, shifting the funding proportions in their favour. He criticised public schools for becoming 'too politically correct and too values-neutral'. In addition, Howard applied a new funding model for private schools, abandoning measures of their private income from fees in a needs formula and using instead the socioeconomic status of students via postcodes (the SES model).

Under Howard, total public spending per student (state and federal) was $10 715 for government schools and $6054 for private schools. But the national government's portion of funding for public schools fell from 42 to 32 per cent during the Howard era.[54] Parents voted with their feet—the shift to private schools reached one in three nationally. On Sydney's North Shore more than half of all students were private.

Howard reversed Labor's opposition to new private schools and saw this as 'enfranchising a whole group of people never able to send their children to an independent school'.[55] In 2004 Howard boasted 'that more than 300 new independent schools have opened in Australia since we came to office'.[56] While Howard's critics blamed him for the shift to private schools, this was reality denial: the evidence showed it was driven by values.

One of the electoral aims was to gather Catholic votes. In 2003 Education Minister Brendan Nelson had to negotiate the entry of the Catholic school system into the SES funding model. Before Nelson met the head of the Catholic Church, Cardinal Pell, Howard instructed him: 'Don't create any problems for us with the Catholic schools.' It was a directive with forty years of history.[57] In 2004 when the Catholic system entered the SES, Howard invoked Menzies for the 'great breakthrough' in private school funding, attacking the critics of school choice, and applauded private education with its belief in 'spiritual and religious values'.[58]

Howard's philosophy had a financial justification: if people enjoying private schools and private health returned to the public sector the strain on government finances would be greater. Howard believed that universal service provision by the state without strong private-sector contributions was an inferior model. In electoral terms the ideology of choice worked for Howard—it lifted his profile in health and education, keeping Labor under pressure on the issues that it owned.

From the pro-market Right, again spearheaded by the CIS, came an accusation made to hurt: that Howard had created the monster of 'big government conservatism'. For CIS analyst Andrew Norton, the contradiction was between Howard's nominal support for small government and his privileging pro-Liberal social institutions, private schools and private health, with a spending agenda that would make a Labor government proud.[59]

As usual, Howard was unmoved. But consultant Henry Ergas sprang to Howard's defence and argued that his ideology of choice was an economic reform in its own right. For Ergas, Howard was promoting genuine competition between public and private school and health systems. 'There was in the Howard years a transformation that offered consumers greater choice and ultimately greater control,' he said. Ergas predicted it would prove difficult for Labor to dismantle.[60]

The final arm of Howard's social conservatism, and the most ideologically provocative, was his claim on the classless society—or, put another way, seizing egalitarianism for the Liberal Party. Brazen in this task, Howard depicted himself as the battler's PM in a fashion redolent of Billy Hughes with the Digger. 'The average Australian believes in a classless

society,' he argued, meaning it not in a Marxist sense but as a social sentiment.[61] Yet Howard had various formulas on class, saying on other occasions that in Australia 'everyone wants to be middle class'.[62]

It is no surprise that he enshrined the battler. In the Fraser government,
Howard was occasionally patronised for his lower social background.[63]
His speechwriter, Christopher Pearson, said Howard had severed the link
between Liberal prime ministers and the Melbourne Club.[64] Without
origins in big business or the land, it is unsurprising that he developed
closer ties with ordinary people. Neither John nor Janette had any traces
of a high Anglo–Australian accent and from the moment they opened
their mouths their middle Australia location was obvious.

Basic to this outlook was Howard's commitment to a highly redistributive state. To be precise, he sought a fusion between a competitive
economy geared to the globalised age and a state pledged to redistribution to maintain egalitarianism. When the Rudd government received the
Treasury's 2008 preliminary paper on Australia's tax-transfer system it was
told Howard had presided over a 'highly re-distributive' arrangement.[65]
Treasury chief Ken Henry labelled the Australian system 'extraordinarily
progressive'. The 2006 Warburton–Hendy tax review, reliant on Treasury
analysis, found that Australia's redistributive system was the second most
progressive among ten OECD nations.[66]

Professor Ann Harding, Director of the National Centre for Social
and Economic Modelling (NATSEM), concluded in 2005 (analysing the
first half of the Howard era) that the top 40 per cent of earners were
supporting the bottom 60 per cent and, in particular the bottom 40 per
cent due to Howard's redistribution. Summarising her NATSEM work,
Harding said:

> We believe that the distribution of final income over the period
> from the mid-1990s to 2001–02 remained much the same. That
> is, we don't believe that Australia became more unequal … There
> is strong growth at the bottom—the bottom hasn't been left
> out. Our welfare state has been very successful at re-distributing
> income from the rich to the poor. The transfers involved are
> substantial.[67]

These conclusions were modified in the latter Howard period.
NATSEM research found that, due to ongoing strong growth in private incomes and tax cuts at the top, there was an increase in the national income
flowing to the top 10 per cent of Australians in the decade to 2005–06. But

this did not gainsay the highly redistributive nature of the Australian state. The redistribution to the bottom 20 per cent remained huge.[68]

Former OECD analyst Professor Peter Whiteford analysed welfare spending and concluded:

> Even though Australia spends less than the OECD average on social security benefits, the formula for distributing benefits is so progressive—and the level of taxes paid by the poor is so low—that Australia appears to redistribute more to the poorest 20 per cent of the population than any other OECD country.[69]

In a range of more recent studies NATSEM identified a series of redistributions: from childless households to households with children; across the life-cycle from younger people without children to older retired people; in income terms the redistribution was pronounced from the top 20 per cent to the bottom 60 per cent; but the largest gainers from redistribution were aged people and sole parents, not mainstream families. Indeed, NATSEM's research found that couples with children were essentially holding their own, with their benefits being offset by their taxes—strong evidence that showed the need for Howard's family support payments.[70]

The political implication is obvious—the most contentious aspect of Howard's redistribution was not to battler families (so-called middle-class welfare) but to the aged, the over-55s on whose votes he depended so much. Towards the end of Howard's era Grey Power become the big sleeper issue.

Interviewed in retirement, Howard said: 'I followed this issue of redistribution closely. I was proud of those quintiles showing people in the low income brackets were doing so well under us. It was a deliberate policy of my government.'[71] But Howard stressed that he had always had two overriding objectives: to encourage people to be successful and to look after the less well-off. It was in pursuit of his first objective that Howard halved the capital gains tax and abolished end taxes on superannuation payouts, both regressive steps.

Most of this structure of redistribution was not Howard's creation; it came from past governments—in particular, from Hawke and Keating. It mirrored the Australian practice of a means-tested welfare system, an idea that won its greatest momentum in the previous Labor era. The strategy of a targeted welfare state to complement a deregulated economy was the heart of Hawke–Keating policy. Their purpose was to keep public support for their pro-market economics by distributing the benefits. While Howard relaxed some of the means tests, he kept this a broad, bipartisan Australian strategy.

The pivotal aspect of Howard's equity profile, however, is that he created so many jobs. This is the most vital and yet unremarked aspect of his commitment to the fair go. It is Howard's job creation record that guarantees his government will be seen as a supporter of egalitarianism. Howard, in effect, flew a new banner telling Liberals to become the party of both deregulation and equity—or, in Howard's terms, of economic liberalism and social conservatism.

The 'mainstream mob' and Howard delivered for each other over a decade. Eventually the model collapsed. Howard left a complex and contradictory edifice of social conservatism, both a gift and a burden for his successors.

22

WORKPLACE DEREGULATION:
THE FINAL CRUSADE

If they want war, we'll have the full symphony.
—Bill Kelty in 1996 on the Howard government

The Howard government dreamt of the most formidable assault on industrial orthodoxy and trade union power in Australia's history—but was mostly checked by the Senate and Howard's instinct for caution. For Howard, deregulation of the workplace was his deepest economic faith. This cast him as a political radical. The campaign against union power to achieve a more productive Australia was integral to John Howard's character.

In eleven years Howard introduced two reforms of the system—the Reith/Kernot 1996 compromise and the full bodied 2005 *WorkChoices* package. In retirement he is unrepentant. Anybody who thinks Howard anguishes in private about the folly of *WorkChoices* misreads him. Leaders such as Howard and Keating do not disown the ideas that have governed their careers.

'I wasn't going to dingo out,' Howard said of his *WorkChoices* decision. 'I actually believed in it. I was determined to do IR reform. I had always thought that further industrial relations reform was critical.'[1] This is the answer to one of the strangest questions posed in politics: why did Howard risk his government in 2007 on the *WorkChoices* package? The answer is that it sprang from conviction. Howard broke from the Liberal tradition of Menzies and Fraser that accepted the workplace status quo.

Howard always felt Labor was trapped on the wrong side of history, defending an obsolete industrial system. He had plenty of encouragement—his economic advisers in the Treasury, along with big and small business, backed labour market deregulation. Howard's judgement was that Australia was moving towards a less class conscious, shareholding society where collective power was less relevant. By and large, these were sound judgements.

For Howard, workplace reform had two epic results that provided its political and moral justification.

The first was jobs, jobs, jobs. Labour market deregulation was integral to the Howard government's economic model and its effort to create a more dynamic growth economy. The Treasury told Howard and Costello it would create activity and jobs. Before Howard came to power Ted Evans warned, in a comment that became famous, that 'for the nation as a whole the level of unemployment is a matter of choice'.[2] It was a strike at the dishonesty and hypocrisy of the jobs debate, the refusal of politicians to implement policy to create jobs and the media's reluctance to hold them to account. Evans said unemployment was not mainly an economic question but a political one. He warned that society was 'not prepared to contemplate the issues that are involved in increasing the growth rate'—and he meant economic reforms, including a more flexible labour market.[3]

Howard came to end this hypocrisy. He was proud of his 1980s role in converting the Liberal Party to labour-market deregulation. This transition was one of the most important in Liberal history. Over eleven years Howard saw unemployment fall from just under 9 per cent to 4.2 per cent due to a sustained growth economy. This reflected a political priority for job creation, with labour-market reform integral to the strategy. Costello said: 'One of the decisive things about our fourth term is that we set ourselves the goal of full employment. That had been out of Australia's lingo since the Chifley and Menzies days.'[4] This is what *WorkChoices* was about—a full employment economy.

In retirement, Howard argues the policy's merits, pointing to hefty job creation after the introduction of *WorkChoices*. 'It contributed to the accelerated decline in unemployment that occurred,' Howard said.[5] In the eighteen months *WorkChoices* operated about 500 000 jobs were created and the new laws played some role in this.

His second justification was winding back trade union privileges. This was probably Howard's objective from the time he pumped petrol as a kid. He had never made any secret of it. 'I certainly saw this as finally removing the privileged position of the trade union movement,' Howard said of *WorkChoices*. 'Of course, it's a huge thing, I thought wholly legitimate as a civic goal. I don't think any section of the community should have a privileged position.'[6]

Union leaders knew this was an elemental struggle for power. 'The thing about Howard is that he hates unions,' Bill Kelty said. 'He inherited an industrial system that was working. He didn't have to do much to it.'[7]

This highlights the extent of Howard's project: he sought to impose a Liberal Party model on the workplace. In effect, he was raiding the inner sanctum of the Labor Party and trade unions, an act of audacity rare in political history. It was an assault on the privileges and legitimacy of the labour movement, the aim being to diminish forever the power of the trade unions. The union retaliation was fierce and unrelenting.

WorkChoices, however, opened another window on Australia's future—onto the landscape of nationalism. It proposed a national industrial system for about 80 per cent of employees based on the corporations power of the Constitution. For Howard, this was the fatal blow to state industrial systems he had come to loathe. The High Court's 2006 decision upholding the validity of his *WorkChoices* law against the challenge by state governments became one of his defining achievements as prime minister. It was the most important consolidation of Commonwealth constitutional authority at the expense of the states in Howard's era. Finance Minister Nick Minchin said of the High Court decision: 'I'll never forget that day in cabinet when John Howard was passed a note saying the High Court had defeated the challenge. He almost leapt from his chair. I had never seen him so excited.'[8]

For Howard, faith in labour-market reform came from his family origins, his experience during the 1970s as Business and Consumer Affairs Minister dealing with unions, and his views about the internationalisation of Australia's economy from the 1980s. Costello, a barrister in the famous Dollar Sweets industrial case, was a tougher and purer advocate of deregulation than Howard. One of the four founders of the HR Nicholls Society, Costello was usually to Howard's right when the subject was debated in cabinet. Industrial Relations Minister Peter Reith was a formidable apostle for the cause. His successors, Tony Abbott and Kevin Andrews, carried the torch. The Liberal Party conversion was comprehensive.

In May 2005 Howard met ACTU chief Greg Combet in Howard's Sydney office to review the planned *WorkChoices* reforms. Combet had requested the meeting to seek to modify Howard's stance. 'I was genuinely concerned about how far they would go,' Combet said. 'I was coming to realise they were going the whole hog and would try to put the award safety net on the conveyor belt to extinction.' It was a private meeting between reasonable men conducted in a cordial fashion. And it was a dialogue of the deaf.

Combet said: 'Howard put a bit of time into it. He was across the detail. He knew from an ideological and principle position what he wanted to achieve and we basically couldn't agree on anything. I just felt he had an entrenched ideological position.'[9] Howard said: 'Most of the discussion revolved around his idea that if a majority of people in a workplace voted in favour of a collective agreement then that collective agreement should bind the minority. I said, "I can't possibly agree to that."'[10]

The deadlock was built on a decade of political dispute. Howard knew that it takes time to change a culture. He knew that industrial relations was the point of fiercest defence of the old Australian Settlement edifice. The unions were weakened in 1996 when Howard came to power. But they regrouped over time to secure an uneasy stalemate. It was in Howard's fourth term that *WorkChoices* gave the unions a fresh opportunity. Spearheaded by Combet, they staged one of the most brilliant campaigns in Australia's history to inflict a crushing defeat on Howard in a significant contribution to his 2007 election loss.

The upshot is that Howard's industrial legacy is equivocal. His final crusade became a bridge too far. It meant that the Rudd government won the opportunity to define Australia's industrial model for the new century. In the end Howard was broken at his ideological essence. This was an abject defeat with consequences likely to be far-reaching. The extent of labour-market re-regulation proposed by Rudd and Julia Gillard seemed to be formidable.

The important lesson from Howard's 2007 failure lies in his mis-judgement of the trade union movement and the public's mood. Combet said: 'It was a point of no return for us had Howard won.'[11] While Howard was implementing a reform, Combet was fighting for survival. Howard conceded later that his weakening of the 'no disadvantage' test—opening the way for an erosion in employment conditions and pay—was a mistake.[12]

The point is that genuine workplace reform requires a change in political culture to be accepted. Howard got his new policy but he did not convince the public. It was the gulf between policy and culture that left him in ruins. The problem, long recognised by Howard, was that reform was seen as un-Australian for violating the 'fair go'. This was the origin of the powerful coalition against workplace reform that involved unions, the ALP, welfare groups, media, churches, celebrities and community leaders.

It went to values; they believed that the values in *WorkChoices* violated the egalitarian ethic.

Evans, with unforgiving candour, had long before put the equity case—reform might widen the wages distribution but it would create more jobs and 'a major source of inequity in a modern society is the inability to obtain employment'. Of course, this argument was more powerful in 1996, when unemployment was nearly 9 per cent, than it was a decade later, when it had been halved. In 2007, however, Australia's public rejected Howard's stance that fairness could be effected by wage flexibility plus jobs, a decisive judgement.[13]

Howard's related difficulty was that, for all his talk about the classless society, his law was based on a transfer of power to employers.

The justification for Howard's bill began with Menzies. Political scientist Judith Brett explained that Menzies' use of the notion of Forgotten People was an appeal to middle-class morality based on the values of the home as opposed to the workplace where Labor values were dominant. Howard genuflected before the Menzian dictum that 'we don't have classes here like in England'.[14] Howard, like Menzies, saw the Liberal Party as drawing support from all strata of society.

Yet, unlike Menzies, Howard sought to transform the workplace to give effect to this Liberal philosophy—to undermine class so the workplace, as well as the home, could become a source of Liberal values. No Liberal PM before Howard had conceived of such a vision.

Howard's aim was more dynamic and radical than Menzies' framework of a protected economy and a middle-class home-maker morality. Howard strove for a more entrepreneurial outlook tied to the death of class consciousness. Indeed, he was obsessed with this idea. On the eve of becoming prime minister, Howard declared that 'the greatest thing about this country is still its essential classless mobility'.[15] In his 1995 first headland speech Howard wanted to realise 'the great Australian inheritance of a classless society'. Several years later he tried to insert 'mateship' into the constitutional preamble. Howard would often say that Australians valued the 'classless' society. It pointed to one of his most ambitious aspirations: to strike at Labor's originating mission and institutional foundations.

While Marx's predictions had been disproved, Marx's ideas had not died—the workplace was still a study in class power. And Howard was aiding one side of the class divide. It was a contradiction he failed to resolve.

From Howard's 1996 victory a showdown with the unions seemed assured. During the campaign, Kelty had issued a declaration: 'If they

want to fight, if they want war, we'll have the full symphony—with all
the pieces, all the clashes, all the music.'[16] It was classic phoney tough.
But it exposed a movement sliding towards crisis. The unions, hostile
to Howard yet disillusioned with the Accord, faced a new PM with a
popular mandate to introduce more employer–employee bargaining with
reduced trade union powers. The Howard–Reith 1996 policy was still
substantial reform.

Neither the unions nor the Labor Party had the slightest interest in
conceding Howard's election mandate. From its inception, it was a battle
for survival. The loathing of Howard was tangible, the contest visceral.
The trade unions felt that if they did not destroy Howard's government
then he would probably destroy them.

The thirteen-year-old Accord between the Labor government
and the ACTU was terminated with the federal election that brought
the Liberal Party to power. The ACTU was in trauma—it had lost its
government and its seat at the cabinet table. The Accord had concealed
the decline of union authority and grassroots coverage. Within days of his
win Howard said the people had voted 'in the full knowledge that we are
going to make changes to the industrial relations system [and] it will be
one of our very top priorities'.[17]

Kelty quit the Reserve Bank board to begin a campaign with threatening overtones. The ACTU vowed to fight with the Maritime Union
of Australia in any showdown on the waterfront. With Howard's first
Budget, the ACTU launched an assault on the government's economic
policies. The unions had no strategy to deal with a successful Coalition
government.

Aware that he lacked a Senate majority, Howard needed an approach
that was formidable but pragmatic. Peter Reith, a born intimidator with
a friendly smile, was made for this assignment. 'My view about politics
is that your future is always in your own hands,' Reith said.[18] Reith
was Howard's first and best Workplace Relations minister. Combet said
Reith was 'smart, he was bullying, dogged and aggressive, you didn't
want to be shy'.[19]

Reith and Howard had bonded. Reith was the sort of politician
Howard loved—he would fight for his beliefs and take responsibility for
his mistakes. Always a Howard supporter, Reith had an ease with Howard
that Costello would never enjoy. 'Howard and I got on like a house on
fire,' Reith later reminisced. 'We nearly always agreed.'[20] Reith's reform
credentials were almost unrivalled. As the shadow treasurer for *Fightback!*
he had a killer instinct that ran to serial dimensions.

A pragmatist, Reith saw that the era of 'big bang' reformism was over; he now dressed for moderation and negotiation. Reith's 1996 election policy kept the award system and had a 'no losers' pledge. 'Howard and I were at one on this,' Reith said. In particular, Reith devised a new 'no disadvantage' test—that no worker would lose pay in his deregulatory reforms. This came at Howard's insistence with his eye on the 1996 election.[21] For the first three terms Howard's 1996 pledge informed his workplace tactics. Without the Senate, his hand was contained. His agenda was evolutionary, with one exception—the 1998 confrontation on the waterfront.

Reith introduced the *Workplace Relations Act* in May 1996 after a herculean drafting feat. Its philosophy was to give 'primary responsibility for industrial relations and agreement-making to employees and employers at the enterprise and workplace levels' and reduce the award system to 'a safety net of minimum wages and conditions'.[22] A parliamentary analysis said: 'There is little in the Bill which should take observers by surprise and, accordingly, the government can feel relatively comfortable in arguing its mandate to press ahead with the changes it has planned. On the other hand, the breadth of the changes involves significant departures from the traditional arbitral model which has been supported by both sides of politics in government for the better part of this century.'[23]

Introducing his bill, Reith said the turning point in the intellectual debate had been Keating's 1993 speech to the Institute of Directors calling for a new model of industrial relations based on enterprise bargaining with arbitrated wage rises relegated to safety net status. Reith came to inject red blood into Keating's model. He praised Keating in order to damn him. For Reith, Labor's failure was its inability to cross the bridge from collective to individual rights. He saw Labor as 'torn between its nominal embrace of reform and its political dependence upon the unions'.[24]

The economic legitimacy for this bill was irrefutable—it lay in Australia's atrocious high unemployment and weak real wages. Unemployment in the fifth year of recovery was still 8.9 per cent and 27.8 per cent for youths. For Howard, Costello, Reith, the Treasury and the Reserve Bank a reformed labour market would lead to higher productivity, more jobs and higher real wages. Reith argued that the United Kingdom and New Zealand had moved beyond Australia towards a decentralised industrial system.

'Australian farmers produce some of the cheapest high-quality beef in the world,' he said. 'A steer at the farm gate costs 60 per cent of the cost of an equivalent beast in the United States. But by the time it gets to Tokyo it actually costs more, and the main reason for this is because in the meantime it's been through an Australian meatworks and an Australian port.'[25] He had a litany of examples.

The role of the Australian Industrial Relations Commission (AIRC) would be limited to safety net decisions. New awards would be simplified and restricted to a specified number of matters.

The heart of the policy lay in employee–employer agreements. First, there would be enterprise agreements on a collective basis with or without unions. Second, individual statutory contracts called Australian Workplace Agreements (AWAs) would be introduced, to be negotiated directly between employers and employees.

Reith said the aim was choice without discrimination 'in favour of one form of agreement over another'. There was teeth in the 'no losers' election pledge and pay rates under any new agreement had to be 'no less than prescribed under the relevant award'. There were new measures to end union monopolies, limit the right to strike and strengthen the secondary boycott provisions by returning them to the *Trade Practices Act*. A new unfair dismissal scheme would reduce pressure on small business.

Reith's pragmatism was revealed during the cabinet debate when he was defeated on one vital aspect: the cabinet preferred an 'all or nothing' approach and knocked out his option for non-union collective agreements. It was an effort to force the more radical AWA agenda. For Reith, this was a blunder. He felt it was essential to offer a full variety of options in the shift to an enterprise culture. Usually depicted as an ideologue, Reith was a pragmatist. He wanted this decision softened and he lobbied Howard and other ministers on an individual basis. He got the issue re-submitted to cabinet and had his original view endorsed.

The trade unions were hostile and the Labor Party fought the bill. The severance of the ALP–ACTU Accord was an historic opportunity for Labor to redefine its relationship with the unions—but Labor declined to take this plunge. It would march with the unions for a decade through to the 2007 poll. Kim Beazley's tactic was to regain the Labor base vote lost at the 1996 election. It was a safety-first approach that meant backing the unions.

Combet dismissed those innocents who pretended this was a mild reform. Combet saw the AWAs as a new strategic beachhead in Australian politics. 'These were significant changes,' he said.

There's no doubt about that in my mind. Anything that introduces a statutory individual contract for the first time in the national system is a big thing. This is not just some iconic union movement view. Statutory individual contracts don't exist in other advanced economies as far as I am aware. It was an ideology driven by the mining industry to de-unionise and destroy collective bargaining. The whole thrust of the Liberal Party philosophy that started here and continued through to *WorkChoices* was to ensure that individual contracts became the legally dominant form of workplace agreement making.[26]

The evidence, however, is that Combet's analysis was exaggerated. The actions and rhetoric of the Howard government throughout its life reveal that it wanted to change the workplace by introducing AWAs but that it saw collective bargaining as the main instrument of agreement making. Indeed, there is no evidence to the contrary.

The Democrats industrial spokesman, Andrew Murray, said:

I felt the trade union opposition to AWAs was based on self-interest. The abiding feature of a statutory instrument is that it provides greater certainty, greater relevance and easier understanding than jurisprudence. Statute is a good thing. My view has been that providing individual statutory agreements are constructed in a fair environment and there is a strong regulator then an employee is often better off with an individual statutory agreement than you are with a common law individual agreement.[27]

It is a position that Labor rejected continuously, from Beazley in 1996 to Rudd in 2007.

The ACTU's opposition to AWAs was bitter and unabated. 'They were used to disadvantage people even though they had the award safety net under them,' Combet said of the 1996 model. 'It was impossible to police them and they were secret.' For Howard, the AWAs transcended economics—this was a political right in a modern democracy that purported to be free and civilised.

But the unions played into Howard's hands. Keating's defeat had left the unions with a taste for direct action. Determined to confront Howard over his economic policies, ACTU leaders helped to organise the 19 August 'Cavalcade to Canberra' demonstration. A crowd of about 10 000 unionists gathered in the main ACTU rally but a separate, more radical group of about 3000 Aboriginals, unionists and students came together on the forecourt directly in front of the building. As a confrontation began between police and Aboriginals, the crowd grew angry and became a mob.

Journalist Brad Norington described these events:

> Some used a delivery trolley and a flagpole to prise open the doors and gain access into the foyer. Others used a stanchion ripped from one of the doors as a battering ram to smash their way through a thick side window into the adjoining Parliament House bookshop which they ransacked and used as another access into the building. Altogether about 100 people broke through, running amok in the foyer until they were either arrested or forced outside by police reinforcements with helmets and shields. At least 40 people were taken into policy custody. When cleared, the entrance to Australia's place of representative democracy was a mess of blood and broken glass.[28]

The main rally continued some distance away, most people initially unaware of the violence, with speeches from Beazley, Jennie George, Lowitja O'Donoghue and Bob Brown. George said the perpetrators of the riot came from 'outside the mainstream rally' but it was later confirmed that several officials from one of the Australia's largest unions, the CFMEU, had been involved.[29] Combet said years later that it did untold damage to the union movement and 'I am still angry about it'.[30]

George and Kelty had an appointment with Howard to seek concessions on the industrial bill. After inspecting the damage, Howard saw them briefly. Later he said the violence was 'un-Australian' and that 'never under any circumstances will my government buckle to threats of physical violence or behaviour of that kind'. The ACTU was in denial, angry with Howard's implication that it was responsible.[31] Aboriginal leader and ATSIC Commissioner Terry O'Shane said: 'I'm not proposing that we go to war but if they declare war on the workers then we'll declare war on them.'[32]

It was a template for the times—those groups privileged by Keating were struggling with their loss of access, filled with misplaced self-righteousness and denying Howard's legitimacy. The self-delusion of ACTU leaders thinking direct action might 'rattle the confidence' of Howard was staggering.[33] Howard said that these events 'will be greeted with revulsion by mainstream Australia', exploiting a divorce between union power and popular sentiment that he would manipulate until *WorkChoices*.

The bill's fate lay with the Senate. Given Labor's opposition, Reith needed the Australian Democrats for its passage. That made Democrats leader Cheryl Kernot a pivotal player. Kernot was campaigning against Howard's policy to privatise Telstra and was hostile to the Budget spending cuts. But she needed to differentiate the Democrats from Labor and wanted to project them as an economically responsible force. So Kernot decided the Democrats would amend but not defeat the industrial reforms.

Reith found Kernot to be sensible and pragmatic. 'She saw the process as a genuine discussion on the merits,' he said. 'That impressed me greatly.' Kernot said: 'It's a tribute to Peter that in all those talks he didn't come the heavy at all.' There were three Democrats involved—Kernot, Murray and John Cherry. 'Make no mistake,' Reith said. 'We got this bill because of Cheryl Kernot.'[34]

Reith salvaged about 70 per cent of his initial measures. The unions took a hit but it could have been worse. Murray, who did the technical work for the Democrats, said: 'We restored a much fairer balance between the rights of employers, employees and unions.' In a pivotal stand, the Democrats backed a system of AWAs tied to a non-disadvantage test. The AWAs, later to become a political bogy, were created on Coalition–Democrats votes.

Howard delegated the entire negotiation to Reith. Murray said: 'I found Reith to be intellectual and able, with a wide understanding of industrial law. While he held to an ideology he was not an ideological politician but practical. My staff found him to be unfailingly polite. When he phoned the office he would [do so] himself.'[35]

This bill saw the first critical decision of the Howard era on parliamentary strategy: to compromise with the Senate, not to confront it. It was an insight into Howard's judgement. He did not want to run the bill onto a double dissolution list.

Howard's survival, not just his program, would be threatened by the Senate during his first three terms. Despite sustained provocation, he kept his nerve and, on each occasion, chose to compromise. In 1996 Howard and Reith were united—they saw this decision as a no-brainer.

But Costello was the hawk. He was dismayed that the Australian Democrats would decide the extent of reform and that a hard-won mandate would be compromised. Costello argued his case in cabinet. He said: 'My view was that the government was fully entitled to insist on its policy. We had a mandate for it. We had campaigned for reform for years. We should stand by our bill and, if necessary, make it a double dissolution bill and an election issue. I actually thought this was our position.' When Costello said this publicly he was stunned that Howard convened an immediate doorstop to contradict him.[36]

For Howard and Reith, Costello was on another planet. When Reith was negotiating with Kernot she was furious at reports that Costello wanted a double dissolution election. 'Don't take any notice of him, Cheryl,' Reith told her dismissively.[37]

Psychology and politics told Howard to cut a deal. Having fought so long to become prime minister, Howard did not fancy dashing to a double dissolution election. 'Good judgement is to know when to settle and when to hold out for more,' he said. 'A double dissolution would have been very foolhardy. People would have thought: why is he doing this? We got enough out of the deal with Kernot.'[38]

Howard wanted to purge any lingering Hewson tag. 'One of the assets I brought to the leadership when I returned,' he said, 'was that, although I had a strong philosophical base, people didn't regard me as a radical or an extremist. There was a tinge of that attitude towards John Hewson.'[39] Howard was purging the last remnants of Hewson's brand. This was Howard the agent of stability—it was the image he craved. He believed it was the key to his 1996 victory and to being a leader for the long haul.

The speculation about Howard as an early-election-plotting Machiavellian occurred from one term to the next as predictably as a drum beat. The facts are that Howard never called an early poll, he never triggered a double dissolution when he had the grounds, he never had any interest in early elections—he felt the public disliked them.

The Treasury supported Howard's reform, arguing that Australia faced two structural problems—a deficiency of national savings and a rigid labour market. It predicted 'substantial' benefits from Reith's law.[40] Both Ian Macfarlane and Ted Evans gave their public support.

Macfarlane said Australia was doomed to high unemployment unless it reassessed its cultural outlook. He said that over the past six years Australia had been the third-fastest growing economy in the OECD after Ireland and Norway—yet its unemployment rate was still 8.7 per cent, higher than a range of nations with an inferior or equal growth performance, notably the United States (4.9 per cent), the United Kingdom (6.1 per cent) and New Zealand (6.4 per cent).

In order to combat unemployment Macfarlane said 'growth alone will not be the answer'. The key was the extent of workplace reform. A regulated IR system protected those in work at the expense of those without work. For Macfarlane, the issue was not whether Howard had gone too far but whether he had gone far enough. Referring to Howard's 1996 reforms, Macfarlane said that Australia's labour market flexibility was in the middle—better than the large European nations but inferior to the United States, United Kingdom and New Zealand. He lamented the quality of public debate, warning that many of Australia's attitudes towards fairness flowed from another age when the level of unemployment was 2–3 per cent. He said: 'While income inequality may not seem fair, unemployment is not very fair either.'[41]

Evans said labour market reform was 'crucial to achieving higher economic growth and high employment growth and to reducing unemployment' and he warned it would 'require changes in behaviour and attitudes'.[42] Evans said workplace reform was 'far more than an ideological' obsession. It was 'a practical response to what we know about how labour markets work'. For Evans, the onus should be on opponents of labour-market reform to justify their position. He said the correct policy was to pursue equity through the tax and welfare system, not by workplace regulation that lifted unemployment.[43]

These were unpopular arguments but they offered an insight into the public debate. Media coverage about inequity was driven by interest groups—the Labor Party, the ACTU, and welfare and church groups—that were hostile to reform. Individuals who benefited from reform because of better productivity or more jobs were voiceless—though Howard sought to empower them as his battlers. A decade later unemployment was just above 4 per cent, an outcome beyond the 1996 expectations. In reaching this goal it would be as wrong to exaggerate the role of workplace reform as it would be to deny its impact. Murray's conclusion is undeniable when he says the reform became a 'significant success' that enjoyed 'wide community acceptance'.[44]

Combet said of the 1996 reform: 'At the safety net level they constrained awards to 20 employment conditions. You'll note that this now is a position reflected in Forward with Fairness [Rudd's 2007 policy] in that awards will have ten conditions but in the legislated minimum there will be another ten conditions. Reith's law set the scene for that.'[45]

There were many critics. Mike Keating said Howard's reform was more about 'reducing the power of trade unions and did not really promote a productivity agenda'.[46] Dedicated to abolition of the Commission, the HR Nicholls Society was furious. Its guiding philosopher and Hugh Morgan's former adviser, Ray Evans, wrote: 'After nearly 18 months in office the Howard government has reached a low point in public esteem and self confidence. The principal cause of this slump is the complete failure of the government to move towards restoration of full employment. It would have been more honest and more accurate if he [Reith] had reported "Mission Abandoned".[47]

Reith replied:

> I think it would be fair to say that you did not want us to be a re-run of the Fraser government and we haven't been. I suppose it is more likely that you had hoped that we would be an instantaneous Thatcherite clone. Thatcher gave good government to the UK over 11 years but if you had compared her first two years with our first two years I reckon she was a slow starter.[48]

Despite their mutual tensions Beazley had tied Labor to the unions. His friend Tony Blair had taken the opposite path, distancing New Labour from the unions and lecturing that 'we have nothing to lose but our dogmas'. Beazley, however, was attached to dogmas. In mid-1998 Labor released an IR policy turning the clock back to the 1980s—it wanted restoration of the Commission's powers, abolition of all AWAs, strengthening of the award system and support for industry-wide agreements.[49]

Keating's former economic adviser, John Edwards, said:

> The Labor platform now marches back to the late eighties and early nineties. There is no reference in the policy document … to the goal of fostering enterprise bargaining as the predominant method of determining wages, an explicit goal of the Keating government. This return to the past comes at a time when around 40 per cent of the workforce is covered by enterprise bargains. The consequences of reverting to an arbitral system are so alarming and dangerous that Labor is unlikely to do it.[50]

Labor's retreat vindicated Howard's strategy—he was cast as the moderate reformer while Labor was defending the old order. For Howard, it was the perfect position.

23

AN INDEPENDENT BANK AND
THE DEATH OF INFLATION

Macfarlane wouldn't have done that.
—John Howard on Governor Glenn Stevens' interest rate
increase decision during the 2007 election campaign

The Howard government would thrive on the death of inflation—
this was an execution felt in every household and a welcome
bell at each election. No decision in the Howard years was more
pivotal than making the Reserve Bank independent in the cause of
low inflation. Ian Macfarlane's 1996 elevation as governor was the most
significant appointment made by the government in its eleven years. It
made Howard's reputation as a low-interest-rate prime minister.

Macfarlane was born and raised for this job. A bank veteran, smoother,
more worldly and better dressed than Bernie Fraser, Macfarlane was a
technician and a strategist. He inspired confidence in markets, politicians
and the media. Macfarlane had sound judgement of interest rates and a
good nose for politics—like Fraser he realised that bank independence
was a gift that had to be vindicated by the bank's own performance.
He served as governor for ten years and during this time Howard won
three elections, choosing in the 2004 poll to enshrine low interest rates
as the main proof of his political virtue. Little was said at the time that
Macfarlane, not Howard, set interest rates.

In 2006 Glenn Stevens was appointed governor as Macfarlane's
successor and faced more difficult global conditions. But relations
between the government and Stevens were not the same. The flashpoint
came in the middle of Howard's 2007 losing campaign when the Bank
raised interest rates, much to Howard's anger. The Finance Minister,
Nick Minchin, said: 'John Howard was absolutely enraged about the

Reserve Bank's decision to lift interest rates in the campaign. It had to be seen to be believed. Howard thought this was one of the greatest acts of treachery that had ever been committed. His attitude seemed to be "We've appointed all these people, don't they understand that?"[1]

Peter Costello said: 'There was no urgent reason that required a rate rise in November 2007.' But Costello, unlike Howard, felt that the focus on interest rates was a plus. 'It helped us. Every time we got the campaign onto economic management we went up,' he said.[2]

Howard conceded later that 'I'm a bit dirty on the Bank for doing that.' He said Stevens 'could easily have waited' until the next month after the poll and, unlike Costello, he believed the government had been hurt. He felt Stevens' mistake was to become trapped into thinking he must assert his independence. Howard said Stevens was 'quite different' from Macfarlane, more rigid and doctrinaire. 'I don't think he's worldly,' Howard said. Then he made the killer comment: 'Macfarlane wouldn't have done that.'[3]

These remarks herald a revolution in Australia's politics explicit in the rise of the Reserve Bank and its ability to make and break governments. This is new territory for Australia. The independence of the Bank was seeded by Keating and achieved by Howard and Costello—but Costello was more relaxed about independence than Howard.

Over the years Howard would grumble when Macfarlane raised rates but he knew the model was working—Macfarlane believed in early medicine for a long life. His purpose was to deny the next recession and, in a singular feat, it came neither on his ten-year watch nor on Howard's eleven-year watch. Macfarlane's skill at smoothing the growth curve helped to transform Sydney's skyline and keep Howard at Kirribilli. Macfarlane was free from reassessments that doomed the standing of former US central bank chief Alan Greenspan, once seen as 'master of the universe'.

Monetary policy cannot create wealth. Its task is to deliver stability by curbing potential booms and busts. Its task is to start the party but keep the punchbowl under control. The Bank's monetary management was directly responsible for the post-1991 growth cycle that ran throughout the Keating–Howard era. During this time the Bank successfully negotiated a series of lethal threats—the Asian financial crisis, the 2001 US recession and the domestic housing bubble, and, finally, it waged a long campaign (with limited fiscal policy support) to halt the inflationary surge provoked by the post-2003 terms-of-trade boom.

It was an impressive effort but not a perfect one. By global standards it was probably unrivalled. Howard's technique was to take credit when the Bank was cutting rates and blame the Bank when rates were being increased. The centrality of interest rates to his fortunes was manifest in the 2007 election loss that occurred amid rising inflation, higher interest rates and household price pressures as the Bank struggled to manage the resources boom.

Bank independence was Costello's triumph over Hewson. There was one certainty about Costello in 1996: he came to bury Hewson's 1993 policy legacy. Their acrimonious personal relations were reinforced by profound policy rifts. Costello dismissed Hewson as a reckless amateur whose ineptitude had ruined an election victory three years earlier and whose judgement on interest rates had been a proven failure.[4]

'We had an economic model in the 1990s and an independent central bank was fundamental to that model,' Costello said.[5] Treasury chief Ted Evans advised Costello to adopt more ambitious reform: an amendment to the *Reserve Bank Act* to buttress low inflation. But Costello stuck by the pre-election policy. That meant a written agreement for an independent bank with an inflation target in the 2–3 per cent range, the informal target its governor, Bernie Fraser, had adopted.

There was no magic about Costello's policy but there was judgement. In reality, Howard and Costello seized Fraser's model, they polished it, they codified it, they removed it from the unfathomable mystique that surrounded central banking and they implanted their new pride in the economic policy daylight. It was clever beyond their wildest dreams. The idea of Reserve Bank independence became sanctified in the Liberal Party credo, glorified by unfolding election victories. There were two frustrated spectators: Keating and Hewson.

The paradox of the Reserve Bank is that it had been independent by law but subservient by practice. The 1959 *Act* vested the bank with monetary policy responsibility—subject to an ultimate override by the government provided it notified the parliament of the disagreement. But for decades monetary policy had been run by Treasury, whose postwar legendary chief, Sir Roland Wilson, assumed that the Bank 'amounted almost to an irrelevant outpost and insisted that there was only one real line of advice to the Treasurer … the Head of Treasury'.[6]

In 1996 Costello was lucky: Fraser's term as governor was about to expire. Fraser had not the slightest interest in renewal. Costello distrusted Fraser as a Keating partisan. The two men had a rough history. In mid-1995 Fraser had attacked the Coalition, publicly rebuking Howard for his 'five minutes of economic sunshine' remark, dismissing it as a 'hollow-sounding throwaway'. Fraser said of Howard: 'His comments pissed me off a lot. They were causing difficulties in the markets and they weren't true, which made it worse.'[7] Fraser had praised the 1990s recovery that had delivered 3–4 per cent annual growth and debunked Howard's hint about its unsustainability.[8]

After his speech Fraser was paged at Melbourne Airport: he took the message that the shadow treasurer, Costello, wanted to talk to him immediately. But Fraser had a busy schedule and didn't regard Costello as top priority. He returned to his Sydney office. There was another message from Costello. The next day he was in Brisbane and Costello phoned through direct. Fraser said:

> Costello was very unhappy with me making those comments about the Leader of the Opposition. I told him 'Those remarks aren't true and there're causing problems in the markets.' He kept saying but this is the Leader of the Opposition and I said 'I don't care who he is.' We went round and round in circles. But there was an implied threat from Costello or what I took as an implied threat. His words were, to the effect, 'If we don't like this, we can do something about it.'[9]

When Fraser returned to Sydney he made a file note of the discussion.

Costello went public to say that, under a Coalition government the governor would be expected to operate independently and avoid any partisanship. For Fraser, it was water off a duck's back. Years later Costello conceded that, while Fraser was close to Keating, he was 'his own man and made his own decisions'.[10]

Fraser and Howard had worked closely twenty years earlier. 'We were very close when I was in the Treasury and he was Treasurer,' Fraser recalls. Occasionally in the 1990s, when Howard was in Opposition, they would bump into each other at the football. But that changed after an incident between Fraser's wife and Howard.

> My wife confronted him at some public gathering. She raised this line [of Howard's] that Bernie Fraser is Keating's man. She said to him, 'You should know better than that. People know Bernie is his own man.' And Howard was saying 'Did I say that?' And she said: 'Yes, you did. Oh, you said it alright.' And there was a sort of freezing of relations.[11]

The 1996 election was the pathway to lower inflation. Howard and Costello were superbly placed. Over the previous five years, 1991–96,

Australia's average underlying inflation rate had been 2.5 per cent—the best result in such a five-year period for thirty years—while GDP growth had averaged 4 per cent a year for the previous three years.

In their brief time together relations between Costello and Fraser were cool but proper. Costello was struck by the Fraser whisper, saying 'bank governors are Delphic enough but when they whisper they are doubly hard to penetrate'.[12] Once in office, Costello told Fraser that the wars between the Coalition and the Bank were over. And Fraser's initial intervention helped the government.

With the lapse of the Accord and a dysfunctional union movement threatening wage claims, Fraser rang the bell. 'I speak, as you know, as a consistent supporter of the Accord process,' he said. 'If wages growth continues to pick up, rather than come back a notch, there will be little option but to raise interest rates.' It was a reminder that the world had changed. The Accord was dead but the Reserve Bank was armed—it would enforce the wage restraint. Power had passed from the Accord to the Bank.

There was more good news for Howard and Costello: it was time to unwind Fraser's 1994 monetary tightening. Costello, as a new treasurer, wanted the first interest rate cut to follow his Budget as a reward for his fiscal responsibility. It would reflect well on the new government.

Treasury Secretary Ted Evans agreed and told Fraser: 'I don't think Costello's request is unreasonable and it's clear we are getting a very good Budget from him.' Fraser was unmoved, but at least he didn't call Costello a dickhead.[13]

However, Fraser did something unusual—he cut rates half a percentage point three weeks before the August Budget, contrary to Costello's plan. This was Fraser defying the new Howard government. Macfarlane was taken aback. 'It was Bernie saying, Up yours, and it should not have happened,' he said.[14]

Fraser's defiance caused a rupture within the Reserve Bank board. For the first time under Fraser's governorship the board split. A vote was required. Interviewed for this book, Fraser was unrepentant.

> The argument was that the decision could wait. It wasn't explicit but the sense was that if we wait until after the Budget this would be an endorsement of the Budget. It became apparent that this was what Costello had wanted. But he hadn't raised it with me. I was surprised. I thought there was a case to move then and there.

When the vote was taken the board split 4–4, with Fraser having the casting vote to secure the rate cut. Fraser felt the Bank was being pressured for political reasons and he got his back up. Macfarlane was distinctly unimpressed. He felt Fraser had lost his judgement. Macfarlane said: 'I voted against the rate cut. So did Ted (Evans). All the ones with any knowledge voted against it. Bernie was just shoving it up them as he went. He could have done it after the Budget. It was a silly little episode.'[15] Costello claimed the credit anyway, saying the cut was a 'down payment' on a good Budget.

Costello's critical task was to select a new governor and the choice seemed obvious. Fraser believed Macfarlane, as deputy, was the best candidate. Costello concluded that Macfarlane was strong on economics, neutral on politics and personally affable. What more was left? But the appointment was tied to Costello's plan for an independent Bank.

Fraser was critical of Costello's vision. For Fraser, the bank was already independent, and fiddling about with new letters would make no difference. In addition, Fraser felt that an exclusive 2–3 per cent inflation target, even though it was 'over the cycle', was too rigid. Costello did not put any proposal to Fraser, thereby denying him the chance to reject it.

Macfarlane had a different view—he backed both the target and the formal agreement. He believed this was a desirable revolution. But Costello was methodical—he established that Macfarlane would endorse the agreement as a prelude to his appointment as governor.[16] It was an agreement between the Treasurer and the Governor, a mutual compact, released on 14 August 1996 with the announcement of Macfarlane's appointment.

It recognised 'the independence of the Bank' as provided by statute, said the Bank would focus on price stability while taking account of economic activity and endorsed the goal of keeping 'underlying inflation between 2 and 3 per cent, on average, over the cycle'. Interest rate decisions would be announced by the Bank, not the government. The government recognised its obligations for a disciplined fiscal policy to assist these objectives. In order to promote transparency and accountability the Bank would release six-monthly statements and the Governor would report to parliament twice a year.[17]

Fraser said:

> When the draft letter arrived, Ian showed me and asked me what I thought. I said 'It is for you to decide.' I mentioned my two concerns. The first was that this was a letter between the Governor and the

Treasurer while the *Act* said it is the Bank board that sets interest rates and I always strove for consensus with the board. Second, it was a letter about inflation and inflation targets—there was no mention of other objectives—and that made me uncomfortable.

Fraser says he would have required significant changes before signing the letter.[18]

In his public swan song Fraser said the agreement was unnecessary. Dismissing claims that the Bank had been political under his leadership, Fraser said 'No hard evidence has ever been advanced—there is none'. The only evidence was 'concocted, based on "impugned sinister motives" to my mateship with Paul Keating'.[19]

How important was this agreement? Evans said:

It is a formal transfer of power from government to the Reserve Bank. It is most unusual for politicians to formally surrender power. It got the government out of interest rates and this is a big step. If the agreement didn't exist then human nature suggests the politicians would have intervened more and tried to intervene more.[20]

Access Economics founder Geoff Carmody played down any suggestion of Australia as a central bank pioneer. 'This wasn't some magic Australian invention,' he said. 'There had been a history of overseas policy development in central banking that was in advance of Australia.'[21]

But Macfarlane's view is the most illuminating. He puts great weight on the 1996 agreement, far more than the other players. Macfarlane asserts that the Bank's standing was transformed in the shift from Keating to Howard. In retrospect, the Bank under Keating had been kidding itself. Macfarlane said that, in the Keating era, the Bank felt it was independent but it wasn't—the final decision on interest rates rested with the prime minister.

'People underestimate how much change has occurred since 1996,' Macfarlane said ten years on. 'It is a different world now. There is a very big difference between giving advice and being responsible yourself. It means you act differently.'[22] Interviewed for this book, he reflected:

The Reserve Bank didn't really have international standing under Paul Keating, even though he was a good guy to work with. I mean, the institution just did not have international standing. We really only got it after we had formal recognition of our independence in 1996.[23]

Former Westpac chief and Treasury official David Morgan said:

Central bank independence introduced by the Howard government in 1996 was a very big deal for Australia. This helped to transform Australia from one of the most inflation-prone economies to being one of the least inflation-prone. That transformation has been important for our competitive position.[24]

Bank independence generated a new relationship between the Bank and government—but this change is widely misunderstood. Independence is a gift the politicians gave the Bank. It is neither absolute nor does it override the statute. Its makes the Bank more autonomous as an institution. It creates a contradiction, in that the Bank takes the decisions but the politicians are responsible before the people. This means, as a consequence, that the Bank by its performance must retain the support of the political class. Independence must be validated by the Bank's performance in the long run. This dictates that the Bank must not just operate in the financial market but manage both its political relations with government and public relations with the people to retain confidence in the model. The Bank has a more important and sensitive political role but a role it must discharge with great subtlety. The pressure on the Bank in financial and political terms is far greater than before.

Labor's blunder in August 1996 was to attack the agreement rather than claim joint ownership. There was nothing in this deal to offend Labor principles. Keating became a public critic. Beazley suggested that it might be illegal and attacked the agreement for subverting the Bank's charter on jobs. It was a shocking call. When Kevin Rudd came to power twelve years later the agreement was retained.

In 1998 Macfarlane said: 'There is still a lingering misconception in Australia that parties of the political right support central bank independence and that those of the left oppose it ... it is not true at present, was not at an earlier date and has not been the case in other countries.' He pointed out that in New Zealand, France and the United Kingdom it had been parties of the Left (represented by the Lange, Mitterrand and Blair governments) that achieved central bank independence.[25]

Macfarlane's monetary policy became Howard's golden political thread. Howard, even on his darkest nights when his fortunes were gloomiest, could take solace in the fact that the cash rate at the 1998, 2001 and 2004 polls had been 5 per cent, 4.5 per cent and 5.25 per cent respectively, enabling people to borrow for their homes and then borrow again and, at these rates, still meet their repayments.

The Howard–Costello experience recalled the prudence with which RG Menzies had handled the central bank after his 1949 victory. He retained, as Governor of the Commonwealth Bank (with its central bank responsibilities), the prominent Keynesian economist, Dr HC 'Nugget' Coombs, who had been close to outgoing Labor Prime Minister Ben Chifley. The gulf between the Howard government and Fraser was too great to permit any such accommodation. But the parallel does exist—it lies in the astute handling of the bank by the Menzies and Howard governments to reap economic and political dividends.[26]

Once the model was in place, it functioned beautifully for Howard and Costello. As Costello advanced along the trajectory of a budget surplus, Macfarlane regularly cut interest rates. The first Budget was rewarded with two 0.5 per cent rate cuts in late 1996; the second Budget was rewarded with another two 0.5 per cent rate cuts. Any analysis of Howard's 1998 re-election on a difficult tax package must include the interest rate factor. In Howard's first term, the cash rate was cut five times—from 7.5 per cent to 5 per cent—a significant easing.

Macfarlane was getting the precise effect he wanted: higher growth and lower rates. In August 1997 the Governor's optimism moved to a new threshold. He declared himself 'confident' that the model would deliver a long expansion. Macfarlane said: 'With inflation tamed and with some slack available, we should be quite capable of growing by 3.5 per cent, 4 per cent, 4.5 per cent (or possibly even faster) over the next couple of years without any significant detrimental effect on inflation.'[27]

The test in Howard's first term was the Asian financial crisis. Arriving in Howard's re-election year, central banks began to raise rates to stabilise currencies. Howard went on the alert: the mix of a GST package and rising interest rates was a lethal cocktail for him.

On 20 May 1998 Howard called Macfarlane to a private meeting in his Sydney office to discuss how the bank saw the outlook. This was Howard's most important meeting with Macfarlane in his first term. Howard came with a message—the Bank should beware of lifting interest rates as other central banks had done. He urged that the exchange rate should take the impact despite the depreciation this involved.

Australia's dilemma would centre upon its collapsing dollar. Macfarlane's strategy was to hold the line on interest rates yet the Bank was under intense pressure to lift rates to defend the dollar. On three occasions in 1998—January, June and August—the Bank responded with foreign exchange intervention to try to steady the falling exchange rate. In Martin Place, the bank's home, the nervous tension was palpable. At this meeting the Prime Minister and the Governor were on the same wavelength—they both had their reasons for opposing interest rate increases.

Macfarlane told Howard that inflation remained within the Bank's target, so there was no rationale to change policy. But the pressure to lift interest rates was immense. He advised Howard that the government's best response was to run a responsible fiscal policy, to play down talk about tax cuts and to avoid any suggestion that ministers were happy with the extent of the currency fall. The management of expectations would be vital, Macfarlane said.

'We have to get the rhetoric right,' he told Howard. 'We have to stop saying the exchange rate is behaving in exactly the right way because this gives the impression we approve of its fall and hence gives the impression we will be comfortable with further falls.' Howard agreed. He explained to Macfarlane that his own language had been geared to this message. The Prime Minister was pleased with the Governor's view—this was exactly the steel that he wanted from the Governor.

Macfarlane said he welcomed the signs of changing market sentiment: expectations of a rate cut were evaporating and the next trend would be expectations of a rate rise. That would be a good thing. He told Howard that, 'while we need not encourage this view, we should not dispute it' because such expectation 'will help to put a bit of stiffening into the exchange rate'.[28] This was Macfarlane trusting that expectation of a rate rise would eliminate the need for any action.[29]

On each occasion in 1998 when the dollar overshot on the downside, the Bank kept its nerve. Macfarlane said later that the option for a rate rise was 'on the table ... and financial markets knew this'. Indeed, the Bank wanted them to know.[30] Howard was very happy with this meeting. His senior adviser, Arthur Sinodinos, felt that Howard's political support at this meeting helped to steel Macfarlane in the crisis. 'I think that this helped the Bank,' Sinodinos said.[31]

This meeting revealed that Bank independence did not preclude critical dialogue between the Prime Minister and the Governor. It showed that Australia's monetary response to the Asian crisis, while conducted by the Bank, was endorsed by Howard. And it showed that Howard was prepared to initiate talks with the Governor when he felt the government's interests were at stake. 'My memory is that we both went away reassured,' Macfarlane says.[32] The strategy worked—interest rates were not lifted.

Howard, having to sell a GST election package, averted the extra problem of higher interest rates.

This discussion was really about the politics of the float. It was the floating currency that made possible Australia's relatively smooth adjustment to the Asian crisis. Australia now had an economic model able to handle such external disruption—a huge step towards deeper national maturity. The dollar took the impact and the economy moved forward. As Asia succumbed, Australia sailed onwards. Keating studied the results with pride. Howard observed them with relief. Macfarlane was a governor who grasped the glory implicit in the float. 'I think in pure economic terms it was enormously valuable for Australia that we got through it and got the international credit,' he said.[33]

There was, however, a second meeting in 1998 between Howard and Macfarlane, a classic in Howard's approach to political strategy. On the morning of 28 August, Howard asked Macfarlane to see him. When they met the Prime Minister asked Macfarlane to brief him on the outlook for the Australian dollar and global currency markets. Macfarlane explained that the worst of the Asian crisis was behind. There was no discussion about an election but Macfarlane was convinced that this meeting was 100 per cent about an election.

This was Howard giving the Governor a chance to alert him to any dangers over the coming six weeks for the dollar and interest rates. Macfarlane understood the code. He did not issue any such warning. By default, Macfarlane gave Howard a signal—to the best of his knowledge there were no nasty shocks coming. And Howard called his 1998 election two days later.[34]

24

THE CULTURAL TRADITIONALIST
AS POPULIST

I think my main achievement in the culture debate
was to rekindle a pride in the old Australia.
—John Howard, December 2008

'I am an Anzac Bradman Australian,' John Howard declared in October 2007, the month before his defeat.[1] It was an identity Howard had carried with honour. He had come to power in 1996, certain that his victory had a deeper meaning—as a chance to rekindle belief in traditional Australia. Howard tried to launch a cultural counter-revolution.

He came to power sure that a culture war was being waged against Australia's traditions, the targets being patriotism, God and family. Howard saw the enemy insurgents as scattered across the Labor Party, universities, and public, cultural and legal institutions. He believed they had made progress in hijacking and trashing the nation's traditions. For Howard, this was an attack on the values that had made Australia a successful nation and the values loved by ordinary people. It was a war on many fronts.

It was also a personal issue for John and Janette Howard. Janette's role as a high school teacher in the generation before postmodernism began to infect the curriculum was a pervasive influence on the Howard family.

This decision had two consequences. It defined Howard's government as the enemy of the culturally progressive Establishment and it invited people to put a 'use by' date on Howard. He was defining himself by the symbols of the past, not the future. There was a further complication: Howard didn't know how to fight this war. His policy response as a cultural traditionalist was woeful compared with his resolute action as a social conservative. These were overlapping yet different battles.

After his retirement Howard said his main achievement in the culture wars 'was to rekindle pride in the old Australia after it had been devalued by Keating'.[2] He saw this as a political, almost a spiritual, mission. Yet rekindling pride, while a palpable result, was an elusive achievement and it concealed more substantial failures.

The scale of the cultural conflict was vast and disorganised. From Howard's perspective, it was easy to discern. He saw Australian history under assault in a campaign to discredit the nation's past; the Western canon under attack in the educational institutions; the traditional family being devalued in the cause of a false tolerance; the Christian virtues that had constituted the moral foundations of society being systematically dismantled; patriotism under assault as an idea whose time had passed and traduced as progenitor of twentieth-century violence; and the recruitment of multiculturalism to argue that Australia was no longer a society bonded by a single unified culture residing in the Western tradition.

Howard tried to position the Liberal Party against these trends. It was a risky tactic given the power of interest groups that he was targetting and their ability to sway votes. But Howard interpreted his election victory as evidence that Australian progressivism was at a moment of historic weakness.

For Howard, this was a chance, but nothing was guaranteed. 'Over recent times, a new constituency has galvanised around new issues and in support of Liberal priorities,' he declared in the 1996 Menzies Lecture.

> This new constituency does not represent a permanent re-alignment in Australian politics. Its continued support for Liberal priorities cannot be taken for granted—it must be earnt. Liberalism now has an opportunity unparalleled for almost fifty years, to consolidate a new coalition of support among the broad cross-section of the Australian people.[3]

Liberal research and his political instinct told Howard that the battlers had viscerally distrusted Keating's cultural agenda. But culture is deceptive terrain and Howard often had a poor understanding of the ground on which he was fighting.

The Howard project would involve economic liberalism, social conservatism and cultural traditionalism. This mixture, unseen before his leadership, would not be replicated after his demise. It was a reminder that Howard was interested in political ideas—he articulated them not as an intellectual advocate, in the mould of Whitlam or Keating, but as a politician talking to people over a cup of tea.

In his 1988 manifesto *Future Directions*, Howard gave his cultural traditionalism its first comprehensive exposure. But he did not use this term; in office he gave no speeches offering an outline of this philosophy; and he appointed no minister to discharge this task. Indeed, he often had trouble conceptualising what he meant. Yet the term 'cultural traditionalism' is the best description of the pervasive outlook he brought to virtually every aspect of public policy for his eleven years as prime minister. Howard had no doubt that 'the cultural war stuff is very important'.[4]

The essence of Howard's cultural traditionalism lay in his patriotism—his view of a united, strong Australian nation, dedicated to its Western values and fostering this tradition in its institutions and symbols. There was a bizarre alternative idea that gained traction among his critics—that Howard was driven mainly by religion. The truth is that he wasn't interested in religion, never talked religion and saw it as a strictly private domain.

As a cultural traditionalist Howard upheld the constitutional monarchy; he championed traditional approaches in the education curriculum and transparency in assessing school performance; he fostered patriotic sentiment, almost a civic nationalism, in his emphasis on Australian achievement, the Anzac commemoration and displays of the flag; he opposed apologies based on a disreputable view of the nation's past; he privileged national identity as a unifying force and he rejected contemporary campaigns to enshrine identity based on sub-groups of class, sex or ethnicity with their potential to create division; he felt that stable family values assisted a stable nation; he insisted that multiculturalism be limited by support for national laws, values and loyalty to a single Australian identity founded in its Western inheritance; he claimed that national sovereignty entitled a democratic Australia to resist refugees self-selecting the country and he opposed the influence of American culture and championed instead Australian folklore. Most of these positions could be traced back to his patriotism.

Howard came to these debates only as a politician, never as a theorist. This is the key to his cultural traditionalism—he was a populist. Week after week on talkback radio he spoke to the common man in the language of the common man.

In Australia's pluralistic democracy Howard had political power— but he did not have cultural power. This meant that in cultural, as well as social, terms he was an anti-Establishment figure. The centres of resistance to Howard's cultural traditionalism were easily listed in private discussions with the Prime Minister and his senior colleagues. It was a frighteningly long list and it began with two institutions: the ABC and the universities. They were followed by the teacher unions, the Fairfax papers, progressive lawyers and judges, the culture sector, the green lobby, the so-called 'multicultural industry', most of the indigenous political leadership and the diverse interests campaigning for human rights and a Bill of Rights. It was remarkable how much private discussion with ministers returned to the culture war. It was ever-present.

As his last and best speechwriter, John Kunkel, said, Howard came to 'challenge many of the comfortable verities of late twentieth-century Whitlamite progressivism'. Unlike many other Liberals, Howard had the courage for this task.

His government, formally or informally, was pitted against many centres of cultural and intellectual life guided by various ideologies that Howard distrusted, such as secular humanism, postmodernism, assertive multiculturalism, indigenous self-determination, environmental alarm-ism, demands for a codified entrenchment of rights and ideas of 'post-national' identity.

One of Howard's blunders is that he defined what he was against more than what he was for—against the Aboriginal apology, the republic, gay marriage, Kyoto, boat arrivals, multiculturalism and, finally, he was viscerally against Keating's identity agenda. Kunkel said: 'I felt the balance was wrong, that it took too long to shake off the shadow-boxing with Paul Keating.'[5]

Strong on populist messages, Howard was weak on intellectual argu-ment. He failed to integrate his cultural traditionalism into a persuasive statement of beliefs and philosophy. This weakened and even crippled his project. 'You have to look for coherence in the Howard project, it doesn't come naturally,' Kunkel says.[6] It is a telling criticism.

There was a strategic risk for the Liberal Party in Howard's agenda—he was isolating the Liberals from important institutions and social movements, literally severing their ties. Under Howard, the Liberals lost traction with the tertiary-educated professional classes that possessed much of the nation's brain power. Too often, he was hostile to them. Political analyst Ian Marsh argues that the rise of these social movements 'is arguably the single most significant change in the character of postwar politics'. The danger was that Howard, by seeking the community voter, was alienating the Liberals from these movements for a long time.[7]

Howard's inability to speak in moral terms and recruit moral arguments to explain his positions became a serious flaw. Whether the issue was the Aboriginal apology, Hansonism, boat people, truth in government or industrial relations reform, Howard lacked the skill of Tony Blair or Bill Clinton to put a moral framework around his policies. This conceded the moral 'high ground' to his opponents and threatened his legitimacy. He became known as a 'wedge' politician—one whose positions had no integrity but were motivated by irresponsible self-interest. By successfully branding Howard with this polemic his cultural opponents defeated him.

Howard's moral sin was 'inexcusable'—he actually believed the morality of the people was in no way inferior to the morality of the cultural elites. The hallmark of the cultural critics who campaigned against Howard was their obsession with morality—he was depicted as a liar, intimidator, murderer, racist, sexist and war monger. This list, eventually, said more about his critics than about Howard.

In his 2008 memoirs Peter Costello described a play, *Two Brothers*, performed by the Melbourne Theatre Company and supported by the Australia Council, that drew on the SIEV X tragedy when hundreds of asylum seekers were drowned at sea. Costello wrote:

> Evil is personified by the brother who is a senior minister ... he is also a liar and an adulterer ... The playwright claimed that I was the inspiration for the character. In the play the minister orders the navy to let hundreds of illegal asylum seekers drown rather than rescue them at sea. It turns out the minister is a mass murderer too ... My daughter Madeleine was taken with her secondary school class to see it. One can imagine the lesson in class the next day: 'Your father is a mass murderer. Discuss.'[8]

Australia's cultural debate was primitive by American standards. In the United States, prominent conservatives had been fighting the 1960s legacy for decades. Indeed, this was origin of the American neo-conservative movement. In 1993 its godfather, Irving Kristol, said the end of the Cold War against the Soviets meant that 'the real cold war has begun'. This was the culture war at home—against American-style left-liberalism and its campaign to 'ruthlessly corrupt American life' sector by sector with its ideology of moral anarchy. For Kristol, this was a great test, a more challenging cold war, with America more vulnerable to insurgents from within.[9] Numerous American writers, such as Francis Fukuyama, had dissected the struggle for the social order between traditionalist and progressive movements originating in the 1960s.[10] A participant in this revolution, US writer Todd Gitlin, said in his history of the decade that every US election since 1968 had been 'at least on its symbolic plane, a cultural referendum'.[11]

Christopher Lasch, in his bestseller *The Revolt of the Elites*, identified the fault line in America that Howard sought to exploit in Australia, saying:

> It is the working and lower middle classes, after all, that favour limits on abortion, cling to the two-parent family as a source of stability in a turbulent world, resist experiments with 'alternative lifestyles' and harbour deep reservations about affirmative action … the new elites, the professional classes in particular, regard the masses with mingled scorn and apprehension.

Lasch said the cultural elites believed the term 'Middle America' had 'come to symbolise everything that stands in the way of progress: "family values", mindless patriotism, religious fundamentalism, racism, homophobia, retrograde views of women'.[12] In a similar fashion Howard in 1996 knew that the arrogance of the progressives had given him an opening.

For a decade patriotism was Howard's main weapon in this struggle. He invoked the 'national interest' to justify every major decision. 'I felt we had wasted a decade in this endless seminar about our national identity,' Howard said. 'The great mistake Keating made on nationalism was to give the impression there was no longer room for the old Australia and people who believed in the old Australia. Noel Pearson often said that Keating had a "repudiational approach" to our past.'[13]

For Howard, Australia's nationalism was mature. He felt that any notion that nationhood was unfulfilled until the republic or reconciliation arrived was plain lunacy.

Asked when he felt that Australia became an independent nation Howard immediately replied that 'emotionally' this happened in World War I.

> We fought as an Australian army. We fought in an Australian military tradition. I still have a memory of seeing an old diary of my father's from World War I with an entry written in September 1918 and the line simply read 'Relieved by a Pommy division'. I mean this was a private in the Australian army unit in France in 1918. That's what he wrote.[14]

This is one of the most revealing statements in Howard's political life. It shows that he interpreted the nation through the lens of his own family. He saw Anzac as the foundation idea; he believed in the power of nationalism among the people; he was convinced that his father in 1918 was an Australian nationalist. He was as sure about Australian nationalism as he was about his own family. Keating's claim that this same Australia was crippled by colonial deference turned his stomach.

Howard would honour the people's patriotism that he saw in his own family. He would not seek to reinvent it. This is the rock of Howard's stubbornness on cultural issues—his family experience told him he was right. In retirement he said:

> I felt the national identity issue Keating had raised was a phoney issue. I had always felt Australians had a very strong sense of national identity. My knowledge of the distinctive character of the Australian forces in World War I and World War II told me that it was never hard to define yourself as an Australian. If there is an argument for this country to become a republic it is not that we get confused with Englishmen. We don't. And we haven't for generations. Australian nationalism was something I felt instinctively, so I had no trouble identifying with it.[15]

In his fourth 1995 headland address, Howard signalled his intent to smash the Keating construct.

> The suggestion that we have yet to develop a proper identity, or that government can deliver us a new and improved one, treats us like children. It smacks of Big Brother. It also suggests that we need someone else to dream our dreams for us ... The current prime minister must be one of the few leaders from any era, anywhere in the world, who appears to have so little respect for his own country's history that he is attempting to rewrite it.[16]

National identity, Howard insisted, belonged to the people, not the leaders. It transcended political manipulation. It was 'our common inheritance', something 'no political party can expect to monopolise or turn into its plaything'.

However, this was an exercise in sophistry. Howard would recruit identity to his own cause. He came not to bury the identity debate but to win it. By vesting identity in the people Howard signalled his technique—he would govern as a conservative populist, the synthesis most likely to confound Labor. An aggressive Howard would seize nationalism as the banner for his prime ministership. Meanwhile a deluded media still saw him as an unimaginative 1950s pro-British Menzian reactionary.[17]

Howard was obsessed with repudiating Keating's 'claim that the Coalition is, and always has been, a bunch of lickspittles with a servile attitude towards Britain'. Howard quoted historian John Hirst, saying that if Keating wanted to attack the supporters of Empire he would have to include Curtin and Chifley along with Menzies and RG Casey.[18]

Howard had been encouraged by historian Geoffrey Blainey, just as Keating drew sustenance from Manning Clark. In 1993, in the John Latham Lecture, Blainey attempted a balance sheet of Australian history, concluding that Australia, despite its blemishes, was 'one of the world's success stories'.

Reflecting on Australia's intellectual life Blainey laid out his accusation that would echo for the next decade:

> To some extent my generation was reared on the Three Cheers view of history. This patriotic view of our past had a long run … There is a rival view which I call the Black Armband view of history. The black armbands were quietly worn in official circles in 1988. The multicultural folk busily preached their message that until they arrived much of Australian history was a disgrace. The past treatment of Aborigines, of Chinese, of Kanakas, of non-British migrants, of women, the very old, the very young, and the poor was singled out, sometimes legitimately, sometimes not … The Black Armband view of history might well represent the swing of the pendulum from a position that had been too favourable, too self congratulatory, to an opposite extreme that is even more unreal and decidedly jaundiced.[19]

Blainey had written the text for Howard's prime ministership. Coming a year after Keating's Redfern speech and the High Court's Mabo decision with its condemnation of Australia's past, its brilliance was to throw the progressive intellectuals onto the defensive. 'The Black Armband' entered the language.[20]

The following year Howard enunciated his political strategy: 'Liberals should become the party of Australian achievement.' He would stand for achievement, not shame. The people felt 'that legitimate expressions of pride about the past have been stifled'.[21] Howard was on the march.

Moving onto the offensive in his 1996 Menzies Lecture, Howard wanted the Liberal Party to define itself by cultural issues. The Black

Armband polemicists, he charged, said Australia's past was a 'disgraceful story of imperialism, exploitation, racism, sexism and other forms of discrimination'. Howard, by contrast, declared that 'the balance sheet' was 'one of heroic achievement'. He would not deny the assault on the Aboriginal people, nor other sins. But Howard wanted to end the national seminar of guilt. He would live the story of Australian achievement—refusing apologies for the past, refusing to condemn Pauline Hanson.

He defended Menzies as an icon of tradition, not because he had the slightest wish to replicate Menzies' society in the late 1990s; this idea, advanced by his critics, was absurd. 'We do not yearn for some lost golden age,' Howard said. Australia, he said, was a 'more diverse and better' nation than it had been under Menzies. The point was obvious: he saw Howard's Australia as superior to Menzies' Australia.[22]

The gulf between Keating and Howard was apparent—Keating drew inspiration from his vision of Australia's future while Howard drew inspiration from the past. Their conflict had several subtle dimensions. Keating was more the patriot, Howard was more the nationalist. The flaw in Keating's approach was his view of Australia's past; this is where he was vulnerable and it is where Howard attacked him for promoting a 'divisive, selective and inaccurate' history.[23] Yet the strength in Keating's approach was his quest to find a modern patriotism geared to evolving social and economic realities. Both men were deep patriots; but their visions were in competition.

However, cultural change is more elusive than economic change. In totalitarian systems the state dictates the culture, while in democracies culture must transcend state power. There are serious and desirable limits on the ability of governments to shape national culture, a point Howard realised. His record is clear—as a cultural traditionalist he was a rhetorical success and a policy failure.

There is no cultural institution that Howard reformed—as distinct from having stifled—not the ABC, SBS, the National Museum of Australia or the Australia Council. His government seemed inept and confused dealing with such institutions though it did throw them on the defensive. It was addicted to appointing loyalists, of one sort or another, to chair the boards—Donald McDonald to the ABC, Carla Zampatti to SBS, Tony Staley to the National Museum—but it had no strategy for reform.

Howard suffered the worst of both worlds. He was under attack for subverting cultural institutions, notably the ABC, yet his government failed to implement strategies for effective cultural change. It fiddled, instead, with financial stringencies, bureaucratic intimidation, serial appointment of political loyalists to boards and periodic venting of its frustrations. Howard's former office chief, political commentator Gerard Henderson, reviewing a decade of Howard's government, lamented: 'John Howard has had little success in overturning the impact of what has been called the Left's long march through the institutions.' While praising Howard's role in the public debate, Henderson said he had failed to have a significant impact in the cultural arena. He argued that Howard, like Menzies, had won elections yet, after a decade, the Left still prevailed in many of the halls of institutional power.[24] A similar critique was made by Howard's biographers Wayne Errington and Peter Van Onselen: 'The paradox of Howard's participation in debates about history and culture is that his rhetoric was not matched by a systematic plan to reform Australia's educational and cultural institutions.'[25]

These are core insights. Howard's problem was that Australia's universities, as speechwriter Kunkel said, were 'a wasteland for conservative ideas'. Howard had few intellectual allies and seemed disinclined to muster many more. He recruited few people direct from universities to assist his project. Pru Goward, drawing on her experience as a journalist and Liberal politician, said:

> Conservative governments don't have natural supporters who are articulate and philosophical writers. The conservative intellectual group is very small in Australia. So the politicians are lonely and they are joked about all the time. I had a saying that the only way to win an argument was to put a right-wing proposition in a left-wing way.[26]

The contrast with Kevin Rudd was stunning. Within six months of winning office Rudd hosted a 2020 Summit with 1000 prominent Australians, many from the nation's intellectual centres, co-chaired by his long-time friend, University of Melbourne Vice-Chancellor Glyn Davis. The participants were not universal Labor supporters but they revealed either an intellectual rapport with Rudd or a sympathy for Labor aspirations, in sharp contrast with the Howard years.

Howard offered support to the think-tanks where he felt comfortable: speaking at the Centre for Independent Studies, at *Quadrant* dinners and at the Institute for Public Affairs. He welcomed the growing number of conservative columnists in Murdoch-group newspapers that contributed to a more pluralistic climate and the influence of conservative intellectuals in think-tanks. But, for many conservatives, the great progressive edifices stood unconquered.

On schools policy Howard waged an eleven-year war with the teachers' unions but his ability to influence school curriculum was strictly limited. This was a state responsibility and state governments made few concessions to Canberra.

The epic failure was university policy. Aware that the academy was a furnace of hostility towards his government and conservative culture, Howard took a stance that was defensive and aloof. He rarely visited a university campus; it was 'enemy' territory. It was not his nature to engage the academy in debate. He wasn't willing to commit the time and he assumed that the intellectual class was beyond persuasion. This view, probably correct, hurt Howard and damaged Australia's higher education sector. The mutual distrust was pervasive.

Howard's government failed to deregulate universities, deliver institutional autonomy and promote more diversity, specialisation and consumer power. By contrast, Menzies had made university policy a priority. Howard did not seem to grasp that breaking down rigid government control of universities was the catalyst to changing the academic culture that he loathed. It is the greatest failure of institutional reform in his era.

The judgement of Howard is that he refused to cultivate support for his cultural vision among Australian opinion makers and institutions. He rode with his supporters and tried to ignore his opponents. Often he seemed reduced to gestures such as appointing that robust conservative warrior Keith Windschuttle to the ABC board, earning hollow cheers but perhaps signifying his impotence. The hostility of his intellectual opponents convinced Howard that there was no basis for dialogue. The truth is that he was comfortable with the people but uncomfortable with cultural leaders. This gulf remained unbridged and Australia remained the poorer.

This is not how Howard sees the story. He claims that it was under his prime ministership that Australia was reoriented towards traditional values. He argues that by 2001 the trend was manifest: the Keating identity debate was being eclipsed, the republic had been rejected, multiculturalism had been softened, the Anzac commemoration had become a patriotic resurgence and Australia's military tradition had been rekindled with Australia's leadership of the UN intervention in East Timor. Disputes over 'toadying to Britain' were fading outside the tokenistic play or film. The refrain Howard used was that 'the things that united Australians were infinitely more important than the things that divided Australians'. It had the virtue of truth.

In his 2001 Centenary of Federation address on Australia Day, Howard said social cohesion was 'arguably the crowning achievement of the Australian experience over the past century'. It was a landmark asser-tion. For twenty-five years he had worried that multiculturalism might pull Australia apart. He had warned about Asian migration, he had fretted about becoming a nation of tribes. Now he saw the nation in his own image, a trait of all prime ministers.[27]

Over time new currents supported Howard. In much of Europe and North America, as Fukuyama described, old-fashioned multiculturalism was replaced 'by more energetic efforts to integrate non-Western populations into a common liberal culture'. People saw that immigrants had to be treated as individuals, not as members of a cultural sub-group.[28] Howard had once declared that under multiculturalism 'it is impossible to have a common Australian culture'. Now he had changed—he felt multiculturalism was subordinated to Australianness and he believed Australia was integrating migrants into a common culture.[29] In retirement, he rhetorically asked: 'How many people now talk about multiculturalism?'[30]

'The truth is that people come to this country because they want to be Australians,' he told a National Press Club audience in 2001. 'Australia is a magnet for people from all corners of the globe not because of what it might become but because of what it has become.' While he was careful never to quote the figures, a total of 1 086 000 migrants had arrived under Howard's government.[31] Howard's abiding belief in Australian unity was seen more clearly—it was driven by nationalism, not race. And it was shared by most Australians.

In the end, Howard used culture to cultivate his leader's profile. He worshipped three images: the sportsman, the Digger and the bushman. This is where his populism reached its zenith. Howard was hopeless at sport, had little contact with the military before becoming PM and was city born and bred. But each morning Howard walked in his Australian tracksuit; he became the Diggers' PM at home and in war zones; his 'lis-tening' trips to regional Australia with awkwardly fitting hat and country clothes became a ritual.

He recruited the icons of nationalism to Australian conservatism—it was naked political theft. Even worse for Labor, Howard stole the mateship brand. Having once boasted that he was the 'most conservative' leader in the Liberal Party's history, Howard finished as the most 'common man' Liberal leader. The extent to which Labor misread him over his first three terms was astonishing.[32]

Howard raided Labor's inner sanctum where mateship had been a sacred symbol, embodied in Henry Lawson's poems and intellectualised by Russel Ward in his *Australian Legend*. But Howard decoupled mateship from its ideological tie to Labor. So intense was this assault that Howard, in a truly comic event, tried to insert mateship into the new preamble for the Constitution only to discover that the people were not quite so populist! He had to withdraw.

His constant suggestion was that mateship defined his government. 'Our policies have mirrored the Australian character, Australian priorities—in short, the Australian way,' Howard said.[33] Mateship was the door to patriotism, egalitarianism and civic nationalism. Howard, the failed leader of the 1980s, rebadged himself as a populist symbol of the nation. It is one of the greatest jokes played on Labor since Federation.

His cultural traditionalism probably had a greater impact than his critics concede. It regularly exposed the shallowness and absurdity of his progressive opponents who metaphorically blew their brains out. The examples are almost limitless but witness the *Age*'s star cartoonist, Michael Leunig: '[Howard's] from the silvertail tribe and everybody knows it … he's from the nepotism culture: secret handshakes, Machiavelli, networking; he speaks fluent spin, but mateship and its language are not really in his bones.'[34] Ordinary Australians flying the flag on their cars or homes were attacked by a Left retreating to what Gideon Haigh called an 'effete cosmopolitanism'.[35]

At the peak of his influence in January 2006, Howard declared victory in the cultural battle with Keating. 'Australia's standing in the world has never been higher,' he said. The identity debate 'has been finally laid to rest'.[36] In retirement Howard said: 'In 2007 I said that Australia had become a stronger, prouder, more prosperous country than in March 1996. I felt this very much. I felt Australians had become a lot prouder of their country.'[37]

Howard's declaration of victory was a self-serving exaggeration.[38] Australia became a prouder and more patriotic nation because of the joint efforts of Keating and Howard. Both leaders have a shared stake in that project, despite their differences. Resolution of the competing Keating–Howard patriotic visions will be decided by history and that history began with Kevin Rudd's election.

Rudd shares Keating's passion for a modern patriotism, geared to the future, Asia-literate, reconciled with the indigenous peoples, culturally diverse and informed by an international outlook. Yet Rudd, as a church-attending Christian and supporter of family values, shares Howard's beliefs in the Western canon, personal responsibility, the Anzac ethos and a united Australia anchored to its cultural traditions. Rudd borrows from both visions. The path of patriotism will carry the imprint of both Keating and Howard.

25

RECONCILIATION: THE LOST OPPORTUNITY

Only you, or a leader very similar to you, can achieve reconciliation.
—Noel Pearson to John Howard, 17 September 2007

John Howard's Aboriginal policy is the missed opportunity of Australian conservatism. It was only in his dying months of office that Howard finally perceived his real mission—that with the trust of conservative Australia behind him he could transform the reconciliation debate for the entire nation. For over a decade Howard squandered an opportunity to successfully redefine indigenous policy. It was a failure of politics, morality and imagination.

Reconciliation was conceived in a paradox. Its politics were owned by the Labor Party due to the Keating legacy. But the nation was divided over its meaning. As reconciliation evolved in both its symbolic and practical dimensions, it became a natural position for a conservative leader. Labor was in denial of this truth; the Liberals were blind to their opportunity.

Keating's control over indigenous issues as prime minister had left the Coalition defensive and confused. It had little initial strategy beyond cheap exploitation of Keating's pro-indigenous unpopularity. The problem was identified by Arthur Sinodinos: 'We had not thought through our position on reconciliation prior to the 1996 election.'[1] Howard would pay for this oversight.

On Aboriginal policy, Howard was too fixated on his own dogmas. He was unable to break down the hostility towards him from indigenous leaders and use his influence as prime minister to broker a new political bargain with Aboriginal Australia.

In retirement, he was regretful.

Should he have visited more Aboriginal communities as an MP before becoming prime minister? 'Probably, yes,' Howard admits. What of his 1998 election-night pledge to advance reconciliation? 'It was probably an example of an idea to which I hadn't given enough thought,' he concedes. Why did he take so long to devise a coherent Aboriginal policy? 'It's fair to say I would have done better if I gave a clearer definition to practical reconciliation,' he laments.[2]

In the end, it came in a rush. In 2007, Howard became an activist. He staged an intervention in the Northern Territory. He delivered an emotional speech conceding past failings. He pledged a new politics of reconciliation based on a constitutional referendum and a commitment to practical action. His indigenous affairs policy at the 2007 election was far more ambitious than Kevin Rudd's—but it was too late.

Howard's problem was that for too long he had no Aboriginal allies. Trust was never established. Council for Aboriginal Reconciliation chair Pat Dodson was unable to deal with him and resigned. Aboriginal and Torres Strait Islander Commission chair Lowitja O'Donoghue found him 'cold and unsympathetic'. Howard had difficulty relating to indigenous leaders at a personal level. During 2007 he had two leaders, Sue Gordon and Noel Pearson, to dinner at the Lodge. Pearson said: 'I was told later he felt it was the best time he had had with indigenous people. It struck me how sad that was, how isolated and removed he had been.'[3]

Max Moore-Wilton said:

In 1996 you had an indigenous leadership in mourning for the loss of the Labor government. People such as Dodson and O'Donoghue were not willing interlocutors with the Howard government. There was a great sense of frustration. Howard had inherited a Labor framework. There wasn't any alternative indigenous leadership. The government struggled along until towards the end it did the [Northern Territory] intervention because there was enough public concern to break out of this Labor framework.[4]

The real problem, however, was different. Sinodinos nails it squarely: 'Howard seemed to be saying that Black Australia had to accommodate itself to the government and the mainstream, while Aboriginal leaders were saying to Howard, "No, you've got to change".'[5]

The gulf was ideological, political and personal. Howard's sensitivity about 'One Australia' meant he distrusted the political and legal infrastructure built around reconciliation—he rejected an official apology, rejected the notion of a Stolen Generation, was sceptical of communal land rights, felt Aboriginals must find their future in the mainstream economy, never really accepted ATSIC, opposed a treaty, rejected the notion of cultural separatism, was against the High Court's Wik decision, opposed acceptance of Aboriginal customary law and worried about the meaning of self-determination.

This is a long list. But it has a conspicuous feature—on each issue public opinion was with Howard. The indigenous policy framework that Howard had inherited was unsustainable. It was a house built over thirty years on good intentions, legal innovation and respect for indigenous culture with a strong bias towards a separate though shared Aboriginal destiny. Sooner or later, it needed to be renegotiated. Howard's instinct told him this—he was prescient and correct.

A new political bargain was required. It was a chance for conservative Australia but the opportunity was squandered for too long.

Howard took years to recover from his humiliation at the May 1997 Reconciliation Convention in Melbourne, when much of the audience stood and turned their backs and he succumbed to anger. 'I appeared to lose focus and control,' he concedes.[6] The wounds were deep and self-inflicted. He carried them privately but his confidence was damaged. This is the psychological origin of Howard's surprise 1998 election-night pledge to make reconciliation a second-term priority, proof this brooding failure had lodged in his brain.

Howard's second departmental head, Peter Shergold, said:

> I think it severely shook his confidence in dealing with Aboriginal leaders. He was always wondering what sort of reception he might get. As a professional politician Howard knew how to behave but with Aboriginal leaders he was often apprehensive, you saw it in the body language. Once he was treated with politeness, then it was different and he would respond.[7]

With the Melbourne humiliation, the distance already separating Howard and Aboriginal leaders became a chasm. This diminished the nation and polarised opinion. 'The reason Aboriginal Affairs was such a difficult area for me was that my own thinking was out of step with the majority of informed thinking on both sides of politics,' Howard said.[8]

But this avoids the heart of the problem: that Howard failed to devise a constructive conservative framework for indigenous affairs and reconciliation. A litany of 'negatives' does not constitute a policy. Reconciliation demanded a proactive response from Howard. The entire nation knew what he was against and, to an extent, this won him votes. But that was short-term politics. Howard's real task was to draw the elements together, identify the concessions he would make and the gains he would require, and negotiate a new political compact. He approached this point over the final 2004–07 term but his political capital was too expended.

The stumbling block for Howard was the apology to Australia's indigenous people. It seemed so small, yet he made it so large. Unable to surmount his resistance to an apology Howard, in the end, wore it as a curse. It became his baggage, carried from one term to the next, an abiding denial of an idea whose time was overdue. By 2007 it had become testimony to his obsolescence. His stubbornness confounded many of his followers, who whispered 'Get it over and done with'. That was not Howard's way. His refusal to apologise was a gift he handed Kevin Rudd, who extracted its capital in full and with brilliance.

'There is an instinctive rejection of the notion of an apology within conservative Australia,' Howard said.[9] Yet his stance transcended politics. It was not in his heart. He believed it was the wrong thing to do. Progressives attacked him for exploiting prejudice when Howard was really upholding his beliefs. This was the true Howard and it will count against him in the toll of history. In the sunset of his prime ministership, lapsing into an unusual introspection, Howard seemed to regret this void. 'I'm the first to admit that this whole area is one I have struggled with during the entire time that I have been prime minister,' he told the Sydney Institute six weeks before losing the election.[10]

In the end, a black man became his friend: it is that simple.

Noel Pearson reached out to Howard. 'Pearson had a great influence on him,' Sinodinos said. 'The shame is that it didn't come sooner.'[11] Pearson's magnetism gave Howard the confidence to make a big leap. 'From 1996 to 1998 I was febrile with dislike of Howard.' Pearson said. 'Despite my grief about Keating's demise I wrote to Howard in 1996 saying he should add to Keating's rights agenda with a full-blown responsibilities agenda. I don't think Howard got it.'[12]

Pearson was a compelling orator, an intellectual able to sway opinion and a leader who studied the fate of his Cape York community. He was a man of two worlds. Inspired by the works of Henry Reynolds, he became a pro-Keating advocate of land rights. Once denouncing the Howard government as 'racist scum' yet observing the destruction within his own community, he pledged to smash the Progressive Left's rights paradigm that had governed indigenous policy for thirty-five years. After the 1998 election Pearson reached two conclusions: Howard was a long-term PM, and his social philosophy was right.

From the start Howard had focussed on practical improvements in Aboriginal communities—housing, health and education. It was a technique to deny the campaign for indigenous political rights and it was denounced by most Aboriginal leaders. This sullen deadlock seemed entrenched.

However, it was shattered by a political whirlwind out of Cape York in 1999 when Pearson, declaring he was 'worried for my mob', attacked the Aboriginal policy orthodoxy for its welfare dependency, saying 'it has torn our society apart, it has made a proud and decent people helpless', leading to an 'inferno of social disintegration'. As a practical visionary Pearson came to lay blame: it was the fault of the Progressive Left, he charged. This was the pro-Labor middle-class political movement that had dominated Aboriginal affairs since Whitlam. Pearson told them bluntly: revise your thinking or get out of indigenous affairs.[13]

If Pearson's critique was valid for the poorest section of Australia, then it had a universal validity. His attack became the most sustained assault on Progressive Left social thinking for a generation and had credibility because it was empirically based. Pearson was saying that Howard's conservative emphasis on individual responsibility and practical action was the right approach—and he wanted an alliance with Howard. The Labor Party was incredulous.

Its shape took years to unfold but the deal was obvious—Pearson would back Howard's practical reconciliation but he wanted Howard to cross the Rubicon and convert to symbolic reconciliation. Offered such a deal, most politicians would seize the gift. But Howard waited too long, unsure and suspicious. Their personal ties developed only in Howard's final term. Pearson set out to persuade Howard, a concept foreign to indigenous leadership.

Pearson said:

I sensed in 2007 there was a chance he could be persuaded. I wanted to grab the opportunity we had lost in 2004 when I had tried to put together a coalition of Aboriginal leaders to deal with Howard but it came to nought. People's aversion to the man had blinded them to political reality. I mean, if you want to carry the Australian people for Reconciliation then you need Howard or somebody like him. I was thinking long-run. We had to get the conservatives pledged to our cause.[14]

Pearson's message to Howard was about the power of conservatism. The upshot was that Howard in his eleventh year pledged a referendum for a 'new settlement' of black–white relations. His aim was to add the conservative vote to the 'reconciliation' vote. 'I don't believe Labor could unite conservative and progressive Australia on this issue,' he said. He wanted to duplicate the 1967 referendum landslide when the 'Yes' vote topped 90 per cent, a fantastic notion after a decade of division.[15]

It was Pearson who opened Howard's eyes. He had put his ideas first in a face-to-face meeting, then via the staff, Sinodinos and Kunkel, and then by letter. His first letter, 6000 words couched as a re-election strategy, was penned from Cairns on 17 September 2007.[16] It will stand as the most remarkable letter written by an Aboriginal leader to a Prime Minister. Pearson was leading Howard towards a conservative commitment to reconciliation.

Dear Prime Minister,

I believe that Australia needs your leadership during the next term of government. You are uniquely positioned to secure the following inspirational agenda for the country:

To move Australia fundamentally but prudently:

1. From 'symbolic and practical reconciliation' to 'recognition of Indigenous people within a reconciled, indivisible nation'

2. From a 'repudiational republic' (which is Australia's current default direction) to an 'affirmational republic'

3. From a 'welfare state' to an 'opportunity state'

You have declared that you will resign during the next term. You need a narrative for Australia that dispels the notion that the work of your public life is done. It must engage the most knowledgeable commentators as well as ordinary people.

The electorate must be convinced that your election programme, if realised, would represent a major part of your life's achievement, and that your achievements during your last term in office will represent a rich legacy in its own right. The voters must believe that your programme lays the best ground for Australia's future, that you will deal with unfinished business that *will need to be dealt with by the country*—if not by you then by a some future prime minister—and that you are the only leader who is able to oversee the implementation of this agenda.

Pearson wanted Howard to defeat Rudd. He offered encouragement, flattery and political advice.

You will recall that I spoke to you about my rating of Australia's prime ministers. I asserted that Australia has never had a Tier 1 leader. If you formulate a vision—that will make the electorate think of you as a potential Tier 1 prime minister, you can win this election. Your aspiration will need to be this ambitious if you are to win …

There is much complacency in the electorate about the idea of a Rudd prime ministership, but there is too much cynicism or scepticism about you…

Your agenda for Australia must be able to achieve two things: first, it must be astonishing (but credible) in order to make the whole electorate and the whole commentariat listen. Your agenda must afford you temporary hegemony in media and public debate …

I do not believe it is possible for the Government to inch its way back through a traditional election campaign. Only a program that contains fundamental policy shifts will be able to attract the full attention of the media and the public.

Presuming an intimacy with Howard, Pearson spoke to him with unusual frankness. He came as a sympathiser who felt Howard could actually help indigenous people and make a difference.

If there is one issue which defines you as a combative Right over Left warrior, it is indigenous policy. Movement to the centre in this area will therefore be the most impactful.

The way to do it is to base the case on your own life story and your own relationship to Indigenous Australians, including your feelings about the 1997 Reconciliation Conference in Melbourne, an event in your prime ministership which you have averred, has troubled you. It will be in the personal telling of your story that you will be able to dispel any sense that there is any insincerity in what you are doing. You must bare your soul.

You did not grow up with black fellas. You did not know any Aboriginal Australians. The important thing about your relative

discomfort and lack of relationship is that you share this experience
with 90 per cent of non-indigenous Australians …

You accept the fact of mistreatment of Aboriginal people, but
you could not accept that reconciliation required a condemnation
of your identity and heritage and a repudiation of our British
heritage and of what has been achieved in Australia.

Pearson now moved to the crux of his argument. He offered an
intellectual foundation for what he believed to be Howard's natural
position on reconciliation:

indigenous misery will not be resolved with current policies. I
believe it is possible and also necessary to reconcile national unity
with indigenous peoplehood …

Almost all sovereign states are shared states. There are 193
states but several thousand distinct peoples. Most countries have
significant minorities that are culturally and historically distinct.

You and I agree on two things:
- The number of sovereign states will not change: only a
  handful (if any) of new states will be recognised.
- It is better that sovereign states have a united (undifferentiated) public citizenship.

The latter of these opinions is probably one that you have held
all of your life. For me it is a position I have arrived at after many
years of grappling with my people's predicament and studying how
other states have fallen victim to (or avoided) internal conflict. I
have come to the conclusion that we must reject a differentiated
public citizenship.

However, the universal challenge is, how do states reconcile a
united public citizenship and peoplehood?

As strongly as I believe in national unity, I believe that
cultural diversity has to be accommodated for nations to reach
their potential. The distinctness, the peoplehood of Australia's
indigenous peoples is not a progressive political construct. It is
a real social and historical force that needs recognition. Failure
to settle this issue will in the long term lead to prolonged social,
political, cultural, spiritual and economic losses and problems.

We need to reconcile the principle of an undifferentiated
national citizenship with indigenous people's rights to land,
language, culture and identity on the following bases:

   i. The supremacy of individual choice and human rights
      ahead of group rights

  ii. The imperative of all Australians to speak English

 iii. The imperative of all children to obtain full, mainstream
      educations so that they can exercise real choice

 iv. The imperative for land reform to enable economic de-
      velopment whilst preserving communal title

For Pearson, this was the basis for a political compact between indigenous and conservative Australians on how to live in harmony. He said these principles highlighted the failure of the recent United Nations Declaration of the Rights of Indigenous Peoples. Damning the Declaration as 'unworkable and disappointing' Pearson said its defect was the inability to accept that group rights must be subservient to both national unity and individual freedom, a critique Howard shared. Analysing indigenous identity Pearson invoked economist Amartya Sen to argue that individuals need to be seen as possessing 'layers of identity'.

> In a reconciled Australia, an indigenous Australian would see herself as an Australian, a citizen of Australia; a member of her clan and indigenous people; a custodian of her traditional culture and language(s), and a member of the Western and British cultural community.

Here was the Pearson synthesis. It was an ideal yet who was to assert it was impossible? But Pearson's vision was at odds with a generation of progressive indigenous policies advanced by Australian governments. He urged Howard to action:

> Denial of peoples' right to retain their identity is morally wrong and will retard social and economic development.
>
> Successful Australian reconciliation would demonstrate two things:
>
> • First, that culturally different peoples with very different histories can live peacefully within a unitary nation state with an undifferentiated citizenship.
>
> • Second, that it is possible to overcome serious problems of under development.
>
> I am talking about constitutional recognition of Aboriginal and Torres Strait Islander people as an indigenous people of the country, and a recognition of their right to keep their culture, language, traditions and identity …

Only you, or a leader very similar to you, can achieve reconciliation.

Pearson now took his exposition on to a new plateau:

Australia is built on two foundation stones: one foundation stone is the indigenous heritage, and on top of that was laid the British heritage. And these foundation stones still exist. They endure, they should endure for the future.

Reconciliation and the affirmational republic need to be linked together conceptually as well as politically. I think that reconciliation alone will not be enough for your re-election bid—you must reconsider your position to a republic as well.

The necessary constitutional amendment requires 'Nixon to go to China'. Only a conservative leader can change the constitution by carrying the conservative constituency and delivering the 80–90 per cent strategy that is needed so that the majority of electors in a majority of the states is achieved. This is something that cannot be successfully me-tooed, because the maths won't allow that. Labor can only prosecute a 51 per cent strategy on constitutional change: only a highly conservative leader can prosecute a 80–90 per cent strategy that has any chance of success.

Howard rejected Pearson's republic proposal. But in a remarkable decision he accepted Pearson's advice on constitutional recognition for the indigenous peoples and pledged to a referendum, proof of Pearson's persuasion.

But Howard was unable to link the two concepts as Pearson proposed and, as a result, lost the necessary impact. He accepted Pearson's flattering contention that he could mobilise conservative voters to change the nation—witness Howard's talk about a 90 per cent vote in his proposed referendum. In his Sydney Institute speech four weeks later, Howard tried to follow Pearson's advice to 'bare your soul', an act contrary to his nature.

In Pearson's second letter, dated 10 October but transmitted the day of Howard's Sydney Institute speech,[17] Pearson wrote:

Dear Prime Minister,

In my discussions with Patrick Dodson and other indigenous leaders in the past three years we articulated the following goal for our people:

'For Aboriginal children to have the same expectations of life as their fellow Australians—to develop their unique cultural, social and economic capital—secured by a new framework of Aboriginal rights and responsibilities, embraced in a national settlement.'

I strongly urge your use of the phrase 'unfinished business' because (i) it resonates with what indigenous people have often described as being the challenge and (ii) because it explicates your candidature for a fifth term: you have important unfinished business to complete for the country's future.

We discussed the question of the apology and it being subsumed by this project. I have never been passionate about the apology and I think I have understood your position on this. I think that present day leaders who apologise for actions taken by actors in history are vulnerable to charges of moral vanity, but nevertheless expression of sorrow and empathy about historical injustice or inhumanity is appropriate.

Indigenous governance institutions are important—however it is their interface with Australian governments that is the nub question. The point of ATSIC was not to establish an interface with governments, rather it established an indigenous affairs ghetto away from the main game.

The key to reform in indigenous affairs is for governments to be obligated to act both diligently and honourably:

- to support the rebuilding of indigenous responsibility
- to honour indigenous rights

The Australian Welfare State induces the most crippling sclerosis in indigenous society because its programs invariably displace responsibility from those who should really be vested with relevant responsibilities (individuals, families, communities).

The recognition of indigenous people-hood requires constitutional amendment. I suggest amendments in two areas, one symbolic and the other substantive:

- In the preamble, Indigenous people's special status is symbolically recognised.
- A new head of power is needed to provide the Commonwealth with jurisdiction to make laws 'with respect to the cultural, social and economic development of Aboriginal and Torres Strait Islander peoples and the achievement of reconciliation between indigenous and non-indigenous Australians.'

In my discussions with John Kunkel from your office we discussed the concern that, in laying out your commitment tonight, you must strike a balance between 'baring the soul' and avoiding an impression of excessive 'introspection'. My advice is to err on the side of passion on this.

Yours sincerely

Noel Pearson

In his speech Howard announced a bill within the first 100 days of his fifth term for a reconciliation statement in the Preamble of the Constitution. He pledged a referendum within eighteen months, saying reconciliation could not be a 51–49 or even a 70–30 project. Admitting the low points in his dialogue with many indigenous leaders Howard said: 'I fully accept my share of the blame for that.'[18]

But Howard was doomed and his belated reconciliation leap died along with his political career at the 2007 poll. As Pearson said, this progress came only after 'years of lost opportunity'.[19] It was Howard's leadership failure not to move sooner; a leader with prescience would have put the referendum idea at the 2004 election and put the referendum to the people in 2005 as part of a new strategy that involved practical and symbolic reconciliation. For Howard, it was the final saga in a story of emotional and political inability to construct a viable indigenous affairs position.

When he arrived in office Howard was trapped by the storm of the *Bringing Them Home* report delivered to his government in April 1997. This report, resulting from a national inquiry into the separation of Aboriginal and Torres Strait Islander children from their families last century, created a sense of grief and hysteria that exposed Howard's emotional and political limitations in Aboriginal policy.

The report was Howard's inheritance from Keating. It had been backed by Labor's Aboriginal Affairs Minister, Robert Tickner, a New South Wales left-wing lawyer who wore his heart on his sleeve, and federal Attorney-General, Michael Lavarch. Tickner knew about the Stolen Generation and unlike most MPs had read academic Peter Read's original path-breaking work on the subject. But Lavarch had the carriage—he found that the Human Rights and Equal Opportunity Commission (HREOC) was pushing to conduct an inquiry.

This was prompted by HREOC President Ronald Wilson and Aboriginal and Torres Strait Islander Social Justice Commissioner Mick

Dodson. 'Wilson and Dodson were advocates for the inquiry, they wanted to do it,' Lavarch said.[20] 'I saw this as a nation-shaping report,' Tickner said.[21]

The inquiry's terms of reference mirrored Labor's mindset. This was not a dispassionate and historical examination of the law, administration and policy surrounding the removal of Aboriginal children based on evidence from Aboriginals, public servants, police and missionaries with a view to documenting for the entire nation the history of how governments had come to such policies and what were their consequences. Such an inquiry was deserved by the nation. But Labor commissioned a different inquiry.

Wilson and Dodson were crusaders, though Wilson had a skeleton in his cupboard. As a High Court judge Wilson had been in the 4–3 minority in the Mabo (No. 1) judgment that made possible the subsequent substantive Mabo and Wik judgments. As Jesuit priest Frank Brennan said: 'If Wilson had had his way then the Mabo case would never have gone anywhere.'[22] Pearson was scathing. 'I was sceptical of Ronald Wilson,' he said. 'He was a classic case of moral vanity with this late-career exercise. If he had his way there was no Mabo, yet the Left lionised him.'[23]

The terms of reference dealt only with removal by compulsion, duress or undue influence. The report's first paragraph said: 'Throughout this report, for ease of reference, we refer to "forcible removal".' The report explained that voluntary removals were not covered. It interpreted 'forcible' removal to include government and police action under legal authority as well as court orders. It found that from 1910 to 1970 'between one in three and one in ten Indigenous children were forcibly removed.'[24] In fact, HREOC did not know the numbers affected, a serious flaw. Earlier survey work by the Australian Bureau of Statistics had suggested a figure of 10 per cent covering voluntary and forcible removals. This pointed to serious defects in methodology.

The document was a literal cry from the heart. It was an oral polemic of tragedy, injustice and grief based on personal stories that moved readers to tears and shock. It was powerful because most Australians had been unaware of this history. 'Grief and loss are the predominant themes of this report,' were the opening words. Kim Beazley wept in the parliament when speaking to its findings.

The report recommended reparations that consisted of an apology from all parliaments and from the churches, restitution, rehabilitation and monetary compensation. The reparations were to cover individuals forcibly removed, family members who suffered, communities that were damaged and descendants of those removed who suffered damage. Individuals were to be entitled to a minimum lump-sum payment from a new National Compensation Fund with proof based on the balance of probabilities. Such payments were not to displace common law rights through the courts. It was an untenable ambit claim.

The report found the removal policy was 'genocidal' within the meaning of the 1948 Convention on the Prevention and Punishment of the Crime of Genocide. It said genocide did not necessarily mean physical destruction but could refer to the aim of eliminating indigenous cultures. It argued that genocide did not need to be motivated just by animosity—even if one motive was to look after the better interests of the child, that did not rule out genocide. This fudged the line between assimilation and genocide.

Wilson said four years later in an interview with the *Bulletin* that it was a 'mistake' to use the word genocide. He said the authors debated the term and decided the word would 'lend greater force to the reparations'—a concession that the genocide charge was a political tactic and an insight into the 'rights culture' techniques. Wilson said the report heard 'stories' rather than testimony and listened to 'story tellers' rather than witnesses. He claimed the report revealed 'the truth' but the test of proof used was short of a court of law. He said the inquiry was careful to ensure that it was 'in line with indigenous aspirations because, after all, it was indigenous sources who were agitating for the inquiry'.[25]

Noel Pearson said:

> It wasn't a history; it was moral advocacy. I knew from the history of my own community that this story was very complicated. Some children were stumped up at the missions by their mothers, some were delivered by troopers, others were saved from terrible situations and some were arbitrarily taken. The characterisation of this history by the word 'stolen' simplified a more complex story. It generated the 'rescued' generation concept and that had some validity.[26]

The report had two consequences. First, it entrenched the idea of a Stolen Generation in popular discourse and this featured prominently in Rudd's formal apology. Second, it guaranteed an unresolved political dispute over the motives, administration and scale of the policy because the report was neither objective nor a reliable comprehensive history of what happened. It was an agonising yet therapeutic experience for many Aboriginals who had lived in silence with their child removal.

But the report's polemical nature—together with its 'genocide' finding, inadequate rules of evidence, sweeping reparations agenda and inability to interview many of the public servants involved who believed they were diligent in looking after the interests of the children— guaranteed a sceptical or negative response from wide parts of the Australian community. Wilson failed to bring the country with him. Indeed, the nation was polarised between those moved by the scale of the injustice and those rightly suspicious of the politics involved.

With usual timing, Howard's speech to the Australian Reconciliation Convention in Melbourne to honour the thirtieth anniversary of the 1967 referendum coincided with the HREOC report and Howard's Ten Point Plan in response to the High Court's Wik decision. Arriving to reorientate reconciliation from a Labor to a Coalition framework, Howard misjudged his presentation.

The intriguing aspect of Howard's speech, however, is forgotten. He came close to delivering what Aboriginals wanted: he made a personal apology but not an apology on behalf of his government. Howard told the meeting that reconciliation must primarily confront 'the true causes of Aboriginal and Torres Strait Islander disadvantage' and this was the 'cornerstone' of its meaning. It was a mistake to apportion 'blame and guilt' for past injustices. As he spoke, several dozen people stood and turned their backs—but some turned around, a few even sat down and many clapped when Howard surprised his audience.

'Personally, I feel deep sorrow for those of my fellow Australians who suffered injustices under the practices of past generations towards indigenous people,' he said. 'Equally, I am sorry for the hurt and trauma many here today may continue to feel as a consequence of those practices.' And Howard, momentarily, seemed surprised by the flash of warmth from a critical audience.[27]

This moment hung in the air—both sides shocked at what might be possible—before it was lost. Howard's next line warned that 'we must not join those who would portray Australia's history since 1788 as little more than a disgraceful record of imperialism, exploitation and racism'. Before he finished the audience had rejected him. 'I reacted to interjections on Wik,' Howard said. 'It looked bad and I accept that.'[28]

At the Convention's close, Brennan joined with Reconciliation Council chair, Pat Dodson, and the audience to express a collective apology. The next week in parliament Howard said: 'My government does not support a formal national apology.' His reason was that the current generation cannot 'be held accountable for the errors, wrongs and misdeeds' of past generations.[29] He kept this position for a decade.

It was an untenable excuse. Howard accepted that governments apologise for past wrongs: witness Japan and Germany over World War II. He confused the obligation on governments to acknowledge their nation's past with imposing guilt on the current generation for historical wrongs. The public understood the difference. Every state government, Labor and non-Labor, would apologise.

One of Howard's senior advisers at the time offered a sharp analysis: 'The Prime Minister felt these policies at the time had the support of government, churches and the public and were done from good motives. He believed it was wrong to condemn them in retrospect as racist and exploitative by applying the values of a latter age. The point is, Howard felt the apology was wrong.'[30]

This is a sounder explanation. Yet Howard seemed unable to explain his position. In 2007 he said: 'The challenge I have faced around indigenous identity politics is in part an artefact of who I am and the time in which I grew up.'[31] It was a tempting line, but untenable. After all, Paul Keating was a 1950s child. When Howard and Keating first entered parliament their attitude towards Aboriginals was similar—unsympathetic and uninterested. But Keating grew and Howard stultified.

'I don't believe in apologising for something for which I was not personally responsible,' Howard said. 'It's as simple as that.'[32] Yet almost nobody saw the apology in these terms. When Rudd extended the official apology in February 2008 he avoided any such interpretation. The real issue was not guilt but responsibility—it was accepting that governments had committed past wrongs.

Howard's real motive lies in his view of history and identity. He had a passion for the idea of Australia as a virtuous settler society. It was an ideology, originating in Howard's family life, and it was to be defended as though any breach would render irreparable damage. His fixation was Australian achievement and he was reluctant to accept the parallel story of official racism. Howard had no trouble admitting there were misdeeds—but he rejected the revisionist view that these 'misdeeds' required official redemption.

Historian Bain Attwood wrote of the psychological threat to conservative Australia arising from the growth of Aboriginal history that shook 'the comforting map of the past'. For some people this reinterpretation 'threatened to strip the nation of its moral legitimacy and draw into question whether it was worthy of anyone's love and loyalty'.[33] Howard seemed apprehensive that this door, once opened, might unleash forces leading to reparation and separatism. Speaking at the Sydney Institute, Howard said: 'I have always acknowledged the past mistreatment of Aboriginal people ... Yet I still feel that the overwhelming balance sheet of Australian history is a positive one. In the end, I could not accept that Reconciliation required a condemnation of the Australian heritage I had always owned.'[34] He would not violate his own faith in Australia.

This is Howard's epitaph, for better or worse. There was nothing in Liberal Party ethos that dictated its rejection of an apology. The party took this stance because it was Howard's party. Like Saint Peter, Howard had three opportunities to apologise—in 1997, 1999 and 2000—and he refused on each occasion. It was Howard who invested the apology with more significance than it warranted. The more Howard refused, the more important the apology became and the more support it won.

To calm his fears, Howard should have read Henry Reynolds, spearhead of the new history. He would have been surprised to find common ground between them over the rooted sense of Australian-ness:

> In writing about dispossession I haven't myself felt dispossessed. I cannot remember a time when I didn't feel at home in Tasmania ... you either feel you belong or you don't. And once that sense is there it can't be given up, willed away or reasoned out of existence. Almost thirty years of writing revisionist history changed my views about many things but never touched my sense of where I had come from, where I belonged and where since early childhood I had known the wind, the sky and the silver slanting light.[35]

It was a metaphor for the nation's ability to transcend admission of past wrongs.

Many of Howard's colleagues, including Peter Costello, were shocked on election night in 1998 when Howard, in his victory speech, suddenly pledged himself 'to the cause of true reconciliation'. He saw the unfinished business. Yet, as Sinodinos said, Howard was expressing 'an aspiration, not a policy agenda'.[36]

The next year, after Australian Democrats Senator Aden Ridgeway became the second Aboriginal to be elected to the parliament, Howard negotiated a new motion with him. The parliament expressed 'its deep and sincere regret' and Howard said he hoped the community would see the motion as 'a genuine, generous and sincere attempt to recognise past errors'.[37] As Brennan said, 'the motion was a significant improvement on nothing'. Howard had shifted position but the issue was stalemated.

The 'Stolen Generation' debate saw both sides in denial. The government was unable to confront the depth of official racism in the past, particularly in its pre-war phase when half-caste children were removed on the assumption that mixed blood Aboriginals would eventually be absorbed into the white population. The assumption was that Aboriginal culture was worthless, becoming white was a reprieve and such children were to be educated 'at white standard' in order to move onto 'an equal footing with whites'.[38]

On the other hand, many of Howard's critics seemed unable to grasp that the policy was based in law, public administration and the values of the age. Child removal began when the idea of racial equality was rejected internationally as well as domestically. It was a welfare policy as well as a racial policy, a point many could not admit. In his August 2000 Federal Court judgment, Justice O'Loughlin provided an historical overview showing the policy applied to part-Aboriginal children, that they were educated as a government responsibility, that it was assumed that such children, left in the camps, would be treated as outcasts and that parental consent had not been needed. By the 1950s Sir Paul Hasluck was the responsible minister and his test for removal was what best delivered 'a happy future for the child', rather than any hard and fast rule.[39]

The Howard government rejected financial compensation, as did the Rudd government. It was unrealistic to think any national government would do otherwise given that the policy was lawful. But rejection of compensation was a further argument for an apology.

However, Howard's nadir came in May 2000 with culmination of the decade-long reconciliation process. The Centenary of Federation was the artificial deadline for achieving reconciliation. The symbolic climax came in Sydney over 27–28 May with ceremonies at the Opera House and an estimated 200 000 people crossing the Harbour Bridge.

Before the event Howard moved to protect his back He raised the bridge walk in cabinet. Costello recalls:

> He said I hear that some of you might be walking and this won't look good, so we had better have a collective decision … I just said if we have to have solidarity why not all show solidarity by walking. I said this would be a very powerful statement, a real story … When you think about it: who can be against reconciliation? Even to this day, I can't figure why you wouldn't walk. My view is that we grossly mishandled this.[40]

'I think Costello was isolated,' Peter Reith said. 'Howard had made clear that he wouldn't join the walk. The cabinet wasn't going to humiliate the Prime Minister. Costello's plan was never going to be agreed.'[41] Howard said: 'I don't ever remember Peter Costello arguing in favour of a formal apology. A majority of cabinet was against us marching. I largely took the view this was an opportunity for public expression; it wasn't something a prime minister did.'[42]

Because negotiations over the final declaration between the Howard government and the Council for Aboriginal Reconciliation broke down, the entire event was fractured. In the end, the Council endorsed an assertive document unacceptable to Howard. The Council's earlier draft, penned by David Malouf, was an effort to find common ground. It should have been the basis for a settlement. The sticking point was the apology—again.[43]

It was a mistake for Howard not to reach agreement on the declaration, even if that meant conceding the apology for everything else he wanted. The draft unacceptable to Howard had read: 'One part of the nation apologises and expresses its sorrow and its sincere regret for the injustices of the past, so the other part accepts the apology and forgives.'

At an uplifting Opera House ceremony the declaration was presented to all of Australia's political leaders, the end of a ten-year process. Howard took the document but did not embrace its words. The ceremony became a bizarre Australian tragedy. Most of the Aboriginal leaders rose to the occasion, feeling obliged to manage Howard's limitations. A dignified Evelyn Scott, Council for Aboriginal Reconciliation chair, worked to contain the difficulty created by a man of power. Howard, on stage with six premiers, the Opposition leader, the Democrats leader and the Governor-General, was a lonely figure. The next day he declined the bridge walk.

At this point Howard became the symbol of a divided nation. On this weekend he seemed a prime minister isolated, irrelevant and lacking legitimacy. His method of reconciliation with its focus on practical outcomes seemed to have lost traction despite its necessity.

Howard, in fact, was deeply troubled. 'He knew he looked heartless,' one of his closest advisers said.[44] Howard had lost the politics—it was obvious that the next prime minister, Labor or Liberal, would apologise. He had converted the apology into a mammoth issue against himself. Polls at the time suggested that the public was with Howard. Newspoll showed voters dividing about 60–40 per cent against an apology.[45] But

Rudd would show that a prime minister who led with the apology would pull opinion in his favour.

However, Howard's position did evolve and by 2005 he was pledged to both practical and symbolic reconciliation. In retirement, he argued that he had been finally vindicated. 'In the end, ironically, public opinion settled closer to my position,' Howard said. 'This was illustrated by public support for my Northern Territory intervention.'[46]

Howard did leave his landmark. But he bears responsibility for much of the delay, division and demoralisation that marked indigenous policy during his time in power. For too long he lacked the means of persuasion.

Surveying Howard's era, Pearson offered a balanced judgement:

I have a sense of loss. We haven't completed the circle—bringing the responsibilities and rights agendas together properly. You know that Keating could have done it—with a longer political life he would have been comfortable with a responsibilities agenda together with rights. Had Howard moved earlier and had the indigenous leaders been more acute, then Howard, I believe, would have united the two positions. But the big event under Howard was the responsibilities agenda. There's no hope for indigenous people without this tectonic shift and Howard forced it through with his obduracy.[47]

PART V

THE CRISIS OF
LEGITIMACY

26

THE PERILS OF PAULINE

We've obviously not in favour of Pauline Hanson, so we may as well say so.
–Alexander Downer to John Howard, 1996

It was John Howard's strongest censure of Alexander Downer—an angry Prime Minister rang to complain about his Foreign Minister's stand against Pauline Hanson. 'Why are you saying this?' Howard asked of Downer's criticisms. 'The trouble with your comments is that they look as though you're responding to Hanson and I'm not.' Howard was on the warpath.[1] His sensitivity about Hanson was extreme—but his judgement was flawed.

The exchange had been triggered by Asia's backlash against Hanson's September 1996 maiden speech explicitly injecting race into Australian politics and Howard's equivocal response. In reply to Howard, Downer defended himself—he was speaking as Foreign Minister and for Australia's national interest. Downer recalls:

> I said to Howard, 'I think this is the line we should be running. As Foreign Minister I've got to take into account where we are in the world and this isn't helping. We're obviously not in favour of Pauline Hanson so we may as well say so.' But Howard wasn't very happy. It was one of only two or three occasions when he ever rang me direct to complain.[2]

Crossing Howard was not done lightly. Downer was unnerved but he held firm. 'We've done it now,' he told his advisers as he put the phone down. 'But it's the right thing to do.'[3]

The diplomatic service was in shock at Howard's behaviour. It is revealing that in Downer's dealings with Howard over nearly twelve years the dispute between them that most sticks in his mind was not over war, terrorism or high policy—it was over Pauline Hanson, an amateur populist with a 'Viagra in the bush' sex appeal.[4]

For Philip Flood, Secretary of DFAT, the issue was a nightmare. He asked missions in Asia to document the local reaction; Australian ambassadors were ready to comply. Flood wanted Howard's office to sight as much of this adverse reaction as possible. On occasions Flood took the cables and newspaper clippings direct to Howard's office chief, Grahame Morris. But Morris was unimpressed—he had no intention of allowing such ripples to disrupt Howard's domestic strategy.

Flood raised the issue with Howard once during a phone call. He recalled:

> I said to the Prime Minister the position he was taking on Hanson was damaging our relations with South-East Asia. I also argued it was damaging the strategy he had asked me to pursue from the start—to progress relations with Asia on our own terms. I said 'You want me to do this but your position on Hanson undermines our efforts.' But he wasn't interested. His reply was terse, something like 'Philip, you're wrong' and that was about it. He dismissed what I was saying.[5]

Flood was almost incredulous at the Hanson saga. Appointed by Howard to run DFAT, Flood felt that Howard was compromising his responsibility as prime minister. He said: 'There were real principles at stake. In my view what was happening was reprehensible. Howard's comments about political correctness and a relaxation of past censorship gave a green light to Hanson. The Prime Minister's attitude towards Hanson was a serious lapse on his part.'[6]

As 1997 unfolded without any coherent anti-Hanson strategy from Howard, Flood grew more alarmed. He saw no sign that Howard read the material he provided. 'Grahame Morris didn't seem to be swayed at all,' Flood said. 'Can't you see, Philip, that we risk losing these voters?' Morris said on one occasion.[7] They were talking past one another. Flood felt Howard was acquiescing in a position close to racist. 'I thought this was a serious problem for Australia and it worried me a lot,' he said. 'It clearly worried Tim Fischer and Alexander Downer. Our position was being damaged in the region and we seemed unable to devise an effective reply.'[8]

Howard's position contrasted with that of Trade Minister Fischer. Branding Hanson 'dumb and divisive', Fischer said: 'I reject the comments of any individual who would prejudice our trade, investment and tourism, whether they live in Ipswich, Ingham or Innamincka.' He recalled:

> I said we had to get real. I was standing against the agenda of Pauline Hanson and I made that clear. Howard didn't say anything to me. As National Party leader I was in a different position to Downer. I believe Grahame Morris was loading Howard up with the 'softly, softly' tactic.[9]

Peter Costello was appalled by Hanson. He said: 'My view was that she represented the far right whose ambition was to discredit and undermine mainstream conservative parties and, in time, replace them.' The Victorian Liberal Party could not comprehend Howard's weakness on Hanson.[10] It was a double problem—Howard was reluctant to confront Hanson and he was upset when other ministers challenged her.

Yet Downer and Fischer held their beachhead—their criticism of Hanson became a feature of their profiles. 'I use my language, they use theirs,' Howard replied testily. Flood felt Downer had a streak of toughness concealed by his looks. Yet the Hanson affair also showed Downer's loyalty. There were strict limits to how hard Downer and Fischer pushed; they would not let Hanson destroy their relations with Howard.

Ashton Calvert, who succeeded Flood as DFAT secretary, said:

> The Hanson issue was damaging because it was seen as an example of the way Howard thought. He saw Hanson in narrow domestic terms, not in foreign policy terms. It was damaging because it enabled people in the region to say that Australia was not meeting the test required of a neighbour. I find it hard to believe the Howard of 2003 would have made the same mistakes as the Howard of 1996 and 1997.[11]

In mid-1997 Downer sent Howard a summary of the views of Australia's Asian ambassadors from a Canberra meeting where Hanson became a dominant topic. It said ambassadors were 'uniformly concerned' that the Hanson debate had 'already done some damage to our national interests in the region and had the potential to do further serious damage ... and specific damage to our political and commercial interests'. The meeting believed that 'a strong and prompt government response to Hanson was vital'.[12]

The power of Hanson lay in her racial chauvinism, isolationist purity and economic nationalism. Her party, One Nation, offered a phoney but plausible vision, a manipulation of grievance, exploitation of rural resentment, funny-money quackery and racism. Usually such protest movements flicker across the terrain and extinguish. But a conjunction of elements gave Hanson political ignition.

'She had the potential to destroy the government,' said Morris.

> Most of the difficult periods in Howard's life are when he's under attack from the Right. The Coalition doesn't have any idea about how to deal with an attack from the Right—whether it's Joh Bjelke-Petersen, or a John Elliott business type or a Pauline Hanson. Howard always feels comfortable when his right flank is solid. But if the right wing is in trouble then you get terrible instability.[13]

'She was a mortal threat to the government,' said Minchin, who backed Howard's management of the issue.[14]

The Hanson affair was a sweeping Australian failure—of leadership, of media and of popular culture. It is wrong to sheet the entire blame to Howard. It is incredible that Hanson, despite limited electoral support, became the most identified and discussed Australian in Asia and, from this profile, projected an image of Australia to the world as mean, ignorant and racist.

Hanson came close to destroying the Howard government at the 1998 election when One Nation polled more than 8 per cent of the primary vote or more than a million votes. This was the most dramatic third-party eruption in Australian history. Hanson represented a unique Howard failure—he misread the morality and the politics, a rare double. Howard misjudged the threat Hanson constituted to his government and he misjudged the threat she represented to Australia.

Though he survived, Howard was tainted. Hanson sought to re-inject race into politics and the first obligation on the prime minister was to repudiate this attempt. Because of Howard's equivocation the shadow of race overhung his prime ministership and the accusation that he played racial politics became gospel among his critics. This was not a case of Howard sacrificing principle for electoral gain—with Hanson he sacrificed both.

Hanson was a populist breakaway from the conservative base. She stole Coalition primary votes in greater proportion than she returned via the preference system. This meant that in two-party-preferred terms Hanson was a vote transfer machine from the Coalition to Labor. Labor denounced

Hanson but thrived on her presence. She realised the Coalition's worst nightmare: a battle on two fronts. 'The skyrocket was going to flame out but it took a lot longer than we thought,' Morris said.[15]

As the Liberal Party candidate for the safe ALP seat of Oxley, based in Ipswich, Hanson was disendorsed during the 1996 campaign for racial remarks. The decision was taken by Howard, Andrew Robb and Morris. The upshot was that Hanson, as a disendorsed Liberal, became an independent and, without any Liberal candidate in Oxley, defeated the sitting ALP member. She was elected entirely by accident. Hanson was an opponent of the Howard government, having been thrown out of the Liberal Party.

Petite, with red hair and quavering voice, she introduced herself as a mother of four, a sole parent and a businesswoman with a fish-and-chip shop. Her maiden speech began with her complaint that 'governments are encouraging separatism in Australia by providing opportunities, land, moneys and facilities available only to Aboriginals'. Hanson was sick of the view that 'Aboriginals are the most disadvantaged people in Australia'. Claiming the nation was 'being divided into black and white' Hanson said 'I am fed up with being told, "This is our land." Well, where the hell do I go? I was born here … I am calling for ATSIC to be abolished. It is a failed, hypocritical and discriminatory organisation.'

The second half of her speech provoked an even greater reaction:

> I and most Australians want our immigration policy radically reviewed and that of multiculturalism abolished. I believe we are in danger of being swamped by Asians … A truly multicultural country can never be strong or united … Immigration must be halted in the short term.

Hanson attacked international capital, calling on government to end 'kowtowing to financial markets, international organisations, world bankers, investment companies and big business people … The government should cease all foreign aid immediately.'[16] Some of her grievances were legitimate and Howard saw this. Yet Hansonism from its inception sought to repudiate Australia's position as a liberal, non-racist, immigrant nation.

Initially, however, Hanson was not big news. It was Howard who gave her momentum. In one of his worst judged speeches, to the Liberal State Council in Queensland on 22 September 1996, Howard signalled sympathy for Hanson and contempt for her critics. He saw Hanson entirely within the context of his election victory—as an extreme reflection of the tides that had carried him to power. He backed her right to free speech, as though this was the issue. He gave a mocking denunciation of Keating—saying he was defeated because he lost touch with mainstream Australia and listened only to 'the flatterers and the fawners' in the press gallery who had become 'a self-deluded political elite'.

'One of the great changes that has come over Australia in the last six months is that people do feel able to speak a little more freely and a little more openly about what they feel,' Howard said. 'In a sense the pall of censorship on certain issues has been lifted … I think there has been a change and I think that's a very good thing.'

Howard offered an example. Three years earlier, during the native title debate, the *Age* carried a cartoon of himself and Peter Reith on horses shooting Aboriginals above a caption 'The second dispossession'— merely because, Howard said, 'we disagreed with the government'. He felt his election 'has done something to make that kind of neo-McCarthyist zealous prejudiced reaction' a little less acceptable.[17]

Howard was sympathetic to Hanson not for what she *supported* but for what she *opposed*. Hanson attacked the Aboriginal industry, political elites, divisive multiculturalism and ATSIC, and Howard agreed with each of these views. When Howard looked at Hanson voters he saw Howard battlers. He could not shake the notion that she was part of his success, not his failure. Yet this proved to be folly. He was appeasing a movement that would seek his destruction. As late as April 1997 Howard said dismissively: 'I take the gloves off to real opponents … I believe that by the time of the next election … she will have disappeared.' Meanwhile the National Party in Queensland was collapsing.[18]

Seven weeks after Hanson's maiden speech the government and Opposition unanimously voted in parliament a motion that upheld Australia's commitment to equal rights 'regardless of race, colour, creed or origin', support for a non-discriminatory immigration policy and rec- onciliation with the indigenous peoples.[19] But the Hanson genie had escaped.

Howard was less prepared to take a stand on moral principle because he was less convinced that great principle was at stake. It was one thing for Hanson to critique political correctness; it was entirely another thing to embrace racist policy. The difference was basic, yet Howard missed it. This confusion was fundamental to his leadership failure. Turning a blind eye was no answer. This was a challenge to non-negotiable principles of Australian society.

The revival of racist positions would damage Australia's interest in Asia, yet Howard seemed to have no comprehension that the White Australia policy legacy dictated that Australia could afford no quarter on race issues. Howard had been vulnerable on race since his 1988 suggestion about cutting back on Asian immigration in the cause of social cohesion.[20] While he admitted in 1995 that these remarks were a mistake, they had not been forgotten.

From the moment of Howard's Queensland speech the story changed—the issue was not Hanson but Howard's equivocation over Hanson. The tactical blunder was staggering. Morris said:

> The strategy was really to starve Hanson of oxygen. As it turned out, we couldn't. The media kept chasing her and giving her publicity. So Howard's strategy of not picking on her was probably right but it didn't work. We genuinely thought if the Prime Minister picks on this woman we'll just make her more popular.[21]

The tactic missed the greater logic—that Howard's refusal to reject Hanson would make her a far bigger story.

Minchin defended Howard's integrity. 'He wasn't going to insincerely criticise Hanson as a witch and I respect him for that. John felt Hanson was a reaction to the excess of the Keating era and it would have been insincere on his part to condemn her.'[22]

It was inevitable that Howard's attitude would become a test of his standing in the region. The magnitude of the blunder was staggering— Howard allowed himself to be defined in Asia by a prejudiced political amateur.

The result was predictable—the progressive media launched an assault. Hanson became the mechanism to delegitimise Howard. By 1998 Hanson had become notorious worldwide, chiefly the result of overseas media following the Australian media. This was a fantastic distortion of her importance and news value. It betrayed the myopia of a media class that was self-righteous and devoid of perspective. It is difficult to imagine other comparable nations where a solitary right-wing populist occupying one seat in the national parliament for one term would achieve such status.

ANOP pollster Rod Cameron said the Hanson machine was driven by 'criticism from the elites, the more criticism she gets, the better she travels'. Liberal Party Director Lynton Crosby reported: 'Our research found that every time the media or others focussed on Pauline Hanson her support—and One Nation's—would rise in the polls.' It didn't matter whether the publicity was good or bad. Journalist Nicolas Rothwell said that each insult, fascist, racist or Nazi, 'is a recruiting cry'. He warned that constant harping on her voice, dress and past liaisons was counterproductive and that the phalanx of media critics applied an 'emotional bite' absent from the coverage of other parties, a factor that people noticed.[23]

But Hanson was a compelling story. Having left school at fifteen, she had survived two broken marriages, four children, two angry former husbands and two alienated older sons.[24] She did not live poorly. Journalist David Leser, who interviewed her at home wrote: 'Hanson's house is a hacienda of polished floorboards and wood panels on 65 hectares of grazing country boasting 25 head of cattle and a number of Arabian horses.'[25] On another occasion Leser saw a woman beset with her 'creeping realisation that it has all spun out of her control'.[26]

Meanwhile the stories from Australia's media rolled across Asia like a thunder clap. Some of the most influential papers in Asia covered the Hanson phenomenon at length, including the *South China Morning Post* in Hong Kong, the *Asian Wall Street Journal, The Nation* and the *Bangkok Post* from Thailand, and Malaysia's *New Straits Times*. The themes were Howard's refusal to repudiate Hanson's racism and Hanson's support from the Australian people. Australia's ambassador to Thailand, Cavan Hogue, said: 'The Australian media line that Howard was too slow to react was taken up in Thailand's media. The local angle was "Has the leopard really changed its spots?" It was a reference to White Australia.'[27]

The *Jakarta Post* warned that 'racist views in Australia are still alive and well' and said Asia felt that if Australia was 'genuine about valuing its relations with Asian countries, Hanson's remarks would have been repudiated immediately' by Howard.[28] *The Nation* in Thailand said that Howard's silence 'endorses Australia's racist fringe' and accused Howard of having a history of exploiting racism. The *Asian Wall Street Journal*, in a more sophisticated view, said Australia's record on democracy, human rights and multiculturalism meant that it would be held to a higher standard.[29] The *New Straits Times* said that more alarming than Hanson was 'the groundswell of support she is receiving from middle Australians' and people crying out 'we love you'. The paper said a survey revealed that two out of three Australians supported Hanson.[30]

Many publications, including the *South China Morning Post* and *Bangkok Post*, reported that the Asian student market and Asian investment in Australia were at risk. The Malaysian Government had a field day. Trade Minister Rafidah Aziz appealed to Malaysians in Australian to

return home if they were being discriminated against.[31] Dr Mahathir
Mohamad said students would be recalled if they became racist targets.[32]
Long articles appeared on the history of the White Australia policy, its
abolition and its resurgence. The letters to regional papers were filled
with frequent reports of racist incidents and Australia's retreat towards
White Australia.

The debate was often surreal. Queensland Premier Rob Borbidge,
on a visit to Hong Kong, insisted that his state was still a safe place for
Asians to visit and to live. But Australia was depicted as a country in
dysfunctional decline, with *The Nation* saying that unless Australia
tackled this issue 'it will be a small backward-looking land influenced by
[xenophobia] … in a region which most pundits predict will become the
economic center of the world'.[33]

The government's decision to cut the immigration intake by 8 per
cent in 1997–98 was depicted as a response to Hanson. In August 1997
the *Asian Wall Street Journal* had the honesty to editorialise that 'the Asian
press is one medium that has blown up Ms Hanson's allegation that her
country is being "swamped" by immigrants into a major, largely bogus,
story about "racist Australia"'.[34]

Reflecting on Asian attitudes towards Australia, Hogue wrote:

> While racism in Australia has been reduced quite fundamentally
> over the last fifty years it remains strong in much of Asia. Many
> ethnic Chinese migrate to Australia from Southeast Asia to escape
> racism in the countries of their birth. There have been no anti-
> Asian riots in Australia for well over a hundred years; they are still
> going on in some parts of Asia.[35]

This perspective was rare during the Hanson surge.

Flood saw there was much confected outrage from Asia. The region
'was being two-faced given the extent of racism that is tolerated in a
number of countries'.[36] The point was Australia's vulnerability to the
racism charge. Fischer said Hanson 'gave strength to our enemies and our
commercial competitors'.[37] From Bangkok, Hogue sent a cable titled 'The
Perils of Pauline', arguing that 'Australia had to tackle Hanson's impact
in the region as quickly as possible because once the media perception is
established it is very hard to alter.'[38]

Morris had read many cables, including those that Flood forwarded
to him. As a journalist he quickly saw the pattern. 'Most of the cables
were reporting newspaper articles from Asia based on articles originally
published in Australia,' he said. It was obvious to Morris that the Australian

media was driving Asia's reaction. 'We were going around in circles,' Morris said. 'Everyone was saying "we're going to be ruined because nobody will trade with us". But when we actually spoke to Asian leaders they pretty well understood this person was a maverick.'[39]

Downer argued that the Left had to share part of the blame. 'You don't want people slagging off at Australia saying we're racists,' he said. 'But this was being said in Australia and being replayed into Asia. The Left in Australia was portraying it as though Hansonism was created by John Howard. I kept explaining to people in Asia that Hanson had been expelled from our party. She was our political opponent. They were often surprised at this.[40] Hogue affirms this point: 'People thought Hanson was part of the Howard government.'[41]

In April 1997, at Ipswich Civic Hall, Pauline Hanson's One Nation was launched as a political party. In her speech Hanson pledged to restrict foreign ownership, restore tariffs, curb immigration, restore equality and reject the Aboriginal industry and multiculturalism. 'We have been pushed far enough,' she said.[42] A Newspoll survey taken over the 2–4 May weekend showed One Nation's support at 7 per cent, a new threshold. Howard had to respond.

It was on 8 May, in his speech to the Australia–Asia Society, that Howard offered his first sustained critique of Hanson. He said:

> She is wrong when she suggests that Aboriginals are not disadvantaged. She is wrong when she suggests that Australia is in danger of being swamped by Asians ... Every Australian, regardless of colour, race or creed, is entitled to walk our streets, ride our buses and trains, play sport on our fields and pursue their work with confidence, utterly free of discrimination, vilification or insult. Every Australian, regardless of background, is entitled to be treated with total respect and total dignity ... Those who propose putting up the shutters could not be more wrong.[43]

Engagement with Asia, Howard said, would depend on 'a deep and greater understanding of the region's people'. There was 'no geographic linkage more important' to Australia than Asia and 'we are forever part of this part of the world'. Yet Howard also argued that, because Australia was a long-term partner to the region, 'we do not come as a supplicant'. His message was that mutual respect 'has to be a two-way thing'.[44]

The Sydney dinner was a glittering event. After Howard sat down Morris walked over to Flood's table and said: 'Philip, are you satisfied now?' Flood replied: 'Yes, Grahame, but it's nearly a year too late.'[45]

Why had it taken Howard so long? From the start there had been one obvious tactic—respect for Hanson as a person and a cool criticism of her policies. That criticism was not hard to make. On the economy, she sought resort to protection and trade retaliation, a reversion to a Fortress Australia. She showed no desire to accept Asians as friends, let alone as economic and security partners. Her policies would mean slower growth, more unemployment and new social divides. The strategic implications were that Australia would be left without friends or genuine partners in Asia, the Pacific and America. Under Hanson's agenda Australia would become a pariah nation. It was not hard to campaign effectively against Hanson—but it was not done.

Hanson exploited multiple grievances, her targets being Aboriginals, Asians, immigrants, banks, foreign money, multiculturalism and the established parties. Her real target was the political system. Almost everybody would agree with one or another of her sentiments because she shook the cage into which Australia had consigned its past. Hanson wanted the old monoculture and the old economy and she won support among victims of change—rural communities, blue-collar workers and unemployed older males. She became a political metaphor for a deeper dysfunction—the risk that Australia would lose its nerve on the bridge between past and future.

Beneath his rejection of DFAT's concerns, Howard made a tough judgement—that Australia's relations with Asia would not be damaged by Hanson. Howard was focussed on hard power, not soft power. He believed Australia's economic, trade, financial and security ties would not be hurt and that Asian media reports about Hanson would fade. After a great fright, this view was largely vindicated.

When Hanson was a distant memory, Downer sided with Howard. 'At the end of the day, did Hanson have any practical consequence?' he asked. 'Probably not.'[46] Drawing the line on Thailand, one of the countries most affected, Hogue said: 'Hanson had little impact at government level. There was no drop in Thai student numbers or trade. The damage finished up being restricted to Australia's corporate image—and for a while, this was substantial.'[47]

Downer's excuse for Howard is too convenient. The truth is that damage was done and it was largely unnecessary. Howard's focus was on the domestic political equation.

The ALP National Executive decided in mid-1997 to place Hanson last on voting tickets at federal and state elections. Labor became the anti-Hanson party. A succession of senior Liberals demanded that One

Nation be put last on Coalition tickets. This was critical because the only way One Nation candidates, including Hanson, would be elected was by Coalition preferences. In May 1998 Costello said that One Nation would be put last in his seat 'because I want to make it entirely clear that is not the future for Australia'.

When Howard saw this interview he rang Costello. 'He was angry,' Costello reported. 'I replied that I had every right to decide how preferences were going to be allocated in my seat … the longer we let the issue run, the more damaging it would become.' Costello had exposed Howard's lack of leadership.[48]

Yet Howard had credible concerns. His calculation was that he would win the 1998 election provided he got a good share of One Nation preferences. Howard's golden rule of politics was to safeguard the conservative base. 'He was always focussed on this, almost obsessed by it,' said David Kemp.[49] Minchin said: 'Right-wing breakouts without an exchange of preferences pose a mortal threat. I knew that One Nation could destroy the government. It was for this very reason I thought it was a mistake to put them last and invite their retaliation against us.'[50]

The dilemma, however, would be resolved by the Queensland state election of 13 June 1998 that saw the defeat of National Party Premier Rob Borbidge, bringing to power a new ALP premier, Peter Beattie. Hanson's party had the strongest vote among conservatives, polling 23 per cent compared with 15 per cent for the Nationals and 16 per cent for the Liberals. The election proved that One Nation had the potential to destroy a conservative government.

This result followed the decision of the National and Liberal parties in Queensland to preference One Nation ahead of Labor.[51] Hanson's party won 11 out of 89 seats and eight of these were delivered because of this preference decision. The Coalition was feeding the monster that would devour it.

The election revealed two big trends: One Nation stole the National Party base in regional Queensland, and urban Liberal voters hostile to the Coalition's preference deal with Hanson defected to Labor. The Liberals lost nearly a third of their Brisbane vote. It was a double blow. Borbidge's tactic, in effect, had been to offer One Nation a deal. With the National Party under assault, he saw Labor as the enemy and One Nation the potential ally.

At the national level Labor could oppose Hanson on moral grounds yet profit from her party at the ballot box. The Nationals were under direct threat and their instinct was appeasement—this put Fischer under

Paul Keating began a regular association with former New South Wales premier Jack Lang at age twenty. Theirs was a much misunderstood relationship since Keating, in power, became the classic anti-Lang leader with his deregulatory agenda. (© Newspix/News Ltd)

The Prime Minister Bob Hawke and his Treasurer Paul Keating during the 1985 Tax Summit. (© Newspix/News Ltd)

Annita and Paul Keating. (© Newspix/News Ltd)

Leading Aboriginal intellectual Noel Pearson. (© Newspix/Campbell Scott)

Prime Minister Paul Keating at Redfern Park on 10 December 1992. Keating wanted his speech to make an act of recognition; while given to a black audience, it was an appeal to white Australia. (© Newspix/Bob Finlayson)

Keating and Indonesian President Soeharto shared a special relationship, the most audacious example of which was a formal security pact with Indonesia. (© Newspix/ Michael Jones)

US President Bill Clinton and Keating in Jakarta for the 1994 APEC meeting. (© Newspix/News Ltd)

The men from the
Reserve Bank: former governors
Bernie Fraser (above) and
Ian Macfarlane (right).
(Above: © Newspix/David
Crosling; right: © Newspix/
Richard Cisar-Wright)

Paul Keating and Bill Kelty shared a most remarkable partnership between a Labor leader and a union chief. (© Newspix/Michael Potter)

John Howard and his family celebrate his 1996 election win at the Wentworth Hotel. More than a change of government, it changed the Liberal Party. (© Newspix/News Ltd)

Howard, with an outline of what appears to be a bulletproof vest underneath his suit, tries to placate a hostile pro-gun rally in Sale, Victoria. (© Newspix/News Ltd)

Prime Minister Howard and Treasurer Peter Costello at the Liberal Party's 47th Federal Council meeting in Canberra. (© Newspix/Michael Jones)

Alexander Downer. The Howard–Downer partnership was critical to the government's success; Downer would become, eventually, the minister closest to Howard.
(© Newspix/Michael Jones)

Arthur Sinodinos, John Howard's Chief-of-Staff. (© Newspix/John Feder)

Dr Ashton Calvert, Secretary of Department of Foreign Affairs and Trade.
(© Newspix/Ray Strange)

Prime Minister Howard and wife Janette with Sir John Carrick, Howard's mentor.
(© Newspix/David Sproule)

Howard with Australian Ambassador Andrew Peacock and Chairman of the US Federal Reserve, Alan Greenspan, in Washington. (© Newspix/David Crosling)

Prime Minister Howard with Chinese counterpart Li Peng in Beijing during his 1997 China tour. Howard was happy to survive the trip without mishap. (© Newspix/News Ltd)

Left: *Prime Minister Howard farewells the Australian troops in Townsville as they prepare for deployment in East Timor. (© Newspix / Jason Weeding)*

Below: *Howard with INTERFET Commander Major General Peter Cosgrove. (© Newspix / Michael Jones)*

Peter Reith, an instrumental member of Howard's team, and his first and best Workplace Relations minister. (© Newspix/Michael Jones)

Greg Combet replaced Bill Kelty as ACTU Secretary. When he orchestrated the 2005–06 union campaign against WorkChoices, he drew directly on his lessons from the 1997 waterfront struggle. (© Newspix/ Richard Cisar-Wright)

Left: *Cheryl Kernot, who spearheaded the Democrats' discussion with Peter Reith on workplace reforms, to whom Reith attributes full credit for their passage. (© Newspix / Anthony Weate)*

Below: *Indonesia's strongman, President Soeharto, signing the humiliating IMF agreement for his nation in 1998 during the Asian financial crisis while the Fund's boss, Michel Camdessus, looks on. This became the defining image of the Asian crisis—it shocked Asia and swore it to new policies that would forever deny the West another chance to impose its will on an entire region. (AFP / Getty Images)*

Howard with the Queen at Yarralumla. (© Newspix/News Ltd)

Dr BJ Habibie, Indonesian President. (© Newspix/ News Ltd)

Independent MP Pauline Hanson.
(© Newspix/Patrick Hamilton)

On 9 September 2001 Prime Minister Howard was in Washington with wife Janette and son Tim. It was a significant trip: just thirty-six hours later America would be attacked in New York and at the Pentagon, inaugurating a new age of terrorism and foreign wars. (© Newspix/John Feder)

Howard with his brother-in-arms, George Bush. The 9/11 attack invested their relation-ship with an emotional bond and a shared strategic conviction. (© Newspix/John Feder)

Kim Beazley, with his wife Susie Annus, concedes defeat at the November 2001 election. (© Newspix/Tom Rovis Hermann)

immense pressure. Yet there was still a seat-by-seat logic in the federal Nationals seeking a targeted preference exchange with One Nation in order to fend off Labor.[52] The self-interest of the Liberal Party was obvious—it was to preference Hanson last.

Former Liberal Party director Andrew Robb said that Labor had an interest in attacking Hanson. He said: 'Repeated demands by the anti-Hanson forces for the Prime Minister to metaphorically "take Hanson out" strengthen Labor's hand by making a martyr of Hanson, further increasing her appeal and further splitting the conservative vote.'[53]

The Queensland result unleashed a political cataclysm. There were demands for Howard to review his stand on tax reform, competition policy and the full sale of Telstra. The National Party president, Don McDonald, said that Howard would be 'mad' to proceed with his GST. National Party Senate leader Ron Boswell said Howard was 'in a desperate situation'. Election analyst Malcolm Mackerras warned that on this vote Hanson could win eight or nine Senate seats at a double dissolution.[54] After the poll Hanson, deluded yet intoxicated by success, said Fischer had to be removed as National Party leader.[55]

Malcolm Fraser called for the Liberal Party to preference One Nation last. 'I cannot conceive of the Liberal Party giving any comfort to Pauline Hanson,' Fraser wrote, alarmed at exactly this prospect.[56] Tony Abbott said the Liberals must preference Hanson last, arguing that One Nation 'could destroy the Howard government and give responsible conservatives a bad name'.[57]

The conclusion was apparent: if Howard preferenced Hanson in the federal poll, that decision would dominate the campaign. The Liberal Party would split, a political civil war would ensue and many Liberal voters would defect to Labor.

After the state election, Fischer and his deputy, John Anderson, re-signed their positions and were re-elected unopposed. With his own party intimidated, Fischer played a courageous hand over the next several months. 'The battle is now going to be writ large across Australia,' he said.

On the big policy issues Howard kept his nerve—he declined to compromise on tax or the Telstra sale. 'You don't react by panicking,' he said.[58] Aware that any major policy retreat would signal a rout, Howard launched a critique of Hanson's economic policy, saying it would 'endanger the jobs of many tens of thousands of Australians'. He never called her a racist.

Yet Howard refused to follow the advice of Costello, Fraser and Abbott to lead the Liberal Party into a position of unambiguous opposition to Hanson. His attack was a study in tactical ambivalence. The reason was obvious—Howard aimed to win back the defectors to One Nation—or, at least, to win their preferences. He would not attack those whose votes he sought. Over the coming months each Liberal Party state division decided to preference Hanson last.

In retrospect, the Queensland poll was Hanson's high tide. From mid-1998 her limitations became more apparent, as did her reliance on others, such as minder David Oldfield and organiser David Ettridge. One Nation was constituted as a business, not as a political party, and this defect proved fatal. When Abbott launched his campaign against Hanson—without telling Howard—it was on the grounds that her party was not validly registered for public funding. Abbott saw this successful campaign 'as the most important thing I have done in politics'.[59]

Ultimately, Howard survived Hanson but got a terrible fright. 'I have no doubt I handled it the right way,' he said. 'I knew she was appealing to many people who were traditional supporters of the government. I believed that if you overreacted to her, then she'd attract more publicity.'[60]

Yet Hanson got saturation publicity anyway. The truth is her rise was not inevitable and reflected a complex Australian failure. Hanson was a revolt against Australia's modernisation championed by Keating and, far more cautiously, by Howard. The traumas arising from this reinvention were real and manifested in many ways—from attacks on so-called economic rationalism to fears that Australia might degenerate into a 'nation of tribes'. Such sentiments ran through much of Australia's public debate.

This is the reason firm leadership was needed to rebut Hanson over the racial and economic prejudices she upheld. The case against Hanson was based in morality and national self-interest, a powerful nexus. Yet Howard was too reluctant to advance it.

The media failure over Hanson was integral to the malaise. Its values of celebrity, confrontation and entertainment were prominent. Hanson was made a celebrity by the popular media and a demon by the quality media—and she thrived on both counts.

It cannot be said that a different response from Howard would have produced a better result. But it could hardly have produced a worse result. The 1998 election was not just a Coalition–Labor contest; it became a test of whether One Nation would derail Australia's economic and social modernisation and entrench a new bitterness.

27

CONFRONTATION ON THE WATERFRONT

Very few politicians will risk their career for their beliefs,
but that's what Peter Reith did.
—Chris Corrigan, April 2008

Peter Reith's tragedy is that of a man who lost his dream, his clout and finally his career. In Shakespearean fashion Reith was compromised by the weapons he used on the waterfront: the negotiator of 1996 became the agent of confrontation of 1998. For the Howard loyalists, Reith was the hero who lost control of events.

It began with Reith's drive to reform the Australian waterfront and break the power of the Maritime Union of Australia (MUA), an icon of monopoly union power. The upshot was a reprise of class warfare, a conflagration where the government lost the propaganda contest and provoked adverse judgments from the Federal Court. This brought Reith to a 1998 career crisis. He said:

> The Howard government was feeling very fragile. The truth is that when it comes to a real fight few people are ready to commit. I was pretty isolated. When we discussed the situation in cabinet I was surprised that Peter Costello attacked me over the [Federal Court] decision. It's probably the only thing I cannot forgive him. Unfortunately Downer wasn't there that day and Amanda Vanstone was just about my only backer [apart from] Howard.[1]

Reith was the last man to offer his head but he needed a signal of Howard's support. 'It was one night at Kirribilli House,' Reith said.

> I reviewed the options with Howard. I trusted him and could talk to him about my own and the government's situation. I put before

him all the options, including my resignation if that was the best political course. Of course, I didn't think it was the best option and I didn't think Howard would either.[2]

Howard would not countenance the loss of Reith. 'You are not going to resign under any circumstances,' he replied.[3] These men were warriors of many years and Reith was probably the minister closest to Howard. The Prime Minister would not tolerate giving Reith's political head to the detested MUA—hell would have to freeze over.

Interviewed nearly a decade later, Howard was unrepentant. 'Reith was doing the will of the government,' he said. 'We wanted this reform. Peter felt embarrassed about the way the court action went. We did very badly. I said we are not going to lose an outstanding minister on that account. I think Reith did a fantastic job with the waterfront dispute.'[4]

For Reith, who saw himself as a future leadership contender, the waterfront offered a contrast with Costello. The cautious Costello would never exhibit the risk and confrontation that Reith entertained.

In an equivocal outcome Reith won a far more efficient waterfront, while the MUA kept its monopoly and lost its bargaining power. Reith was defined as a polarising agent of division, a minister identified with 'dogs and balaclavas' for night enforcement. He was seen as ruthless rather than strong. Reith canvassed the resignation option with Howard because, at the time, he had become a liability.

The waterfront battle frightened moderate opinion. '[It] was now seen as a government of confrontation,' said Democrats industrial spokesman Andrew Murray. 'The waterfront reinforced a loathing among some people for Reith and Howard that lasts to this day.'[5] For Labor's True Believers and the trade unions, Reith became a target. In the end, Howard survived but Reith fell—and the story of his downfall began on the docks.

Australia's waterfront in 1997 was an employer duopoly and a union monopoly. It was a strict cost-plus business—the stevedoring companies passed on excessive labour costs to port users. The two companies were P&O Ports, an international operator, and Patrick Stevedores, run by a self-made former chief of Bankers Trust Australia, Chris Corrigan. New to the waterfront business, lanky, ambitious and driving, Corrigan had borrowed heavily to get established and his survival depended on structural reform of labour practices.

The key to the waterfront crisis was the combination of Corrigan's lines of credit and Howard's 1996 election pledge to end the MUA monopoly and introduce competition on the docks.

The MUA ran a closed shop that dictated poor waterfront productivity, a high-wage labour force (workers averaged about $75 000 a year, with some earning up to $95 000, more than a university professor) and meagre hope of reform through negotiation. The MUA and employers knew the system was inefficient. The former Labor government had invested large funds in reform but after some progress the gains were eroded due to the sacrosanct status of the MUA.

Its predecessor, the Waterside Workers Federation, had a long history of radicalism, communist control and confrontation with government. Few institutions had been more loathed by Australian conservatives. The MUA was a small, tribal and highly political union still seen as flag bearer for the solidarity that once branded Australia's trade union values. The MUA's history and its monopoly provoked an almost irrational hostility from the Liberal Party.

Even the most rational union leaders saw the MUA as a symbol to be defended at all costs. Bill Kelty said:

> Lindsay Fox told me that Howard was going to fuck us over. I said to him, 'Put your money on us, mate.' You see, I wanted Howard to go after the MUA. That was where we were strong, but I couldn't believe what they eventually did.[6]

The MUA's ethos was obsolete in an internationalised economy. Union leaders would tolerate neither the end of their monopoly nor non-union labour. Yet ACTU leaders saw the MUA's immunity as a test case of trade union authority, a mindset that guaranteed a showdown.

In September 1997, sensing the coming climax, Kelty declared: 'To weaken the Maritime Union of Australia is to weaken the union movement as a whole. The day we give away that support is the day we rip out our own heart and leave it pumping in irrelevancy.' If Howard moved against the MUA, Kelty threatened 'the biggest picket that's ever been assembled in this country'.[7]

Corrigan was frustrated to discover that the loyalty of his employees was to the union, not to the enterprise. 'I naïvely believed for some years we could improve the waterfront by consensus,' he said. 'I assumed reasonable people might reach reasonable compromises. By the end of 1996 I had discovered there was not a chance in hell this would occur without an upheaval.'[8]

Howard concluded that agreed reforms were a pipe dream. If Hawke and Keating failed to extract them, what hope did he have? From the time he came to power, Howard accepted the inevitability of this battle. 'I was always going to do the waterfront,' he said. 'I knew that eventually we'd have to have this fight.'[9]

The fight was not just about waterfront productivity. Howard, like Kelty, saw the MUA as a test. For him, it was an offensive union monopoly and its abuse of power needed to be broken. It became an elemental struggle.

Transport Minister John Sharp put the economic case: world best practice for comparable-sized ports was upwards of thirty containers an hour while the average in Australia was seventeen, with Sydney at fifteen containers per hour.[10] Australia's waterfront was notorious and its reputation was international. But Sharp's resignation over travel accounts left Reith as the decisive player.

Drawing on both his department and external advice, Reith settled on an interventionist strategy—the government would become an agent for change on the waterfront. It would go beyond mere encouragement of companies to take action under the Coalition's new 1996 IR laws. Howard authorised the interventionist strategy in writing in April 1997. This meant that Reith and Howard had become reform agitators, a fateful decision. Reith said that, if Margaret Thatcher had written such a letter, the HR Nicholls Society 'would declare her to be a gutsy and determined leader'.[11]

What did intervention mean? There was a variety of options but the critical step was to replace the workforce with non-union labour. That could only occur with a willing employer and Corrigan was more than willing. The defect in the Howard/Reith interventionist strategy was that government became hostage to Corrigan. The government would not be in control. An interventionist strategy meant reform would be sub-contracted to a formidable business leader with his own objectives. But Corrigan, unlike Reith, was not running for office.

During late 1997, Corrigan planned to replace his MUA workers with a non-union team trained in Dubai. He relied on former Australian SAS operatives to recruit this force. It was a fantastic notion betraying a desperation and naïvete. But it revealed the rock of Corrigan's strategy. 'If I attempted any reform without an alternative workforce I was destined to fail,' he said. 'I needed alternative labour. The unions could just shut you down and force negotiations where you would be handed your arse. You'd get nothing.'[12]

For Corrigan, secrecy was the key to this operation, though a few government officials had been made aware of the Dubai scheme.

Unsurprisingly, the MUA discovered the plans and passed material to the Labor Party, leading to explosive questions to Reith in the parliament on 3 December 1997. He replied, in obvious confusion, that he was unaware of any Dubai operation. 'I definitely did not know about it,' Reith said later. 'The day before, I had briefed a cabinet sub-committee on waterfront reform and there was nothing about Dubai. That afternoon I rang the employers to ask them about it and Corrigan denied it. He told me that it wasn't him.'[13] Corrigan said later that, in planning the Dubai operation, he 'never told anybody in government'.[14]

Reith looked like a mug. Two days earlier his senior officials had held a meeting with Corrigan and his legal adviser, Graeme Smith, to discuss options. 'Neither Mr Corrigan nor Mr Smith referred to any training of workers in Dubai or anywhere else,' his deputy secretary, Robin Stewart-Crompton, said in a subsequent memo.[14]

The story was a public relations masterstroke for the MUA in that it established a conspiratorial setting for the waterfront showdown. In their book on the crisis, journalists Helen Trinca and Anne Davies capture the media's response to Dubai:

> The baby boomers who ruled the Australian media, the university educated children of Vietnam, had little collective respect for soldiers. The involvement of service personnel in a plan to bust a union was seen by the media as laughable. Not to mention being only one step short of the old bogy of putting troops on the wharves.[16]

It was the MUA that killed Corrigan's plan. Its chief, John Coombs, flew to London and persuaded the International Transport Workers Federation to threaten to target Dubai. When its Ports Authority pulled the plug in December 1997, the trainees looked like fools, Corrigan was humiliated and Reith was typecast.

At the outset Kelty deputised his assistant secretary, Greg Combet, equipped with degrees in engineering and economics, to run the ACTU's waterfront strategy. It was a pivotal decision with long-run consequences for Howard's survival. Kelty said: 'I'd said to him [Combet] in early 1997 … we're planning for a dispute. You've got responsibility for it … This is a dispute that is going to make you the leader of the ACTU.'[17] The dispute would be a ferocious initiation for Combet, who was just turning forty. He had worked for the MUA for years and was a protégé of the legendary union leader Tas Bull.

His role gave Combet an insight into the tactics required to defeat the Howard government in an industrial showdown. When Combet, as ACTU secretary, orchestrated the 2005–06 union campaign against *WorkChoices*, he drew directly on his lessons from the waterfront struggle.

After the Dubai fiasco, Combet and Coombs met Reith in his Melbourne office for a bruising encounter. Attacking Reith, Combet waved a departmental document that canvassed sacking the working force. Reith produced his own document on appalling productivity figures. He goaded the unionists, asking: 'What are you going to do when the farmers come down to the wharves to take your jobs?'[18]

This alluded to the more serious option being discussed by Corrigan, the National Farmers Federation (NFF) and the Howard government: for the NFF to establish a stevedoring company to operate Webb Dock in Melbourne on a lease from Corrigan to train and employ non-union labour.[19] The government committed to the plan. 'It had to be a radical plan to have any chance,' Corrigan said. He asked Reith to provide funds for redundancy costs and the government agreed on a loan arrangement. 'This was the key,' Corrigan said.[20] It became full-blooded intervention.

For two decades the NFF had spearheaded campaigns against union power—it believed the docks were squeezing the lifeblood out of Australian farmers. With his Dubai option lost, Corrigan needed the NFF. When he invited them to take over Webb Dock, NFF President Donald McGauchie and his industrial director, James Ferguson, agreed. Their operating assumption was that any improvement on the waterfront depended on inflicting a defeat on the MUA.

NFF consultant Paul Houlihan said the plan was possible only because of Reith's 1996 industrial law. Houlihan said: 'The biggest single factor was Reith's law establishing AWAs separate from the award stream. It meant you could employ labour on the waterfront without bring roped in to the existing industry standard.'[21]

Democrats spokesman Andrew Murray was aghast at the strategy. 'It was close to midnight one night when Peter Reith rang to brief me on his proposals,' Murray said. 'I told him immediately we couldn't support it.'[22]

For Combet, the revolution was astonishing. 'The industry was essentially a duopoly,' he said. 'If the union won gains they just went into the price and everyone was happy. But we saw that Corrigan was an iconoclast. By mid-1997 we knew we were going to face something big.'[23] But Combet never imagined its scale. Howard had given Corrigan the government's bottom line. 'We will back waterfront reform subject to one condition—that it complies with Australian law,' he said.[24]

In late January 1998, in driving rain, the MUA was evicted from Webb Dock and a shaken Combet universalised the dispute—he said it was a threat to the entire union movement in Australia. Reith praised Corrigan for his courage. The NFF leaders were ebullient. Over coming days the MUA pickets were intimidating, rocking minibuses, spitting, throwing urine and taunting NFF employees with 'we know where you live, we know where your kids go to school'.[25]

But this was merely the prelude. Corrigan, driven by financial imperatives, was a man for the big leap. His game plan was far larger: he wanted to replace his entire MUA workforce across the nation's wharves with non-unionists. A week before Easter 1997, Howard foreshadowed an epic encounter. 'It is one of the defining moments in the industrial relations experience of any country,' he said, asking for public support.

On the night of 7 April, Corrigan moved.[26] Hired security men took control of Patrick facilities as a prelude to Corrigan's deployment of non-union labour. The process was a public relations blunder—dogs and balaclavas were the order of the day while Corrigan presided from his Point Piper home. The MUA was being locked out. The dogs were Corrigan's idea because he believed 'these people, if they were allowed to stay there for very long, would set about vandalising the equipment', which meant the waterfront would be shut down.[27] Corrigan said he was sorry for workers who had been betrayed by their union. Combet said the action was 'disgraceful and unAustralian', pledging that the union movement would 'stand behind the sacked workers'.

Launching a well-prepared media blitz, Reith predicted a 'complete turnaround' on waterfront productivity within twelve to eighteen months. He said Corrigan had been 'pushed too far'.

But Corrigan and Reith had no hope in the public relations war. They suffered an abject loss to the MUA and the unions. 'They made a huge mistake with the Dubai scam and the dogs and balaclavas,' Combet said. 'There was an 84 per cent public opposition to our cause early on, but sentiment shifted almost overnight.'[28]

The story was dominated by means, not ends—an alleged conspiracy to smash the MUA was a superior story to improving crane rates or fixing monopoly power. The main risk for the unions was the behaviour of the pickets and the television images of small children being recruited into a violent picket line. But the media largely accepted the union story.

'We had to unite the movement, and we did,' Combet said. 'The MUA wasn't our most popular union in the movement.' His message was that 'if employees can have their collective bargaining rights and their union smashed in a core industrial area, then anyone is vulnerable and we had all better stand up and fight.'[29]

This was coupled with another tactic pitched at public opinion—the fear of job insecurity, the idea that would destroy *WorkChoices* nine years later. Its trial run came on the waterfront with Reith as master tutor. Combet said:

Our research showed a growing dissatisfaction with economic change, its pace, pressures it was creating and an acute sense of job insecurity across the community. I realised this was the best way of building support and that's what we focussed on. Job insecurity affects everyone, not just the unions. Reith had got out ahead of us in 1996 and 1997 when he was banging on about crane rates, feather bedding and bludgers. I learnt a great deal from him—you get out of the blocks early.[30]

Corrigan's coup, however, would be undone by the courts. Drawing on advice from Melbourne lawyers Julian Burnside QC, Herman Borenstein and Josh Bornstein, the MUA alleged an Australia-wide unlawful conspiracy to sack workers because they were unionists. One advantage, in union eyes, is that this case went to the Federal Court, not the Victorian Supreme Court. Another was that Justice Tony North was drawn to hear the case. As a barrister, North was 'from the union side of the industrial law divide'.[31]

North issued a temporary order that Corrigan had to take back his union workers. This was the turning point for Coombs and Combet. By this order the bench gave the MUA the moral high ground. Corrigan said of North: 'From the time he was the selected judge, it was inevitable that we would get a decision unhelpful to our case.'[32] On appeal, North's judgment was upheld in the Federal Court and then by the High Court.

The Federal Court decisions were a searing blow for Reith. It seemed he had led the government into a confrontation with catastrophic consequences. The cabinet was distinctly cold towards him. This was the context for his Kirribilli House talk with Howard when Reith offered his political head. 'I never budged,' Reith said. 'But I had Howard behind me. That made all the difference.'[33] But years later, when interviewed,

Reith signalled that doubts about Howard's commitment had crossed his mind. 'I was very revved up,' Reith said. 'What would I have done if Howard hadn't supported me? I think I would have gone after him.'[34]

A worried Howard spoke to Corrigan. 'I could fully understand that Howard was concerned and nervous,' Corrigan said. 'I mean, things never went to plan. We went from plan A to B to C and then invented new plans. He was worried that our legal strategy kept failing.'[35]

In *Patrick Stevedores v MUA*, the High Court judgment meant that the union won the battle but lost the war. The court upheld its right to return and the MUA monopoly stayed. On 7 May 1998 a victorious MUA marched back to the docks as ACTU chief Jennie George wept for joy. Yet the court set up the conditions for a negotiated settlement and these were driven by the banks, which threatened to foreclose on Corrigan and put his company into receivership.

'In practice, the High Court decision forced the union to negotiate, so we didn't lose the last legal peg,' Corrigan said.[36] Coombs said: 'The banks got a message to us: if you are going to pursue the conspiracy [court case] we will foreclose on the company … so there was nothing else but to negotiate some settlement.'[37] For Reith, the High Court judgment meant, in effect, 'that if one of you goes down then both of you are going down'.[38]

The union lost half its Patrick numbers to redundancies. In their summary of the dispute Trinca and Davies conclude: 'The real loss, however, was to the union's day-to-day power on the docks and the erosion of the workers' wages and conditions … For Corrigan, the exercise had been extremely positive. [He] cut his workforce and wages bill in half. Better still, he broke the culture of overtime.'[39] But the NFF had been sidelined and its non-union labour force left without jobs.

On the docks, management seized the upper hand from the MUA. Over time it became possible to employ non-union labour. The Howard government contributed $150 million to cover redundancies. Howard and Reith claimed victory on the back of a more efficient waterfront but they were angry with the Federal Court and state governments for their lack of support. The Productivity Commission found five years later that net crane rates had 'improved markedly', rising to 25 containers an hour.[40]

The MUA success in the courts was not replicated with the ACCC. The Howard government had sharpened the secondary boycott provisions to curb irresponsible industrial action. Costello, having watched the MUA on television engage in what he was sure was a secondary boycott, had rung Allan Fels and asked what he was doing. Costello's position was simple: he wanted the law applied fairly. But there was a personal factor at work: Fels and Kelty had been close personal, family and political friends for twenty years.

Fels initiated action against the MUA over its attempt to stop vessels that had been loaded by non-union labour at Patricks from leaving Australia. It was not an easy decision for him. Kelty was incensed. The ACCC won a temporary injunction involving hefty fines against the MUA. But when the overall waterfront dispute was being settled all sides wanted an end to the ACCC action as part of a wider settlement. Fels refused to abandon his action. The upshot was that Fels and Kelty met at a friend's house in South Melbourne.

Fels said:

> Kelty wanted me to withdraw the action because, he argued, the union had been responding to illegal behaviour. I pointed out that his argument didn't stand up. My job was to enforce the law. Kelty proposed a range of alternatives. But when it became clear that I wouldn't back down he got very upset and abusive. He told me what a bastard I was. Then, at the end, he said: 'We are no longer friends.' And that became the end of our friendship. Our families had been very close for so long. We'd go to the movies together, I used to play in the ACTU cricket match, everyone at the ACTU knew about our personal friendship. It was difficult for our family.

Eventually the case was settled on the ACCC's terms and Corrigan paid the MUA's damages bill.[41]

Corrigan's view is that each of the three players had wins.

> I got a viable business. A majority of employees remained members of the MUA. I think the union achieved its objective, but more in form than substance. The reality is that most employees welcomed the changes. The government, I think, got re-elected in 1998 partly because Howard showed he had backbone. I think Howard could claim a success.[42]

As expected, Reith was upbeat about the outcome:

> Their [MUA] numbers have been slashed and their war chest [has been] severely depleted, and they had finally been confronted by

an employer with the guts to say 'enough is enough'. The barriers to entry to the MUA's monopoly have been so graphically lowered that it is now obvious that just about anybody can step over them.[43]

Howard would forever boast about the showdown.

> The waterfront reform is one of the great achievements of the government. It has delivered practical benefits. It sent a very strong signal to people that we are a serious reformist government. It kept faith with that vast army of people who supported the government and who had felt the Fraser government had failed the reform test.[44]

Howard and Reith tried to invest the event with iconic status. Reith said: 'Margaret Thatcher's test came with the miners and with Wapping. Ronald Reagan's came with the air traffic controllers. John Howard's came with the waterfront.'[45]

Combet was dismissive of such triumphalism. He said the winners were the MUA and Corrigan, not the government. 'We ticked every box,' he said. 'Some of my colleagues thought the goal was to destroy Patricks and Corrigan. Well, it wasn't.' Combet said his goals were to get employees' jobs back, finalise a settlement, ensure that entitlements were fully met (including redundancy payments), have all legal costs met and prevent individual contracts in the industry. Significantly, Combet said: 'we recognised the days of closed shops were over'—a recognition that only came after the dispute.[46]

The showdown guaranteed that Combet, from the movement's Left, would become Kelty's successor. And it fashioned his strategy as ACTU leader. Combet said:

> From the waterfront, I learnt the importance of bringing together the arms of strategy and then winning support for it. Bill Kelty used institutional power with a Labor government. But I didn't have that. I needed to use the media to win support. I needed to use not just industrial lawyers but commercial lawyers, the smartest legal brains, that's why I went to Julian Burnside. I learnt about corporate law and insolvency law. I realised after the Accord ended that it was important for the unions to emerge from their shell, to look outward to the community and to reconnect with people in workplaces. It was a values campaign. I felt we were in an

environment more like the US, absent institutionalised arbitration, so we needed to be focussed at grass roots levels and to apply these new techniques.[47]

It was the dry run for *WorkChoices*. Combet would be ready for the great showdown of 2005 over *WorkChoices*, a point Howard missed completely.

What was Corrigan's final take? He said: 'Once people were allowed to behave as individuals rather than as a collective their whole attitude changed. They enjoyed coming to work. I think they enjoyed their liberation.'[48] Murray, a Reith admirer, said: 'The dispute poisoned the well. It tainted Howard's effort to modernise the Australian workplace and bring the community with him.'[49]

A sceptic about politicians, Corrigan gained an admiration for Reith. 'He was willing to sacrifice his career to achieve important things for the country,' Corrigan said. 'I think very few politicians will risk their career for their beliefs. Reith put it to me that "I want to achieve something here, even if it costs my career".'[50]

Reith paid a high price. His home, his wife and his family needed security protection. 'One day the coppers arrived saying there was a bloke with a gun coming to kill me,' he said.[51] Howard confirmed the serious-ness of the threat: 'My federal police told me that they had no more ugly demonstrations to deal with than those against Reith. They were really menacing.'[52]

Reith's former adviser, Peter Hendy, said: 'I think the waterfront dispute was a political success but it took the government some time to reach this conclusion. In the interim it was very worried. One consequence is that it weakened Reith as a future leadership contender.'[53]

The Liberal Party now saw Reith as a heroic but risky proposition. The public saw him as deeply polarising. What was not yet apparent was that his career had entered a blind alley.

28

ESCAPING THE NATIVE TITLE CRISIS

*We were heading into a divisive double dissolution election which would have
torn the fabric of our society and set race relations back forty or fifty years.*
—Senator Brian Harradine, 8 July 1998

In his first term John Howard was driven to the brink of a double dissolution election that would have polarised Australia and sunk his political legitimacy. The crisis was triggered by the High Court's late 1996 Wik judgment on native title that shocked Howard and shattered the conservative side of politics. This decision, by a radical High Court, delighted the Aboriginal leaders, emboldened the Labor Party and unleashed forces that threatened the Prime Minister's survival and reputation.

Howard's response to Wik during 1997 had been to devise a Ten Point Plan to restrict native title—a plan under assault by the Labor Party and facing possible defeat in the Senate. If the Senate denied Howard, then he had only two choices: either a retreat that would ruin his standing with conservative Australia or a double dissolution election on native title that would doom his reputation as a leader playing 'race' politics.

The dilemma was captured in the Prime Minister's declaration of political war to the joint party meeting on 2 December 1997. He said:

> We have vowed in the cabinet and ministry to stick to our proposed legislation. My gut feeling is that it is highly likely that the Senate will make unacceptable amendments. The deadlock provisions of the Constitution are the only way we will get the Ten Point Plan. We won't control both Houses [after an election] so a Joint Sitting is the only course. The talk of a race election is just political bullying. It is grossly offensive and is just calculated to put us off

our course of action. Every instinct in my body tells me we will be held in contempt if we accommodate our critics. We have resolved on a course and we must stick to it.[1]

In this speech Howard invoked Churchill's dictum when he said 'he who feeds the crocodile can take comfort knowing the crocodile will eat him last'. A strange fate had befallen him. Howard was being 'wedged' by the progressive side of politics—a radical High Court, an assertive Labor Party, an aggrieved Aboriginal leadership and a potentially hostile Senate.

Howard's grip on Australia was in jeopardy. The issue transcended native title. It was about Howard's political and institutional authority as prime minister and whether his government would be broken. Given his distaste for confronting the Senate, Howard's serious contemplation of a double dissolution election testified to the gravity of his dilemma.

In the end Howard was 'saved' when Tasmanian independent Brian Harradine, holding the balance of power, negotiated a compromise to pass the bill. The Howard–Harradine compromise was denounced by Aboriginal leaders and by Paul Keating, who said Australia should not fear an election that exposed Howard's racist bias.

Keating felt he knew whom to blame. At 9 a.m. on 3 July 1998 Keating rang St Canice's Presbytery at Darlinghurst, down the road from fashionable Potts Point where he would locate his own office. His target was the Jesuit priest Frank Brennan, an authority on native title, an influential adviser to Harradine, a compulsive social justice campaigner and a man of independent intellect. 'He just went ballistic,' Brennan said later.

'You ought to be ashamed of yourself,' Keating began, 'you ought to be fucking ashamed of yourself.' Keating said Brennan was playing in politics out of his depth. 'You've let Howard off the hook,' he said. 'You had him cornered and you let him off the hook. You should stick to your prayers. You spend too much time slinking around the corridors of Parliament House pretending that you're important.'[2]

Keating's fury boiled down to a single focus. 'You and Harradine have saved Howard from the consequences of his folly,' Keating told Brennan. 'And you have made the Aborigines pay for it instead.' Accusing Brennan of being a meddling priest, Keating said the brand of 'professional Catholic represented by Harradine and Brennan' was a menace. They did not represent Aboriginal interests; only Aboriginals could represent Aboriginal interests, Keating said. Brennan's promotion of a Wik compromise was a 'betrayal' of the Aboriginal cause.[3]

The final straw for Keating had been Brennan's op-ed in the *Sydney Morning Herald* that morning which praised Harradine. 'It's a relief for the whole country,' Brennan wrote. 'Third time around, Wik has been resolved.'[4]

Brennan had been worse than a meddling priest: while calling on Howard to make concessions he had opposed the Labor Party on Wik. He had fought Labor's strategy of confrontation of Howard. He had opposed the strategy of the Aboriginal leaders. He had dined with Howard at the Lodge. He had consulted with Catholic Liberal politicians, among them Tony Abbott, to reach a settlement. He had advised Harradine for many months to cut a deal with Howard over Wik.

For Labor, Brennan had become a public menace—a dangerous menace because Labor, like everybody else, assumed he exercised a decisive influence over Harradine and Harradine would determine the fate of the bill and the nature of the 1998 poll.[5]

On 8 July 1998 Harradine told the Senate why he had negotiated the deal with Howard: 'We were heading headlong into a divisive double dissolution election which would have torn the fabric of our society and set race relations back forty or fifty years. That is where we were heading and everyone in this chamber knows it.' Harradine thanked Howard and also thanked Brennan for whom 'I have had a great regard.' While he acknowledged Brennan's influence, the priest had been abroad when the final deal was done and he was not involved in it.[6]

On Wik, Harradine stood squarely in the centre, an unusual position for him. He assumed native title was neither the panacea that many believed nor the demon that others depicted.

As for Brennan, he was an independent witness. As a priest–lawyer, a prolific writer and an astute networker, Brennan was dangerous because he championed the Aboriginal cause but he was not hostage to indigenous leaders. He incurred Labor's suspicion because Brennan treated issues on merit and not as endless opportunities for Labor political gain as he operated across Northern Australia, East Timor, detention centres and Kings Cross.[7] Brennan was one of Australia's most effective critics of the Wik decision. But there was a more important critic—Brennan's father, Chief Justice Brennan—in the minority judgment.

In 1995 the Keating government had appointed Sir Gerard Brennan chief justice on Sir Anthony Mason's retirement, a widely applauded appointment. Brennan had written the principal Mabo judgment but he was no radical. Frank Brennan had no doubt that his father's Mabo judgment showed he rejected the idea of native title coexisting on pastoral leases, the main issue in Wik.

The Wik judgment released on 23 December 1996 hit the Howard government like a thunderclap. Howard was taken by surprise; his legal advice had been to the contrary. Within hours conservative Australia went into meltdown. Howard, struggling to hold non-Labor politics together in the teeth of Hanson, now saw the populist right-wing forces launch a tirade against native title.

This was not the High Court's finest hour. The main issue was whether land claims by the Wik and Thayorre Peoples on Cape York had been extinguished by the granting of pastoral leases under Queensland land acts. The court found in favour of the Aboriginals in a 4–3 decision, with separate judgments from Justices Toohey, Gaudron, Gummow and Kirby in the majority. They found a pastoral lease did not necessarily confer right of exclusive possession on the pastoralist. They found if there was a conflict in the rights, then the pastoralist prevailed, but if there was no conflict of rights, then rights could coexist.

It was assumed that Wik followed Mabo. But no such assumption was justified. 'What shocked us was that the Chief Justice didn't carry his court,' Tim Fischer said. 'People started asking questions about the court,' Howard said. 'I accepted the decision. But everybody had assumed [that] the grant of a pastoral lease extinguished native title. Now we had this convoluted thing of coexistence.'[8]

Brennan, the main judge in Mabo, had been outflanked. The Chief Justice wrote the single minority judgment for himself, McHugh and Dawson. People praised its coherence but, as Fischer lamented, 'it didn't matter'.

In dissent Brennan said: 'The law can attribute priority to one right over another, but it cannot recognise the coexistence in different hands of two rights that cannot both be exercised at the same time.'[9] The judge said: 'It is too late now to develop a new theory of land law that would throw the whole structure of land titles based on Crown grants into confusion.'[10]

With two new judges since Mabo, it was Justice Gummow's finding for the Aboriginal side that was the balance-shifting decision. An exultant Daryl Melham, Labor shadow minister for Aboriginal Affairs, told Gareth Evans it was enough to confirm his belief in God. 'But you didn't know his name was Gummow,' Evans quipped.[11]

With 40 per cent of Australia's land mass covered by pastoral leases, Howard, in an understatement, said: 'We have a new ball game.' NFF

President Donald McGauchie declared: 'I think this decision has just about ended Aboriginal reconciliation, certainly with the pastoral industry.' Queensland National Party Premier Rob Borbidge said the result was 'totally intolerable' and he wanted immediate extinguishment from Howard. For Western Australian Liberal Premier, Richard Court, the decision vindicated his initial alarm about Mabo.

The president of the national Native Title Tribunal, Justice French, said the decision meant claims on pastoral leases would have to be determined 'on a case-by-case basis' and this meant 'talk about gates and fences and vehicles and camping [rights]'.[12] Howard faced an outcry across conservative Australia for blanket extinguishment of native title in defiance of the 1975 *Racial Discrimination Act*.[13]

Frank Brennan's opposition to Wik would become crucial. He criticised the majority's historical analysis, method and understanding of a pastoral lease. For Brennan, there was now 'a moral necessity' for parliament to confront the issue and strike the balance.[14] He issued two public warnings: he warned Howard that 'legislating in a discriminatory way about native title under the cloak of workability … would be a threat to the well-being of all Australians'.[15] But Brennan also warned the Aboriginal leaders. Convinced that the High Court had over-reached, Brennan believed that this time, unlike Mabo, the Aboriginal win 'had little chance of being translated into a win on the floor of parliament'.[16] Such a win was the exact objective of the Aboriginal leaders and the Labor Party.

The charge of racism against Howard was immediate. Within weeks Noel Pearson said that Howard's flirtation with changing the *Racial Discrimination Act* meant that he 'must be a racist'. Executive Director of the Kimberley Land Council, Peter Yu, said the Howard government's response to Wik was 'steeped in racism'.[17]

Howard had become reconciled to the High Court's Mabo decision. Indeed, he had called it 'completely unexceptionable'. Howard's problem was Keating's *Native Title Act*, and his parliamentary secretary, Nick Minchin, was charged with fulfilling Howard's 1996 election mandate to rebalance that law. The Wik decision only made this task more urgent and increased the political stakes. From the start Howard and Minchin knew the populist blanket extinguishment option was utter folly.

'After Wik we were sitting on a political volcano,' Minchin said. 'The original *Native Title Act* was never designed to accommodate or facilitate the concept of coexisting rights. The National Party just wanted complete extinguishment.'[18]

During a turbulent three months to May 1997 Howard spearheaded his government's lengthy consultations and response. In March 2007 Howard invited Frank Brennan to dinner at the Lodge via an intermediary, the prominent New South Wales state Liberal Kerry Chikarovski, who also attended. At dinner there was a long discussion about Catholics and Protestants that Brennan found outdated. But Howard may have been smarter than Brennan realised: Catholicism would figure in the resolution of native title. Brennan gave Howard a series of points on the way forward. 'He was across his brief and completely unemotional,' Brennan said of Howard. The priest told the Prime Minister that he respected Howard's 1996 mandate to amend the act.[19]

Howard negotiated a fragile holding position within the conservative forces—state and federal, Liberal and National—sealed by a cabinet decision of 7 May in favour of his Ten Point Plan in response to Wik. The key to the politics was locking in Fischer. This decision defied Borbidge, the pastoralists and the populists. Howard dismissed their call for wholesale extinguishment in favour of amendments that modified the impact of the Wik decision and shifted the native title pendulum towards farmers and miners. Aboriginal leaders denounced the Ten Point Plan; Pearson said that its advocates 'are not true Liberals, they are racist scum'.

Minchin said blanket extinguishment was a populist fantasy. It risked exposing the Commonwealth to 'just terms' compensation. Any such law might be unconstitutional; it would not pass the Senate. In a subsequent letter to Howard, Minchin said: 'Far from giving us a fast-track solution, blanket extinguishment would have spelt more years of uncertainty than any other course.'[20] As usual, the populist right was on a political suicide mission.

The showdown came at Longreach in central Queensland on 17 May when Howard and Fischer addressed nearly 3000 people from the front steps of the Stockman's Hall of Fame. 'On that day we faced Armageddon or the Ten Point Plan,' Fischer says. 'It was my call to suggest Longreach and persuade Howard to attend.' He told his backers before the meeting that there were still 'bucketfuls of extinguishment' in the plan. Indigenous leaders were enraged. Howard was ready to allow the states to pass laws rolling back proven native title rights and cut back the right to negotiate.

The Longreach meeting seemed a disaster—Howard was jeered, his plan was voted down and he left shaking his head 'at the level of fear and misinformation' among pastoral interests. The sides were deadlocked. Fischer said Longreach was the point at which 'momentum started to come behind our plan'.[21] But that is not Howard's view.

Howard told the rally:

Under our Ten Point Plan no pastoral leaseholder can lose anything at all under their pastoral lease. Nothing at all … you can't lose your land and people who are quoted around this country saying that native title claimants could have you thrown off your land, could have you dispossessed … that is absolutely 100 per cent wrong.

He offered guarantee after guarantee—pastoralists would not have their rights to sink a dam or build a fence compromised. He attacked the right to negotiate as 'that stupid property right' given to native title claimants that his law would 'completely abolish'.[22] Compensation payments flowing from any resumption of native title rights would be met in the 75 to 25 per cent ratio by the Commonwealth and states respectively. No cost would be carried by the pastoralist. This provision had been essential to lock in Fischer.

Finally, Howard said blanket extinguishment would not work—the potential compensation would be greater, the law would face a High Court challenge, and getting such a bill through the Senate was improbable.[23] He stared down the mad Right's blanket extinguishment bid, an idea fed on racism and unscrupulousness.

The Ten Point Plan, in effect, became a 'peace plan' for the non-Labor side of politics, the key to preserving its unity. It became the mechanism to save Howard, the Coalition and his government. Howard conceded later that he had 'badly mishandled' the issue because 'I allowed the debate to go on inside the party for too long.'[24] Yet the Ten Point Plan became sacrosanct. Major concessions threatened by the Senate would have an incendiary impact within the National Party and the non-Labor states. Howard was a leader with little room for manoeuvre.

Labor's aim was to throttle Howard's bill; it moved about 330 amendments. The Opposition was driven by a shifting array of emotions and calculations—it was weak, divided and angry. Labor remembered the Coalition's refusal to co-operate with the 1993 Keating bill. Its self-image had become that of the native title justice party and it was riven by distrust of Howard yet tempted by the tangible sense of his vulnerability. While Beazley as a Western Australian knew a showdown over Wik would not assist Labor's public standing, there were many in the party convinced that polarisation around native title would ruin Howard's legitimacy to lead the nation.

Given his background in Mabo, Gareth Evans, now deputy leader, was pledged to defend native title rights. At one point Evans said that if Labor could not repair the bill then 'we will vote against the whole legislative package whatever the consequences'.[25] Evans was assisted by two capable left-wingers: shadow minister Daryl Melham and Nick Bolkus, who was impressive leading the Senate debate. 'Our approach was simple,' Melham says. 'We wanted amendments to get the best possible result.'[26]

There were three Wik debates between late 1997 and mid-1998, making the issue the most canvassed in the parliament's history. Harradine signalled his position at the outset: he would pass Howard's bill provided it met fundamental moral principles for Aboriginal Australia, and he wanted to avoid any divisive double dissolution poll. This was the start and end of his position. Harradine spoke for nobody but himself and he was a notorious loner. But he accepted his responsibility as holding the Senate's balance of power. Brennan told Harradine to get his own lawyers and he hired John McCarthy QC and Jeff Kildea.

The first Senate debate produced a bill with 217 amendments and a deadlock. Harradine said Howard had got 90 per cent of his bill; Beazley accused Howard of plunging the nation into a race election rather than taking a fair compromise. There were four issues of dispute: Howard wanted a tougher threshold test for lodgement of a native title claim, a sunset clause on claims, elimination of the right to negotiate and a weakening of the scope of the RDA as it applied to native title.

For Howard, the Senate amendments were 'completely unacceptable'. The government had been 'completely frustrated' by Labor, the Democrats and Harradine. He claimed that 79 per cent of Australia's land mass, in theory, could be subject to a native title claim, a figure rejected by indigenous leaders and Labor. The government, Howard said, will not retreat.[27] This was the context for his party room invoking of Churchill. For Howard, conservative unity and his own authority were at stake.

He announced that the bill would be resubmitted and, if it met the same fate, it 'could be used by the government as the basis of a double dissolution'. This was a statement of intent and a pressure tactic. But he was stung by talk about a race election. 'I have never said I wanted a race election,' he said. 'Some of my critics have said I want a race election. I have not. There will never be, in my lifetime, a race election in Australia.'[28] He told the party room it 'faced a ferociously sensationalised press campaign'.[29] Michelle Grattan wrote that Howard 'appears certain to go to the people in a double dissolution election' in the second half of 1998.

Beazley warned of an unprecedented risk for the nation. 'There'd be a racial tinge in a way that we've not had before in this country,' he said.[30] The next month Beazley told the ALP National Conference: 'This country cannot afford a race election but I promise you this: if we have to confront a race election we will fight it on two fronts—the racial front and the bread-and-butter front.'[31]

Minchin said: 'A double dissolution was a ridiculous option. I feared the consequences for Australia and I didn't necessarily think it would help us. I argued internally against the option. But Howard's difficulty was that it looked as though the government couldn't resolve the problem.'[32]

Brennan advised Harradine to keep working for a compromise. He felt Howard would offer concessions. Brennan wrote to Beazley on 20 March 1998 saying that if pressure was kept up he was confident 'there will be some movement'.[33] But, while Brennan opposed Howard on three of his four 'sticking points', he disagreed with Labor and the National Indigenous Working Group (NIWG) in their tough line on the application of the RDA. Brennan felt that, on the RDA, they were seeking more from Howard in 1998 than they did from Keating in 1993.[34]

The NIWG felt that Brennan was undermining their position. In January 1998 Mick Dodson and the NIWG's lawyer, Ron Castan, visited Brennan to ask him, in effect, to withdraw and keep quiet. On 13 January indigenous leader Peter Yu wrote to Brennan, in effect, asking him to cease his advocacy. 'I will be silent,' Brennan said in a reply the same day, save an article that had already gone to press in the Jesuit-owned public affairs magazine *Eureka Street*.

Brennan agreed to be gagged. He had committed an unpardonable sin—exposing the duplicity of the Labor Party and the NIWG. In a letter dated 31 December 1997 to shadow minister Daryl Melham, Brennan had said:

> There are now two groups in the country anxious for a double dissolution on Wik. First, there are those opposed to native title. They want the election so that the Howard government can implement its plan without the full range of Senate amendments. They especially want to do away with the right to negotiate ... Second, there are the strong advocates of native title who believe that a double dissolution will give the Labor Party a real chance of election with a commitment to a full blooded implementation of the Wik decision. For them, the more draconian the Howard bill, the better in the longer run.

> I am not a member of either camp. I am not a member of the
> second camp because I do not believe Labor has any real chance
> of election in a Wik double dissolution election.

Brennan said any election over native title would finish with defeat for
Labor and the Aboriginal side with disastrous consequences. This path
had to be resisted. He argued it was essential 'for the Senate to return a
bill which is still identifiably a Howard bill but with a redrawn moral bottom line such that the bill is still sufficiently workable and certain'. This
referred to the December 1997 Senate Bill but without the inclusion of
the Opposition's RDA amendment.[35]

Brennan's letter, *Eureka Street* article and further letters to Peter Yu
and Melham exposed a strategic gulf between Brennan and his Labor and
Aboriginal allies. Brennan outlined the legal basis for a compromise. But
he was also attacking the hypocrisy of Labor and the Aboriginal team. His
letter to Yu, dripping with sarcasm, said: 'As you all head down the double
dissolution path, be assured my co-operation through my silence from
hereon in.'[36] On 15 January Brennan again wrote to Melham, saying 'key
Aboriginal leaders and their advisers have temporarily forgotten who is
actually in government'.[37]

A frustrated Melham felt that Brennan was eroding Labor's position.
Yet Brennan's moral standing made him a difficult opponent. Melham, a
practising Catholic, found himself taking communion from Brennan at
mass while working to contain his influence outside church.

Brennan shook his head in disbelief at the Aboriginal tactics.
He noted that the NIWG retained the services of former Labor MP
Warren Snowden. He noted that the NIWG had two counsel, Ron
Castan QC and John Basten QC, and both were also counsel for the
Labor Party. What conclusion was Howard supposed to draw? What
would Keating have done in similar circumstances during the 1993
Mabo negotiations?

'Imagine hiring an ex-Liberal politician as your consultant to deal
with Paul Keating,' Brennan asked. 'Imagine telling Keating in 1993 that
your lawyer was also the lawyer for the Liberal Party.'[38] Brennan's point
was that the indigenous leaders had no viable legislative strategy. They
had given up on Howard. Their plan was 'all or nothing'—an election on
Wik hoping to produce a new Labor government. Veteran correspondent
Alan Ramsey penetrated to the heart of this folly, quoting a source saying:
'We're dealing with the classic politics of disempowerment, of a mob not
used to Labor being out of government … it's utterly loopy stuff.'[39]

On 9 January, Castan wrote to Brennan saying that 'nobody in their right mind' from the indigenous side wanted a double dissolution.[40] Castan, no doubt, was genuine. But this did not deny Brennan's argument that there was no basis whatsoever for any NIWG belief that Howard would buckle before demands from Labor and the Aboriginal leadership. If Howard would not abandon his bill then it would become an election issue. Keating relished this prospect.

'The Labor Party conducted itself as if it were the government,' Brennan said. The scope of Labor's proposed rewrite meant, in effect, a Labor law. Brennan said: 'It was inconceivable the Howard government would dump its own legislation and embrace a legislative package designed by the architects of the 1993 legislation of which the new government was so critical. But the NIWG, Labor and the minor parties took their stand and said they could do no other.'[41]

Melham said later, 'We wanted to force Howard to live with the consequences of his policy.' But he added a proviso: 'I didn't want the nation embroiled in a race election.'[42] Yet the politics were inescapable—despite their doubts, Labor and the NIWG were prepared to risk a double dissolution election. At one point Labor Senate leader John Faulkner gave Harradine's lawyers this explicit message. Brennan wrote to Yu: 'There are many Australians, not stakeholders and some of them churchgoers, who are left wondering why a Senate compromise would not be good for all of us in March 1998.'[43]

That compromise did not eventuate. The bill was lost a second time, just. Howard and Harradine held four or five meetings but Howard bowed to the non-Labor premiers on the right to negotiate. Harradine told Brennan: 'You know, I'm talking to the wrong fella, it's Borbidge and Court that won't let him move.' But Harradine felt it wasn't over.[44]

Harradine remained Howard's only hope for a compromise bill. For Minchin, the Democrats and the Greens were a lost cause, reduced to taking 'riding instructions' from the Aboriginal leaders.[45]

The turning point on Wik was the June 1998 Queensland state election—it eliminated Borbidge and revealed that a double dissolution election would be a disaster for Howard, an open invitation for One Nation to flood the Senate. 'Now is the chance,' Brennan pressed Harradine. 'Howard won't want a double dissolution. Strike while the iron is hot.' Brennan lobbied Tony Abbott on the need to compromise. As Minchin also saw, the Queensland poll had frightened Harradine.[46]

A short time later Abbott rang Brennan, who was in Hong Kong, saying: 'Mate, we want you here.' Sensing the deal was coming the third time round, Brennan stayed away—it was negotiated with the government by Harradine and a bevy of lawyers, including Castan.[47] In the end, Harradine got some concessions from Howard but the government saved its political face. Castan privately told McCarthy, Harradine's lawyer, 'John, it's a great deal.'

The key provisions were carried in the Senate on a 35–33 vote. Yu called it 'a cruel and malicious blow'. Future Democrats Senator Aden Ridgeway said Harradine's role was 'unconscionable and insidious'. Pearson said 'Harradine sold us down the drain.'[48] But indigenous opinion was divided, with ATSIC chair Gatjil Djekurra saying the compromise was 'an advance' on the original bill. The Labor Party rejected the compromise and attacked it.

The Tasmanian said he had won improvements on Howard's bill and had prevented an election that would have been 'frightful, divisive, racial'. He warned that One Nation's likely success at such a poll would have installed an anti-indigenous balance of power in the Senate. Harradine apologised to the Aboriginals for their exclusion from the final negotiations. 'I have prayed about it,' Harradine said of his decision.[49]

Brennan correctly said the bill 'was an improvement on what would have been delivered by a returned Howard government'.[50] He argued that, without the deal, native title would have been an election issue, Howard would have been re-elected and the Ten Point Plan legislated without any Harradine compromise, a persuasive proposition.[51]

This was not Keating's view. In his 6 July article attacking Brennan, Keating said:

> Howard had to choose between a double dissolution and taking a defeat … Howard has managed to get his party down to 34 per cent in the polls. He is, of course, beatable from this position. But Harradine and Brennan have taken the view that Labor, which would take a different approach to Wik, cannot win the election.[52]

Keating hoped the Ten Point Plan might become the key to Howard's destruction. Interviewed for this book, Keating was unforgiving: 'If Howard was prepared to have a race election, well fine,' he said. 'If it was to be so openly on display, then let's have the race election.'[53]

After the compromise, Beazley backed off. Labor had no heart for any ongoing battle. Beazley said Labor would not 'revisit' native title in the campaign. This was sensible—native title was off the national political agenda. The battle would shift to the states and the courts. Beneath his attack on Howard, Beazley was relieved. So was most of the Labor Party.[54]

Ultimately, the decision Harradine took was his own. Advisers can be vital but politicians take the responsibility. While Brennan had no role in the final deal there is no denying his influence on the strategy Harradine had followed from the start. While Harradine won some gains, Howard had achieved his aim—a major shift in the balance of native title law.

Among Aboriginal leaders hostility towards Brennan was intense. In a vituperative exchange with Brennan in 2004, Pearson charged there was 'real and undeniable evidence of your role in getting Harradine to forge an unjust compromise and capitulation with the government … my second point concerns your father … the judge who dissented in the Wik case was your father … [and] it was inappropriate for you to try to act like King Solomon … where your father had ruled that native title was extinguished in pastoral leases'.[55] Interviewed for this book, Pearson said: 'We didn't need Frank Brennan in 1993 and we would have been better off without him in 1998.'[56]

Howard was euphoric with relief, declaring that the outcome would 'allow Australians to feel good about themselves'. Melham said that 'Howard had got out of jail.'[57] Howard slammed Labor for playing a 'negative, destructive' game from start to finish. He never revisited native title again, even when he had Senate control.[58]

Would Howard have gone to a double dissolution? There is no definitive answer but some pointers are obvious. First, Howard didn't like double dissolutions. He avoided this option in both his second and third terms despite having the grounds. Second, there is no evidence whatsoever that Howard was seeking a 1998 election on race or native title—he wanted the bill, not an election. Third, Howard knew a double dissolution would empower One Nation in the Senate as an institutional breakaway from the conservative side and his interest was to prevent that. On the other hand, however, Howard needed his bill. As Minchin said, 'Howard had to keep the pressure on Harradine.' The option of an election was part of that pressure.[59]

Questioned for this book, Howard said: 'I didn't really want a double dissolution. But I kept it there as a possibility. I can't say looking back that I was absolutely determined not to have one. But I thought it would have been very messy and divisive.'[60]

This equivocal answer reveals the essential point—Howard had a strong interest in a deal with Harradine, a vindication of Brennan's advice at that time.

The idea that Beazley would have won an election with Wik
unresolved is fanciful. The inescapable conclusion is that both Howard and
Beazley were relieved by the Harradine deal that allowed them to retreat
from their polarising confrontation. As one insider said, 'Harradine took
the bullet for a political compromise both government and Opposition
were ready to accept.'

This retreat was in the national interest. The extent of institutional
conflict was dangerous. The native title issue, which intersected with
the apology debate, saw Howard's government backed by the non-
Labor states and farmers and miners in conflict with the High Court,
the Senate, the Labor Party, the Australian Democrats, the Greens, the
Aboriginal leadership, the churches and most of the upmarket media.
There is no denying that the legitimacy of his prime ministership was at
risk, as distinct from his popularity.

The Wik debate was about land management and reconciliation—
but Howard, unlike Keating, spoke only one language. Howard said Wik
'is not a racial issue; it is a land management, investment, security of
Australia, welfare of Australia issue'.[61] This was less a tactic than a reflection
of Howard's mind. Gareth Evans declared that Howard 'just does not get
it—he does not seem to understand the demons of hurt and humiliation
and fear and prejudice that are being unleashed'.[62]

Howard's inability to use the moral language of reconciliation meant
he was falsely branded as seeking a race election. Aware of the divide
between the government and Aboriginal leadership, Brennan concluded
'the blame lies on both sides'.[63]

Howard was a winner from the Wik settlement. But it was a negative
gain—he had escaped the Labor wedge. Most people felt his authority
was diminished. Michelle Grattan wrote: 'Nobody now thinks that
Howard will lead into a third election. The likely scenario is that, barring
maintaining his present huge majority, he would leave or be pressured
out next term.' The orthodoxy was that Howard was a divisive prime
minister unlikely to have an enduring impact.[64]

29

THE GHOST OF BILLY McMAHON

My belief was that the government had stagnated. We had to restore momentum.
—John Howard on the most important decision of his prime ministership

During John Howard's second year the whispers began to circulate—he was regressing into his 1980s siege mentality. His polling ratings fell and Australia succumbed to a brooding pessimism. Under assault from the Left and Right, Howard's authority began to deteriorate. At Liberal Party headquarters Andrew Robb saw the ghost of Billy McMahon through the Canberra fog.

Having won in 1996 on a platform of high caution, Howard was left with no governing strategy. His prime ministership was engulfed by uncertainty. Grahame Morris said: 'We genuinely thought it could be a one-term government.'[1] Arthur Sinodinos believed Howard had an agenda crisis. 'There was a sense of drift in 1997,' Sinodinos said. 'The moral was "If you leave a void then others will fill it".'[2]

Howard was facing a resurgent Kim Beazley and the One Nation eruption. During May 1997 Newspoll had the Coalition primary vote bumping along at 41 per cent, down six points from the 1996 victory. Costello's second Budget had disappeared without trace. The media smelt Howard's weakness. Business Council of Australia (BCA) President Stan Wallis said the government lacked 'strategic thinking and vision'. It was a leadership problem.

'A lot of people thought we were going to be a one-term government,' Howard said. 'Many people would say that to me.' Frank Lowy told Howard in 1997 that, at a business lunch he had attended, everyone at the table volunteered that Howard would lose the next poll.[3] With the exception of his election-year defeat, Howard conceded that 1997 was his worst year.

Complaints about the government focussed on two areas: jobs and tax. With unemployment at just under 9 per cent, Australia seemed mired in a jobless recovery while the re-emerging demand for tax reform was blocked by Howard's 'never ever' GST pledge. Howard's inability to cut unemployment and his paralysis on tax reform crippled his authority. The economic writers turned on him. The *Australian*'s Alan Wood said Howard's first term 'has been generally disappointing and a respectable second-term agenda is its best hope of restoring credibility'.[4] The *Sydney Morning Herald*'s Ross Gittins said: 'John Howard is looking more like his old boss Malcolm Fraser as each day passes.'[5]

The nation's mood was surly and disenchanted. In mid-1997 social researcher Hugh Mackay released a grim report:

> The uncertainty of the job market has finally worn us down to the point where we no longer seem to believe that anyone has a serious solution in mind. We know where the jobs are being lost, but we don't really know where the new ones are coming from. We hear about the Information Revolution but that seems to be about shrinking the labour market rather than expanding it. We hear about small business as the potential engine of economic recovery, and we raise our eyebrows in disbelief.

Respect for Howard was eroding. Expectations of his government had been low but there was 'now a palpable sense of let-down'. There was a broader concern—'that the government is weak, that it lacks direction and that it is too beholden to selected business interests'. Howard was seen as 'somewhat out of his depth, too easily influenced by the pressure of public opinion'. The Mackay report, titled 'The Disappointed Country?', found many people regarded the GST as a 'foregone conclusion'; Pauline Hanson's rise was attributed to a leadership vacuum.[6]

As Howard and Costello knew, unemployment would take many years to recover from the 1990s recession. It was not their fault but it was their responsibility. Employment Minister Amanda Vanstone had warned that 'we won't be re-elected' unless unemployment fell. The government's jobs strategy had two arms: maintaining the growth cycle and waiting for its 1996 labour market reforms to impact. It would be a long haul.

Worried by his inability to deliver on jobs, Howard succumbed to populist economics—he cut immigration and he froze tariffs. Howard was reduced to appeasement of a community angst that was beyond his control. The private justification he offered journalists was unconvincing—these were temporary measures to get through the worst.

In Keating's last year, Australia's migrant intake was 82 560. This was reduced to 74 000 in Howard's first year and then to 68 000, a low level historically. The reduction amounted to 20 per cent in Howard's first two years. The second cut was pure Hanson appeasement. Even worse, Howard endorsed Hanson's claim that immigration caused unemployment. While denying that Hanson had driven the cabinet decision, Howard said he had long believed 'there is a link between high unemployment and high immigration'. During a trip to the Blue Mountains in late May 1997 Howard attacked Hanson and then said: 'Could I remind the rest of Australia that my belief that there is a link between certain levels of immigration and high unemployment goes back to 1991, which is five or six years ago, long before anybody had heard of the current occupant of the seat of Oxley.'[7] Immigration Minister Philip Ruddock, unhappy about the decision, was powerless to check Howard.

The resort to a tariff pause showed a prime minister in retreat before mounting electoral hysteria. In mid-1997 a polling report by Rod Cameron's ANOP for the manufacturing lobby said: 'The country is seen to be in the doldrums and there is currently no end in sight. Australia is suffering from economic and social malaise and a lack of confidence in the future … the community already believes it is witnessing the death throes of Australian manufacturing.'[8]

The backdrop was BHP's intention to close its Newcastle steelworks, ending an iconic chapter in Australia's heavy industry. Industry Minister John Moore said 'perhaps no single announcement by a company in recent years has had a greater unsettling impact on ordinary Australians'.[9] In mid-1997 Howard combined with Moore to freeze the reductions in car tariffs for five years.

They rejected the majority recommendation from the Productivity Commission to cut car tariffs from 15 per cent in 2000 to 5 per cent by 2005.[10] The final decision was that the 15 per cent tariff would stay until 2005 and the government would legislate for a step down to 10 per cent from 1 January 2005. The industry purchased a five-year postponement plus a higher end point.

The political pressures on Howard were immense. With a state election imminent in South Australia he wanted to protect John Olsen's Liberal government. Olsen and Victorian Liberal Premier Jeff Kennett were pleading for protection for their respective states, the manufacturing base of Australia's car industry. Kim Beazley was demanding a tariff freeze and keen to wedge Howard if he refused. Within the Labor Party the Keating example of tariff reduction courage was dead. Howard said his motive was a combination of 'politics and industry stability, particularly in South Australia'.[11]

His aim was to cut a deal with car industry chiefs to deny his opponents political oxygen.[12] The car bosses attended Howard's press conference on the announcement. It was an official sign—this was a special 'fix'. The shadow of 'Black Jack' McEwen's protectionism hovered over Howard. It was the old-fashioned Liberal corporate politics beloved by Malcolm Fraser. Howard had worked with the industry and premiers to destroy the Productivity Commission's case.

The economic advisers were appalled. Treasury Secretary Ted Evans said: 'I advised Costello very strongly that we should proceed with these tariff reductions and he agreed.'[13] In cabinet, Costello argued for a sensible compromise—that the tariff be cut by one percentage point each year from 2000. 'There was a good economic argument for that,' Howard conceded.[14]

While Howard did not accept Costello's position, he declined to back Moore's start point—that tariffs be increased before being reduced! After Costello put his case in cabinet, he was surprised to see Moore leave the room. He went to talk to the car bosses located elsewhere in the building; the client group was on hand to sanction the cabinet's decision. Costello felt the cabinet was being compromised. There was strong support for his position from Downer, Reith and McLachlan, who opposed this capitulation. It was a tight decision; the difference was Howard. The Prime Minister insisted on the tariff pause and he got it.[15]

He was trashing his own credentials. Seven years earlier, in 1990, Howard said 'there must be no lapse back into protectionism under the guise of an industry policy'.[16] The contrast with Keating was irresistible. It was Keating who, when unemployment was above 10 per cent and his colleagues wanted tariff cuts slowed or halted, refused to budge an inch. Now Howard, half a decade later, sitting on a huge majority with unemployment lower, imposed a tariff pause.

But Howard felt he was acting to save his government. In mid-year, before Howard's decision, Cameron had identified 'a major sleeping issue that is about to break through and become a dominant theme'—the demand for an active jobs policy. Cameron said the 'great protection debate' was re-emerging. He said: 'The fact that Prime Minister Howard has not done so [taken action] already is proof of one of two things: either he is not the poll-driven prime minister which he has so often been described as or his pollster has been on a long holiday.' Cameron warned that without urgent action Howard would reduce the time 'before this government is voted out'.[17]

No political slouch, Howard saw the trend Cameron identified. So did Beazley. The protectionist coalition was formidable—it comprised the car companies, unions, Liberal state governments, the Labor Party, the Australian Democrats, the Hansonites and the talkback radio jocks led by Alan Jones. Howard said later: 'I was very concerned about the politics and I think I was right.'[18] In Howard's defence, the result could have been worse. Howard legislated for the tariff cut to trigger in 2005, irrespective of conditions—and, in the end, this happened.

It was obvious that Howard and Moore would apply the protection freeze to the textile, clothing and footwear (TCF) industries also being reviewed by the Productivity Commission. The regional structure of the industry and its high level of unskilled workers were perfect for a Hansonite push. Cabinet endorsed the TCF tariff freeze in September. But there was a mini-drama when both Tim Fischer and Costello told the truth in public—that protection did not save jobs.[19]

In the 1997 winter Australia was in danger of losing its way. Howard was too reactive and there was a risk that Howard, Beazley and Hanson would reinforce each other with counterproductive economic policies. Productivity Commission chair Bill Scales warned that tariffs were a tax and lamented that 'arguments that were fought and lost in the 1970s are appearing again'.[20]

Scales said that protectionism would cost Australian jobs by imposing higher costs for the country and reduced competitiveness. He explained that demand for labour would rise if all tariffs were removed. In a reference to Howard and Beazley he said the benefits of trade liberalisation 'must be given unequivocally by our political masters'. His broader argument was that Australia, after its successful 1980s reforms, was now at the crossroads. The tariff debate was a proxy for whether 'Australians really want to be part of the global economy with all its benefits and challenges'.[21]

It was a critique of Howard's failure to provide intellectual leadership and Labor's complicity in this failure. Australia was in the sixth year of recovery. The economy was growing at 3.75 per cent, yet the government was running scared.

On the other hand, the tax challenge was different. Howard was still a GST believer; he had never recanted. The real issue, therefore, was how long he would deny his convictions. The tax issue was pure politics and the politics were changing.

The business lobbies were keen to build a GST consensus. In October 1996 there was a 'politician free' tax summit jointly shared by the Australian Chamber of Commerce and Industry (ACCI) and the Australian Council of Social Services (ACOSS) under the respective leaderships of Graeme Samuel and Robert Fitzgerald. This laid the basis for a resurrected GST. The summit, involving business, welfare, church, professional and community groups, reached a new position: business recognised the need for tax equity and welfare accepted the efficiency case for the GST. A tax forum was created to lobby the government.

By May 1997 Howard sensed tax reform had become too great an opportunity to ignore rather than too great a risk to contemplate. He began to look for an exit strategy from his 'never ever' GST pledge. His plan was to run on tax cuts at the 1998 election and the GST offered him steeper income tax relief. Meanwhile Costello, long a convert to the GST, was irritated by Treasury's unrelenting crusade. On one occasion, when Ted Evans and Ken Henry gave him a long pro-GST exposition, Costello told them: 'You don't need to lecture me. I know this case inside-out. I fought for the GST at the 1993 election and we lost.'[22]

Evans told Costello the GST was a 'critically important' reform. It meant a new revenue base that didn't compromise incentives. The Treasury was frustrated with Costello—it wanted a GST and felt nothing was happening. 'We had given up trying to persuade Costello,' an impatient Evans later told colleagues.

Two days after Costello's May 1997 Budget, Howard and Costello reviewed the disappointing response. 'We both knew the tax side [of the Budget] was in dire need of reform,' Costello said. 'We made a pact. Neither of us would rule out a GST again.'[23] At the end of the week Howard told his advisers at Aussie's coffee shop, at the Paris end of Parliament House, that he had taken the fateful decision to put tax reform on the public agenda. On the Friday, Costello, speaking at a post-Budget lunch at the Essendon Football Club, refused to rule out a GST. He said that 'if we decide to do it in a future parliament I think the fair thing would be to tell the people and seek votes accordingly'. He sent three signals: big tax cuts were coming, a GST had to be considered, and the government would need a new mandate.[24]

Fischer hadn't been told. When an agitated Fischer read the news reports on Saturday he rang Howard. Howard told Fischer he had struck an agreement with Costello. The next day Howard told a Sunday-morning television audience: 'There is no doubt that at some stage, sooner or later, we will have to reform the Australian taxation system.' Asked whether this would involve a GST, Howard replied: 'You can't have reform unless you look at all of the options.'[25]

Howard was pleased with himself. 'I crossed the Rubicon when I did that interview,' he said. 'I had always been heading for Damascus.'[26] Interviewed for this book, he insisted that his embrace of the GST had only been an issue of timing.

ACOSS president Robert Fitzgerald said: 'Doing nothing isn't an option any more. All the main community groups now believe that tax reform involving income, assets and consumption is essential and can be successful.' The ACCI president, Mark Patterson, said the 'existing regime is simply unsustainable'. The chair of the BCA tax taskforce, Fergus Ryan, said: 'The Business Council believes that tax reform will prove to be as defining an issue as Mabo, the republic or the environment.'[27]

From this moment Howard had two options: an inquiry mechanism to transition through the 1998 election or putting a comprehensive GST package on the table for the poll. The media were sure he would be cautious. Michelle Grattan said Howard was 'unlikely to want to spell out a tax reform agenda before the election'. Gittins said 'anyone who imagines that Mr Howard will ever buy the GST is a dreamer'.[28] But Howard was Damascus-bound.

The Labor Party was delighted with Howard's news. Beazley saw his golden chance, declared a GST 'unnecessary' and relished the prospect of another GST election. He dismissed the initial response by shadow treasurer, Gareth Evans, that tax reform might have some merit. But Beazley forgot that history rarely repeats itself.

The Mater Hospital is a landmark on Sydney's North Shore near the Howard family home at Wollstonecraft. Howard was admitted on 25 July when a combination of flu and bronchitis had left him with viral pneumonia. This followed a punishing overseas trip when he failed to strike a rapport with either Bill Clinton or Tony Blair and found the Test match at Lords washed out on the day he attended.

On his return Howard had chaired a two-day cabinet meeting in Canberra, travelled to Townsville for a day, visited Thursday Island and then spent two days in Newcastle, a city facing an historic rethink because of globalisation. Back in Sydney, he succumbed. His fifty-eighth birthday on 26 July was not one of his best, though Howard, in his hospital bed, switched between the fourth cricket Test and the Bledisloe Cup. It would be his only significant illness as PM and he missed two cabinet meetings.[29]

But his political brain functioned at the Mater and during his recovery at Kirribilli. 'I did a lot of thinking over that period,' he said.[30] Isolated from the rush of daily business, Howard confronted a deeper issue: the meaning of his prime ministership.

He had overcome almost insurmountable odds to become PM, but what was the point if he was not true to himself? It was not just about political courage; it was about realising his convictions. Howard decided he had been too timid. He asked himself: would the government's position be stronger if I pushed a GST tax reform package? Howard decided the answer was yes. This led to the most important decision of his first term and, ultimately, of his prime ministership: to commit to a GST-led tax reform and to honour his convictions. It would be death or glory.

Howard said it was 'a personal decision' that flowed from 'my belief that the government had stagnated and that we had to restore momentum'.[31] He had been living off the 1996 victory for fifteen months. Keating had gone and Howard had to win next time in his own right. Political capital, unless renewed, only deteriorates. Howard decided to renew his government.

It was an existential decision and it came from Howard, not his advisers. 'I would have talked to Grahame Morris about it,' Howard said later. 'Grahame would have thought it was a stupid idea.'[32] Howard had never seen himself as a Billy McMahon, yet such talk had been circulating. 'In my view we had to do something big,' Sinodinos said. 'Howard believed in the GST and felt it could be marketed from government. We also saw the mood had changed—there was a business/welfare joint ticket for reform. The PM knew his government needed a big cause.'[33] Liberal Party director Lynton Crosby said: 'The GST was symptomatic of the fact that Howard didn't have any real agenda. The decision to review the tax system was a tactical device to get Howard back on the front foot.'[34]

Howard was handed a lucky break. The High Court, in a 4–3 decision, found against the New South Wales tobacco franchise fee, thereby destroying the states' ability to levy taxes on tobacco, alcohol and petrol. The court, in effect, deemed these to be excise duties and found them unconstitutional. The practical impact was to deny 17 per cent of the states' revenue base. The Commonwealth's indirect tax powers had never been so clear since Federation. For Howard and Costello it was a dream result paving the road to tax reform.[35]

During a series of meetings at Kirribilli over 7 and 8 August with his advisers and with Costello, Howard finalised his historic decision. On

Sunday 10 August he flew to Canberra for his first night at the Lodge in a month and for a two-day cabinet meeting to discuss the economy. He told Reith: 'I've got the majority and I'm going to use it.' On the morning of 13 August, Howard rang the state premiers to inform them of the decision. At a full press conference he announced that the government would 'reform and modernise' the tax system.

A Taxation Task Force, headed by Treasury's Ken Henry and with representatives from Howard's department, the Tax Office, Costello's office and the Cabinet Policy Unit, would prepare options. There were five guiding principles, agreed by Howard and Costello and authorised by cabinet: no increase in the overall tax burden; major reductions in personal income tax, with priority to families; a broad-based indirect tax to replace some or all of the existing indirect taxes; appropriate compensation; and reform of Commonwealth–State relations. Howard promised to release the government's position before the next election.[36]

In his opening sentence Howard defined the issue of the 1998 election—the Coalition's future vision against Beazley as 'yesterday's man chained to yesterday's taxation system'. Howard would campaign as an agent of reform. He argued that there was a 'mood change' on the GST from the 1993 election. He took heart from his phone calls to the premiers. But Beazley reached a different conclusion. 'This is the old Liberal Party agenda,' he said. 'If the GST was an issue [at the next election] we'd fight on that.'[37]

An ebullient Howard now divided his first term into two halves. The first half was the 'repair phase'—fixing the Budget deficit, setting up the central bank, reforming industrial reforms. The second phase was just starting—it was about 'realising the potential of Australia'. Howard's conviction was to achieve 'a significantly lower rate of personal income tax'.[38] Big decisions usually liberate leaders and Howard's defensive body language had surrendered to confidence. He permitted himself an observation—that in 1985 both Beazley and Evans had supported Keating's proposed indirect tax.[39]

Once the process began, it was directed by Costello. 'I worked on the package essentially for twelve months,' he says. 'At the outset I decided the rate for the GST should be 10 per cent.'[40] It needed to be high enough to abolish the existing wholesale sales taxes and deliver cuts in personal income tax. Henry told Costello that the base of the GST must be as broad as possible; he had no need to persuade the Treasurer. Costello had learnt from Hewson's 1993 failure that a broad base delivered a simple tax by minimising exemptions. 'Keeping the design simple meant keeping the answers to questions simple,' Costello said. 'Hewson's failure to master the detail killed him in the last days of the 1993 campaign.'[41]

There was an initial difference between Treasury and Costello. Henry preferred the exercise as an indirect tax reform, keeping to a minimum any switch from direct to indirect taxes. But Howard and Costello insisted that the GST must raise the overall indirect tax burden to create 'space' for the income tax cuts they needed. Henry bowed to this necessity. But they listened to Henry on compensation when he told them 'you should compensate to buggery', saying this had been a defect in Keating's 1985 model.

Henry's team, physically separated from the Treasury building, worked closely with Costello. But Henry knew Howard was the driving force and that Howard would preside. It made the officials slightly uneasy. What idea might Howard dream up?

At the start there was a meeting involving Howard, Costello, Henry and Sinodinos to discuss the parameters. Howard surprised by saying: 'I'd like to look at a two-rate income tax scale, 15 cents and 30 cents.' For the first time the Treasury had an interactive computer model in the cabinet room that could show the full impact of tax, benefits and welfare payments for any rate scale. The keyboard was placed between Howard and Costello with the screen in front. The 15/30 scale was punched in and the screen rolled out winners and losers across the income spectrum. 'No, the curve can't go like that,' Howard said immediately. The curve showed that, as income rose, there were significant, then larger, and finally huge gains at the top. 'The curve's got to come down,' Howard said urgently. Then he went further. 'At some point, those gains have got to go negative.' He didn't specify at what point he wanted people to become losers. It showed Howard's mindset—he wanted to prove his equity credentials by being seen to disadvantage the rich.

'If you want that, PM, you can't cut the top rate,' Henry said. 'You can't have that rate at 30 per cent.' That was now fine by Howard. The meeting had lasted ninety minutes. Howard had gone from wanting a 15/30 rate scale to ruling out any cut in the top 47 cents rate.

Costello and Howard decided the GST proceeds should flow to the states. This followed a decision by federal and state treasury officials to work to this result. For the premiers, the gains were obvious. For Costello, this deal had two pluses. It maximised his leverage to get the premiers to abolish a number of indirect taxes and it killed off the scare campaign that the GST rate would be quickly increased. Under Costello's proposal a higher rate would require the unanimous consent of the states (some of which were certain to be Labor) as well as legislation by the national parliament.

The Treasury accommodated Costello's desire to have the GST defined in the Budget papers as a state tax, thereby making the Howard government's tax burden look artificially lower. Ted Evans said: 'I was prepared to recommend the GST be seen as a state tax in order to help the government. The view I formed over many years was that Treasury had to know when to compromise to win on good policy. This was such an occasion.'[42]

It was the biggest tax reform for half a century. The proposed GST, unveiled a year later in August 1998 with few exemptions, swept away a decrepit indirect tax system. A new 30 cents income tax rate would apply to low and middle-income earners, covering 80 per cent of taxpayers. This replaced the 34- and 43-cent rates. The top rate stayed at 47 cents but with a higher $75 000 threshold. Family payments were restructured and increased to target households with children and give the greatest benefit to single-income families. The CPI was estimated to rise 1.9 per cent, with a one-off 4 per cent increase in all welfare payments to guarantee over-compensation for fixed-income earners along with special assistance for the aged. The corporate rate was cut to 30 per cent and a new quarterly system of tax payments for business introduced.[43]

This was far more formidable than past efforts to sell a GST. Howard and Costello proposed winners all round, trying to avoid any winners-versus-losers debate. They staged a massive raid on future budget surpluses to cut income taxes from 2000–01. Their entire tax agenda was made possible because of the first-term restoration of the surplus on which they would draw. They gave the GST revenue to the states, lock, stock and barrel, locking in the premiers to shared responsibility. If this could not deliver the GST, then it was beyond political salesmanship.

The reforms satisfied the tests of equity and aspiration. The major proportionate winners were those on very low income levels (who enjoyed higher social security payments) and middle-income earners (from the tax cuts). The distribution of $13 billion in income tax cuts was weighted to those below $47 800 annually who paid 43 per cent of total income tax and who would receive 48 per cent of the tax cuts. The income tax cuts maintained the progressivity of the system. For example, the top fifth of income earners paying 57.2 per cent of the income tax burden would now pay 58 per cent while the bottom 20 per cent, who paid 2.3 per cent of the tax burden, would pay 2 per cent under the new package.[44]

Costello used PowerPoint presentations in the cabinet room to brief Howard and his advisers on several occasions and later the full cabinet. One occasion became famous. 'Surely you're not taxing golf club memberships?' Max Moore-Wilton asked with alarm. 'Max, we're taxing food,' Evans replied. Max was left shaking his head and some officials felt uneasy. If Max was unhappy, how unhappy would the public be?

But Costello's alarm came with Michael L'Estrange's proposal to Howard, near the end, that an 8 per cent GST might be preferable to appease the welfare lobby and reduce the impact of higher prices. Costello was incandescent with rage. Henry said this would 'seriously compromise' the package. 'This means there are no income tax cuts,' Costello said, astounded. He was ready to defy Howard. 'I had no intention of redoing the proposal,' he said.[45]

The launch date was set. For Henry, the incident confirmed the paradox of the package—it was driven by Howard's courage yet subject to Howard's whims. 'Howard is a risk,' Henry had told his colleagues during the process. Costello felt the 8 per cent kite suggested Howard had lost his nerve—but it was temporary.

The policy launch was 13 August 1998, the day before Costello's birthday. It was a revealing event.[46] There was a Canberra media lock-up, with a joint Howard–Costello press conference. Howard took centre stage. Costello sat in symbolic subservience to his left. Janette Howard was in the audience but not Tanya Costello. Howard spoke for twenty minutes of 'a new tax system for a new century'. He recalled his crusade for tax reform; he had worked for this 'more than half of my political life'. He thanked Costello for 'his fine work', along with the officials. Howard took questions for thirty minutes. Finally, at the fifty-minute mark, he handed over to Costello. Mission accomplished; the political branding was complete. In Henry's view Howard was the political driver of the GST. Costello was the implementing agent.

Howard incurred much media criticism for breaking his 'never ever' GST pledge. The critique became deafening, a classic in the annals of media hypocrisy. The idea that politicians cannot change their minds is absurd. In this case Howard was putting his new policy in comprehensive detail to an election. It was a copybook case of democratic practice.

The risk was huge—and Howard came close to defeat. No prime minister had attempted such an audacity. It defied the lesson of the 1993 election: that the public would not buy a new 'lifestyle' tax. Howard had been driven to this position by a strange mixture of weakness and courage. Ultimately, he chose to cross the Rubicon and risk everything.

The super-cautious leader of 1996 had cloaked himself with audacity for his 1998 re-election.

'In my view this became the making of his prime ministership,' Sinodinos said.[47] Nick Minchin said: 'Howard now had an issue to fight for.'[48] Morris, significantly, put it differently: 'The decision was that if John Howard was going down, he would go down as a reformer who tried to change things.'[49]

Not only had the atmospherics changed, but Howard had changed. He operated better with a defined mission. Tax and the economy were his strengths. As the winter fog lifted from Canberra in August 1998, Billy McMahon's ghost had disappeared.

30

IN HIS OWN RIGHT: THE 1998 ELECTION

It's good to have a mountain to climb.
—John Howard, December 1998, at the government's Christmas party

The 1998 election saw John Howard survive his moment of highest risk while Kim Beazley would be seduced by his near-victory experience. Few elections in Australia's history have been so riddled with contradictions and false trails. Howard emerged numerically weaker, with his majority slashed from 44 to 12 seats, yet he was psychologically stronger. This poll bequeathed an equivocal political climate over 1998–2001 reflected in the leaders—Howard never looked back yet Beazley concluded that the government would be swept out with the 2001 political tide.

Politicians struggled over the meaning of the 1998 election. Had it resurrected the Howard project from its brush with death, or did it doom Howard as a disappointing two-term prime minister unable to match Malcolm Fraser's record? Both sides looked at Labor's 51–49 per cent two-party-preferred margin, normally sufficient for victory, and drew opposing conclusions: Howard would make the most of his reprieve and Beazley felt that Labor had won a moral victory.

But there is a deeper story. The 1998 election gave Howard the governing formula that he had found so elusive; it cured the chaos of the first term. Howard had struggled to resolve two ideas—to be a force for stability and to bring decisive change. The upshot had been a defensive 18 months that saw his poll ratings collapse before the lurch into a death-defying GST crusade. The truth is neither offered a viable model for office.

Having won on his own agenda, Howard's direction became more assured—being a conviction leader yet taking pragmatic decisions backed by a wall of money. It would deliver him another two election wins. The lesson, as Arthur Sinodinos said, was that 'you set the agenda and play to your strengths'. So Howard would become strong but not foolhardy; he would listen but project his convictions. He would refine a governing strategy.

This election saw the revolt of the Howard battlers. The leader who had pledged reassurance in 1996 was now imposing a GST shock. No wonder the battlers were confused. The extent of Howard's first term disaster was shown by the swings—the 1996 pro-Howard swing of 5 per cent was negated by the 1998 pro-Beazley swing of 4.6 per cent. Howard had marched up the hill and nearly marched all the way down again. Many battlers who liked Howard in 1996 were further alienated by the Liberal Party's decision to preference against Hanson. There was still a 'battler' factor in Howard's win but this was no permanent realignment in politics—the battlers had to be won election by election.

It was a poll filled with historic danger for Australian conservatism. Howard faced not just the prospect of defeat but a defeat partly engineered by the extreme Right in the form of One Nation. This would be the worst sort of defeat, guaranteeing bitter recriminations within the rejected Liberal and National parties for years. If One Nation got a foothold in Federal Parliament then conservative politics would be structurally compromised.

There was, however, a grand aspect to Howard's 1998 victory. Won off the GST-led tax reform package in the teeth of fierce Labor resistance, it invested Howard with fresh lustre and seeded the 'Howard as conviction leader' narrative that would reach mythic proportions. The pro-Labor polemicists hated the 1998 election story—it saw Howard as the first leader in the industrialised world to win on such a tax reform package. This victory was about courage, not opportunism. It is probably the most conspicuous election victory on a reform agenda in the Liberal Party's history.

The irony is that Labor's anti-GST populism helped to make Howard a political hero. If Labor had won an election on such reformism, the ABC would have been making documentary dramas about it for the next fifty years. The truth is that the 1998 election changed Howard—he felt a political and moral command over Labor. In Howard's view, he had campaigned for the national interest and Labor had been cheap-jack populists, not a clever play against Howard. Such sentiment was also a potential trap: it was the mindset that would take Howard to *WorkChoices*.

Howard's deepest shock came after the polls closed on election day, 3 October. The exit polls of Liberal Party federal director, Lynton Crosby, predicted Howard's defeat. When Crosby broke the bad news, Howard was shocked—he was expecting to win. 'I delivered the last rites to the family at Kirribilli House,' he said. The poll was devastating. For a short time Howard's career turned to ashes.[1]

Beazley got his own shock the night before. 'I thought we were going to win,' he said. Kim saw the door opening on high office. 'It was only on the Friday night that Robert Ray and Gary Grey briefed me on our tracking poll and told me I'd win 17 seats but that I would not be governing,' he recalled. 'I was very depressed. And they were right.'[2]

It was a knife-edge campaign. For much of the election Newspoll showed a Labor win. Insider opinion was divided—the view that Howard could not win on the GST was offset by incredulity that he would be rejected after one term. But at mid-point the Liberal strategists, Crosby and researcher Mark Textor, had survey results pointing to their defeat. Crosby says: 'We thought we were confronting an election defeat. In the end, we found enough seats to firewall. That meant relying on good MPs, putting more resources into local campaigns including television advertising and sorting out what seats we could hold. These decisions were necessary because defeat was a real prospect.'[3]

Howard's timing had been right. Having released his tax package on 13 August he called the election on 30 August for 3 October. He knew the longer the GST sat on the table, the more corrosive it would become. The competing tax packages dominated the election in a 1993 replay but tax was also a metaphor for the economy—Howard's strategy was to win on economic management. He played to Australian pragmatism, shunning any utopianism.

In the campaign the government kept its nerve—just. Its victory reflected the power of incumbency, a superior marginal seats campaign, the sense in New South Wales that prosperity was returning and the triumph of marginal seat Liberal MPs such as Jackie Kelly, Danna Vale and Trish Draper, who reflected the 'Howardisation' of the party. Familiar and durable as old boots, Howard now presented himself as a believer. In the final week he said of his GST gamble: 'I know it is risky. I know it is against the conventional wisdom, but whatever the result is I will have no regrets.'[4]

The election witnessed a remarkable yet misleading Labor revival. Aware that the 1996 defeat posed great dangers for Labor, Beazley's purpose over 1996–98 was to keep Labor united, ensure its relevance and hold Howard to account. But he was gifted by events—Howard's blunders, the rise of One Nation and Howard's GST initiative. Seeing

Howard's vulnerability, Beazley had made a calculated lunge for a 1998 victory.

Although an Oxford-educated intellectual with a compelling grasp of global political and military history, Beazley was a Labor traditionalist and tribalist. His conservative mindset was allied to a personal decency and projection as a credible prime minister. The opposite of Keating in most respects, Beazley was also different from Hawke with whom he enjoyed a 'father/son' political bond. Beazley was a Labor loyalist, an Australian traditionalist and a modern leader steeped in old-fashioned ideas.

Operating as Defence Minister in the 1980s, Beazley had not allowed the policy innovation of the Hawke–Keating era to touch his soul. In a remarkable self-analysis Beazley said:

> I'm an ideological Social Democrat. I'm about the world view of the Labor Party in a way that they [Hawke and Keating] were not. I think in a way both Bob and Paul were … not necessarily within the Labor Party tradition. They have a radical perspective on the world—a view that wants to change things … Bob's a bit less than Paul that way. I am more conventional in the sense of having a view in the first instance which is an ideological, Social Democratic view.[5]

Howard saw Beazley as a throwback to old Labor. He had opposed Howard's Budget cuts, rejected his industrial reforms and rallied Labor's class consciousness during the waterfront dispute. Beazley threatened to bring home Labor's base after the Howard burglary. He was repair man after Keating's indulgence, a leader of policy caution and political attack able to better Howard in television debate.

Given Beazley's strategy, the GST was political manna. By the 1998 election Beazley had convinced himself that Howard was a palpable threat to Australia's egalitarianism. Replying to the Budget on 14 May 1998 Beazley said: 'The Labor Party believes that John Howard has forfeited any right ever to claim a mandate for this GST. And our opposition will be there whether we win or lose the next election. A vote for Labor is a guaranteed vote again the GST. If we are elected, you will not get one, and if we are in Opposition, we will oppose this in the Senate.'

This appeal was as old as politics—a stand against a new tax; it was that simple. It gave Labor a cause to disguise its policy vacuum.

The GST had no ideological significance as an anti-Labor policy. It had been championed by Keating in 1985; such indirect taxes were near universal in social democratic Europe; the GST was radical politics but conventional economics. Bill Kelty said 'It's a socialist tax because it gets a lot of revenue.'[6]

The Rudd government would accept the tax and enjoy its benefits. There was no intellectual basis to the view that it would ruin Australia's way of life or its egalitarianism and such frenzied claims, though widely held, were baseless. But Labor wanted to finish Howard. So the great 1998 paradox was born—Beazley needed the GST as his demon as much as Howard needed the GST as his saviour.

The truth about the GST has been buried by Howard's victory. 'When you researched the GST virtually nobody thought it was a good idea,' Crosby said. 'As a policy, it was a negative. People didn't want it. When we pressed people further and asked "Why is Howard doing this?" the answer was usually along the lines "It must be the right thing for the country."'[7] This became the device to sell an unpopular product.

Beazley's package, called 'A Fairer Tax System—With No GST', invites two judgements: it was pitched to consolidate Labor's base but it misread the rising tide of middle-class aspiration that Howard was cultivating. Labor's policy misjudged Sydney and provoked a series of tactical disputes with New South Wales Labor Secretary John Della Bosca. Sydney's values were being shaped by rising home prices, falling interest rates, more jobs and the quest for Howard-type incentives. Beazley had missed the trend.

Beazley sought to make fairness the issue of the election. Without a GST he used tax credits to target his redistribution. He outbid Howard for both single-income and dual-income families up to $55 000 a year. A dual-income family with two children on a total income of $40 000 a year would gain $63.46 a week from Beazley and only $21.30 from Howard. But above $55 000 a year most families would be better off under Howard.

Labor's policy was replete with symbols of upwards envy—indirect taxes would be levied on caviar and business jets, tariffs would be increased on four-wheel-drive vehicles and capital gains tax exemptions would be eliminated. Such symbols were interpreted as evidence of redistribution or class resentment.[8] The New South Wales branch disagreed with the strategy and felt federal Labor was out of touch with income realities in Sydney. The Coalition accused Labor of assuming that any household with an income of more than $50 000 a year was rich. Post-election, former New South Wales ALP Secretary Stephen Loosley said Labor's tax package missed the upward mobility dynamic in New South Wales.[9]

In his launch Beazley attacked the Howard government as 'hard, chaotic and incompetent'. He unveiled a 5 per cent unemployment target but failed to offer any plan on how to achieve it. In macro policy, Labor was highly responsible. Its package was revenue neutral—proof that Labor had learnt from the Howard–Costello campaign over the 1996 deficit.

On tax, Labor was positioned to the left of the Australian Democrats, the striking yet unremarked feature of the election. In an historic move, the Democrats had accepted a GST but 'with compassion'—a victory for leader Meg Lees and Andrew Murray. They demanded a range of exemptions enshrined by the removal of food. This was a spectacular shift to the centre that divided the party but, from the moment of its announcement, raised the prospect of a Howard–Lees GST without food.

Lees described as 'irrefutable' Howard's argument that the indirect tax system needed reform. Branding Beazley's policy as 'tired, tokenistic and tentative tinkering', Lees said Labor changes were 'a pathetic piece of patchwork'. She said the Democrats had non-negotiable plans for a fair GST. This became a momentous event for Howard and Beazley.[10]

The Democrats' criticism of Labor's policy as obsolete suggested that attitudes towards the GST had changed since 1993. Labor's Senate Leader, John Faulkner, had warned that 'opposing a GST from Opposition is a lot more difficult than defeating it from office the way Keating did'.[11] In a more rational climate Labor would have adopted the Democrats stance as its own. But the Labor Party, though trying to distance itself from Keating's image, was still entranced by Keating's spell and his 1993 victory. There was no stomach within Labor for anything but an anti-GST crusade.

This obsession would run throughout the 1998 and 2001 elections and eventually ruin Labor's credibility. On policy merits, Labor should have accepted a GST without food plus measures to target progressivity. That would have made the election contest Howard's GST versus Beazley's fairer GST. It was obvious in 1998 that this was Labor's best hope and equally obvious that it was totally unachievable given the internal mood of the party and its determination to purge Howard outright.[12]

The Democrats policy, however, created an angst within the government. The adviser most familiar with the GST debate was Peter Hendy from Reith's office, who had lived through *Fightback!* Hendy saw the conundrum: would Howard lose the election on an unpopular GST that had no hope of passing the Senate anyway? He wrote a memo to Reith ten days before the vote, urging a policy change:

> The Government may need to make a dramatic announcement to 'save the day'... With respect to the GST and food my consistent view in recent times has been to exempt it or charge it at a concessional rate. As argued in 1992 but not agreed by Hewson any announcement on dropping food should be done at the last possible minute. I would suggest [if we had to have a big bang] on the Thurs of the last week … If the price of delivering the most significant reform since WWII was to negotiate on food he [Howard] should consider it … Even if we won the election I think it is odds on this is what will happen in any case. It is better to get an electoral benefit out of it now than not win.[13]

This reveals the sheer alarm about defeat. As campaign director, Crosby recalls being approached a fortnight before the poll by Robert Hill about removing food from the GST. 'I certainly thought about it,' Crosby said. Hill was unable to recollect this event but said he would have had 'serious reservations' about a last-minute change.[14]

Reith knew Howard was beyond concession. The unity of cabinet over the tax package, bound by Howard and Costello, meant that reopening the package was too dangerous. Costello felt that 'the GST gave us a cause—and that was better than just defending our record'.[15]

The key to the Howard–Costello handling of the GST was to avoid any fatal mistake. 'We could have had a birthday cake,' Costello said of Hewson's immortal blunder. 'I believe that if there had been a single stumble the package could have unravelled.' For Costello, it was yet another triumph over Hewson. At each point he depicted Hewson as the example to avoid.[16]

Apart from the GST, the election was defined by One Nation. This party did not exist at the 1996 election yet won 8.4 per cent of the primary vote in 1998. It was a third-force eruption without precedent. The essential story of the 1998 election is forgotten—most of the defections from Howard went to Hanson, not Beazley. The arithmetic is irrefutable—the Coalition lost a huge 7.4 per cent of its primary vote and Labor lifted its primary vote by only 1.3 per cent.

The paradox is that One Nation gave Labor a whiff of victory but also denied that victory by becoming the main vehicle for Howard defectors. Howard's frustration assumed a personal dimension on voting day outside Gladesville Public School. A One Nation worker said to him: 'I hope you win.' An exasperated Howard pointed to the preference recommendation against him in his own seat and asked: 'Well, what are you doing this for?' The One Nation worker said he had to follow the preference allocation against sitting members. Howard said: 'How can you do this and say you want me to get back?' He felt there was a collective madness at work.[17]

It was fighting on two fronts that took Howard to the brink of destruction. He faced a Beazley-led revived Labor base and a Hanson-led regional populist revolt. Crosby calculated that 67 per cent of One Nation voters came from the Coalition and only 53 per cent preferenced the Coalition in return—a net voting transfer from Coalition to Labor.[18]

After the election a relieved but bitter Crosby said that 'Labor apparatchiks saw One Nation as Kim Beazley's vehicle to the Lodge. Labor was hoping to create its own DLP.' Crosby said that Labor preferenced One Nation last 'at absolutely no cost' when the same decision by the Liberal Party came at a price—that angry former Coalition voters having already defected with their primary vote were tempted to defect with their preference vote in retaliation. Crosby's exit poll found that 60 per cent of Coalition defectors to One Nation expected Howard to win. They tended to be protesters, not Beazley believers. It was Crosby's first national campaign against Labor; he would not forget its strategy.[19]

The related issue raised by One Nation in 1998 was whether Hansonism would derail Australia's modernisation. This was the historic risk posed by the election—a test that Australia passed.

Hanson lost her seat and was removed from the parliament, a pivotal outcome. Her party won just one Senate seat in Queensland, not the swag of Senate seats earlier threatened. One Nation preferences did not determine the election result yet the decision of the major parties to preference against Hanson was vital. Another factor was the heroic anti-Hanson campaign waged by Fischer in possibly his finest service to the Coalition. Despite the fall in the Nationals' vote, Fischer was ebullient in the tally room on election night, anxious to see that Asia's newspapers carried the message of Hanson's loss.

The truth is that Labor wasted its vote. It stockpiled majorities in safe Labor seats and failed to win marginal seats. 'It's the election that got away,' Faulkner said. He knew that winning 51 per cent of the vote yet losing the election spelt a tactical campaign failure. Faulkner's lament was that Labor started from so far behind: if only Keating had done better in 1996.[20] Crosby verified this, saying: 'The principal reason we won was because of the big margin we inherited from the 1996 victory and our ability to present the GST as a symbol of John Howard being prepared to take a stand as a conviction politician doing the right thing for the country.'[21]

The technique Beazley deployed to reclaim the heartland cost him in the marginal seats. As former ALP politician Rodney Cavalier said: 'The return of the traditional in 1998 was more than matched by the forfeiting of the middle.'[22] This explanation fits with Beazley's policies. The view that Labor was 'robbed' is wrong. Labor was unable to win a House of Representatives majority. 'In the end, it was a bridge too far,' said Beazley.[23]

In Queensland the ALP finished with 8 seats out of 27 and in New South Wales 22 seats out of 50. It was still crippled in the two big eastern states. Beazley picked up only two seats in New South Wales. At no stage did New South Wales ALP headquarters believe Beazley would pull a significant swing. Howard was saved by a dozen sitting Coalition MPs in marginal seats, many on narrow margins, who resisted the pro-Labor tide.

The result was more equivocal than it seemed later. Howard's primary vote, at 39.5 per cent, was weak; the Coalition's Senate vote, at 37.7 per cent, was appalling; despite Fischer's euphoria, the National Party's future remained dubious; and the Democrats won the Senate's balance of power. An unspoken decision awaited the Liberal Party: whether to trust Howard at another poll or move to Costello.

This result could have become the escalator to Howard's defeat. The reality, however, was the opposite—Howard invested his 1998 victory with more momentum than it justified on paper. That is the art of incumbency.

As Crosby and Textor saw, the GST had a paradoxical impact—it was unpopular with voters yet it created the Howard legend. Howard and Crosby would cultivate this legend, part myth, part truth. Crosby boasted: 'John Howard was completely aware that no other political party in the Western world had been successful in promoting an entirely new tax system during an election campaign. We used the GST and the victory to build the idea of Howard as the political strong man.'[24] In a cruel barb that stung Beazley, Howard said he had 'no ticker'—it was also an invitation to see Howard as a leader with the courage of his convictions. This cultivated profile of Howard would assume colossal dimensions over next two terms.

Despite Howard's litany of first-term blunders, the public was unconvinced about Labor. Cavalier said: 'Not one commentator wrote in favour of a change of government, the memory of the recently fallen was too fresh for them, they felt the government deserved more than one term to prove its mettle.'[25]

Labor drew the wrong conclusion from the 1998 election. One Nation's erosion of Howard's vote cast a spell of false optimism over Beazley. 'It's within reach,' he said late on election night about Labor's prospects next time.[26] The day after the election Beazley told the *Australian*'s Matt Price: 'I will feel good going into the parliament with a majority of the Australian people behind us.'[27] Howard said:

> Beazley concluded that, 'I'm on the way back.' He felt that if he played safe then he would win next time. Beazley totally misread this result. The 1998 election did not represent the rebirth of Labor. It was One Nation that made Labor look so good.[28]

While the 1998 election would empower Howard in psychological terms, Labor concluded that he was seriously wounded. Even worse, it decided to rely on Howard's weakness. Six years later, after its 2004 loss, Paul Keating said: 'The Labor Party doesn't understand how much Australia has changed and what the economic reforms have delivered.' This problem was seeded in 1998. Keating's lament that Labor had retreated to focus on low-income earners and its traditional base was correct. Howard's comment about Labor being fooled by One Nation was also correct.[29]

At their December 1998 Christmas party Howard said to Reith: 'It's good to have a mountain to climb.' But Howard wouldn't risk any repeat of his 1998 GST election mountain.

PART VI

JOHN HOWARD
DISCOVERS THE WORLD

31

THE AMATEUR WITH ATTITUDE

Foreign policy cannot be conducted over the heads of the people.
—John Howard, 2005

John Howard came to power as a novice destined for an adventure—his discovery of the world as prime minister. Although a politician for twenty-two years, Howard was a stranger to most world leaders, without regional networks and inexperienced in diplomacy. Yet there was a conundrum: he had deep foreign policy instincts.

His initial inclination was a delusion. Howard felt that Keating had indulged too much in foreign affairs, so he would avoid this mistake. 'Foreign policy isn't my highest priority,' he told his new Foreign Minister, Alexander Downer. It was naïve and self-effacing. 'Initially he just left it to me,' Downer said.[1] But Howard learnt it was impossible to succeed as prime minister without succeeding in foreign policy.

When he focussed, there was no gainsaying his intent—Howard came to reorientate Australia's place in the world. He was an amateur with attitude, passionate about his beliefs yet unsure of his policy, a dangerous juxtaposition.

The magnitude of his amateurism was disconcerting. Before Howard's first APEC meeting, DFAT chief Philip Flood said: 'My concern was getting him to see that APEC was a worthwhile initiative, that this was an important body for Australia.'[2] Former DFAT chief Dick Woolcott said: 'I have the impression that Howard didn't relate easily to Asians. He tended to be uncomfortable with them, particularly with the Indonesians, who spoke a different language.'[3] Veteran ambassador Cavan Hogue said: 'Asia was not John Howard's comfort zone; that was with the good old Anglos.'[4]

Howard dismissed the notion of foreign policy as an exotic art form. He felt it was about common sense. He shunned the trappings, distrusted utopianism and loathed diplomatic tokenism at variance with public sentiment. He was suspicious of DFAT for its affinity with past Labor governments. Initially, he had little conceptual grasp of foreign policy or empathy with Asia, such impressions being almost universal among the officials who advised him, including later admirers.

His early goals were modest—to signal a new approach, stay out of trouble and disprove Keating's campaign slur that 'Asian leaders won't deal with Howard'. Howard was divorced from the foreign policy 'club' or Establishment, that loose group of specialists, many of whom had left their imprint on Australian policy as diplomats, academics and advisers but who had mostly retired by 1996. Because Labor had governed for two-thirds of the period since 1972 it is unsurprising that the Foreign Policy Establishment view was geared more to Labor than Liberal. Howard wanted to rebrand Australia's policy with notions often unmentionable in polite company—traditionalism, nationalism and populism, ideas seen as a touch 'uncivilised' for Australian foreign policy.

After the election Howard told Flood about the style he would bring to meetings with foreign leaders, saying: 'We are proud to be Australian, proud of our culture and traditions—we do not grovel to foreign leaders. I will be defiantly Australian without being gauche or provocative.'[5] The sense of nationalistic pride was almost rampant.

Howard's attitudes were elemental. His belief in tradition meant fidelity to the United Kingdom and United States; his search for economic dividends guaranteed an obsession on trade and investment gains from Asia and America; with fewer inhibitions about military power he was more prepared to authorise ADF deployments; and his suspicion of the multilateralism of the United Nations saw him convinced that foreign policy was about getting the best deal from other heads of government.

Like Keating, he believed in realpolitik. Howard saw foreign policy as a strict national interest project, as distinct from a morality exercise. The DFAT chief whom he dismissed, Michael Costello, said: 'On foreign policy Howard was no extremist, just a conventional, very conservative orthodox Liberal rather like Menzies.'[6] Many pundits claimed Howard lacked foreign policy convictions, a complete misreading of the man.

While never a sophisticated rhetorician, Howard knew what he believed—that the American alliance was our special national asset; that Japan was our best friend in Asia and China was our greatest opportunity; that Australia's success originated in its British heritage; that our national values were beyond compromise and that national identity was beyond political engineering; that Indonesia was a flawed giant that should not monopolise our attention; that Europe cared little for Australia and had entered its afternoon twilight; that Israel must be defended for its values and its history; that nationalism, not regionalism, was the main driver of global affairs; that economic globalisation was a golden opportunity for Australia's progress; that Australia's prestige in the world would be determined by the quality of its economy and society and not by moral edicts to satisfy the human rights industry; and, finally, that Australia's tradition of overseas military deployment reflected a timeless appreciation of its national interest.[7] Each view was held with passion.

They constituted an amalgam of ideology, judgement and prejudice. Many were contentious and seen as obsolete within intellectual circles. During eleven years Howard refined his policy, but his attitudes remained untouched.

Howard operated in partnership with Downer, the politician he had replaced as Liberal leader, a collaboration unrivalled for trust and longevity between a prime minister and a foreign minister. Downer became Australia's longest serving foreign minister. Despite losing the leadership in 1995, Downer was not black of heart. His former aide, Greg Hunt, said: 'Not only did Alexander not have any rancour towards Howard, he genuinely liked Howard. He committed to Howard for the long term. I don't think Howard ever forgot that.'[8]

Partly educated in Britain, where his father had been High Commissioner, Downer was a former diplomat with a receptive mind, a friendly disposition and a schoolboy sense of humour that careered from self-parody to petulance and that, combined with a plummy accent, became a target for Australia's anti-British media prejudice.

'Downer didn't have the brainpower of Gareth Evans but he had more jokes,' Flood said. 'He knew that Evans was a figure of great substance and he told me that he respected Evans' achievements as Foreign Minister. He was very conscious that he was following Evans. I remember Downer's first visit to Indonesia and his talks with Ali Alatas, whom Evans knew well. When the meeting went well, Downer was on cloud nine.'[9]

Howard wanted his own stamp on the content, style and direction of foreign policy. He needed help from officials who shared his sentiments and could limit the unintended damage.

Howard had chosen Flood as DFAT chief but his two most influential advisers became Michael Thawley, a former diplomat, straight-backed and clean cut, a front that disguised seething policy passions, and Flood's successor, Ashton Calvert, an Asianist, a Japanese expert and a linguist. Calvert had been close to Keating, while Flood and Thawley had been senior public service advisers to him.

There were two views Thawley and Calvert shared with Howard: they were pro-American and they felt that Australia had got too obsessed about South-East Asia. They were revisionists in their rejection of the 'South-East Asia' DFAT school whose intellectual leader was Australia's greatest contemporary diplomat, Dick Woolcott, who had run the department under Hawke and whose role had been vital in the creation of APEC.

An unrivalled diplomat with a long series of postings spanning Russia, Africa, Asia and New York, Woolcott was a peerless networker whose skill in dealing with politicians was matched only by his genius at moulding public opinion through media briefings of a frankness that would have provoked the slaughter of any ordinary diplomat. Few who saw Woolcott in action could imagine a better national representative. Diligent, energetic and urbane, he seemed to be known to everybody who mattered in a range of Asian capitals.

But Howard's arrival was the drum beat for change. 'Very early on, we had a big debate within the government,' Thawley said. 'There was a divide. The Establishment wanted Howard to reach out to South-East Asia and to Dr Mahathir and I was very antagonistic about that. I told Howard—and this is a crude encapsulation—that he could align Australia with America and Japan or he could drift away towards South-East Asia. This was a choice to be made.'[10]

The middle years of Howard's era were influenced by Calvert, whose intellectual conclusions were as deep as they were dogmatic. Interviewed in 2003 as DFAT chief, Calvert described the DFAT mindset he sought to rectify:

> It had got to the stage where deepening our ties with South-East Asia was seen almost as our moral duty. It almost became an obligation that transcended strategy; an end in itself. This was associated with a post-Vietnam scepticism about the United States, a feeling that America wasn't very reliable. We had convinced ourselves we should be careful about being too reliant on America and too close to America.[11]

As professionals, Thawley and Calvert were focussed on North-East Asia and America, ready to give intellectual weight to Howard's instincts to modify the Labor legacy and rebadge Asian engagement.

The stakes were high because Woolcott was close to Howard and Downer. Indeed, he was escorting them into the corridors of power. While formally in retirement, Woolcott, at Downer's request, had advised the Coalition on its 1996 election policy and won changes to strengthen the pro-Asia line.[12] For Howard and Downer, he was a figure of reassurance. After the change of government, Woolcott made separate trips as their personal envoy to Malaysia and Indonesia to prepare for the initial Howard and Downer meetings with South-East Asian leaders. They recruited Woolcott to prove themselves in Asia.

'When Howard came to office he felt he had to show he could deal with the region,' Thawley said.[13] Downer kept Woolcott as chair of the Australia–Indonesia Institute, a post from which he could monitor Australia's relationship with Indonesia. Woolcott was put on the advisory board for the government's foreign policy White Paper. When Howard left his consultancy post with Clayton Utz, he even suggested that Woolcott take up the vacancy.[14]

But this 'love affair' would turn to ashes. Woolcott was the arch-symbol of the Foreign Policy Establishment that had grown comfortable with Hawke and Keating. The tension inherent in Woolcott becoming personal adviser to Howard and Downer would have a convulsive resolution. Over three terms Woolcott, their advance man into Asia, would become disillusioned and then emerge as a lethal critic of Howard/Downer foreign policy. The breach was personal and comprehensive. It symbolised Howard's break from the foreign policy orthodoxy espoused in the advisory, academic and media centres where policy was debated and evaluated.

Over the years Woolcott criticised Howard over Hanson, for down-grading Asian ties, opposing the republic, fawning before Bush's security policies, retreating from multilateralism and joining the Iraq War. A few months short of the 2004 election, Woolcott, along with former military chief Peter Gration, organised the statement of the group of forty-three former senior officials and military chiefs attacking Howard's Iraq policy.

After the government's 2004 re-election Downer, in response to a conciliatory letter from Woolcott, replied in these terms:

> I can never forget that you participated in an action that was deliberately planned to portray the Howard government as being dishonest. You and your 42 colleagues timed and executed your intervention in a manner not designed 'to foster a deeper

understanding of Asian countries and cultures' but to perpetrate maximum political damage to the government in the lead-up to an election. It was an orchestrated and calibrated campaign whose only saving grace, in my view, was its failure … It does not surprise me that you encounter negative views of Australia in your travels. Given your activities, I expect you have become something of a lightning rod for such views.[15]

Woolcott became a permanent symbol of the chasm between Howard and the previous generation of Australian policy makers. In 2006 he said:

Australia today is not the country I represented with pride for 40 years. I travelled extensively in 2005 and I observed how our standing has been undermined in much of the international community and some important countries in our own region. Out standing is suffering because of a recrudescence of those atavistic currents of racism and intolerance that we have inherited from our past. With our participation in the Iraq War, the Howard government has also reinforced the image of an Australia moving back to the so-called Anglosphere.[16]

His critique was shared by much of the policy-making generation across the Whitlam to Keating period.

The 'orthodox' backlash was intense but had several different flashpoints. At the end of 2001 a statement from three Australian National University academics deeply versed in government policy rolled across Lake Burley Griffin. It came from one of the most influential academics on Australia's external policy over the past fifty years, Hawke's adviser and former Beijing ambassador, Ross Garnaut, former DFAT chief Stuart Harris, and trade policy and Japan specialist Peter Drysdale. The force of their assault was remarkable:

Australia's official relations with the Asia–Pacific region are more fragile and less productive than at any time for several decades. This has jeopardised Australia's national security. It also threatens the prosperity that has accompanied productive economic relations with countries in our neighbourhood over the past decade … Our failure in the Indonesian relationship is now well known internationally. It weakens our standing throughout East Asia. There it compounds the doubts created by the 'deputy sheriff' episode … the awful reality in November 2001 is that we are less effective in advancing the interests in Asia of Australia and its allies than for a generation.[17]

Howard's determination to break from the past had been visceral. Its manifestations were his appeasement of Hanson, his promotion of East Timor's independence, the low priority he attached to Asian regionalism, his instinct to align closer to America and his punishment of asylum seekers. The idea of Howard as 'dismantler of the orthodoxy' took hold.

But Howard's departure from the orthodoxy did not constitute a strategic revolution—this is the fundamental point about his policy. It is a point many people were slow to grasp. Because Howard did not explain his policy effectively and because it evolved in response to unpredictable events, the confusion about its nature was pervasive.

The reality is that Howard came neither to revolutionise nor to reverse Australia's foreign policy direction. At the end of four terms, the judgement was incontrovertible—Howard's continuity with Keating on Australia's strategic outlook was far greater than his discontinuity. This point was often rejected by the Establishment and denied by Labor, but the historical evidence was overwhelming.

'My goal was one of rebalancing,' Howard said. 'I felt the relationship with the United States and the Brits had slipped under Keating for no good reason. I felt you could have the lot—the money and the box. And that was really what I had in mind. It wasn't in any way to retreat from the emphasis on Asia.'[18]

Howard, like Keating, believed that rising Asian prosperity was assisted by a strong US role in the region with its alliances acting as a stabilising force and its economy providing a market for Asian exports. For Howard and Downer, therefore, a strengthening of US alliances in Asia including ANZUS would only reinforce the security of the region and Australia's ties in Asia.[19] This was the bipartisan Australian way. There was no zero-sum game. Downer's adviser, Greg Hunt, said: 'Once relations with the region are strong, then it's easier to get closer to America.'[20] The judgement on Howard and Downer is that they altered the balance, priorities and style of Australian policy inherited from Keating but did not change its fundamental strategic basis.

Like most new prime ministers, Howard exaggerated his break from the past. In fact, he was beset by a contradiction—he wanted to distinguish himself from Keating yet he didn't want to unsettle other nations by ditching Keating's policy. He was both agent of change and a champion of continuity. It confused many people and sometimes it confused Howard himself.

In the end, he brought three big ideas to foreign policy: to redefine Asian engagement, to achieve a closer strategic alignment with the United States and to operate as an Australia-first nationalist sceptical about multilateral arrangements. Each of these generated fierce resistance.

The greatest confusion lay in his Asian policy. 'He came into office with the idea we had gone overboard on Asia,' Thawley said. 'He thought Paul Keating had gone beyond what the public will accept. He felt we looked too keen and lacked self-respect in dealings with Asia.'[21] Howard believed close ties with Asia were essential, yet he approached Asia as a cultural traditionalist. He dismissed Keating's view that Australia would best succeed in Asia by changing to become a republic, more multicultural and more independent.

Howard was running a foreign policy and fighting a culture war and the two became hopelessly entangled. 'I have never seen the need to adjust anything about Australia or Australia's internal ambience to accommodate Asia or any other country,' Howard said. 'This is part of my rejection of the Keating republican push and the ludicrous statements that we had to take the Union Jack out of the flag.'[22]

In response, Howard offered an alternative doctrine: that Australia faced no conflict or choice between its history and its geography. It could remain a Western nation yet succeed in Asia. For Howard, engagement could never be about Australia's identity; it could only be about foreign policy. Howard sought to capitalise on Australia's Western heritage, not to compromise it. He said that Australia would only succeed in Asia by being itself, not by trying to be somebody else.

Howard set out to smash Keating's nexus between engagement and identity. He felt this coupling was a blunder for Australia's foreign policy and its ties with Asia. The proposition was simple: if Australians announced they were a second-rate country until the republic arrived, then Asians would treat them as a second-rate country.

The year Howard became prime minister, the American scholar Samuel Huntington released his book arguing the pre-eminence of culture in politics. Huntington wrote: 'While a country could avoid a Cold War alignment, it cannot lack an identity. The question "Which side are you on?" has been replaced by a much more fundamental one, "Who are you?" Every state has to have an answer.'[23] Howard rejected Huntington's 'clash of civilisations' thesis; but he knew Huntington's question demanded an answer.

Howard had detected the trend Huntington predicted—that glo-balisation would provoke the rise of nationalism and cultural assertion. While Gareth Evans had argued a cultural convergence in the Asia–Pacific, Howard reached the opposite conclusion—that Australians were more assertive of their Western origins and Australian patriotism. 'He [Keating] couldn't get traction with his policy because people did basically think he felt we had to change the character of Australia to accommodate Asia,' Howard said. 'This was the thing that Keating totally misread in the Australian community. I think Australians are very happy to be close to Asia but not at the price of altering our character.'[24]

It was a distortion of Keating's position—his real message had been that Australia had to adapt by having a culture that 'is shaped by, and helps to shape, the cultures around us'.[25] That meant acquiring the social and intellectual skills to progress in Asia.

But there was another side to Howard/Downer policy: their desper-ation to match or outbid Keating in Asia. Within four hours of Howard's 1996 swearing-in the push began—with the announcement that Woolcott would visit Malaysia's prime minister, Dr Mahathir Mohamad, to encourage him to visit Australia en route to a planned New Zealand trip.[26] 'We wanted to show that we could do things with Asia that Labor couldn't,' says Greg Hunt.[27] On Howard's first day, he tried to outsmart Keating on Asia.

The Howard–Mahathir meeting took place and the Malaysian played along. In retrospect, it is amusing. Howard and Downer would repent at length as they endured years of barbs from Dr Mahathir who disliked Australia regardless of who was prime minister. A sheepish Downer con-fessed later, 'There's always a downside with Dr Mahathir, no matter how hard you try.'[28]

But Downer took no risks with Asia. Knowing what was required, he said on the eve of his first ministerial visit to the region: 'I want to give an unequivocal message to the region: closer engagement with Asia is the Australian Government's highest foreign policy priority.' There was no qualification. 'This government will be building on, not tearing down, the previous government's work,' he said. It was the ultimate tribute to Keating's success in Asia.[29]

On Asia, Howard would pose as a statesman, as he did in New York in mid-1997, and say that Asia policy was largely bipartisan.[30] Yet he could not resist playing politics for electoral gain, with his accusation that Keating had run an 'Asia only' foreign policy—it was the sort of nonsense that made Howard look a fool in Asia. Calvert complained that

Howard defined himself by reference to Keating for too long. Eventually he grew up.

In reality, Howard followed a conventional Asian engagement policy. 'I worried that on his first trip he might want to visit the US and Britain, but I was wrong,' Flood said.[31] Howard honoured the conventions. He went to Asia before America, Japan before China—and he went to Indonesia first. 'It proved he wasn't junking the past,' Thawley said.[32] President Soeharto was the first foreign leader he met abroad.

Not for a second did Howard believe Keating's formula that 'no country is more important to Australia than Indonesia'.[33] 'I don't share that view,' he told Flood.[34] Howard offered the Indonesians neither insight nor intimacy. At the banquet he pursued his cultural obsessions, pompously declaring 'we do not claim to be Asian' (as though Indonesians were in doubt) and saying that neither nation was being asked 'to deny its history, principles or cultures' (as though this had ever been a worry for Soeharto).[35] He was far too defensive.

But years later—when Howard found an Indonesian leader he liked, Susilo Bambang Yudhoyono—he outdid Keating with visits, dialogue and initiatives. Having virtually invited himself to Yudhoyono's inauguration, Howard showed brilliance in offering Indonesia $1 billion aid after the 2004 tsunami and created a personal bond with Yudhoyono. By this stage he was declaring 'Our home is this region'. Visiting Jakarta after the disaster, Downer had Yudhoyono approach him. 'Grasping my hand with both of his hands and with tears in his eyes, he said "I will never forget what you have done for us."'[36] At Calvert's initiative, in 2006 the two nations negotiated a new Lombok Treaty replacing that old Keating–Soeharto agreement that Jakarta had ripped up over East Timor.

Years later Calvert said: 'Howard/Keating differences towards Asia weren't great at all. Most of this was inflated; it tended to be about identity. The differences were over domestic and cultural issues, not policy.'[37] Interviewed for this book, Howard said the differences with Keating on Asia were more about culture and 'the foreign policy approach had not been all that different'.[38] Keating rejects such views.

The message was that Howard, if given the opening, was a dedicated exponent of Asian engagement. Downer negotiated Australia's entry into the East Asian Summit and declared that his 'greatest achievement' as Foreign Minister was to terminate the squabble about Australia's role in Asia.[39] By the time Howard left office Australia's relations across Jakarta, Tokyo, Beijing and New Delhi were, taken collectively, as good as they had ever been.

On the US alliance, Howard's views were uncomplicated and old fashioned—the alliance was an invaluable link with the world's greatest power and should be utilised as a national asset. Howard wanted to add value to the alliance—by moving closer to the United States and becoming a stronger partner, an idea that was heresy to the Foreign Policy Establishment. Howard saw the alliance in strategic and cultural terms—as Australia's security insurance and an expression of shared Western values. The latter assumed saliency after 9/11 inaugurated a worldwide ideological struggle.

Howard's entire life told him the Liberals were better alliance partners. Despite effective Australia–United States ties under Hawke and Keating, Howard was suspicious. Thawley encouraged him, saying: 'He felt we had to regain US confidence and he sensed, rightly, that it had diminished a bit. Howard wanted a shift and I agreed with him.'[40] Howard was convinced that success in Asia was tied to Australia's links with America.

His essence, however, was a radical interpretation of US power—Howard was a believer in virtually permanent US primacy. Asked about his philosophy of Australia–United States ties, he said: 'It is based on my very strong view that in fifty years' time the United States economy will still far and away be the strongest in the world. In a hundred years' time it will be too. America is going to remain the strong economy in the world, that's my view.'[41] His faith in Western and US primacy was unshakeable, possessing an almost mystical quality. Howard did not entertain notions of US decline. While impressed by China's economic rise, Howard never drew the strategic conclusion that Australia had to distance itself from America.

Calvert and Thawley encouraged him. 'The Foreign Policy Establishment underestimates the significance of US strategic and economic pre-eminence,' Calvert said. It was one of his favourite themes.[42]

As a consequence, Howard believed that America would become more, not less, important to Australia in the post-Cold War age, an idea fiercely contested by much of Australia's foreign policy community. They believed Asia, not America, had become top priority. The orthodoxy said Australia must maximise its independence within the alliance for strategic reasons and because the Australian people were hostile to any hint of 'all the way' subservience.

Kim Beazley, one of the most sophisticated exponents of alliance orthodoxy, explained the calculation:

> The essence of policy under Hawke was to create 'space' in dealing with the US—to have Australian initiatives such as APEC, the

South Pacific Nuclear Free Zone, the Cambodian peace initiative and to develop our doctrine of defence self-reliance. This was the direction of our thinking. But Howard came and changed everything. He had a completely different view—he didn't want this distance from the US for Australia to develop its own initiatives. He just wanted to get close to the Americans.[43]

This penetrates to the different alliance conceptions of Labor and Liberal. Labor was happy with the alliance but Howard wanted to improve it. Labor believed the main value of the alliance was to help Australia achieve its ambitions within Asia (witness Keating's APEC diplomacy), not to use the alliance, as Howard intended, to get closer to the United States in political, economic and military terms. Nor did Labor embrace Howard's passion about shared Western values. For a nation close to Asia, this seemed too static in cultural terms. In addition, residual anti-Americanism within the ALP Left (let alone ALP leader, Mark Latham) was given fresh licence by the Bush presidency, making shared values an unpalatable idea.

Howard's outlook originated in his feel for Australia's role as a do-minion in the Empire age. His alliance thinking would have been familiar to Billy Hughes and Menzies who knew Australian statecraft was about extracting the best deal from the 'great and powerful friends'. Howard said: 'I am an Australia-first nationalist. But I am also an "Americaphile" and an Anglophile. And I have never seen any lack of congruence be-tween these three attitudes.'[44]

While true, such faith went unredeemed during Howard's initial visit to London as PM, when the Australian High Commission was told to arrange his meeting with Tony Blair around Howard's cricket timetable. He demanded to be in London for the first day of the Lord's Test. It was a bad time for Blair, who had many commitments and wanted Howard's visit postponed. When Howard insisted, Blair obliged, yet felt he had been inconvenienced—he gave Howard a short meeting and no joint media conference. Flood said: 'Howard went into that first meeting not realising how much he and Blair had in common.'[45]

It was a serious mistake with a funny side. At one point Howard, trying to be clever, asked Blair: 'What are you going to do with the Thatcher legacy?' Blair paused, he sat up straight, extended his arms and broke into a huge grin. 'I'm going to take the lot,' he chortled. Blair laughed, but Howard seemed stunned. It wasn't the answer he expected. On his return to the hotel, Howard was fuming. 'That man's a bloody chameleon. He doesn't stand for anything,' Howard declared.[46] In time, they became friends, admirers and war allies.

By this stage Thawley was aware Howard had a physical limitation. 'His deafness really affected the way he talks, his reactions, his tone on the telephone,' Thawley said. 'His ability to engage with people immediately is limited. It often takes him more time to build trust in others.'[47]

Howard's third break with Labor and the 'orthodoxy' lay in his conception of state power—he felt globalisation was empowering nations with new responsibility and opportunity. For Howard, it was nations that mattered. He had a distaste for the social democratic internationalism of the United Nations, he distrusted the EU and ASEAN as regional bodies, believing they produced 'lowest common denominator' results, and he was suspicious of international innovations such as the Kyoto Protocol and the International Criminal Court.

He was driven to these conclusions by his nationalism, realism and Burkean conservatism. Faith in state power permeated every aspect of his policy. The key to a better world, Howard believed, lay not in the UN but in competent national governments. This was the story of Asia's rise; it was the story of Australia's success. He felt the age of globalisation was making national power more important while making necessary multilateral agreements more difficult.

This philosophy had stark consequences. It meant Howard was ready to wage war in Iraq without UN sanction; he refused to rely solely on the World Trade Organization and resorted to bilateral trade agreements; and he doubted whether any global climate change compact along Kyoto lines would ever work. Unlike Keating, his mind was not drawn to regional architecture. The notion of Howard proposing APEC as a regional body would have been inconceivable because his mind was geared to bilateral action.

More than any leader since Menzies, Howard saw foreign policy as an extension of domestic politics. 'Foreign policy cannot be conducted over the heads of the people,' he said. Rejecting the argument of luminaries from Alexis De Tocqueville to George Kennan that pandering to popular opinion threatened sound foreign policy, Howard said the leader's job was to 'promote the values of the people'.[48]

The world changed dramatically on Howard's watch. The Asian financial crisis altered perceptions in Australia's favour; the China boom tied the nations together on a mutual gain basis; the arrival of President Yudhoyono and demise of Dr Mahathir opened new windows into Asia; and the election of George W Bush saw a fresh rapport with America. 'Howard has been lucky because the world changed in ways that suited him,' Calvert said. 'He is naturally cautious but when the time comes to respond, he usually acts boldly.'[49]

As a pragmatist, Howard adapted the Hawke–Keating inheritance but did not dismantle it. In foreign policy, he is best seen—as he saw himself—as an agent of rebalance and adaptation. He operated within, rather than against, the Australian foreign policy tradition. The key to his policy and its contradictions was that he sought greater international engagement from his platform as an Australian nationalist.[50]

32

GLOBAL FOLLOWER AND REGIONAL LEADER

In 1998 John Howard was ready to put Australian boots on the ground against
Saddam Hussein and ready to deploy the F-111s to drop bombs on Iraq.
—Hugh White, Defence department Deputy Secretary

In early 1998 the Howard government pledged a ground forces
military commitment to join US President Bill Clinton in an attack
on Iraq—a decision that stunned the Defence department and
terminated the 'peace culture' of Australia's strategic community. It was
the first sign of John Howard's mettle on the US alliance. His 'boots
on the ground' decision became a new benchmark. At this point, five
years before the 2003 Iraq War, officials realised Howard's support for the
alliance was different from Labor's.

Howard said: 'I remember this situation clearly. Clinton rang me
about this. There had obviously been feelers put out at a State Department
and Pentagon level. I felt this [commitment] was the sort of thing a close
ally of the United States would do. I felt very strongly about it. And
I didn't have any opposition [in cabinet].'[1]

An insider to this decision, Defence Deputy Secretary Hugh White,
said: 'In 1998 John Howard was ready to put Australian boots on the
ground against Saddam Hussein and ready to deploy the F-111s to drop
bombs on Iraq. Bob Hawke did neither of those things in the 1991
Gulf War.'[2]

The Defence department had prepared a submission for Cabinet's
National Security Committee with a list of seven escalating recom-
mendations for Australian military support. Howard's preference quickly
became obvious. He wanted the firmest of the seven options—the commitment of 110 special forces. This option was last because it was not

taken seriously by the department—it was an 'extreme' option designed to point ministers towards more 'sensible' decisions. But Howard got firm support in cabinet from Defence Minister Ian McLachlan.

After the decision there was a phone discussion between McLachlan's aide, Peter Jennings, and White. 'Have you guys seriously thought about this?' White asked. 'You know that people could die?'[3] The point is that Howard had thought about it.

McLachlan said: 'My view was that Australia had to make a substantial contribution and John Baker, as Chief of the Defence Force, agreed with this. The SAS were our best.'[4] In describing Howard's approach, White said: 'Howard was particularly cautious and measured in coming to his decision. There was no hint of any "all the way with the USA" mindset. In the end, however, he was deliberately tougher than Labor. He wanted to increase the size and tempo of Australia's role and this was a change in our military priorities.'[5]

Howard wanted to marginalise Labor's strategic culture. He believed that Hawke's limited yet contentious commitment of three ships during the 1991 UN-sanctioned Gulf War to liberate Kuwait had been far too weak. When Labor Defence Minister Robert Ray had said the commitment could be lifted from three to five ships, Hawke declined, saying the contribution was both 'substantial and proportionate' and he worried about putting 'young Australians at risk'. Hawke was aware, in seeking caucus and cabinet approval, that the commitment 'might appear to go against some cherished Labor principles'. Hawke saw this as 'the first commitment of Australian forces to combat since the Vietnam War'. He had to argue against ludicrous claims by some Labor figures comparing the planned operation to Vietnam.[6]

This 1991 commitment provoked a huge debate over a small deployment. It testified to a 'peace mindset' that dominated Australia's strategic outlook. Indeed, for the last twenty years of the Cold War, Australia had virtually no military role with its US alliance partner. Its focus became peacekeeping and stabilisation in Cambodia, Somalia, Rwanda and Bougainville. But the success of the Gulf War had eroded the post-Vietnam timidity. The transformation in the political climate from 1991 to 1998 was dramatic and Howard's assertive outlook was backed by public opinion.

When Howard came to power the political limitation on Australian Defence Force (ADF) deployments was conspicuous. One senior defence official said: 'In 1996 the Defence department regarded the deployment of 100 personnel to Bougainville as a major operation yet a decade later

Australia had nearly 4000 personnel abroad in about 10 operational missions. The transformation was profound.'[7]

The truth is that the ADF, to a considerable degree, had been unready for combat. The notion of military power projection had faded from the political culture. Howard tried to rectify this problem, though his success should not be exaggerated. Testimony to Howard's impact came in 2005 when the Chief of the Army, Lieutenant-General Peter Leahy, said: 'Over my thirty-four years in the Army we have never enjoyed such a high degree of respect and support from the government. Nor have we been accorded such a relatively high priority within the overall scheme of Commonwealth resources as we are today.'[8]

The force Australia deployed to the Gulf comprised 110 members from the Specialist Air Services Regiment, two Boeing 707 aircraft for air refuelling support and about 80 RAAF personnel. Other nations with commitments included Britain, Canada, Argentina, New Zealand, Poland and Germany. The Australian deployment did not commit to active operations—that would require a further decision that Howard was ready to make. In the end, it proved to be unnecessary. Opposition Leader Kim Beazley supported the decision. It was announced by Howard after a 10 February 1998 cabinet meeting. On 17 February, Howard and Beazley farewelled the force from Perth.

This decision reveals Howard's true nature. His commitment was to the US alliance, not to George W Bush. In 1998 in support of President Clinton, whom he hardly knew and with whom he had no meaningful relationship, Howard stuck out his political neck. His commitment mocked Labor's 1991 effort. It sent the message that Howard would make greater ADF deployments on behalf of the alliance. McLachlan said: 'It was a statement to Clinton that while we couldn't contribute in numbers we would offer our best people. It meant we were serious. Internally, it sent a signal to the "softly, softly" foreign affairs brigade.'[9]

This was the first in a series of decisions that defined Howard as a national security prime minister. He would preside over the most intense period of activity by the ADF since the 1960s Vietnam era. It was totally unplanned; Howard was merely responding to events. The main events that transformed Australia's strategic outlook were the 1999 East Timor crisis and the 9/11 attack on America by Islamist terrorists. But Howard's strategic intentions were signalled during his first term for anybody with their eyes open.

They were revealed in two events that presaged the dual nature of Howard's outlook—global follower and regional leader.

First, the 1998 Iraqi crisis saw Howard's interpretation of ANZUS to include Australian commitments in support of the United States in the Gulf and wider region. He wanted such commitments to be niche yet meaningful. This would stamp Australia as a strategic follower of US policy outside our region and supporter of US global objectives. The commitments to Afghanistan and Iraq flowed directly from this view. In a wider sense, this reflected an Australian tradition that had run for a century. As White said: 'Beyond the immediate neighbourhood Australia is a follower.'[10]

Second, when mercenaries were introduced into the region and the constitutional order was threatened in Papua New Guinea in the 1997 'Sandline' crisis, Howard took a firm decision: Australia must operate as regional leader, prepared to intervene and safeguard its sphere of influence. Within the region Howard pioneered a strategic leadership—witness the 1999 East Timor commitment, the 2003 Solomon Islands intervention and 2005 East Timor intervention. This was tied to one of Australia's emerging challenges apparent since the late 1980s Fiji crisis—that Australia lived in a zone of potential failing states.

This gave the Howard era its hybrid brand—regional leader and global follower. For Howard, it had a calculus: that Australia's support for US global projects would entrench US support for Australia's regional projects.

The irony of Howard's life is that he became a strategic and war leader. This defied his past career but was consistent with his family tradition. Howard's character as an armed forces prime minister was implanted from youth. He had a profound respect for the ADF. He exempted defence, but not health, education or welfare, from the 1996 Budget cuts. In retirement he boasted: 'I was very big on defence spending. It rose by 47 per cent in real terms over my period and I am proud of every dollar. I don't apologise for any of it.'[11]

The 1998 Iraq crisis was triggered by Saddam Hussein's defiance of UN weapons inspectors. This came eight years after his invasion of Kuwait and followed the uncovering by the inspectors of a vast WMD program—the work of a gangster regime that had gassed its own people. From late 1997 Saddam had taken the offensive and, in response to his breach of Security Council resolutions, Clinton ordered a US build-up in the Gulf and asked other nations to help. UN Secretary-General Kofi Annan sought a diplomatic solution to prevent another war. Clinton wanted military action. US Secretary of State Madeleine Albright was a hawk.

The NSC decision involved SAS forces and aircraft. Howard had wanted to send F-111s. When told this was not feasible because they lacked adequate electronic warfare self-defence, he was furious. Australia's frontline air capability was not fit for combat. He gave immediate instructions for the upgrade to be installed. The deployment decision went to the full cabinet with White and the Chief of the Defence Force, John Baker, briefing. The only minister to query its consequences was Environment Minister Robert Hill.

Active operations were not triggered. On 23 February Annan announced that he had negotiated a settlement and made the fatal comment that Saddam was 'a man I can do business with'. When he returned to the UN's New York headquarters Annan was cheered in the foyer by assembled staff. A sceptical Clinton abandoned the military option for the time being.[12] It was Annan's diplomacy that pre-empted a Clinton–Howard 1998 military partnership against Iraq.

Six months later Saddam betrayed Annan and cracked down on the inspections. 'Even people sympathetic to him [Saddam] in the Security Council are fed up with him,' Annan said. In private Annan said it was incredible that Saddam was still in power, eight years after his humiliation over Kuwait. US Defense Secretary William Cohen toured eleven Middle East nations to rally support for a US military strike. By November 1998 an aerial bombardment of Iraq was close.[13] At this point, it was Albright who briefed Downer on Clinton's military plans and asked for Australia's help. Downer's response was immediate: 'Australia would stand by the US.'

The Albright–Downer meeting was on 15 November 1998 in Kuala Lumpur before the APEC meeting. 'My mind is on Iraq,' Albright began. She condemned Iraq for flouting conditions imposed by the UN, saying 'The US would not put up with it.' Iraq's behaviour was 'totally unacceptable'. The Iraqis 'were seeing how much diplomatic traffic the situation would bear before the US acted.' She told Downer that the US was 'set to act' and claimed to be talking to Clinton 'every five minutes'.[14]

Downer replied that Australia would support the United States and make an appropriate statement on US military action against Iraq. Albright apologised to Downer that Clinton could not attend the APEC meeting because he faced a war decision. But Vice President Al Gore would come and he was 'very smart' and 'likely to become President'. Albright and Downer engaged in a mutual criticism of Annan for giving in to Iraqi pressure in February. Albright said Iraq had been 'jerking the US around' for eighteen months and the time for diplomacy had passed. She had spoken to the Chinese foreign minister who did not accept the use of force. Albright said: 'The US will be screamed at by the international community and would welcome a statement of support from Australia.' Downer stressed that 'the US should not look weak'.

Interviewed later, Downer said: 'In my view we must play a part on the global stage. The Labor Party is about "little Australia"—bring the troops back, don't get involved globally, don't do too much. But the American alliance is about being global.'[15]

This time the US planes were in the air and the attack was just over an hour away—but Saddam backtracked in his 'cat and mouse' play. With up to 300 cruise missiles set to be fired, Clinton aborted the attack. After more provocation Clinton launched a four-day bombing campaign, Operation Desert Fox, in December 1998. It terminated the role of the UN inspectors in Iraq and revealed the West's weakness in dealing with Saddam Hussein.

These 1998 events, however, were a 'dry' run for Howard and Downer. They had committed totally to Clinton and Albright—in military and political terms. It was inconceivable they would not commit to Bush when that test came.

There was little realisation in Australia that the Gulf had become a priority area within the umbrella of the alliance. Successive Australian governments had made three separate bipartisan commitments—in 1987, 1991 and 1998. The first, driven by Beazley, was Labor's despatch a team of divers for mine clearance; the second was the first Gulf War; and the third was Howard's commitment to Clinton. Since the late 1980s Australia's military commitments in the Gulf and Middle East had become the main arena of alliance obligations. This showed, despite the words of the treaty, that the alliance tied Australia and America into a global partnership.

Beazley said: 'A paradox of Australia's strategic history is that its alliance with the United States, convened in a Pacific context, has for the last twenty years seen direct military collaboration focussed on the Persian Gulf and its hinterland.'[16] For Howard, the game plan was apparent—Australia went to the Gulf in support of the United States. He would uphold the tradition but offer a lot more military grunt. This was the Liberal way.

The previous year, in Papua New Guinea, a flashpoint had occurred that Flood identified as 'an important shift' in Australian strategic thinking and a vital step in the education of John Howard. For Howard, the saga began on 18 February 1997 when the Office of National Assessments briefed him that the PNG Government had signed a $36 million contract with a British-based consultancy firm Sandline International for the supply of arms and mercenaries to destroy the Bougainville Revolutionary Army and re-open the Panguna mine on Bougainville.[17]

The effect on Howard was enduring. This constituted the injection of mercenaries into Australia's sphere of influence. It threatened the stability of PNG, a nation backed by $300 million annually plus defence support from Australia. It risked Australia's regional interests as well as 10 000 Australians living in the country. In the Papua New Guinea crisis Howard enunciated a policy of pro-active intervention as the metropolitan power to persuade and threaten PNG to eliminate the mercenary force. As Flood saw it, these were omens of a new era.

Howard summoned Baker and White to his office to brief him. As they drove to Parliament House together, Baker and White, convinced of the need for a tough Australian response, speculated in the car about whether the rookie PM would be firm enough. But they were surprised by Howard's determination. 'We found a prime minister prepared to take whatever action was necessary to stop Sandline getting a foot in PNG,' White said.

> The thing that struck me was Howard's spontaneous belief that in its immediate region Australia had to assert itself. There was no mistaking his determination. Although the issue did not arise, I sensed he would have been prepared, as a last resort, to use the ADF to stop Sandline.[18]

The NSC decided that Australia should stop the mercenaries deploying to Bougainville and then remove them from PNG. It decided, as Flood said, that 'the ADF should look at options for assisting in this operation'.[19] The terms of this cabinet decision were tough, though it said the objectives should be attained with 'the least damage' to PNG relations. Ian McLachlan said: 'We were absolutely firm on this point. We weren't having mercenaries chopping up Bougainville. Everyone agreed on this.'[20]

While Australia opposed any Bougainville secession, PNG Prime Minister Sir Julius Chan had misjudged Australia's reaction to his scheme to bring Bougainville to heel. Regional specialist Mary-Louise O'Callaghan wrote that Howard's 'unequivocal opposition to the Sandline contract was a watershed.' Chan, 'so used to Canberra's rubbery line' that usually 'bent to accommodate the PNG position', failed utterly to grasp that the game had changed.[21] O'Callaghan argued that Chan's resort to mercenaries 'was the greatest threat yet to the region's stability and Australia's role as the leading power'.[22] Howard, in addition, had Beazley breathing down his neck saying it was time to 'turn up the Bunsen burner' on PNG.

A meeting at Kirribilli House between Howard and Chan failed to resolve the issue despite Howard's firm line. Thawley said: 'We didn't want a confrontation. The stuff with Chan was done privately. But Howard was very firm and aid was on the line.'[23] But there was no resolution; Chan was more stubborn than Australia anticipated.

In mid-March the crisis worsened when the Commander of the PNG Defence Force, Brigadier General Jerry Singirok, launched an operation to remove Sandline and threaten the Constitution. He demanded the resignations of the Prime Minister and senior ministers. A stand-off threatened between the army and the government. In this situation Howard's reaction was to support the elected government but stress the need to remove the mercenaries.[24] It had become a double crisis—to stop the mercenaries and prevent a coup. The ADF was on alert.

Howard despatched a team of emissaries—Flood, White and Alan Taylor, a senior official—to meet the aloof and autocratic Chan in Port Moresby.

Acting on Howard's instructions, Flood said:

I told Sir Julius that, if he did not abandon the idea of using mercenaries, Australia would take drastic action and that it would affect both the aid program and the Defence Co-operation Agreement. He was taken aback. He was then offered additional assistance if he walked away from the Sandline deal.[25]

Chan tried to bargain but Flood wouldn't budge. The delegation left with the talks in deadlock.

Within twelve hours Chan had buckled to Australia's intimidation—with his political position collapsing, he killed the Sandline deal. The mercenary side of the crisis was finished. But at Townsville, 1000 kilometres south, the third brigade was ready for deployment to PNG. O'Callaghan wrote: 'The Howard cabinet, with one word, could have had troops pouring into PNG by the planeload.'[26] The original mission was to evacuate Australians, if necessary. But the alert was serving another purpose—to increase pressure on Singirok to avoid any threat to the constitutional order.

At this point the task for Australia's High Commissioner, David Irvine, required high diplomatic skill. He would need to frighten Singirok off military action with the threat of ADF intervention but play down Chan's hopes that the ADF would intervene to save his political neck. Interviewed on Australian television, Foreign Minister Downer refused to confirm or deny the circumstances under which the ADF would be deployed—his aim being to keep both Singirok and Chan worried for different reasons. In the end, Chan resigned and the constitutional order was preserved.

The final symbolism in this saga saw two RAAF F-18s 'escort' the Russian plane that contained Sandline's lethal armoury into a smooth landing at Tindal base in northern Australia after it had been diverted from Port Moresby, another demand imposed by Howard's government.

For Flood, the resolution 'demonstrated Australia's capacity to bring considerable leverage to bear in regional diplomacy'. Flood had no doubt Howard had changed Australia's policy—he moved towards 'breaking the mould in terms of official forbearance towards PNG'.[27] This was Australia's sphere of influence and it had to enforce its dictates. Howard was free from the postcolonial 'guilt' that had long restricted Australia in dealings with PNG. In the region, it was the opposite of being a US 'deputy sheriff'.

White agreed with Flood's analysis but he felt there was a deeper significance. He said: 'PNG's constitutional order had been threatened. I think Howard would have resisted any coup and that he would have deployed the ADF if necessary.'[28] The point is that Howard wanted to avoid any such decision. Interviewed about this in retirement, he was non-committal, saying the situation had not got to that stage, a classic Howard response.[29] But the ADF option was available and palpable.

The upshot was obvious. Despite far-flung commitments backing the United States outside the region, Howard saw the immediate region as his strategic priority. His instinct was that Australia had to become more interventionist as regional leader. As Flood and White suspected, these views would soon have bigger consequences.

33

THE CHINA SHOCK

You see, it's much better face to face, isn't it.
—Jiang Zemin to John Howard, November 1996

In John Howard's first year China taught him a lesson that he never forgot: even the most conservative pro-United States Australian leader had to succeed with Beijing. The shock of Howard's first year was the collapse in relations with China, an event that worried Howard and had the potential to ruin his prime ministership. From this moment of peril came a journey—Howard took Australian conservatism on a new road to Beijing.

It was China's pressure tactics that forced Howard's rethink. Conceding the magnitude of his initial blunders, Howard made the rare admission that 'things got off to a bad start'.[1] This was the wake-up call that saw Howard decide that a partnership with China was essential for his success in office. As the most pro-US leader since Menzies, Howard would become convinced that the rise of China was good news for Australia and had to be managed parallel with the US alliance. This led directly to his greatest foreign policy achievement: bringing Australia into closer relations with both America and China.

The crisis with China came in September 1996 when, after six months of Howard government ineptitude, China put relations with Australia on a diplomatic freezer. It was a calculated move. Australia's ambassador, Ric Smith, was unable to secure appointments with Chinese officials. 'As Ambassador I was worried,' Smith said. 'How serious was it? As a policy issue, on a scale of trouble from zero to ten, it was about a seven. China was going to teach us a lesson.'[2]

But there was a deeper risk. How long would the freeze last and might China decide to wait out Howard? Downer's former adviser, Innes

Willox, said the situation was 'very serious, a potential disaster for the government'.[3] Smith conceded the gravity but said 'we did assume it would pass'.[4] Howard had to deal with China; otherwise his credibility would be crippled and Keating's taunt would be vindicated. It was one thing to squabble with Malaysia's Mahathir Mohamad; being snubbed by China was quite another.

The crisis was multifaceted. At one point even Downer's future as Foreign Minister seemed shaky. Howard and Downer had no standing with China. Parading their American credentials, they exposed their failure to give serious attention to China, still emerging from the shadow of its 1989 Tiananmen slaughter of its own people. 'China didn't know the Howard government,' Smith said.[5]

It took time, but Howard finally turned his weakness into success. Philip Flood said: 'In the end, Howard did very well with China and with Asia. I disagree with Dick Woolcott that these were lost years for us in Asia. I don't think that's right at all.'[6]

In 2004 Howard told the Asialink forum: 'I have worked very hard to build an enduring relationship with China.' In 2006, a decade after he had taken office, Howard, at a joint press conference with Chinese Premier Wen Jiabao, said:

> Of all the relationships that Australia has with other countries, none has been more completely transformed than the relationship with China over the last ten years. Now I don't seek to invoke language such as special relationships and so forth, but I simply make the point that the transformation of the relationship with China has been remarkable.[7]

It was an exaggerated claim but revealed Howard's ambitions. During his final term, a confident Howard offered a view of China that differed from that of George W Bush. 'China's progress is good for China and good for the world,' Howard told the Asia Society in New York in September 2005. 'Australia's strong relationship with China is not just based on economic opportunity. We seek to build on shared goals and not become obsessed by those things that make us different.'[8]

In August 2004, after talks with Premier Wen in Beijing, Downer said the two greatest political events of the past half century had been the collapse of the Soviet Union and the rise of China. He praised China's pragmatism, noted that China had passed the United States as an export market for Australia, and said Australia and China had agreed to build a 'bilateral strategic relationship', a phrase that beckoned but was never satisfactorily explained.[9]

With the Howard era receding into history, Hugh White took the logic of these words and events to a persuasive conclusion:

> The popular perception of Howard is that is his main legacy was to strengthen ties with the United States. However, the biggest difference he made was the transformation of relations with China and that was Howard's personal achievement. He did this by identifying the economic opportunities at an early stage. He then proceeded to ignore the strategic dilemma posed by the development of a close economic relationship with a China destined to become America's main rival in Asia.[10]

In fact, Howard was more adroit. He used his personal ties with Bush and his pro-American credentials to purchase a degree of political immunity from the Americans in pursuing a more independent Australian approach to China. His attachment to Bush's America blinded nearly everybody to the obvious nature of Howard's diplomacy—a deepening of ties with both China and America together. This will be his main foreign policy legacy.

For Australian conservatism, it was a threshold event. The rise of China presents Australia with a challenge unique in its history because, for the first time, our major trading partner, China, will be a strategic rival to our main alliance partner, the United States. As Allan Gyngell has said, managing relations with China and America is now 'the central task of Australian foreign policy'.[11] Howard made it look easy but such a conclusion is highly deceptive.

The origins of Howard's China policy lie in his response to the 1996–97 crisis that saw an extraordinary series of bilateral mishaps. It began with the US alliance: in March 1996 there was a Taiwan Strait trauma when China launched provocative missile tests and Clinton sent two carrier battle groups to the area. Downer waited until he was sworn in and then made a public declaration of support for the United States. While Australia was the only government in Asia to make its support public, many other governments had the same views. 'They knew it would cost with China,' said Downer's adviser, Greg Hunt. 'But they felt it was critical, as a new government, to take a stand.'[12]

In the 1996 Budget the government abolished the Development Import Finance Facility (DIFF), a concessional finance scheme for help-ing developing nations which had been benefiting China. Beijing was

angry and protested. Downer told parliament that Beijing had not complained, but this served only to expose him and the furore undermined
his position.

Meanwhile the Howard government was re-orientating towards
the United States in its public declarations. *The People's Daily* accused
the United States of using Japan and Australia like 'the claws of a crab'.
Howard met the Dalai Lama, exciting a hostile Chinese reaction. 'China
was getting lots of negative signals,' Smith said. 'The Chinese feared a
policy change was underway.'[13] Their alarm was that Australia's policy
was undergoing a deliberate shift from Keating. It was an understandable
view, but it was wrong.[14]

Howard and Downer had not thought through the China relationship. They were unprepared and exposed as amateurs. Howard's senior
ministers were confused, unsure whether China was friend or rival.
Defence Minister McLachlan took a hawkish stand on Taiwan. Flood
was alarmed at the lack of any 'coherent' position. There was no over-
arching framework for the China relationship—Howard's urgent job was
to discover it.

Behind the scenes Downer was almost frantic. Years later he said:
'I think they wanted to see how strong we were.'[15] It is a neat rationalisation. His first meeting with China's Foreign Minister, Qian Qichen, did
not occur until 25 July. Downer tried to explain away the problems. He
said Australia's policy was 'to encourage the United States to continue
its security role in the region' but we had 'no intention' to seek contain-
ment of China. He was concerned this 'perception may have grown up
in Beijing'. ANZUS, he said, was not directed at China.[16]

Such reassurance had no impact. Some people began to ask in whispers: was this the new status quo? Eventually Downer summoned the
Chinese ambassador. 'I said all this has gone on long enough and I think
it's time to start building a positive relationship,' Downer recalled.[17]
Beijing felt its tactic was succeeding.

These events warrant deep examination because they reveal the
extent of China's political leverage over Australia and they raise doubts
about the ability of Australian governments to withstand serious pressure
from Beijing. The idea that Howard's arrival had damaged Australia–China
relations was a political embarrassment for him. Any notion that it would
prejudice future economic gains would be lethal. At this point Howard
took one of the strategic decisions of his prime ministership—that he
must succeed with China. The decision was never articulated in these
terms but this is how Howard's mind functioned. He had to succeed for

domestic political reasons and for his foreign policy to be credible. Once Howard reached such conclusions he acted ruthlessly on them. Yet the recovery took time.

It began in the corridors of the 1996 APEC meeting in Manila, when Howard had his first meeting with China's President, Jiang Zemin. With his task being an urgent repair job, Howard has never forgotten this meeting. He said this was 'one of the most important' foreign policy meetings of his time in office. Before the meeting Howard said he recognised that China 'will be a fundamental world player' and that he wanted a 'practical, positive relationship'.

In the meeting Howard delivered the message that Australia's 'One China' policy was unchanged. Howard, devoid of any Republican pro-Taiwan sentiment, was unequivocal. He wanted to deal with China on the same basis as the previous government. He sought a practical and constructive relationship. Howard said his message was 'pragmatic, a kind of let's build on our points of agreement'. He told Jiang the US alliance 'is not directed against you, it is part of our history, our democracy'.[18] The meeting was in translation. The breakthrough came at its conclusion. As they stood to leave, Jiang Zemin took Howard by the arm and said in English with a smile: 'You see, it's much better face to face, isn't it.' Howard understood.

'I liked him a lot,' Howard said. 'He was very pragmatic.'[19] In the first half of his prime ministership, Jiang was the foreign leader Howard met the most often. 'This meeting was the ice-breaker,' Smith said. His access was restored. Jiang invited Howard to visit China. The meeting's significance, Howard said, was that a framework for Australia–China relations was canvassed. It would be consolidated when he visited China.[20]

Meanwhile Downer was framing benchmarks to sustain the China relationship. In December 1996 he told visiting Minister of State Security Jia Chunwang that Australia 'didn't just look at China as an economic partner but also as a security partner'. The task for the current generation was to develop a new security architecture for the region. He wanted a dialogue with both the People's Liberation Army and with China's intelligence agencies. On trade policy, Australia believed it was a 'geo-political imperative' to have China in the World Trade Organization despite any US reservations.[21]

In March 1997 Howard made the second-most important visit of his prime ministership—his inaugural visit to China—ranking in significance only behind his September 2001 meeting with George W Bush. He had never prepared for a visit so thoroughly, consulting Bob Hawke and Ross Garnaut and sending Flood on an advance mission. He had a long working session at the Lodge one Sunday night with Moore-Wilton, Flood, Thawley, Ric Smith and Morris. While his lack of knowledge of China was conspicuous, Howard began to absorb the China paradox—it was communist controlled yet economically open, offering limitless opportunity for Australia.

On the first night in his Shanghai hotel suite Howard was surprised when the curtains were drawn to reveal the most dynamic construction vista in world history. 'How long has this been going on?' he asked, standing close to the glass. The answer was that Shanghai's economy had been growing at 14 per cent for five years. Howard was having a 'crash course' in modern China.

Flood had advised Howard that he was going to be treated well. Because the Chinese would scrutinise every word, he should rely on prepared texts as much as possible. The message from Flood and Smith was that Howard must invest more in the China relationship and seek a long-term partnership. Consistency of message would be vital.

In a clever move, Howard took a delegation of senior Australian businessmen with him, proof of his economic partnership vision. This invested the visit was a strong economic momentum. The government also accepted the deal Smith had negotiated with the Chinese—Australia would withdraw from the ritualistic US-led United Nations condemnation of China's human rights record, provided China agreed instead to enter into a human rights dialogue with Australia. Smith had told former DFAT Chief Michael Costello before the 1996 election that Australia needed a different strategy on human rights. He judged that Howard would 'buy' the deal, given his distaste for UN gestures, and Smith was right.[22] Albright later rang Downer to complain; the Chinese were happy.[23]

In Beijing, Howard offered the Chinese a political compact, agreed before the trip—a relationship based on 'mutual interest and mutual respect'. Mutual interest meant they would focus on the shared positives, notably economics and trade, and play down their differences. Mutual respect meant an acceptance that they had different values, political systems and cultures—the implication being that Australia, unlike America, would not hector, lecture and moralise. Howard would respect China's right to run its own society and he expected China to respect Australia's values.[24]

Howard wanted a professional 'national interest' relationship based on practical gains, not an exercise in mystique or hyperbole. The word *friend* never passed his lips. He never feigned intimacy and he never forgot he was dealing with communists prepared to shoot their own people. When Howard repeatedly invoked 'national interest', he was speaking a language invented by the Chinese. Beijing's leaders did not raise the US alliance but they got Howard's signals—Australia was a democratic nation allied to the United States and such conditions of its national life were non-negotiable.

At the Great Hall of the People, the Chinese had turned on a typical high-voltage welcome ceremony. Howard's face was red and his body stiff during the patriotic spectacle with national anthems, military guard and inspections of the guard. Then followed talks with a frosty but cordial Li Peng at a table that seemed to extend forever. The Chinese were masters at suggesting their power would match their civilisation. They were also brilliant at getting foreign leaders to treat them today as the assumed great power they expect to become tomorrow, a masterful ploy. Howard was happy to survive without mishap; he learnt about China's priority for sovereignty, respect and consistency.

Howard had another good meeting with President Jiang, who spoke in English over some of their lunch and detoured into the Western canon, Dickens and Mozart. Jiang affirmed that China would follow its export-based 'open' economy strategy; the scope for mutual benefit was vast. One of Howard's best meetings was when he took the business delegation to an audience with dynamic Vice-Premier Zhu Rongji. It highlighted another aspect of Howard's emergence. He presented himself in a way inconceivable at home—as chairman of Australia Inc. pushing a corporate relationship between the nations. Smith told Howard that Zhu was expected to become the next premier.[25]

Howard left China feeling that an operating framework had been established. Grahame Morris said: 'He felt he was on a winner.' Smith saw two stages in Howard's evolution: 'The first on this trip was learning how to get on with China and the second came later—taking the political dividends from the relationship.'[26]

'Howard followed in Hawke's footsteps and that is the reason he succeeded,' Garnaut volunteered. But Howard, unlike Hawke, never got emotional about China. His emotional detachment from the wild currents that had guided Australia's approach to China over past decades seemed to beget realism. On the return journey Howard said he wanted to be judged 'by one criterion and one criterion only—was it good for Australia?'[27]

He established with Beijing a 'national interest' framework that delivered a decade of expanding links with China. Howard said he was an 'optimist' about China's economy and the Australia–China economic partnership. A few months later Zhu visited Australia, toured the resources areas and enjoyed a lunch with Howard. 'This was very good—we can do business,' Zhu told Smith.[28]

Assessing Howard's China policy, Smith said:

> It was directed towards practical benefits. This reflected his own style but distinguished his line from Keating's loftier, more regionally based approach. Howard persuaded the Chinese they could trust him. On that basis he helped win a good bit for Australia in economic terms. And he conceded nothing on the US relationship.[29]

In retirement, Howard said: 'Jiang Zemin and I, in a sense, built the contemporary relationship between the two countries. I think the Chinese understood our American dimension. I don't think we have to choose between the Americans and the Chinese. I don't think that at all.'[30] The reality is that Howard stood on the shoulders of Whitlam, Fraser, Hawke and Keating.

From the moment he had arrived home in April 1997, 'optimism' became Howard's defining message about China. It never wavered for a decade. Howard flew a new flag for Australian conservatism: keeping the US alliance and making China a new partner. It was a different path from that taken by most American conservatives.

34

FAREWELL TO POOR WHITE TRASH

Suddenly we became a country that had shown
it was the strong man of the region.
—Peter Costello, February 2007

On 15 January 1998 a photograph flashed around the world signal-ling the subjugation of Asia to the West. Indonesia's strongman, President Soeharto, was signing the humiliating International Monetary Fund (IMF) agreement for his nation while the Fund's boss, a lapsed French socialist, Michel Camdessus, stood behind him, arms crossed, dominant and haughty.

This became the defining image of the Asian crisis—it shocked Asia and swore it to new policies that would forever deny the West another chance to impose its will on an entire region. The clash between Soeharto and the IMF, backed by the US Treasury, became a watershed moment in the late 1990s Asian financial crisis.

This crisis, along with East Timor and the 9/11 attack on the United States, was one of the three most important external events that shaped the first half of the Howard government. On 23 February, five weeks after Soeharto's humiliation, cabinet's National Security Committee (NSC) met in Sydney to finalise Australia's position. It was briefed by Reserve Bank Governor Ian Macfarlane and Treasury Secretary Ted Evans, who offered opposing views of the crisis.

In one of the critical stands in its history, the Reserve Bank declared war on the IMF. Its intellectual steel came from Macfarlane and Deputy Governor Stephen Grenville who, in a singular twist of fate, was an Indonesian specialist. 'From January 1998 we concluded that the IMF basically didn't know what it was doing in Indonesia,' Grenville said. 'This was a capital account problem and the IMF was treating it as a current account problem. Their diagnosis was completely wrong.'[1]

Macfarlane and Grenville would not sit this out. Convinced that the IMF package was a recipe to destroy Indonesia, they appealed to Peter Costello. Costello and Macfarlane had two long phone calls in mid-January on Indonesia's plight. The problem was that Costello's department, the Treasury, reflected the IMF orthodoxy. 'Costello's department was telling him that the IMF was right and we were telling him that they were wrong,' Macfarlane said. 'Our argument was that the Fund, under influence from the US Treasury, had completely misread the crisis.'[2] The stakes were high—going to war against the Fund meant a confrontation with the Clinton Administration.

Under Reserve Bank pressure, Costello convened a meeting of his senior officers—Treasury and the Bank—to hammer out the issues in front of him. He did not show his hand at the meeting, but Costello agreed with Macfarlane and Grenville. 'The IMF program was particularly harsh,' he said. 'It was plain that whatever the IMF wanted them to do, Indonesia did not have the capacity to do.'[3]

When the NSC met, Indonesia was facing one of the sharpest financial collapses of the twentieth century. The number of people below the poverty line was expected to double to 50 million. Sentiment at the senior reaches of Howard's government had turned against the Fund. Michael Thawley has spoken to Grenville about his concerns while Ross Garnaut and other ANU economists had launched a public critique of the IMF.

But Downer and DFAT had a new strategic concern—that the US-backed Fund was threatening Indonesia's thirty-year-old political stability, with the risk that Soeharto would fall. By this stage Australia knew that some US motives were malevolent. There had been a highly secret phone conversation in January 1998 between a senior Australian official and his US counterpart in Washington when the American had said 'the quicker the fucking regime goes the better'.[4] Australians knew that senior Americans had a political motive—they wanted the liquidation of Soeharto. No wonder Paul Keating became so enraged.

Meanwhile, in a comic episode, Camdessus was apologising for the photograph. He explained that his mother had told him as a boy it was best to avoid 'the Duke of Edinburgh' stance of arms behind back, so he had folded them and 'this is the only time my mother's principles have betrayed me'.[5] If only the problem was about posture.

In his opening remarks to the NSC meeting, Howard stressed the seriousness of Indonesia's plight and the need for Australia to take what action it could to help. Howard's sympathies were apparent. The meeting was dominated by the financial matters. Macfarlane issued a lengthy critique of the IMF's stance, with Evans more muted in his support for the Fund's position.

Downer supported Macfarlane and criticised the IMF. The most startling intervention came from Defence Minister Ian McLachlan, who launched a withering assault on the IMF, saying its behaviour in Indonesia was outrageous. Costello said little but was getting the result he wanted. The consensus was that Soeharto would probably survive and this was the best result for Australia. There was alarm that BJ Habibie was his running mate and potential successor.[6]

The meeting saw the demise of the Treasury line, with full support for Macfarlane's position. From this point Australia began planning its diplomatic offensive on behalf of Indonesia and against the IMF. This would involve representations in the United States by Costello, Downer and Macfarlane and bring the Australian Government into conflict with the US Treasury run by the two 'masters of the universe', Bob Rubin and his deputy, Larry Summers. These officials, smart and famous, had assumed the status of global giants during the 1990s, a golden age of US economic influence, as lesser nations—from Russia to Brazil—sank into crisis and had to be 'saved' by the Washington system on terms negotiated by Rubin and Summers.

The landmark decision by a conservative cabinet—to stand against the IMF and its US backers on behalf of a friendless Indonesia—was embraced by the three key ministers, Howard, Costello and Downer, but the passion came from the Treasurer and Foreign Minister. According to Philip Flood, 'Peter Costello was the key.'[7] It led to some of the toughest meetings Costello and Downer had in their careers, both with Summers.

Macfarlane felt sure the IMF was not gunning Soeharto as an objective but he saw the US Treasury in a different category. In 1998, when Macfarlane attended a meeting of central bank governors and criticised the IMF over Indonesia, the governor of France's central bank, Jean-Claude Trichet, told him: 'It wasn't about economics, it was about regime change.' When Macfarlane asked how he knew this, Trichet said, 'My friends at the Quai d'Orsay have told me.'[8]

Downer didn't need the French to tell him. Recalling his 18 March showdown meeting with Summers, Downer said:

I warned that if the IMF keeps pushing this line it will just bring down the whole Indonesian structure and he said, 'Well, that would be a good thing wouldn't it?' I said, 'We live next door to them. You live in Washington, mate, all the way across the Pacific. It doesn't matter much to you. For us, it's a catastrophe waiting to happen on our doorstep. This is about a revolution in Indonesia.[9]

However, Australia's defence of Indonesia was not the main story in this crisis. The 1997–98 Asian crisis needs to be seen in strategic and psychological terms, as well as financial. This was the 'coming of age' of the Howard government. After the Asian crisis Australia was a different country. Its impact, now lost in the mists of time, was transformative for Howard, Costello and Downer and they carried this 'liberation' until their 2007 defeat. Its stamp was on everything they did—it left them with a sense of empowerment, a belief in American supremacy off the back of Asia's weakness, and a new confidence in Australia's strength. Interviews with Costello and Downer about this event are remarkable.

'This was the watershed for Australia,' Downer said in 2006. 'I could feel this dealing with Asian ministers. It is when Australia went from being a political mendicant in the region to being a country with real strength.' Downer reported that when he became Foreign Minister he was patronised in Asia. 'I did find them [Asian ministers] quite patronising when I first met them. I found them, very much, you know, here's little Australia turning up and "What do you want today?" kind of attitude. Look, I was new and they'd been dealing with Gareth [Evans] for a long time.'[10]

After being appointed treasurer, Costello felt this Asian hubris. 'You have no substantial lessons to offer us,' was Asia's attitude as he detected it. 'The attitude was "You won't be part of the future economic development of this region, your best days are well and truly behind you,"' Costello says.[11] Recalling his first trip to the region to the APEC Finance Ministers meeting, he said: 'We were given a polite welcome but we were not respected. Australia was tolerated much as a fading uncle is tolerated at Christmas dinner: there out of politeness and past association rather than present or future expectation.'[12]

Such comments must be seen in context—Costello and Downer were unknown commodities replacing a well-known Labor government. Their remarks are self-serving. Hawke, Keating and Evans were highly respected in the region, a fact with a long documentation.

Yet Asian hubris towards Australia was authentic. The ASEAN members had fooled each other about their successes. The region's brilliant statesman, Lee Kuan Yew, became a crusader for Asian values and a critic of Western decadence, saying the liberal political tradition where people 'do their own thing ... has not worked out'.[13] Lee's famous taunt was that Australia was 'the poor white trash of Asia', a line he repeated as recently as 1994.

Interviewed in 1992 Lee said:

Ten or twelve years ago Singapore opened a consulate in Sydney hoping to build up economic links with Australia. After a few years we shut it down. You were living in a capsule industrially. You were not going at the same speed as the rest of East Asia. As we were upgrading our economies you were carrying on with your old ways ... Culture here [Australia] means a comfortable protected way of life that has bred a certain complacency.[14]

Visiting Australia in 1994, three years before the Asian crisis, Lee was even more dismissive. He said: 'Deep-seated problems of work ethic, productivity, enterprise, bloody-minded unions protecting unproductive work practices, feather-bedding and inflexibility in wages are neither quickly nor easily cured.'[15]

As the region's chauvinist, Malaysia's Dr Mahathir Mohamad boasted that Asia's model was superior to that of the West and that its government-directed capitalism (or developmental state) was surpassing laissez-faire. In Kuala Lumpur, the twin towers of the Petronas state oil company were the world's tallest buildings, a symbol of Asia's assertion. Mahathir treated Australia with contempt, exploiting the country's neurosis and reinforcing the idea of Australia as a society marginalised in its own location.

Lee and Mahathir did not speak exclusively for South-East Asia but their voices were loud and Lee spoke enough truth to sting. Costello said: 'Lee's statements struck a great deal of fear into Australians. The fear was that he could well be right.'[16] Yet Lee and Mahathir had misjudged the gains from Australia's post-1983 economic reforms.

The so-called Asian miracle had become a landmark in world economic history. In 1998 economist Joseph Stiglitz said: 'No other economic system has delivered so much, to so many, in so short a span of time.'[17] Yet the economic contractions from the crisis were some of the most severe since the Great Depression. Indonesia's GDP shrank by 13 per cent, Thailand's by 11 per cent and South Korea's by 7 per cent.[18] It took Indonesia seven years for per capita income to return to its mid-1997 level. East Asia's downturn was part of a global crisis over 1994–99 that also afflicted Mexico, Russia and Brazil and, in the fall of 1998, threatened the stability of US markets.[19]

The crisis was a psychological gift to Howard because Australia remained strong while the region sank into recessions and depression. Its financial system was fire-proofed from contagion and its export sector was flexible enough to find new markets outside Asia. The orthodoxy of decades had been reversed—as Asia succumbed, Australia thrived.

This was a crisis of Asian governance—the region's financial, economic, legal and political systems were too weak to manage the demands of globalisation. The Asian model had to be redefined. For Howard, this insight was stunning—it proved that the utility of Australia's British-derived institutions, legal system, market economy, public policy and culture had been under-estimated by Asians and Australians alike. At this point Howard, Costello and Downer became seized with the idea that would dominate their government: Australia's model was geared for success in the globalised age. There was no more important economic idea in their time and it became the origin of a new Australian hubris.

The Asian crisis was caused because global capital flows had outpaced the institutions of the Asian state. Capital flows to emerging markets rose from about US$9 billion annually during the 1980s to more than US$240 billion before the crisis, the modern version of fool's gold.[20] Asia failed in two areas—the financial systems had defective supervision and the political systems buckled when a firm policy response was essential.

Three nations, Thailand, South Korea and Indonesia, were forced into IMF bail-out packages. The IMF, created as part of the 1944 Bretton Woods conference decisions, was dominated by the West, notably by the United States. Its charter is to promote global monetary co-operation and stability and, with its headquarters in Washington, the Fund was close to its allies in the US Treasury and US Federal Reserve. It was governed by its faith in the financial market model, far distant from East Asia's model. By the 1990s the Fund was champion of liberalised capital flows.

It operated as financial doctor and credit union. When nations were caught living beyond their means and foreign lenders went on strike, the IMF was the only body able to extend a hard currency loan. As a trade-off, it became business planner for such hapless nations, laying down its terms to ensure economic recovery. It was a global enforcer of Western ideals. The conventional crisis facing the IMF was caused by a current-account deficit, the result of government overspending, with the Fund remedy being all-round fiscal and monetary austerity.

But the Asian crisis was different. In Asia, nations suffered a sudden withdrawal of hard currency because the capital markets, typified by the herd mentality, lost faith in the banking system and its ability to repay foreign loans. This was a private debt crisis. It was this second type of crisis—a capital account crisis—that afflicted Asia in the 1990s.[21] One of the reasons the IMF struggled is because, initially, it used old remedies for a new problem. This was the origin of the criticism levelled against the IMF by Australia's Reserve Bank.

During the Asian crisis the IMF managing director was Michel Camdessus, a senior official under François Mitterrand. His driving deputy was Stanley Fischer, raised in Africa, educated in Britain and America, close to the US Treasury. They were a formidable duo.

The Reserve Bank's initial alarm was triggered at the 1997 IMF and World Bank meeting in Hong Kong when the Fund's policy committee concluded that free capital flows were 'an essential element of an efficient international monetary system in this age of globalisation'. This meeting invited the IMF's executive board to amend the Fund's articles to 'make liberalisation of capital movements one of the purposes of the Fund'.[22] It was a major change in the rules of world finance.

Macfarlane saw this as destabilising folly for developing nations exposed to short-term speculative capital. It was an invitation for capital account mayhem. 'It was being pushed even after the onset of the crisis,' Macfarlane said with incredulity.[23] The Reserve Bank resisted what it saw as a 'huge push' by the IMF and the US Treasury to amend the IMF articles to impose capital account liberalisation on nations. Macfarlane said: 'The US runs the IMF and it made the mistake of encouraging nations to liberalise their capital accounts too early. This is also the view of Paul Volcker.[24]

The crisis had begun on 2 July 1997 when Thailand's currency collapsed, triggering the contagion that spread to Malaysia, Indonesia and the Philippines and extending to South Korea, Taiwan and Hong Kong. The origins of the Thai crisis lay in the intersection of three factors: excessive and volatile capital inflows based on high levels of short-term debt, a fixed exchange rate system that would be forced into a float in the worst possible situation and a weak financial sector without proper regulatory and prudential provisions. Too many bad loans had been made that threatened, ultimately, borrower and lender.

Appalling management by the central bank saw it forced into a belated float, with the currency losing 60 per cent of its value in three months. The government prevaricated, 'struck dumb by the size of the fall in the currency'. Everyone wanted to evacuate their capital to avert an even greater loss, thereby maximising the currency collapse.[25]

Thailand initially resisted IMF intervention and the IMF had no power to intervene unless invited by the host government. But Fischer ordered a team to Bangkok, saying, 'in the time it takes you to get there, I'll persuade them.'[26] On 5 August the government cracked and Thailand agreed to an austerity program in return for an IMF package to stabilise the currency. Negotiations were bitter and the Fund misjudged the depth of Thailand's crisis. The downturn was brutal and the government fell.

A short time later, IMF and central bank officials met in Tokyo to discuss the rescue package. Australia was represented by Grenville and a senior Treasury officer. They had approval for Australia to contribute US$500 million as a loan to the Thai bail-out. The funds would come from the RBA's balance sheet and appear as a central-bank-to-central-bank swap. When the Malaysian official pledged US$1 billion, Grenville saw the political problem. Australia could not offer half as much as Malaysia, a nation less than a third of its size. Grenville spoke to Macfarlane and they agreed to recommend a doubling in Australia's contribution to US$1 billion. This needed ministerial approval and they went to Costello.[27]

'We were aghast at trying to do half a billion and making a fool of ourselves,' Macfarlane said. 'The Treasury only wanted to do half a billion and we wrote an alternative memo saying we had to do a billion. Trying to be cheap-skates would be disastrous, and Costello and Downer agreed with us.'[28]

Costello and Downer saw the politics. Downer called it a 'must' for Australia. They decided Australia had to help, its help had to be commensurate, and it must be part of the overall IMF effort.[29] Thailand's bail-out was a total of $US17 billion, conditional on structural reforms. The main contribution was Japan's $US4 billion to compensate for America's refusal to contribute.

At this point Costello looked past his department and rode with the Martin Place mob. It was a political statement by Australia that it would help Asia during the crisis. Once the decision was taken, Downer felt a change in the political current from Asia. Australia was operating as a creditor power.[30]

Thailand was a significant ASEAN nation under-weighted in Australian media coverage. The decision reinforced Australia's ties in a relationship that would prosper under Howard. The following year the Thais would provide Australia with a deputy commander for the East Timor force and a few years later negotiate a Free Trade Agreement with Australia.

In October 1997 the panic reached North-East Asia, striking Hong Kong first and then South Korea, an economy larger than that of all ASEAN nations combined. Korea was vulnerable. It had massive corporate debts; a financial sector where loans were based on collateral size, not financial return; and a socialisation of bankruptcy risk. The share market and the currency collapsed and many banks were technically insolvent. Newly elected president Kim Dae-jung accepted an IMF package and, critically, under the leadership of the US Federal Reserve, action by international banks to roll over $24 billion of short-term loans, thereby averting the prospect of default by an OECD nation. The Korean bail-out was a huge US$58 billion, with Australia contributing another US$1 billion. The IMF's conditions were tantamount to 'a radical transformation of the Korean economic model'.[31]

Costello recalls: 'I had to go to my office on Christmas Day to authorise Australia's US$1 billion. My wife said, "Who's working on Christmas Day?" and I said it wasn't Christmas Day in Korea because they don't celebrate it.'[32]

The significant feature of the Korean bail-out was the renegotiation of short-term debt, an action beyond the IMF's authority that required the US monetary authorities to drive the agreement on the debt rollover. This happened for two reasons: a Korean failure would hurt the world economy and America had huge national interests in South Korea's stability. Costello said: 'The Americans were really concerned strategically. They thought if Korea went down it could tempt the North Koreans. They were much tougher on Indonesia than they were on Korea.'[33]

Indonesia was the nation worst hit. Its capacity to respond effectively was the least and its fallout was the greatest. For three decades Indonesia's economic success had buttressed the legitimacy of Soeharto's regime. The World Bank said in a 1994 report: 'The evidence clearly suggests that the poor have been doing well, and far better than in most other developing countries.'[34] By the mid-1990s life expectancy at birth in Indonesia was 65, in contrast with 49 a quarter of a century earlier. But there was no doubting Indonesia's problem with 'KKN'—corruption, collusion and nepotism—starting with Soeharto's family. Despite such corruption, Soeharto was no 'kleptocrat' like Zaire's Mobutu Sese Seko and President Ferdinand Marcos of The Philippines.

The key to Indonesia's crisis was that Soeharto's political system was broken, in effect, by the global capital flows of the 1990s. Once the issue in Indonesia became governance, then Soeharto was doomed. The World Bank later said: 'No country in recent history, let alone one the size of Indonesia, has ever suffered such a dramatic reversal of fortune.'[35] The collapse was one of the worst in twentieth-century history. Why was Indonesia punished far beyond the extent of its economic problems? The answer is 'domestic policy mismanagement, which culminated in a total loss of confidence in the regime'.[36]

In the best account of the crisis, American journalist Paul Blustein said: 'The Indonesian crisis is a tale of error piled atop error, with each side's bad moves—both the Fund's and the Indonesian's—compounding the other's and dragging the country's economy to depths nobody had previously imagined possible.'[37]

Indonesia floated its currency in August 1997. But the problem was whether, as the *rupiah* fell, Indonesia could repay foreign loans in hard currency. When Soeharto saw this vicious circle he was alarmed and confused. It was a challenge beyond his ability to devise any solution.[38]

The first IMF agreement of October 1997 was a US$35 billion bail-out, with Australia again contributing US$1 billion. The deal included the closing of sixteen banks, a step that undermined confidence in the banking system. From the start, however, Soeharto's government showed signs of early backtracking on the agreement.

The Indonesian Budget of January 1998 was criticised by the IMF as 'insufficiently austere', an irresponsible attack by the Fund that triggered a new collapse in financial market confidence.[39] Soeharto was trapped between the streets and the market; stranded between, on the one hand, social alarm over hyperinflation for food and, on the other hand, recognition that the IMF package had failed and must be renegotiated.

At this point Clinton moved decisively. On 8 January he rang Soeharto from Air Force One urging him to embrace more reforms and to work with IMF chief Camdessus, who was arriving in Jakarta the next week. Japan's Hashimoto and Howard rang with the same message. The US Federal Reserve and the US Treasury were in close touch with the IMF on a revised package. 'We were told that we must have Soeharto sign—it won't mean anything if the finance minister signs,' said Fischer of the new agreement. The night before the signing, Camdessus went to Soeharto's house for several hours to explain the document.[40] The upshot was the dramatic 15 January new IMF–Indonesian agreement, sealed in one of the public relations disasters of the late twentieth century: the Soeharto–Camdessus photograph.

The IMF package constituted an economic revolution that transcended measures to stabilise the exchange rate. It was a socio-economic redesign of Indonesian society according to Western values of economic liberalism. The agreement dismantled the networks, corruption and subsidies built into the economy. Blustein wrote:

> Tommy Soeharto's National Car project would lose all of its subsidies and his control over the clove trade would be abolished. BJ Habibie, the nationalistic technology minister, would lose government funding for his cherished project to build commercial aircraft. The president's daughters would suffer the cancellation of power-plant projects they had invested in. Tycoons close to Soeharto who controlled cartels or monopolies over the trade in palm oil, plywood, paper and a host of other products would be forced to face the chill winds of competition.[41]

Camdessus and his economists were thrilled.

'If this doesn't surprise the markets, nothing will' was the sentiment. The IMF was sure such shock therapy would halt the *rupiah's* fall. But it had misjudged and the collapse continued. How had the IMF miscalculated?

First, the package lacked credibility. It ignored the immediate debt problem and imposed a structural reform test that Soeharto's Indonesia would never meet. Soeharto signed without belief, and people familiar with Indonesia knew this. Former US Federal Reserve chairman Volcker read the IMF program and gruffly asked its officials what the hell clove monopolies had to do with Indonesia's crisis.[42]

There was no plan to address the heart of the problem—huge foreign debts of Indonesian companies and banks that had escalated by multiples with the currency collapse. There was no scheme to suspend or reschedule repayments. This was precisely the arrangement negotiated for Korea in December 1997, spearheaded by the United States. The difference was that Korea mattered to the United States and Indonesia was unimportant. An arrogant IMF said that 'Indonesian firms should sort out their own problems with their foreign creditors'.[43] The IMF package was renegotiated yet again in April 1998 to address some of these issues.

Before Soeharto saw Camdessus he had welcomed another visitor, Paul Keating. Out of respect for their friendship, Keating came to tell Soeharto that he should step down. As Keating left, his last words were: 'If you wait until March, you will wait until it is too late.'[44] Soeharto ignored his advice.

The most influential Australian critic of the IMF package was Grenville. Certain the IMF had gone off the rails, Grenville told Costello the IMF plan 'is not working and won't work'. The issue triggered a split between the Reserve Bank and Treasury, aligned historically with the

Fund, with Evans having once served as an IMF executive director in Washington.

Macfarlane said:

> We thought the IMF model was causing huge damage in Indonesia and we questioned their entire competence. Our argument was that the IMF, under pressure from the US Treasury, was treating Indonesia as an old-fashioned Latin American crisis caused by profligate fiscal policy leading to excessive monetary growth leading to inflation and to a balance of payments crisis. That's the IMF's bread and butter and 90 per cent of the problems they face are like that.[45]

The Bank said the problem was massive short-term capital flows. The Reserve Bank/IMF rift reflected a split about how to manage globalisation. The Fund favoured freedom for capital movements while Macfarlane and Grenville saw sanctioning short-term flows as the heart of the problem. The old Reserve Bank would not have launched this frontal assault; the new Reserve Bank was ready to test its political influence.

'Privately Costello said scathing things to me about the IMF and the US Treasury,' Macfarlane said. 'I don't think he had faith in his department on this. Ted loved the IMF. He instinctively supported the IMF and the US Treasury'.[46] Costello said his stance was 'more the view of Grenville than the view of Ted' and that 'Grenville believed the IMF package was too onerous and I reached that view. Ted's view was that the IMF should be supported.'[47]

Soeharto should have retired but in March 1998 he was reappointed by the People's Consultative Assembly for a seventh five-year term. It was the old man's fatal blunder. He selected BJ Habibie as his vice-president and gave his cronies and his daughter jobs as ministers. It was obvious he had no heart for the IMF package he had just signed. Many companies had lost 90 per cent of their value, capital inflow had virtually ceased, food shortages and riots had begun.

Meanwhile the Howard government's campaign against the IMF met an immovable obstacle: a triple alliance of Clinton, the US Treasury and the Fund. Clinton had complete trust in Rubin and Summers at the Treasury but their power created havoc within his administration.

Talking about Indonesia, Rubin said: 'I am no longer confident that economic reform alone will work. There has to be political reform as well.' The US Treasury consulted former US ambassador to Jakarta Paul Wolfowitz and recycled his arguments about the need for political reform in Jakarta.[48] There was uproar at State, Pentagon and National Security Council level over the Treasury line. The former US assistant secretary of state for Asian and Pacific Affairs, Stan Roth, warned about the risks in deposing Soeharto. The US Ambassador to Indonesia, Stapleton Roy, 'denounced as a fantastic conceit the suggestion that Washington could tell a leader as proud as Soeharto how to run his country's internal political affairs'.[49] The Clinton Administration never committed to regime change but senior economic officials talked as though it was necessary.

In mid-March Macfarlane visited New York and Washington to present Australia's position. On 16 March he saw Camdessus and Fischer and offered a sustained critique of their agenda, saying 'they needed to back off and cut back the conditions on Indonesia'.[50] Macfarlane told Camdessus that America had misread Indonesia.

> A lot of people in Washington seem to think that Soeharto's the same as Marcos, that he took a rich country and impoverished it. In fact, he didn't. It's true he charged too high a management fee but during Soeharto's time there was an enormous improvement in living standards in Indonesia. I think people in America don't get this.

But Camdessus said to him, 'No, they don't. They think he's the same as Saddam Hussein.'[51]

The main Australian representations came from Downer during his March 1998 visit to Washington accompanied by Australia's Jakarta ambassador, John McCarthy. Downer came on a doomed mission. He saw Camdessus and World Bank chief James Wolfensohn, but the decisive meeting was with Summers on 18 March. It would generate much dinner party gossip in Canberra and Washington. The US side included Tim Geithner, later to become secretary under President Barack Obama.

Downer said Australia supported the IMF package but wanted a 'proper sequencing of reforms'. He warned:

> There is no point trying to impose a package on Indonesia that the government will not implement. If the international community takes action which tears up Indonesia's social fabric then the IMF program would be counterproductive. The problem is that it is believed in Indonesia that implementation of the package would break the back of the country socially.[52]

Summers was unimpressed. He spoke with a slow American drawl and an intellectual precision meant to intimidate. Saying he did not dispute much of what Downer said, Summers remarked: 'If a country descends into hyperinflation and capital flight then there will also be no stability for the society.' Downer's views 'were similar to those held in Poland in 1990, in Russia in 1994 and in Mexico in 1995', Summers said. 'I feel very deeply about the need for success in Indonesia.' He said this would have consequences for 'stability across a large part of the world' and then revealed 'that Secretary Rubin has told the President that this was probably the most important issue … he would have to deal with for the rest of the term'. Characterising the Australia–United States disagreement, Summers said 'what had to be balanced was Australia's concern that a stick can be bent only so far before it breaks, with the equally valid concern that if confidence and stability were not restored then the system would break. In every successful IMF stabilisation major voices had said that the program was going too far and that society would be destroyed.'

Summers damned Soeharto—he had not run monetary policy properly, he had not reformed monopolies, he had not restored economic credibility. 'Discussion of this issue should begin with defining the right tactics to encourage Indonesia to take the right steps,' he said. Downer was stunned to find that Poland was Summers' constant reference point. He felt it was as though Indonesia revolved around Warsaw. Summers and Downer had a different perspective on Soeharto; Downer felt the US Treasury deputy would be happy to see Soeharto politically liquidated.

Downer found that Summers challenged his argument on the need for sequencing. 'Is Australia suggesting that there should be a rescheduling of reforms that the Indonesian Government has twice agreed to undertake immediately?' Summers asked. Downer said Australia wanted immediate action on monetary policy; it backed structural reforms but not 'too fast or else nothing would work'; and it wanted food subsidies maintained. Summers was sympathetic about food subsidies but returned to his theme—what would Indonesia do to restore economic confidence?

He warned there was a real risk of damage to the IMF. It would be 'disastrous for the paradigm of negotiation with Indonesia to be how much Indonesia can stand rather than what needs to be done to restore credibility.'

At this point, Downer, growing exasperated, said Australia was trying to be constructive by 'explaining what would and would not work in Indonesia'. Australia had 'particular insights' into Indonesia and Australia 'had not always agreed with all of the US actions on Indonesia'; the photo of Camdessus standing over Soeharto had been 'most unfortunate'.

Soeharto's resilience had not always been factored into decisions. America and the G-7 had to 'understand that Indonesia had to be handed sensitively'. Downer said that 'Australia would pursue its own interests, not the interests of others'—a reference to the IMF and the US Treasury.

In reply, Summers said that in 1995, over Mexico, 'every one of the arguments that Australia had been making was made *mutatis mutandis* in support of a lax policy approach'. The United States 'stood behind the IMF' and 'the Fund needed to negotiate a strong program' that 'was based on economics, not geopolitics'. Summers said: 'Ultimately, it is the Fund's imprimatur that is important, not its money. The US position is not driven by political considerations such as East Timor, a desire for greater pluralism in Indonesia or human rights.' He wanted to nail the claim the US Treasury was playing politics.

Proceeding to his repudiation of Australia's position, Summers said 'it was important that the unrealistically idealistic diplomatic perspective not be conflated with a consideration of what, financially, was most likely to succeed.' He said: 'While the Indonesian landscape is not encouraging it is useless for the international community to want stability and confidence more than a government or its people.' Downer shot back that 'the Indonesians wanted stability and confidence restored'. Summers agreed, but asked whether they were prepared to 'take the necessary steps to achieve it'. Downer highlighted two pitfalls—if there was 'a divorce between the IMF and Indonesia then the Indonesian economy would go through the floor' but equally if there was 'a dishonest marriage between them, the Indonesian economy would implode'.

They agreed on the need for food aid and trade financing. But they disagreed on the pivotal issue of restructuring Indonesia's debt. Downer said this was 'critically important' but Summers said there could be no movement on corporate debt restructuring 'until Indonesia had agreed a macroeconomic framework with the IMF'. Downer lamented this delay. Summers suggested that Australia might need to put more pressure on Indonesia but Downer replied that Australia saw no point in 'sending anyone to Indonesia to read Soeharto the riot act' since 'everyone else was doing that and it wasn't working'. Summers thanked Downer for coming and said he better understood Australia's perspective. He hoped Downer better understood the US view.

There was no bridging the gulf. Summers was unreceptive to Downer's argument that Indonesia's political chemistry had to be appreciated—the purpose of Downer's visit. Summers had a global view that he was imposing on Indonesia and he would not be halted by Australia. Costello saw Summers a month later and had a similar row with Evans telling Costello afterwards he had never witnessed a meeting like it.[53]

Did Australia's campaign have any effect? None, judging from the Summers–Downer encounter. 'We had no impact,' Grenville says. 'There is no evidence we made any difference.'[54] Macfarlane said: 'If we did, it was indirect. The Americans would have been startled to be challenged from Australia. But it's true that by the time our message was getting across it was too late [for Indonesia].'[55]

Could Australia have done more? Keating attacked the Howard government for failing to prosecute the case more vigorously. Keating, unlike Howard, would have run the issue as prime minister. 'Keating would have flown to Washington himself,' Allan Gyngell said.[56] But the damage by financial markets outpaced the rate at which politicians could take decisions. April saw the announcement of a new IMF program heading in the direction Australia wanted.

The story of Indonesia in 1998 was a study in financial markets destroying a political leader of once unrivalled authority. Soeharto resigned in May, two months after his re-election. One of his cabinet ministers, Yuwono Sudarsono, said: 'It was his presence and his stare. He looked right through you. Every five years, 1000 people met in a congress and there was not one who was brave enough to stand up and say "Enough".'[57] Hal Hill wrote: 'There were no institutional checks on his authority and, conversely, no safeguards in the event of his failure in a crisis.'[58]

Soeharto's fatal defect was his static conception of the Indonesian state and his inability to recognise that his New Order must submit to the needs of the successful modern nation. His biographer, Robert Elson, wrote:

> Soeharto in important senses had been the state … The fundamentally important questions about the identity and trajectory of the Indonesian nation were not addressed in any meaningful way; they were simply ignored out of fear of what the consequences of addressing them might bring.[59]

In the end, Soeharto was responsible for his own demise. There is no evidence the IMF tried to eliminate him. Sections of the US Government felt Indonesia would be better off without him—and that judgement proved to be correct. The January 1998 IMF program was not a cunning plot but rather 'the upshot of an international rescue attempt gone badly, embarrassingly and tragically awry'. The judgement on the IMF came from Camdessus's successor, Horst Kohler, who declared: 'I will not have another Indonesia'—meaning that future structural reforms will be built into IMF programs only with the genuine support for the country's leaders.[60]

The crisis had several pivotal consequences. First, Asia became critical of the West and decided on a current-account 'fortress' strategy. It said, in effect, 'never again'. Led by China, it took out insurance on a scale without precedent, building reserves off low exchange rates and generating vast financial imbalances in the global economy. This was a decisive factor in provoking the 2008 global financial crisis.

Grenville said: 'Each time we fix a crisis we seem to sow the seeds for the next crisis. I think the current global financial crisis, starting in 2008, is linked to the solutions drawn from the late 1990s Asian crisis.'[61] In 2006, before he retired as governor, Macfarlane issued a warning: 'We are still paying for the Asian crisis. The price is Asia's solution. And what worries me is that it runs current-account surpluses year after year and builds up massive international reserves which are the biggest single contributor to international imbalances.'[62]

Second, a weakened South-East Asia became more introspective and chose to buttress Asian solidarity. ASEAN took a strategic decision to invite the three powers of North-East Asia—China, Japan and South Korea—to meet in a new forum known as the ASEAN plus 3. The first such meeting was in Manila in 1999. In effect, it was the triumph of Mahathir's 'Asia for the Asians' idea that he used to undermine Keating's APEC vision. Asian nations bonded as victims. Macfarlane said: 'There was huge resentment in Asia about how the crisis happened, resentment against the IMF and the US as its supporter.'[63] There was not the remotest suggestion that Australia—or America—would have a place in the ASEAN plus 3.

Third, the crisis left an empowered China, a result satisfactory for Howard. China enjoyed new respect as a responsible player. When exchange rates across Asia went into free fall, China decided not to devalue and offered itself as the region's saviour. Post-crisis China took advantage of a demoralised region that was critical of America and unconvinced by Japan.

Fourth, Indonesia was a short-run loser but a long-run winner. Its economic demise shot its regional influence. In Australia, business wrote off Indonesia and its fading star was reflected in the abandonment of Indonesian studies in Australian universities. Despite the sceptics, however, the transition to democracy progressed better than many expected. Downer said: 'In our hearts we always wanted a democratic Indonesia and that's what we got. Who would have guessed that Habibie would have turned into midwife of Indonesian democracy and human rights?'[64]

Fifth, the crisis revealed the might of the United States—its economy, technology and animal spirits. Consider the record—within ten years the world had seen America's triumph in the Cold War, Japan's slump and Asia's crisis. The constant theme was the superiority of the US model. For Howard, it was absolute proof that his strategy to 'rebalance' closer to America was vindicated.

The Howard government became intoxicated by the idea of America as unchallenged global power. The irony is that the US 'unipolar moment' was so short. It lasted from the mid-1990s to 2004, the years of Howard's rule, only to be eclipsed by the disastrous economic and security policies of George W Bush at home and abroad. There is, in the American triumphalism surrounding the crisis, the 'beginning of the end' for US unmatched dominance.

Why did Australia survive the Asian crisis? The answer is because of its economic reform model. 'It was the float that got us through,' Macfarlane said. 'If we had had a fixed exchange rate then we would have had a crisis like Asia. There's no doubt about that.'[65] The Reserve Bank let the dollar depreciate rather than defend it with higher interest rates—Asia's response that throttled its economies.

This provoked an atmospheric change between Australia and the region that was obvious to any Australians visiting Asia. The effect on senior ministers was visceral. It was a time of passion for Howard, Costello and Downer. Australia had proved to be a stronger nation than its politicians, businessmen and media had ever realised. Howard said: 'There had been business people rattling on about how the Malaysian model was desirable for Australia to follow. They would be embarrassed to be reminded of that now.'[66]

Attending the 1999 APEC Finance Ministers Conference, Costello reported:

> We were no longer the fading relation. Many ministers I had met at previous meetings were unable to attend—some were in jail, some were under house arrest, many had been dismissed. Nobody ever came into my office again suggesting I follow the Asian economic model. Asia was now urged to follow the Australian model. The consensus was that there was no substitute for open markets, strong institutions, the rule of law, competition policy,

balanced budgets, independent central banks. Australia became the pin-up boy. Suddenly we became a country that had shown it was the strong man of the region.[67]

Downer said: 'Asian attitudes did change. They [Asians] became more interested in what we had to say. Australia looked a strong country with strong institutions. We finally buried the poor white trash of Asia idea.'[68]

'There was always this suspicion that we were a bit of a boom and bust economy,' Macfarlane said. 'But we started to get articles about the miracle Australian economy.'[69] The crisis had vindicated the Hawke–Keating–Howard model involving the float, fiscal responsibility, low inflation, bank regulation and sound governance.

For Howard, the region's tragedy was Australia's opportunity. Australia and Japan were the only two nations to commit to the three IMF bail-out packages. Howard set out to show that Australia was a permanent partner in bad times as well as good. For the first time, Howard and Downer felt ownership of Asian engagement.

The crisis led to the creation of the G-20, the major powers plus others involved in the crisis, its first meeting being in Berlin in 1999. This was the institutional creation from the crisis—Australia's membership was achieved only because of its crisis diplomacy. 'This was a breakthrough point for Australia,' Costello said. 'We only got this seat because of our active stand during the Asian crisis.'[70]

After the crisis a senior DFAT officer, John Dauth, chatting to Howard, remarked about the role of the economy in foreign policy. He was startled by the reaction. Speaking with conviction, Howard said: 'Australia's success in the world depends upon its strong economy.'[71]

PART VII
HOWARD UNLEASHED

35

EAST TIMOR: THE TURNING POINT

I think there is now a very good chance that East Timor will be independent by the end of this year and we intend to go along with this.
—Alexander Downer at Davos, January 1999

East Timor was John Howard's coming of age—the point at which the novice was transformed into a national security leader. This was Australia's most important military involvement since the Vietnam War. It was an unprecedented event for the country—for the first time Australia took the leadership role in a United Nations operation. The crisis empowered Howard, who not only deployed the Australian Defence Force (ADF) but assumed the posture of a war leader.

The combined impact of Howard's 1998 re-election, passage of the GST tax reform and the successful East Timor intervention raised Howard's political authority to a new plateau. Before East Timor, Howard hardly launched a foreign policy initiative; after it, he was proven in negotiation. The crisis saw Howard in sustained negotiation with the US President, the UN Secretary-General, regional leaders and, for the first time, engaged in close decision-making with the ADF.

From this point, Howard became a bolder prime minister. His actions after 9/11 cannot be comprehended without reference to East Timor.

DFAT Chief Ashton Calvert, an architect of the policy, said: 'John Howard's diplomacy over East Timor was the most impressive example of head-of-government international advocacy that I saw in my career.'[1] US Assistant Secretary of State Stan Roth said: 'I believe John Howard played a leadership role in convincing President Clinton and his team that this was a security issue and not just a humanitarian issue. I give Howard great credit for having bitten the bullet and said we will put our forces in harm's way at the head of a coalition.'[2]

The East Timor story is riddled with myths. Three of the benchmarks should be defined at the outset. First, in early 1999 Howard and Downer recognised that an independent East Timor was likely and they worked to achieve this result in an extraordinary reversal of Australian foreign policy. Second, the crisis became an example of Australia–American alliance co-operation and not the disaster often depicted. And third, the Australian-led intervention was successful because of Jakarta's acquiescence and its decision not to contest Australian forces in a theatre where pro-Indonesian forces had a massive numerical superiority.

Asked about the damage to the Indonesian relationship, Alexander Downer said: 'They loved us a lot less but respected us a lot more.'[3] The intervention was universally seen as one of the most successful in the UN's fifty-year history, and Australia's prestige around the world, with the exception of Indonesia, was enhanced in a way most Australians did not comprehend. 'A lot of people were surprised and didn't believe we would ever do this sort of thing,' Downer said.[4] In private, senior ASEAN ministers were impressed by Australia's actions but disliked Howard's hubris.

Describing his feelings on the eve, Howard said:

> My wife and I went up on the Sunday before to the Lavarack barracks and talked to a lot of the troops. They were sitting about in small groups. I'd never been through anything like this before. You thought 'Heavens above, you just don't know.' You could have had fifteen or twenty wiped out in an attack by a patrol. That would have altered the whole complexion of the thing. I certainly accepted there was a real possibility of casualties of that order. I just expected there would be and feared there would be.[5]

The East Timor story was dominated by risk, unpredictability, confusion and changing objectives. There was uncertainty within the Australian Government about the real goals. This policy was conducted by Howard and Downer in a hall of mirrors. Its essence was their decision to work towards an independent East Timor, a point still not appreciated and a strategic objective that could never be openly conceded because of the hostility it would generate with Indonesia.

The bigger question was whether the creation of a small, new, unstable East Timor nation 'owned' by Australia was in the long-term national interest, an assessment bound to alter over time. The truth, however, is that keeping East Timor part of Indonesia would have guaranteed its own tale of unresolved woes, with even greater risks for

Australia–Indonesia relations. The evidence suggests that Howard and Downer made the best call.

They struggled to reconcile two competing objectives: to secure the path to an independent East Timor and to preserve relations with Indonesia. That meant, ultimately, avoiding war with Jakarta. This was the most lethal risk—it would have been a catastrophe for Australia and its regional standing and it would have destroyed Australia–Indonesia relations for decades. In the end, war was avoided but relations went into 'freeze' for several years as a result of Howard's policy.

Howard and Clinton, after an initial jolt, worked effectively together. The US role was vital—its political pressure on Jakarta made the intervention possible and US military backing of Australia helped to deliver Indonesian compliance. The extent of such US support is scarcely recognised. There is no doubt, however, that the United States taught Australia a sharp lesson: that it was Australia's job to look after its own neighbourhood in any crisis. The operation became a threshold for Australia's assumption of greater regional responsibility. It changed the way Australia saw itself. As the metropolitan power, Australia moved towards a greater security and military responsibility in an immediate region plagued by weak and unstable states.

The irony is that the intervention was authorised under the UN umbrella. Howard, the UN sceptic, insisted that UN authorisation was the only basis on which he would intervene. Yet the operation exposed Howard's character as a populist whose embrace of the Anzac legend now had a real-time example. Howard orchestrated that Australian ritual—the departure of the troops, their progress in foreign lands and their triumphant arrival home. His presentation of the intervention by downgrading its UN status and highlighting Australia's 'way of war' ethos distorted its essence and left the impression that it was an intervention against Indonesia, an irresponsible message.

For Howard, East Timor became a political weapon to be used against Labor—he depicted the intervention as a repudiation of Keating's appeasement of Indonesia and a restoration of Australia's honour, a false and disreputable ploy. It fanned Howard's arrogance in a way that damaged ties with Indonesia more than was necessary and saw his bending of foreign policy for electoral gain at the cost of the national interest.

Despite this critique, Howard showed a judgement superior to his critics in the Labor Party and the Australian media, many of whose prescriptions would have been disastrous. At each stage of the East Timor story the political and military risks were high. Howard demonstrated an ability to balance competing goals, to improvise and to avoid absolutist solutions. Howard conceded that the East Timor episode was 'important' for his foreign policy and his maturation as PM. 'It was certainly the biggest single foreign policy issue,' he said. 'It was the first time I'd had a major interaction in a personal way with the military. I had a lot of contact with Kofi Annan and with Clinton.'[6]

In an almost miraculous coincidence, the Australian commander, Major-General Peter Cosgrove, could not have been bettered in a global search by John Howard Central Casting. To say that Cosgrove was Howard's perfect choice understates the situation. Cosgrove was an able military leader, a down-to-earth Australian with a common touch, media flair and a political nose. His military leadership vindicated Howard's political decision.

The origins of East Timor's transition lay in the Indonesian revolution that forced Soeharto's resignation in May 1998 in favour of BJ Habibie. The Australian orthodoxy was that Habibie would be a weak and erratic stopgap. Even a brief meeting with Habibie would reinforce such pessimism—a bizarre figure, small, talkative and a technologist with a touch of the mad scientist, he had become president by accident. Though denied popular legitimacy, Habibie was an internationalist who grasped that the situation called for decisive action—he pledged free elections for Indonesia.

It was Habibie's decision to review East Timor's status that forced Australia's policy reassessment. The sequence is critical—it was Howard who followed Habibie. The mantra that Australia liberated East Timor is false, though Australia's intervention was decisive. In 2006 Downer said: 'I told some Indonesians that one day you guys will build a statue to Habibie because he is the father of Indonesian democracy. He was a bright guy, very Westernised and easy to deal with.'[7]

Aware that a democratic Indonesia could not keep East Timor enchained, Habibie said he would grant the province a special status, later confirmed as autonomy, as a trade-off for international acceptance of Jakarta's sovereignty.[8] This posed a strategic test for Australia. The deepest faith among Australia's strategists was that East Timor must not compromise ties with Jakarta, its political leaders and TNI (the army). For analysts such as Defence Deputy Secretary Hugh White, the main issue was a successful regime transition, not East Timor.[9]

In his 1996 and 1997 dealings with Soeharto, Howard followed in Keating's footsteps. 'We went along with the integrity of the Indonesia line and I've never pretended otherwise,' Howard said.[10] The realism that drove Australia's stance from 1975 onwards—that pressure on Soeharto would not win any concessions on East Timor—proved true to the bitter end. Yet the Australian public, fed by a relentless media campaign, was distrustful of this East Timor policy for three decades.

Such distrust was founded on two factors. Over thirty years Indonesia's military was unable to pacify the province, with an estimated 200 000 East Timorese deaths during this time. The 1991 Santa Cruz massacre had become a powerful testimony to Jakarta's failure. In addition, there had been a campaign against Jakarta by much of the Australian media, with the deaths of five journalists at Balibo in 1975 being framed as a template of Indonesian aggression and duplicity. Suspicion of Indonesia was entrenched in Australian public attitudes. By 1998 East Timor remained mired in poverty, domestic divisions and a resistance movement fighting Jakarta.

It was Downer and Calvert who initiated Australia's policy change. Downer saw that once Habibie had opened the door on East Timor it would not be closed. This gave Australia a chance—but only a chance—to resolve the East Timor issue. Downer's aim was to improve relations with Indonesia by removing what Indonesia's foreign minister, Ali Alatas, had called the 'pebble in the shoe'. Domestic politics was also driving Howard and Downer. Labor's shadow foreign minister, Laurie Brereton, had pioneered a reversal of ALP policy and was campaigning for an act of self-determination. In short, domestic politics in Indonesia and Australia meant that the status quo was unsustainable.

During his July 1998 visit to Jakarta, Downer launched his push. He told Alatas that Jakarta must change its approach—it should negotiate directly with East Timor's leaders in preference to UN-orchestrated dialogue. He urged that independence leader Xanana Gusmao be freed from gaol. He offered Australia's support to help procure a consensus within East Timor, yet Alatas was reluctant. During their dinner in Jakarta, Downer therefore suggested that DFAT sample worldwide the opinion of the East Timor leadership diaspora. 'We stayed at dinner until midnight talking,' Downer said. He won a grudging approval from Alatas to proceed.[11] It would prove decisive.

This survey result, provided to Downer in August based on interviews with twenty-nine East Timorese leaders, found that the majority favoured autonomy only as a bridge to a referendum on independence within three to five years. There was only token support for Habibie's position—autonomy as a basis for international recognition. The survey proved that Indonesia's new flexibility had radicalised sentiment within East

Timor and that Indonesia's leadership needed to move further to win a settlement. Australia's veteran ambassador to Indonesia, John McCarthy, in several meetings with Gusmao, was told that only a referendum on self-determination could bring any lasting solution. Downer wrote to Alatas with the survey's results but Alatas declined to act.[12] This turned Australia's attention to Habibie.

Downer was profoundly influenced by this survey. It convinced him that autonomy alone was not an answer and that Habibie's new position was doomed. There had to be a ballot at some stage, despite Jakarta's denial. Once Downer reached this conclusion the edifice of Australia's previous East Timor policy began to collapse. 'The only path for Indonesia was to accept wide-ranging autonomy followed by a referendum,' Downer said.[13]

But the survey had a deeper meaning. Downer recalls: 'I said to my department after the survey results that "Much as you may not like this, one day that place will be independent." That's what the survey really meant.'[14] For Australia, this was a revolutionary idea. The notion could only be expressed in whispers but it became implanted in Downer's mind.

On 3 October the Howard government was re-elected and Downer was taken to the edge of defeat in his seat of Mayo. 'I want to be a lot more active on East Timor,' Downer told Calvert after the re-election. He was talking to the right man—Calvert had been waiting for this opportunity. In response he recommended the idea of intensifying Australia's pressure on Indonesia through a letter from Howard to Habibie.[15] Calvert had never served in Indonesia and had long distrusted the East Timor policy. He disagreed with the pro-Indonesia stand of former department head Dick Woolcott, who had influenced so many politicians. Calvert felt that Australia should have made a better effort to steer a middle course in 1975. The more Calvert reflected on the events of 1975, the more he concluded that Woolcott, then ambassador to Indonesia, had compromised Australia by becoming too close to Indonesia's leaders. Calvert believed that Australia had finished with an untenable stance—'In public we had to criticise Indonesia's conduct yet in private we were largely supportive of Indonesia's policy.'[16]

By 1998 Calvert saw twenty-three years of Indonesian failure. Keen to oblige Downer, he said Australia had to 'lance the boil' that infected relations with Indonesia. This was urgent since events had their own momentum; Australia must not be left behind.[17] Under Calvert's guidance, DFAT prepared a cabinet submission for Downer and a draft letter to Habibie. Downer's former adviser, Innes Willox, said: 'The initial idea was shaped in Downer's office—it was a necessary policy shift and a sharp break from the former Labor government.'[18]

On 30 November Calvert sent Downer a memorandum marked 'secret' with a draft letter from Howard to Habibie attached. This letter would be reworked and despatched from Howard's office nineteen days later.

Calvert's note signals the new thinking in East Timor policy. He wrote:

> You will note that it [the draft letter] picks up on your thought that, in effect, there are only two realistic scenarios for the future of East Timor—either full independence (and probably sooner rather than later); or some form of free association with Indonesia, achieved as the end point of a process, the model for which might be the Matignon Accords which the French achieved in New Caledonia.

The letter, Calvert wrote, 'commends a Matignon-type process to the Indonesians'. This meant 'an act of self-determination held at some reasonably distant point in the future'. Calvert said this would be an 'important' change in Australian policy that was now 'more conceivable than at any time since the Indonesian invasion in 1975'. With his eye on electoral politics, Calvert said an 'important advantage' for Howard and Downer, if they proceeded, would be the 'much stronger' alignment of their position with the Australian public.[19]

This note reveals the true Downer/Calvert position—that unless Indonesia could legitimise its incorporation, the radicalisation of East Timorese opinion would lead, one way or another, to independence. The note made clear that Downer saw independence as a real possibility. But independence, at this point, was not their policy—they preferred to see the Indonesian incorporation succeed and become legitimised. This was Australia's firm position. The letter offered Habibie a mechanism to settle East Timor's status as part of Indonesia. 'It was designed as a warning to Indonesia and to encourage it to make a far better effort in East Timor,' Calvert said.[20]

The reality, however, is that by proposing a ballot, even a far-off ballot, Australia was opening the door to independence. This duality was embedded in the Downer/Calvert position. They knew that independence was just as likely an outcome as autonomy in any self-determination process. Dressed up to help Habibie, the beauty and the trap in their position was its ambivalence—and Habibie saw through it.

Downer and Calvert were being definitive not about the solution but about the method. The change in Australia's position was about process—but this flexibility within the letter caused utter confusion within the Australian Government. The Defence department, for example, was never told what the letter really meant. Indeed, among senior officials there was a variety of interpretations about its meaning.

Howard liked the idea. Michael Thawley said:

> Howard had been thinking of a change of policy, though not the letter ... He had kept coming back to this point in NSC discussions. There had been talk between Howard and Downer about what we would have to do. Howard had been very uneasy about our East Timor policy.[21]

Indeed, to this day there is rivalry between the Howard and Downer camps for ownership of the initiative.

Howard, as usual, proceeded with caution. He spoke with his advisers, Thawley and Peter Varghese, and rang Flood, then UK High Commissioner, who encouraged him. Howard's advisers wrote the final version. Thawley says of the letter:

> It recognised our existing policy wasn't sustainable. The real issue was for the Indonesians to actually deal with the East Timorese which they were reluctant to do. At that point our view was probably a more sensible outcome in the longer run was autonomy for East Timor [within Indonesia] and potentially independence later. In the back of our minds was a process that would postpone the decision on independence—you would have a vote at the end of five or ten years or, if the Indonesians had been brilliantly generous, you might have some other deal reached.[22]

For Howard, the domestic politics were important. Downer's adviser, Greg Hunt, says:

> Public opinion probably ran at 90 per cent that Australia had done the wrong thing by East Timor. There was a moral unease, a sense that something should be done. I know Alexander felt this. Howard and Downer did not want to be compromised by the policies of the past on East Timor.[23]

From the start, this was a Howard–Downer operation. John Moore was Defence minister, but the Defence department was sidelined; it assumed the aim was to consolidate the status quo. Downer, via his relationship with Howard, now began to dominate Defence in shaping Australian strategic policy—and this would apply from East Timor to Iraq.

In early December cabinet's National Security Committee (NSC) approved the policy change and the letter. It was both an evolutionary and a radical shift.[24] There was no objection. At the end, Howard turned to Downer and said, 'This is a big step.'[25]

Deputy Prime Minister Tim Fischer was excited. 'This was the most important letter written in the Howard years,' he said. 'There were two letters written last century that led to nations being created: the Balfour letter and the Howard letter.' The Balfour letter, written in 1917 by Britain's foreign secretary Arthur Balfour, pledged a homeland for the Jewish people in Palestine. 'I would argue that the Howard letter was as important as the Balfour letter,' Fischer said. 'Howard took this to the NSC, he did not take it to the full cabinet and I believe that was the right call.'[26]

The final version, signed by Howard on 19 December, was sharper than the Calvert draft. Howard began by offering Habibie reassurance. 'I want to emphasise that Australia's support for Indonesia's sovereignty is unchanged,' he wrote. 'It has been a longstanding Australian position that the interests of Australia, Indonesia and East Timor are best served by East Timor remaining part of Indonesia.' He then moved onto the mechanism. Howard applauded Habibie's autonomy offer but argued, in effect, that it was obsolete and wouldn't work. 'Attitudes in East Timor are hardening,' he warned. 'On the substance of the negotiations, the advice I am receiving is that a decisive element of East Timorese opinion is insisting on an act of self-determination. If anything, their position—with a fair degree of international support—seems to be strengthening on this.' Supporting self-determination but acting as sympathetic friend, Howard suggested a 'review mechanism' be built into the autonomy package along the lines of the Matignon Accords in New Caledonia that would defer 'a referendum on the final status'. This would give Jakarta 'time to convince the East Timorese' of the benefits of staying with Indonesia. Ending on an optimistic note, he told Habibie, 'we believe that a solution is within your grasp'.[27]

Howard reflects:

> When we talked about writing to Habibie the feeling was that the time had come to encourage some change in policy. In addition, there was always that latent sympathy in the Australian community

towards East Timor, a rare combination of the right and the left, the old Diggers and role of the Catholic Church, which was strong.[28]

But Australia had misjudged the letter and misread Habibie. The execution of its policy shift was inept. Downer should have travelled to Jakarta and broken the news personally.

Habibie received the letter initially through ambassador John McCarthy during a ninety-minute meeting in the President's office on 22 December. McCarthy found Habibie agitated and contradictory. He dismissed immediately Howard's proposal of autonomy followed by a distant referendum. Habibie was angry about the reference to the Matignon Accords, a mechanism to resolve a French colonial issue that offended Indonesia's pride as an anti-colonial nation. But Habibie took a dramatic position, summarised in McCarthy's cable the next day: 'If autonomy in the form the Indonesian Government provided was not acceptable to the East Timorese, he was inclined simply to grant independence.'[29]

Habibie said that if East Timor was going to end up independent, it should happen quickly; there was no point in Jakarta retaining responsibility for the province only to find that years later it became independent. Habibie told McCarthy that 'Indonesia will not die without East Timor.' He dismissed Howard's proposal for a deferred referendum as a 'time bomb' for his successor.[30]

He spoke at length about Indonesia's wider problems, arguing that he could not give East Timor too much attention and he refused to become victim to the 'tyranny of a minority'. Indonesia's economy was still in crisis and there was resistance to assistance for East Timor. At one point, when McCarthy raised the option of the UN force if there was internal conflict in East Timor, Habibie at once replied: 'I can't do that.' McCarthy left feeling that, while Habibie had rejected the referendum, there was a lot of flexibility in his position.[31] At the end Habibie said he welcomed Howard's approach. The message was that Habibie was receptive to a policy change but his instinct, if put under pressure, was to cut East Timor loose.

When McCarthy met Alatas a fortnight later he was told that the military, headed by General Wiranto, would never accept independence and that Habibie could only act with the approval of his ministers. This proved to be extremely bad advice. Alatas was being isolated as Habibie hijacked Jakarta's decision-making. He was influenced by his ministerial confidant, Adi Sasono, a former head of the Indonesian Association of Islamic Intellectuals, who was prepared to see East Timor's separation, and his own foreign policy adviser, the astute Dewi Fortuna Anwar, who felt Jakarta had to be liberated from East Timor.

On 21 January, when Habibie read the original of Howard's letter (as distinct from the cable), he wrote a notation on the letter, saying: 'If, after 22 years the East Timorese people cannot feel united with the Indonesian people' then it would be best to seek an honourable separation.[32]

Habibie, a transition president with supposedly little authority, had made up his mind. In late January the Indonesian cabinet took its remarkable decision: East Timor, in effect, would be offered a consultation (later established as a referendum) on autonomy or independence. Such a decision would have been inconceivable just a couple of months earlier. This was Habibie's personal decision; it was impetuous, audacious, dangerous and utterly stunning, made more remarkable because he had carried his ministers and the armed forces, TNI.

Habibie had called the bluff of the old pro-Soeharto establishment and the army. Two factors underwrote this decision: the financial crisis had shaken the certitudes of Indonesian politics by exposing the nation's vulnerability and the reality that holding the province against its will had become untenable in a polity of democratic elections. There was a sense of spite directed at the East Timorese—if they refused to be reconciled then they would be discarded like a rotten branch.

Alatas and Defence Minister General Wiranto submitted to the momentum for change. But the motives behind this cabinet decision were contradictory. Some ministers such as Alatas were deluded that Indonesia would prevail in the ballot. In the cabinet Wiranto demanded just two conditions: that there be no admission that the 1975 decision was wrong and no recriminations against the military over events in the province.[33] Habibie was reconciled to separation, though not preferring this. Finance Minister Ginandjar Kartasasmita told Downer that Indonesia could no longer afford the costs of sustaining East Timor. Habibie announced the new policy in Jakarta on 27 January 1999.[34]

The criticism that Habibie had moved too quickly and failed to win genuine support from TNI and other power centres is valid. As a consequence Indonesia remained profoundly divided over the referendum. It was incapable as a nation of preparing adequately for East Timor's ballot.

It is, however, too easy to condemn Habibie's haste. This was window-of-opportunity politics—Habibie seized the moment and the moment might not have lasted for long. Postponing the ballot for several years would only have created another set of problems. There was never going to be a smooth separation between Jakarta and Dili. The defect in

Howard's letter was that it misjudged Indonesia's vulnerability: a ballot down the road from autonomy, as he proposed, was not tenable.

Howard said he felt his letter had been 'a very big influence' on Habibie.[35] Calvert said it was 'an essential catalyst'. While Habibie's instincts predated Howard's letter, it is doubtful whether Habibie would have moved when he did, the way he did, without this provocation.

The cabinet decision stunned opinion in Jakarta, Australia and the world. There was initial suspicion that it was a trick, especially as the mechanism to test East Timorese opinion had yet to be formalised. While Howard and Downer were surprised by Habibie's leap they were not dismayed. Indeed, they were in advance of many of their officials.

Careful in public, Downer was delighted in private. Attending the World Economic Forum meeting in Davos in January 1999, just after Habibie's announcement, Downer was excited by the unexpected path taken by Habibie. Ruminating at length over coffee, Downer said: 'I think there is now a very good chance that East Timor will be independent by the end of this year and we intend to go along with this.'[36] Happy with the prospect, he attributed the main influence to Howard's letter. Of Habibie's response, Howard said: 'We were surprised he went that far but not displeased.'[37]

Interviewed after the East Timor crisis, Downer said: 'We certainly didn't think it [Habibie's] was a bad idea. It was not our preferred path. But, in the end, it did provide a solution to the problem.' Downer ridiculed the notion, advanced by many people, that Australia should have withheld its support from Habibie's new position.

> That would have had a number of consequences. It would have sent Habibie ballistic. That would have created a meltdown in our relations with Indonesia. You'd have the Indonesians saying they were prepared to have an act of self-determination and Australia saying 'Oh, not so fast'. We would have been in conflict with Indonesia and in conflict with the East Timorese who knew exactly what their public opinion wanted. Finally, it would have created a most gigantic hiccup in Australia which meant I probably couldn't have remained Foreign Minister. The Australian public would not have accepted such a position.[38]

Howard did not foresee Habibie's reaction. Australia would never have proposed an immediate ballot. It is false, however, to think that Australia was forced to accept an Indonesian policy that it did not want.

For Howard, it was a 'no-brainer'. Howard and Downer became willing parties to this new direction and soon became proud of their role in provoking it. At this point they decided to torch the Keating monuments and make history.

Australia's position became support for a UN-supervised ballot later in 1999—while telling Indonesia that autonomy would be the best result from the ballot. This was the essential condition to maintain effective relations with Indonesia. As 1999 advanced, Howard and Downer were sure that independence would be the outcome. By their position, they became, in effect, willing backers of an independent East Timor.[39]

This undermines the critique of the East Timor episode made by White after his retirement from the Defence department—namely, that an independent East Timor arose from a blunder, not an intention. White said:

> The outcome [independence] that was hailed as a triumph in December [1999] differed in every respect from the government's objectives at the start of the year … Was Howard's letter a good idea, then? Prime facie it seems to have provoked a response that Australia did not expect and did not welcome. That provides strong grounds for criticising the decision to send it.[40]

It is true the goals of Australian policy changed. But they did not change as much as many people believed, given the duality in the original Downer/Calvert position. Howard believed the major change in Australia's policy came in his December 1998 letter—and that backing Habibie's new position of January 1999 was a momentous yet a relatively easy decision.

'The referendum was only going to go one way, though not all the Indonesians could see that,' Downer said.[41] This was Howard's view. Interviewed for this book, he said:

> I felt that once Habibie had agreed to it [a referendum] that the result would probably go the way of independence. I accepted that would happen. Rather than it being a contestable goal it seemed to me inevitable. But one had to be careful about handling that publicly because we had to work with the Indonesians and, in the end, you had to get the Indonesians to agree. They had to agree.[42]

It is the pivotal insight so many Australians refused to accept. East Timor's independence would occur only with Jakarta's consent. This point, so elementary, would be furiously resisted in the forthcoming Australian domestic debate.

So there was a gulf between Australia's public and private positions and a blurring between them. This generated internal confusion among the main players. 'I don't think anybody was campaigning for independence,' Thawley said.[43] White said: 'I never had the sense in any NSC meeting that Howard or Downer wanted an independent East Timor.'[44]

During February 1999, Downer visited Bali, Jakarta and Lisbon. He met an Indonesian government in dysfunction, torn between relief and resentment over East Timor. Downer met Gusmao for the first time while he was in detention. He told Jakarta to allow East Timor to make its decision in a peaceful environment. Speaking to Habibie, Downer said of a ballot: 'Our hope was that they would choose autonomy but our sense was that they were more likely to choose independence.'[45]

Downer advocated a UN role, including a police presence for the ballot, with a transitional UN administration after the ballot. Australia did not favour a UN peacekeeping force before the vote. This reflected both false optimism and hard realism. The optimism was the hope that Indonesia would keep the peace; the realism was knowing that Indonesia would not tolerate peacekeepers before the vote. Downer said, 'Because we felt East Timor would choose independence, we were worried the Indonesians would just walk out and leave the place in flames.'[46]

On 11 March 1999 the NSC took a far-reaching decision based on advice from the Defence department and the ADF—to bring an additional brigade to thirty days' readiness from mid-year. This meant Australia would have two ready brigades. The drivers behind this decision were White and Chief of the Defence Force (CDF) Chris Barrie. White said: 'Our thinking was that a peacekeeping operation might be needed and, in this situation, that Australia would be expected to lead.'[47] Barrie said: 'This was a critical decision. If we hadn't had that extra brigade, could we have done the job in East Timor? Frankly, I doubt it.'[48]

The decision was designed to cover several possible contingencies— withdrawal of Australians, stabilisation of East Timor if Indonesian forces withdrew, or participation in an international peacekeeping operation.

There was, however, abject internal confusion about Australian Government objectives. White, the leading strategist in Defence, defined in a series of official level meetings what he believed were Australia's objectives. They were having East Timor remain part of Indonesia; ensuring that ties with Jakarta were put before the fate of East Timor; retaining Australia's military ties with Indonesia; and avoiding any ADF deployment, if possible.[49] These were White's benchmarks—each of them was trashed before the end of the year, proof of the violation of policy orthodoxy that Howard and Downer would entertain.

In early 1999 Jakarta was beset with a chaotic president, a divided government and a bitter TNI. Two future presidents, Megawati Sukarnoputri and Abdurrahman Wahid, said that East Timor should remain within Indonesia. In a wild outburst, Habibie called Indonesia's occupation an act of 'charity' and asked: 'What did they give us? Natural resources? No. Human resources? No. Technology? No. Abundant gold? No. Rocks? Yes.'[50] Jakarta was ready to punish East Timor and Howard would underestimate the depth of its rancour.

At this point militia violence backed by elements of TNI erupted against independence supporters, provoking alarm internationally and uproar in Australia. The Howard government misjudged its potential and was slow to comprehend Indonesia's duplicity. General Wiranto promised Australia, publicly and privately, that the army would not play any intimidatory role. He spoke with a forked tongue. Habibie controlled neither Wiranto nor TNI. Jakarta offered rhetorical support for a free ballot while running a covert campaign to defeat an independence vote.[51]

The TNI had an investment in East Timor of blood and treasure. For years TNI had relied on locally raised paramilitary forces to enforce security, mainly East Timorese who backed integration with Indonesia. From early 1999 these militias were mobilised with a new agenda: to defeat the ballot by murder and violence. The terrorism was supported from the local TNI command via weapons, transport and direction.

In this situation, it was inevitable that the charge of appeasement of Jakarta would be laid against the Howard government. The accusation was made by Labor and much of the media—the issue was the need for an international peacekeeping force in East Timor before the ballot. The first incident in what became a long and spurious saga were media reports of a split between the Howard and Clinton governments over peacekeepers.

This arose from a February 1999 State Department 'brainstorming' session in Washington when there were sharp differences between Calvert and the senior state official Stan Roth. Calvert argued that the first priority was to pressure Indonesia into keeping the peace—while at the same time recognising that an international intervention may be needed in a worst-case scenario. Roth, by contrast, argued that 'a full-scale peacekeeping operation would be an unavoidable aspect of the transition'.[52]

When the record of this meeting was leaked, the idea took hold of a split between a reluctant Australia and a keen America over confronting Jakarta in the name of peacekeepers. In fact, there was no such split. Interviewed for this book, Roth said:

> This was not a US Government position and I was not making a request on behalf of the US Government. The issue had not been raised in any US Government policy making circles. This was two officials trying to think ahead. Media accounts of this meeting are rubbish. In hindsight you have to say Ashton was right about the political difficulties of getting peacekeepers.[53]

At the meeting Roth expressed a personal view. It was neither Albright's position nor the Clinton administration's position. There was no support within the Pentagon, the US military or the White House for a peacekeeping force in East Timor before the ballot. This was never going to become US policy and it had no advocates—yet the idea of Australia rebuffing America on the issue became an Australian media orthodoxy.

It was assisted by Downer's incompetence. In an outrageous remark, Alatas told Downer on 23 February that Indonesia's arming of the militias was a 'legitimate' exercise. Instead of taking a public stand, Downer offered a pathetic excuse that the violence was caused by 'rogue elements' within Indonesia's military, thereby accepting Jakarta's own line. After Downer's comments White rang John Dauth in DFAT. 'Mate, this is wrong. We know it's wrong,' White said, a reference to intelligence. White said the violence was connected to elements in TNI's command structure.[54]

At subsequent officials meetings White asked: 'Can we trust the Indonesian army to maintain security for the ballot? No. TNI is a main supporter of the militias. And we know what they are doing.'[55] White said peacekeepers before the ballot were essential. But DFAT, obsessed with the need to keep Habibie 'locked' into the process, dismissed this position. Calvert argued that Jakarta would never tolerate it—and his judgement proved to be correct.

On 6 April in the seaside town of Liquica several dozen East Timorese were slaughtered in an open display of links between TNI, police and the militias that did the killing.[56] Senior TNI commanders only 100 metres away were conspicuous in taking no action. A report by the Australian Defence Intelligence Organisation said the Indonesian army was 'culpable whether it actively took part in the violence or simply let it occur'.[57] The ghastly politics were obvious—the ballot could only occur with Jakarta's support yet Jakarta's instinct was to intimidate a vote against independence. Australia's protests had no impact.

Ten days later there was another massacre, in Dili itself, after a militia parade in front of the governor's office. Militia leaders Joao Tavares and Eurico Guterres presided and Guterres called for 'a cleansing of all those who have betrayed integration and to capture and kill them'.[58] A convoy of twenty to thirty trucks and an estimated 1000 militia then circled Dili and launched attacks on the homes of independence leaders, notably, Manuel Carrascalao whose son they killed. The death toll was at least twelve, with some estimates double this. The militias were encouraged by Indonesia's administration in Dili.[59]

The blind eye that Wiranto turned to the violence signalled that his motive was to defeat the independence campaign. Wiranto told a 3 May Jakarta cabinet meeting that the integrationist cause would prevail at the ballot. In their account of these events, Australian journalists Don Greenlees and Robert Garran argue that Wiranto and the minister for Political and Security Affairs, Feisal Tandjung, authorised an elaborate covert operation to defeat the independence movement.[60] Habibie lacked the authority to challenge TNI and any such action would have been most unwise because it was imperative for the democratic cause within Indonesia that the army acquiesce in the transition to free elections. Any Habibie showdown with the military would have been disastrous.

The Liquica and Dili massacres were a turning point. Howard had read Australian intelligence assessments that implicated TNI with the militia resistance. Facing irresistible political pressure to act, Howard rang Habibie on 19 April, warned that TNI had to be brought into line and asked Habibie for a meeting at Bali. Downer told Howard, 'You have got to get him to agree to more than 50 UN police, this is hopeless because there is too much violence.'[61] The Bali meeting was a gamble on Howard's part. He was driven not just by the killings but by outrage within Australia and Labor's campaign that he was appeasing Jakarta. Yet Howard had no game plan whatsoever. He was improvising as he went.

The following day a delegation of Australian newspaper editors visiting Jakarta had an hour with Habibie. 'We will separate in peace, in honour, as friends,' a talkative Habibie said of East Timor. Quizzed about the militias, he replied: 'It's almost impossible for him [Wiranto] to disarm them.' It was an admission of Habibie's impotence.

At one point Habibie went off the record to reject any peacekeeping force before the ballot. He said he had told Howard on the phone that if a peacekeeping force was imposed on Indonesia then it would abandon

East Timor and the ballot and unilaterally withdraw. Habibie was adamant on this point. Indonesia's sovereignty meant it would never submit to foreign troops on its soil. His threat would have doomed East Timor to civil war between integrationists and separationists.[62] This warning could not be dismissed lightly. It was not the first time the threat had been issued. Downer said: 'One of Habibie's constant secret messages to us, as he put it, was that if there is too much violence we will abandon this ballot and just give it away.'[63] For Australia, it was a nightmare scenario—a civil war on the doorstep.

Indonesia's opposition to peacekeepers before the ballot was based on principle and politics. The principle was a refusal to have its sovereignty compromised while East Timor was part of Indonesia; the politics sprang from Indonesian nationalism, the stance of TNI and aversion to such an unpopular move on the eve of Indonesia's own elections.

By going to Bali, Howard accepted that Australia was the principal regional power with responsibility to secure an acceptable outcome. This assumption, implicit in his December 1998 letter, was now made explicit. It became the basis on which Howard acted from this point. While he was en route to Bali and before the meeting, the differences within Australia's delegation were stark. White argued that Australia must demand a peacekeeping force before the vote. Calvert disagreed, insisting that neither Habibie nor the Indonesian political system would tolerate peacekeepers.[64]

On 27 April, Howard began the Bali talks with a private meeting with Habibie that lasted nearly ninety minutes. This was the critical encounter. Howard had to extract concessions from Habibie yet keep his confidence, a difficult act. Howard raised the prospect of a peacekeeping force and three times Habibie rejected it. 'No, no, no,' he told Howard. Habibie said that as a politician his position would become 'untenable' if he accepted such a force.[65] 'He told Howard that he would not survive as president if he made such an agreement,' Downer later recalled.[66] Dewi Fortuna Anwar said Howard pressed Habibie 'a number of times' about the peacekeepers with Habibie rejecting him. Habibie repeated his threat to quit East Timor in line with his statement to the Australian editors.[67]

'I tried very hard,' Howard said of this meeting.

> I raised the question of getting peacekeepers in before the referendum took place. But Habibie was absolutely emphatic that it wasn't acceptable. I pressed him, but I also accepted that it was

an impossible ask. I didn't expect him to agree. He basically said to me 'I'd be dead politically if I agreed to this' and he was right.[68]

They began to discuss, instead, how to strengthen the police numbers and this became Howard's main hope. But Habibie agreed to Howard's request for an Australian consulate to be established in Dili.

After the private meeting the Australians retreated to Howard's hotel suite. 'It's not going too well,' he told them. The task now, Howard said, was to press in the plenary session for the best deal possible on more police. Howard felt they could get such a deal. 'What about troops?' White asked. But that cause was lost.[69]

The plenary meeting was large, with fourteen representatives from each nation. The Indonesian performance was filled with brazenness, intransigence and mendacity. The official Australian record of conversation shows that Habibie began with a summary of agreement now finalised between Indonesia, Portugal and the UN. It required a secure environment for the ballot on 8 August. The critical point was that Indonesia would be responsible for security surrounding the ballot. The police would have charge of law and order and TNI would be neutral.

Habibie said the troublemakers were 'not numbered in the hundreds but in tens'. He accepted that a number of international police would come as advisers, with numbers to be determined by the UN. The main source nations would include Australia.

In response, Howard said Habibie's change of policy was 'courageous' and that Indonesia had not won the international appreciation it deserved. Australia believed the best outcome for all parties was that East Timor should remain part of Indonesia but that Australia would accept the result of the ballot. Howard told Habibie the recent 'violence and loss of life' had been caused by people who had 'been out of control'. He welcomed the commitment of Habibie and Wiranto to restore order. He urged them to disarm people. Howard said:

The world needed to be satisfied that it [the ballot] was done in a free and democratic manner. There needed to be adequate police involvement under the supervision of the UN to achieve both the reality and the appearance of integrity in the process … a way needed to be found to handle that.

Habibie pledged to 'do everything to make sure the process in East Timor was successful'. But he would 'not be guided by the opinions of the press'. Whatever the decision, he said, 'East Timor would always have problems. If integration was chosen, those who wanted independence would cause problems. If it separated, those who preferred integration would cause problems.' If East Timor before the consultation became uncontrollable, he would make a unilateral decision to give East Timor back to the UN. He had to concentrate on Indonesia. Habibie told Howard he would not be 'insulted and embarrassed because of 700 000 people in East Timor'. He added that he 'doubted whether they would have a very bright future as an independent country given the small size and population of East Timor'. His contempt was palpable.

However, Howard now returned to the pivotal question. He warned Habibie that if the ballot lacked integrity then 'Indonesia's international standing would be damaged'. He pleaded from an Australian perspective to increase the numbers of international police advisers. The record says:

> He [Howard] did not think it was realistic to expect 40–50 police advisers, as had reportedly been suggested, could do the job. Australian personnel would also be participating. He needed some assurance about their safety. He would be asked by the media and others if he was satisfied with security arrangements. He wanted to be able to say that an adequate number of police would be involved to ensure safety. He meant no disrespect to Indonesia sovereignty but he needed room to move on this issue.[70]

White said: 'I was shocked when Howard said this. His argument was for Habibie to save him from political embarrassment at home. He wanted Indonesia to solve his own political problem.'[71]

The Indonesians remained intransigent. Despite the formality of the plenary, Wiranto, sitting next to Habibie, cut his hand across and above the table, saying to Habibie yet not looking at him, 'No, no.' He was giving Habibie his orders even in front of the Australians.[72] 'Habibie got very aggressive about it,' Downer said. 'But remember, he was speaking in front of Alatas and Wiranto. Our position was that 50 civilian police was completely inadequate.'[73]

Habibie told Howard the agreement on security had been finalised with the UN and Indonesia did not wish to change it. Wiranto intervened to say he intended to increase Indonesian police numbers in East Timor. He added: 'If Australian citizens did not trust the Indonesian military and police to maintain peace and security, then they need not come to East Timor.' Howard ignored this gratuitous comment and directed his remarks to Habibie. He said he was not trying to alter the UN agreement.

He was seeking, with Indonesia's support, a way 'to express confidence that the numbers of police involved would be adequate'. But Habibie was stubborn and intransigent. He did not want to reopen the issue. Indonesia, he said, had completed this discussion. In a typical Habibie ploy he made a threat—if the 'current arrangement was not adequate to maintain security he had a safety valve—he would talk to the UN about moving directly to the separation of East Timor'.

The bedrock position had now been reached. Howard, in effect, was making a personal appeal to Habibie. Howard continued:

> The question of adequacy of police numbers was a reasonable one for the Australian public to ask him about. The numbers could be worked out by the United Nations but he wanted to be able to say that Indonesia recognised the need for adequate numbers. The Prime Minister asked whether, if the UN were to propose a police contingent of several hundred, this would be acceptable to Indonesia.

Alatas was alarmed by this notion and rejected Australia's concerns. He said if Howard was this worried he should talk to Kofi Annan. Habibie said it would be 'difficult' to have such numbers and claimed, incredibly, that 'even without increased police numbers the current security situation in East Timor presented no problems … It was not the case that an international crisis was occurring in East Timor.' Here was Indonesian denial at intolerable levels. But Habibie said he was planning a significant increase in the number of Indonesian police.

Howard replied that 'we have a right as a contributor to express views about the need for an adequate number of police advisers'. And with this formula Howard, suddenly, broke through. The mercurial Habibie said 'he now understood the Prime Minister's point'.

They quickly agreed on a form of words for use in the joint conference, namely, that the numbers would be 'adequate'.[74] Howard said Australia would contribute $20 million to the East Timor consultation process. At the end Habibie mentioned, just in passing, the situation in Irian Jaya and Maluku, reminding people that if anybody 'tried to disturb Indonesian sovereignty, they would have to face TNI'. It was a friendly threat. For Habibie, East Timor would not become the first domino in the break-up of the Indonesian state.

The Australians had said informally that the increase in police advisers should be 200 to 300 so Howard had more flesh for the meagre bones. Downer said: 'We then went straight to the Americans and the UN and

said we needed at least 200 to 300. I spoke to Albright about it.'[75] Howard
left Bali with extremely limited concessions—the minimum needed to
look tenable. Howard had not raised peacekeepers during the plenary; he
extracted no pledges about disarming the militias.

Bali proved the limited leverage Australia had over Indonesia and
the futility of trying to threaten or intimidate the Indonesians, a point
Howard realised. By appealing to Indonesia as a friend, he probably used
the best tactic. 'We came out of the meeting with enough to argue that
the process should advance,' Downer said. 'This was the judgement we
had to confront.'[76]

The lesson from the Bali meeting was that peacekeepers were viable only when Indonesia had agreed and the UN Security Council had
mandated the operation. Neither condition was going to be met before
the ballot. The veto would be applied in the Security Council if any
such attempt was made without Jakarta's consent. Such realities had little
impact in Australia, where the demand that peacekeepers be injected immediately into East Timor had its own momentum, fuelled by the media,
the Labor Party and public opinion. Downer said: 'Are these people silly
or are they just dumb? It would have been better to have peacekeepers
but the Indonesians would never agree. These people don't understand
the mindset of a country that has been colonised.'[77]

Asked a decade later if a peacekeeping force before the ballot was
tenable, Kim Beazley said: 'Not really. But it was worth trying to get
it.'[78] CDF Chris Barrie said: 'You couldn't put a military force into East
Timor without getting the agreement of the Indonesian Government.'[79]
If foreign forces had entered East Timor without Jakarta's consent it
would invite war with Indonesia. Most influential Australians demanding
peacekeepers did not grasp this reality; but others did and they constituted,
in effect, an Australian war lobby against Jakarta.

On 5 May, in New York, agreement was signed between Indonesia
and Portugal, ending seventeen years of talks with provision for the
8 August ballot. The United Nations Mission in East Timor (UNAMET)
would be created to supervise the ballot. Speaking at the ceremony, Kofi
Annan said it was imperative that the UN be allowed to implement the
agreements freely. The defect in the agreement was that Indonesia, a party
to the dispute, was in charge of security. 'What would you suggest we do?'
Annan replied when quizzed about this conflict.[80]

The Clinton administration endorsed this approach. Deputy
Assistant Secretary of Defence for Peacekeeping and Humanitarian
Affairs Dr James Schear said:

There were no advocates within the US Department of Defense or the White House for peacekeepers to be sent to East Timor before the ballot. US concerns about the risk of violence were reflected in appeals to the government in Jakarta. In 1999 Kosovo was the main focus of US activity. This was the NATO air campaign conducted against Slobodan Milosevic that eventually saw the Serbian capitulation in June of that year and a surge of 50 000 NATO-led peacekeepers to help stabilise the province. Kosovo consumed enormous amounts of high-level US attention and energy. Washington's reluctance to play a major role in East Timor needs to be seen, in part, against that background.[81]

Downer went to the US in June.

We did our best to keep the Americans engaged. But it was bloody hard to get Clinton and Albright and [Defense Secretary William] Cohen focused on this issue. At the UN I told them it was very silly to send out this message that if the violence continues, it will put off the ballot. That just encourages the militias to get the thing cancelled.[82]

Downer told Kofi Annan that 'It was important that the Indonesians were made to understand that other countries knew what their security forces were up to in East Timor and that they be made to stop.' He said Australia would be making fresh efforts in this regard.

The flag over the UN mission was raised on 3 June. The mission was headed by an experienced British official, Ian Martin, with Annan's representative being Jamsheed Marker from Pakistan, and comprised 210 international staffers, 422 UN volunteers, 271 civilian police, 50 military liaison officers and 4000 local staff. Australia mounted a major logistical operation from Darwin to make the operation feasible.

From its inception UNAMET was a target of the militias, with threats made against its staff and its compound, including threats to kill Martin and Marker. UN staff were attacked during June and July, forcing Martin to travel to Jakarta to protest that TNI was working with the militias with impunity. Howard protested by letter to Habibie but Australia's position, as conveyed by Downer to Annan, was that the ballot should proceed on time.[83] Annan agreed, but it was delayed three weeks until 30 August.

Australia took a deliberate decision that the ballot should proceed despite flawed security. This responsibility fell upon Howard and Downer.

The moral justification, ultimately, is that this is what the East Timorese leaders wanted. Downer said:

> Our point was that the ballot, whenever it was held, was going to be a bloody risky exercise. And if you kept putting it off because of the level of violence, well, on that basis, it would never happen. It was not only our position that the ballot should go ahead—it was the position of Xanana Gusmao, Ramos-Horta and CNRT (National Council for Timorese Resistance).[84]

In response to the mantra that peacekeepers were essential, Howard said: 'Insisting on a peacekeeping force would have meant no ballot … We did not have the right to take that [a vote] away from the people of East Timor.'[85] As Downer said, the real issue was whether the violence justified the abandonment of the vote. His fear was that the UN would lose its nerve and put the ballot off. Downer said:

> The critics will say I was wrong, but I was absolutely determined that the ballot was going to take place. I spoke to Ramos-Horta about it when the violence was growing and growing. I told him that if you don't take this ballot now it may not come again for another ten or twenty years. And he said, 'We need the ballot now.'[86]

On the eve of the vote Habibie took calls from Annan and the leaders of the United States, Japan and Australia, all seeking a peaceful ballot. During Howard's 29 August phone call he again raised the issue of peacekeepers and Habibie said that he would only consider this after Indonesia's parliament had formally voted to ratify post-referendum separation. Meanwhile some prominent Indonesians were deluded until the end. 'Ali Alatas and General Wiranto thought that they might vote to stay with Indonesia,' Downer said. 'I have reason to believe that.'[87]

The 30 August vote was a triumph for the people. They queued from as early as 4 a.m., with whole families carrying food and bedding, some in their best clothes. An extraordinary 98.6 per cent of registered voters went to the polls. The result, announced four days later, was 21.5 per cent (94 388) for autonomy and 78.5 per cent (344 580) for independence. In announcing the outcome Annan said 'There were no winners and no losers today.' He spoke to Habibie and appealed for calm. Gusmao, still imprisoned in Jakarta, preached reconciliation. The vote was a vindication of the 35-year-old independence struggle but it showed a divided society, with one in five East Timorese wanting integration. 'I was very excited about how well the ballot had gone,' Downer said.[88]

Gusmao called for an international security force, warning that East Timor was on the brink of 'total destruction' from the Indonesian generals. The cheering in Dili soon surrendered to gunfire. Houses were burnt, thousands fled to the hills, the residence of independence supporter Bishop Belo was destroyed, people were being marched out of Dili by militias, Ambassador McCarthy's car was shot at, UN staff were being attacked and hundreds of East Timorese fled to the UNAMET compound. The Australian Consulate at Dili reported that 'TNI is allowing militia violence and intimidation to continue almost unchecked.' Wiranto and Alatas were sent to East Timor on 5 September and on their return Wiranto insisted that the situation was under control. This prompted a biting reply from McCarthy: 'I can't believe that Wiranto … didn't know what was happening. He did go into town … and the town was in chaos that day. It was in absolute chaos and yet no attempt was made to stop it.'[89]

Events now moved quickly. Annan spoke to Habibie about an international force but met resistance. Discounting this, Annan promptly rang Howard to ask if Australia would be prepared to lead a multinational force in East Timor. Howard was ready for the UN request.

Howard told Annan that Australia could deploy 2000 troops within forty-eight to seventy-two hours' notice. Howard said:

> I did indicate to Kofi Annan [that] it had to be understood that Australia would take the lead role. I wasn't going to commit large numbers of Australian forces unless we were effectively in charge. I made that clear. He [Annan] was asking us to provide the bulk of the troops and I had the idea that the leadership might end up being a bit negotiable. I made it clear that I wouldn't accept that.[90]

From this point Howard became a sustained advocate for intervention, lobbying the Americans and the Asians. Initially there was very little international support for a peacekeeping force. At the weekend Downer said publicly that Australia would be wiling to lead 'a coalition of the willing' with UN approval.

At this stage Australian intelligence was alarming. There was an urgent need to evacuate personnel. The intelligence suggested that killings might be occurring in large numbers, people were being loaded onto trucks and taken away, ships were being loaded with people and leaving port. The NSC met on the Monday and Tuesday after the ballot and authorised an evacuation of UN personnel.

More importantly, however, cabinet specified the conditions under which Australia would act: a Chapter VII UN Security Council mandate (stronger than peacekeeping, it permitted military 'enforcement'), a force with a strong ASEAN component, the prior consent of Indonesia's government, support from the United States, and Australian leadership. From the time of the ballot Howard took control of Australia's decision-making; his grip on these fundamentals was the key to Australia's firm response.

The bigger point is that Australia was on alert—it had the capability to deploy quickly. White said no planning had been done for an Australian leadership mission—yet Australia had forces on readiness for deployment before other nations. Moreover, post-ballot Howard had the political will. Australia's role in East Timor has been misinterpreted—far from preventing the injection of an international force, it was Australia's commitment that made such a successful intervention possible in September 1999. Roth understood this. 'My personal belief is that thousands of Timorese are alive today because of John Howard,' he said.[91]

The ballot had transformed the politics. The loss of East Timor fatally undermined Jakarta's opposition to an international force. The ballot was also critical for world opinion because, as Howard explained, it was only the 78 per cent independence vote that galvanised disinterested UN members towards an intervention. Annan, having authorised the ballot in the UN's name, knew the UN had to find a solution—quickly.[92] But the Indonesian Government remained the problem. 'We were ready to go but Habibie had to be persuaded to agree,' said Downer.[93]

By 7 September there was abundant evidence of a population relocation, with militias forcing East Timorese from their homes—more than 100 000 were being taken to Indonesian West Timor and the UN estimated that by 14 September only 200 000 of a total of 800 000 people were still in their homes. UNAMET reported that the purpose was 'to give the impression of a large-scale dissatisfaction with the vote'. The destruction of infrastructure seemed to be raw vengeance aimed 'at teaching the East Timorese a lesson'. This was a 'scorched earth' tactic that would leave 80 per cent of Dili's buildings destroyed. The violence was deliberate—to ensure that East Timor began its new life in misery and ashes. Water, electricity and communications were shut off and there were numerous massacres. Australia's army attaché from Jakarta, in East Timor at the time, described his impression as 'Nagasaki'—'virtually everything was burned.' Conditions in the UN compound, a de facto refugee camp, became desperate.[94]

'The violence was a lot worse than I anticipated,' Downer said.[95] Howard and Downer had misjudged grossly. Yet they had wanted to misjudge, to justify the ballot.[96] Meanwhile a resistant Habibie told a UN Security Council Mission urgently visiting Indonesia that he would not contemplate an international force until Indonesia's parliament had approved the separation.

Public opinion in Australia was outraged. It was a dangerous moment, with much commentary calling for unilateral military action, the most important stance of this kind coming from the *Sydney Morning Herald*. Explicitly endorsing a 'whatever it takes' approach, it editorialised:

> Australia, however reluctantly and without waiting for others must lead the way—in force. Mr Howard talks of up to 2,000 Australian troops, but still the talk is conditional on receiving international support and Indonesian agreement. The time for such talk has passed … Australia should end this dangerous period of uncertainty. It should declare its intention to move troops into East Timor if Indonesia doesn't restore order immediately and if, in that event, the UN Security Council fails to call together urgently a peacekeeping force.[97]

That would have invited war with Indonesia. It violated Howard's defined principles for a successful Australian intervention and it revealed not just the depth of aggravation caused by the East Timor slaughter but the irrationality towards East Timor and Indonesia embedded in much of Australia's media. Howard said later that such a move 'would have been tantamount to declaring war' against Indonesia and that 'it was an option no responsible government could have contemplated'. The idea was divorced from any military or political reality. It was an insight into the East Timor saga, where the judgement of the Howard government was superior to the media that assailed it so relentlessly.[98]

Years later, an incredulous Howard said: 'I was basically being attacked by everybody for not invading the place. I said you can't do that, you've got to get a United Nations mandate. It was elementary. It seems bizarre in the light of all the later comments that have been made about me and the United Nations.'[99]

For Clinton, East Timor was not on the radar. Misjudging this, Howard expected Clinton to support the international force not just in political terms but with a US troop commitment. It was his elemental view of the alliance—that 'we support each other'. But the United States was reluctant and Howard would be disabused. Clinton's national security adviser, Sandy Berger, had made the notorious remark that 'my daughter has a very messy apartment up in college, maybe I shouldn't intervene to have that cleaned up'.[100] The Australians were appalled.

Howard rang Clinton to ask for a commitment of combat troops, only to be turned down. 'We're very heavily stretched. We can't offer troops,' Clinton said. Howard was caught out. He said: 'I was taken aback. Clinton said, "We're very stretched, you'll find it hard to believe but we are very stretched and there's a lot of resistance to us committing ourselves any further, we've got many thousands in Kosovo." I expressed my intense disappointment. We made our position very clear.'[101] For Howard, this was a violation of the alliance's spirit. He felt that Australia was being dumped, given its unbroken military support for the United States. There is no question that he pushed Clinton hard.

This was Howard's miscalculation. Australia's Defence department did not expect US 'boots on the ground'—it wanted US political, logistical, intelligence support and a US military underwriting of the operation. Howard, in effect, misjudged Australia's needs and US politics. His personal preference was for US troops.[102]

Dr James Schear, Deputy Assistant Secretary of Defence for Peace-keeping and Humanitarian Affairs in the Clinton administration, said: 'There was never any plan within the US Government to put combat personnel on the ground in East Timor. Our focus was logistical support.'[103]

But Howard and Downer were charged up. Howard gave a media briefing that included his 'boots on the ground' request and Clinton's rejection. It was a highly unusual action, revealing his resentment. For forty-eight hours there was a frosty tension from Howard's office towards the White House. As usual, Downer was on the same wavelength. He went public on CNN to criticise the administration and on 7 September he took a call from US Secretary of State Madeleine Albright, who had watched him from her Hanoi hotel room. She rang to express her anger. 'You're not as angry as we are about your attitude,' Downer shot back.[104]

Downer said Australia was trying to 'put together a coalition of the willing countries for an early UN security presence' but the US military 'had indicated that it did not want to provide assistance'. He reminded Albright that Australia had been 'a very supportive ally to the United States' but 'the messages coming out of the Pentagon about preparedness to assist with a coalition force were completely negative and this was disappointing to Australia'.[105] Albright agreed to help. 'She became our champion,' Downer said. 'The problem had been Clinton's National Security Adviser [Berger].'[106] It was, at best, a half-truth. No one in the US system wanted combat forces—Pentagon, State or White House.

The tension with Clinton was quickly resolved. On 8 September the White House decided to support a peacekeeping force and Clinton rang Howard to say the United States would make a 'tangible contribution'. America was committed in political terms; this was more important than troops.

Clinton now moved to smash Habibie's resistance to a UN force by mobilising the might of the United States. The IMF and the World Bank threatened Indonesia's economic lifelines; the State Department went public; the commander of US forces in the Pacific, Admiral Dennis Blair, went to Jakarta and threatened Wiranto to his face; Clinton warned that Indonesia's economy was at risk and declared from the White House lawn that Habibie had to fix the problem or 'invite' the international community to fix it.[107]

Meanwhile a Canberra–Washington video conference was conducted linking Russell Hill and the Pentagon with White and senior US Defense official Kurt Campbell (a veteran of the Australian American Leadership Dialogue) as co-chairs. 'From the moment the picture came up and I saw the level of US representation I knew we were okay,' White said. White told the United States that Australia needed airlift, intelligence support and logistics. It was not chasing any infantry. After the conference, on returning to his office, he was rung by a senior Pentagon official, Walt Slocombe, who said: 'We will provide that support.' White thanked him and said: 'There's one more thing. It is very important for Australia. If our forces face TNI we would value a statement from the United States to TNI that it will be supporting Australia.' There was a pause. 'You've got it,' Slocombe said.[108]

From the Pentagon's perspective, Schear said: 'After it became clear that Canberra wanted more, the US decided to augment key enabling capabilities such as communications, planning, intelligence and airlift.'[109]

By a lucky coincidence the annual APEC leaders' meeting was taking place in Auckland, with Clinton, Howard and most Asian leaders (not Habibie) in attendance. Howard's challenge was to use APEC to rally regional support for the intervention. As Clinton flew across the Pacific towards New Zealand his focus tightened. He spoke to Howard from Honolulu and firmed up the US message. When the two leaders met in Auckland, they were in concord. Clinton confirmed the US contribution. Howard was satisfied.

The Auckland APEC meeting was a dream event for Australia; all the leaders Howard needed were on hand. The meeting became living proof of Keating's originating vision. Clinton was now engaged in the regional action, not Kosovo. 'I don't know what would have happened without this APEC meeting,' Downer said. 'Keating was completely right about APEC's value.'[110] Before he left Auckland, Clinton praised Australia and, significantly, said it was taking 'the lion's share of the role'. Having got a fast answer from Clinton, Howard embarked on a diplomatic drive at Auckland to put together a multinational force, lobbying the region, including the leaders of Thailand, Singapore, the Philippines, Brunei, South Korea, Japan, New Zealand and Canada. The atmospherics, with APEC leaders focussed on the crisis, maximised Howard's leverage.

As the world held a gun to Jakarta's head, Habibie and his senior ministers met on 12 September and invited the international community to send a force to East Timor. At an Auckland media conference that began at 1.30 a.m. the next day, Howard called it 'a tremendous step forward' and showered Habibie with praise.

On 15 September the UN Security Council passed the resolution authorising the intervention force with three tasks: to restore peace and security, to protect the UN mission and to assist humanitarian operations. Under this resolution Australia would deploy more than 5000 personnel to East Timor and have command of a force that would exceed 13 000, with more than a dozen nations represented.

Thailand provided the deputy commander. In a futile move, Habibie tried to deny Australia leadership, telling Thai Foreign Minister Surin Pitsuwan that he wanted an ASEAN commander—only to be told that ASEAN nations did not have the resources or budget for the task.[111]

Major General Peter Cosgrove, a Vietnam veteran, was appointed to command the international intervention. Despatched to Canberra for final preparations, Cosgrove was struck by the anxiety in Defence HQ. He recalls: 'The question being asked was: Are we stumbling into a war?' Cosgrove's reaction was 'Not if I can bloody well help it.'[112]

But Barrie and White were doing their job. Barrie said: 'Ministers had to know. I wrote an appreciation for the NSC that went through all the possibilities—war with Indonesia, casualties, hot pursuit, legal issues. I said there would be casualties because there would be pockets of militants.'[113] For Australia, there were two critical tests: would the militias contest the UN force and would elements of TNI contest in defiance of Jakarta?

Australian intelligence estimated there were 30 000 Indonesian troops in East and West Timor. Barrie said:

We were very lucky. Had a fire fight started, I think the outcome could have been different. If you had had a few dead on each side, then it could have got out of control. I went there on day four—you had 20 000 TNI soldiers waiting to be evacuated and their demeanour was one of anger and disappointment.[114]

White said: 'Howard's decision had left some serious gaps. We were very exposed. This operation looked good because our potential adversaries chose not to contest us. If the militias had resisted we would have had trouble. If backed by TNI, we would have been defeated.'[115]

Estimating the likely casualties issue, Cosgrove said: 'Early days, perhaps scores of casualties, we're talking here some dead and some injured.'[116] He said later:

If someone had told me before we started there'd be no casualties, my response would be that is madness. We had some people wounded. One soldier died. Before these operations the military does what amounts to an actuarial assessment—we are obliged to do this. We had the casualties figured to be much higher and that's because we assumed the militia, from time to time, would fight it out.[117]

On the eve of the operation US Secretary of Defense William Cohen went to Jakarta for meetings with Habibie and Wiranto. Schear, who accompanied Cohen, said he went 'fully prepared' to deliver a firm message.[118] Cohen told Habibie and Wiranto that the world expected Jakarta to co-operate with the Australian-led UN operation. He said: 'This deployment must not be contested. Any Indonesian forces that contest them will meet US forces.'[119] This was a reference to a 2000-strong Marine group in the Pacific. 'The Marines were just offshore and everyone knew they were there,' Cosgrove said.

Calvert had no doubt about the importance of Cohen's visit. Calvert said: 'The message Cohen conveyed was "If you touch the Australians, the United States will come after you."' It was reinforced at the US–Indonesian military level. 'This gave John Howard a lot of assurance,' said Calvert.[120] Schear said: 'The Pentagon's top leadership was of the view that if Australian forces got into serious difficulties then the US, as an ally, would unquestionably act to assist them.'[121] In addition, the United States re-organised its satellite intelligence to give the Australians enhanced coverage of any pro-Indonesian military action.

This puts an entirely different light on the US role in East Timor. It accentuates the utility of the alliance and the US backup that guaranteed the operation.

Cosgrove's first decision was 'to get there fast'. He grasped at once the political–military dynamics. Cosgrove managed the vital balance—he projected military authority against the militias yet he conciliated the Indonesian officers. The evidence came at the outset with Cosgrove's change of the deployment plan—instead of arriving in Blackhawks flying low and hard before dawn, he switched to a more orthodox arrival, by C-130 Hercules transport aircraft, acting on advice from Colonel Ken Brownrigg, army attaché in Jakarta. His judgement was that 'a horizon filled with helicopters' might unnerve the Indonesians and provoke a military exchange. 'I didn't want to spook them *à la Apocalypse Now*,' Cosgrove said.[122]

At Darwin on the morning of the deployment, Cosgrove met Howard for the first time, the start of a mutually beneficial bond. In East Timor, Cosgrove delivered for his men and for Howard. The absence of combat casualties put Howard in Cosgrove's debt and won his admiration. Cosgrove's career, in turn, would be transformed—he was appointed Chief of Army and then Chief of the Defence Force.

The opening days of deployment were the most dangerous of Howard's prime ministership to that point. Howard expected casualties. Habibie refused to take his calls. Australian troops were told they would be targets.

Cosgrove emphasises the Australian responsibility.

> The US gave us diplomatic and political assistance and there was episodic logistical aid. As the force commander, however, I was unaware of any military contingency plans as such for the US to assist us if there was a particular problem. Of course, I never had any doubt that if we had got into serious trouble, the Yanks would have had no choice.[123]

For Cosgrove, the military-to-military ties with Indonesia would now pay off. 'At every level we kept bumping into people who had personal contact, personal knowledge of [Indonesian] officers present somewhere in the East Timor construct.'[124]

The intervention's impact on Australia's political and military leadership exceeded any other event since Vietnam. Drawing on his own career, Cosgrove says: 'In more recent military history, we had been a nation of followers. East Timor created the need for us to lead—we had not only to give the orders but provide the bulk of the force, the energy and the logistics.'[125] Barrie summarises the operation:

> East Timor was a watershed. First, this was a UN leadership position for Australia for the first time. Second, we were in charge of the military coalition when ordinarily we were minnows. Third, it meant the caution of the Howard government's early days disappeared. Frankly, I think there was an unwarranted sense of triumphalism.[126]

In retrospect, Howard said, 'it was perhaps a good thing they [the United States] didn't offer troops on the ground' because 'it meant Australia had to confront doing this in a lead role'.[127] East Timor saw Australia's acceptance in psychological, political and military terms of a stronger regional security responsibility. 'This was the first time we had done this without American combat forces,' Howard said.[128]

The operation is underrated in US alliance terms. East Timor's legacy may be greater than that of Iraq—pioneering a regional leadership model as distinct from perpetuating the global follower model. But this event changed US views of Australia. From the State Department point of view, Roth said:

> It is one thing for the international community to react with horror and hold debates at the UN and call for action; we see this on many occasions. It is another thing to become head of a coalition and place your own troops in danger. Howard helped to get the United States to do the right thing in terms of supporting Australia diplomatically and in its logistical support to the coalition forces.[129]

From the Pentagon's perspective, Schear said, 'In my view the Australian–American co-operation was very close. Peter Cosgrove deeply impressed the Americans that he dealt with. The US view was that his conduct of the East Timor operation was high quality.'[130] Howard said later that Clinton had been 'very helpful' in dealing with the Indonesians and the US role overall had been 'very important'.[131] The Howard–Clinton spat, ultimately, was not important.

As a foreign policy exercise, there is no agreement on Howard's venture. Being a participant and a critic, White said the upshot was a fractured relationship with Indonesia, the severance of military ties, a huge

ADF commitment and the creation of a new nation on Australia's doorstep yet to be viable. Branding it 'an operational success but a strategic failure', White argues that the story cannot be seen as an Australian triumph because 'the final outcome [independence] was the opposite of what was intended' in the Howard letter. 'The real story,' he said, 'is that events got out of control.'[132]

But Howard and Downer did not seek East Timor's independence by accident or mistake—their aim was to remove the main obstacle to better ties with Indonesia. Their critics misjudge three critical factors. Once Indonesia accepted democracy, retaining East Timor became a most unlikely proposition given 80 per cent of its people opposed incorporation; once Habibie decided to force a ballot the only practical Australian option was to support his decision and try to make it work; and once Australia accepted its responsibility and led the UN force there was inevitably going to be damage done to Australia–Indonesia relations. The judgement, on balance, must favour the Howard/Downer policy.

However, Howard had a choice as to how he presented East Timor's transition: as part of the democratisation of Indonesia, with Canberra and Jakarta working together, or as the act of a popular Australian Government finally confronting Jakarta and repudiating thirty years of gutless appeasement. Howard chose the second path of cheap populism. Damning his predecessors, Howard said: 'It has been left to a Coalition government to reverse twenty-five years of over-accommodation to Indonesia … governments of both political persuasions have got it wrong.'[133]

But Howard, using this test, also got it wrong. Indeed, he had waited until Habibie opened the door. If his predecessors were guilty, then Howard was guilty. The truth is that the crisis revealed, again, the limits to Australia's influence with Jakarta. This had been the story since the 1975 Indonesian incorporation of East Timor. The reality about this event was unspoken in Australian politics and its media—that if Australia had wanted to stop the 1975 invasion it had to resort to war, an option the public would never have countenanced. Distortion and dishonesty about the real options facing Australia in 1975 was the foundation of the media-cultivated appeasement mythology.

Howard and Downer now turned this sentiment against their opponents. 'There was much gnashing of teeth among the Left,' Downer said with relish. 'You know: Oh my God, the fascist Howard government can't have liberated East Timor. The Left in Australia was humiliated by the whole exercise.'[134]

The synthesis of the Asian financial crisis and East Timor intervention generated a bizarre Howard government hubris—part truth, part delusion. In a series of improvisations, Howard had turned the East Timor crisis into an operational example of Australia's military capacity, diplomacy and values, sanctioned by the UN, a remarkable event. He then declared Australia to be in a position of 'immense strength' in the region. Downer loved to describe Australia as a 'significant country', dismissing the torpor of the 'middle power' label used by Labor ministers. 'We are the thirteenth biggest economy,' Downer said. 'We should be doing things in the world.'[135]

Often an undiplomatic foreign minister, Downer said of the intervention: 'We showed that Australia is a player in the region and worthy of respect. I mean, the others [regional nations] could never have done this. They know that but they are not going to put out a press release saying that.'[136]

Howard's ebullience cost Australia's national interest. The same month as the intervention, in an interview with the *Bulletin*'s Fred Brenchley, Howard, while not using the term himself, endorsed Brenchley's description of Australia as a 'sort of deputy' policeman to America in the region.[137] It was one of his worst rhetorical mistakes. This was not his regional policy and the East Timor operation saw the reverse process. But it didn't matter—Australia as a 'deputy sheriff' to the United States became the message transmitted at home, in Indonesia and in Asia for the next seven years. It was one of Australia's worst 'soft power' blunders after Hansonism.

Interviewed later, Howard said: 'I should have disowned it the next day. I left it too long. That wasn't my idea at all.'[138] It was inconceivable that such a mistaken remark could have come from Keating.

But it was not the only blunder. A few days earlier Howard was dismissive of the Keating–Soeharto Security Agreement—an invitation for an angry Jakarta to abrogate the Agreement. Dewi Fortuna Anwar cited Howard's comment as a reason for the decision. Indonesia now became a regional opponent of Australia, shifting from security partner to antagonistic neighbour. The structure of bilateral relations continued but it was an empty shell. White was correct in saying Howard's presentation of the intervention 'failed to offer the Indonesians any respect'.[139]

Most of Australia's public, however, saw the truth. Unable to confront either its moral or political failures in East Timor, a weakened Indonesia preferred the dishonest course of blaming Australia. Howard became a scapegoat for Indonesia's deep malaise. He took heart because domestic opinion was behind him. On East Timor, Howard created the nexus between military action and populist politics that would henceforth mark his leadership.

It saw him bond with the ADF and the elevation of the ADF on the national horizon. Cosgrove said:

> Before the Howard period, we were, if you like, seen in traditional terms—turning out on Anzac Day—but from 1999 onwards we came to front of mind as an ever-present arm of government doing all kinds of things. We were in East Timor, Solomon Islands, responses post-Bali, post-tsunami, you name it and the ADF would be involved. It became an ever-present institution, a vigorous arm of government and with that went money and resources.[140]

While the East Timor intervention was a 'one-off,' it marks the threshold of Howard as a National Security prime minister. It is the turning point. This status, entrenched after 9/11, originated in 1999. That was when Howard turned cabinet's National Security Committee into a powerhouse, when he sampled the thrill of strategic power and liked its taste, when he identified himself with the ADF, and when he opened a new chapter as prime minister.

36

DEFEAT OF THE REPUBLIC

The Governor-General is the effective head of state of Australia.
—John Howard, 25 October 1999

In 1999 John Howard refused his chance to become father of an Australian republic, throwing his support instead behind an alternative conservative model of prime ministerial governance. Howard stood by his beliefs and scored a triple success: he defeated the republican push initiated by Keating, exposed a schism among republicans that threatens to doom their project, and kept his government united despite different views on the question.

Howard did more than repel the republic—he cleared the path towards his own radical-conservative Australian model: a strong prime minister, weak Governor-General, absent head of state. The appeal of this model for any Australian prime minister, Liberal or Labor, is immense. The story is not just about the republic's defeat—it is about Howard's progress over a decade to entrench an alternative model that reflects the utility of Australia's conservative political tradition. This aspect of Howard's response went almost unremarked.

In the 1999 campaign Howard declared the Governor-General to be 'effectively our head of state', deliberately marginalised the Crown, and insisted the 'independence' wanted by republicans had already arrived.[1] Howard's response to the republican push was subtle and underrated. He declined to champion the Queen. Howard championed instead Australia's conservative 'crowned' republic where the Governor-General, a distinguished Australian who represents the Queen, performs virtually all head-of-state functions. The more the community accepts Howard's argument, the more it drains the energy from the republican push.

Howard knew that the magic of the Crown was tarnished—his answer was to fill the vacuum not with a president but with a stronger prime minister. Howard didn't need the people's consent; he merely needed to defeat the republic. This opened the door on his vigorous Australian Conservative model defined by the rising power of the national government, the weakening of the states, opposition to a Bill of Rights that would enhance the judiciary, and elevating the prime minister's role as a synthesis of chief executive and unifying symbol, despite its inherent contradiction. Kevin Rudd seemed attracted by the Howard model he inherited.

Stung by the performance of Sir William Deane as Governor-General, Howard would not tolerate an assertive figure or political personality in the post. He believed Deane had pushed the boundaries too far—using his office to promote reconciliation, taking a different position from Howard and provoking media stories about their differences. Howard's bizarre appointment of Archbishop Peter Hollingworth to Yarralumla as Deane's successor seemed an effort to find an acquiescent conservative with moral authority, but it ended disastrously when Hollingworth had to stand down. Howard then went for a safe choice with a retired military man, Major General Michael Jeffrey. Along the way, Howard often became the ceremonial figurehead where the Governor-General would have once presided.

The key to Howard's model was to deny an Australian president, with a fresh constitutional and political legitimacy, operating from Yarralumla as a rival centre of power and prestige to the Prime Minister. His objection went to both symbolism and powers. On symbolism, Howard dismissed the argument for an impartial president as an over-arching agent of unity, saying in rebuttal: 'I don't think that can ever happen in this country. We are too individualistic to ever find one single person who is going to interpret the nation to itself.'[2] On powers, Howard said creating a presidency would compromise the separation between executive and ceremonial functions: the president would encroach on the prime minister's authority. This would 'destabilise' a system that 'has worked so well and helped give us such stability'.[3]

So when republicans demanded an Australian as head of state, Howard argued that a presidency was the wrong answer to their question.

For Howard, there were sharp risks in honouring his 1996 election pledge to pursue the republic process. 'I knew if the republic got up, it would be used against me with people saying I was yesterday's man,' he said. 'I was prepared to wear that risk.'[4] Arthur Sinodinos argues that

Howard's position would probably have become untenable. 'It would have been nearly impossible for him,' Sinodinos said.[5] National Leader Tim Fischer, a republican, says that, after family factors, the referendum was instrumental in ending his career. 'It was the time bomb,' Fischer says. 'I was not going into this referendum lying to myself.' With the Nationals pledged to reject the republic, Fischer felt his position was untenable.[6] Within the Liberal Party, the republic was the template for Howard–Costello generational differences.

Offering a persuasive case for change, Peter Costello demolished Howard's position. He said the Queen's inability to open the Sydney Olympics proved that the ceremonial role of the head of state was broken. He said the idea that the Governor-General was effectively the head of state was spurious and he recalled the recent dinner for the South Korean President when 'the poor Governor-General [William Deane] was sitting there all the time being head of state but not knowing it'.[7]

The Queen is Australia's head of state—but Howard represented a tide of conservative opinion keen to suppress this constitutional reality. In effect, he wanted to enhance the Governor-General against the Queen but weaken the Governor-General against the prime minister. Howard's position cannot be understood without reference to both aspects.

The 1999 defeat of the republican referendum did not settle the issue. The republic remains in suspension, awaiting another inevitable shift in the political current for a relaunch. Keating remains confident that his ignition of the republic will be vindicated. 'The country is still ambivalent about its future,' he said after the defeat. With radiating optimism Keating dismissed 1999 as a 'warm-up for the real event'. Casting beyond Howard, he declared that the republic is 'truly inevitable, as an idea it's overpowering'. For Keating, it must be 'celebrated' as an event. 'It's important that we don't just wimp over the line by a vote, with a prime minister who doesn't want it,' he said.[8]

But Keating rightly identified the nation's ambivalence. Keating's 'celebrated' republic remains some time away; just how far defies prediction. The 'No' vote in the referendum was 54.9 per cent. This invites two possible conclusions: a 'Yes' vote of 45.1 per cent is a solid base for a future effort; yet it is in the bottom third of 'Yes' votes of Australia's forty-four referendums since Federation, hardly a promising outcome. Not one state had a 'Yes' majority and four states must vote 'Yes' to carry the proposal.

The result vindicated Howard's assessment that the question would be defeated. The people were not ready for the republic. This was despite opinion polls showing, with a rise in patriotism in the 1990s, that republicans strongly outnumbered monarchists. These polls had given republicans great heart. Yet they were misleading. Howard said having 'no significant section of the population opposed' was probably necessary for success.[9] In private conversation he suggested that 80 per cent poll support was the sort of figure needed to carry a referendum.[10] Indeed, history showed that, before Menzies' referendum to ban the Communist Party had been defeated, it enjoyed support in the polls running at about 80 per cent.[11]

The referendum, along with the related question for a new preamble, was unlikely to prevail given the tradition of hostility to constitutional change, with only eight out of forty-two previous questions having been approved. Beyond this, it failed for three reasons that pose a permanent challenge for the republican camp. It did not enjoy bipartisan political support, at the minimum from the Prime Minister and Opposition Leader; it saw the republican movement fatally split, with 'direct election' republicans joining the monarchist cause; and it saw the people responding to the 'No' campaign against an 'elitist' or 'politicians' republic' being imposed on them. All three problems need to be rectified for a future referendum to have any hope.

From the start, the best prospect for the 'Yes' case was to recruit Howard, given his sway with conservative Australians. The most concerted effort to persuade Howard was made by Noel Pearson in 2007, in person and by letter, arguing that 'only you, or a political leader very similar to you, can solve' the republic issue. Pearson and Howard had a long discussion in Sydney. Recalling that meeting, Pearson said:

> Australians don't want to repudiate their past. I believed the problem with the republic was the sense that it represented a repudiation of the British heritage. This was Keating's message. Howard got this point. It was his view. It's why people were uneasy. This is the reason I devised the difference between the repudiational and affirmational republics. I thought I got close to persuading him.[12]

But Howard was only being polite.

Pearson asked Howard on the eve of the 2007 election to support two referendums: constitutional recognition of Aboriginal and Torres Strait Islander peoples; and an affirmational republic that kept the British heritage. Howard accepted the first and rejected the second. Pearson argued that only a leader such as Howard could carry the conservative vote for a republic and deliver 'the 80–90 per cent strategy that is needed'.[13]

Pearson said: 'On one occasion I asked Tony Abbott "Are you just going to defend the citadel every time the barbarians have a go?" I think Howard found the argument compelling. But Howard told me "I can't find this in myself." I felt he understood the arguments but his own feelings were too deep.'[14] Asked about his talk with Pearson, Howard says: 'He made this suggestion and it was a very warm discussion. But I didn't believe in the republic.'[15]

Howard knew his own supporters. Out of 80 Coalition-held electorates, 63 voted against the republic. Out of 64 Liberal Party seats, 47 voted against. On referendum eve, Newspoll showed Coalition voters split 62:35 per cent against. About 80 per cent of National Party voters were in the 'No' camp. Conservative scepticism about the republic ran deep and wide.[16] Howard, proud of his career consistency on the issue, never gave serious thought to changing.

For Howard, putting the question proved rewarding beyond his dreams. The campaign destroyed the façade of republican unity, shattered the Keating momentum and opened a political Pandora's box of unresolved horrors for republicans. Howard's legacy is that future governments will move with reluctance and caution on the republic front, a truth many republicans fail to comprehend.

Howard showed that the fundamental issue is no longer the Queen. The issue is the nature of an Australian Republic—a more formidable problem. The moral from 1999 is that the 'No' case commands a natural majority based on monarchists and republicans who oppose the model on offer. This is Howard's legacy; it is the fortress that sustains his model of prime ministerial governance unburdened by any president.

The mask concealing the real debate is now ripped away. The republic debate is about two issues—Buckingham Palace and Westminster democracy—and this is the irrevocable lesson of the 1998 Convention and the 1999 Referendum. It is the reason the debate is so complex and progress will be so difficult. Any question on the republic, such as the 1999 question, by definition deals with both issues: do people want a republic and do they want the republic on offer? The 1999 model rejected Buckingham Palace (by embracing a president) but kept Westminster democracy (by opposing a popularly elected president)—and the public threw it out.

This model was close to Keating's 1995 position. With some modifications, it was the Turnbull-led Australian Republican Movement (ARM) model—this involved a non-executive impartial president, elected by a two-thirds majority of national parliament, replacing the

Governor-General and becoming head of state with the severance of ties to the Crown.

The 'Yes' case was a study in restraint and rationality. It was merely about having an Australian as head of state. It would be 'a small step, important and safe'. The focus was on symbolism and reassurance. Former Chief Justices Gerard Brennan and Anthony Mason gave their approval. It was faithful to Keating's vision and Labor's preference. The ARM mantra was minimal change; the tactic was to prevail by offering a conservative republic. The model kept Westminster purity where governments were formed with the confidence of the House of Representatives and where the president acted on the prime minister's advice. As constitutional authority George Williams said, Australia 'was not a People's Constitution'.

But the public was unpersuaded. This model never enjoyed majority support. Opinion polls consistently showed that only a 'direct election' republic would prevail and that the chosen 'minimalist' model would be defeated. The split among republicans on the convention floor carried over into the 1999 campaign. The ten-member official 'No' team consisted of eight monarchists and two 'direct election' republicans: Ted Mack and Clem Jones, belonging to a self-styled Real Republicans group.

Branding the chosen model a 'suicide course', Mack attacked its elitism and, above all, its denial of popular sovereignty by allowing the politicians, not the people, to elect the president. Basic to the strategy of the 'No' campaign was its hybrid monarchist–republican character. This meant it could not campaign for the monarchy—it could only campaign against the republic model on offer. This was the key to its success.

The head of Australians for Constitutional Monarchy (ACM), Kerry Jones, said 'The "No" campaign was the people's protest'—it became a populist bandwagon. The 'No' case was waged against 'the politicians' republic' tapping into disdain of politicians and exploiting their alleged 'grab for power'. The monarchy, hardly ever mentioned, seemed to be irrelevant. This penetrated to the great campaign farce: the 'No' case abandoned the Crown. During the campaign Jones actually called for consideration down the track of a 'direct election' republic model. This prompted Costello to quip that the 'No' case was offering to both save the Crown and deliver a popularly elected president 'and both propositions can't be right'.[17] As part of its tactics, the 'No' case said there could be a future referendum after the current model was defeated, a manifest fraud, yet many people thought this feasible.

Howard stayed aloof from most of the campaign until the end. Happy to benefit from the disreputable tactics of the 'No' case, he refused to endorse them. He made clear his total rejection of the 'direct election' republic. For Howard, this was a repudiation of Buckingham Palace and a threat to Westminster democracy. It was the worst of all worlds. 'This would produce rival power centres in our political system,' Howard said. 'Under such an arrangement both the prime minister and the president would claim popular mandates. Even if the president's powers were carefully laid out in the Constitution, the adversarial nature of Australian politics would ensure that tension between the two would arise.'[18]

This concern united much of the political class. Howard, Keating and Costello were together, fearing that a president with a popular mandate would collide with a prime minister's parliamentary mandate.

There is, however, no denying the paradox of the referendum—it was defeated by a campaign that invoked popular sovereignty, not the value of constitutional monarchy. Howard, as usual, focussed on the result, not its deeper meaning. In fact, the significance of the campaign was the success of the 'No' case in keeping Australia a monarchy when monarchists are outnumbered by republicans. This achievement should not be underrated. A majority of the 55 per cent who voted 'No' identified themselves to pollsters as republicans. This is the monarchist vision of the future: they do not require a majority to succeed; they need only to defeat any particular republican model on offer. The strategy is ready to be repeated for another republican model by forging another temporary alliance with disaffected republicans who oppose whatever model is offered. It is a destructive tactic because it describes a society with diminished faith in its monarchy yet without agreement on an alternative.[19]

This tactic will be potent because passions over Westminster democracy are likely to be as potent as passions over Buckingham Palace. After the 1998 Convention, constitutional authority Greg Craven said: 'What the Convention exposed was a great gap between conservative and mainstream constitutionalism in Australia, and its radical opposite: a chasm between broad (if qualified) confidence in representative parliamentary government, and its rejection as a fraud on the popular will and the rights of citizens.'[20] This rift between republicans is profound and passionate.

The effect of Howard's victory will be to radicalise the republican position. The rejection of 'minimalism' means that republicans must examine a 'direct election' model. This is the result's irrefutable political logic. 'The next model for an Australian republic should be a popularly created, direct election model,' Williams said.[21] This is the new republican orthodoxy.

It is fuelled by the 'two Australias' nature of the 1999 result. The vote split along income, education and socioeconomic status. The rich seats voted republic and the poorer and regional seats voted against. The most prosperous 34 seats voted 'Yes' more than two-to-one. Inner city seats voted republic, while the further from the central GPO, the higher the number of people who voted against. Despite Labor's complete unity for the republic it delivered only 57 per cent of Labor voters. The regional factor was huge, with the 'Yes' vote being only 37 per cent in Queensland, 41.5 per cent in Western Australia and 40 per cent in Tasmania.

This analysis betrays the shallowness of the republic's support. It is a fair-weather cause affirmed in opinion polls that are meaningless but, when there is a proposal on offer, such support fractures over the model. Australians are hopelessly divided on what the republic means—whether it should directly empower the people or merely deliver an Australian as head of state.

After the vote, Howard said: 'Remember that the "Yes" case had on its side the whole of the Labor Party, most of the Australian Democrats, 30–40 per cent of the Liberal Party, every premier with the exception of Richard Court, and you know, putting it mildly, 95 per cent of the Canberra Press Gallery and the editorial support of all newspapers except the *West Australian* and the *Weekend Financial Review*.'[22] Given its poor vote, this betrays a deep flaw in the republican cause.

Accepting the result's logic, that great servant of the republic, Professor George Winterton, began the task of codifying the reserve powers in an effort to render the 'direct election' model safe, so that an elected non-executive president would not threaten the Westminster system. The issue, however, remains riddled with contradictions. The vulnerability of a 'direct election' model, when scrutinised in any referendum, is obvious— it means a politician for president and it compromises the 'unifying' nature of the office.

After the 1999 result, it was easy to say that Keating's republican push was premature. The reality, however, is different—this will be a long journey and the only way to surmount the obstacles was by starting out.

There was no gainsaying Howard's victory. There are now two futures for the republican cause—a long period of 'storage' because no government has the incentive for a rematch or an imaginative effort to find a viable 'direct election' method. In the interim—and that could be long—the Howard model of prime ministerial power is the practical inheritance that his successors will evolve and refine.

37

SURVIVING THE GST AND AVOIDING RECESSION

*If I had left it to him [Costello], he'd never have negotiated
a deal with the Democrats, or talked to the Democrats.*
—John Howard on his government's 1999 survival crisis

During his second term John Howard faced two threats to his survival—one from the protracted GST struggle and one from a possible recession. Howard's economic credentials, his strongest political asset, came to the brink of eclipse. The battering Howard endured was an unpredictable cocktail—rising interest rates, a domestic downturn, a currency collapse, skyrocketing petrol prices and the bursting of the global IT bubble. Like Houdini, Howard escaped in the nick of time.

Ruthless in his pursuit of a third election victory, it was before the 2001 election that Howard's true economic character took shape. His supreme goal was to maintain the growth cycle. He began the pragmatic plunder of the budget surplus to 'buy' an electoral majority, and having touched defeat over the GST, he curbed any further instinct to expansive economic reform. The GST reformist of the 1998 election went into political hibernation.

On the economy, Howard became a methodical opportunist. The spending policies he later followed with success were pioneered and proven in 2001. Self-interested pragmatism was unleashed—speculation about Howard as a neo-liberal or free market ideologue was revealed as utter delusion. Yet the economic policy shocks that mounted over 1998–2001 nearly ruined him, so that by March 2001 he was staring down the gun-barrel of election defeat on the economy.

Consider the landmarks along this path. In May 1999 Howard's GST faced either defeat or major surgery in the Senate; he was forced to watch, often in anger, as Reserve Bank Governor Ian Macfarlane raised interest rates in five successive steps; in July 2000 the GST was introduced into an economy where confidence was weakening; the 2000 December quarter was the first quarter of negative growth for nine years, with an election-year recession a real threat; in March 2001 the dollar fell below US$0.50 for the first time since the float in 1983 amid a growing panic about Australia as an 'old' economy; the same month Howard faced a grassroots revolt over petrol prices, and unemployment was on the rise. In autumn 2001 Howard's credentials as superior economic manager were in jeopardy, and threatened his survival.

The second-term economic crisis and Howard's escape left an indelible mark—it revealed Howard's tenacity as a fighter and his political versatility. He switched from conservative to populist to liberal according to events. During these crises Howard's differences with, and ascendancy over, Peter Costello became decisive. There was, however, one constant—the Howard–Costello economic model of fiscal surpluses, independent central bank and flexible labour market stayed in place. The model held together and emerged stronger, not weaker, from this exacting test.

Any idea that the 1998 victory settled the tax reform issue was a myth. The GST had new potential to destroy the Howard government, first in 1999, then in 2001. Howard was tormented by the GST for most of his second term—the struggle sapped the government's energy and deluded Kim Beazley into believing that Howard would not last beyond two terms.

Post-election, speed was of the essence. Costello took charge of the tax bills and the plan was to legislate the package before mid-1999 when the new Senate was constituted. That meant relying, again, on the votes of the independents, Brian Harradine and Mal Colston. Because Colston suggested he would either support the government or abstain, Harradine's became the pivotal vote. The new taxes would take effect from 1 July 2000, allowing more than a year for their bedding down ahead of the late 2001 election. The project would occupy the entire second term.

Within hours of the 1998 election, Labor resumed its GST war. Beazley said Howard had a mandate 'for nothing other than good government'.[1] The party that once believed in election mandates was trashing the notion. The GST had served Beazley to great effect in the 1998 election and he saw no reason to avoid a replay. Convinced by Howard's woes and Labor research, Beazley by autumn 2001 was measuring the drapes for the Lodge. As early as 7 December 1999, he told the ALP caucus that Labor would 'surf into office on the back of the GST', infuriating the government and prompting Costello's sneer that he must be a 'modern Midget Farrelly'.[2] It reflected a new Labor faith—governments that introduce GSTs lose the next poll.

In the first half of 1999, Australia was engulfed in a hysterical public debate dominated by special pleading, the culprits being the Senate and the media. Australian Democrat Andrew Murray, a key player in the Senate GST debate, recalls:

> The whole thing shocked me. What I thought was a perfectly ordinary and reasonable policy which had been accepted all over the world was creating turmoil in Australia. I just didn't understand it. I remember people on chat shows shouting about it. I would ask people, 'Have you travelled to Greece or anywhere else? Do you know they have a GST?' It was as though Australia was hanging the wrong person. I know New Zealanders just couldn't believe the immaturity of the Australian community and the media over the GST. It was introduced in NZ without trouble.[3]

Four Senate committees investigated the tax reform. Costello said: 'The idea of the committees was to find every aggrieved lobby group and air every grievance in an attempt to create public opposition to the tax reform.'[4] Facing a virulent campaign to ruin the reform in the Senate, Costello recalled:

> Horror stories of businesses that had decided to close rather than make the effort to implement the GST were everywhere. The National Tax and Accountants Association president claimed the GST would cost jobs. 'Truck drivers could die from unwarranted pressure to cut costs on the back of the GST,' said the Australian Trucking Association. The left-wing Australia Institute issued a press release: 'At least sixty-five more people will die each year due to increased air pollution and traffic accidents if the government's proposed changes to fuel prices in the GST package go ahead.' The Queensland Minister for Energy claimed that increases in electricity bills from GST 'will lead to cold showers and cold meals.[5]

Costello's aim was to secure the full package with its broad GST base. He tried to appease Harradine, whom he knew was an opponent of market-based economics in the BA Santamaria mould. 'He would never name his precise demands when he was negotiating,' Costello said.[6]

The Treasurer was in the air en route to Singapore in May 1999 when Harradine told the Senate he would vote against the GST. 'I apologise,' he said. 'I know my name will be mud but it has been mud before today.'

Nick Minchin had to break the news to Howard. 'We were devastated,' Minchin said. 'This was very serious for the government. Having relied on Harradine, we were now at the mercy of the crossbenches.'[7] Costello was gutted. 'We had won an election on it [and] we were now faced with the complete defeat of the package,' he said.[8] Inability to validate the reform would be a failure of Australia's political system.

The cabinet met at Longreach when Costello was still overseas. It had no stomach for a double dissolution election. Any such resort would have been a disaster, with Howard inviting defeat the second time around. The pragmatist in Howard took command. 'We had to sit down with the Democrats and get the best deal possible,' Howard said.

> I had half a dozen calls the next day [after Harradine's speech] from friends and leading figures in the business community saying, 'John, I know it's a disappointment to you, but you've got to get the best you can.' When I look back on it, to do otherwise would have been catastrophic. That would have been the end.[9]

That is Howard's admission that his survival was in jeopardy. Defeat of the tax package would cripple the government, the prelude to its demise.

In a most unusual event, Howard was saved by the new Democrats leader, Meg Lees, who had spearheaded the Democrats' embrace of a 'fairer' GST for the 1998 election. Howard and Costello negotiated with Meg Lees and Andrew Murray for seven days. Howard's main concession was to abandon the GST on food—in return he saved the GST and saved the new 30 cents marginal tax rate for the 80 per cent of taxpayers earning less than $50 000 a year.

'Costello was averse to the concessions,' Murray remembers. 'But there was no way in heaven our party would hold to any deal if food had stayed taxed. Food had to come out. Howard saw that.'[10] 'I played bad cop while Howard played good cop,' Costello said.[11] But Howard repudiates this view with contempt.

Howard's criticism of Costello is deliberate and lethal. Interviewed for this book, he said: 'If I had left it to him [Costello], he'd never have negotiated a deal with the Democrats, or talked to the Democrats.' Howard found Costello resistant to political reality and the government's dilemma.[12] This view is confirmed by Lees. 'If Costello had been in charge there would have been no agreement,' she said.[13] Lees says:

Early in the piece we had a meeting with Costello in his office. At the start he stood up and declared that the GST on food was 'off the table'. I said 'Well, if that's where we're at, there is no point in going on.' And we walked out. I went back to the Democrat offices and said 'look, we need a press release to announce we're saying no as Mr Harradine did. But John Howard rang me, that same night, with a different message. He said, 'Don't do anything, let's all have a talk, come down to Melbourne and we'll go through this.'[14]

Concerned to keep the integrity of the tax, Costello strove to limit the exemptions. But Howard distrusted Costello's judgement and could not fathom his purpose. Years later, Howard was almost lost for words at Costello's effort and said: 'You know, this is our big deal. We go to the election, we win the election, we lose a swag of seats in the process. And then, because we don't get precisely everything we want [shaking his head] … he [Costello] was an enigma.'[15]

Howard said Costello did a good technical job with the GST, but he criticised what he saw as one of Costello's fatal flaws. 'The actual policy came from me,' Howard said of the political commitment behind the GST. 'The policy drive on the waterfront came from me and Reith … He [Costello] was not a driving policy person on a lot of things.' It was a characteristic of Costello that Howard was never able to understand.

Lees led the Democrats' negotiating team to Melbourne. 'From the start it was clear Howard wanted an agreement,' she said. 'We began on the easy issues where we agreed. It wasn't until the end that Howard made the concession on food. Costello was grumpy and mightily pissed off—he seemed to feel the GST was his personal policy.'[16] At one point Howard rang Reith. 'There's no issue of principle here,' Reith told him. 'Taking food out will be a political plus. It would be absurd to lose the entire package over food.'[17]

Announcing the compromise on 28 May 1998 Howard said it was 'truly a historic moment in the economic modernisation of Australia'. He would live off this triumph for the next nine years. At the time it was unquestionably the greatest policy achievement of Howard's career and crucial to saving his political legitimacy. Howard argued that 85 per cent of the package had been kept. Reconciled to the deal, Costello said: 'Eighty-five per cent sure beats zero.'[18] The final package was loaded with concessions for families, the bush, pensioners, and self-funded retirees. Howard praised Costello for his 'great skill' and damned Labor for its 'vituperative negativity'.

The concessions to the Democrats were significant—exclusion of food at a cost of more than $3 billion, restructuring the diesel fuel rebate for environmental purposes, reduced tax cuts for people above $50 000 a year, more generous compensation for pensioners and further GST exemptions in education and health. It was tempting to interpret the result as a Lees–Murray effort to bury the Democrats' 'fairies at the bottom of the garden' image and become a more serious political party. Lees won more of the Democrats platform in one negotiation than the party had achieved over the previous thirteen years. More than a decade later she said: 'This gave Australia a better tax system and from the perspective of the global financial crisis in 2009 you can see how important this tax base is for the country.'[19]

But Lees became a target. 'Labor just played politics and leaked all sorts of rubbish against me,' she said. Lees misjudged her own party and the ideological fixations of the Left. Much of the Democrats rank and file never forgave her dealing with Howard. The Democrats were branded as the party that gave life to the GST. 'We were left high and dry,' Murray said. 'We were poor at selling our GST position. Some of the community reaction was extraordinary—it was criminal in terms of the threats. I've operated in the worst sort of environments imaginable, wars and so on, but this was something else. It's an ugly side to Australia.'[20] The Democrats would not recover from this deal, which helped to fracture the party. 'The GST was a major source of antagonism within the Democrats but it was not the cause of our demise,' Murray said. 'That cause was the acute dissension in the party room that exploded in 2002.'[21]

At Treasury, Ted Evans was satisfied, dismissing the economists who denigrated the value of the GST reform. 'I thought the GST was a critically important reform,' Evans said. 'It delivered a very significant revenue base that didn't interfere with incentives to labour force participation. We haven't seen the best of it yet. If we didn't have it, then income taxes would be higher. Down the track it will be important to lift the GST rate so it does more.'[22]

This was not the view of first-term Labor MP Kevin Rudd, who told the House:

When the history of this parliament, this nation and this century is written, 30 June 1999 will be recorded as a day of fundamental injustice—an injustice which is real, an injustice which is not simply conjured up by the fleeting rhetoric of politicians. It will be recorded as the day when the social compact that has governed this nation for the last 100 years was torn up.[23]

There was almost no limit to Labor's indulgent denunciations.

The Howard government was phasing in a new tax system. Every business had to register for GST and obtain an Australian Business Number (ABN) to quote during transactions. More than two million ABNs were issued and companies, notably small businesses, had to keep records many had never kept before. This required businesses to complete a quarterly Business Activity Statement (BAS) showing their transactions and GST. The initial complexity of the system provoked a rebellion within small business and another Howard–Costello flashpoint.

Arthur Sinodinos recalls:

> We allowed the bureaucracy to get away on this one. It was a failure on my part, a failure on the part of Howard's office and a failure by Costello's office. I had never seen a proposed BAS form until the political crisis hit us. We were punishing small business, our core constituency. Howard got very involved on this. He was personally engaged in redrafting the form. He wasn't taking any chances.[24]

It was a blatant Howard invasion of Costello's terrain. Once again Howard, baffled by Costello, was frank in his critique: 'I got very frustrated with him [Costello] at the beginning of 2001 over this. I had to really push and shove to get him to shift on the BAS. That was absolutely critical to our [political] recovery.'[25] The top reaches of the government were consumed with chatter contrasting Costello's aloofness with Howard's 'fix-it' pragmatism. Howard got his simpler BAS. One adviser said: 'Costello seemed to think it wasn't his job to micro-manage the problem.'[26]

Howard felt Costello had outsourced a highly sensitive political problem to his bureaucrats and was reluctant to make repairs. The issue came to a head with the second BAS to be filed in early 2001. Costello said later that people were upset at having 'extra bookwork over the summer'.[27] The truth is that Howard went on the warpath against his treasurer. These potentially fatal events were decisive in convincing Howard that Costello's judgement was faulty.

But Howard also had another target—the Reserve Bank. In November 1999, responding to a stronger local and global economy, the Bank initiated the first interest rate increase of the Howard era. Over the next ten months it lifted the cash rate by 1.5 points to 6.25 per cent in a total of five adjustments. Howard was disconcerted, then alarmed. He was fortified by Treasury opposition to the rate rises, led by Evans. The

Bank board was split over the tightening. That was when it saw the first real heartburn over Reserve Bank independence.

'It was an open and shut case for a tightening,' Macfarlane said.

> Actual inflation was going up. Our forecast was that it would go up further. The cash rate at 4.75 per cent was the lowest in 20 years or so, a maximum expansionary setting. Obviously, it wasn't helpful to have the Treasury Secretary argue the opposite case. But on every occasion enough of the Board voted in my favour for the decision to go my way.[28]

In late January 2000, Howard, on a listening tour of the bush, publicly doubted the need for interest rate increases when playing to his 'battler' constituency. But the message went around the world like a thunderclap. In a stunning retort, the dollar plunged nearly 3 cents in New York against the US dollar. The *Australian*'s Alan Wood reported: 'It was a deliberate dumping of the Australian dollar. What was really disturbing to the monetary authorities was the implication that markets still suspected the bank was subject to political influence. Financial markets still do not trust Australia.'[29]

An angry Howard dismissed as 'stupid, ignorant and wrong' anybody who blamed him for the currency plunge.[30] But the Bank blamed him. 'It is undoubtedly true,' Macfarlane said of Howard's culpability. 'We knew it because our people were sitting there.'[31] Bank officials plotted exactly what happened. The dollar tanked on Friday afternoon New York time, missing the Saturday papers at home and repressing any political furore. It came directly from the PM's comments; Howard was the guilty man. 'It makes us look like a banana republic,' Macfarlane said of Howard's performance. 'It makes it look as though this isn't a serious currency. I know he [Howard] didn't set out to do it. But we were very upset.'[32]

Howard had two concerns: he disagreed with the Bank and he wanted the public to know these decisions were the Bank's and not the government's. But Macfarlane would let the world know that John Howard didn't run Australia's monetary policy. The Bank lifted rates 0.5 per cent in February and another 0.25 per cent in April. For Macfarlane, this was the living expression of the 1996 agreement on Bank independence.

Suddenly, the paradoxical nature of that independence hit Howard – the Bank took the decision but Howard took the consequences. Macfarlane, safe with his seven-year term, never went to an election, but Howard did. Howard knew that the voters would liquidate any prime minister who let an independent bank ruin the economy—and Macfarlane knew that being independent was no guarantee of his success.

Meanwhile at Treasury, Evans, a veteran hardliner and former protégé of John Stone, was ending his career as an optimist. Impressed by the reform-induced productivity of the economy and its ability to expand without provoking a price shock, Evans was a monetary policy dove to Macfarlane's hawk. Evans' message was that 'even a 1 per cent tightening these days is a big deal'.[33] It was a matter of fine judgement, but Howard and Costello liked Evans' judgement.

'It became a Canberra view,' Macfarlane said. 'The idea was that Treasury or its political masters had achieved so much structural reform that the old rules no longer applied.' Macfarlane was surprised at Evans' stand. 'When I told Bernie Fraser that Ted had moved to the expansionary side, he was astonished,' Macfarlane said.[34] The Bank's policy provoked growing unease. 'Howard didn't like the tightening,' Macfarlane said. 'He had a lot of trouble coming to grips with it. I'm sure his economic staff told him it wasn't needed.'[35]

The long and spectacular decline of the Australian dollar now became a factor in the Bank's interest rate increases. As the dollar fell to a new low below US$0.58, Macfarlane said a weak exchange rate was not benign. Australia was trapped between rising interest rates and a collapsing dollar, with the Bank under constant pressure to follow the US Federal Reserve as it lifted rates.[36] At Treasury, Evans was unimpressed. 'The fact is the Bank was chasing the exchange rate,' he said. 'That's why I was worried. They were targeting the exchange rate.'[37]

In April 2000, Howard called Macfarlane to a meeting with Costello, Evans and Max Moore-Wilton. 'Why should the currency be so weak when we have good growth, low inflation and a budget surplus?' Howard asked. He was dismayed about the harsh judgement on Australia. Macfarlane gave the standard reply: it was the interest rate gap between Australia and the United States that led to a strong US dollar and weak Australia dollar. This was one reason the Bank was lifting interest rates.[38]

But Evans decided to bell the cat. He told Howard that his interest rates comments were unhelpful and had undermined confidence in Australia. Evans and Macfarlane were united on this. 'It doesn't matter what we believe,' Evans said. 'The markets think the government is back into the interest rate business because of your comments.'[39] Howard seemed shocked by such old-fashioned 'frank and fearless' advice. Over the next couple of days Sinodinos had to smooth relations. But Sinodinos, an old Treasury hand, would tell Evans he agreed with him.[40]

Macfarlane delivered the same message, but politely, telling Howard:

> There is a residual reservation about the Australia dollar because of suspicions about the Reserve Bank and the Australian Government. It might surprise domestic opinion but the Bank is seen internationally as less of an anti-inflation hawk than its peers. There are also doubts about the government's resolve on central bank independence—a relatively new thing in Australia—and achieved without the legislative fanfare of other countries.[41]

'I am strongly in favour of central bank independence,' Howard told the meeting. Recalling his time as treasurer in the 1970s and 1980s, Howard said he hated setting interest rates. On Macfarlane's point about interest rate differentials, Howard doubted that raising short-term interest rates was effective in defending the currency.

They agreed it was best for Howard to saying nothing about the currency fall, but if he had to make a comment, Macfarlane urged him to avoid any impression that he was unconcerned about the dollar's slide. 'That attitude would be interpreted as benign neglect and would be an open invitation to a speculative attack,' the Governor warned. The debate moved to the critical issue—would the Bank keep increasing interest rates?[42]

'It is extremely unlikely we have seen the last increase,' Macfarlane said. Howard and Moore-Wilton said rising interest rates were more damaging than further falls in the dollar but Costello had the opposite view—he was more worried about the falling exchange rate, saying it undermined confidence and the government's standing. If Howard hoped to deflect Macfarlane then he was wrong. 'I went back out and raised interest rates two more times,' Macfarlane recalled.[43] Asked later if he felt under pressure at this meeting, Macfarlane said: 'No, I didn't. Howard never put me under direct pressure on interest rates. He never did that.'[44]

In this highly charged climate the Bank indulged itself once too often. In its quarterly review in early May 2000 the Bank had a lethal reference buried in its analysis, complaining that 'political comments about interest rates' in January had encouraged the sudden fall in the exchange rate. It had fingered Howard. The review said the dollar had not recovered and had entered instead 'a long downward trend'. The

Australian's economics correspondent, Ian Henderson, published the story on page one of the weekend edition under the headline 'RBA blames Howard for dollar's fall'.[45]

There was a flurry of Saturday-morning phone calls. An angry Howard rang Costello to complain. Costello rang Macfarlane, who said the story was a 'beat-up based on a few words in a fifty-page document'. Costello began to tell the Governor to ring Howard but was interrupted when Howard called Macfarlane on another line. 'He was very angry about the article, which he thought was out to get him,' Macfarlane recalls. Howard told the Governor: 'If you didn't like my comments then it was your responsibility to tell me and not to allow this criticism to appear in the document.' In his defence Macfarlane said the Bank was reporting a view held in the market about what happened to the currency. He said only the *Australian* had the story on page one.[46] 'The PM was not very satisfied with this answer and asked if I would be prepared to put out a denial,' Macfarlane says. 'I said that would not help the matter, but may make things worse.' Macfarlane was right.[47]

In mid-May, after the US Fed raised rates, an unrepentant Howard went public again, declaring that Australia didn't need a 'knee-jerk' response to 'everything that happens overseas'. He said it would be 'absurd' if the 'democratically elected Prime Minister of Australia could never say anything about monetary policy'. Howard sided with Treasury against the Bank—citing remarks by Evans disputing the nexus between the Australian and American economies.[48] Commentator Brian Toohey said the problem was that 'one arm of executive government, the RBA, is allowed to operate independently of the other arms'.[49]

The tension between the Bank and Treasury was undisguised. Macfarlane said: 'I can state categorically that Ted Evans in the board meetings argued against each one of these interest rate increases. I knew what was happening—from the start of the tightening Ted was worried that I would push too far.'[50]

But Evans has a somewhat different recollection. 'I wasn't opposed to any tightening as such,' he said. 'My concern was that we were going too far, that the Bank would repeat its mistake of 1994 and push rates too high.'[51]

The pressures originated in the new world of Reserve Bank independence. This spurred the cultural shift between the Bank and Treasury. Macfarlane argued that the transformation of the Bank had come under Howard, not Keating—because real independence arrived only in the 1996 formal agreement between the Treasurer and the Governor.

'You take a very different view when you are responsible for the policy,' Macfarlane said of the Bank's new position. 'It's different if you are going to be the scapegoat. It is not the same as just giving advice.'[52]

In its May 2000 Budget papers the Treasury nailed its optimism to the wall, declaring that higher productivity growth meant Australia could sustain lower unemployment than in the past generation under the discredited regimes of Whitlam and Fraser. Evans would never use the term, but it implied a new golden age.[53] Howard and Costello felt that, if the risks could be negotiated, the rewards would be great. The immediate task was to manage the price impact of the GST from 1 July 2000. Macfarlane's 0.25 per cent increase in August, the final tightening in this cycle, was widely seen as insurance against GST-induced inflation.

Meanwhile global capital markets were killing Australia. In October the dollar fell below US$0.52 and Howard called Macfarlane to another meeting—this time a meeting of minds and shared frustrations. 'The politicians, including the Prime Minister and Treasurer, were worried,' Macfarlane recalls. 'A constantly falling exchange rate makes people think What is wrong with us?' Macfarlane, by now, felt the markets had made a serious mistake about Australia and were acting irrationally.

'The reason the dollar has got so low is this stupid infatuation with the new economy and the idea of Australia as an old economy,' he told Howard. They contemplated their fates as the share-market craze for the dot.com boom drove capital away from Australia and into nations with strong ICT manufacturing. Macfarlane told Howard 'we couldn't do anything about it'.[54] Macfarlane remains scathing about the 'new economy' cult, saying:

> The NASDAQ peaked in March 2000 and started to fall quite sharply. That should have given everyone the signal that the new economy stuff was overdone. People were getting out of the new economy shares. The bubble had burst but the exchange rate still seemed to react to a damning view of Australia as an old economy. And that lasted until March 2001.[55]

The chairman of the US Central Bank, Alan Greenspan, was dazzled by the productivity impact of the hi-tech revolution. After deciding in the bathtub one morning in 1997 to brand it 'irrational exuberance', Greenspan had long since surrendered to the market frenzy. Financial markets indulged the dot.com boom and Howard's Australia was out of fashion. But Howard and Macfarlane knew that fundamentals, not fashion, would prevail.

When the bust came the change in global sentiment was electric. Macfarlane identifies the exact date—3 January 2001, when the US Federal Reserve cut rates in a sudden reversal. America was en route to recession. Macfarlane said the Fed decision 'had a big impact upon us'. While the NASDAQ would fall by 70 per cent, the retreat in the US share market was more orderly—at about 20 per cent. The dot.com companies were in meltdown; the masters of the universe were meeting credit calls.

Australia's Reserve Bank, convinced of the urgency, began a new phase of cutting interest rates in February 2001 with a 0.5 point reduction—an opening to election year. The US slowdown quickly fed into Asia and Europe. The confidence-sapping September 11 attacks on the United States came when the downturn was entrenched. With interest rates being slashed around the world, Macfarlane followed with more cuts in March, April, September and October. 'Our reductions were relatively quick,' he says. 'That's because the world recession came quicker than we thought.'[56]

For Howard and Costello, however, there was a new and more immediate sledgehammer: the sudden threat of a domestic GST-induced recession. The shock was delivered on 7 March 2001 when statistics for the December quarter showed that the economy had contracted by 0.6 per cent. It was the first negative quarter since the 1991 recession. A second quarter contraction would meet the technical definition of a recession—it would mean a 2001 election-year recession caused by Howard's GST implementation.

The negative December quarter had been caused by the unexpected collapse in house building in the second half of 2000, a response to the GST. It was a sharp recession within one sector of Australia's economy. 'We were dealing with a once in a lifetime or once in a generation change,' Macfarlane said, conceding that nobody had picked it. Howard attacked Macfarlane, saying his interest rate increases during 2000 were 'an error of judgement' that had weakened the economy. Costello agreed but was more restrained.[57]

Costello knew he would be blamed. He felt a recession would be 'fatal' for the government and would destroy his reputation and probably his career.[58] The horror was almost unimaginable—as a recession treasurer, Costello would be doomed; every line he had used for years against Keating would be resurrected and thrown at him. In this situation the Lodge would rapidly recede.

Costello's dilemma was that the March quarter was nearly over— and this was the quarter that would make or break him. The situation was compounded by two further factors—the world oil price was rising, driving up domestic petrol prices, and the dollar had reached its nadir, falling to US$0.48 cents, its lowest level since the Hawke government had floated the currency in 1983. This accentuated the risk that confidence would be sabotaged. Howard and Costello were facing a perfect storm. In public Costello kept his nerve, saying the 'transitional effects' of the GST should be over by mid-year. In private, he had one shot in the locker.

Costello called Evans and Ken Henry to his office. 'We can't have a second negative quarter,' he told them. 'Treasurer, there's only three weeks left in the quarter,' they reminded him. But Costello didn't care; the issue was survival. 'I want advice from you about what can be done to guarantee that this quarter won't be negative,' he said. Evans and Henry told him very little could be done; there were no guarantees. But Costello wanted an urgent fiscal stimulus despite the fact that it was three minutes before midnight. Two days later, the First Home Owner Grant, worth $7000, was doubled to $14 000. Evans and Henry had seen the whites of Costello's eyes. But Costello was not alone.

From February to early May 2001, seven successive Newspoll surveys showed Labor's primary vote lead over the Coalition averaging 8 percentage points, equating to a huge ALP victory. During March–April, Beazley briefly moved ahead of Howard in the 'better PM' polls. Knowing that he faced defeat, Howard revealed a methodical ruthlessness, seen first in March 2001, that defined the rest of his career. Sinodinos said: 'Howard's mood was grim and determined. He demanded that we identify and work through all our political problems.' Lynton Crosby said: 'We had alienated some of our core constituencies, older voters and small business.'[59]

The recovery began with petrol. Costello drew up two options to ease petrol prices: cutting the excise 1.5 cents per litre; and abolition of the automatic half-yearly indexation of fuel excise. Howard seized them both, at a cost of $630 million over four years. 'Costello wasn't pushing for this,' Sinodinos said.[60] It became a symbolic point in Howard's march—the sacrifice of a long-term revenue position for a short-term political gain.

On 17 March the Liberal Party lost its prized Brisbane seat of Ryan in a federal byelection dominated by petrol prices, anger over GST implementation, and small business alienation, with a pro-Labor swing of just under 10 per cent. The premonition of Howard's defeat grew stronger— but in retrospect Ryan became the lowest mark in a turning tide.

For Howard and Costello, the recession reprieve came on 6 June when the March quarter showed a healthy 1.1 per cent growth, an exaggerated high. It verified the government's narrative—the perfect storm had been a passing phenomenon and the GST phase-in had not wrecked the economy. The previous month Costello's 2001 sixth Budget became a showcase for Howard's methodical plugging of his electoral weaknesses. The government showed fidelity to its most loyal constituency, Grey Power, delivering an array of tax breaks, handouts and health benefits for 2.2 million pensioners and self-funded retirees. The surplus over the forward estimates was comprehensively raided with new tax and spending measures costing $12 billion over four years while the government declared that a 'moderate' fiscal stimulus was justified in the coming year.

In fact, the Budget slipped into a modest deficit for 2001–02, testimony to the recession scare and lower than expected revenue during the year. ALP National Secretary Geoff Walsh said the impact of the Budget was 'to shift the Coalition from a desperate position to one where it was back in the fight'.[61] These events were the guiding star to Howard's final two terms when he would resort to raiding ever-bigger surpluses to buttress the votes of households.

The point is that the Howard–Costello economic model was coming through. As Howard drew upon the surplus to calm public agitation, his nerves were settled by the pace of Macfarlane's interest rate cuts during 2001. After the October reduction, Howard went to the 2001 election with the cash rate at 4.5 per cent, the lowest for 30 years. The economic engine was humming for action after two years on a terrifying roller-coaster. Macfarlane conceded that 'maybe' his August 2000 'final' rate increase had been 'one too many' but he insisted that didn't matter. The Bank had got the big trends right—it had contained inflation in 2000 and helped to prevent the international recession from claiming Australia in 2001.[62]

Despite tensions, Macfarlane and Howard had worked effectively together. Macfarlane had delivered for Howard and Howard, in turn, saw the value of Bank independence. Macfarlane learnt that independence meant the Governor had to retain political confidence in the Bank's authority. 'We accept that independence had been delegated to us,' he said. 'We knew it could be taken back. You are very conscious, therefore, to keep the confidence of people. You want the government to keep its side of the agreement.'[63]

In Howard's second term the conventional wisdoms were broken: Australia emerged as a more resilient economy. It would escape, for the first time, an American recession. Macfarlane said the 2001 recession in most G-7 countries 'was the first international recession in recent decades that Australia has managed to avoid'. He saw this as 'an important event' where 'our reputation went up again'.[64] Australia benefited because it had missed the speculative dot.com asset price boom and because of its more reform-based economy. It was time, Macfarlane said, to abandon the 'historical determinism' that Australia was chained to the US economy.[65] It was also time to abandon Australian pessimism about our economic prospects—the current expansion had lasted beyond a decade and was superior to expansions of the 1970s and 1980s.[66]

There was a discernible Australian economic model: the Keating–Howard–Costello model. Its aspiration was a sustained growth cycle and it was delivering.

Howard, although battered, had kept intact his economic credentials based on low inflation, low interest rates, more jobs and tax cuts. After threatening a bloodbath, 2001 opened the door to the sunlit uplands. Howard was ready to fight on the economy. But an unpredicted event now occurred that would eclipse the economy as the main issue.

38

TAMPA: THE ULTIMATE PORTRAIT

My objection to Howard was more about method than principle.
—Kim Beazley, April 2009

From 1998 the Howard government faced the largest influx of boat people in the history of modern Australia—a movement that mocked its border security and deepened its anxiety about Australian sovereignty. More than 8300 people arrived in the three years before the *Tampa*, a small figure by global standards but large for Australia. John Howard believed that Australia was under siege, yet his repeated efforts to deter the boats had failed. At this fateful moment in August 2001, on the eve of the election, the Norwegian freighter *Tampa* sailed into sight filled with asylum seekers. It was a problem for the Howard government but it also became something else—it turned into the solution that Howard craved.

The dilemma raised by the Tampa saga would pivot on a clash of principle—the right of the liberal democratic state to protect its borders and decide who becomes part of its community, and the principle of universal human rights that obligated rich nations to welcome asylum seekers who arrive on their doorstep escaping persecution. The modern world has devised no answer to this conflict of principle. It is a struggle not between good and evil but between the competing interests of the nation state and the international order.

The politics of Tampa were primal. Howard used Tampa to stage a crisis and deploy the full armoury of the state—diplomatic, legal, financial and military—to terminate briefly the third wave of boat people since the Vietnam War. The extreme solution Howard authorised was successful in halting the boats but its cost was disproportionately high in human and financial terms and, as a policy, it was tenable only for a short time. It helped to win Howard an election victory. But its extremism bequeathed the legacy that there must be a better way.

Tampa offered the sharpest insight into John Howard of any event on his watch. Every contradiction embedded within Howard was on display—the conservative offended by boat people upsetting the established order, the nationalist pledged to defend sovereignty, the radical keen to deploy every organ of executive power and the populist mobilising massive public support.[1] The Labor Party, despite its loathing of Howard, was surprised by the speed, resolution and brutal simplicity of his moves. Labor took years to recover from these events.

The Tampa saga brought to a zenith the conflict between Howard's values and those of Australia's educated progressive class. It polarised the nation in favour of Howard's majority but gave the minority an enduring moral polemic against Howard that was prominent in his 2007 defeat.

There was one moment in the saga that ignited Howard, his senior ministers and his advisers—when they realised the captain of the *Tampa* had lost control of his ship. This became the trigger for Howard's fierce resistance. If there is a single moment that became the flashpoint, this is it.

Just hours after *Tampa* captain Arne Rinnan picked up the 433 asylum seekers from their stricken vessel and set course for Indonesia, he was confronted by five men who came to the bridge making demands and threats that he alter course for Christmas Island. Rinnan told the ABC's Sally Loane: 'I got five people up here on the bridge and they was talking in aggressive and highly excited voices and was really threatened a little bit'.[2] He told a senior Australian official: 'I have lost control of my ship. I am frightened.'[3] Howard said: 'They were forcing this bloke [Rinnan] to sail for Australia. He'd lost control of the vessel. Under pressure, he agreed to come to Australia. We couldn't tolerate that.'[4] Asylum seekers, having paid smugglers to get to Australia, were now, in effect, hijacking a merchant ship.

The mood at senior reaches of government was incandescent—at this point Howard decided he would stop these people, whatever it took. Max Moore-Wilton said: 'The Prime Minister saw this as the stage where Australia had to draw the line as a nation.'[5]

The weakness of Howard's policy over the previous two years was his inability to address people smuggling at its source—to strike an effective agreement with Indonesia. History taught that this was the only certain solution. The region was complicit in the boat traffic. The strategic lesson of the Tampa is Australia's absolute reliance on Indonesia for border security and for its domestic peace of mind. Howard's objective was to stop the boats; his problem was the limited means to achieve this end.

Recent history had proved this point. Malcolm Fraser's success in accepting the first wave of Indo-Chinese boat people rested on stopping the boats. About a million people left Vietnam in the late 1970s heading for a shocked region, prompting Malaysian Prime Minister Dr Mahathir Mohamad to threaten to 'shoot on sight' intended arrivals. The first decisive test since the abolition of the White Australia Policy, it became a triumph for Fraser. It is largely forgotten that this was an offshore program— unannounced boat arrivals numbered just over 2000 while about 56 000 came via offshore processing with total offshore numbers swelling to 190 000 with family reunion. The critical event was the agreement that saw refugees held in South-East Asian camps pending resettlement to the United States, Canada and Australia. The key to this Australian triumph was converting the intake from onshore to offshore.

The Keating government, in a different situation, applied the same technique with China. A few years after the introduction of mandatory detention Australia was faced with an influx of Sino-Vietnamese boat people from Beihei province in China. This was managed through the negotiation of a Memorandum of Understanding that enabled the people to be returned to China without bringing any onshore refugee claims. It was a diplomatic solution at source.

Paul Keating said Howard's problem with border protection 'is that he doesn't have the region on side, he can't negotiate an agreement with Indonesia and that means he can't solve the problem'.[6] In the end, Indonesia did help. The bigger point, however, is that Howard was locked into an escalating series of punitive decisions because there was no agreement with Jakarta.

From 1998 onwards Howard was confronted by an influx of boat people that had been brought from outside the region into South-East Asia by people smugglers. These people had fled the Middle East and South Asia—mainly Afghanistan, Iraq, Iran and Pakistan. They travelled through several countries to reach Australia—often flying to Malaysia and being put on boats in Indonesia with Australia as their destination. The appeal of Australia was strong—it was a prosperous nation that had a high success rate for onshore refugee claimants, residence for refugees and family reunion.

Howard and the Immigration Minister, Philip Ruddock, reacted in the Australian tradition—they launched a comprehensive campaign of resistance. Howard saw such arrivals as an insult to his authority as prime minister and a negative with the public. But in the year before Tampa a total of seventy-five boats carrying more than 4100 people were intercepted off Australia's coast. By 2001 this pattern was entrenched, despite their best efforts.

The Howard government's resistance strategy had three main elements. First, in 1999, cabinet approved Ruddock's plan for the Temporary Protection Visa (TPV) for unauthorised arrivals, mainly boat people. Those found to be refugees won a three-year visa, not permanent entry. They had to reapply three years later. It created two classes of refugee in Australia. Those on temporary visas were denied any family reunion rights or a right to travel outside Australia and return. Australia became one of the few nations to deny permanent status to people deemed to be refugees.

Ruddock rejected the accusation that this was Hanson's policy. 'She wanted all refugees placed on TPVs,' he said. 'That's everybody. Our policy applied only to those who came unlawfully.'[7] One consequence, given the denial of family reunion and the untold grief caused, is that TPVs only caused more boat people and increased the numbers of women and children with risk of sickness, detention and death.

The second element was that the government intensified the role of detention as a deterrent. It established a new and isolated centre at Woomera because Port Hedland was full, along with the Baxter centre near Port Augusta and a new facility at Christmas Island. Ruddock stressed the continuity of detention policy from Keating's time: 'When we came to power mandatory detention was already in place, for men, women and children. There were no buts or maybes. Family groups were being held.'[8]

This view was rebutted by former Immigration Department head, Chris Conybeare, who said detention was toughened under Howard. 'Under the Coalition, detention meant incarceration,' Conybeare said.

> Detention centres were deliberately set up to look more like jails, imposing a type of penal regime, with the aim being a total segregation from the community. The Coalition privatised the running of the centres, an idea that was never considered under Labor.[9]

Frank Brennan argued that detention was immoral and a failure as a deterrent. The irony is that the government could not admit that deterrence was a motive—because the High Court, in its 1992 decision validating detention, had limited its application to the processing of claims as distinct from being a permanent policy. Brennan said that, while it had operated for a decade, detention did not deter the wave of boat people from 1998. It was 'self-evident' that asylum seekers were unlikely to abscond while their claims were being processed. Therefore, the 'only possible advantage' was having failed claimants on hand for deportation. But the utility of this looked weak when in 2000–01 there were only 177 boat people removals, in contrast with 60 000 people in the country who had overstayed their visas.[10]

Pressed about the justification for detention, Ruddock said:

> There isn't a country in the world that, in relation to unlawful movements, just allows people to become immediately lawful. In Kenya I visited a detention centre holding 90 000 people. I've visited detention centres in Malaysia that were like an Australian battery hen farm. I've visited facilities in Britain, France, Greece, Denmark and Sweden. The major difference is the Australian policy of holding people until you find whether they have a proper entitlement or they should be removed. A lot of European countries hold people for a limited time frame. I spent a lot of time studying this. I concluded the weaker your legal framework, the larger is the pool of people you will have to deal with.[11]

The Howard government was overwhelmed by sheer numbers. Howard and Ruddock got trapped. The policy became untenable in its administration and detention facilities could not cope because the system was flooded with too many people. Detention became a rigid, almost an ideological, stance; in practice, it was indefinite detention, including initial screening, processing of claims and awaiting removal. The system should have been reformed with a more limited brief. Its deterrence value under Howard remained questionable. Only in its final term did the Howard government grudgingly concede that detention had gone too far, and offered alternative arrangements for children.

The third element in Howard's resistance was the campaign to lock out judicial intervention in refugee determination. After Ruddock became minister the department recommended a 'privative clause'. As Commonwealth Ombudsman John McMillan explained, the advice was that such a clause 'was the only mechanism that would effectively contain judicial review of immigration decision-making'.[12] It signalled the collapse of executive–judiciary relations on migration. The bill said privative clause decisions 'must not be challenged, appealed against, reviewed, quashed or called into question in any court'. It was a radical law, struck down by the High Court in 2003.

Refugee law specialist Mary Crock said that, in a sense, 'refugees threatened to bring Australia's judicial system to its knees'. By 2002 there were more than 4000 applicants involved in class actions before the High Court as the conflict between executive and judiciary became a 'gargantuan struggle'. In May 2002 over 54 per cent of all full Federal Court decisions were immigration cases. Crock said judges were imbued with the idea 'that the courts stand between the individual and administrative tyranny'.[13] The so-called tyranny was the law of the land. Offering an insight into judicial thinking, Federal Court judge Marcus Einfeld said a law can be 'fundamentally immoral' no matter how many politicians vote for it.[14]

The constitutional position was conceptually simple—judges cannot review an administrative decision on its merits; they can only review a decision to ensure that proper process was followed by the executive. From the High Court bench, Sir Gerard Brennan had expounded the doctrine: '[The] court has no jurisdiction simply to cure administrative injustice or error … If judicial review were to trespass on the merits of the exercise of administrative power, it would put its own legitimacy at risk.'[15] This was the separation of powers doctrine.

The reality, however, is that judicial review became a highway to an Australian refugee policy crisis. An industry was built on this highway constituting lawyers, NGOs and refugee activists. Judicial review was frequently used as a device to keep asylum seekers in the country for years and sometimes to win from judges a merits decision denied at the executive level. Judges required that 'natural justice' be upheld but they did not define what that meant. Before becoming ombudsman, McMillan found that judicial review had been 'over-reaching'. He warned that judicial pursuit of 'absolute justice' blurred the line between law and policy. He found 'countless' examples of judicial assumptions 'that are wrong or highly contestable', that judges looked to sources outside Australia to interpret what the laws of the Australian parliament meant and that this 'distortion' of national priorities meant that 'we spend considerably more each year on litigating about 12 000 refugees' places than we spend on our foreign aid budget to deal with the 22 million or so refugees and displaced persons'.[16]

The Federal Court and the High Court tried with varying success to negotiate through the minefield of claims by non-citizens. By 2003–04 migration litigation constituted 52 per cent of total work of the Federal

Court, a gross failure of Australian priorities.[17] Some judges had become crusaders. McMillan's critique, however, went further. He concluded, after detailed analysis, that judicial activism in refugee decisions 'ends up producing a worse rather than a better system of administrative law'.[18]

Judicial activism on migration became a political cause—it began to be justified by lawyers, intellectuals and media on the grounds that ministerial accountability had declined. It was one thing to argue that judges should protect individual rights under the law; it was entirely another to argue that judges should become activists to remedy defects in ministerial accountability. This constituted a radical project to change Australian governance.

Ruddock sponsored various measures to limit judicial review, with little success. The main move, the privative clause, was blocked by the Labor Party for four years until 2001, when it was passed in the legislative flood after Tampa.

The overall story up to August 2001 is that Howard was losing his war with the people smugglers. The weapons of TPVs, tougher detention and curbing judicial review had caused a huge political row for little practical gain. Growing alarm drove the executive to assess the ultimate solution—deployment of the Australian Defence Force (ADF) on the water. Such a ruthless policy needed a ruthless man and such a man just happened to run the Prime Minister's Department—Max Moore-Wilton. In 1999 Moore-Wilton moved to centre stage and he never left. He acted in Howard's name in a display of executive power that intimidated anybody who experienced it.

Aggressive, usually effective, charming when required, a former boss of ANL and deeply hostile to the boat people, Moore-Wilton in 1999 organised a People Smuggling Task Force to better police the nation's coastline. Initially a civilian operation, the taskforce was the origin of an evolving whole-of-government approach that, in 2001, would consume the Howard government and the nation.

The mechanism involved a number of agencies—the Prime Minister's department, the Defence department and the ADF, DFAT, the Department of Immigration, the Department of Transport, Customs, the Attorney-General's department, the Australian Federal Police, Maritime Safety, Protective Services and the Australian Quarantine and Inspection Service. There were no specific terms of reference but everybody knew the mission. The taskforce coordinator was a senior officer from Moore-Wilton's department, Jane Halton, with a reputation for diligence and candour.

Moore-Wilton came to end the defeatism on the water:

The Immigration Department was making continuing demands that we had to provide more and more detention facilities. This meant detaining people for long periods of time and detaining more people. In my view no politician, it doesn't matter who they are, is comfortable having lots of people behind wire. So there was a huge problem building up. If people could get a boat, then the Australian border control authorities were collecting them and taking them to detention centres. At Ashmore Reef we had officers just waiting around for the next boat to collect. In my view and in the Prime Minister's view this was defeatism.[19]

Howard and Moore-Wilton would not settle for defeat; they were going to crack this problem. In 2001 the issue became the focus of the cabinet's National Security Committee (NSC) and the Secretaries Committee chaired by Moore-Wilton that serviced it. Moore-Wilton now demanded a focus on one question: how to stop the boats? There were two ways—giving the Australian Federal Police authority to work with Indonesian police to try to limit departures, and putting the ADF on the water.

Moore-Wilton was pushing and pushing. 'We debated this endlessly in the Secretaries Committee,' he later said. 'Papers went back and forth to cabinet. The view essentially was that it's very difficult to stop the smuggling trade unless you can turn the boats back. There was a great reluctance on the part of the navy to address this.'[20]

At one point a naval blockade was assessed but Chief of the Defence Force (CDF) Chris Barrie dismissed the notion. 'No one at that stage thought it was worth a candle,' he said. 'The boat still gets through, you all look like a bunch of dills.' Barrie stressed the limits to the use of force.[21] But Moore-Wilton wasn't fooled; he knew force had to be used. And Barrie knew that, sooner or later, Howard would order the ADF into action. 'Dealing with people smuggling has been a classic navy responsibility for centuries,' Barrie conceded. 'It's very dirty work and navies don't like it. But there's no denying it's a classic navy role.'[22]

In the first five months of 2001 boat arrivals reached a new tempo, landing more than 1600 asylum seekers at Ashmore Reef. A vortex of issues now came together. The detention centres were full. Riots had broken out among inmates. In mid-2001 Ruddock went to Jakarta to seek better co-operation and was rebuffed. 'The Indonesians told me bluntly they weren't prepared to detain people for Australia,' he says. 'I think they were amused that instead of them being blamed Australia was now being blamed for detention. It was only after 9/11 and the Bali bombing that Indonesia started to rethink.'[23]

In mid-August, a fortnight before the Tampa crisis, Howard visited the new Indonesian president, Megawati Sukarnoputri. In private Alexander Downer had damned her as useless; DFAT jokes about her incompetence were legion. Howard proposed that Australia finance 'a very large detention centre in Indonesia', the idea being that Indonesia 'would hold people there rather than allowing them to leave and come to Australia on boats'. Megawati was unmoved.[24] Howard was stymied— criminals were bringing refugees to Australia but Australian authorities could not counter them. Howard had no friends in Jakarta; the East Timor crisis was too recent.

By this stage Peter Reith was Defence Minister and Moore-Wilton knew that this lifted the chance for serious action by the ADF. In early August 2001 Howard asked Barrie at an NSC meeting about a role for the military. It was agreed that options would be prepared.[25] Howard was ruminating on the military option but he remained cautious. On the eve of *Tampa*'s arrival, Howard said that using the armed forces 'for a humanitarian nation … really is not an option'. As usual, Howard would resort to boldness only when given an opening.

'I was encountering concern in the community,' Howard said. 'It had come up on talkback radio. People were worried that we were losing control. It wasn't the dominant thing on my mind, but it was on my mind. It was a rising issue.'[26]

The timing of the Tampa crisis was extraordinary—it arrived when the Howard government faced, at best, a stalemate with the boats and, at worst, a defeat. This is verified by cabinet secretary Paul McClintock, who saw the mood from the inside. McClintock says: 'It was by no means clear that the government could win this battle to curb the boat arrivals. Indeed, there were some sceptics within government who actually felt the battle was being lost.'[27]

'The Tampa wasn't something the government manufactured,' Moore-Wilton says. 'It happened, as these things do, through serendipity.' It was a surprise, yet an event for which Howard was prepared, in psychological and political terms. Moore-Wilton says: 'We had been working on these issues for months. The Prime Minister was totally conscious of the issues. I think it brought to a head in his mind that this was time for decisive action.'[28]

On August 26, the *Tampa* was travelling from Fremantle to Singapore. In response to a search and rescue broadcast, it intercepted an Indonesian vessel and took aboard the asylum seekers who were heading for Australia's remote Christmas Island and what they hoped would be a new home. The pick-up occurred within the Indonesian rescue zone. Captain Rinnan set course for the port of Merak on the Indonesian island of Java 400 kilometres away. Indonesian authorities had given permission to land.

But within the hour Rinnan was told by the asylum seekers 'either take us to Christmas Island or go to any Western country'. There were threats of suicide and jumping overboard. Asked by Sally Loane if he felt under threat, Rinnan said: 'Oh, yes, ma'am, with 434 of them.' Under questioning he said: 'This could have been turning to a really ugly situation if we was heading for Indonesian water.' He had been at sea for forty years but this event was the 'first time in my life'. With his crew of twenty-seven vastly outnumbered, the captain headed for Christmas Island. It was the responsible decision.[29]

Moore-Wilton said:

> The boat people told the captain they'd cause hell if he didn't turn around. We said to ourselves 'If this happens, not only do we have boats coming to Australia but they'll use any merchant ship that's going past as well.' It was a massive potential escalation.[30]

Acting on Howard's authority, Moore-Wilton ordered the *Tampa* to turn around. Messages to this effect were rung to Rinnan. But Rinnan held course. Behind him he had the authority of the Wilhelmsen Line. Its Oslo headquarters had taken a decision—the *Tampa* would unload its cargo at Christmas Island and continue its voyage. Moore-Wilton says: 'The shipping line told us "The master's in charge of the ship and he's decided to go to Australia." It's this maritime culture. We then told the company "In that case the ship will be stopped."'[31]

As the *Tampa* approached the island Australian authorities ordered it to remain twelve miles offshore, outside territorial waters. Rinnan agreed. That night the asylum seekers could see the lights of freedom flickering on Christmas Island. On the morning of 27 August senior ministers and officials—legal, military and diplomatic—met in Parliament House. Cabinet decided before noon that Rinnan would not be given permission to land his people.

Howard was not for turning. He would not tolerate these asylum seekers, mainly from Afghanistan, having targeted Australia from halfway across the world, having got to Indonesia and paid smugglers for a boat, having been rescued by the *Tampa*, having intimidated its captain to reverse course, finally achieving their aim and, disembarking on Australian territory, winning access to its refugee determination process.

While Howard spearheaded the response, his senior ministers were united. Howard never acted alone. 'The cabinet was rock solid,' he said.[32] This was an agreement of conviction that spanned Costello, Downer, Reith, Abbott, Ruddock and others. Costello said:

> I have no doubt it was the only decision that could have been responsibly made. To have allowed the ship into Australia, when it had been turned around on the demands of the passengers taken on board, would have been to give a clear signal that Australia had an open-door policy.[33]

Cabinet moderate Michael Wooldridge says: 'The turning point in this meeting came when Ruddock said he had intelligence that thousands more were in Indonesia waiting to leave. He was telling us this is just the start. This had a big impact on cabinet.'[34]

Asked about his advice, Ruddock said:

> We had intelligence at one point [that] there was a pipeline of 10000 people waiting to come from the Middle East and Indonesia. This was before the *Tampa*. We were already looking at how we could use the military to intercept vessels. We were under attack from people smugglers. They were putting together more and more boats and people were introduced to the process a bit like seeing a travel agent.[35]

Capturing cabinet's mood, Sinodinos said:

> The critical point came when the *Tampa* was turned around. This provoked a sense of outrage from ministers. The feeling was that it was so blatant, such a direct defiance, an in-your-face action. Ministers felt 'If we cave in to this how could we possible explain it to the Australian people?'[36]

McClintock said: 'The Tampa represented another "hole" in the system: boat people arriving by merchant ship. For the cabinet, there was only one issue—how to stop the boats.'[37]

In retrospect, Howard said: 'I knew it was a risky decision. There was always a risk you'd have physical violence, or people on the boat not accepting it, or a death. But I also knew unless we took a stand we were in a lot of trouble.'[38] Howard felt that to give landfall to the *Tampa* was an act of surrender; it would brand him as a weak leader.

Howard and Ruddock announced the position at a 12.50 p.m. joint media conference. 'We simply cannot allow a situation to develop where Australia is seen around the world as a country of easy destination,' Howard said. This was the principle on which he stood. But Howard had no viable policy. He improbably declared that the crisis must be resolved between the governments of Indonesia and Norway and that such views had been conveyed to them. It was a fantasy world. Who, pray, would take the asylum seekers: Indonesia or Norway?

Howard's problem was that these souls could not be cast adrift forever. Yet he had not the slightest prospect of finding another country to take them, a reality that dawned too slowly. Indonesia was the only option and that was never viable. It would be too polite to brand this policy-making on the run because the policy did not yet exist to warrant the label. Beneath Howard's projection of strength was only chaotic improvisation.

For Howard, the Tampa matter was a challenge and a gift. Denying landfall was filled with unpredictable hazards. Yet it would provoke a crisis with the chance to transform a contest that Australia had been losing. Fortified by the belief that he was right and the judgement that Australian opinion would back him, Howard chose confrontation. For him, it was an issue of will and sovereignty. From this moment the task of his ministers, advisers and public servants was to 'make the policy work'.

This was not a stunt to win the 2001 election. Repeatedly raised as Howard's motive, this misconceives the issue. Stunts are trivial actions taken for personal gain. Halting the *Tampa* was the cumulative logic of Howard's border protection policy. This was a deadly exercise in prime ministerial power. Howard did it to stamp himself as a strong man knowing this was the key to electoral victory. He would have done the same any week, month or year the *Tampa* arrived. Those who mistakenly think it was driven by election timing misjudge Howard and the enduring urgency of the border protection issue. All his close advisers at the time verify this point: Sinodinos, McClintock, Moore-Wilton, not to mention the senior ministers.

'This was about maintaining the integrity of our asylum seeker, refugee and immigration policies,' Sinodinos said.[39] McClintock said: 'Howard believed his government would be judged by its ability to stop the boats and end the trade. He knew the *Tampa* would become the major test of his success or failure. Howard was determined to prevail and, once he took this decision, he was determined to win the politics.'[40]

There was a strong case for saying Howard should have let the
Tampa land and use this event to tighten his border protection policy. This
argument, significantly, was not put within the government. This testifies
to a mood—it would have been seen as defeatist. The future head of the
Department of Prime Minister and Cabinet, Dr Peter Shergold, said: 'The
boat people generated an extraordinary reaction within the government.
Max Moore-Wilton was driven by this issue. In my memory of meetings
of departmental secretaries this was the subject on which his views were
the strongest.'[41]

Tampa became the decisive event in Australia's refugee policy—the
power shifted from Ruddock to Howard, the Pacific Solution was devised,
and the ADF was ordered onto the ocean. Once Howard committed, he
readied to punish Labor, convinced that sooner or later the party's nerve
would crack. Denying the *Tampa* meant Howard had to discredit its boat
people. Asylum seekers had two possible identities: as brave refugees who
should be met with compassion or as 'queue-jumping' interlopers self-
selecting Australia. Howard chose to propagate the second identity.

At 11.30 a.m. the same day, lawyers representing the ship's owners
and Captain Rinnan told a senior immigration official, confirmed by fax,
that 'the medical situation on board is critical'—'If it is not addressed
immediately people will die shortly.' The message said four people were
unconscious. The *Tampa* 'has now run out of the relevant medical supplies
and has no way of feeding these people', it said. 'If the situation is not
resolved soon more drastic action may have to be taken to prevent loss
of life.'[42]

Howard seemed almost indifferent to the plight of the boat people,
sick and suffering in the Indian Ocean sun. He promised to provide
food and medical supplies, but insisted this would not 'compromise the
validity of our refusing permission for the vessel to land in Australia'.[43]
Meanwhile Rinnan told the media that the situation on his ship was
deteriorating, with a hunger strike and threats to jump overboard.

Australia's only hope was for Indonesia to accept the ship. Downer
told cabinet that the chances of Jakarta's co-operation were 'not good'.
On the afternoon of 27 August, Australia's ambassador to Indonesia, Ric
Smith, called on the Indonesian government and reported back that its
attitude was negative.[44]

Indonesia's rebuff was a potential turning point. Without an
alternative port, logic suggests cabinet would retreat from its day-old
stance and allow the *Tampa* to land. It would have been an embarrassment
for Howard, who would look a vacillating leader, but a speedy resolution

would have killed the news story, with the political agenda moving on. Yet there is no evidence that Howard contemplated retreat. On this issue, he had become an unreasonable man.

The next day, 28 August, he told *A Current Affair*:

> Every situation has its 450 souls, every situation has stories of hunger strikes, every situation has the threat of people doing self-damage and jumping overboard and even suggestions of throwing children overboard ... but on the other hand, I have to worry and my colleagues have to worry about a situation where we appear to be losing control of the flow of people coming into this country.[45]

There was a further fallback position—for Australia to give the *Tampa* landfall at Christmas Island and then transmit the asylum seekers to Indonesia for processing. Such an arrangement would have to be negotiated between the leaders, with United Nations High Commissioner for Refugees (UNHCR) approval, and with Australia offering Jakarta enough incentives. Of course, it was not possible—every path led to Jakarta and that was a dead end.

That afternoon the NSC asked Barrie to prepare a maritime plan to detect, intercept and warn vessels carrying unlawful arrivals. The government correctly believed more boats would follow.

Faced with a stalemate, the Wilhelmsen Line decided to defy Australia and enter territorial waters. The *Tampa* was a ship in distress and Australia provided no solution.[46] Downer made a futile call to Norway's foreign minister, Thorbjoern Jagland, urging him to get the *Tampa* to sail to Indonesia. But Jakarta and Oslo had shut the door. After dawn on 29 August, Rinnan issued a mayday and headed into Australian waters. Howard had lost another and a decisive round.

The Prime Minister's response was to escalate the conflict—the NSC decided that morning to take military action. There was no dissent. Downer rang Jagland again at 9.30 a.m. to deliver Australia's first military ultimatum to Norway. Downer said that 'entry would be in breach of international law and Australia would take whatever action was necessary'.[47] After the *Tampa* entered Australian waters at 11.39 a.m. Canberra time, the SAS boarded and took control of the ship. The SAS commander told Rinnan that the ship was to be removed from territorial waters but Rinnan refused.[48] Howard spoke to Norway's prime minister, Jens Stoltenberg, only to be frustrated by Stoltenberg's response that he had 'no responsibility' for instructing Rinnan. This, Howard said, was despite the fact that 'it is a Norwegian flagged vessel, it is a Norwegian captain and it is a Norwegian company'.

At 2 p.m. in parliament Howard announced the ship was 'in the control of the SAS'. Describing the situation as 'unprecedented' Howard drew the line, saying: 'Every nation has the right to effectively control its borders and to decide who comes here and under what circumstances, and Australia has no intention of surrendering or compromising that right.' The government would take 'whatever action is needed—within the law, of course' to stop the boat and its occupants from landing in Australia. He offered no solution whatsoever to the stand-off.[49]

In reply Kim Beazley expressed his gratitude to the SAS. 'This country and this parliament do not need a carping Opposition,' he declared. Backing Howard, he said 'landfall should take place in Indonesia'. The government, he said, 'has acted lawfully'. The problem was substantial and 'the government is seeking as best it can to resolve it'. Rarely has an Opposition been more supportive of the government.[50]

But Beazley would be broken. Howard was on the political warpath; his blood was up. He could smell the political fear in Beazley's conciliation. Now he moved with a mix of threat and bluff—against the *Tampa* and against Labor. At 5.50 p.m. Howard called Beazley to a meeting. He had a bill, he wanted to brief Beazley, it would be in the House within the hour. They met promptly with senior advisers and Beazley read it with dismay. 'I can't support this,' he told Howard. 'We'll block this in the Senate.'[51]

Called the Border Protection Bill, it was designed to intimidate the *Tampa* and test Labor. It validated retrospectively the military action taken against the *Tampa* and the ship's intended removal from territorial waters. The bill authorised Australian personnel to remove vessels from territorial waters, to board them, to remove boat people, to make arrests and to take action against any attempt to resist 'by jumping overboard'. All such actions would be excluded from challenge in any Australian court and any boat people involved in such incidents would be denied any claim for refugee status. These powers were not *Tampa*-specific.

The Labor Party was in stunned dismay. National Secretary Geoff Walsh warned Beazley that 'this could finish us'. But Beazley and his top aide, Michael Costello, were adamant. 'The bill was draconian and Beazley was completely right to refuse to accept it,' Costello said.[52] In the House, a liberated Beazley was soon roaring: 'Drag the boat out, sink it, people die. That is what this bill permits.' Australia, Beazley said, faced a serious problem, not a national catastrophe. Accusing Howard of 'wedge politics', he denounced the bill as unconstitutional. Beazley had much merit on his side but he lost the politics.[53]

The bill was defeated in the Senate and three weeks later a modified bill was passed, a vindication of Beazley's stance. But Howard's message stuck—that Beazley was a 'flip-flop' leader. 'There was a profound conviction that John Howard was taking a stand on principle,' said Beazley, 'and that the Labor Party was playing politics.'[54]

On the ocean, however, Howard took another defeat. The *Tampa* would not move, despite every threat he could muster. That left one final unpalatable but inevitable option—if he could not move the boat, he would move the people. In order to prevent the asylum seekers being processed in Australia, Howard would move them by boat to Pacific nations for processing. It would become known as the 'Pacific Solution', costly and tortuous, with the main candidates being East Timor, Papua New Guinea, Nauru and New Zealand.

This solution was procured by Australia's influence as the metropolitan power. At this moment of high risk, it was the Howard loyalists— Downer and Reith—who delivered. A desperate Downer tried to impose the *Tampa* people on East Timor before Kofi Annan vetoed the idea. He pleaded with the New Zealanders and Prime Minister Helen Clark agreed, evidence of her sound relationship with Howard. Reith and Downer worked in tandem on Nauru's President, Rene Harris, with Australia offering the bankrupt island state an initial $30 million, an outright bribe.[55] Under agreements with Nauru and Papua New Guinea, within weeks detention and processing facilities were established in those nations.

Nauru accepted 280 asylum seekers and New Zealand took 150. The latter were the lucky ones: they were processed and given refugee status in New Zealand, while the Nauru refugees had to be relocated to other nations, including Australia, as agreed by Howard. Howard stuck to his principle in defiance of the UNHCR: none of the *Tampa* people would land or be processed in Australia. Six days into the crisis, Howard and Ruddock unveiled the Pacific Solution, launching a bizarre chapter in Australian public policy. It meant that Australia could outsource detention. But it went further.

The Pacific Solution was tied to the September 2001 law to excise certain offshore territories from Australia's migration zone. Such territories could be determined by regulation decided by the minister. The initial excisions were Christmas Island, Ashmore Island, Cartier Islands and then

Cocos (Keeling) Islands. Boat people arriving at these islands (this meant most boat people) were deemed not to have entered Australia's migration zone and, as a result, they fell outside Australia's refugee protection system and the jurisdiction of Australian courts. They were shipped to Pacific islands to have their claims processed by the UNHCR and Australian officials.

Excision meant asylum seekers arriving in Australia could be expelled to other nations for processing, undermining the global regime of refugee acceptance. It had multiple consequences—it eased pressure on Australia's detention centres, removed the courts from the process and provided a disincentive to boat arrivals. Such people, even if found to be refugees, would not be eligible for permanent residence in Australia and entitled only to a TPV. Excision eases pressure on the legal system—it denies non-refugees access to the system and penalises genuine refugees.

'We worried the pipeline was getting so large it would over-run our capacity,' Ruddock said. 'So we moved on all fronts.'[56] Mocking claims that he was playing to the mob, Howard said: 'I didn't want this to happen. I didn't plan it. I didn't design it. I didn't time it. It came and I've had to deal with it and it's got nothing to do with wedge politics or racism or Hansonism.' Then he savaged Beazley for 'walking both sides of the street'.[57]

On 1 September Howard unveiled Australia's military strategy—it was the inception of Operation Relex, a fateful step for his own reputation and a victory for Moore-Wilton. The ADF would conduct surveillance, patrol and response operations in international waters between the Indonesian archipelago and Australia. It would involve five naval vessels and four P3 Orion aircraft. An ADF mission was in Jakarta to brief the Indonesians. Howard said the ADF would not engage in 'acts of belligerence' but it was 'designed to deter and [to] encourage deterrence'. The purpose, Howard said, was to stop boat people leaving Indonesia.[58]

It was a strategy of interdiction—asylum seekers would be met on the high seas and asked to turn around. If they failed then the navy was instructed to board vessels once they reached Australia's contiguous zone, take control and return the boat to international waters. If the boat people began to disable their vessels the operation would become hazardous.

Australia had never previously deployed the ADF against refugee boats; such action inflamed opinion within the UNHCR and was contrary to Australia's international obligations. Barrie was apprehensive and put his concerns to Howard:

The NSC ordered us to begin operations. I wasn't opposed to the operation. But I said in terms of the rules of engagement, nobody should lose their life. I told them this is not a military operation, we are not shooting people. If that means we don't succeed in stopping these people, than that's what it means. I made a number of points. One, we are never going to be totally successful. Second, there is a humanitarian aspect. I told the cabinet 'This is dreadful work, people have paid a lot of money to get on these boats and they will stop at nothing to get here.' If you read the records of the British blockade of Palestinian it's all there about what the Jews did.[59]

It was a warning about violence and self-harm.

Howard told the public the navy would behave with decency. 'We are Australian,' he said. 'We don't behave barbarically. We don't shoot people, we don't sink ships, but our generosity should not be abused.' It showed his genius for articulating exactly what the public wanted to hear.[60]

Operation Relex came from a prime minister confident about the exercise of power. Howard would never have done this in his first year of office, but he was different after East Timor. Under pressure the navy co-operated: it focussed on stopping the boats being disabled and getting the Indonesians to accept the boats back. For a while the towback policy was effective. Moore-Wilton praised them. 'The Indonesians, by their silence, were co-operating on the boats being towed back,' Howard said recently. 'This is how we resolved it.'[61]

But the strains were immense—within the navy, between civilians and the military, and between politicians and the military. Operation Relex did stop the boats. 'There's no doubt, the strategy worked,' Barrie says.[62]

Meanwhile Howard was humiliated by President Megawati, who refused to take his phone call. He fluctuated between resentment and restraint. 'We do not have the co-operation of countries that should be co-operating,' Howard lamented. Attributing the breakdown to the East Timor legacy, he said the relationship 'will never be the same as what it was in the Keating years', claiming it was unbalanced in those days. Howard admitted that Australia needed a Memorandum of Understanding with Indonesia and said 'we have been endeavouring to negotiate that now for months'.[63]

At this point the Federal Court intervened and found against the Howard government. An action was taken by the Victorian Council for Civil Liberties and a private solicitor, Eric Vadarlis. They had no instructions from the asylum seekers but they were given standing before the court on the basis that they were acting in the public interest. In a script worthy of Shakespearean farce the judge was Tony North, the judge from the waterfront case, and one of the barristers was Julian Burnside, who had represented the waterfront union. As David Marr said, the contest was unchanged.

North found the rescuees were being detained by the SAS and their proposed expulsion from Australia was illegal. He ordered that the *Tampa* boat people be returned to Australia and be allowed to lodge their refugee claims—a ruling that would have destroyed the entire edifice created by Howard. The government was unsurprised by North's decision. An appeal went to the full Federal Court. The day of North's ruling was 11 September 2001.

The government won the appeal 2–1, with Chief Justice Black in dissent. This decision boiled down to an issue of executive power: whether government had the power to control its borders. Justice French for the majority, later appointed Chief Justice of the High Court by Rudd, found such a sovereign power was embedded in the Constitution residing in the executive. For Howard, the final hurdle was passed. His policy would be unfurled. The lawyers had failed to stop his Tampa crackdown.

Howard and Ruddock had another temporary victory when, with Labor's nerve smashed, it gave passage to the resubmitted privative clause bill to restrict judicial review. Ruddock was ebullient. But the Gleeson High Court brought the issue to finality in February 2003 when it unanimously threw out the privative clause law. It was a humiliation for Ruddock and the executive. The High Court made clear that its jurisdiction to grant relief 'cannot be removed by or under a law made by the parliament'. Facing a genuine problem with the courts, mainly the Federal Court, Ruddock had gone for overkill and been humiliated.

After the 2003 judgment, Frank Brennan said that Ruddock had been warned and asked how he could he get it 'so wrong'. Brennan said the crisis revealed the indispensable constitutional role of the High Court whose jurisdiction cannot be contained by government.[64] The message was clear: judicial review of migration decisions would remain vigorous.

In his post-Tampa policies, Howard led public opinion. There had been almost no popular demand to stop all the boats; it grew in response to Howard's action. The policy created its own demand, igniting elements of nationalism, populism and racism, all given prime ministerial sanction. It was a stunning ten days in Australia's political history: it polarised the nation into Howard haters and Howard admirers, with a majority in

Howard's favour. It cast him as a leader of nationalist strength almost in the Billy Hughes mould and it broke Beazley's self-confidence.

Ruddock conceded that the pre-Tampa policies had been failing. 'I would have preferred that the incremental approach we took had worked and this situation [Tampa] hadn't arisen,' he said. 'That's what I would have preferred. We made incremental decisions, like the TPVs. One expects them to work. But they didn't work.'[65] Moore-Wilton saw the exercise as a triumph. He said Tampa became a 'circuit-breaker'—it enabled Howard to turn defeat on the water into victory.[66] For Howard, Tampa was the ultimate test of border protection and leadership mettle— he wanted his election campaign defined by this issue.

After the election Howard was open about the politics. 'I believe the asylum seeker issue was a major issue during the campaign,' he said, stressing that people had seen Labor as weak on border protection and the government as strong.[67] Reith said: 'To me the Tampa was an open and shut case. The government decides who comes to this country. I don't think any Australian government would take another position. I was totally comfortable with what we did.'[68]

Australia's 2001 clash over refugee policy was one of the most intense ever in a liberal democracy. But it was not unique—the Clinton administration invaded Haiti largely to curb its refugee outflow and European nations had been forced into debates about their core constitutional values in meeting the asylum seeker challenge.[69]

For half a century the organising principle of Australia's refugee policy has been control—the Howard government upheld this principle but applied it more ruthlessly. Since World War II Australia had been generous in accepting more than 500 000 refugees. They came largely via offshore processing in co-operation with the UNHCR, not arriving destitute on the country's coastline. Australia had accepted refugees from all races and religions with little aggravation, the only exception being unauthorised boat arrivals.

The prejudice against boat people had two origins: the unique Australian political compact sustaining its immigration intake that government was to control all people movement to Australia in the national interest and the public expectation that Australia, because it was an island continent, would safeguard its borders. Both were entirely reasonable public expectations. Those refugee advocates who espoused an 'open door' for boat arrivals challenged Australia's traditions, national interest and political culture.

A classic statement of contemporary Australian practice came from former DFAT chief Michael Costello:

> The world is awash with refugees. My view is that we should take as many migrants and refugees as possible. But we have a duty to ensure we don't just reward those who get here by boat and we have an obligation to the Australian people to ensure that any refugees we accept meet the standards we require as a country. This is a Labor position and a proper position. There can be no open door to Australia.[70]

When Howard became prime minister he kept the refugee and humanitarian intake at 12 000 people. But the Coalition structured the program as a zero sum game so that any upsurge in 'onshore' arrivals meant the same cut in the 'offshore' program. It was to prove that the government, not boat people, determined the total number of refugees.

The numbers of refugees estimated by the UNHCR at the start of 2001 was 12 million worldwide.[71] The communications revolution and rise of a global people-smuggling industry means that significant numbers of asylum seekers travel thousands of miles to reach their preferred destinations. This trend will only intensify.

The international instrument governing refugee flows is the 1951 United Nations Convention Relating to the Status of Refugees and it defines a 'refugee' as a person with a 'well-founded fear of being persecuted for reasons of race, religion, nationality, membership of a particular social group or political opinion'. Obligations are imposed when a person who claims refugee status arrives in a country that is party to the convention. The main obligation is 'non-refoulement'—not returning the person to possible persecution and not penalising asylum seekers who enter a country illegally.

Having prohibited refoulement the Convention offers no assistance to host nations that incur such obligations. It takes no account of the political or social impact of accepting asylum seekers in large numbers, nor does it impose sanctions on nations that persecute or expel their own people.[72]

The politics surrounding this convention have been transformed over the past half-century. Most Western states would probably not sign it today, because the convention was written for events that no longer exist—a world shocked by the Nazis and the Holocaust and gripped by the Cold War.[73] The Convention was a powerful instrument during the Cold War when refugees were relatively few in number, when they served as propaganda pawns in the conflict and when refugee flows in the developing world remained within the region of origin, hardly affecting Europe, North America or Australia.[74]

The end of the Cold War changed everything—industrialised nations faced 'floods of people of all ages, skills and backgrounds', with criminals and undesirables joining with 'normal citizens seeking asylum in the West where they would be greeted with as much enthusiasm as a plague of locusts'.[75]

The political rationale for the 1951 Convention no longer exists. It has been replaced by a humanitarian rationale. The absence of a national interest policy for accepting large numbers of refugees is fundamental to the current global debate. At the same time, the lines between economic migrants and refugees have blurred in a way that the 1951 Convention did not anticipate. The Australian public can hardly be blamed for concluding that asylum seekers who travel halfway around the globe and through many nations to reach Australia are also seeking a migrant outcome.[76]

The Convention's definition of persecution as a hostile act by the state against the individual has been overshadowed by a new paradigm: the contagion of failed states. Many asylum seekers since the 1980s have fled not because of state persecution but as a consequence of state failure and do not strictly meet the Convention's definition.

The Convention, however, remains the only instrument short of global anarchy. Professor William Maley says:

> The claim that the Refugee Convention is not working as it was intended in 1951 is spurious. Unquestionably, more people now fall within the definition of refugees in the Convention than its originators expected. The refugee crisis is actually a crisis of moral failure as states seek to shed obligations which they freely entered.[77]

In her speech marking the fiftieth anniversary of the Convention, Erica Feller, a senior UNHCR official, warned that 'resolute leadership is called for to de-dramatise and depoliticize the essentially humanitarian challenge of protecting refugees … Responsibility for such a trust must be shared by many, or it will be borne by no one.'[78]

Ruddock branded as 'obscene' the attacks on Australia's border protection when Australia was one of only eleven nations taking an annual quota of refugees from UNHCR camps. Howard said: 'We, of course, take more refugees on a per capita basis than any other country in the world after Canada, so nobody can accuse Australia of being hard-hearted.'[79] But the accuracy of this claim did not stand up.[80] Its moral presumption is dubious. It is no answer, as Brennan argued, to say 'we close the door on the asylum seeker at our doorstep in order more readily to assist the refugee in the faraway camp'.[81] If Howard's Australia was so filled with compassion, he would have increased the offshore program—yet that remained largely frozen.

The longer Ruddock spent studying the issues, the more obsessive he became. 'We had a lot of intelligence,' he said.

> Smugglers were saying we can get you into Australia. People would be briefed on the questions that our interviewing officers would ask. As part of the 'natural justice loop' we gave former detainees their interview tapes and these tapes were sold on the black market in the Middle East. People would turn up knowing what questions were going to be asked. When we changed the questions, they started to object. If I care about refugees then giving places to people who fabricate a story serves no public policy.[82]

Moore-Wilton saw the entire process as a criminal fraud.

> There's no doubt what our judgement was. It was largely a criminal process with an economic basis, not a refugee basis. Now, the refugee advocates never accepted that. But many of the people coming basically wanted to escape to a new life in Australia.[83]

'If you look at these populations in Teheran, Damascus and Amman, when the UNHCR did the processing you had about 10 per cent accepted as refugees,' Ruddock says.

> By the time these people got through Australia's processing the figure was about 90 per cent. It built an expectation that nobody knew how to prove whether or not you were a refugee. While refugees have a right to protection, they do not have a right to choose the country that provides the protection.[84]

The fate of the *Tampa* people reveals the uncertain nature of refugee determination. Virtually all of the 131 who went to New Zealand were found to be refugees. Of the remaining 302 on Nauru, a total of 115 were found to be refugees and were resettled, with Australia taking 28 people.

But a majority, a total of 186, returned voluntarily to the home country, mainly Afghanistan after the fall of the Taliban regime. They either did not succeed with their claim or abandoned their claim in frustration.[85]

There was a non-negotiable reality. Any Australian government, Liberal or Labor, will seek to halt asylum seeker boats. This is the lesson of history and it will not change. The Australian public accepts a large and controlled annual migration intake—and it is unlikely to tolerate significant numbers of boat arrivals self-selecting Australia. Such voyages to Australia are hazardous and promote a sinister industry. They constitute a failure of international and regional agreements.

Asked what he would have done as prime minister, Beazley says:

> The *Tampa* would have made landfall and the people would have been processed in Australia. But the main thing is we would have done whatever was required to keep agreement with Indonesia. If we had had to pay big money, then we would have paid. I believe in effective border protection. A hard line is essential for Australia. My objection to Howard was more method than principle.[86]

At the 2007 election Kevin Rudd took a hard line against boat people. He said a Labor government would take rescued asylum seekers to Christmas Island and, in relation to seaworthy vessels, 'you'd turn them back'. Committed to the idea of orderly migration, Rudd said he would not allow people 'who do not have a lawful visa in this country to roam free. That's why you need detention.' In office, however, he made significant reforms—he abandoned the Pacific Solution, abolished TPVs and softened the detention regime. It was the latest quest to find a better balance.[87]

In 2001 Australia was trapped in a universal conflict: refugee rights were being expanded by lawyers, statutes, constitutions and judicial decisions in the name of human rights—yet governments were limiting such rights via detention, visa restrictions, greater border controls and judicial crackdowns.

The Tampa affair penetrated to this challenge facing the nation state. It is a contest between competing rights—the right of democracies to decide who joins their societies and the right of refugees to find a better life. There are no absolute answers, just a recurring struggle of politics, law and public opinion to find the balance.

The art of statecraft is to manage this contradiction. The extremity of Howard's solution betrayed an over-reaction and a departure from the enlightened self-interest that guides Australian immigration policy at its best. His response elicited some of the worst, not the best, in the Australian community. Menzies once said of immigration, referring to White Australia, that 'it is our duty to ourselves to handle this policy so that it is presented to the rest of the world in its proper terms and in its true light'. It was a wise principle that Howard breached.[88]

Beazley was right to say that Australia did not face a national catastrophe. It was Howard's action that exaggerated the crisis and his punitive policies were necessary primarily because Australia had not negotiated adequate regional agreements, notably with Indonesia. Despite this, Howard's critics were conspicuous in their failure to offer an alternative solution that would halt the boats—this remains their enduring weakness and the ultimate vindication that Howard will claim: he did the job. The lesson for his successors is to show that a better path exists.

39

THE SEDUCTION OF BUSH

This is a guy you can go on a long patrol with.
—Richard Armitage, describing George W Bush's
initial reaction to John Howard

John Howard saw George W Bush coming. During the 2000 US election he secretly cheered Bush on, convinced that Bush would be his type of president. The Howard cabinet was totally and not universally discreet in its partisanship. 'He's our kind of guy,' Downer had told Howard after meeting Bush when he was governor of Texas.[1]

Howard and Downer were appalled by future Democrat nominee Al Gore. They saw Gore as far to Bill Clinton's left, unsympathetic to Australia, a quasi-protectionist, weak on Asia and hostile to Coalition values. 'Gore had shown no interest in Australia,' Downer said. 'He was cold, aloof, distant and unfriendly.'[2]

During his visit to the United States in 1999, Downer flew to the Texas capital, Austin, to meet Bush, acting on Andrew Peacock's advice. He was accompanied by his aide, Greg Hunt. Bush had a huge office with floor-to-ceiling wood panelling and shelves without a single book, just sporting memorabilia. 'Downer and Bush clicked over two items,' Hunt said, 'free trade and East Asia policy.'[3]

Downer recalls: 'We got on like a house on fire. He was enormously positive about Australia. We had more than an hour together and I nearly missed the plane back to Washington. I reported back to Howard. It helped to generate our enthusiasm about Bush.'[4]

Howard and Downer had picked Bush a long way out. Peacock, with his excellent Republican ties and links to the Bush family, had made a superb call. Howard was keen to see a Republican succeed Clinton, and Bush had obvious advantages. While Howard had not met Bush, he was known within Bush's political constellation. 'I got on well with his father,' Howard said. 'I had met his father way back in 1986 when I was Opposition leader and he was vice-president.' But Howard knew Bush's running mate, Dick Cheney, and they had three or four meetings between 1996 and 2000 when Howard was PM. 'Every time Cheney came he asked to see me. He was a useful contact,' Howard said.[5]

Australia would have no greater friend in the Bush administration than Deputy Secretary of State, Richard Armitage. 'I dealt with John Howard on and off for twenty-five years,' Armitage said. 'I met him first in the early 1980s when he was not in government and I briefed him on the "Star Wars" concept. I decided he was a small man in stature who had real balls.'[6]

Howard felt sure he could do business with George W Bush—and he was right, beyond his dreams.

Howard and Bush would create a New Intimacy, verifying that Australian–American relations were shaped by the personal bonds between leaders as well as enduring national interest. They would forge the closest personal relationship between an Australian prime minister and a US president, closer than that of Harold Holt and Lyndon Johnson in the 1960s. The New Intimacy was about politics. Howard and Bush were political soul mates who saw more of each other and spoke more with each other than any of their predecessor pairings. It became a mutual loyalty.

'I liked Bush,' Howard said. 'I am by nature somebody who doesn't run away from friendships with people. I found him a highly intelligent, well briefed person whose public communications skills were not as strong as I am sure he would have wanted but who privately was a well organised person with a relatively clear view of the world and of people.'[7]

From the start, Howard's aspiration had been to bring Australia and the United States closer together. He said: 'From the moment of our election in 1996, as a deliberate act of policy, my government intensified Australia's post-Cold War relationship with the United States.'[8] But the dream had not been realised.

'Bill Clinton wasn't his kind of American,' Philip Flood said. 'Howard got on much better with Republicans than Democrats but he got on best with British Tories.'[9] Years later Howard was sensitive to claims about a poor relationship with Clinton. 'It was better than has been recorded,' he said. 'Our relationship was friendly.'[10]

The truth is that Howard and Clinton never clicked, though they worked effectively together over East Timor. Beyond this, Howard seemed lost for any strategy to actually bring Australia and America closer together. 'Howard had great trouble giving effect to this aspiration,' Hugh White said. 'He didn't have a good personal relationship with Bill Clinton, didn't mount any substantial initiatives and very little happened in the first few years.'[11] Reflecting on his appointment as Ambassador to the United States in 1999, Michael Thawley said: 'Howard wanted to consolidate the relationship but he didn't have in mind any great initiative at that point.'[12]

The first meeting with Clinton came during the President's 1996 visit. The Howards, John and Janette, seemed out of their depth. Clinton delivered a brilliant speech to the Australian Parliament, flew to Sydney where he praised Australia's multiculturalism and then repaired to Port Douglas to make a scarcely veiled criticism of Howard's reticence about global warming. The lack of rapport between the Howards and Clintons was apparent during the dinner on Sydney Harbour and was conspicuous between Janette and Hillary.[13] These wives came from different planets.

In mid-1996 the Howard government had window-dressed a Sydney Declaration for the annual Australia–United States ministerial talks— it upgraded a series of activities begun under Labor, branding them a 'reinvigoration' of the partnership. The Americans played the game under the Sydney sunshine at Watson's Bay. 'The Sydney Declaration came from the advisory system,' White said. 'It wasn't a Howard initiative at all.'[14]

Downer said later: 'When I first met Warren Christopher, the Secretary of State, he said to me: "I'll call you Alex, you call me Chris." I thought, "Fuck, what's this?"' But he was a charming guy. You know, we were pro-American, we believe in democracy, freedom, the liberal market and capitalism. We believe in the US role in East Asia through its alliances. This is emotional and intellectual. The Clinton administration was very warm to us.'[15] Downer was happier when Madeleine Albright, feisty and engaging, moved into State.

White was struck by Howard's lack of curiosity about the security aspects of the alliance. When White briefed senior ministers on Pine Gap he sensed their surprise at Labor's boldness in being willing to upgrade its functions from intelligence to war fighting. The Howard government signed on the dotted line.[16]

During the Clinton administration, Howard made two unremarkable visits to Washington, conspicuous for their lack of content, ideas and political orchestration. He had little to offer and the Australian Embassy effort was woeful.

Howard failed to grasp that Clinton was an 'ideas' politician. 'I think we hadn't realised just how clever and how intelligent Clinton was,' Flood said of the 1997 visit. 'It wasn't a warm meeting.'[17] It was, however, the sort of meeting where Keating would have thrived. Clinton ranged over global issues with great authority while the Australians did not impress; Howard seemed an amateur.[18] Michael Gordon wrote that 'he stuck to an agenda so narrow as to hint at a diminished role for Australia in international affairs'.[19]

Despite his alliance posturing, Howard was more comfortable on the economy. His hopes for this first visit were not realised despite good meetings with new Defense Secretary William Cohen and Republicans such as Trent Lott and Colin Powell. The cynics said Howard preferred seeing the out-of-power Republicans.

The 1999 visit was derailed by a dispute over Australia's lamb exports to the United States. 'We got a message saying "Do you want to be hit with lamb tariffs before Washington or after Washington?"' Thawley said. 'I told Peacock he should tell the Americans this was an appalling way to treat us and we would be very aggressive, that it would become a focus of Howard's meeting with Clinton.'[20] It went downhill from this point. Clinton's political friends in the United States Senate needed their lamb market protected, so the barriers were a given.

But Clinton was late for the meeting; Howard was kept waiting in a car in the rain. The talks hardly lasted thirty minutes. An Australian official who attended said: 'There was no time for any real discussion, no Rose Garden event. It was polite but nothing more. The Clinton White House was very self-absorbed.'[21]

The White House had beforehand refused any joint media conference. 'It was clear Howard would get stuck into them and the Americans were quite agitated,' Thawley said.[22] Howard said later: 'We were cranky about lamb. Whereas the Bush administration within thirty-six hours fixed the problem with steel tariffs, the Clinton administration did nothing about lamb. It sort of makes the point.'[23] It revealed Australia's lack of sway with the Clinton administration, the political failure of the Australian Embassy and the absence of any Clinton–Howard commitment to manage the relationship to avoid such damaging 'optics'.

This was a Conservative Australia adjusting to a Democrat America, with the periodic tribulations it entailed. Howard came to the alliance absent of any of the romantic, literary or historical infatuation with the United States displayed by Labor Party luminaries such as Bob Carr, Kim Beazley and Stephen Loosley. As Howard remarked, he was not living a love affair with America. 'I am not as sentimental about America as some Labor people,' he said. 'America is a "good in parts" country. I like their cordiality and politeness, particularly the North-Easterners, but I can't abide their lack of a decent social safety net and their gun culture. I do hold the view that we have similar values and I guess someone of my generation is influenced by the attitudes I formed towards America in World War II.'[24]

Howard's style, unlike Keating's, was to avoid grand initiatives. He knew there would be no bold schemes with Clinton. So he waited on events. His instincts told him Bush was the US partner that he needed.

Howard and Downer's hopes for Bush were vested in two areas that had seen problems with Clinton: free trade and Asian policy. Ashton Calvert said: 'We felt the Clinton administration lacked a sure touch dealing with Asia. But the big event was Clinton's failure at the Seattle WTO meeting. This was a turning point.'[25]

The 1999 Seattle meeting was the zenith of the anti-globalisation street protesters but it has a far greater importance. Hosted by America, the talks were the chance to establish a new global trade round ('the Clinton round') but they collapsed under accumulated rifts between the United States and the EU. The Australians never forgave Clinton. For Howard, Downer and Trade Minister Mark Vaile, it was inexcusable weakness. A believer in free trade, Clinton abandoned any claim to global leadership by championing the insertion of labour rights in the negotiations, the main demand of the US trade unions and their mechanism to retain protectionism.

The ever-cautious Vaile branded the meeting 'a debacle—we could have run the thing a lot better in Australia; in fact, it could have been run a lot better in many parts of the world.'[26] The cause of world trade liberalisation seemed unlikely to recover.

Failure at Seattle would help give Howard what he had needed and had been missing—a big idea with America. Howard would not just *support* Bush; he would have a radical idea to put to Bush, a Free Trade Agreement (FTA) between Australia and the United States after the World Trade Organization (WTO) failure. It was a dramatic departure from Australia's strategic tradition. There was a strange beauty to the politics— in the mechanism where Clinton had failed, the Howard government discerned the key to its approach to Bush.

The eighteen months before Bush's victory saw a radical rethink of Australia's trade policy driven by several forces.

For fifteen years under Labor and the Coalition, Australia's trade diplomacy had been dedicated to multilateral liberalisation—the achievement of legally binding lower trade barriers implemented on a universal basis involving all WTO nations. For Australia, the fourteenth largest economy with a tiny domestic market of 20 million people and no trade bloc to join, a liberal global trade system was fundamental. Australian ministers, officials and academics had made this a national priority and Australia's role in such negotiations had been substantial. Labor's successes were its establishment of the Cairns Group of agricultural nations, its role in the Uruguay Round, which produced significant liberalisation, and its APEC trade initiatives. While global liberalisation was the superior path, it had become more difficult to win unanimous support from all WTO members to realise this agenda. Seattle told the Howard government that support for a new global deal was weak.

In its 1997 White Paper the Howard government had committed to the principle of bilateral trade agreements as well as regional and global negotiations. Within the Asia-Pacific there was growing interest in bilateral deals as insurance against a multilateral failure. Japan, Singapore, New Zealand, South Korea, Chile and Canada were pushing these alternatives.

Another factor driving Howard to a trade deal with America was an Asian 'closed door' against Australia. In October 2000 in Chiang Mai, ASEAN ministers rejected a recommendation from a region-wide officials committee that negotiations should begin on a free trade area that encompassed the ten nations of South-East Asia, Australia and New Zealand. This idea, predating Howard, would come to fruition finally under Kevin Rudd. In the late 1990s it was strongly backed by Downer, who was keen to see Australia integrated into ASEAN's trade system. But this recommendation was rejected by Asian ministers on blatant political grounds, with Malaysia and Indonesia leading the rejection.

Australia would keep trying, but Downer drew the lesson. 'You can't keep running a policy that doesn't work,' he said. 'You have to find a policy that makes progress.'[27] Asia had shut the door on Australia. So Howard and Downer would ride with America.

The final factor driving Howard to an FTA initiative was the hyper-power status of the United States. Howard was a believer in the rise and rise of America. He said the Americans 'are still the best exponents of capitalism and they are going to be the strongest economy in the world until the end of time, that's my view'.[28] This remarkable comment meant Howard had no time for weighty analysis of what may or may not happen to the United States over the next ten or twenty years—his instinct told him America would be Number One forever. He made policy on that basis.

For Howard, Downer and Vaile, the chance to institutionalise closer US links was a plus. The National Party knew agricultural access would be hard but it would take whatever access was available. A champion of the FTA, former Australian trade ambassador Alan Oxley said: 'In the twenty-first century the US will be the pumping, throbbing heart of the world economy. The benchmarks for global competitiveness are now being set and constantly revised in the US economy.'[29] This was Howard's song.

In the vast literature on this subject, the US 'revival' was dated from the fall of the Berlin Wall to the Clinton-era IT-driven boom on Wall Street. Information age industries were seen as a 'third industrial revolution' that would keep America the dominant nation for another century. Historian Paul Kennedy, who had previously written of US decline, said its combined economic and military power, in relative terms, exceeded that of the Roman Empire. Howard felt that the US alliance was looking a better investment than ever.

The pipe-player in the seduction of Bush would be Thawley. Appointed as Washington ambassador, Thawley came with diplomatic experience, lots of energy and intellectual passion. At his farewell party, Howard said to Thawley and his wife, Debbie, 'Don't forget our association, will you.' It struck Thawley as odd. After all, he was going to Washington to work for Howard. Yet it was typical of Howard's understated style: in effect, he was authorising Thawley, as a public servant, to contact him directly as required.[30] For Thawley, all the planets would come into alignment.

When Thawley arrived, the Democrats were in the ascendancy. But Thawley was not so convinced. Six months into the presidential election year, after surveying the landscape, Thawley wrote a note to Howard:

> I said the election was Gore's to lose but that he might lose it. If Bush won, there were things we would have to think about. By that time I had held a couple of conversations with Condi Rice. The message was they would take us seriously and, therefore, they would have expectations of us. I said Bush would have a more strategic interest in Asia than Clinton. The third point was trade. I said Bush would be a free trader, he would go for regional and bilateral stuff and he would put an emphasis on South America and Mexico. We would have an opening to pursue a trade relationship. The issue for Australia was whether we wanted to pursue that in a group or bilaterally.[31]

Events now moved quickly. The contest looked tight, but Thawley's hope was that Bush could win. While staying in contact with the Democrats, he invested in the Republican 'brains trust'—Rice, Bob Zoellick and Armitage, the latter two veterans from past Republican administrations. This is where the value of Phillip Scanlan's Australian American Leadership Dialogue became manifest—Armitage and Zoellick were not just participants, they were believers; for years they had given the Australian relationship their time and energy, attending repeated dialogue meetings in both nations and, in the process, establishing wide contacts among Australians as well as becoming invaluable contact points for a range of Australians.

Thawley canvassed views with senior Republicans and then reported to Howard. As the year advanced, Thawley's optimism was based on two signals Bush was sending—he wanted to champion free trade and to strengthen US alliances in the Pacific. This was Australia's script. Somewhere in that complex of streets between the Australian Embassy on Scott Circle and the locations of the Republican players hoping to assume executive power, Thawley found his own road to Damascus—he became a convert. He decided a free trade agreement with the United States was 'absolutely essential'.[32] This would become the purpose of his ambassadorship.

At the 2000 Australian American Leadership Dialogue in Washington, senior Republicans close to Bush were open about his plans. Philip Zelikow, who had worked for George H Bush and who would become principal architect of the 9/11 Report, said: 'In a George W Bush administration there will be a significant initiative of some kind on free trade. The Governor has a personal commitment to this. Bush and his advisers are open to regional and bilateral trade agreements.' It was more than an invitation; it was a warning that if Australia didn't act, it would be left behind.[33]

In Canberra, Downer and Vaile were enthusiastic. Calvert was a strong supporter. But Thawley's advice to Howard and Howard's conclusion were the key. Thawley judged it was achievable. 'Many people thought we were mad,' he said. 'They thought we'd never get it.'[34]

In late 2000, before the US election, the Howard cabinet decided to seek an FTA with America. It was not contingent on Bush, but realism dictated it could only occur with Bush. It revealed Howard's priority in economics—after four years in power his major initiative with America was not security-based but economic. But it gave Howard a strategic focus—the seduction of Bush was about persuading him to an FTA.

This decision made the Howard 'insiders' even more pledged to a Bush victory. 'Nobody knows how much we wanted Bush to win,' Downer said.[35] Hunt said: 'I think the Bush project helped to bring Howard and Downer closer together. They had a shared vision that others didn't see.'[36] When Gore, as Democratic nominee, began campaigning on environmental policy and labour rights, the Howard cabinet was horrified. 'We felt a Gore presidency would be very bad for Australia,' Downer said.[37]

This was not, in pure form, a trade decision for trade reasons. Downer had put the case: 'An FTA would be an opportunity to render our economic relationship with the United States on the same sort of footing as our political relationship, which is expressed overwhelmingly—and highly successfully—through our security alliance.'[38]

It repudiated the Australian tradition of separating the alliance from trade. Given the resentment of the US farm lobby towards Australia, trade tensions were seen as a threat to the security partnership. Now Howard wanted to reverse the model—to extend the formal partnership into the economic and trade area.

For Thawley, the FTA was more about investment than trade. He argued that the advantage of getting closer to the United States was 'the technology, the competition, for our entrepreneurs and professional classes, of being part of the wider world'.[39] He attacked the narrow focus on agriculture when dealing with the United States. Australia's exports to America were weak but investment was strong, with Australian business US-fixated. The United States was Australia's largest source of foreign investment while Australia was the eighth largest investor in America. Australians were deeply involved in News Corporation, Cola–Cola, Ford, Philip Morris and the World Bank.[40]

There was a history to the FTA idea that had seen Ross Garnaut killing it off. The idea had arisen periodically as a US initiative, then in 1985 US Deputy Special Trade Representative Mike Smith spoke to Garnaut, as Hawke's economic adviser.[41] Smith said that the United States might be interested in a bilateral FTA and would take the issue further 'if Australia were interested'. The Hawke government commissioned a paper by a prominent multilateral free trader, Professor Richard Snape, which dismissed the concept. The upshot was that Garnaut and Smith agreed that both nations should stick by a global strategy in what became the Uruguay Round.[42]

In 1998, the US Special Trade Representative in the Clinton administration, Charlene Barshefsky, raised with Tim Fischer the notion of the

P5, a free trade agreement involving the United States, Australia, Chile, New Zealand and Singapore. The P5 trade ministers met to discuss the concept. Fischer was interested but Thawley said it wasn't going anywhere. He told Howard to wait for Bush.[43]

The cabinet decision would run into hostility from the Trade Policy Orthodoxy, located at the ANU. 'This would be an historic and false step for Australia,' Garnaut said immediately. Unfazed by vague talk about getting closer to the United States, he insisted on a trade analysis and concluded that the gains were small. He warned that the United States would not permit access to agriculture—the principal benefit for Australia—and warned that the FTA would discriminate against Asia, our main trading partner, and was therefore a 'no-brainer'. Garnaut said: 'It is the wrong moment to compound a drift in regional sentiment against Australia by introducing discrimination against East Asia into our trade relations with the US.'[44]

A different perspective came from Keating's former aide and Washington ambassador Don Russell, a free-trader like Garnaut. While Russell was sceptical about the benefits, he saw a political logic: convinced the United States would go the path of special deals corrupting trade policy, the real case for the FTA was defensive, to help buttress Australia's market share in the United States from political assault by others.

From this point Howard's long run of luck kicked in. Bush beat Gore in a tight election and he appointed Zoellick as the United States Special Trade Representative. On Thawley's advice, Howard formally wrote to Bush in March–April 2001 proposing the FTA. A few weeks later Bush replied, saying that any FTA had to be comprehensive, a promise that he later broke. The Australian campaign had begun; it revolved around Thawley.

Given the concern of the US farm sector, Zoellick was initially wary. 'He told me he was committed to getting there but he wanted to do it at his own pace,' Thawley said.[45] But Thawley had his own timetable— Howard was planning to visit the United States around September 2001 to meet Bush for the first time and Thawley knew an agreement to negotiate the FTA must become the centrepiece of that meeting. 'My aim was a commitment by September,' he said.[46] This was ambitious but Thawley's judgement was correct: there was always a long queue in Washington, and Australia had to be aggressive.

In March, Downer visited Washington, where he found a congenial climate; the potential for a deeper partnership with Bush was palpable. The Bush administration looked more capable (a misleading perception) and many were friends of Australia. Bush was supported by Cheney, Defence Secretary Donald Rumsfeld, Secretary of State Colin Powell (with Armitage as his deputy), National Security Adviser Condoleezza Rice and Zoellick at trade. Downer's first impression was their greater interest in the Asia–Pacific.

The United States saw the FTA in alliance terms. Powell said that Australia was one of America's 'very, very best friends in the world', praised its East Timor role and said he would never call Australia a deputy sheriff. He branded the FTA 'a good idea', saying that when Howard visited 'it will be one of the top items on the agenda'.[47] 'I did whatever I could on the FTA,' Armitage said.[48] It was treated as the request of a close ally, unlike a similar request from New Zealand.

But Zoellick had to manage the business end—and it was riddled with traps. He told Downer that Bush had an ambitious free trade agenda linked to broader economic and security aims. Success, however, depended on domestic politics since under the US Constitution the trade power rested with the legislature. The pivotal decision was to persuade Congress to grant the executive the required trade authority—called 'fast track', it meant that once trade deals negotiated by the administration went to the legislature for approval, amendments were not allowed. The deal had to be accepted or rejected. This process empowered the executive—but everything depended on prior Congressional approval. For Zoellick, nothing could prejudice his Congressional campaign for 'fast track'.

Downer said:

> I spent a lot of time persuading Powell the FTA was a good idea. When I saw Zoellick I pushed very hard. The truth is that these were political decisions. They weren't really trade decisions. They involved political judgements based on our relationships with Bush, Powell, Armitage and Zoellick. We knew them all.[49]

Zoellick had two related aims. First, coming to power after the Seattle debacle, Bush wanted to launch a new global trade round. This would be achieved at Doha in 2002 with Australian support. Second, Bush wanted to initiate new regional and bilateral FTAs off the back of the highly successful North American Free Trade Agreement (NAFTA) and his priority area was Latin America. Zoellick called this dual strategy 'competitive liberalisation'.

While under pressure from the US farm lobby, Zoellick gave Downer a provisional commitment on the Australian FTA. 'I'm pleased with the way it's going,' Downer said after their meeting. 'There's no doubt they were nervous about us pushing ahead too fast,' Thawley said. 'The White House wanted us to build Congressional support and a business coalition and we did these things.'[50] Downer went to Capitol Hill to raise the FTA direct with the Congress, a prelude to Thawley's intense campaign on the Hill over the next two years.

The groundwork for Howard's 2001 US visit was the most elaborate since his 1997 visit to China. This was facilitated by the arrival in Canberra of a new US ambassador, a business intimate of Bush and a former Texas politician, Tom Schieffer, whose brother Bob was a prominent US journalist. Schieffer, more a personal envoy, was batting for the FTA. 'It wasn't easy, it was the only point of contention in the lead-up to the [Howard–Bush] meeting,' Schieffer said.[51] A lot of preliminary work was done at trade minister level.

After Howard's arrival in Washington, Thawley hosted a barbecue of Australian lamb at the residence on Sunday evening, 9 September, under the magnificent trees at the onset of fall. It was an A-list of guests, a sign of Howard's growing status—the Cheneys, the Powells, the Rumsfelds, military chiefs, Supreme Court judges, nearly a third of the cabinet and White House staffers. Howard's transformation in Washington from outsider to valued guest was complete. No Australian leader had ever pulled such a Sunday-night gathering of the great and powerful. Weary with jet lag, he was keen to follow the tennis. At one point, Howard retreated inside to watch the coverage as Lleyton Hewitt defeated Pete Sampras to win his first US open. The Howards were euphoric. One Australian observer was unimpressed: 'It soon became apparent that the Prime Minister had nothing to say to one of the most influential audiences he will ever have.'[52]

Many Washingtonians would recall this evening with a nostalgic sadness—it was the final curtain on an age about to die. Just thirty-six hours later America would be attacked in New York and at the Pentagon. It would inaugurate a new age of terrorism, foreign wars, domestic security, repressive national security laws and, within America, a sense of embattlement. Thawley said: 'I would often meet people who would raise that evening with me, saying how much they enjoyed it and lamenting that it was the end of the era.'[53]

The next morning Howard went into his meeting with Bush with confidence. 'I think that's true,' he said when asked if he sensed beforehand they would click.[54] They had spoken on the phone—once before Bush had become president and once more recently, when Bush had called Howard the day after Don Bradman died.[55]

It was the fiftieth anniversary year of ANZUS and Howard met Bush at the naval yard when the President handed over the bell of the USS *Canberra*, named by Franklin Roosevelt after the HMAS *Canberra* was sunk by the Japanese in 1942. They had a chat and drove back to the White House together for formal talks, a joint appearance at the White House Rose Garden and lunch.

Howard spent about three hours with Bush, an unusually long time for such an encounter, longer than Rudd's initial meeting with Barack Obama. The contrast with Howard's two meetings with Clinton was stark. For Thawley, they connected, finally, in the White House talks. 'Up to that point they'd had some conversation but they hadn't actually clicked,' he said.[56] Bush and Howard saw they were fellow conservatives, free traders and values politicians. 'He was obviously briefed and he had worked out that it would be a very important relationship,' Howard said.[57] Howard liked Bush and was impressed by him. That Bush's father was invited to lunch was a tribute to Howard.

Armitage said: 'I was at the lunch and it was clear to me that either 41 [Bush Snr] had told his son "this is a guy you can go on a long patrol with" or 43 [George W] had already figured that for himself. There was no lull in this conversation.'[58]

In the Rose Garden, Howard declared that he and Bush were 'very close friends'. For Howard, always cautious about personal rapport, it was an unusual sign of his confidence. Bush said 'if there is any place that is like Texas, it's Australia', a highly dubious claim. The Bush–Howard show was rolling.

This was a different Howard because it was a different America. During these 10 September talks Howard saw Bush, Powell, Zoellick, Rice and Armitage. He later told the media the relationship 'couldn't be in better shape'. The Republicans were his political companions. They seemed more interested in Australia and the region than the Democrats. And Howard felt more comfortable with them.

Australia knew beforehand that Bush could not commit formally to the FTA at this meeting. Zoellick had to get Congressional approval for 'fast track' before any commitment to a negotiation with Australia. But Howard was confident; Bush gave him a positive signal. A joint statement said the trade ministers would report back before the end of year on progress. There is no doubt that Howard exaggerated the gains for Australia in an FTA and underestimated the ferocity of the American negotiators. 'We paid a price for the FTA but there will be benefits,' Russell said later.[59] For Howard, the FTA was a bigger project—a strategic initiative as well as an economic initiative. Unaware what the next day, 11 September, would bring, the FTA was the tangible expression of his success with Bush.

Years later Downer had no doubt who made the FTA possible. 'Bush delivered this himself,' he said. 'It had his stamp. Nothing would have happened with Gore. These were political decisions based on our relationships with Bush, Powell, Armitage and Zoellick.'[60]

Howard had bonded with Bush on 10 September, signalling a new era for the alliance. That evening he dined with Rupert Murdoch at the Occidental Grill, adjacent to the Willard Hotel, around the corner from the White House.

40

BROTHERS-IN-ARMS

Of course, it's an attack on all of us.
—John Howard, 12 September 2001

T he bond John Howard and George W Bush created on 10 September took a gigantic leap the next day—they became brothers-in-arms after Islamist terrorists attacked the American homeland. Howard's political life, from Earlwood to Kirribilli, had been a preparation for this moment. His heart and brain were in alignment—John Winston Howard was going to war alongside George W Bush.

The 9/11 attack on the United States is the origin of Australia's commitments to Afghanistan and Iraq and its closer strategic, military and intelligence ties with the United States. Having pondered about how to bring Australia and America into a closer strategic partnership Howard got his answer in the most brutal manner. The 9/11 attack enabled Howard to realise his strategy.

A few days later Howard said: 'There's no point in a situation like this being an 80 per cent ally.'[1] Howard chose to become a 100 per cent US ally. It was fatuous to think he would support the United States in Afghanistan but avoid Iraq—that would have been a violation of Howard's history, character and faiths.

This crisis ignited Howard's three beliefs about the US alliance— that it was about national interest, it was about the values of Western civilisation and it meant either side must support the other in war. He projected confidence in a setting of alarm, death and grief.

The significance of Howard being in Washington at this time has been misunderstood—Howard would have made the commitments to Afghanistan and Iraq anyway. Moreover, his meetings with Bush had been completed the previous day. The significance arises because

Howard responded in an act of supreme prime ministerial authority that dramatised and personalised Australia's reaction and placed it on an open-ended strategic basis.

Howard was the only allied leader in the US capital. This put him in a unique situation. He responded not just as a US ally but as a leader expressing personal empathy with the American people and its leaders—and Howard was conscious of this mission. Ashton Calvert said: 'He understood this was America's hour of need and he was aware, being in Washington, that what he said as a US ally would be very important, the form of words would be important.'[2]

Working from the sub-basement of the Australian Embassy after the attack, Howard drafted a short message for Bush, offering 'Australia's resolute solidarity with the American people at this most tragic time'. But when the US Ambassador to Australia, Tom Schieffer, arrived in the basement, Howard's response as an individual was far less restrained. Schieffer said: 'When they told him I was there, he literally ran out of his office, came over and embraced me and said "we're with you on this, we're going to help you". Well, it was very emotional. I can't remember exactly what I said. It was only later I realised how unusual it was for John Howard to do something like that.'[3]

It was Schieffer who captured the proximity of the crisis for Howard: 'You never had to convince John Howard afterwards that this was a real threat to civilisation, this was a real threat to Western values and ideas. He saw that and he understood that.'[4] It is one reason he was always so supportive of Bush—Howard had been there.

The 9/11 attack invested the Howard–Bush relationship with an emotional bond and a shared strategic conviction—they became warriors together. Although they did not see each other in the days after the attack, Howard felt America's grief, sensed its will to retaliate, shared its horror at the attacks and pledged to fight alongside its forces. Being there made Howard aware of American vulnerability. Max Moore-Wilton said:

> The thing was so brutal, so large, so encompassing. Nobody had seen America destabilised like this. On 9/11 and the next day, Washington closed down, the bureaucrats were told to stay home, the streets were empty, there were no aeroplanes in the sky. This had never happened before. The impact on American psyche was huge.[5]

Schieffer articulated what must have flashed across Howard's mind:

What if those guys had decided to do this yesterday instead of today? We would all have been at the White House and you don't know whether the plane that went down in Pennsylvania would have gotten through, we would have had the President, the Vice-President, the Prime Minister all there at once.[6]

There is a near-consensus on Howard's personal response to the crisis—that it was effective, controlled and instinctual. Its impact on the Americans he saw was enduring. It was as though the crisis applied a magnifying glass to his entire visit—everything loomed much larger, the memories were sharper, the emotions were more engaged, the personal ties ran deeper.

In a rare moment, the 9/11 attack annihilated domestic politics. Howard's response was endorsed by the Labor Party and the Australian public. For a few weeks he acted as leader of the nation until, gradually, domestic politics was resumed. When this happened, however, the political climate had been transformed—from 9/11 Howard would become a National Security prime minister. National security dominated the 2001 election campaign and it would dominate his third term over 2001–04, creating a new narrative.

Howard was in his room at the Willard Hotel preparing for his press conference when American Airlines 11 smashed into the North Tower of the World Trade Center at 8.46 a.m. He was conducting his press conference when United Airlines 175 hit the South Tower at 9.03 a.m. Two minutes later, in a Florida schoolroom, Bush's aide, Andrew Card, told the President about the second plane, saying 'America is under attack.'

When Howard returned from his press conference he looked out the window of the Willard and saw smoke rising from the Pentagon where he had been the previous afternoon for talks with Donald Rumsfeld. He was informed about the fate of American Airlines Flight 77 that crashed into the building at 530 miles per hour. Rumsfeld, in his office at the time, had left immediately to help the rescuers. The Secret Service evacuated Howard and his party to the basement of the Australian Embassy, ten blocks away. Meanwhile Bush was boarding his plane at Florida. He told Cheney: 'We're at war … somebody's going to pay.'

Meanwhile Reagan National Airport in Washington detected an unidentified flight en route to the capital. When asked, Cheney authorised fighter aircraft to engage and shoot down, if necessary, the incoming flight and confirmed this order by phone with Bush. At 10.03 a.m. the plane,

United Airlines Flight 93, crashed in Pennsylvania with the hijackers chanting 'Allah is the greatest' after an attempted interception by a group of brave passengers. Its target had been the Capitol or White House. The official 9/11 Commission Report concluded it was by no means certain this plane would have been shot down and found that the passengers 'may have saved either the Capitol or the White House from destruction'.[7]

Australian businessmen, diplomats, Howard's staff and journalists were relocated to the embassy. In the short message he drafted for Bush, Howard said that 'I feel the tragedy even more keenly being here in Washington.' He spoke to deputy PM John Anderson about security arrangements in Australia. Howard said the initial disbelief gave away 'with a rush' as he saw 'this was an event that was going to change the way we lived'.[8]

The scene in the sub-basement was calm. More officials arrived and Howard rang senior colleagues in Australia. He went upstairs to conduct his first media conference since the attack. His themes were determination and empathy.

Howard said 'to our American friends who we love and admire so much, we really feel for you'. He used Franklin Roosevelt's words after the 1941 Pearl Harbor attack, saying it was 'a day of infamy'. Howard called the attacks an 'outrageous act of war'—stressing it was not directed at military targets, as was Pearl Harbor, but at civilians: men, women and children going about their daily lives. Addressing 'our American friends' Howard said: 'We will stand by them. We will help them. We will support actions they take to properly retaliate in relation to these acts of bastardry against their citizens and against what they stand for.'[9]

The implication, though not explicit, was that Australia would participate in any future military action by the United States against the perpetrators of the attack. Issued on the afternoon of September 11, Howard did not have to make such a call. He could have limited himself to sympathy and support for America. There was a deliberation in Howard's tone and intensity in his expression. In a rejection of the weasel words later adopted by many lawyers, Howard branded 9/11 for what it was: an 'act of war'.

That afternoon, Howard was reinforced by an American warrior. From the sub-basement he spoke to Richard Armitage by phone. Calvert said Armitage told Howard they suspected Osama bin Laden. The United States was working on a strong response—leaders in key nations would be given twenty-four hours to make up their minds whether they were with the United States or siding with the terrorists. Calvert said: '[It] was reassuring to us that America was on the game.'[10]

'I think I would have probably made it pretty plain, even at that stage, that we'd been a good ally in the past and we'd be an ally in the future,' Howard said of his talk with Armitage.[11] He was telling the Americans that Australia would fight with them—a statement before sunset on 9/11.

That evening the Howards dined with the Thawleys and other Australians at the residence. They discussed how Howard might leave the United States; it was impossible for the time being, with no planes in the sky. His planned speech to the Joint Session of Congress, where he would have mentioned the FTA, had been cancelled. But Congress would be debating the attacks and the decision was taken that Howard would go to the Hill the next morning. 'I said to Michael [Thawley] I feel like I should go as an expression of support,' Howard said.[12] It would be an informal, low-key gesture.

The move was a masterstroke. 'Howard felt we had to express solidarity with the Americans,' Thawley said. 'But none of us realised how important this would be.'[13]

Congress had been in session throughout the night. Howard's party was driven through empty Washington streets and, on arrival, was escorted to the Speaker's sitting room to meet Speaker Dennis Hastert and House Minority Leader, Richard Gephardt. Howard's party of four, including Janette, was taken to the visitors' gallery where they were the only audience.[14] At this point, the Speaker announced the presence of the Australian Prime Minister to the chamber. One of the Australian officials, Andrew Todd described the situation:

> All 435 members stood, pivoted and gave a standing ovation … truly an emotional moment. He [Howard] physically started shaking. Mrs Howard … patted [him] and [the applause] went on for a while … I think his decision to go, to go quietly and without fanfare … none of this was scripted … I think it achieved more with Congress than the best speech we could have ever prepared for him … And it was all his decision, about only him and Janette, no hangers-on, no media, low key. He was not to be [in] the spotlight and my assessment is that clearly resonated with the Americans and that was the reason for the response from Hastert and Gephardt, and the warm, warm response by members of the Congress.[15]

Thawley said:

> The Americans saw this as an extraordinary gesture of friendship. The applause, even by Americans standards, went a long time. A

number of members of Congress came to the gallery to thank him for coming. Some said to me, 'You don't know how important this is. It means there are people who understand our feelings.' These were some of the most influential figures from the US Congress. They were feeling very vulnerable.[16]

When Howard went to the Senate, a recess was taken, and in a rare gesture, he was escorted onto the Senate floor to express his sentiments. Trent Lott took him around and introduced him to Senators. Asked about this congressional visit, Howard said: 'I think it was quite important an event. I think it had quite an impact on some people in the Congress and it had an impact on me.'[17] Howard noted the sentiment of the Congressional speeches—condemnation of the attacks and demands for retaliation. When the Australian–American FTA came before the Congress several years later, it was passed by a record majority.

That afternoon Howard conducted a longer media conference where his pledge to support the United States in retaliatory action was explicit. Howard said:

> I've also indicated that Australia will provide all support that might be requested of us by the United States in relation to any action that might be taken. Like everybody else I'm hopeful that those responsible will be hunted down and treated in the same manner that their despicable behaviour deserves and brought to justice.

The United States had not requested Australian backing. When pressed, Howard said: 'We would provide support within our capability.'[18]

His instinct was to see 9/11 as an epoch-changing event that had implications for other nations, including Australia. For Howard, it 'marked the end of an era' after the Cold War. He warned that 'Australia is not immune from this kind of possibility'. For Howard, a true friend of America must take an unequivocal stand at this point. It was time to 'stand shoulder-to-shoulder with the Americans'.[19]

In his first interview after the attack, with 2UE's John Laws, Howard let his emotions surface. 'It is just a monstrous thing and I just can't overstate the sympathy, the solidarity, the empathy I feel for the American nation and the American people at the present time … it is an appalling, wilful act of bastardry.' It was, he said, 'in some respects worse than Pearl Harbor' because it was an attack on civilians.[20]

Howard's response was governed by two convictions that lasted for the rest of his time in office. First, he saw the attack as transcending the United States and constituting an assault 'on the way of life that we hold dear in common'. This established a link between Australia and the 9/11 assault. The depth of this conviction was striking. 'Of course, it's an attack on all of us,' he said. This was prescient given the global scope of al-Qaeda's operations, the universality of its Islamist conception and the threat from Islamist terrorists to Australians at home and in South-East Asia that would emerge.

Howard never wavered from this interpretation—on returning he told the public that 9/11 was also 'an attack upon the people and the values of Australia'.[21]

His outlook as a cultural traditionalist dedicated to Western civilisation was basic to this reaction. Howard said the attack 'will leave a lasting impression on the psyche of the free world'.[22] His belief that the US alliance was about values was ignited.

Second, Howard's strategic view of the US alliance was that Australia's national interest dictated unity with America—this was not the time to hedge bets or wait until more was known. His strategic outlook was, as usual, uncomplicated—Australia was allied to America; this was the worst attack on America in its history; Australia, therefore, should declare its unqualified support.

It was a response driven by values and interests. When asked to rate them, Howard said: 'I think it is half and half.'[23] This testifies to a conservative ideology of remarkable depth anchored in realpolitik and cultural faiths.

Reflecting on these events five years later Howard said:

> Being in Washington that day had a huge impact on me. And it has never left me. I can still understand the attitudes of Americans which a lot of Australians can't quite understand. I say to people, just imagine if planes had flown into the Harbour Bridge or into the Opera House, how we would experience a permanent change in attitudes to the people who were responsible.[24]

This statement is easy to misinterpret. Being in Washington on 9/11 did not change Howard's war decisions but it injected them with a greater intensity.

Howard's statements in the forty-eight hours after the attack constitute some of the most important in the history of ANZUS. This was no rush of blood to the head; Howard knew what he was saying. Indeed, he repeated these refrains for years. They came from within, as distinct from being the work of advisers or a cabinet collective. They showed a bold leader, sure of his domestic authority, confident after East Timor. 'I was very deliberate,' he said. 'I believed the majority of the Australian public would support what I said. I was articulating, if you like, an orthodox Australian conservative view. It was something I believed very strongly.'[25]

That afternoon Howard attended a memorial service in the national cathedral to hear the Reverend Eugene Taylor Sutton quote St Matthew in his lesson of conciliation. 'I listened very carefully,' Howard said. 'But the people have got to be brought to justice and I think the preacher used the words "hunted down".'[26] Retaliation was on Howard's mind.

'The world has changed forever,' he told *60 Minutes* before leaving Washington.[27] In subsequent years strategic analysts in Australia would argue that the impact of 9/11 had been exaggerated. Howard had no time for such views. He responded to 9/11 as a political leader, not an academic. He saw that US politics and public opinion had been transformed. He grasped that Bush must launch a retaliation that might not be limited in time or targets and his instinct told him the rules and norms that had governed international behaviour would change. For Howard, this was obvious, though the details were not discernible.

Thawley said: 'He knew instantly this was going to change the whole scene. He knew we were entering a different period. He also recognised that it was going to change American attitudes to almost everything.'[28]

The embassy organised for Howard to leave America, courtesy of the Vice-President, on Air Force Two. On board was US Ambassador Schieffer, emotional about the fate of his country and impressed by Howard's performance. 'Through it all the PM had been very focussed, calm and resolute,' Schieffer says. 'He was very compassionate towards the Americans. His attitude was "My mate's in trouble and I'm going to be there."'[29]

Air Force Two flew across an empty American air space. There were only F18s in the sky. 'We were in regular communication with the White House,' Schieffer recalled. En route Thawley sent a message to Howard that the NATO Treaty was going to be invoked as a sign of support for America.[30] It prompted an obvious question: what about ANZUS? Howard spoke by phone to Downer. 'In a sense I had invoked ANZUS at my news conference in Washington,' Howard said. 'But I think it was Downer who actually thought of the idea of saying we were going to invoke ANZUS. I spoke to him from Air Force Two.'[31]

Downer said: 'I got the department to look at the legal issues and rang Howard back a bit later. I told him I felt we should do it.'[32] Howard spoke to Schieffer; invoking the treaty could only be done by mutual consent and this had to involve the White House. Armitage said later: 'There is no thinking American and no policy-maker who does not swell with pride at Prime Minister Howard invoking ANZUS after 9/11.'[33]

Cabinet formalised the decision on 14 September on Howard's return. After the meeting, he announced that Australia stood ready to assist the United States 'within the limits of its capability'. Howard repeated that 'at no stage should any Australian regard this as something that is just confined to the United States'—a warning validated at Bali thirteen months later.[34]

The invoking of ANZUS was a political act, not essential for Australian military action. Asked whether the idea came from Australia or America, Howard said 'it sort of happened simultaneously'. Questioned on its meaning, he said the decision had 'symbolic resonance' but also 'substance'. Australia's pledge to join a retaliatory war with the United States under the authority of the treaty was an assertion of its living relevance. This decision covered the Afghanistan conflict but not Iraq since Saddam Hussein was not involved in the 9/11 attack. While Bush said America was 'at war' Howard avoided such a formulation, in recognition that the Australian and American positions were not identical.[35]

The decision meant that an alliance written for the Cold War in Asia and seen by Australians as an insurance guarantee for their nation was invoked for the first time as a result of attacks on the US East Coast by a non-state actor representing Islamist terrorism. Nothing could have been more remote from the 1950s vision of Percy Spender and John Foster Dulles who negotiated the treaty. This result was equally a surprise for an Australian public, psychologically unprepared for this event yet sympathetic towards America.

The decision, in effect, signalled that the legal provisions of ANZUS had declined in importance with the creation of a political, advisory and military infrastructure of institutional co-operation and shared purpose. It verified the proposition of Australian historian, Peter Edwards, that 'the alliance is a political institution in its own right'. It was a milestone for ANZUS. It was also formal confirmation of a known truth—the treaty was global as well as regional; bonded by values as well as interests; and related to threats to America as well as to Australia.

The treaty was not limited to the Pacific, a reality long accepted by Australian governments via their military contributions to the Gulf region. The pre-9/11 Bush administration view was outlined by the Director of Policy Planning in the State Department, Richard Hass, who said in mid-2001 that the United States saw ANZUS not so much as a regional alliance but as 'two countries joined in a global partnership'.[36]

For the Australian public, the idea that ANZUS could involve Australia in the defence of America was a novel view. It was, however, embedded in Australia's strategic community and explicit in the 2000 Defence White Paper.

The attack on the United States was conducted by a fanatical enemy, the Islamist global terrorist group al-Qaeda under the leadership of a Saudi exile, Osama bin Laden. In 1998 bin Laden and an Egyptian fugitive, Ayman al Zawahiri, issued from their Afghan headquarters a *fatwa* calling for the murder of any American anywhere on earth as the sacred 'duty for every Muslim who can do it in any country in which it is possible to do it'. While bin Laden had strategic grievances against the United States, such as America's military presence in Saudi Arabia, they merged into an over-overarching ideological claim—that American was the enemy of Islam and was conducting a global war against Islam. This became the justification for Muslim martyrdom and the killing of civilians as well as US forces. For bin Laden, America could save itself only by abandoning the Middle East and, as a bonus, converting to Islam.[37]

After the weekend at Camp David with his advisers, Bush issued a series of directives on Monday 17 September—an ultimatum to the Taliban to produce bin Laden and close its Afghanistan terrorist camps; the development of a plan to attack the Taliban and al-Qaeda; a program of support for Pakistan following President Musharraf's agreement to US conditions to became its ally rather than its enemy; and the launch of a global campaign against terrorism.[38]

This constituted a transformation in US global strategy. Addressing a Joint Session of Congress on 20 September, Bush announced his 'war on terrorism' that 'will not end until every terrorist group of global reach has been found, stopped and defeated'. The defect lay in its open-ended nature. This betrayed a reluctance to focus the campaign just on al-Qaeda and mutations of Islamist terrorism and the risk that it would extend more widely to 'rogue' nations with no link to the attack.

The Australians had no idea that an internal debate had been conducted within the Bush administration in the week after the attack about whether to strike Saddam Hussein. On the morning of 15 September at Camp David the first assessment and decision was not to strike Iraq—Cheney said it would be a mistake to pursue Saddam immediately but did not rule out the option later. Al-Qaeda and the Taliban became the targets.[39] Because Rumsfeld's Pentagon had no military blueprint for Afghanistan, the CIA took the lead. Cofer Black, head of CIA counter-terrorism, told Bush that al-Qaeda fighters did not surrender or negotiate but 'when we're through with them, they will have flies walking across their eyeballs'.[40] It was not until early October that regime change was agreed as the goal in Afghanistan, with the US tactic being to outsource much of the fighting to the anti-Taliban United Front.

In early October, Chief of the Defence Force Chris Barrie held talks in Washington with his military counterparts, including chairman of the Joint Chiefs, Richard Myers, and the commander, US Central Command, Tommy Franks. On 3 October Ambassador Schieffer showed Howard US intelligence material that tied bin Laden to the 9/11 attack. On 4 October Howard announced that his government was authorising a range of military assets to be made available. The next day, 5 October, Howard called a federal election for 10 November. The campaign would see the return of security and foreign policy as a frontline election issue.[41]

After speaking to Bush on the night of 16 October, Howard an-nounced the Australian commitment the next day—a 150-strong special forces detachment, two P3 long range maritime aircraft, two B707 tanker aircraft, retention of a guided missile frigate, a naval task group, one frig-ate with helicopter capability and four F18A aircraft for a total commit-ment of about 1550 personnel. Howard reported Bush to be 'very, very grateful'. Describing the danger as 'much greater' than in East Timor, he said the deployment had to be seen as a 'significant further stage' in Australia's role in the war against terrorism. Howard warned this would be 'a very long, drawn-out campaign'. Refusing to rule out casualties, he said 'some could be killed'.[42]

For Australia and for its US alliance, this was a war against a new enemy—Islamist terrorism. It was a dramatic departure in the alliance's history, more significant than initially recognised, given that Australia lived in an Islamic geography adjacent to Indonesia. This raised a core strategic question: would Australian and American interests be as united against the new enemy as they had been united during the forty years of Cold War? There was no easy answer; yet the question was fundamental. As junior partner Australia would be deeply affected by the wisdom of Bush's strategy. Yet Bush's doctrine of pre-emption, the targeting of 'axis of evil' rogue states and invasion of Iraq, would see America plunge into a strategic quagmire.

This penetrates to the deeper meaning of 9/11—Howard's pledge made him hostage to Bush as a war president and Bush proved to have serious limitations. This would shape the final half of Howard's prime ministership.

Downer said the legal basis for the US-led action rested on the self-defence provision of the UN Charter, Article 51. He reported that there was a 'universal' view within the Security Council that this was sufficient. In addition, the US action was buttressed by a Security Council Resolution condemning 9/11 as an act of terrorism and calling for perpetrators and sponsors to be brought to justice.[43] This meant the Afghanistan campaign was sanctioned by the US alliance and by the UN, thereby guaranteeing bipartisan support from the Labor Party and public opinion.

Within days Howard and Beazley, in the midst of the campaign, spoke at farewell ceremonies for the troops at Campbell Barracks, Perth. Howard told the departing Australians that 9/11 had been, 'in a very direct sense, an attack on Australia and what we value'. He said that Bush had spoken to him about the quality of the SAS and they were now part of 'a very great Australian military tradition'. They went with 'our prayers' and wishes for 'a safe return'.[44]

The Taliban was deposed by a combination of US air strikes, CIA bribery of its commanders and attacks by the United Front forces. A moderate Pashtun, Hamid Karzai, was handpicked by the CIA as Afghanistan's new leader and sworn in 102 days after 9/11. But peace did not return to Afghanistan. In a battle in the Tora Bora mountains that the United States outsourced to Afghans and Pakistanis on their respective sides of the border, bin Laden escaped on foot or by mule into Pakistan. The man behind 9/11 eluded capture or death, proof that Bush's bark was worse than his bite. Australia's forces were withdrawn soon afterwards.

The episode revealed Howard's complexity as a politician. His technique was full-scale rhetorical support for the United States but niche military commitments of limited duration and a quick withdrawal. Hugh White said: 'Howard's rhetoric after 9/11 pointed to a fundamental threat to the global order. He invoked Pearl Harbor on a number of occasions. But look at what he does—he sticks to the pattern of the past twenty years, sends relatively modest forces for a low duration to the Gulf and Afghanistan. Some time later the same process is repeated with Iraq.'[45]

This is Howard's gap between rhetoric and action. For Howard, it is hard-headed political realism. It mocks critics who depict Howard as an emotional, pro-American romantic who got carried away. It is hard to imagine a worse misreading of the man.

The US military view was that Australia's forces made a difference. Downer said: 'They killed a lot of Taliban. While their number was small, our profile was high. This had a direct impact on Bush. I have heard him say we are one of the few countries prepared to do real fighting.'[46] Over the years, however, there would be internal criticism about Australia's gap between rhetoric and action—talking big but not doing too much. One of the critics was Dennis Richardson, Thawley's successor in Washington, who was unafraid to raise the issue with Howard.

The climate created by 9/11 had another bonus for Howard that took years to discern—with Bush fighting Islamists terrorists, it diminished the US focus on China. This gave Howard more 'space' for his China policy. White said:

> It made Howard's China policy a lot easier. Howard kept saying that Australia didn't have to choose between Washington and Beijing—as though such a discretion was ever in Australia's decision-making ability. But 9/11 meant the United States would be preoccupied for years with a new enemy. It gave Howard more scope for his China policy.[47]

The 9/11 attack opened a remarkable new chapter in Australia–United States ties. Within a year Howard had seen a different America—governed by Bush and under attack. Howard thrived in a climate removed from Clinton's self-obsessions. With Bush, he became a political ally, a personal friend and a brother-in-arms.

Their concord would produce tighter military ties, greater defence force inter-operability, closer intelligence sharing, a better economic partnership formalised in the FTA and an intimate political bond. Having waited four years for his opportunity, Howard used Bush and 9/11 to realign towards America. The irony, however, is that Bush was a dangerous senior partner.

41

INTEGRITY OVERBOARD

Peter Reith came into the office and got us together and said: 'I have been with the Prime Minister and nothing else matters now except winning the election. Nothing else matters.' And that was the direction to the office.
—Mike Scrafton, Peter Reith's military adviser

John Howard's deployment of the Australian Defence Force (ADF) to enforce border protection meant that boats would be boarded and turned around during the 2001 election campaign. The 1 September announcement set the Australian state against the asylum seekers. Where there is a threat, there is an enemy—and the Howard government succumbed to demonising the boat people. That tactic would haunt the government for the rest of its days.

In an astonishing coincidence, cabinet's decision came ten days before al-Qaeda's attack on the United States. It meant Operation Relex coincided with a mood of apprehension that infected the Howard government and public opinion. The boats were framed in an 'invasion' context, resisted by the Australian Navy as the world contemplated the smouldering ruins of New York. For Australians, there were two paradigms on display: Muslims as terrorists and Muslims as asylum seekers.

By raising the stakes so high the government sent multiple messages: not only were the boats unwelcome but, at a more subtle level, the people were undesirable. This reflected the government's view that boat people were customers of a criminal industry with dubious refugee credentials. If, by contrast, they were family-loving people who were innocent victims of persecution then Howard's policy might be judged as inhumane.

Deployment of the ADF became the greatest experiment in border control in Australia's history, with interdiction being a highly political project. The Howard government would not surrender control of these operations to the navy. There was competition between the navy chain of command and the civilian authority centred in the Prime Minister's Department, servicing Howard and driven by Max Moore-Wilton. Because every naval encounter with a boat had electoral sensitivity, the government felt compelled to exploit any encounter as quickly as possible.

These elements culminated in the 'children overboard' affair, a saga that became notorious and implanted the idea of the Howard government's lying pathology. Liberal Party Federal Director Lynton Crosby concedes this point. 'Children overboard wasn't a 2001 campaign issue,' Crosby says. 'But where Labor was successful was spinning the story after the election that Howard's victory was won on a lie.'[1]

Starting at midnight on 3 September 2001, Operation Relex saw the Navy encounter twelve boats (called 'suspected illegal entry vessels' or SIEVs) over nearly four months. A total of twenty-five navy vessels were involved in the operation. The chain of command was from the naval ship commander to Brigadier Silverstone (Commander Northern Command) to Naval Component Commander, Rear Admiral Smith, to Commander Australian Theatre, Rear Admiral Ritchie, to the Chief of the Defence Force (CDF), Admiral Barrie, who reported to Reith. In parallel with this military chain was the People Smuggling Task Force headed by Jane Halton in the Prime Minister's Department. It was the daily clearing house for information about Operation Relex, for setting policy and for directing events. It reported to Moore-Wilton and Howard's office.

The policy changed at the mid-point of the operation. Until SIEV 4 the policy was to intercept, board and hold the boat people in the hope of transfer to another country. From SIEV 5 the aim was to return the vessels to Indonesia. This meant trying to prevent vessel sabotage by the crew and boat people. Critical to the operation was keeping the people aboard their own vessels as long as possible since, once transferred to a naval ship, they would become Australia's immediate responsibility. Of the twelve boats, four were escorted back to Indonesia and three sank during interception, with the people taken to detention in the Pacific. People from the other boats were held in custody for processing.

Rear Admiral Smith explained that, because the aim was to deter boats, there were 'numerous instances of threatened or actual violent actions against ADF personnel' as well as 'various acts of threatened or actual self-harm and the inciting of violence'. The ADF had not previously faced this situation. The risk was rapid escalation into violence or a safety issue that was life-threatening. The people were hostile to

Howard government policy and to a navy commissioned to stop them. Having travelled so far, they expected to reach Australia. Naval officers said a response 'pattern' grew—threats, violence, self-harm—including threats to children and sabotage of boats.[2]

On 6 October HMAS *Adelaide* intercepted SIEV 4 heading to Christmas Island and in international waters. It sent warning notices by various means but all were ignored. *Adelaide*'s commander, Norman Banks, reported signs of 'visible and oral aggression'. After the boat entered Australia's contiguous zone and ignored further calls to 'heave-to', Brigadier Silverstone in Darwin directed Banks to make an 'assertive boarding'. Shots were fired ahead of the vessel, further loudspeaker warnings were ignored and a boarding party took control and changed its course to Indonesia. It was 4.45 a.m. The people were reportedly 'irate, aggressive and to some extent hysterical'. Banks reported that a number threatened to commit suicide, gesturing with wooden sticks, and a total of fourteen jumped overboard. All were recovered by navy personnel. At 6.01 a.m. a second boarding party was inserted. Medical aid was offered but Banks reported that occasional force was needed to keep control. Water that was offered was thrown overboard. Vandalism and arson were being attempted as eighteen naval personnel tried to maintain order on a small boat with 223 people. But it was taken north and pointed towards Indonesia.[3]

However, Silverstone said that, before this happened, in a conversation at 7.20 a.m. Banks told him that 'a child was thrown over the side'. Banks later disputed this account, saying he saw a child being held over the side and that he had recounted this to Silverstone. While conceding that Silverstone's version might be correct, Banks refused to accept it.

SIEV 4 was the first boat to be intercepted since Howard had called the election. Its handling would be a test of the government's credentials. Reith demanded to be informed. Silverstone later told the Senate his call to Banks that morning arose primarily from the need to keep the People Smuggling Task Force informed and that, had he followed normal practice, not spoken to Banks and relied on the signal traffic, then the 'so-called children overboard issue would never have arisen'.[4]

Once the navy had intercepted a boat, Rear Admiral Smith said 'everything that occurred after that in terms of major decisions, such as boarding, removal of people or whatever it happened to be, actually came from Canberra'. The remote micro-management was extreme.[5]

Silverstone had passed the information about a child being thrown overboard to Canberra, briefing both Air Vice Marshal Titheridge and

Rear Admiral Smith. At 9.30 a.m. Titheridge briefed Halton to this effect. But somewhere along the chain, 'child' had become 'children'. When the taskforce met that Sunday morning Halton reported on the SIEV 4 situation, saying there had been fourteen people in the water and 'they were throwing children in'.

That same day, Philip Ruddock was scheduled to speak in Sydney on the border protection issue. At 9.51 a.m. he rang his department chief, Bill Farmer, who took the call from the taskforce meeting. Farmer told Ruddock that children had been thrown in the water. A short time later, Ruddock announced to the media at his public forum that 'a number of children have been thrown into the water' and described the action as 'disturbing, planned and premeditated'. Ruddock rang Howard and Reith to brief them on the situation. This was when Howard was first informed that children had been thrown overboard. It had been less than five hours since the incident on the water. The media would ignite the nation with the false news.

The misunderstanding probably lay with Banks, but he was a commander under pressure giving a verbal report on a rocky boat while a chaotic situation was unfolding. The real problem was the system— the military chain of command was being intercepted by government imperatives, and those imperatives, in turn, were translated into immediate electoral needs. This was the edifice of prime ministerial power that Moore-Wilton had constructed.

For years Ruddock was forced to defend himself.

> I spoke to Farmer and the report was explicit. They were throwing children overboard. That was the advice. Look, I'll take the blame. I made the decision. I was standing up to brief a press conference and I decided to be upfront. Why did I do it? I was defending the government's policy. I said to journalists later: what would you expect me to have done? Said nothing?[6]

That evening the taskforce authorised an options paper for Howard that included a reference to 'children thrown overboard'. For the bureaucrats, focused on bigger questions, it had little significance. The document was faxed to Reith at home at 8.31 p.m. and also to Howard. But the falsehood had entered the ministerial paper chain. It was now only fourteen hours since the events on the water.

The next day Howard turned the 'children overboard' event into a polemical device to delegitimise the boat people. 'I don't want in this country people who are prepared, if these reports are true, to throw their children overboard,' he said. His message was that genuine refugees did not act in this manner. It was an assault on their moral claims, a declaration that they were not fit to join the Australian community.[7]

'I used the information at the start of the campaign but then I stopped talking about it,' Howard said later.[8] That's true—but it cannot gainsay Howard's use of the story to brand the boat people as unworthy.

Two days later the Office of National Assessment (ONA), in a report for ministers dated 9 October, referred to the *Adelaide*'s interception, saying that 'asylum seekers wearing lifejackets jumped into the sea and children were thrown in with them'. It would become a fateful document. The falsehood had entered intelligence assessments for Howard. And it was only two days since the incident.[9]

While Howard's comments were qualified, he acted on this false advice, having no reason to dispute it. He said later that he had relied on what Ruddock told him. For years Moore-Wilton was angry about the issue, saying: 'It was Murphy's law. Philip Ruddock, for whatever reason, decided to make it an issue that day. It became a monster. The taskforce had to take responsibility for that information being passed to the minister. It was a failure of process.'[10]

SIEV 4 met a predictable fate. Unconvinced that the boat would make for Indonesia, Banks had waited in the vicinity only to find that at 12.19 p.m. on 7 October the vessel was observed dead in the water. A boarding party found the engine sabotaged, with the obvious aim of being taken to Australia. Banks spoke to Silverstone about towing the boat to Christmas Island. The boat people were delighted. The tow proceeded without incident until the afternoon of 8 October, when a problem with the bilge pumps arose. At 4.30 p.m. as the navy was serving the evening meal on SIEV 4 and at 5 p.m. it began to sink, with men, women and children entering the water. The *Adelaide* launched six life rafts and everybody was rescued.

There was a row between Barrie as CDF and Moore-Wilton about where the people should be taken. For Howard and Moore-Wilton, the goal was to prevent their arrival on Australian territory. Barrie said: 'The rule is that nobody loses their lives. When the boat sank Max told me they weren't going to Christmas Island. I told him, "Max, we intend to save their lives, whatever it takes."'[11] Barrie insisted that he, not Moore-Wilton, would decide on the destination. 'The Defence force was asked to mount this operation,' Barrie said. 'Yet we had other departments and Jane Halton's taskforce thinking they ran the show. I reminded people they didn't give me orders.'[12]

While applauding Barrie's role, Moore-Wilton was scathing of naval culture. 'They never saw this as a problem for the government,' he later said. 'It was all about towing people into a port. The maritime industry culture in Australia was essentially a Left attitude.'[13]

A total of 420 digital photos were taken during *Adelaide*'s four-day encounter with SIEV 4, but two became infamous—they depicted navy staff in the water assisting people after the boat's sinking. These photos had nothing to do with the false 'children overboard' event. They demonstrated, instead, the courage of naval personnel. It was a 'good news' story. But there was a critical communications blunder between Defence and Reith's office: when the photographs arrived in Reith's office they were assumed to be evidence not of the rescue but of the 'children overboard' incident.[14]

Reith was under media pressure to release photographic evidence of children being thrown overboard. He rang Barrie to 'cut through' and get quick clearance. The minister's office told him there was also a video of the 'children overboard' event. Officials in the defence system reported to subsequent inquiries that they felt under pressure from Reith's office with the key player being press secretary, Ross Hampton.[15] The upshot is that the photos were not released via the usual Defence channels with its checking procedures. On 10 October, Reith's office, acting under a misapprehension, gave the photos to the media to illustrate the fictitious 'children overboard' incident.

In an interview late that day Reith referred to photographs and said there was film as well, declaring: 'It is an absolute fact: children were thrown into the water. So do you still question it?'[16] The photographs were shown that night on ABC TV's *7.30 Report*. With this 'proof', the circle was closed on the 'children overboard' story. Fiction had become reality.

In fact, a hasty campaign-driven political intervention had interrupted normal procedures, resulting in a grievous blunder. Operation Relex was being maximised for Howard's electoral benefit. Yet there was a parallel story unfolding.

As soon as the photos were shown, much of the military chain of command realised the mistake—this was the 8 October rescue, not the 7 October incident. On the evening of 10 October Barrie was told by the Chief of Navy, Vice Admiral Shackleton, and by Ritchie that the photographs were not the 'children overboard' event.

Barrie, as CDF, told Reith on 11 October that the photos had been misrepresented. 'I do recall that our conversation was testy,' Barrie said.

'He [Reith] got very angry about it.'[17] Reith said: 'I don't recall any such testy conversation.'[18] Barrie had no doubt that Reith got the point. 'I had no reason to believe that he [Reith] did not understand,' Barrie said.[19]

Reith and Barrie had no discussion about correcting the record. 'We had an agreement,' Barrie said. 'We would drop this matter and it was not said but it was my understanding that he [Reith] would deal with the consequences.' Asked why he didn't press Reith on this issue, Barrie said: 'The Minister directs and I advise … I have not really met one [minister] that really appreciated me telling him what his job was.'[20]

The head of Defence Public Affairs, Jenny McKenry, told the minister's military adviser, Mike Scrafton, that the photos had been misrepresented. 'I spoke to the minister,' Scrafton said.

> I explained that we didn't think they were the right photographs. He refused to accept that, pretty much. It was as though there were always stuff-ups in Defence and why should we accept one set of advice against another set of advice.[21]

Reith and his office chief, Peter Hendy, declined to be corrected by the Defence department.

Reith took refuge in a formula that would define the entire affair—the evidence was not strong enough to compel a retraction.

In the first few days the embarrassment of a retraction would have been minor; the longer the denial persisted, the greater the problem became. Hendy said Reith decided 'within 24 hours that he would not change the public record until he had conclusive advice about what had actually happened with the original reports and the photos'.[22] Scrafton said: 'Everybody in Defence knew the photographs didn't represent that event.'[23] For Scrafton, Reith's office 'considered the political solution was "not to raise" the issue'.[24] Interviewed for this book, Scrafton said: 'The government had feedback on the border protection stuff, it was a winner for them, painting the refugees as bad was a winner.'[25]

The story seemed to be too sensationally convenient to be denied. On 14 October, Reith told Channel 7's *Sunday Sunrise* program that he was happy to have Defence release the photographs 'because there was a claim we were not telling the truth about what happened'.[26]

At the same time the military chain of command didn't just expose the false photos—it was correcting the false story. This began when Silverstone and Rear Admiral Smith worried that they had no written confirmation of the 'children overboard' event that had received such prominent media coverage. Silverstone established that there was no such written advice from the *Adelaide*. On 9 October, Smith contacted Commander Banks, who said that he did not witness such an event. Smith instructed Banks to interview his crew at once and sworn statements were taken. By the next day, 10 October, Banks conceded that 'no children had been thrown into the water'.[27] Alarm bells rang in the navy's hierarchy.

The same day Smith passed the message up the line that he was convinced the incident never occurred. Rear Admiral Ritchie reached the same conclusion. This message reached Barrie's office that day. In summary, by the evening of 10 October, when the photos were being released, the navy hierarchy knew that no children had been thrown overboard.[28] The story was a furphy.

On 11 October, Ritchie told Barrie there was no evidence for the claims. At this point Ritchie had copies of the crew's statements, Silverstone's advice and Smith's advice. The evidence was unequivocal. This became a critical discussion since Barrie believed the message from Ritchie to him had been equivocal. Barrie's response was astounding.

He told Ritchie 'I would not change my advice to the Minister' until conclusive proof was provided that the original advice to Reith was wrong. 'I offered the commanders an opportunity to come back and convince me that I was wrong,' Barrie said. [29] It was the Reith formula. Even if Barrie was unconvinced, his obligation was clear—he should have asked Ritchie to 'resolve it once and for all and report back'. But Barrie was a CDF who did not want to be convinced the story was wrong.

Interviewed for this book, Barrie said: 'I was not going to change my advice until I was shown evidence this event did not occur. As it turned out there was a signal message from the *Adelaide* in the system saying it didn't happen. I never saw that. But that was the evidence I needed.'[30]

Around 17 October, Barrie told Reith that the Chief of Navy, Vice Admiral Shackleton, and Ritchie felt there were 'doubts' whether children had been thrown overboard. He told the minister he indicated to them 'until evidence was produced to show the initial report to me was wrong, I would stand by it'.[31] Barrie neither accepted the Navy's advice nor ordered a definitive clarification. It was this decision by the CDF that allowed the 'children overboard' story to stand.

This became the foundation of Reith's position. 'I took note and believed what Chris Barrie had told me and I repeated it,' he said. 'My view throughout was that the incident had happened. And I relied on that advice.'[32] Asked about the responsibility of the CDF, Barrie's successor, Peter Cosgrove said: 'The only duty of the CDF is to tell the government the truth.'[33]

The demands upon the CDF at this time should be appreciated. Barrie told the Senate Committee the ADF 'is under more stress in terms of operations about to be conducted and being conducted than at any time since I have joined the outfit—in 41 years'. He elaborated:

> We were barely three weeks out from the brutal images of aircraft smashing into the World Trade Center in New York and we were about to join the launch of a dangerous mission to Afghanistan. I was focused on the imminent war in Afghanistan and the urgent need to safeguard our homeland from a possible terrorist attack … as well, we were in East Timor … and we are in Bosnia, the Middle East, Cyprus, Egypt, Sierra Leone and Solomon Islands.

In this context, he said, 'children overboard' was 'not uppermost' in his mind.[34] Interviewed for this book, Barrie said: 'From where I sat the "children overboard" issue was nothing. And I had seen no evidence that it did not occur.'[35]

Yet the issue was pivotal to the credibility of the ADF and the Howard government. It had been briefly dominant in the media. Any pretence that it was unimportant is ludicrous. It was obvious what should have happened. Moore-Wilton's successor, Peter Shergold, said: 'The wrong message had got into the system. It should have been corrected immediately. The public service got the government into this mess and the public service had an obligation to get them out as fast as possible.'[36] That task fell to the CDF but Barrie declined it.

There was genuine anger within the navy about the failure of superiors to correct the record. 'Any other CDF would have found out the facts,' Scrafton said. 'If it had been John Baker [Barrie's predecessor] people would have been nailed to the wall to get them. Baker would have gone straight to the commander.'[37]

The majority view of the 2002 Senate inquiry was that 'the chain of command had made the relevant inquiries and assessed the relevant messages, signals, statements, video footage and chronologies and had reached its verdict: the original report was mistaken'. Ritchie had no doubt that he made the position clear to Barrie. The responsibility rested with the CDF.[38]

Interviewed for this book Barrie said:

> I had made fulsome reports to the Minister. What Reith does then is not my business. Reith heard what I had to say—does he want to interrupt Howard and tell him it might all be wrong? No. He

doesn't ... I think Reith was committed 150 per cent to get John Howard re-elected.[39]

Scrafton said: 'From my discussions with Reith, he was aware of the doubts. I find it difficult to believe that such an intelligent, highly political and good minister wouldn't have seen this was a very weak story.'[40]

Reith was an intimidating practitioner of the Howard government's public administration culture—utilise the system for maximum political gain. Barrie said: 'Allan Hawke and I saw Reith about mid-2001 and proposed to him new arrangements for factual reports from the field direct to the media. But he said, "No, we do it my way" and his way was to manipulate the process.'[41] This meant that information from the interdiction of boats would come from the government, not the ADF. 'Reith's people sought to control the information from the chain of command and this is where the problem was created,' Scrafton said.[42]

Yet the problem was more serious. The Australian Defence Organisation has a leadership diarchy—with the head of the Defence department and the CDF providing a dual civilian and military leadership. The CDF has command of the defence forces and the Defence department head has responsibility for policy, resources and accountability. During the 1970s legendary departmental head Sir Arthur Tange laid the foundations for the diarchy and consolidated the authority of the civilian wing. But from the mid-1980s, when the new office of CDF was created, the influence of the military leadership has been enhanced significantly.

The 'children overboard' affair was notable for the passivity of Defence department chief, Allan Hawke. While informed on 11 October that the photographs were a misrepresentation, Hawke did not raise this with Reith. He conceded later that 'in retrospect, I should have discussed that issue directly with and provided clear written advice to Minister Reith'. Hawke said he asked his officers to send a written brief to the minister but that he failed to ensure it was sent. This failure was sufficient for Hawke to offer his resignation post-election to new Defence Minister Robert Hill. He remained in the job.[43] It is difficult to imagine a Defence chief such as Tange would not have given prompt written advice.

The 'children overboard' issue was not central to the 2001 election campaign. For most of the campaign it was not mentioned, a reality too easily forgotten. However, the situation from mid-October was remarkable: the belief in the navy and the Defence department was that the event was fiction, yet the cabinet did not doubt its veracity—the exception being Reith who, at the least, had to harbour private doubts beneath his public conviction. This parallel reality prevailed for several weeks because of campaign logistics—but the parallel universes were unsustainable.

Towards the end of the first week of November the issue started to regain media interest. Scrafton rang Howard's international policy adviser, Miles Jordana. 'It was adviser to adviser,' Scrafton said. 'I said "You need to know that nobody in Defence thinks the event happened".'[44] Scrafton said his advice was 'categorical'.[45]

It was an omen: the 'correction' was moving closer to Howard. The dam wall began to break on the morning of Wednesday 7 November, three days before the election, when the *Australian* published a page-one story saying the published photos were of the sinking and not of any 'children overboard' incident.

Air Marshal Angus Houston was acting CDF while Barrie was overseas. Given the story, he promptly spoke to the head of Defence public relations, Brigadier Gary Bornholt, who showed him the signal traffic and Houston quickly saw the story was false. When Houston rang Reith to correct the record he was methodical yet firm. He ran through the events and advised Reith that 'there was nothing to suggest that women and children had been thrown into the water'. He said the photos were of the sinking the next day and the video, while inconclusive, offered no evidence for the story. 'There was silence for quite a while,' Houston reported. 'It seemed to me that he was stunned and surprised.' But Houston felt Reith was getting news he didn't want to hear. The acting CDF was giving the advice that Barrie had declined to give. It put Reith under the gun. 'I think we'll have to look at releasing the video,' Reith said.[46] It was an omen of denial.

Interviewed for this book, Reith had a different version.

> My recollection is that Angus said he had doubts about the incident. He wasn't categorical. There's no doubt I told him that I'd have to speak to Chris Barrie about it. The last thing I was going to do on the basis of what Angus told me was turn around and change the public record of these events. Frankly, I didn't put a lot of significance in what Angus Houston had told me and I definitely did not convey to Howard anything Angus had told me.[47]

This was an extraordinary position. Its key lies in the context— the election was three days away, Reith was not standing, his career was finished, but his loyalty to Howard and the government was intense. Since his ship was sinking, Reith would bring the entire political baggage unto himself, shield Howard and take the blame. By refusing to pass on Houston's advice, Reith saved Howard from a politically impossible position. It was in keeping with his character.

But this discrepancy between Houston and Reith highlights another point—Houston should have put his advice in writing as soon as he informed Reith. Arthur Sinodinos says: 'Sir Frederick Wheeler wouldn't have just relied on a phone call to say the incident hadn't happened. If this was the view of the CDF or the Secretary of the Defence department then it should have been put in writing.'[48]

It was not the first time Reith had been told the story was false. A week earlier, on 31 October when he was at Northern Command Headquarters, Silverstone had told the minister that the navy had 'concerns that no children were thrown overboard and we have made an investigation of that'. Silverstone reported that, after making this remark, he 'paused, expecting to hear a "yes". He [Reith] then said, "Well, we had better not see the video then" and left my office.'[49]

On the morning of 8 December, Houston rang Hawke to say he had told Reith that the story was false. But Hawke declined, again, to get involved in providing advice to the minister even when it became clear that Reith was not correcting the record. Asked why he did not intervene and offer Reith advice, Hawke said: 'This is a chain of command issue; it is an operational issue.'[50] In short, it was not his job—it was the CDF's job.

But after speaking to Hawke, Houston made another call—to Moore-Wilton to inform him of the situation, a call not mentioned to the Senate committee. 'I certainly contacted the Prime Minister immediately,' Moore-Wilton said in describing his follow-up action. 'I telephoned him. I may have gone to see him, I'm not sure. But I certainly communicated to the Prime Minister at once that Angus Houston had contacted me. I told the Prime Minister that Angus had formed the view that no children were thrown overboard.'[51]

There is no doubting Moore-Wilton's statement about informing Howard. He made it unequivocally to the author on 13 June 2008 during a two-hour interview for this book. It was the first time Moore-Wilton had revealed these details. Its significance, taken at face value, is that it points to Howard being told before the election that the story was false. It triggered an unusual 2009 dialogue between Howard and Moore-Wilton over what really happened and about their conflicting accounts to the author. Moore-Wilton insisted on his position in three separate phone interviews with the author solely about this event and despite a discussion in which Howard tried to persuade Moore-Wilton that his recollection was wrong and urged him to reconsider.[52]

'Obviously, I couldn't ignore what Angus had told me,' Moore-Wilton told the author.

> That's why I informed the Prime Minister. I wasn't giving him formal advice and I wasn't inserting myself in the chain of command. I was passing on what Angus had said and I wasn't in a position to test its veracity. That was the job of the Defence Minister when he spoke to Howard.

Howard denies this implacably. In an interview for this book he said:

> I could not be more explicit on this. Max did not speak to me along these lines. I am as certain about this as I can be on anything. This did not happen. I have a clear recollection of when I first heard about the doubts expressed by Angus Houston. This was February 2002 when Max rang me to tell me the evidence that Angus would be giving to the Senate Estimates committee. I believe Max has confused these two phone calls.[53]

Howard told the author this was such an important issue going to his integrity that he intended to pursue the matter with Moore-Wilton. He subsequently spoke to Sinodinos and urged the author to contact Sinodinos.

When the author put Howard's denial to Moore-Wilton, he was unmoved. 'That's my recollection,' Moore-Wilton said. 'I know that John Howard is very concerned about this. It is not my intention to cast doubt on the former prime minister's integrity. I don't see how we can reconcile this. My recollection is that I informed John Howard of Angus Houston's position on the "children overboard" issue at the time after Angus spoke to me. I can say no more.'[54]

Sinodinos spent these final campaign days in close proximity to Howard. 'If Max had that conversation with the PM we would have known about it,' Sinodinos told the author. 'It would have become part of our discussion on tactics. But there was no inference the PM got this information from Max and I don't believe this conversation happened prior to the election.'[55]

Several weeks later on 9 July 2009, on the eve of this book going to print, Moore-Wilton rang the author to report that he had reflected on the situation and had spoken to Sinodinos and McClintock as well as Howard. He now wanted to change his story. 'As a result I formed the view that my recollection was not sound and that I could not stand by that recollection,' Moore-Wilton said in his fifth discussion of this issue with the author. 'I can find no supporting evidence for it. I have spoken with Mr Howard previously and it is entirely possible that my recollections relate to the conversation I had with him in February 2002 after the election.' Moore-Wilton said Sinodinos and McClintock felt his recall had been inaccurate. Howard had asked him to reconsider and this is what he had done. 'I had a conversation with John Howard yesterday,' Moore-Wilton said. 'It was to inform him that in the light of his strong views I was giving consideration to my position.' Moore-Wilton told the author that in their previous discussion Howard, while pressing him, had said: 'Whatever differences of memory you and I have on this issue Max, it will not affect our friendship.'[56]

There is, however, no confusion on the next point. Reith as Defence Minister did not inform Howard of Houston's rejection of the story. Reith spoke to Howard at least once and probably more than once on 7 November. 'Reith didn't tell me about his discussion with Angus Houston,' Howard said. 'I can only draw the conclusion that Reith gave on television: he felt he ought to discuss it with Barrie. I never found Reith to be dishonest or duplicitous.'[57] Even though Houston had corrected the record, Barrie's advice was the rock upon which Reith would maintain the deception.

With the election imminent, Reith's response, far from correcting the record, was the opposite: to search for evidence to sustain the public falsehood and save the government from immediate embarrassment. That afternoon he asked Scrafton, who was in Sydney, to go to Maritime Headquarters to view the video tape, the other piece of 'hard' evidence apart from the photographs. En route with a companion for a dinner at Leichhardt, Scrafton viewed the tape twice and rang Reith to report it was inconclusive. Reith told him to expect a call from Howard later that night.

Meanwhile Jordana had been ringing the bureaucracy on the same mission—he asked both the department and ONA what evidence they had to sustain the story. With his appearance at the National Press Club the next day (8 November) in mind, Howard wanted whatever fresh evidence was available to buttress the existing story. The department's cupboard was bare. During his queries Halton told Jordana that the Defence department believed the photographs were not of the 'children overboard' incident. At about 7 p.m. ONA's Kim Jones faxed to Howard's office the ONA report of 9 October but coupled it with a warning that the reference to children overboard 'could have been based on ministers' statements' and not an independent basis. It was a correct and important caveat.[58]

That night the Howards convened a working dinner at the Lodge with the main staffer—Sinodinos, McClintock, Tony Nutt and Tony O'Leary—to prepare for the Press Club speech. But the dinner was derailed by an issue that Howard had scarcely considered or addressed over the past month. It became a prolonged debate about tactics for children overboard.

In the first part of the meeting Howard betrayed no unease. 'We had no sense of doom whatsoever,' McClintock said. 'Howard was not acting like a PM whose Defence Minister had just told him the entire story was wrong.'[59] The problem, however, was that evidence for the story was melting away.

Scrafton was about to start his entrée when Howard rang. He thought it was the first of three calls but Lodge records later showed that Howard rang twice. According to Scrafton he told Howard in these calls that the tape was inconclusive; the photographs were of the boat's sinking and not from the day before. He sensed Howard's surprise and was encouraged, so 'with my heart in my mouth' he then said 'that no one in Defence that I dealt with on the matter still believed any children were thrown overboard'.

'It appeared to me from the Prime Minister's responses that he was surprised at what I was telling him,' Scrafton later said. It was Howard's sense of surprise that encouraged Scrafton to volunteer the fact that sentiment in the Defence department was that the incident did not occur.[60] Between Howard's calls Scrafton finished his entrée and began his main course.

Scrafton's recall is that in the second conversation Howard asked about the ONA report and Scrafton said the impression was that it was based on ministers' statements, not separate evidence. 'How could that possibly be?' Howard asked. Scrafton sensed he was perturbed. Scrafton suggested that Howard talk to Kim Jones. He returned to his meal, leaving a prime minister with growing worries.

Howard disputed Scrafton's version of their conversation. He insisted he had spoken to Scrafton 'entirely about the video'.[61] 'I'm not attacking the man,' Howard said. 'His recall of that discussion is different from mine.'[62] Howard insisted that, during the Lodge talks, he 'didn't have any reason to doubt it [the story]'.[63]

However, at the bare minimum, Howard had to be aware that there were significant doubts about the story. Sinodinos said of the Lodge meeting: 'By this stage we were uncertain whether the incident had occurred or not. Our focus … was about defending the PM's position and the government's standing.'[64] This is the vital point.

Howard was not searching for the facts. He was a PM bent on sustaining his position. The meeting decided to release the video the next day. While it was inconclusive, Howard wanted to avoid any suggestion of cover-up. The meeting knew that the government's credibility was on the line. The weakness of Howard's position is that the only fresh evidence he could produce for the Press Club was the ONA report and Scrafton had just told him it was second-hand.

The next morning, driving back from Sydney, Scrafton spoke to Jenny McKenry from Defence Public Affairs about releasing the video. He reported to her that he had told Howard the 'children overboard' event did not happen, a point confirmed by McKenry.[65] The video was released just before noon and Howard arrived at the Press Club half an hour later.

Under questioning by the media, Howard said that he had acted originally on advice from Ruddock and Reith in saying children were thrown overboard. He quoted from the ONA report that Jones had faxed to Jordana the previous night—revealing this document for the first time but saying nothing of Jones's qualifications. Asked about uncertainty surrounding the 'children overboard' incident, Howard said: 'In my mind there is no uncertainty because I don't disbelieve the advice I was given by Defence.' The next morning he said: 'At no stage was I told that advice was wrong and in fact to this day nobody is saying that that advice is wrong.'[66]

In virtually every reference Howard made to 'children overboard' in the final three days of the campaign he referred to 'advice'. Scrafton was not in any position to offer Howard formal advice and he did not try. Reith had not changed the advice because Barrie had not changed the advice. And Reith had not told Howard about Houston's advice. It was Reith who was holding together the slim fabric of credibility to get over the election line.

If Howard had been given correcting 'advice' he would have been compromised on election eve. The initial cover-up in October had forced Reith into a bigger election-eve cover-up.

Howard's answers, however, were misleading. By this stage he knew the photos were not evidence and that the video was not evidence. As Sinodinos said, the Howard camp did not know whether the incident had occurred. Jordana's discussions suggested that, as a senior adviser, he must have had severe doubts. If Scrafton's account is accepted, Howard would have had serious doubts.

Asked about his state of mind when he went to the Press Club, Howard said: 'I didn't think the story was concocted.'[67] After the election Howard made a comprehensive statement: 'At no stage was I told by my department or was I told by any member of my staff or was I told by any minister or was I told by any official in any other department that the original advice tendered was wrong. I had no grounds to believe it was.'[68]

These comments are buttressed by Moore-Wilton's contemporaneous evidence to the Senate Estimates Committee in February 2002. On at least four separate occasions during several hours of evidence, Moore-Wilton said he had had no knowledge that the story was wrong and that he provided 'no such advice' to Howard.[69] 'To my certain knowledge,' Moore-Wilton said, 'I did not brief the Prime Minister or any minister' on "children overboard" during the campaign.'[70] At another point, he said: 'Let me be clear again … I have never been told that children were not thrown overboard until I read General Powell's report.'[71]

Howard had referred Moore-Wilton to this evidence when asking him to reconsider his position. When Moore-Wilton changed his story with the author on 9 July he confirmed that he had re-read this critical evidence.

Pointing to this evidence, Howard said:

> Max Moore-Wilton made it clear to the Senate Committee at the time that he did not tell me the story was wrong. His evidence is unequivocal on this point. It is not credible to think that if Max had told me in November before the election that he would have allowed me to make these denials after the election and not raise it with me.[72]

There is, however, an obvious point that transcends forensic efforts to discern how much Howard knew. As prime minister, Howard had the ability to order his ministers and senior officials to quickly establish what had happened. Indeed, it could have been clarified within a few hours and Howard given the total truth. Because it was not in Howard's interest, he did not ask.

This is unsurprising. It is fatuous to think any other prime minister would have behaved differently three days before the election. The point, as Hugh White said, is that a better served PM would have avoided this dilemma. 'I don't think Bob Hawke would have found himself in this position,' White said. 'Under Hawke the relationship between the defence structure and ministers would have meant that the story was corrected at an early stage.'[73] It is hard to imagine these events happening under Beazley or Robert Ray as Defence Minister.

Scrafton did not reveal his side of the 7 November discussion with Howard until 2004—after he had left the public service. There were two internal inquiries into the 'children overboard' incident in 2002. Scrafton conceded that parts of his statement to the first inquiry established by Moore-Wilton were untrue because he had not been prepared to reveal the substance of his conversation with Howard at that time.

In relation to the second inquiry conducted by Major General Powell, whom Scrafton knew, he revealed details of the Howard conversation on the basis that they remained confidential. Powell and his assistant, Commander Noonan, later confirmed that the confidential material Scrafton provided to them in 2002 was consistent with his 2004 comments—namely, that Howard was told that the events as recounted were unlikely to have occurred.[74]

The final fiasco in this saga, as Howard surged to the election line, came on the afternoon of 8 November. Shackleton, as Chief of Navy, told the media that the navy's advice to government was merely that people were 'being threatened' about being thrown into the water. The wire story ran, naturally, as Shackleton contradicting Reith. Hendy promptly spoke to Shackleton to request a clarifying statement, and this was subsequently negotiated. The navy chief said later that he was 'surprised' to find Hendy did not seem to know that 'the original report was incorrect'.[75]

After the election the truth was revealed in a series of inquiries, with Labor's chief inquisitor being Leader of the Opposition in the Senate, John Faulkner. The turning point came at Senate Estimates when Houston, under Faulkner's questioning, put on the public record his correcting advice to Reith the week before the election. Faulkner said this was the most important question he had asked in his political career. Howard insists that he only discovered the story was wrong on the eve of Houston's evidence.[76]

In the interim, Reith and Barrie had continued to square the circle. When Barrie returned from overseas Reith told him: 'While you were away Angus looked at this issue and told me it didn't happen. But he didn't convince me. I intend to rely upon what you said.' Weeks later, when Barrie finally rang Howard to concede that the story was wrong, he recalled: 'Howard said "I've been waiting for you to ring me." He said "I don't want anybody hung out to dry on this matter."'[77] Some time later Howard bumped into Houston. 'I told him his evidence wouldn't have any impact on the way he was treated—and we kept that pledge,' Howard said. [78] After Barrie and Cosgrove, Houston became CDF.

There are four conclusions to the 'children overboard' story. First, it had no sustained prominence in the election campaign despite being a high profile issue at the end.

Second, it revealed a profound failure of accountability within the Defence structure. The civilian and military chiefs, Hawke and Barrie, failed to give the minister firm oral and written advice. This exposed a defect in the diarchy and the Defence department's weakness in dealing both with the CDF and the minister.

Justifying his inaction, Hawke said he took a 'pure view' of the civilian/military demarcation of responsibilities in the diarchy. Hawke said SIEV 4 'was an operational matter run by the CDF … he was providing the advice and discussing these matters with the minister, not me. I do not think I have a role in it'. [79]

This is unsustainable given the political accountability onus that resides within the Defence department for the conduct of policy. As late as 25 March 2002, Hawke told the Senate he still did not know whether or not children had been thrown overboard. [80] Yet the Defence system knew the story was false. Hawke told the Senate committee that he 'could' have done more but it was 'an open question' whether he 'should' have done more. [81] The next head of the Prime Minister's Department, Shergold, told colleagues he believed Hawke had gone 'missing in action'. [82]

'The Howard government inherited a culture with the military having a rising dominance and they found they liked it,' Scrafton said. [83] Howard gravitated towards the CDF, whether it was Barrie, Cosgrove or Houston. He was less taken by the principle of a powerful Defence secretary but probably would have been happy if one had materialised.

Third, the incident documented the Howard government's management of the civilian/military system for its political benefit. This was embodied by Reith, who dominated both the CDF and the Defence secretary. In the end, Reith's overkill proved fatal. It was his early October decision to stick with the story that was the pivotal factor—it gave life to a false event. The gain for the government was insignificant: it didn't need 'children overboard' to win the election, yet its notoriety would damage Howard's integrity forever. The story became the threshold for Labor's accusation of a lying pathology that would plague the Howard government in its final two terms.

The saga is a reminder that ministers 'decide' and that 'advice' is a private and public instrument to be used or abused. In this case, Reith used advice as a shield to protect the government. The public service, on the other hand, was wary about offering advice that it felt ministers did not want.

Fourth, Howard's approach was dictated by election realpolitik. The 'system' failed Howard at the outset by not correcting the story. In the final days Howard must have had real doubts about the story. But the evidence is against his knowing conclusively that the story was wrong—primarily because he did not ask. Howard's tactic in the final three days —to relentlessly defend his position—was unremarkable. This was the action of a political leader on election eve. However, Howard, as prime minister, must take responsibility for the fact that the Australian people were misled on this issue for the entire campaign.

It was Reith's swansong. Years later Barrie would enjoy having dinner with him in London. 'Reith's a very personable guy, I liked him as a person to work with. But whatever it took was what Reith would do,' Barrie said.[84] 'I have worked with a dozen or so ministers,' Scrafton said. 'Reith was the most analytical, a stickler for getting as much advice as possible, very bright, very loyal. I saw, when he had inadvertently misled parliament, he couldn't get back into the chamber fast enough to correct the record, but once it became political, absolutely no scruples.'[85]

ELECTION 2001: THE HOWARD CONSOLIDATION

Should Howard be re-elected, I believe the country will pay an enormous price.
—Paul Keating, October 2001

I n November 2001 John Howard won his third and most satisfying election. This was the turning point in his prime ministerial career—his authority reached a higher plateau, his dominance over Labor intensified and he stamped Australia with his imprint. At this stage, Howard moved into the category of influential prime ministers.

The election unleashed the authentic Howard—the GST reformer, sponsor of economic growth and household aspiration, expansive vote-buyer off the Budget, executioner of the republic, warrior-in-arms with Bush, arch-protector of borders and orchestrator of a defensive cultural unity. With the biblical injunction of three victories, it became untenable to assert that Howard was a political aberration.

'It was the 2001 election that made us into a long-term, seriously successful government,' Howard reflects. 'To win three times in a row when you've run an activist, on occasions controversial, government is a huge achievement.'[1] The victory answered the question that had plagued Howard's second term: would he succumb as a two-term PM or recover from his 1998 poll fright to become a long-run incumbent?

His re-election came not just on the 'old' Howard agenda but on a 'new' Howard agenda of national security against Islamist terrorists and border security against boat people seeking asylum. The new agenda, unforeseen three months before the election, would prevail for the next five years and shift the structure of politics in Howard's favour.

In retrospect, it is surprising Howard's win was not greater. Given a losing deck, Kim Beazley campaigned with unflagging commitment.

Howard won in a two-party-preferred swing of 1.9 per cent, increasing the government's majority from 12 to 14 seats. Not a single sitting Coalition MP lost to Labor. Yet it was a status quo type result that contrasted with the volatility in the polls over the previous nine months.

'The way to see this election is that Howard had everything handed to him and still nearly lost,' Beazley said. 'At the start of the campaign I was told by party headquarters we were gone and that I would struggle in my own seat.'[2] His office chief, Michael Costello said: 'Look at the issues—refugees, the 9/11 attack, the anthrax scares, the deployment of Australian troops in Afghanistan. Howard should have destroyed Labor for a generation. But Kim campaigned brilliantly and kept Howard's gain to a very modest level.'[3]

Howard became the fourth prime minister since World War II to win a third election, following in the footsteps of Menzies, Hawke and Fraser. This victory created the conditions for him to become Australia's second longest-serving prime minister. The pro-Howard swing was the most substantial to any incumbent government since Harold Holt's 1966 landslide over Vietnam.

While Labor was demoralised, the numbers meant it had avoided subjugation in the next parliament. The reality, however, is that Labor's strategy over the previous five years—offering a small target and trying to win off Howard's negatives—had failed. In the end, Howard proved too formidable and opportunistic while Beazley looked too unconvincing and negative.

Howard's consolidation came from three events—the May Budget, the Tampa/border protection drama, and the 9/11 attack on the United States. Before the Budget the omens pointed to a Labor win, with Howard's position almost irrecoverable.

It was the giveaway Budget saw Howard return to a competitive situation. The two Newspolls post-Budget, when averaged, had Labor and the Coalition each on 40.5 per cent of the primary vote, pointing to a modest ALP win on preferences. Yet Howard's recovery implied a Labor vulnerability. This was verified on 14 July 2001 at the Aston byelection in Melbourne after the death of the sitting Liberal MP. Needing a 4.1 per cent swing to secure the seat, Labor fell short with 3.4 per cent, a weak effort that failed to mobilise real anger against the Howard government.

Six weeks later the Tampa produced a sharp shift in the polls, with Howard moving into a winning position. The only two Newspolls—post-Tampa yet before 9/11—when averaged, had a Coalition primary vote lead of 44.5 per cent to Labor's 39.5 per cent. It was a decisive shift that meant Labor was facing defeat. Suddenly, Labor had become the underdog and Howard was in the ascendancy.

The bigger event, however, was the terrorist attack on the United States. In the history of Australian polling its impact was virtually unprecedented. The first two Newspolls post-9/11 recorded the same result: a Coalition primary vote lead of 50–35 per cent—a Howard landslide. The Labor vote fell by the same margin as the Coalition vote rose—a double blow. The net gain to Howard was 10 percentage points. The AC Nielsen poll also showed the big leap in Howard's position came as a result of the 9/11 attack. This was the situation on 5 October when Howard called an election for 10 November. It is doubtful whether there has been a greater election eve turnaround in history and it penetrates to the perennial dispute about the 2001 election.

'We would have won without Tampa, no question,' says Liberal Party Director Lynton Crosby. 'Our fortunes were on the turn before Tampa.'[4] This reflects the post-election contest, the government insisting that Tampa was not the decisive event and Labor claiming that Howard won the election on the disreputable Tampa tactic of xenophobia and racism. However, Beazley argues persuasively that Tampa and 9/11 issues merged in political terms. 'In my view the Tampa issue on its own would not have brought them home,' he says. 'We would have overcome that. It was the conflation of two issues, Tampa and 9/11, that mattered. While Tampa and 9/11 were separate issues they became blurred in the public mind.'[5]

Crosby's explanation follows a similar line. It finishes with Howard's leadership. 'Tampa and 9/11 were part of the same process,' Crosby says. 'They made national security into a frontline election issue. This put a premium on leadership: the public wanted a strong leader able to handle these unpredictable challenges. This is where Howard had the edge over Beazley.'[6] For Crosby 'more than anything else, the election was about leadership', with Tampa reinforcing 'an existing perception' of Howard's strength and determination.[7]

Professor Ian McAllister from the ANU, drawing upon the 2001 Australian Election Study, concluded that the combined issues of Tampa and 9/11 cost Labor the election and that, of the two, 'terrorism was the more important' in the result. He argued that if 9/11 had occurred but not Tampa 'the Coalition would in all probability still have won the election'.[8]

The government did not need to fabricate links between boat people and 9/11 but Peter Reith and Howard tried. Defending the ADF interdiction, Reith said there could otherwise be 'a pipeline for terrorists to come in and use your country as a staging post for terrorist activities'.[9] On election eve, in an interview with the *Courier-Mail*, Howard said: 'Australia had no way to be certain terrorists, or people with terrorist links, were not among the asylum seekers trying to enter the country by boat from Indonesia.'[10] Beazley has never forgiven him these statements. He said: 'Howard and I received the same briefing from ASIO chief Dennis Richardson, who said there were no terrorists on the boats. It was absolutely clear.'[11] Government efforts to blur the distinction ran contrary to its national security advice.

While Tampa and 9/11 merged in electoral terms, they were clearly different events. The 9/11 attack revealed a new global threat from Islamist terrorists while the boats showed that many Muslims sought escape from persecution in their homelands. The 9/11 attack was beyond Howard's control yet it was his decision that made Tampa an issue. Whereas Howard and Beazley were united on the 9/11 attack, they were initially divided over Tampa. Whereas the 9/11 attack united Australian opinion, Tampa polarised opinion between a large majority and an active minority. Because Tampa was the initial event that ruined Labor, it was seen by many Labor supporters as an immoral act for electoral gain. It is impossible to dissect the emotional tides of 2001 without recognition of these forces.

The evidence overall strongly suggests that Howard would have won with either Tampa or 9/11 behind him—either would have done; he did not need both. The combination reinforced Howard's position yet the election result may not have been much different had there been one, not two, such incidents. Beazley and Howard agree that 9/11 had a greater impact than Tampa.

Yet Howard argues another more contentious line: 'I feel that, without Tampa and September 11, we still would have won the election.'[12] This is a stretch and Labor dismisses the view outright. In reply, Beazley says: 'I saw our polling post-2001. There was 9 per cent of the vote that moved from Labor to Liberal. Of that, 2 per cent went due to Howard's leadership and 7 per cent on a variant of the security/defence/immigration theme.' In short, Beazley says Howard won the election on Tampa and 9/11. Yet this is an obvious conclusion—it does not necessarily mean that Howard, in normal circumstances, would not have won on the economy. But Howard was behind and would have needed to bridge the gap.

Much of Labor's mythology enshrines the Tampa as the pivotal event. The best exposition of this view came from ALP National Secretary Geoff Walsh, drawing upon Labor research. Three weeks after the poll,

Walsh said: 'Political veterans say they have never seen an issue like Tampa. Tampa effectively knee-capped One Nation and anointed John Howard. Three-quarters of the One Nation vote loss went straight to the Coalition.'[13]

Walsh argued that post-9/11 it was still Tampa 'that remained the reference point and driver for voters switching to the Coalition'. He said there were three elements in vote switching triggered by Tampa: fear about more boats, the perception of Howard's response as popular and strong, and the fact that Labor was judged to have 'played politics' on the issue. Walsh reported that Labor MPs felt Tampa had been the killer. In the last week of the campaign government advertising relied heavily on border protection. Newspaper ads featured a clenched-fisted Howard above the words: '*We* decide who comes to this country and the circumstances in which they come.' This pledge from Howard's policy speech became the most memorable phrase of the election.[14]

Walsh said that, as late as June 2001, ALP Labor research showed a 4-6 per cent two-party-preferred swing to Labor in outer metropolitan marginal seats, with the Coalition primary vote falling. He said Tampa produced an 8-point turnabout against Labor in two-party-preferred terms and slaughtered this winning position. 'Tampa remade John Howard's image,' Walsh said. 'Before Tampa, he was seen as tired, out-of-touch and the architect of an unpopular tax.'[15] This testifies to Labor's shock at seeing victory stolen.

The quality media was weak in assessing the reason for Tampa's impact and fell back on the racial stereotype. This was justified given the government's demonisation of boat people, stoking xenophobia, manipulating the 'children overboard' deception and linking boat people with terrorists. But attributing the public reaction to race was wrong and misjudged both the Australian public and the border protection issue.

In his analysis of the issue Ian McAllister tested why Australians were so intense, in a ratio of 3:1, in support of turning back the boats. After assessing four factors he found that the explanations (in priority order) were: opposition to higher immigration levels, national identity and pride leading people to believe the asylum seekers were affronting the norms of accepted Australian behaviour, a perception of the boat people as rule-breakers (or 'queue jumpers') who refused to follow the proper channels to enter Australia—a response likely to be strong among first generation immigrants, and, last of all, racial prejudice.[16]

Implicit in these factors is Australia's tradition that all people movement to this country should be authorised by government in the national interest. History shows this has applied whether the people involved were European, Asian or Middle Eastern. It went to issues of Australian security and identity that were prominent in the decision of the six colonies to federate in 1901.

An inability to grasp the cultural foundations of the border protection issue was conspicuous in the 2001 disputes over Tampa. While Beazley initially disputed Howard's bill, he embraced a hard-line border protection stance during the campaign, provoking criticism that he had 'sold out'. Yet Labor's vote would have been lower had Beazley fought Howard on border protection and no responsible Labor leader would have taken such a position. Former NSW Labor minister Rodney Cavalier said: 'You do not engage in equivocating postures on a matter as fundamental as the territorial integrity of the nation.'[17]

But Labor's alarm about Tampa conceals another story: that of its protracted strategic blunders. For too long Tampa has been used to excuse Labor's multiple deficiencies. During 1998–2001 Labor chose the path of caution, confident that Howard would ebb out of office. It relied on hostility to the GST, household pressures, petrol prices, Howard's alienation of his constituencies and grass-roots retail politics to mobilise a coalition of the disaffected. By March 2001 Beazley was riding high on this tactic.

Labor's confidence reached its symbolic zenith in Melbourne in early May 2001 at the centenary celebrations to honour Australia's first parliamentary sittings. These celebrations also involved the centenary of the Labor Party caucus. Howard presided over the historic commemoration in the Royal Exhibition Building, Melbourne, but Labor hijacked the week: the most memorable event in a week of celebration was Labor's gala dinner to honour its own 100 years, with speeches from its three former prime ministers—Whitlam, Hawke and Keating—along with Beazley, who was introduced as 'our next prime minister'. On display were the exuberance and power of the modern Labor tradition originating with Whitlam. The evening glowed with Labor confidence about its history, present and future, with the impulse transmitted to Beazley.

After the event Beazley was euphoric. He congratulated John Faulkner for his efforts in organising the Melbourne events and upstaging Howard. But Faulkner was shocked and, as a professional, offended at Beazley's supreme confidence that he would win the election. This was the period defined by many ALP advisers as the 'small target strategy'. Faulkner rejected the notion; for him, there could be no such thing. He didn't believe this was the way to win an election. Yet Beazley was fixated on Walsh's marginal seat research. Labor was getting the swing in the seats it needed, unlike the 1998 election. 'We've going to win this,' Beazley told his Labor intimates and the political media before leaving Melbourne.[18] And most people agreed with him. Howard would be swept away as an insignificant prime minister who had simply been lucky enough to beat Keating at his nadir.

In March, when things were blackest, Howard told Beazley across the chamber: 'it may be easy pickings today, but there will come a time when you actually have to tell the Australian people what you stand for'.[19] Howard and Crosby were betting on leadership. Howard had studied his opponent—he knew Beazley was a decent man, a gradualist, a traditionalist, neither bold nor an innovator and pledged to winning on yesterday's agenda.

'The biggest single weakness with Beazley is that he has not argued for three or four causes in his political life,' Howard said, presenting himself, by contrast, as a conviction politician. 'My positions go back to the 1980s. Now whether this proves decisive in the election I don't know. But as I look at my opponent he doesn't have the policy definition that I believe I had in 1996.'[20]

Former ALP national secretary Bob Hogg believed Labor had misread both Howard and the political climate. Hogg said:

> Instead of a hard-headed assessment of John Howard's political skills and policy limitations, the ALP leadership's analysis was coloured by its intense dislike of Howard … the ALP is desperately trying to establish the Beazley 'persona' in these last campaign weeks which itself is an unintended self-criticism. The period since the 1998 election should have been used to achieve that objective. This election was there to be won provided Beazley fought continuously on a positive policy framework. That would have established his credentials as a leader of stature rather than a figure of uncertainty. Instead, the Opposition adopted a purely negative strategy.[21]

In private, Keating was a critic, convinced that Beazley had failed to project an image of policy authority or strength. Former New South Wales general secretary John Della Bosca had publicly criticised Beazley's fixation on GST rollback. Walsh conceded that Labor's big lead in early 2001 was too reliant on preferences, with the primary vote 'not as solid as we would have liked'.[22]

Howard was lucky the Tampa issue materialised—yet Tampa did not produce a rogue result. On the contrary, the issue fitted perfectly into the politics Howard had cultivated since his 1996 victory: support for blue-collar values, validation of 'mainstream' beliefs, championing Australian nationalism and, more recently, presenting as a prime minister pledged to halt the boats. Tampa allowed Howard to demonstrate that most Australians, given the chance, would rally behind his banner. It exposed Labor's uncertainty where Howard was most certain.

Labor's 'small target' strategy was premised on Howard as a weak leader. As Hogg said, Beazley assumed 'that Howard would become as unpopular as Paul Keating and that nothing unexpected would derail his campaign'.[23] One reason Labor hated Tampa was because it destroyed the view of Howard that Labor had enshrined in its winning game plan. Having ridiculed Howard for being 'out of touch', Labor was shocked at how 'in touch' Howard became.

During the campaign Howard planted his convictions centre-stage. Asked to nominate his main achievements over five years, he shot back: 'Undeniably the broad economic achievements, particularly bringing the Budget back into surplus, tax reform and IR reform, East Timor and guns. Put them together.'[24] But they didn't fit together. And they fitted together even less when border protection was included. Howard's was not a coherent ideology. Its only organising principle was as a list of Howard's convictions—and this became the bedrock issue of the 2001 election: it was about Howard's convictions and leadership.

Howard went to the poll with a tactical mix of defence and attack. While a proponent of economic change, he sought to ameliorate its harsh impacts by limiting competition policy, bolstering the social safety net, freezing tariff cuts and denying bank mergers. He was the pragmatist who cut petrol excise and ditched automatic price indexation. Crosby's successor, Brian Loughnane, said: 'The petrol decision was critical—it ensured petrol wasn't an issue and told people Howard was listening. If we hadn't done it, the consequences would have been disastrous.'[25] When this prompted the media to question his convictions, Howard scoffed: 'It would be a major policy shift if I tried to roll back the GST.' Fixated by the need to combat Labor's strengths in health and education, Howard backed Medicare, delivered a private health insurance rebate and poured funds into private schools.

Beazley waited too long to release his policies. As Howard gradually recovered between March and August, there was no core change in Labor tactics. Spooked by Costello's technique of updating the Budget estimates at the start of the campaign, Labor refused to release detailed policy ahead of this fiscal update. It meant that Howard dictated events.

For Howard, the politics of surplus budgets now reached its zenith. Howard and Costello had Labor trapped. They raided the Budget first, leaving a small surplus of only \$500 million projected for 2001–02. This meant Beazley had few funds for his promises since he was not prepared to tolerate a deficit and was not prepared to raise taxes. His two stellar pledges—GST rollback and Knowledge Nation, the precursor to Rudd's Education Revolution—looked feeble. After campaigning for years on 'rollback', in his final policy Beazley kept 97 per cent of GST revenue after three years, which meant rollback was mainly symbolism. The exemptions where Beazley offered relief were limited to energy bills and items such as funerals, nappies, caravans and tampons. Beazley insisted that the tactic worked, saying the GST was the biggest single factor for voters switching from Liberal to Labor.[26] No doubt he did win votes, but Labor's ignominious policy presaged the end to its 'rollback' travesty.

Knowledge Nation was neither a genuine reform nor backed by a hefty financial commitment. Under Beazley's policy, during the first four years he would spend four times as much to finance 'rollback' as he did on universities. If Knowledge Nation had been the priority, Labor would have kept the GST intact to maximise education funding.

At the 2001 poll Labor handed the Hawke–Keating glory of superior economic management to the Coalition. It was now owned by Howard and Costello. Beazley ran as a Labor traditionalist offering better health and education and more fairness. The lethal attack on Howard's economic policy came not from the Federal Opposition but from Keating in his Fairfax campaign columns. An isolated voice, Keating refused to surrender the economy flag:

> In terms of economic outcomes, the government has lived almost exclusively off the policy reforms of the previous Labor government. Its one major structural change was the policy championed by the Socialist Party of France: the GST ... Let's check the government's economic performance. Growth is at a 10 year low. Productivity has fallen sharply from the 3 per cent a year bequeathed to the Liberals by Labor. The dollar? You almost need a pair of binoculars to find it. Today it is US50 cents ... a banana republic exchange rate. The growth in full time jobs has been paltry and unemployment is rising ... the Howard government is the

heaviest taxing Australian Government ever. And the top marginal tax rate is still 48.5 per cent.[27]

Keating attacked Howard for abandoning Labor's plan to boost award-based superannuation beyond 9 per cent, saying the government had dodged 'the one major task left in Australian economic policy: to finally lick the national savings problem'. He mocked Howard and Costello over debt, pointing out that foreign debt had risen from $190 billion to $311 billion under their government. He ridiculed their Budget surplus as 'negligible' and lamented that annual increases in Australia's sharemarket had been greater under Labor than under Howard.[28]

This attack on Howard and Costello came in the name of pro-market liberalism. It fingered their economic vulnerabilities and the modesty of their reforms. But Keating's stance said as much about Labor as about the Coalition. It was a position that Labor—occasional tokenism aside—had deserted. Labor, unlike Keating, had to focus on winning the election. Yet Keating had nailed the Howard–Costello defects—under their policies Australia's savings were too weak, its productivity was slipping and it needed to do more on incentive, jobs and tax. Such views had no role in the campaign.

In truth, campaign 2001 was filled with delusional nostalgia. Howard had a refugee policy that was unsustainable and Beazley's GST rollback was a fraud that kept most of Howard's tax. Two conclusions were obvious: the next prime minister would have to abandon Howard's Pacific Solution and the next Labor leader would have to accept the GST 100 per cent.

Howard, however, had already cast a shadow over his political future. This had come in his sixty-first birthday radio interview with Phillip Clark on 26 July 2000. Before the interview Clark said: 'I'd like, if I could, to talk about being in your sixties and what it means for you.'[29] An astute Clark got under Howard's guard and Howard, in effect, said he would consider his future when he reached 64 in three years' time. Costello saw this as a sign that Howard would belatedly honour his December 1994 'McLachlan-witnessed' statement to leave after a term and a half.

At this moment Howard created expectations that the 2001 election would be his last. While Howard had spoken honestly to Clark, this interview was a serious mistake. Howard had put a self-imposed timetable on himself and raised Costello's hopes. 'Nobody advised me to do it,' Howard said. 'There was no motive. I shouldn't have. It was ill disciplined. Strewth, when I'm 64, yes, the irony of that didn't hit me until afterwards.'[30]

On polling day, Howard lifted the Coalition's two-party-preferred vote from 49 per cent to 50.9 per cent, the second-best result for the Coalition in the previous twenty years. But it remained far below Howard's 1996 benchmark of 53.6 per cent. The One Nation aberration was being unwound; the halving of its vote against the Tampa backdrop guaranteed Howard as beneficiary. His success lay in uniting the conservative base. Howard calculated that any progressive Liberal voters he lost would be outweighed by the conservatives he gained, a judgement true in 2001 but not in 2007.

Preferences delivered the Labor Party a respectability that concealed its alarming vulnerability. While Labor's parliamentary numbers were reduced from 67 to 65 seats, its primary vote was only 37.8 per cent, the lowest for nearly seventy years. In New South Wales and Queensland, it polled even worse. Howard and his Liberal strategists had reason to believe that Labor's structural problems would deepen over the next term.

The 2001 election was notable for Howard's assertion of his true self. His evolution as prime minister, for better or worse, had reached a new plateau. The tactical caution of 1996 was stripped away and the GST reformer of 1998 had surrendered to a fuller, more authentic, more ruthless Howard. For the first time, Howard was free: Howard campaigned as Howard—and, in the process, he took Labor by surprise.

Howard went to the election seeking final endorsement of the GST, having defeated the republic, steadfast in his rejection of the Aboriginal apology, triumphant in a military deployment to underwrite East Timor's independence, undisguised in his scepticism about the label of multiculturalism, resolute about going to war in Afghanistan along with George W Bush, having launched a border protection crackdown spearheaded by the ADF, and as champion of a resurgence 'common man' nationalism.

He was a more populist, tougher and more assured leader. It is hard to imagine a more comprehensive assault on the icons of the progressive Left. For the first time Howard's full political persona was on display— the strange policy amalgam of economic liberalism, social conservatism, cultural traditionalism and national security vigilance. It was the full Monty.

Within Howard, there was a tangible sense of vindication. He was contemptuous of claims that he manipulated the Tampa issue to stoke racism and xenophobia. He anticipated victory along with the defeat of those critics who claimed he was an illegitimate prime minister. 'Obviously, it will be much harder for my critics to write me down if

I win,' he said a fortnight out. 'Much harder. They could have explained it away in 1996 or even in 1998 but it will be much harder this time.'[31]

Later he said: 'I think there was a view throughout the first part of 2001 that the government would probably lose. I think the point about legitimacy is a very fair observation in relation to the commentariat, but it's not a fair observation in relation to the public.'[32] Many Australians were growing comfortable with Howard. Hogg said: 'The Prime Minister talks of his "commitment to the land I love" and says that what drives him most in public life is [the] "spirit of the Australian people". These sentiments appear to be genuine.'[33]

In a rare event Howard discussed his personal adjustment to the office. 'I don't brood as much about whether something is the right decision,' he said. 'There is something to the theory that the best leadership years are later ones. I think you handle things better. In many respects I feel more on top of it now than at any time since I became prime minister. I have got better.' Reviewing his entire career and his battles with Fraser, Peacock, Bjelke-Petersen and Hewson, Howard said: 'I have never been broken.' The 2001 victory instilled in Howard new authority and longevity.[34]

With Labor sticking by a disciplined campaign message, it was Keating who launched the ultimate accusation—that Howard had betrayed Australia by surrendering to its dark side. For Keating, Howard had proved even worse than he had expected. He said:

> On one occasion, Howard said that he was the most conservative leader the Liberal Party had ever had … I knew Howard would down the republic … I said at the time that Asian governments would meet him but would not seriously deal with him because I knew he would soon show form and turn his back on effective regional engagement. And I knew given half a chance, he would abandon any wider notion of reconciliation with our Aborigines. But what I didn't know is that he would give a wink and a nod to Pauline Hanson's first intolerant utterances … This government, in pursuit of electoral gain, will play fast and loose with the country's conventions and, I believe, with its moral substance … Should Howard be re-elected, I believe the country will pay an enormous price. Those in the region around us who, until now, have regarded Howard's two victories as an aberration will, I believe, sullenly bed down for the long-term in their dealings with Australia. Our marginalisation, now advanced, will accelerate.[35]

Keating's hostility towards Howard was unabated. His polemic was a mixture of validity, exaggeration and delusion. Howard's record is more complex in its successes and defects than Keating would tolerate. But Howard had buried too many Labor dreams. Keating forgave neither Howard's policies nor his 1996 victory. This was Keating as perpetual warrior, refighting old battles and contesting Howard over the nation's direction, dismayed that Labor seemed unable to prosecute this job. His unifying idea was Howard's infamy but this argument had been lost: Howard had won two elections and was about to win a third. Any notion that in Australia's democracy repeated election victories were aberrations was fanciful. This idea nourished Labor's heart but did not assist its grasp of Howard's achievements or how he might be defeated.

After the election, Les Carlyon, in a memorable article, described the alienation of the intellectual class from Howard:

> Howard, they say, is an interloper and Keating had greatness in him. Howard sees postcards and Keating painted great frescoes in our minds. Howard is mean-spirited and Keating was all about kindness and goodness. Howard is suburban and Keating had a large mind … The trouble with the anti-Howard brigade is that they keep delivering the same twee sermon. *Why we should all feel guilty. This is not the Australia I love. How can I tell my children what Howard did to [tick box] Aborigines/republicans/refugees/the broad-faced potoroo?* … The song has been playing on the op-ed pages of our broadsheets for years now, and with Howard's third election win it has become shrill. It may be time to give it up on the grounds that it is irrelevant to the world we live in.[36]

Crosby saw that economic prosperity, border protection and 9/11 had put steel into Howard's leadership brand—he looked credible, popular and strong. The government would live off this brand for a fourth term. By the election, the economy had bounced back. June quarter growth in 2001 was a strong 0.9 per cent. The recession scare was long gone.

The 2001 election opened a new phase of politics. It moved beyond the 1980s agenda that had seeded the Howard–Keating rivalry; it invested Howard with command over Conservative Australia and the Liberal Party that doomed any Costello challenge; and it gave Howard a unique opportunity—the chance for a successful prime ministership and retirement on his own terms.

Its legacy led directly to the decisive February 2003 discussion on the leadership between Howard and Costello. They have different views of this meeting but the 'bottom line' seems that Howard's intention was to stay unless his leadership was ruined by the Iraq war starting the next month. 'He told me that he had not yet made up his mind but he wanted to give his successor time to establish himself before the 2004 election,' Costello said.[37] But Howard's recall is different. 'I made it very clear to Peter that I was not keen to go,' he said. 'We had a very lengthy meeting. I kept a record of that. I made it very very clear that he shouldn't assume I was going to go.'[38] According to Howard, he was preparing Costello for his mid-year decision to stay as PM.

There was, however, one situation in which Howard concedes he would have resigned—if the Iraq war went badly. Howard says he indicated this to Costello.

> I do think we accepted that if the thing in Iraq had gone really badly for us ... I'd have accepted that and gone. I know both of us said at the time 'Look, you know, we're about to be engaged in a military conflict and we'll have to sort of see what happens. I had at the back of my mind and I suppose it was something I would have discussed with Janette—if the thing went very badly in Iraq and it got all ugly then I would accept responsibility. And that might make my position very difficult because I didn't know how that [Iraq] was going to go, you know, whether we'd have a lot of fatalities.[39]

This shows Howard felt that a bad campaign against Saddam Hussein would probably cost his job and deliver the leadership to Costello. It is the first time Howard has conceded this point. It confirms Costello's account of this discussion—that Howard had told him 'if Iraq goes badly it [the party] would want me to go'.[40] In retrospect, Howard's position after the 2001 election was so strong that only a disaster in the Iraq campaign proper would have forced his exit.

After the election, Howard's relations with new National Party leader, John Anderson, solidified the Coalition. The Liberal moderates, Hill and Ruddock, were tied to Howard. His 1996 promise of a voter realignment based on the Howard battlers now gained fresh credence. Howard's use of economic, cultural and security issues to detach a section of the Labor vote had spanned three election victories. 'I think there was a mood change when we went into 2002,' Howard said.[41] Labor was psychologically damaged by the defeat. Beazley resigned the leadership in favour of Simon Crean.

It is false, however, to think Howard had taken command of the country. While beaten, Labor stayed competitive. As Walsh said, it had a 'real chance' of winning the next election. It had political dominance within the states. Howard's majority was modest rather than large and he did not control the Senate. Beazley had beaten Howard during the campaign debate. Howard had polarised the country with Tampa, refugee policy and 'children overboard', prompting a community resistance that would grow over the next two terms.

Despite Labor's rage, the policy differences between Howard and Beazley had been minor. While Labor hated Howard, his success had pulled Labor into his orbit. Beazley backed Howard over the 'war on terror', invoking ANZUS and border protection; he had virtually conceded the GST; they agreed on the Budget surplus, an independent central bank and the open economy; their differences were over a series of programs hardly substantial in dollar terms. More significantly, Labor opposed Telstra privatisation, wanted to do more on education and took a symbolic position that became decisive later—promising to ratify the Kyoto Protocol.

This was a reminder of the historical truth unpalatable to both Labor and the Liberals: Australia in 2001 remained a Keating–Howard project. The policy continuity between them still defined national progress while their differences were sharper and more intense than ever, despite Keating's exit from politics five years earlier.

The 2001 election left Howard emboldened with a fresh agenda. His final two terms would be dominated by his partnership with Bush in the 'war on terror', the China boom that transformed Australia's national income and the rise of climate change.

In 1994 Howard had said that one and a half terms would be enough—but he had forsaken such modesty. Howard was now aiming higher. He was like a mountaineer who, having climbed to a level beyond his dreams, was empowered by success yet vulnerable to hubris.

NOTES

Introduction: The March of Patriots

1   See Paul Kelly, *The End of Certainty*, Allen & Unwin, Sydney, 1992, Introduction.

2   This paragraph draws in part on discussions with former NSW Labor Minister, Rodney Cavalier. See John Edwards, *Curtin's Gift*, Allen & Unwin, Sydney, 2005.

3   Kelly, *The End Of Certainty*.

4   See John Edwards, *Quiet Boom*, Lowy Institute Paper 14, 2006.

5   Peter Whiteford, 'The Welfare Expenditure Debate: Economic Myths of the Left and the Right Revisited', *Economic and Labour Relations Review*, vol. 17, no. 1, 1996.

Two Men

1   For accounts of childhood and family background see John Edwards, *Keating: The Inside Story*, Penguin, Melbourne, 1996; Fia Cumming, *Mates, Five Champions of the Labor Right*, Allen & Unwin, Sydney, 2001; Wayne Errington and Peter Van Onselen, *John Winston Howard: A Life*, Melbourne University Press, Melbourne, 2007; and David Barnett, *John Howard Prime Minister*, Viking, Ringwood, 1997. For newspaper accounts of Howard see Milton Cockburn, *Sydney Morning Herald*, 7 January 1989; Roy Masters, *Sydney Morning Herald Good Weekend*, 7 April 1990; and Robert Wainwright and Tony Stephens, *Sydney Morning Herald*, 18, 20 and 21 September 2004.

2   Edwards, p. 38.

3   Cumming, p. 12.

4   Barnett, pp. 5–7.

5   Cockburn, *Sydney Morning Herald*.

6   Errington and Van Onselen, p. 13.

7   Cumming, p. 58.

8   Cumming, p. 57.

9   Edwards, p. 53.

10   Howard, interview, February 2005.

11   Cumming, p. 12.

12   Edwards, p. 68.

13   Edwards, p. 62.

14   Cumming, chapters 1–3.

15   Howard, interview, February 2005.

16   John Howard, address at gala dinner for 50th anniversary of the election of the first Liberal government, 9 December 1999.

17   Errington and Van Onselen, pp. 29–37.

18   Sir John Carrick, interview with the author, November 2008.
19   This view is based on personal discussions with Paul Keating during the 1970s.
20   Errington and Van Onselen, pp. 29–37.
21   John Howard, discussion with the author, December 2008.
22   Sir John Carrick, interview with the author, November 2008.
23   John Howard, Tribute Dinner, Sydney, 7 May 2008.
24   Carrick, interview, November 2008.
25   Masters, *Sydney Morning Herald*.
26   AW Martin, *Robert Menzies, A Life*, vol. 2, Melbourne University Press, Melbourne, 1999, p. 125.
27   See Errington and Van Onselen, chapter 1.
28   Don Watson, *Recollections of a Bleeding Heart*, Random House, Sydney, 2002, p. 4.
29   His earlier ambition for Banks was thwarted due to a redistribution.
30   Edwards, p. 70.
31   Edwards, Chapter 3.
32   House of Representatives, *Hansard*, 17 March 1970, p. 515.
33   Errington and Van Onselen, p. 28.
34   John Howard, interview with the author, February 2005.
35   John Lukacs, *Churchill*, Scribe, Melbourne, 2002, p. 178.
36   Martin, p. 504.
37   Robert Wainwright and Tony Stephens, *Sydney Morning Herald*, 18 September 2004.
38   Barnett, p. 15.
39   Barnett, p. 15.
40   Wainwright and Stephens, *Sydney Morning Herald*, 18 September 2004.
41   Howard, interview, February 2005.
42   Errington and Van Onselen, chapter 2.
43   Paul Keating, interview with the author, May 2008.
44   Keating, interview, May 2008.
45   Paul Kelly, *The End of Certainty*, Allen & Unwin, Sydney, 1992, p. 247.
46   Kelly, p. 247. For a recent debate on my Australian Settlement argument see *Australian Journal of Political Science*, vol. 39, no. 1, March 1994.
47   Keating, interview, May 2008.
48   Keating, interview, May 2008.
49   Keating, interview, May 2008.

1   A New Leadership

1   Paul Keating, discussion with the author, January 1992.
2   John Edwards, *Keating: The Inside Story*, Penguin, Melbourne, 1996, p. 465.
3   Don Watson, *Recollections of a Bleeding Heart*, Random House, Sydney, 2002, p. 19.
4   Stephen Smith, discussion with the author, March 2003.
5   Mark Ryan, interview with the author, November 2008.
6   Watson, p. 25.
7   Bill Kelty, interview with the author, April 2008.
8   John Dawkins, interview with the author, December 2008.
9   John Button, *As It Happened*, Text Publishing, Melbourne, 1998, p. 402.

10 Edwards, p. 467.

11 Ryan, interview, November 2008.

12 Paul Keating, Canberra Press Gallery speech, 7 December 1990.

13 John Dawkins, discussion with the author, December 2008.

14 Neal Blewett, *A Cabinet Diary*, Wakefield Press, Kent Town, 1999, pp. 30, 101.

15 Don Russell, speech on the tenth anniversary of the Keating government, 20 December 2001.

16 Ryan, interview, November 2008.

17 Tony Cole, discussion with the author, April 2005.

18 Michael Keating, interview with the author, February 2009.

19 Michael Costello, interview with the author, March 2009.

20 Edwards, pp. 467–9.

21 Michael Keating, interview, February 2005.

22 Allan Gyngell, interview with the author, December 2008.

23 M Keating, interview, February 2009.

24 Russell, speech, 20 December 2001.

25 See Mark Ryan (ed.), *Advancing Australia, The Speeches of Paul Keating,* Big Picture Publications, Sydney, 1995.

26 Paul Kelly, *The End of Certainty*, Allen & Unwin, Sydney, 1992, p. 658.

27 Watson, p. 25.

28 Based on personal discussions with Paul Keating, 1998–91.

29 Paul Keating, interview with the author, May 2005.

30 Ryan, interview, November 2008.

31 P Keating, interview, May 2008.

2 Big-bang Liberalism

1 John Hewson, interview with the author, December 2008.

2 Hewson, interview, December 2008.

3 Peter Hendy, The Politics of a Goods and Services Tax, unpublished paper, 1997, p. 57.

4 Norman Abjorensen, *John Hewson, A Biography*, Lothian Books, Port Melbourne, 1993, p. 130.

5 Paul Kelly, *The End of Certainty*, Allen & Unwin, Sydney, 1992, p. 598.

6 John Howard, interview with the author, February 2005.

7 Hewson, interview, December 2008.

8 Peter Costello with Peter Coleman, *The Costello Memoirs*, Melbourne University Press, Melbourne, 2008, p. 57.

9 Hewson, interview, December 2008.

10 Geoff Carmody, interview with the author, June 2005.

11 Peter Hendy, interview with the author, January 2005.

12 Hendy, chapter 6.

13 Hendy, chapter 6.

14 Hendy, p. 98.

15 Hendy, pp. 94–9.

16 Don Watson, *Recollections of a Bleeding Heart*, Random House, Sydney, 2002, p. 18.

17 Peter Reith, interview with the author, January 2009.

18 Howard, interview, February 2005.
19 See Ross Gittins, *Sydney Morning Herald*, 4 December 1991.
20 Kelly, p. 615.
21 Helen Trinca, *Australian*, 22 November 1991, and *Australian*, 23–4 November 1991.
22 John Howard, speech, 20 October 1992.
23 John Howard, National Press Club speech, 7 October 1992.
24 *Jobsback*, The Federal Coalition's Industrial Relations Policy, October 1992.
25 Howard, speech, 7 October 1992.
26 *Australian*, 21 October 1992, and *Age*, 21 October 1992.
27 Peter Hendy, interview with the author, March 2005.
28 Hewson, interview, December 2008.
29 Peter Reith, interview with the author, January 2009.

3 The Price of Survival

1   John Dawkins, interview with the author, December 2008.
2   Michael Keating, interview with the author, February 2005.
3   This chapter draws in part on the best historical account of these events, that given by Laura Tingle in *Chasing the Future*, William Heinemann Australia, Melbourne, 1994.
4   Dawkins, interview, December 2008.
5   Paul Keating, discussion with the author, January 1992.
6   Don Russell, interview with the author, December 2008.
7   John Edwards, *Keating: The Inside Story*, Penguin, Melbourne, 1996, p. 456.
8   Rod Sims, interview with the author, January 2005.
9   John Dawkins, interview with the author, January 2009.
10 Tony Cole, interview with the author, February 2005.
11 Russell, interview, December 2008.
12 Ric Simes, interview with the author, November 2008.
13 John Hewson, interview with the author, December 2008.
14 Cole, interview, February 2005.
15 Tony Harris, interview with the author, January 2009.
16 M Keating, interview, February 2005.
17 Dawkins, interview, December 2008.
18 Tingle, p. 163.
19 Harris, interview, January 2009.
20 Paul Keating, *One Nation* speech, 26 February 1992.
21 M Keating, interview, February 2005; Cole, interview, February 2005.
22 Tingle, p. 161.
23 Harris, interview, January 2009.
24 Dawkins, interview, January 2009; Edwards, p. 486.
25 Dawkins, interview, January 2009.
26 Dawkins, interview, January 2009.
27 Don Watson, *Recollections of a Bleeding Heart*, Random House, Sydney, 2002, p. 272.
28 Watson, p. 272.
29 Ric Simes, *One Nation* memorandum, December 2008.

30   Cole, interview, February 2005.
31   Simes, *One Nation* memorandum.
32   Michael Keating, Comparison of *One Nation* Forecasts and Outcomes, March 2005.
33   Harris, interview, January 2009.
34   Paul Keating, interview with the author, May 2008.
35   Greg Smith, interview with the author, March 2005.
36   Cole, interview, February 2005.
37   Cole, interview, February 2005.
38   *Australian*, 6–7 February 1993.

4   Keating Launches the Culture War

1   Among Australian historians and academics there had been differences over history for some years, often branded a culture war. But it was Keating's intervention that implanted this debate in the centre of politics.
2   Paul Keating, interview with the author, May 2008.
3   Paul Keating, speech, 24 February 1992.
4   This accounts draws on Don Watson, *Recollections of a Bleeding Heart*, Random House, Sydney, 2002, pp. 114–16.
5   House of Representatives, *Hansard*, 27 February 1992, p. 373.
6   Paul Kelly, *100 Years: The Australian Story*, Allen & Unwin, Sydney, 2001, chapters 1 & 5.
7   Kelly, p. 224.
8   Neville Meaney, 'Britishness and Australian Identity', *Australian Historical Studies*, vol. 32, no. 116, April 2001.
9   James Curran, *The Power of Speech*, Melbourne University Press, Melbourne, 2004, p. 197. In developing the argument about Keating's nationalism I have drawn on the ideas in Curran's book.
10   Manning Clark, *A History of Australia*, vol. VI, Melbourne University Press, Melbourne, 1987, pp. 495–6; see also Curran, pp. 211–13.
11   Manning Clark, *Time*, 25 January 1988.
12   House of Representatives, *Hansard*, 28 May 1991, p. 4032.
13   Clark, *A History of Australia*, p. 499.
14   Curran, Chapter 5.
15   Watson, pp. 122–3.
16   Watson, pp. 127–8.
17   Watson, pp. 111–15.
18   House of Representatives, *Hansard*, 28 April 1992, pp. 1833–8.
19   *Hansard*, pp. 1841–9.
20   Keating, interview, May 2008.

5   The Death of Neo-Liberalism

1   Kevin Rudd, *Monthly*, February 2009.
2   John Hyde, *Dry—In Defence of Economic Freedom*, Institute of Public Affairs, Melbourne, 2002, p. 195.
3   *Australian*, 15 March 1993.

4   Andrew Robb, Address to the National Press Club, 1 April 1993.
5   Peter Hendy, The Politics of a Goods and Services Tax, unpublished paper, 1997, p. 153.
6   John Howard, interview with the author, February 2005.
7   Peter Costello with Peter Coleman, *The Costello Memoirs*, Melbourne University Press, Melbourne, 2008, p. 58.
8   Michael Wooldridge, interview with the author, January 2009.
9   Malcolm Fraser, *Quadrant*, May 1993.
10 Fraser, *Quadrant*, May 1993.
11 George Dangerfield, *The Strange Death of Liberal England*, Serif, London, 1997, p. 14.
12 Francis Fukuyama, *The End of History and the Last Man*, Penguin, London, 1992.
13 David Henderson, *The Changing Fortunes of Economic Liberalism*, Institute of Public Affairs New Zealand, Business Round Table, February 1999, p. 58.
14 Gregory Melleuish, *A Short History of Australian Liberalism*, Centre for Independent Studies, St Leonards, January 2001.
15 Don Russell, interview with the author, December 2008.
16 Hendy, p. 132.
17 Hendy, pp. 132–3.
18 Don Russell to Prime Minister, 12 November 1992.
19 John Hewson, interview with the author, December 2008.
20 Hendy, p. 136.
21 *Australian*, 11 December 1992.
22 Hendy, p. 136.
23 *Australian*, 19–20 December 1992.
24 Hewson, interview, December 2008.
25 Laura Tingle, *Chasing the Future*, William Heinemann Australia, Melbourne, 1994, p. 222.
26 *Australian*, 3 March 1993.
27 Fraser, *Quadrant*, May 1993, and *Australian*, 15 March 1993.
28 Robert Manne, 'Has the Liberal Party Lost Middle Australia?' in Brian Costar (ed.), *For Better or Worse—The Federal Coalition*, Melbourne University Press, Melbourne, 1994.
29 *Australian*, 7 March 1993.
30 This draws on two different articles by Hyde: *Australian*, 16 March 1993, and *Quadrant*, May 1993.
31 Howard, interview, February 2005.
32 Peter Costello, interview with the author, April 2005.

6   Econocrats and Bleeding Hearts

1   *Independent Monthly*, April 1993.
2   Don Russell, speech at the tenth anniversary of the Keating government, 20 December 2001.
3   *Australian*, 9 June 2008.
4   Allan Gyngell, interview with the author, December 2008.
5   Don Russell, interview with the author, November 2008.

6   Mark Ryan, interview with the author, November 2008.

7   Gyngell, interview, December 2008.

8   Paul Keating, address to staff, 12 March 1993.

9   Don Watson, *Recollections of a Bleeding Heart*, Random House, Sydney, 2002, pp. 333–4.

10   Deborah Jones, *Australian*, 1 March 1993.

11   *Independent Monthly*, April 1993.

7   The Open Economy

1   Paul Keating, interview with the author, May 2005.

2   See John Carroll and Robert Manne (eds), *Shutdown: The Failure of Economic Rationalism*, Text Publishing, Melbourne, 1992.

3   Bill Kelty, interview with the author, April 2008.

4   Paul Keating, *One Nation* speech, 26 February 1992.

5   Michael Keating, interview with the author, February 2005.

6   Paul Keating, 26 March 1992.

7   This version of the meeting supplemented with interviews draws on John Edwards, *Keating: The Inside Story*, Penguin, Melbourne, 1996, pp. 478–81.

8   Edwards, pp. 479–80.

9   Kelty, interview, April 2008.

10   The account of this meeting is based on Edwards, pp. 479–81.

11   P Keating, interview, May 2005.

12   Paul Kelly, *100 Years: The Australian Story*, Allen & Unwin, Sydney, 2001, p. 139.

13   Paul Keating, speech, 10 November 2004.

14   John Dawkins, interview with the author, January 2009.

15   Tony Harris, interview with the author, January 2009.

16   Edwards, pp. 488–9; Don Russell, interview with the author, May 2005.

17   Don Russell, interview with the author, December 2008.

18   Dawkins, interview, January 2009.

19   Russell, interview, December 2008.

20   P Keating, interview, May 2005.

21   Russell, speech on the tenth anniversary of the Keating government, 20 December 2001.

22   Paul Kelly, *The End of Certainty*, Allen & Unwin, Sydney, 1992, p. 682.

23   *Australian*, 27 August 1992.

24   Russell, interview, May 2005.

25   Russell, interview, December 2008.

26   John Hewson, interview with the author, December 2008.

27   P Keating, interview, May 2005.

8   Empowering the Bank

1   Bernie Fraser, interview with the author, December 2008.

2   Ian Macfarlane, interview with the author, February 2006.

3   Fraser, interview, December 2008.

4   Craig McGregor, *Sydney Morning Herald*, 23 November 1991.

5   McGregor, *Sydney Morning Herald*, 23 November 1991.

6   Fraser, interview, December 2008.
7   Macfarlane, interview, February 2006.
8   Fraser, interview, December 2008.
9   Macfarlane, interview, February 2006.
10 See John Edwards, *Keating: The Inside Story*, Penguin, Melbourne, 1996, pp. 331–2.
11 Paul Kelly, *The End of Certainty*, Allen & Unwin, Sydney, 1992 p. 489.
12 *Sydney Morning Herald*, 23 November 1991.
13 Fraser, interview, December 2008.
14 Macfarlane, interview, February 2006.
15 Fraser, interview, December 2008.
16 Macfarlane, interview, February 2006.
17 Macfarlane, interview, February 2006.
18 Ian Macfarlane, Shann Memorial Lecture, 15 September 1998.
19 Macfarlane, Shann Memorial Lecture, 15 September 1998.
20 Paul Keating, interview with the author, May 2005.
21 Stephen Grenville, 'The Evolution of Monetary Policy: From Money Targets to Inflation Targets', in Philip Lowe (ed.), *Monetary Policy and Inflation Targeting*, Reserve Bank of Australia, Sydney, 1997.
22 *Sydney Morning Herald*, 23 November 1991.
23 See Stephen Bell, *Australia's Money Mandarins*, Cambridge University Press, Cambridge, 2004, p. 12.
24 Fraser, interview, December 2008.
25 Fraser, interview, December 2008.
26 Macfarlane, interview, February 2006.
27 Bernie Fraser, speech to Australian business economists, 31 March 1993.
28 Grenville, p. 148.
29 Fraser, interview, December 2008.
30 Macfarlane, interview, February 2006.
31 Ted Evans, interview with the author, February 2005.
32 Fraser, interview, December 2008.
33 Macfarlane, interview, February 2006.
34 Keating, interview, May 2005.
35 Macfarlane, interview, February 2006.
36 Fraser, interview, December 2008.
37 Evans, interview, February 2005.
38 Fraser, interview, December 2008.
39 Bernie Fraser, 13 June 1995; 30 March 1995.
40 Macfarlane, Shann Memorial Lecture, 15 September 1998.
41 Tony Cole, interview with the author, February 2005.
42 Fraser, interview, December 2008.
43 Cole, interview, February 2005.
44 Evans, interview, February 2005.

9   Towards a Competitive Australia

1   Paul Keating, interview with the author, May 2008.
2   Graeme Samuel, A Five Year Stocktake, 7 July 2000.

3   Ed Willett, The Future of National Competition Policy, 20 November 2000.
4   Fred Hilmer, interview with the author, January 2009.
5   This chapter draws on Fred Brenchley, *Allan Fels: A Portrait of Power*, John Wiley, Australia, 2003.
6   Allan Fels, interviews with the author, December 2008 and January 2009.
7   Graeme Samuel, interview with the author, December 2008.
8   Fels, interview, December 2008.
9   Graeme Samuel, 2003 Alfred Deakin Lecture.
10 Rod Sims, interview with the author, December 2008.
11 Sims, interview, December 2008.
12 Hilmer, interview, January 2009.
13 Hilmer, interview, January 2009.
14 Paul Keating, interview with the author, May 2005.
15 Fred Hilmer, The Bases and Impact of Competition Policy.
16 *National Competition Policy, Report by the Independent Committee of Inquiry*, AGPS, Canberra, August 1993.
17 Elizabeth Harman, 'The National Competition Policy: A Study of the Policy Process and Network', *Australian Journal of Political Science*, vol. 31, no. 2, pp. 211–16, 1996.
18 Hilmer, interview, January 2009.
19 Paul Keating, National Press Club speech, 22 October 1991.
20 Samuel, interview, December 2008.
21 Michael Keating, interview with the author, February 2009.
22 Ted Evans, interview with the author, February 2005.
23 M Keating, interview, February 2009.
24 Jeff Kennett, interview with the author, January 2009.
25 P Keating, interview, May 2008.
26 Fels, interview, December 2008.
27 Fels, interview, January 2009.
28 Fels, interviews, December 2008 and January 2009.
29 Fels, interview, December 2008.
30 Fels, interview, January 2009.
31 Fels, interview, January 2009.
32 Andrew Parkin and Geoff Anderson, 'The Howard Government, Regulatory Federalism and the Transformation of Commonwealth–State Relations', *Australian Journal of Political Science*, vol. 42, no. 2, June 2007.
33 Samuel, interview, December 2008.
34 Samuel, interview, December 2008; 2004 Sir Wallace Kyle Oration.
35 Review of National Competition Policy Reforms, Productivity Commission, no. 33, 28 February 2005.
36 Sims, interview, December 2008.
37 Fels, interview, January 2009.
38 Hilmer, interview, January 2009.
39 P Keating, interview, May 2008.

10 Enterprise and Savings

1   Bill Kelty, interview with the author, April 2008.
2   Mark Wooden, 'Industrial Relations Reform in Australia: Causes, Consequences and Prospects', *Australian Economic Review*, vol. 34, 2001.
3   Kelty, interview, April 2008.
4   Kelty, interview, April 2008.
5   Kelty, interview, April 2008.
6   Laura Tingle, *Chasing the Future*, William Heinemann Australia, Melbourne, 1994, p. 295.
7   John Edwards, *Keating: The Inside Story*, Penguin, Melbourne, 1996, pp. 420–1.
8   Edwards, pp. 420–1.
9   Wooden, 'Industrial Relations Reform in Australia'.
10   Paul Keating, interview with the author, May 2005.
11   John Edwards, *Quiet Boom*, Lowy Institute for International Affairs, Lowy Institute Paper 14, p. 33.
12   Kelty, interview, April 2008.
13   Greg Combet, interview with the author, February 2008.
14   Kelty, interview, April 2008.
15   Keating, interview, May 2005.
16   Keating, interview, May 2005.
17   Laurie Brereton, interview with the author, May 2008.
18   Kelty, interview, April 2008.
19   Brereton, interview, May 2008.
20   Brereton, interview, May 2008.
21   Kelty, interview, April 2008.
22   House of Representatives, *Hansard*, 28 October 1993, p. 2777.
23   Keating, interview, May 2005.
24   Kelty, interview, April 2008.
25   Michael Keating, interview with the author, February 2009.
26   Andrew Murray, interview with the author, March 2008.
27   Peter Anderson, interview with the author, January 2008.
28   Peter Hendy, interview with the author, March 2005.
29   Kelty, interview, April 2008.
30   Wooden, 'Industrial Relations Reform in Australia'.
31   Kelty, interview, April 2008.
32   Glenda Korporaal, *Australian*, 30–31 December 2006.
33   Kelty, interview, April 2008.
34   Kelty, interview, April 2008.
35   Kelty, interview, April 2008.
36   P Keating, interview, May 2005; Kelty, interview, April 2008.
37   Kelty, interview, April 2008.
38   Kelty, interview, April 2008.
39   John Kerin, Budget speech, 20 August 1991.
40   John Dawkins, interview with the author, January 2009.
41   Tony Harris, interview with the author, January 2009.
42   P Keating, interview, May 2005.

43 P Keating, interview, May 2005; Kelty, interview, April 2008.
44 Kelty, interview, April 2008.

11 The Patriotism Puzzle

1   James Curran, *The Power of Speech*, Melbourne University Press, Melbourne, 2004, p. 192.
2   Quoted in John Hirst, *Australians*, Black Inc., Melbourne, 2007, p. 90.
3   Paul Keating, Australian Writers Guild Awards speech, 10 July 1992.
4   Paul Keating, University of Notre Dame University speech, 8 March 1994.
5   Paul Keating, National Library speech, 13 August 1993.
6   Paul Kelly, *100 Years: The Australian Story*, Allen & Unwin, Sydney, 2001, p. 92.
7   Donald Horne, *Sydney Morning Herald*, 6 May 1995.
8   Rodney Cavalier, interview with the author, January 2009.
9   Paul Keating, Australian Book Publishers Association Awards speech, 26 June 1992.
10 Kelly, *100 Years*, interview with Paul Keating, p. 93.
11 Mark Ryan, interview with the author, November 2008.
12 Keating, speech, 26 June 1992.
13 Paul Keating, Centenary of the ALP speech, 8 May 2001.
14 Paul Keating, interview with the author, May 2008.
15 Paul Keating, National Press Club speech, 7 December 1990.
16 Paul Keating, Anzac Day speech, Port Moresby, 25 April 1992.
17 Don Watson, *Recollections of a Bleeding Heart*, Random House, Sydney, 2002, p. 183.
18 Paul Keating, *Churchill and Australia* launch speech, 30 October 2008.
19 Keating, interview, May 2008.
20 Curran, p. 224.
21 Keating, interview, May 2008.
22 Curran, p. 210.
23 Paul Keating, Asia–Australia Institute Address, 7 April 1992.
24 Keating, interview, May 2008.
25 Keating, speech, 7 April 1992.

12 Asia and America: The Grand Strategy

1   Allan Gyngell, interview with the author, December 2008.
2   Paul Keating, interview with the author, 2000; see Paul Kelly, *100 Years: The Australian Story*, Allen & Unwin, Sydney, 2001, p. 92.
3   Paul Keating, *Engagement*, Pan Macmillan, Sydney, 2000, p. 15.
4   Paul Keating, interview with the author, June 2008.
5   Bob Hawke, *The Hawke Memoirs*, William Heinemann Australia, Melbourne, 1994, pp. 427–8.
6   Keating, *Engagement*, p. 28.
7   Ashton Calvert, interview with the author, May 2003.
8   Keating, *Engagement*, pp. 29–31.
9   John Edwards, *Keating: The Inside Story*, Penguin, Melbourne, 1996, p. 19.
10 Phil Scanlan, interview with the author, February 2009.
11 Scanlan, interview, February 2009.
12 Paul Keating to President Bush, unpublished letter, 3 April 1992.

13 President Bush to Paul Keating, unpublished letter, 29 April 1992.

14 Keating, *Engagement*, p. 33.

15 Keating, *Engagement*, p. 34.

16 Keating, *Engagement*, p. 34.

17 Don Russell, interview with the author, April 2006.

18 Russell, interview, April 2006.

19 Stephen FitzGerald, *Is Australia An Asian Country?*, Allen & Unwin, Sydney 1997, pp. 2–3.

20 Keating, in addition, disagreed with FitzGerald's foreign policy prescriptions.

21 Paul Keating, Asia–Australia Institute Address, 26 October 1994.

22 Kelly, *100 Years,* p. 93.

23 Calvert, interview, May 2003.

24 Kim Beazley, 'Foreign Affairs and Defence', in Susan Ryan and Troy Bramston (eds), *The Hawke Government*, Pluto Press, Melbourne, 2003, pp. 365–6.

25 Keating, *Engagement*, p. 43.

26 'Defending Australia', Defence White Paper, Commonwealth of Australia, 1994.

27 See Michael Evans, 'The Tyranny of Dissonance, Australia's Strategic Culture and Way of War, 1901–2005', Land Warfare Studies Centre, Duntroon, Study Paper no. 306.

28 Gyngell, interview, December 2008.

29 Calvert, interview, May 2003.

30 Keating, *Engagement*, p. 126.

31 Keating, *Engagement*, p. 126.

32 Gyngell, interview, December 2008.

33 Keating, *Engagement*, pp. 132–4.

34 This account draws heavily on Keating, *Engagement*, chapters 4 & 6.

35 Stanley Roth, interview with the author, June 2008.

36 Gyngell, interview, December 2008.

37 Keating, *Engagement*, chapters 4 & 5.

38 Stanley Roth, interview with the author, June 2008.

39 Keating, *Engagement*, p. 296.

40 Gyngell, interview, December 2008.

41 Peter Gration, interview with the author, December 2008.

42 Hugh White, interview with the author, December 2008.

43 Gyngell, interview, December 2008.

44 Keating, *Engagement*, pp. 138–41.

45 Keating, *Engagement*, pp. 140–5.

46 Gration, interview, December 2008.

47 Gyngell, interview, December 2008.

48 Gyngell, interview, December 2008.

49 Paul Keating, press conference, 14 December 1995.

50 White, interview, December 2008.

51 Gyngell, interview, December 2008.

13 Embracing the Republic

1 Paul Kelly, *100 Years: The Australian Story*, Allen & Unwin, Sydney, 2001, p. 82.

2 Don Watson, *Recollections of a Bleeding Heart*, Random House, Sydney, 2002, p. 223.
3 Watson, p. 223.
4 Neal Blewett, *A Cabinet Diary*, Wakefield Press, South Australia, 1999, p. 100.
5 John Howard, interview with Miranda Devine, *Sun-Herald*, 18 November 2007.
6 Don Russell, memo to Paul Keating, 3 September 1992.
7 John Edwards, *Keating: The Inside Story*, Penguin, Melbourne, 1996, p. 527.
8 Watson, p. 331.
9 Paul Keating, interview with the author, June 2008.
10 Mark Ryan, interview with the author, November 2008.
11 Keating, interview, June 2008.
12 Keating, interview, June 2008.
13 Watson, pp. 314–15.
14 Keating, interview, June 2008.
15 Kelly, p. 83.
16 Paul Keating, discussion with the author, 1994.
17 Kelly, p. 83.
18 Kelly, p. 83; Watson, p. 419.
19 Malcolm Turnbull, *The Reluctant Republic*, William Heinemann Australia, Melbourne, 1993, pp. 252–3.
20 Turnbull, p. 249.
21 'An Australian Republic', Report of the Republic Advisory Committee, Commonwealth of Australia, 1993.
22 Prince Charles, interview with Paul Kelly, *Australian*, 7 February 1994.
23 Paul Keating, House of Representatives, *Hansard*, 7 June 1995.
24 Keating, *Hansard*, 7 June 1995.
25 John Howard, House of Representatives, *Hansard*, 8 June 1995.
26 *Australian*, 12 June 1995.

14 Protecting the Borders

1 Frank Brennan, *Tampering with Asylum*, University of Queensland Press, St Lucia, 207, pp. 42–4.
2 Brennan, p. 43.
3 Brennan, pp. 46–7.
4 Paul Kelly, *The Unmaking of Gough*, Allen & Unwin, Sydney, 1994, p. 212.
5 *Chan Yee Kin v Minister for Immigration and Ethnic Affairs (1989)*, 169 CLR 379.
6 Mary Crock, 'A Legal Perspective on the Evolution of Mandatory Detention', in Mary Crock (ed.), *Protection or Punishment?*, Federation Press, Sydney, 1999, p. 32.
7 Gerry Hand, House of Representatives, *Hansard*, 5 May 1992, p. 2370.
8 Gerry Hand, House of Representatives, *Hansard*, 4 November 1992, p. 2620.
9 Philip Ruddock, House of Representatives, *Hansard*, 11 November 1992, p. 3142.
10 Paul Keating, interview with the author, May 2008.
11 *Chu Kheng Lim v Minister for Immigration (1992)*, 176 CLR 1.
12 Keating, interview, May 2008.
13 Chris Conybeare, interview with the author, June 2008.
14 Conybeare, interview, June 2008.
15 Conybeare, interview, June 2008.

16 Hand, *Hansard*, 4 November 1992, p. 2620.

17 Hand, *Hansard*, 4 November 1992, p. 2620.

18 House of Representatives, *Hansard*, 16 December 1992, p. 3935.

19 Crock, p. 32.

20 Mary Crock, 'Refugees in Australia: of Lore, Legends and the Judicial Process', research paper presented at the Seventh Colloquium of the Judicial Conference of Australia, 2003.

21 John McMillan, 'The Courts v The People: Have the Judges Gone too Far?', Judicial Conference of Australia, April 2002.

22 John McMillan, 'Immigration Law and the Courts', address to Sir Samuel Griffith Society, 15 June 2002; Dr Margaret Kelly, submission to the Senate Legal and Constitutional Affairs committee, July 2005.

23 Paul Kelly, *Australian*, 5 September 2001.

24 Crock, 'Refugees in Australia'.

25 Keating, interview, May 2008.

15 A Fractured Reconciliation

1 Paul Keating, interview with the author, June 2008.

2 Sandy Hollway, interview with the author, November 2008.

3 Keating, interview, June 2008.

4 Preliminary Report to Simon Balderstone on political strategy and Mabo, 1992.

5 Sir Anthony Mason, interview with the author, 2000.

6 *Mabo v Queensland (No. 2)* (1992), 175 CLR 1, 57–8.

7 See Frank Brennan, 'The Traumas of Atonement and Opposition in the Law', speech, 11 July 2004.

8 Brennan, speech, 11 July 2004.

9 Keating, interview, June 2008.

10 It should be noted, however, that Keating said subsequently that he planned to move on statutory land rights if the High Court had not intervened with the Mabo judgment.

11 Frank Brennan, interview with the author, January 2009.

12 Hollway, interview, November 2008.

13 Don Watson, *Recollections of a Bleeding Heart*, Random House, Sydney, 2002, p. 290.

14 Paul Keating, Redfern Park speech, 10 December 1992.

15 Patrick Dodson, interview with Paul Kelly, ABC Television, 2001.

16 Noel Pearson, interview with the author, November 2008.

17 Keating, interview, June 2008.

18 Pearson, interview, November 2008.

19 Keating, interview, June 2008.

20 Keating, interview, June 2008.

21 Keating, interview, June 2008.

22 Robert Tickner, *Taking a Stand*, Allen & Unwin, Sydney, 2001, pp. 182–7.

23 Tickner, pp. 187–90.

24 Daryl Melham, interview with the author, January 2009.

25 House of Representatives, *Hansard*, 22 December 1993, p. 4543.

26 Hollway, interview, November 2008.

27 Brennan, interview, January 2009; Frank Brennan, *The Wik Debate*, UNSW Press, Sydney, 1998, pp. 19–20.

28 Hollway, interview, November 2008.

29 Farley to Hollway, NFF, 14 October 1994.

30 Keating, interview, June 2008.

31 Brennan, interview, January 2009.

32 Keating, interview, June 2008.

33 Alan Ramsey, *Sydney Morning Herald*, 15 November 1997.

34 Senate, *Hansard*, 16 December 1993, pp. 5500–1.

35 Pearson, interview, November 2008.

36 Keating, interview, June 2008.

37 House of Representatives, *Hansard*, 22 December 1993.

38 Melham, interview, January 2009.

16 The Betrayal

1 Laura Tingle, *Chasing the Future*, William Heinemann Australia, Melbourne, 1994, p. 231.

2 Mark Ryan, interview with the author, November 2008.

3 Tingle, p. 231.

4 *Australian*, 16 March 1993.

5 Paul Keating, discussion with the author, 14 March 1993.

6 Ryan, interview, November 2008.

7 *Australian*, 16 March 1993.

8 Don Watson, *Recollections of a Bleeding Heart*, Random House, Sydney, 2002, pp. 350 & 360.

9 Don Russell, interview with the author, December 2008.

10 Ryan, interview, November 2008.

11 Rodney Cavalier, interview with the author, December 2008.

12 Bob Hogg, National Press Club speech, 24 March 1993.

13 *Australian*, 19 February 2003.

14 John Howard, interview with the author, February 2005; Shaun Carney, *Peter Costello, The New Liberal*, Allen & Unwin, Sydney, 2001, p. 172.

15 See *Australian*, 10–11 June 1995.

16 John Dawkins, interview with the author, December 2008.

17 John Lyons, *Bulletin*, 30 August 2005.

18 John Edwards, *Keating: The Inside Story*, Penguin, Melbourne, 1996, p. 516.

19 Lyons, *Bulletin*, 30 August 2005.

20 Dawkins, interview, December 2008.

21 *Australian*, 27–28 February 1993.

22 Based on an account by Edwards in *Keating*, p. 509.

23 Ted Evans, interview with the author, February 2005.

24 Tony Cole, interview with the author, February 2005.

25 Paul Keating, interview with the author, May 2005.

26 Paul Keating, interview with the author, June 2008; Dawkins, interview, December 2008.

27 Dawkins, interview, December 2008.

28 Watson, p. 397.
29 Keating, interview, June 2008.
30 Keating, interview, June 2008.
31 Dawkins, interview, December 2008.
32 Dawkins, interview, December 2008.
33 Budget Statements 1993–94, Budget Paper no. 1, pp. 1.1–1.4.
34 Dawkins, interview, December 2008.
35 Keating, interview, May 2005.
36 Michael Keating, interview with the author, January 2005.
37 Don Russell, interview with the author, April 2005.
38 Evans, interview, February 2005.
39 Cole, interview, February 2005.
40 Don Russell, interview with the author, January 2009.
41 Don Russell, interview with the author, April 2006.
42 Watson, pp. 399–402.
43 Edwards, p. 523.
44 John Dawkins, interview with the author, January 2009.
45 Ric Simes, interview with the author, November 2008.
46 Simes, interview, November 2008; Paul Van den Noord, 'The Size and Role of Automatic Stabilisers in the 1990s and Beyond', Economics Department Working Paper no. 230, OECD, 2000.
47 Bill Kelty, interview with the author, April 2008.
48 Dawkins, interview, December 2008.
49 P Keating, interview, June 2008; Dawkins, interview, December 2008.
50 Tingle, p. 351.
51 Cole, interview, February 2005.
52 Evans, interview, February 2005.
53 Kelty, interview, April 2008.
54 Howard, interview, February 2005.

17 Howard: The Final Option

1   John Howard, interview with the author, February 2005.
2   Grahame Morris, interview with the author, March 2009.
3   Howard, interview, February 2005.
4   Michael Wooldridge, interview with the author, January 2009.
5   Don Watson, *Recollections of a Bleeding Heart*, Random House, Sydney, 2002, p. 541.
6   David Barnett, *John Howard Prime Minister*, Penguin, Melbourne, 1997, p. 616.
7   John Hewson, interview with the author, December 2008.
8   See Mike Steketee, *Weekend Australian Magazine*, 23–24 July 1994.
9   Shaun Carney, *Peter Costello, The New Liberal*, Allen & Unwin, Sydney, 2001, p. 189.
10 Carney, pp. 185–91; 205.
11 Peter Costello, interview with the author, February 2008.
12 Andrew Robb, interview with the author, January 2004.
13 Howard, interview, February 2005.

14 Carney, p. 201.

15 Peter Costello, press conference, 10 July 2006.

16 John Howard, interview with the author, February 2008.

17 Ian McLachlan, interview with the author, April 2009.

18 Costello, interview, February 2008.

19 Howard, interview, February 2008.

20 Howard, interview, February 2008.

21 Howard, interview, February 2008.

22 See Barnett, chapter 14; Carney, pp. 200–10.

23 Peter Costello with Peter Coleman, *The Costello Memoirs*, Melbourne University Press, Melbourne, 2008, p. 66.

24 Bob Day, interview with the author, April 2009.

25 Pamela Williams, *The Victory*, Allen & Unwin, Sydney, 1997, pp. 20–3.

26 Howard, interview, February 2008.

27 Howard, interview, February 2005.

28 Howard, interview, February 2005.

29 Alexander Downer, discussions with the author, 2005 and 2006.

30 Peter Costello, interview with the author, April 2005.

31 This account of the discussion is based on the assumption that the issue, now fourteen years old, is no longer of contemporary political moment and has entered the realm of the strictly historical.

32 John Howard, discussion with the author, February 2008.

33 Nick Minchin, interview with the author, February 2009.

34 Wooldridge, interview, January 2009.

35 Howard, interview, February 2005.

36 Howard, interview, February 2008.

37 Wooldridge, interview, January 2009.

38 Robert Hill, interview with the author, June 2009.

39 Wooldridge, interview, January 2009.

40 John Howard, ANU Lecture, 27 June 1996.

41 Arthur Sinodinos, interview with the author, February 2009.

42 House of Representatives, *Hansard*, 2 February 1995, p. 385.

43 *Hansard*, 2 February 1995, p. 381.

44 Peter Reith, interview with the author, January 2009.

45 Howard, interview, February 2005.

46 *Australian*, 9 January 1996.

47 Hugh Mackay, *Australian*, 13–14 January 1996.

48 *Australian*, 24 January 1996.

18 Howard's Battlers: The Crisis of Modern Labor

1   Andrew Robb, interview with the author, January 2004.

2   Robb, interview, January 2004.

3   Gary Grey, interview with the author, mid-1996.

4   Grahame Morris, interview with the author, March 2009.

5   Grey, interview, mid-1996.

6   National Consultative Review Committee Report to the ALP National Executive, August 1996.

7   Grey, interview, mid-1996.

8   Mark Ryan, interview with the author, November 2008.

9   Menzies polled 51.3 per cent of the two-party-preferred vote and Fraser 55.7 per cent while Howard recorded 53.6 per cent.

10 Malcolm Mackerras, 'Statistical Analysis of the Results', in Clive Bean, Marian Simms, Scott Bennett and John Warhurst (eds), *The Politics of Retribution: The 1996 Federal Election*, Allen & Unwin, Sydney, 1997.

11 National Consultative Review Committee Report.

12 Pamela Williams, *The Victory*, Allen & Unwin, Sydney, 1997, p. 309.

13 Ryan, interview, November 2008.

14 Don Russell, interview with the author, December 2008.

15 Williams, p. 330.

16 Don Watson, *Recollections of a Bleeding Heart*, Random House, Sydney, 2002, p. 612.

17 Williams, p. 172.

18 Russell, interview, December 2008.

19 Don Russell, interview with the author, April 2006.

20 Williams, p. 173.

21 Noel Pearson, interview with the author, November 2008.

22 Williams, pp. 173–5.

23 Williams, pp. 173–5.

24 Watson, p. 669.

25 Robb, interview, January 2004.

26 Robb, interview, January 2004.

27 Robb, interview, January 2004.

28 Robb, interview, January 2004.

29 John Edwards, *Keating: The Inside Story*, Penguin, Melbourne, 1996, pp. 514–15.

30 Robb, interview, January 2004.

31 Robb, interview, January 2004.

32 Grey, interview, mid-1996.

33 Paul Keating, interview with the author, May 2005.

34 Rod Cameron, discussion with the author, mid-1996.

35 Morris, interview, March 2009.

36 Paul Keating. Australian Education Union speech, 19 January 1996.

37 Bill Kelty, interview with the author, April 2008.

38 Andrew Robb, National Press Club speech, 13 March, 1996.

39 Robb, National Press Club speech, 13 March 1996.

40 Grey, interview, mid-1996.

41 National Consultative Review Committee Report.

42 Williams, p. 229.

43 Morris, interview, March 2009.

44 Andrew Robb, 'The Liberal Party Campaign', in *The Politics of Retribution*.

45 Ian McAllister and Clive Bean, 'Long-term Electoral Trends and the 1996 Election', in *The Politics of Retribution*.

46 Kelty, interview, April 2008.

47 Grey, interview, mid-1996.

19 A New Political Manager

1   Arthur Sinodinos, interview with the author, February 2009; David Kemp, interview with the author, February 2008.
2   John Howard, discussion with the author, February 1996.
3   Kim Beazley, discussion with the author, February 1997.
4   Based on personal discussions with Grahame Morris and Andrew Robb.
5   Andrew Robb, interview with the author, January 2008; Kemp, interview, February 2008; Michael Wooldridge, interview with the author, February 2009.
6   Paul Kelly, 'A Man in Full', *Weekend Australian Magazine*, 11–12 December 2004.
7   John Howard, speech, 8 September 2005.
8   Sinodinos, interview, February 2009.
9   Kemp, interview, February 2008.
10   Grahame Morris, interview with the author, March 2009.
11   Morris, interview, March 2009.
12   Sinodinos, interview, February 2009.
13   Sinodinos, interview, February 2009.
14   Kelly, *Weekend Australian Magazine*, 11–12 December 2004.
15   Blair's former cabinet secretary, Lord Butler, said: 'The cabinet now—and I don't think there's any secret about this—doesn't make decisions … the government reaches conclusions in rather small groups of people.' See *Spectator*, 11 December 2004.
16   Kemp, interview, February 2008.
17   Howard, interview, February 2009.
18   Sinodinos, interview, February 2009.
19   Kelly, *Weekend Australian Magazine*, 11–12 December 2004.
20   Tim Fischer, interview with the author, November 2008.
21   Max Moore-Wilton, interview with the author, June 2008.
22   Arthur Sinodinos, interview with the author, February 2008.
23   Peter Reith, interview with the author, January 2009.
24   Kemp, interview, February 2008.
25   Peter Costello, interview with the author, February 2008.
26   Costello, interview, February 2008.
27   Sinodinos, interview, February 2009.
28   Costello, interview, February 2008.
29   John Howard, interview with the author, February 2008.
30   The ministers were Assistant Treasurer Jim Short, Minister for Small Business and Consumer Affairs Geoffrey Prosser, Minister for Administrative Services David Jull, Minister for Transport John Sharp, and Minister for Science and Technology Peter McGauran.
31   John Howard, interview with the author, February 2005.
32   Nick Minchin, interview with the author, February 2009.
33   Morris, interview, March 2009.
34   John Howard, press conference, 14 July 2005.
35   Roger Beale, informal farewell speech at retirement, February 2004 .
36   Howard, interview, February 2005.
37   Sinodinos, interview, February 2009.

38 Howard, interview, February 2009.

39 Patrick Weller, *Australia's Mandarins*, Allen & Unwin, Sydney, 2001 p. 193.

40 Sandy Hollway, interview with the author, November 2008.

41 Moore-Wilton, interview, June 2008.

42 Moore-Wilton, interview, June 2008.

43 Morris, interview, March 2009.

44 Peter Shergold, interview with the author, September 2005.

45 Alexander Downer, interview with the author, January 2006.

46 Ashton Calvert, interview with the author, April 2005.

47 Robert Hill, interview with the author, June 2009.

48 Ric Smith, interview with the author, June 2009.

49 Peter Shergold, interview with the author, June 2009.

50 Michael Thawley, discussion with the author, April 2002.

51 Andrew Podger, retirement speech, 30 June 2005.

52 Paul Kelly, Cunningham Lecture, 2005, Academy of the Social Sciences in Australia; Ian Hancock, 'The VIP Affair', Australasian Study of Parliament Group, 2004, and interview with the author, August 2004 .

53 Kelly, *Weekend Australian Magazine*, 11–12 December 2004.

54 For Howard's attitude towards the media, see Michelle Grattan, 'Gatekeepers and Gatecrashers: The Relationship between Politics and the Media', 38th Alfred Deakin Lecture, 2005.

55 John Howard, address at Bowral, 27 August 1996.

20   The Economic Model: A Story of Australian Exceptionalism

1 Bill Kelty, interview with the author, April 2008.

2 Peter Costello, interview with the author, April 2005.

3 John Howard, inaugural John Howard Lecture, Menzies Research Centre, 19 February 2009.

4 Greg Smith, interview with the author, March 2005.

5 Ted Evans, Shann Memorial Lecture, 25 September 2001.

6 Paul Kelly, *100 Years: The Australian Story*, Allen & Unwin, Sydney, 2001, interview with John Howard.

7 Glenn Stevens, Economic Update speech, 4 June 2009.

8 Glenn Stevens, The Road to Recovery, 21 April 2009.

9 David Morgan, interview with the author, April 2009.

10 John Edwards, interview with the author, March 2009.

11 Ian Macfarlane, interview with the author, February 2009.

12 Ian Macfarlane, ASIC Annual Conference speech, 2 March 2009.

13 Kevin Rudd, *Monthly*, February 2009.

14 Rudd, *Monthly*, February 2009.

15 Morgan, interview, April 2009.

16 Ted Evans, interview with the author, February 2009.

17 John Edwards, interview with the author, March 2009. Like Ted Evans, Edwards criticises Howard over inadequate infrastructure, but says this does not bear on the financial crisis.

18 Macfarlane, interview, February 2009.

19 Peter Costello, interview with the author, March 2009.

20 Morgan, interview, April 2009.

21 Morgan, interview, April 2009.

22 Costello, interview, March 2009.

23 Costello, interview, March 2009.

24 Paul Keating, discussion with the author during the 1996 election campaign.

25 Ken Henry, in Peter Dawkins and Michael Stutchbury (eds), *Sustaining Prosperity*, Melbourne University Press, Melbourne 2005.

26 Ian Macfarlane, 'The Search for Stability', Boyer Lecture no. 5.

27 Ted Evans, interview with the author, February 2005.

28 Ian Macfarlane, interview with the author, September 2006.

29 Arthur Sinodinos, interview with the author, February 2009.

30 John Stone, 'Growth, Jobs and Prosperity', *Quadrant*, January–February 2009.

31 Howard, interview, February 2009.

32 The Treasury, Architecture of Australia's Tax and Transfer System, August 2008, Australia's Future Tax System.

33 Howard, interview, February 2009.

34 Treasury, August 2008.

35 A qualification, however, is that OECD comparisons are weighted towards Europe and Australia, when judged by Asia–Pacific standards, would be far higher on the tax/spend spectrum.

36 Michelle Grattan, *Australian Financial Review* magazine, November 1996.

37 Sinodinos, interview, February 2009.

38 John Howard, interview with the author, February 2005.

39 Peter Costello, interview with the author, April 2005.

40 Evans, interview, February 2005.

41 The Treasury statement showed that, for 1995–96, estimated revenue had been reduced by $1.7 billion caused by a downward revision in the growth forecast from 3.75 per cent to 3.25 per cent. At the same time, outlays had risen about $1 billion since the previous budget because of Labor's decisions and parameter changes. Peter Costello, press release, 12 March 1996.

42 Costello, press release.

43 John Howard, House of Representatives, *Hansard*, 1 May 1996, p. 151.

44 Ric Simes, interview with the author, December 2008.

45 Evans, interview, February 2005.

46 Howard, interview, February 2005.

47 Budget Statements, 1996–97, Budget Paper no. 1, 1–9 to 1–10.

48 Sandy Hollway, interview with the author, November 2008.

49 John Howard, interview with John Laws, radio 2UE, 21 August 1996.

50 Peter Shergold, interview with the author, October 2008.

51 Hollway, interview, November 2008.

52 Costello, interview, April 2005.

53 Ted Evans, speech to Australian Business Economists, 2 September 1996.

54 The exception here was the 1996 election pledge to use some Telstra proceeds to create an environmental fund.

55 Peter Costello, National Press Club speech, 14 May 1997; Essendon Football Club speech, 16 May 1997.

56 Peter Costello, press release, 16 May 1997.
57 Evans, speech, 2 September 1996.
58 Evans, speech, 2 September 1996.

21 The Mainstream Mob: Howard as Social Conservative

1   Michael Duffy, *Independent Monthly*, February 1996.
2   John Howard, discussion with the author, January 1996.
3   Duffy, *Independent Monthly*, February 1996.
4   John Howard, interview with the author, February 2009.
5   Howard, interview, February 2009.
6   Mark Latham, *From the Suburbs*, Pluto Press, Sydney, 2002, p. 20.
7   John Howard, speech to the New South Wales Liberal Party State Council Meeting, 20 April 1996.
8   John Howard, policy launch statements, 18 February 1996.
9   John Howard, Menzies Research Centre, 6 June 1995.
10 Duffy, *Independent Monthly*, February 1996.
11 Duffy, *Independent Monthly*, February 1996.
12 John Kunkel, interview with the author, May 2008.
13 Francis Fukuyama, *The Great Disruption*, Profile Books, London, 1999, pp. 5–6.
14 Paul Kelly, *100 Years: The Australian Story*, Allen & Unwin, Sydney, 2001, p. 245.
15 John Howard, launch of *The Conservative*, 8 September 2005.
16 John Howard, Liberal Party National Convention address, South Australia, 8 June 2003.
17 Howard, Menzies Research Centre, 6 June 1995.
18 John Howard, Menzies Research Centre, 3 May 2005.
19 John Howard, speech, 27 June 1996.
20 Kevin Rudd, 'Howard's Brutopia', *Monthly*, November 2006.
21 Howard, Menzies Research Centre, 6 June 1995.
22 John Howard, interview with the author, December 2004.
23 *Australian Financial Review*, 5 September 2008.
24 Paul Keating, interview with the author, May 2008.
25 Tim Fischer, interview with the author, November 2008.
26 George Brandis, 'John Howard and the Australian Liberal Tradition', in Peter Van Onselen (ed.), *Liberals and Power*, Melbourne University Press, Melbourne, 2009.
27 Brandis.
28 Noel Pearson, interview with the author, December 2008.
29 Latham, p. 26.
30 Peter Davidson, 'Family Payments: Australia's Quiet Achiever', Australian Institute of Family Studies Seminar series, 14 August 2008.
31 Peter Costello, 'Tax Reform—Not a New Tax, a New Tax System', August 1998, pp. 50–6.
32 Budget Overview, 8 May 2007, p. 34.
33 Anne Summers, *The End of Equality*, Random House, Sydney, 2003, p. 156.
34 Peter Saunders, 'The $85 Billion Tax/Welfare Churn', Centre for Independent Studies, Issue Analysis, 7 April 2005.
35 John Howard, Menzies Research Centre, 18 April 2006.

36 Howard, Menzies Research Centre, 18 April 2006.

37 Howard, Menzies Research Centre, 18 April 2006.

38 Max Moore-Wilton, interview with the author, June 2008.

39 David McKnight, *Beyond Left and Right*, Allen & Unwin, Sydney, 2005, p. 200.

40 Howard, interview, February 2009.

41 Kate Legge, 'Jumping the White Picket Fence', in Nick Cater (ed.), *The Howard Factor*, Melbourne University Press, Melbourne, 2006, p. 142.

42 Pru Goward, interview with the author, October 2008.

43 Goward, interview, October 2008.

44 Howard, interview, February 2009.

45 Paid Parental Leave, Productivity Commission, September 2008.

46 Goward, interview, October 2008.

47 Ian Hancock, 'John Carrick: The Influence of Head Office', in Ken Turner and Michael Hogan (eds), *The Worldly Art of Politics*, Federation Press, Sydney, 2006, p. 219.

48 Sir John Carrick, interview with the author, November 2008.

49 John Howard, discussion with the author, December 2004.

50 Christopher Pearson, *Australian*, 21 August 2008.

51 Howard, Menzies Research Centre, 3 May 2005.

52 The main factor driving the shift to private health insurance were new financial penalties for those who failed to join.

53 Harper Associates, A Defence of Public Support for Private Health Care Funding in Australia, April 2003.

54 This statistic needs to be seen in the context of the federal government meeting only about 10 per cent of government school running costs.

55 Howard, interview, December 2004.

56 Nick Cater (ed.), *The Howard Factor*, Melbourne University Press, Melbourne, 2006, p. 133.

57 Paul Kelly, *Australian*, 6 March 2004.

58 John Howard, 29 February 2004.

59 Andrew Norton, *Australian*, 13 January 2007; Andrew Norton, 'The Rise of Big Government Conservatism', *Policy*, Centre for Independent Studies, vol. 22, summer 2006–07.

60 *Australian Financial Review*, 30 November 2007.

61 John Howard, launch of *The Conservative*, 8 September 2005.

62 Howard, interview, December 2004.

63 Wayne Errington and Peter Van Onselen, *John Winston Howard: A Life*, Melbourne University Press, Melbourne, 2007, p. 61.

64 Christopher Pearson, *Australian*, 3 February 2007.

65 Treasury, Australia's Future Tax System, August 2008.

66 Peter Costello, press release, 12 April 2006.

67 Ann Harding, 'Recent Trends in Income Inequality in Australia', NATSEM, University of Canberra, 31 March 2005. See Paul Kelly, *Australian*, 2 April 2005.

68 Quoc Ngu Vu, Ann Harding and Richard Percival, 'A Growing Gap? Trends in Economic Wellbeing at the top of the Spectrum in Australia', NATSEM, 29 August 2008.

69 Peter Whiteford, 'The Welfare Expenditure Debate: Economic Myths of the Left and the Right Revisited', Economic and Labour Relations Review, vol. 22, no. 1, 2006.

70 Rachel Lloyd, Ann Harding and Neil Warren, 'Redistribution, the Welfare State and Lifetime Transitions', NATSEM, 24 February 2005; Ann Harding, Rachel Lloyd and Neil Warren, 'The Distribution of Taxes and Government Benefits in Australia', in Dimitri Papadimitriou, *The Distributional Effects of Government Spending and Taxation*, Palgrave Macmillan, London, 2006.

71 Howard, interview, February 2009.

22 Workplace Deregulation: The Final Crusade

1 John Howard, interview with the author, February 2008.

2 Ted Evans, 'The Vision: A Treasury Perspective', 4 August 1993.

3 Ted Evans, speech, 28 October 1993.

4 Peter Costello, interview with the author, February 2008.

5 Howard, interview, February 2008.

6 Howard, interview, February 2008.

7 Bill Kelty, interview with the author, April 2008.

8 Nick Minchin, interview with the author, February 2009.

9 Greg Combet, interview with the author, February 2008.

10 Howard, interview, February 2008.

11 Combet, interview, February 2008.

12 Howard, interview, February 2008.

13 Ted Evans, speech, 23 October 1996.

14 Judith Brett, *Robert Menzies' Forgotten People*, Macmillan, Sydney, 1992.

15 Michael Duffy, *Independent Monthly*, February 1996.

16 Pamela Williams, *The Victory*, Allen & Unwin, Sydney, 1997, p. 297.

17 *Australian*, 9 March 1996.

18 Peter Reith, interview with the author, March 2005.

19 Combet, interview, February 2008.

20 Peter Reith, interview with the author, June 2005.

21 Reith, interview, June 2005.

22 House of Representatives, *Hansard*, 23 May 1996, p. 1297.

23 Bills Digest 96, 1995–96, Parliamentary Library, Parliament of Australia.

24 Peter Reith, Sydney Institute speech, 15 May 1996.

25 Reith, speech, 15 May 1996.

26 Combet, interview, February 2008.

27 Andrew Murray, interview with the author, March 2008.

28 Brad Norington, *Jennie George*, Allen & Unwin, Sydney, 1998, pp. 290–2.

29 Norington, p. 298.

30 Combet, interview, February 2008.

31 Norington, pp. 292–3.

32 *Australian*, 20 August 1996.

33 See Norington, p. 290 for his assessment of the hopes of the ACTU leaders for this event.

34 Reith, interview, June 2005.

35 Murray, interview, March 2008.

36 Peter Costello, interview with the author, April 2005.

37 Peter Reith, interview with the author, January 2009.

38 John Howard, interview with the author, February 2005.

39 Howard, interview, February 2005.

40 Budget Statements 1996–97, Budget Paper no. 1, pp. 2–43.

41 Ian Macfarlane, 'Monetary Policy, Growth and Unemployment', 15 May 1997.

42 Ted Evans, MTIA speech, 1996.

43 Evans, speech, 23 October 1996.

44 Murray, interview, March 2008.

45 Combet, interview, February 2008.

46 Michael Keating, interview with the author, February 2009.

47 HR Nicholls Society, Executive Summary, August 1997.

48 Peter Reith, 'Reflections on the Waterfront Dispute', HR Nicholls Society, 1998.

49 Kim Beazley, press release, 1 July 1998.

50 John Edwards, HSBC Markets, 'A Beazley Government?', 25 September 1998.

23 An Independent Bank and the Death of Inflation

1   Nick Minchin, interview with the author, February 2009.

2   Peter Costello, interview with the author, February 2008.

3   John Howard, interview with the author, February 2008.

4   See Peter Costello with Peter Coleman, *The Costello Memoirs*, Melbourne University Press, Melbourne, 2008, pp. 102–5.

5   Peter Costello, interview with the author, April 2005.

6   Stephen Bell, *Australia's Money Mandarins*, Cambridge University Press, Cambridge, 2004, p. 19.

7   Bernie Fraser, interview with the author, December 2008.

8   *Australian*, 12 July 1995.

9   Fraser, interview, December 2008.

10 Costello, p. 102.

11 Fraser, interview, December 2008.

12 Costello, p. 102.

13 Ted Evans, interview with the author, February 2005.

14 Ian Macfarlane, interview with the author, February 2006.

15 Macfarlane, interview, February 2006.

16 Costello, p. 106. However, Costello and Macfarlane have different recollections on this point.

17 Peter Costello, press release, 14 August 1996.

18 Fraser, interview, December 2008.

19 *Australian*, 16 August 1996.

20 Evans, interview, February 2005.

21 Geoff Carmody, interview with the author, February 2005.

22 Ian Macfarlane, interview with the author, September 2006.

23 Ian Macfarlane, interview with the author, February 2009.

24   David Morgan, interview with the author, April 2009.

25 Ian Macfarlane, Shann Memorial Lecture, 15 September 1998.

26 See AW Martin, *Robert Menzies, A Life*, Volume Two, Melbourne University Press, Melbourne, 1999, p. 136.

27 Ian Macfarlane, Monetary Policy and Economic Growth, 12 August 1997.

28 Howard–Macfarlane record of conversation.

29 The next month, June 1998, Macfarlane took this tactic one step further when, in a London speech, he did encourage the idea of a possible interest rate lift in order to strengthen the currency.

30 Ian Macfarlane, evidence to the House of Representatives standing committee, December 1998.

31 Arthur Sinodinos, interview with the author, February 2009.

32 Macfarlane, interview, February 2006.

33 Macfarlane, interview, February 2006.

34 Howard–Macfarlane.

24 The Cultural Traditionalist as Populist

1 Howard made this statement in his office in front of staff.

2 John Howard, discussion with the author, December 2008.

3 John Howard, Sir Robert Menzies Lecture, 18 November 1996.

4 John Howard, interview with the author, December 2004.

5 John Kunkel, 'Reflections on the Howard Project', *IPA Review*, May 2008.

6 John Kunkel, interview with the author, May 2008.

7 Paul Kelly, *Australian*, 24 September 2005.

8 Peter Costello with Peter Coleman, *The Costello Memoirs*, Melbourne University Press, Melbourne, 2008, p. 166.

9 Irving Kristol, *The Autobiography of an Idea*, Elephant Paperbacks, New York, 1995, pp. 485–6.

10 Francis Fukuyama, *The Great Disruption*, Profile Books, London, 1999.

11 Todd Gitlin, *The Sixties*, Bantam, New York, 1993, p. xiv.

12 Christopher Lasch, *The Revolt of the Elites*, WW Norton & Company, New York, 1995, pp. 27–8.

13 John Howard, interview with the author, February 2009.

14 Paul Kelly, *100 Years: The Australian Story*, Allen & Unwin, Sydney, 2001, p. 246.

15 Howard, interview, February 2009.

16 John Howard, 'Politics and Patriotism', 13 December 1995.

17 Howard, 'Politics and Patriotism', 13 December 1995.

18 Howard, 'Politics and Patriotism', 13 December 1995.

19 Geoffrey Blainey, *Quadrant*, July 1993.

20 Mark McKenna, 'Different Perspectives on Black Armband History', Parliamentary Library, Research Paper 5, Parliament of Australia, 1997–98.

21 John Howard, *Quadrant*, July–August 1994.

22 Howard, Sir Robert Menzies Lecture, 18 November 1996.

23 John Howard, Sir Thomas Playford Memorial Lecture, 5 July 1996.

24 Gerard Henderson, 'The Howard Government and the Culture Wars', *The Sydney Institute Quarterly*, issue 29, August 2006.

25 Wayne Errington and Peter Van Onselen, *John Winston Howard: A Life*, Melbourne University Press, Melbourne, 2007, p. 256.

26 Pru Goward, interview with the author, October 2008.

27 John Howard, Australia Day address, 25 January 2001.

28 Francis Fukuyama, 'Identity and Migration', *Prospect*, February 2007.

29 This argument comes from James Curran, *The Power of Speech*, Melbourne University Press, Melbourne, 2004, p. 254.

30 Howard, discussion, December 2008.

31 John Howard, National Press Club address, 25 January 2001.

32 This draws on Judith Brett, *Australian Liberals and the Moral Middle Class*, Cambridge University Press, Melbourne, 2003, chapter 9.

33 John Howard, 'The Australian Way', 28 January 1999.

34 Nick Dyrenfurth, 'John Howard's Hegemony of Values: The Politics of "Mateship" in the Howard Decade', *Australian Journal of Political Science*, vol. 42, no. 2, 2007, p. 215.

35 Christos Tsiolkas, Gideon Haigh & Alexis Wright, *Tolerance, Prejudice and Fear*, Allen & Unwin, Sydney, 2008, p. 63.

36 John Howard, National Press Club address, 25 January 2006.

37 Howard, interview, February 2009.

38 Curran, p. 265.

25 Reconciliation: The Lost Opportunity

1   Arthur Sinodinos, interview with the author, February 2009.

2   John Howard, interview with the author, February 2009.

3   Noel Pearson, interview with the author, November 2008.

4   Max Moore-Wilton, interview with the author, June 2008.

5   Sinodinos, interview, February 2009.

6   Howard, interview, February 2009.

7   Peter Shergold, interview with the author, May 2008.

8   Howard, interview, February 2009.

9   Howard, interview, February 2009.

10 John Howard, Sydney Institute speech, 16 October 2007.

11 Sinodinos, interview, February 2009.

12 Pearson, interview, November 2008.

13 Paul Kelly, *Australian*, 11 August 1999, 7 August 2002; Noel Pearson, Brisbane Institute speech, 23 May 2000; Noel Pearson, CIS speech, 1 August 2000.

14 Pearson, interview, November 2008.

15 Paul Kelly, *Australian*, 13 October 2007.

16 Noel Pearson to John Howard, 17 September 2007, edited version.

17 Noel Pearson to John Howard, 10 October, 2007, edited version.

18 Howard, Sydney Institute speech, 16 October 2007.

19 Pearson, interview, November 2008.

20 Michael Lavarch, interview with the author, March 2009.

21 Robert Tickner, interview with the author, January 2009.

22 Frank Brennan, interview with the author, January 2009.

23 Pearson, interview, November 2008.

24 *Bringing Them Home*, Commonwealth of Australia, 1997.

25 Patrick Carlyon, 'White Lies', *Bulletin*, 12 June 2001.

26 Pearson, interview, November 2008.
27 John Howard, Australian Reconciliation Convention, 26 May 1997.
28 Howard, interview, February 2009.
29 John Howard, House of Representatives, *Hansard*, 2 June 1997, p. 4559.
30 Former Howard aide, interview with the author, February 2006.
31 Howard, Sydney Institute speech, 16 October 2007.
32 Howard, interview with the author, March 2000; also see Paul Kelly, *100 Years: The Australian Story*, Allen & Unwin, Sydney, 2001, p. 100.
33 Bain Attwood, *Telling the Truth about Aboriginal History*, Allen & Unwin, Sydney, 2005, p. 30.
34 Howard, Sydney Institute speech, 16 October 2007.
35 Henry Reynolds, *Why Weren't We Told?*, Viking, Melbourne, 1999, p. 247.
36 Sinodinos, interview, February 2009.
37 John Howard, House of Representatives, *Hansard*, 26 August 1999, p. 9205.
38 *Bringing Them Home*, Commonwealth of Australia, 1997, p. 32.
39 Paul Hasluck, *Shades of Darkness*, Melbourne University Press, Melbourne, 1988; Kelly, *100 Years*, p. 169.
40 Peter Costello, interview with the author, February 2008.
41 Peter Reith, interview with the author, January 2009.
42 Howard, interview, February 2009.
43 Paul Kelly, *Australian*, 31 May 2000.
44 Former Howard aide, interview with the author, February 2006.
45 Paul Kelly, *Australian*, 3 March 2000.
46 Howard, interview, February 2009.
47 Pearson, interview, November 2008.

26 The Perils of Pauline

1 Alexander Downer, interview with the author, January 2006.
2 Downer, interview, January 2006.
3 Downer adviser, interview with the author, January 2006.
4 This phrase comes from historian Marilyn Lake's article 'Pauline Hanson: Virago in Parliament, Viagra in the Bush', in *Two Nations*, Bookman, Melbourne, 1998.
5 Philip Flood, interview with the author, March 2009.
6 Flood, interview, March 2009.
7 Philip Flood, interview with the author, February 2006 and March 2009.
8 Flood, interview, February 2006.
9 Tim Fischer, interview with the author, November 2008.
10 Peter Costello with Peter Coleman, *The Costello Memoirs*, Melbourne University Press, Melbourne, 2008, p. 151.
11 Ashton Calvert, interview with the author, May 2003.
12 Peter Hartcher, *Australian Financial Review*, 5 June 1997.
13 Grahame Morris, interview with the author, March 2009.
14 Nick Minchin, interview with the author, February 2009.
15 Morris, interview, March 2009.
16 Pauline Hanson, House of Representatives, *Hansard*, 10 September 1996.
17 John Howard, Queensland Liberal Party speech, 22 September 1996.

18   Michelle Grattan, 'Pauline Hanson's Hijack of John Howard', in *Two Nations*.

19   House of Representatives, *Hansard*, 30 October 1996, pp. 6065–71.

20   Paul Kelly, *The End of Certainty*, Allen & Unwin, Sydney, 1992, pp. 418–28.

21   Morris, interview, March 2009.

22   Minchin, interview, February 2009.

23   Lynton Crosby, NPC Speech, 28 October 1998; Nicolas Rothwell, 'Thirteen Ways Not to Think About Pauline Hanson', in *Two Nations*.

24   David Leser, *Sydney Morning Herald* Good Weekend magazine, 30 November 1996.

25   Leser.

26   Leser.

27   Cavan Hogue, interview with the author, March 2006.

28   *Jakarta Post*, 25 October 1996.

29   *Asian Wall Street Journal*, 31 October 1996.

30   *New Straits Times*, 6 November 1996.

31   *New Straits Times*, 10 November 1996.

32   *New Straits Times*, 17 December 1996.

33   *Asia Times*, 2 May 1997.

34   *Asian Wall Street Journal*, 20 August 1997.

35   Cavan Hogue, 'Australia and Asia', *Southeast Asian Affairs*, 2001.

36   Flood, interview, February 2006.

37   Fischer, interview, November 2008.

38   Hogue, interview, March 2006.

39   Morris, interview, March 2009.

40   Downer, interview, January 2006.

41   Hogue, interview, March 2006.

42   Pauline Hanson's One Nation party launch speech, 11 April 1997.

43   John Howard, speech to Australia–Asia Society, 8 May 1997.

44   Howard, speech to Australia–Asia Society, 8 May 1997.

45   Flood, interview, February 2006.

46   Downer, interview, January 2006.

47   Hogue, interview, March 2006.

48   Costello, p. 152.

49   David Kemp, interview with the author, February 2008.

50   Minchin, interview, February 2009.

51   This applied in all seats except Sunnybank.

52   At a federal election One Nation was unlikely to have sufficient support in House of Representatives seats to win on National Party preferences.

53   Andrew Robb, *Bulletin*, 9 June 1998.

54   *Australian Financial Review*, 15 June 1998.

55   Margo Kingston, *Sydney Morning Herald*, 15 June 1998.

56   Malcolm Fraser to Tony Staley, 19 June 1997.

57   *Australian*, 19 June 1998.

58   John Howard, *7.30 Report*, ABC TV, 15 June 1998.

59   Tony Abbott, discussion with the author, May 2008.

60   John Howard, interview with the author, February 2005.

27 Confrontation on the Waterfront

1   Peter Reith, interview with the author, January 2009.
2   Peter Reith, interview with the author, June 2005.
3   John Howard, interview with the author, February 2005.
4   Howard, interview, February 2005.
5   Andrew Murray, interview with the author, March 2008.
6   Bill Kelty, interview with the author, April, 2008.
7   Helen Trinca and Anne Davies, *Waterfront: The Battle that Changed Australia*, Doubleday, Sydney, 2000, p. 5. This account of the dispute draws heavily on this excellent book.
8   Chris Corrigan, interview with the author, April 2008.
9   Howard, interview, February 2005.
10 John Sharp, speech, 15 September 1997.
11 Peter Reith, HR Nicholls Society address, July–August 1998.
12 Corrigan, interview, April 2008.
13 Reith, interview, January 2009. Reith is emphatic about the falseness of Corrigan's statement on ABC TV's *The Howard Years* that he told Reith in this phone call that he was behind Dubai.
14 *The Howard Years*, Episode One, ABC TV, 2008.
15 Memo, R Stewart-Crompton to Dr Peter Shergold, 18 May 1998.
16 Trinca and Davies, p. 82.
17 Ross Martin, 'Bastard Boys, Bill Kelty and Spin', *Quadrant*, November 2008.
18 Trinca and Davies, pp. 93–4.
19 See Trinca and Davies, pp. xiii–xviii.
20 Corrigan, interview, April 2008.
21 Paul Houlihan, interview with the author, March 2005.
22 Andrew Murray, interview with the author, March 2008.
23 Greg Combet, interview with the author, February, 2008.
24 Reith, interview, January 2009.
25 Trinca and Davies, p. 126.
26 Trinca and Davies, pp. 153–67.
27 *The Howard Years*, Episode One.
28 Combet, interview, February 2008.
29 Combet, interview, February 2008.
30 Combet, interview, February 2008.
31 Trinca and Davies, p. 169.
32 Corrigan, interview, April 2008.
33 Reith, interview, June 2005.
34 Reith, interview, January 2009.
35 Corrigan, interview, April 2008.
36 Corrigan, interview, April 2008.
37 Trinca and Davies, pp. 252–67.
38 Reith, interview, January 2009.
39 Trinca and Davies, pp. 252–67.
40 Productivity Commission, International Benchmarking of Container Stevedoring, July 2003.

41 Allan Fels, interview with the author, January 2009. See also Fred Brenchley, *Allan Fels, a Portrait of Power*, John Wiley & Sons Australia, Queensland, 2003, pp. 91–5.

42 Corrigan, interview, April 2008.

43 Peter Reith, 'Reflections on the Waterfront Dispute', HR Nicholls Society address, July–August 2008.

44 Howard, interview, February 2005.

45 Reith, interview, June 2005.

46 Combet, interview, February 2008.

47 Combet, interview, February 2008.

48 Corrigan, interview, April 2008.

49 Murray, interview, March 2008.

50 Corrigan, interview, April 2008.

51 Reith, interview, June 2005.

52 Howard, interview, February 2005.

53 Peter Hendy, interview with the author, January 2005.

28 Escaping the Native Title Crisis

1   Peter Reith's handwritten notes of Howard's speech, 2 December 1997.

2   Frank Brennan, interview with the author, January 2009; Paul Keating, interview with the author, June 2008; Paul Keating, *Sydney Morning Herald*, 6 July 1998; Alan Ramsey, *Sydney Morning Herald*, 11 July 1998.

3   Brennan, interview, January 2009; Keating, interview, June 2008; Keating, *Sydney Morning Herald*, 6 July 1998; Ramsey, *Sydney Morning Herald*, 11 July 1998.

4   Frank Brennan, *Sydney Morning Herald*, 3 July 1998.

5   Brennan, interview, January 2009.

6   *Sydney Morning Herald*, 9 July 1999.

7   Tony Stephens, *Sydney Morning Herald*, 8 July 1998.

8   Tim Fischer, interview with the author, November 2008; John Howard, discussion with the author, February 1997.

9   *Wik Peoples v Queensland* (1996), 187 CLR 1, 87, Brennan CJ.

10 *Australian*, 28–29 December 1996.

11 Daryl Melham, interview with the author, January 2009.

12 *Australian*, 24 December 1996.

13 *Australian*, 24 & 26 December 1996.

14 Frank Brennan, *The Wik Debate*, UNSW Press, Sydney, 1998, pp. 49–50.

15 Frank Brennan, *Sydney Morning Herald*, 4 January 1997.

16 Brennan, *The Wik Debate*, p. 50.

17 *Australian*, 23 January 1997.

18 Nick Minchin, interview with the author, February 2009.

19 Brennan, interview, January 2009.

20 Nick Minchin to John Howard, tenth anniversary letter, 2006.

21 Fischer, interview, November 2008.

22 John Howard, speech, Longreach meeting, 17 May 1997.

23 Howard, speech, Longreach meeting, 17 May 1997.

24 John Howard, interview with the author, February 2005.

25 Brennan, *The Wik Debate*, p. 63.

26 Melham, interview, January 2009.

27 House of Representatives, *Hansard*, 4 December 1997, pp. 12334–40.

28 John Howard, doorstop interview, 5 December 1997.

29 Reith, handwritten notes, 2 December 1997.

30 Michelle Grattan, *Australian Financial Review*, 6–7 December 1997.

31 Kim Beazley, ALP National Conference speech, 21 January 1998.

32 Minchin, interview, February 2009.

33 Frank Brennan, The Traumas of Atonement and Opposition in the Law, Queensland Institute of Technology, 11 July 2004.

34 Brennan, interview, January 2009.

35 Frank Brennan to Daryl Melham, 31 December 1997. See also Frank Brennan, *Eureka Street*, January–February 1998; Frank Brennan, The Racial Discrimination Act, The Native Title Act and the Senate Compromise, 9 January 1998; Frank Brennan to Peter Yu, 13 January 1998.

36 Brennan to Yu, 13 January 1998.

37 Brennan to Melham, 15 January 1998.

38 Frank Brennan, 'Justice for Indigenous Peoples', speech at Bond University, 4 May 2002.

39 Alan Ramsey, *Sydney Morning Herald*, 28 February 1998.

40 Ron Castan to Frank Brennan, 8 January 1998.

41 Brennan, interview, January 2009; Brennan, *The Wik Debate*, p. 67.

42 Melham, interview, January 2009.

43 Brennan to Yu, 13 January 1998.

44 Brennan, interview, January 2009.

45 Nick Minchin to John Howard, 2006.

46 Brennan, interview, January 2009.

47 Brennan, interview, January 2009.

48 Noel Pearson, interview with the author, November 2008.

49 *Australian*, 9 July 1998; Brennan, interview, January 2009.

50 Brennan, interview, January 2009.

51 Brennan, interview, January 2009.

52 Paul Keating, *Sydney Morning Herald*, 6 July 1998.

53 Paul Keating, interview with the author, June 2008.

54 Georgina Windsor and Dennis Shanahan, *Australian*, 9 July 1998.

55 Noel Pearson to Frank Brennan, 10 July 2004.

56 Pearson, interview, November 2008.

57 Melham, interview, January 2009.

58 John Howard, press conference, 8 July 1998.

59 Minchin, interview, February 2009.

60 Howard, interview, February 2005.

61 Grattan, *Australian Financial Review*, 6–7 December 1997.

62 Paul Kelly, *Australian*, 13 December 1997.

63 Frank Brennan to Ron Castan, 5 March 1998.

64 Michelle Grattan, *Australian Financial Review*, 6 July 1998.

29 The Ghost of Billy McMahon

1   Grahame Morris, interview with the author, March 2009.
2   Arthur Sinodinos, interview with the author, February 2009.
3   John Howard, interview with the author, February 2005.
4   *Australian*, 17 May and 3 June 1997.
5   *Sydney Morning Herald*, 19 May 1997.
6   The Mackay Report, 'The Disappointed Country?', July 1997, and *Australian*, 15 July 1997. Hugh Mackay's survey was based on eighteen group discussions with people aged between twenty and seventy years, drawn from the lower-middle to upper-middle of the socioeconomic spectrum and from Sydney, Melbourne, Brisbane, Ballarat, Tamworth and the New South Wales central coast.
7   Paul Kelly, *Australian*, 24 May 1997.
8   *Australian*, 9 August 1997.
9   Michael Gordon and Natasha Bita, *Australian*, 12 June 1997.
10 At the time the Productivity Commission was called the Industry Commission but I have used the better known title.
11 Howard, interview, February 2005.
12 Howard, interview, February 2005.
13 Ted Evans, interview with the author, February 2005.
14 Howard, interview, February 2005.
15 *Australian*, 29 July 1997.
16 Alan Wood, Stan Kelly Memorial Lecture, 1997.
17 Michael Gordon, *Australian*, 30 May 1997; *Australian*, 7 June 1997.
18 Howard, interview, February 2005.
19 Dennis Shanahan and Ian Henderson, *Australian*, 13 September 1997.
20 Michael Gordon and Ian Henderson, *Australian*, 18 July 1997.
21 Bill Scales, Australia—A Nation In Transition, 8 December 1997.
22 Peter Costello, interview with the author, April 2005.
23 Peter Costello with Peter Coleman, *The Costello Memoirs*, Melbourne University Press, Melbourne, 2008, p. 126.
24 Paul Cleary and Alicia Larriera, *Sydney Morning Herald*, 17 May 1997.
25 *Australian Financial Review*, 19 May 1997.
26 Howard, interview, February 2005.
27 *Australian*, 21 May 1997.
28 *Australian Financial Review*, 19 May 1997; *Sydney Morning Herald*, 20 May 1997; *Sydney Morning Herald*, 19 May 1997.
29 *Australian*, 26–7 July 1997.
30 Howard, interview, February 2005.
31 Howard, interview, February 2005.
32 Howard, interview, February 2005.
33 Sinodinos, interview, February 2009.
34 Lynton Crosby, interview with the author, April 2009.
35 Alan Wood, *Australian*, 6 August 1997.
36 John Howard, press release 13 August 1997.
37 *Australian*, 14 August 1997.

38 John Howard, speech to the Queensland Division of the Liberal Party, 14 August 1997.

39 John Howard, speech to the Queensland Division of the Liberal Party, 14 August 1997; Paul Kelly, *The End of Certainty*, Allen & Unwin, Sydney, 1992, p. 161.

40 Costello, interview, April 2005.

41 Costello, p. 123.

42 Evans, interview, February 2005.

43 'A New Tax System', Commonwealth of Australia, August 1998.

44 Treasury figures, refer Paul Kelly, *Australian*, 22 August 1998.

45 Costello, interview, April 2005.

46 Costello, interview, April 2005; Costello, pp. 131–3.

47 Sinodinos, interview, February 2009.

48 Nick Minchin, interview with the author, February 2009.

49 Morris, interview, March 2009.

30 In His Own Right: The 1998 Election

1   John Howard, interview with the author, February 2005.

2   Kim Beazley, interview with the author, April 2009.

3   Lynton Crosby, interview with the author, April 2009.

4   John Howard, National Press Club, 1 October 1998.

5   Peter FitzSimons, *Beazley*, HarperCollins, Sydney, 1998, p. 414.

6   Bill Kelty, interview with the author, April 2008.

7   Lynton Crosby, interview with the author, April 2009.

8   'A Fairer Tax System', Australian Labor Party, August 1998.

9   *Australian*, 5 October 1998.

10 Paul Kelly, *Australian*, 19 September 1998.

11 John Faulkner, interview with the author, March 2009.

12 See Paul Kelly, *Australian*, 28 August 1998.

13 Peter Hendy note to Peter Reith, Election Progress, 22 September 1998.

14 Crosby, interview, April 2009 and Robert Hill, interview with the author, June 2009.

15 Howard, interview, February 2005.

16 Peter Costello, interview with the author, April 2005.

17 Howard, interview, February 2005.

18 Lynton Crosby, National Press Club address, 28 October 1998.

19 Crosby, National Press Club address, 28 October 1998.

20 Faulkner, interview, March 2009.

21 Crosby, interview, April 2009.

22 Rodney Cavalier, 'Campaign Commentary', in Marian Simms and John Warhurst (eds), *Howard's Agenda*, University of Queensland Press, St Lucia, 2000, p. 93.

23 Beazley, interview, April 2009.

24 Crosby, interview, April 2009.

25 Cavalier, p. 95.

26 Matt Price, *Australian*, 5 October 1998.

27 Price, *Australian*, 5 October 1998.

28 Howard, interview, February 2005.

29 Paul Kelly, 'Quest for a Winning Way', *Australian*, 2 July 2005.

31 The Amateur with Attitude

1 Alexander Downer, interview with the author, January 2006.
2 Philip Flood, interview with the author, February 2009.
3 Dick Woolcott, interview with the author, January 2006.
4 Cavan Hogue, interview with the author, March 2006.
5 Philip Flood, Secretary Lecture Series address, 23 November 2006.
6 Michael Costello, interview with the author, March 2009.
7 These views reflect conversations with Howard over the years, his public remarks and speeches and assessments offered by former advisers.
8 Greg Hunt, interview with the author, January 2006.
9 Flood, interview, February 2009.
10 Michael Thawley, interview with the author, March 2006.
11 Ashton Calvert, interview with the author, May 2003.
12 Dick Woolcott, interview with the author, January 2006.
13 Michael Thawley, interview with the author, November 2006.
14 Woolcott, interview, January 2006.
15 Alexander Downer to Dick Woolcott, 23 November 2004.
16 Dick Woolcott, *Age*, 21 January 2006.
17 Garnaut, Drysdale and Harris, *Australian*, 7 November 2001.
18 John Howard, interview with the author, May 2006.
19 Alexander Downer, 'Australia and the United States: A Vital Friendship', 29 May 1996
20 Hunt, interview, January 2006.
21 Thawley, interview, March 2006.
22 Howard, interview, May 2006.
23 Samuel P Huntington, *The Clash of Civilizations and the Remaking of the World Order*, Simon & Schuster, New York, 1996, pp. 67 & 125.
24 Howard, interview, May 2006.
25 Paul Keating, Asia–Australia Institute address, Brisbane, 26 October 1994.
26 Greg Sheridan, *Australian*, 16 March 1996.
27 Hunt, interview, January 2006.
28 Downer, interview, January 2006.
29 Alexander Downer, Foreign Correspondents Association address, Sydney, 11 April 1996.
30 John Howard, Foreign Policy Association speech, New York, 30 June 1997.
31 Flood, interview, February 2009.
32 Thawley, interview, March 2006.
33 Paul Keating, Australia Today Indonesia 1994 Promotion, Sydney, 16 March 1994.
34 Flood, interview, February 2006.
35 John Howard, banquet speech, Jakarta, 16 September 1996.
36 Thawley, interview, March 2006.
37 Calvert, interview, May 2003.
38 Howard, interview, May 2006.
39 Alexander Downer, interview with the author, May 2007
40 Thawley, interview, March 2006.
41 Howard, interview, May 2006.

42 Calvert, interview, May 2003.

43 Kim Beazley, interview with the author, April 2009.

44 Howard, interview, May 2006.

45 Flood, interview, February 2009.

46 Howard adviser, interview with the author, February 2006.

47 Thawley, interview, March 2006.

48 John Howard, Lowy Lecture on Australia in the World, 31 March 2005.

49 Calvert, interview, May 2003.

50 Howard, Lowy Lecture.

32 Global Follower and Regional Leader

1   John Howard, interview with the author, May 2006.

2   Hugh White, interview with the author, March 2006.

3   Peter Jennings, interview with the author, February 2006.

4   Ian McLachlan, interview with the author, April 2009.

5   White, interview, March 2006.

6   Bob Hawke, *The Hawke Memoirs*, William Heinemann Australia, Melbourne, 1994, chapter 28.

7   Senior official, interview with the author, February 2006. In July 2006 figures from the Defence department showed there were 3900 ADF personnel deployed on overseas operations, the main ones being 2000 in East Timor, 1400 in Iraq, 310 to the coalition against terrorism mainly in Afghanistan and about 160 in the Solomon Islands.

8   Lieutenant General PF Leahy, speech to the Centre for Defence and Strategic Studies, 23 March 2005.

9   McLachlan, interview, April 2009.

10 Hugh White, 'Beyond the Defence of Australia', Lowy Institute for International Policy, Paper 16, p. 20.

11 John Howard, interview with the author, February 2009.

12 Refer William Shawcross, *Deliver Us From Evil*, Bloomsbury, London, 2000, pp. 222–50.

13 See Shawcross, pp. 289–99.

14 Record of conversation, Alexander Downer and Madeleine Albright, Kuala Lumpur, 15 November 1998, DFAT cable.

15 Alexander Downer, interview with the author, January 2006.

16 Kim Beazley, 'Operation Sandglass: Old History, Contemporary Lessons', *Security Challenges*, Kokoda Foundation, vol. 4, no. 3.

17 See Philip Flood, in Trevor Wilson and Graham Cooke (eds), *Steady Hands Needed, Reflections on the role of the Secretary of Foreign Affairs and Trade in Australia 1979–1999*, co-published with Australian New Zealand School of Government, August 2008.

18 White, interview, March 2006.

19 Flood.

20 McLachlan, interview, April 2009.

21 Mary-Louise O'Callaghan, *Enemies Within*, Doubleday, Sydney, 1999, p. 236

22 O'Callaghan, p. 81.

23 Michael Thawley, interview with the author, March 2006.
24 Flood.
25 Flood.
26 O'Callaghan, p. 255.
27 Flood.
28 White, interview, March 2006.
29 Howard, interview, February 2009.

33 The China Shock
1   John Howard, interview with the author, May 2006.
2   Ric Smith, interview with the author, April 2006.
3   Innes Wilcox, interview with the author, December 2005.
4   Ric Smith, interview with the author, April 2009.
5   Smith, interview, April 2006.
6   Philip Flood, interview with the author, February 2009.
7   John Howard, joint press conference, 3 April 2006.
8   John Howard, Asia Society address, 12 September 2005.
9   Paul Kelly, *Australian*, 14 August 2005.
10 Hugh White, interview with the author, April 2009.
11 Alan Gyngell, 'Australia's Emerging Global Role', *Current History*, March 2005.
12 Greg Hunt, interview with the author, January 2006.
13 Smith, interview, April 2009.
14 Stephen Sherlock, 'Australia's Relations with China: What's the Problem?' Parliamentary Library, Parliament of Australia, current issues brief 23, 1996–97.
15 Alexander Downer, interview with the author, January 2006.
16 Record of conversation, Alexander Downer and Qian Qichen, 25 July 1996.
17 Downer, interview, January 2006.
18 Howard, interview, May 2006.
19 Howard, interview, May 2006.
20 Howard, interview, May 2006.; Smith, interview, April 2006.
21 Record of conversation, Alexander Downer and Jia Chunwang, Canberra, 12 December 1996.
22 Smith, interview, April 2006.
23 Paul Kelly, *Australian*, 16 April 1997.
24 Paul Kelly, *Australian*, 5 April, 1997.
25 Kelly, *Australian*, 5 April 1997.
26 Smith, interview, April 2006.
27 Kelly, *Australian*, 5 April 1997.
28 Smith, interview, April 2006.
29 Smith, interview, April 2009.
30 Howard, interview, May 2006.

34 Farewell to Poor White Trash
1   Stephen Grenville, interview with the author, January 2006.
2   Ian Macfarlane, interview with the author, February 2006.
3   Peter Costello, interview with the author, February 2007.

4   The Australian official involved briefed the author on this phone call.

5   Michel Camdessus, interview with Paul Kelly and Alan Wood, 1998.

6   Private record of conversation, NSC meeting, 23 February 1998.

7   Philip Flood, interview with the author, February 2006.

8   Macfarlane, interview, February 2006.

9   Alexander Downer, interview with the author, January 2006.

10   Downer interview, January 2006.

11   Peter Costello, interview with the author, February 2007.

12   Peter Costello, The Australian Revival speech, 1 March 2006.

13   Greg Sheridan, *Tigers*, Allen & Unwin, Sydney, 1997, p. 70.

14   Sheridan, pp. 70–2.

15   Sheridan, pp. 70–2.

16   Costello, interview, February 2007.

17   Joseph Stiglitz, 'Restoring the Asian Miracle', *Asian Wall Street Journal*, 2 February 1998.

18   Stanley Fischer, 'The International Financial System: Crises and Reform', The Robbins Lectures, London School of Economics, 29–31 October 2001.

19   Fischer.

20   Hall Hill, 'Indonesia: The Strange and Sudden Death of a Tiger Economy', *Oxford Development Studies*, vol. 28, no. 2, 2000.

21   This analysis draws on Paul Blustein, *The Chastening*, Public Affairs, New York, 2001.

22   Blustein, pp. 48–9.

23   Macfarlane, interview, February 2006.

24   Macfarlane, interview, February 2006.

25   Robert Garran, *Tigers Tamed*, Allen & Unwin, Sydney, 1998, p. 102.

26   Blustein, p. 53.

27   Grenville, interview, January 2006; Macfarlane, interview, February 2006.

28   Macfarlane, interview, February 2006.

29   Costello, interview, February 2007.

30   Downer, interview, January 2006.

31   Garran, p. 128.

32   Costello, interview, February 2007.

33   Costello, interview, February 2007.

34   Blustein, p. 89.

35   World Bank, 'Indonesia in Crisis: A Microeconomic Update', Washington DC, 1998.

36   Hill, p. 129.

37   Blustein, p. 88.

38   Blustein, pp. 100–4.

39   Garran, p. 146.

40   Blustein, pp. 211–12.

41   Blustein, p. 211.

42   Bluestein, p. 212.

43   Blustein, p. 217.

44   Paul Keating, *Engagement*, Pan Macmillan, Sydney, 2000, p. 151.

45 Macfarlane, interview, February 2006.
46 Macfarlane, interview, February 2006.
47 Costello, interview, February 2007.
48 Bluestein, pp. 226–8.
49 Bluestein, pp. 229–30.
50 Macfarlane, interview, February 2006.
51 Macfarlane, interview, February 2006.
52 Record of conversation between Alexander Downer and Laurence Summers, Washington, 18 March 1998, DFAT cable.
53 Peter Costello with Peter Coleman, *The Costello Memoirs*, Melbourne University Press, Melbourne 208, p. 180.
54 Grenville, interview, January 2006
55 Macfarlane, interview, February 2006.
56 Allan Gyngell, interview with the author, December 2008.
57 RE Elson, *Suharto, A Political Biography*, Cambridge University Press, Cambridge, 2001, p. 305.
58 Hill, p. 131.
59 Elson, p. 308.
60 Blustein, pp. 220–33.
61 Stephen Grenville, interview with the author, April 2009.
62 Macfarlane, interview, February 2006.
63 Macfarlane, interview, February 2006.
64 Downer interview, January 2006.
65 Macfarlane, interview, February 2006.
66 John Howard, interview with the author, May 2006.
67 Costello, interview, February 2007.
68 Downer interview, January 2006.
69 Macfarlane, interview, February 2006.
70 Peter Costello, interview with the author, April 2009.
71 John Dauth, interview with the author, March 2006.

35 East Timor: The Turning Point

1   Ashton Calvert, interview with the author, April 2005.
2   Stan Roth, interview with the author, June 2008.
3   Alexander Downer, interview with the author, January 2006.
4   Downer, interview, January 2006.
5   John Howard, interview with the author, May 2006.
6   Howard, interview, May 2006.
7   Downer, interview, January 2006.
8   The account in this chapter of East Timor's transition to independence draws extensively on two books: *East Timor in Transition 1998–2000: An Australian Policy Challenge*, an official history along with relevant documents, DFAT, Canberra, 2001; and the best journalistic account of these events by Don Greenlees and Robert Garran, *Deliverance*, Allen & Unwin, Sydney, 2002.
9   Hugh White, interview with the author, March 2006.
10 Howard, interview, April 2006.

11 Alexander Downer, interview with the author, November 1999.
12 *East Timor in Transition*, Annex 1; Alexander Downer, discussion with the author, 2000.
13 Downer, interview, January 2006.
14 Downer, interview, January 2006.
15 Calvert, interview, April 2005; Downer, discussion, January 2000.
16 Ashton Calvert, discussion with the author, July 2001.
17 Calvert, interview, April 2005.
18 Innes Willox, interview with the author, December 2005.
19 Ashton Calvert note to Alexander Downer, 30 November 1998.
20 Calvert, interview, April 2005.
21 Michael Thawley, interview with the author, March 2006.
22 Thawley, interview, March 2006.
23 Greg Hunt, interview with the author, January 2006.
24 Calvert, interview, April 2005.
25 Downer, interview, January 2006.
26 Tim Fischer, interview with the author, November 2008.
27 *East Timor in Transition,* Annex 2.
28 Howard, interview, May 2006.
29 Greenlees and Garran, pp. xii–xiii.
30 *East Timor in Transition*, p. 32; Greenlees and Garran, pp. xii–xiii.
31 *East Timor in Transition*, p. 32.
32 Greenlees and Garran, p. 93.
33 Discussion with Indonesian Cabinet Minister, Juwono Sudarsono, April 1999.
34 *East Timor in Transition*, pp. 41–6.
35 Greenlees and Garran, p. 93.
36 Discussion with Alexander Downer, Davos, late January 1999.
37 Howard, interview, April 2006.
38 Downer, interview, November 1999.
39 Personal discussions with Alexander Downer, January–June 1999.
40 Hugh White, 'The Road to INTERFET', *Security Challenges*, vol. 4, no. 1, autumn 2008.
41 Downer, interview, January 2006.
42 Howard, interview, May 2006.
43 Thawley, interview, March 2006.
44 Hugh White, interview with the author, April 2009.
45 Downer, interview, January 2006.
46 Alexander Downer, interview with the author, November 1999.
47 White, interview, March 2006.
48 Chris Barrie, interview with the author, December 2008.
49 White, interview, March 2006.
50 Greenlees and Garran, pp. 111–16.
51 *East Timor in Transition*, p. 57.
52 *East Timor in Transition*, pp. 51–2.
53 Roth, interview, June 2008.
54 White, interview, April 2009.

55   White, interview, March 2006.

56   This summary draws on Greenlees and Garran, pp. 120–8.

57   *East Timor in Transition*, Annex 5; Greenlees and Garran, p. 128.

58   *East Timor in Transition*, p. 67.

59   Greenlees and Garran, p. 134.

60   Greenlees and Garran, p. 137.

61   Downer, interview, November 1999.

62   Paul Kelly, *Australian*, 21 April 1999. The author was at this meeting with Habibie.

63   Downer, interview, November 1999.

64   White, interview, March 2006.

65   Greenlees and Garran, p. 145.

66   Downer, interview, January 2006.

67   *East Timor in Transition*, pp. 79, 87

68   Howard, interview, May 2006.

69   Downer, interview, January 2006.

70   Record of conversation between Prime Minister Howard and the President of Indonesia, Dr Habibie, 27 April 1999, Hilton Hotel, Bali.

71   White, interview, April 2009.

72   This is based on the memory of one of the senior Australians at the table.

73   Downer, interview, November 1999.

74   Record of conversation.

75   Downer, interview, November 1999.

76   Downer, interview, January 2006.

77   Downer, interview, January 2006.

78   Kim Beazley, interview with the author, April 2009.

79   Barrie, interview, December 2008.

80   Greenlees and Garran, p. 150.

81   James Schear, interview with the author, June 2006.

82   Downer, interview, November 1999.

83   *East Timor in Transition*, chapter 6.

84   Downer, interview, January 2006.

85   House of Representatives, *Hansard*, 21 September 1999, p. 7619.

86   Downer, interview, January 2006.

87   Downer, interview, January 2006. The final sentence is an obvious reference to intelligence.

88   Downer, interview, November 1999.

89   Greenlees and Garran, p. 205.

90   Howard, interview, May 2006.

91   Roth, interview, June 2008.

92   House of Representatives, *Hansard*, 21 September 1999, p. 7619.

93   Downer, interview, January 2006.

94   *East Timor in Transition*, chapter 8; Greenlees and Garran, chapter 11.

95   Downer, interview, January 2006.

96   Calvert, interview, April 2005.

97   *Sydney Morning Herald*, 8 September 1999.

98   *Hansard*, 21 September 1999.

99   Howard, interview, April 2006.

100 Greenlees and Garran, p. 243.
101 Howard, interview, April 2006.
102 Greenlees and Garran, pp. 240–3.
103 Schear, interview, June 2006.
104 Downer, interview, January 2006.
105 Record of conversation, Alexander Downer and Madeleine Albright, 7 September 1999, DFAT cable.
106 Downer, interview, January 2006.
107 Greenlees and Garran, pp. 240–8.
108 White, interview, April 2009.
109 Schear, interview, June 2006.
110 Downer, interview, November 1999.
111 Greenlees and Garran, pp. 263–4.
112 Peter Cosgrove, interview with the author, February 2009.
113 Barrie, interview, December 2008.
114 Barrie, interview, December 2008.
115 White, interview, April 2009.
116 Paul Kelly and Patrick Walters, *Australian*, 25 June 2005.
117 Cosgrove, interview, February 2009.
118 Schear, interview, June 2006.
119 This is based on discussions with senior Australian and US officials.
120 Calvert, interview, April 2005.
121 Schear, interview, June 2006.
122 Cosgrove, interview, February 2009.
123 Cosgrove, interview, February 2009.
124 Kelly and Walters, *Australian*, 25 June 2005.
125 Cosgrove, interview, February 2009.
126 Barrie, interview, December 2008.
127 Howard, interview, May 2006.
128 Howard, interview, May 2006.
129 Roth, interview, June 2008.
130 Schear, interview, June 2006.
131 Howard, interview, May 2006.
132 White, interview, April 2009; White, 'The Road to INTERFET', pp. 85–6.
133 Paul Kelly, *Australian*, 11 December 1999.
134 Downer, interview, January 2006.
135 Downer, interview, January 2006.
136 Downer, interview, January 2006.
137 *Bulletin*, 28 September 1999.
138 Howard, interview, May 2006.
139 White, interview, April 2009.
140 Cosgrove, interview, February 2009.

36 Defeat of the Republic

1 John Howard, Statement on the Republic Referendum, 25 October 1999.
2 John Howard, press conference, 7 November 1999.
3 Howard, Statement on the Republic Referendum, 25 October 1999.

4   John Howard, interview with the author, February 2008.
5   Arthur Sinodinos, interview with the author, February 2009.
6   Tim Fischer, interview with the author, November 2008.
7   Paul Kelly, *Australian*, 28 October 1999.
8   Paul Kelly, *100 Years: The Australian Story*, Allen & Unwin, Sydney, 2001, p. 83.
9   Kelly, *100 Years*, p. 247.
10   John Howard, discussion with the author, 1999.
11   John Warhurst and Malcolm Mackerras, 'Constitutional Politics: The 1990s and Beyond', in John Warhurst and Malcolm Mackerras (eds), *Constitutional Politics: The Republic Referendum and the Future*, University of Queensland Press, St Lucia, 2002, p. 12.
12   Noel Pearson, interview with the author, November 2008.
13   Noel Pearson to John Howard, 17 September 2007.
14   Pearson, interview, November 2008.
15   John Howard, interview with the author, February 2009.
16   Warhurst and Mackerras, pp. 89–112.
17   Paul Kelly, *Australian*, 13 October 1999.
18   Howard, Statement on the Republic Referendum, 25 October 1999.
19   Warhurst and Mackerras, chapter 8.
20   Greg Craven, 'Conservative Republicanism, the Convention and the Referendum', *The University of NSW Law Journal Forum*, vol. 4, no. 2, p. 18.
21   Warhurst and Mackerras, p. 143.
22   Kelly, *100 Years*, p. 247.

37   Surviving the GST and Avoiding Recession

1   *Australian*, 5 October 1998.
2   George Megalogenis, *Australian*, 10 December 1999.
3   Andrew Murray, interview with the author, March 2008.
4   Peter Costello with Peter Coleman, *The Costello Memoirs*, Melbourne University Press, Melbourne, 2008, pp. 134–5.
5   Costello, p. 135.
6   Costello, p. 136.
7   Nick Minchin, interview with the author, February 2009.
8   Costello, pp. 137–8.
9   John Howard, interview with the author, February 2008.
10   Andrew Murray, interview with the author, March 2008.
11   Costello, p. 138.
12   Howard, interview, February 2008.
13   Meg Lees, interview with the author, May 2009.
14   Lees, interview with the author, May 2009.
15   Howard, interview, February 2008.
16   Lees, interview with the author, May 2009.
17   Peter Reith, interview with the author, June 2005.
18   John Howard, press conference, 28 May 1999.
19   Lees, interview with the author, May 2009.
20   Murray, interview, March 2008.
21   Murray, interview, March 2008.

22 Ted Evans, interview with the author, February 2005.

23 House of Representatives, *Hansard*, 30 June 1999, p. 7889.

24 Arthur Sinodinos, interview with the author, February 2009.

25 Howard, interview, February 2008.

26 Former senior adviser, interview with the author, April 2006.

27 Costello, p. 153.

28 Ian Macfarlane, interview with the author, September 2006.

29 Alan Wood, *Australian*, 1 February 2000 & 20 May 2000.

30 Ian Henderson, *Australian*, 6 May 2000.

31 Macfarlane, interview, September 2006.

32 Macfarlane, interview, September 2006.

33 Ted Evans, interview, February 2005.

34 Macfarlane, interview, September 2006.

35 Macfarlane, interview, September 2006.

36 Reserve Bank of Australia, media release, 5 April 2000.

37 Evans, interview, April 2008.

38 Record of conversation, April 2000.

39 Evans, interview, April 2008.

40 Evans, interview, April 2008.

41 Macfarlane, interview, September 2006.

42 Record of conversation, April 2000.

43 Macfarlane, interview, September 2006; Evans, interview, February 2005.

44 Macfarlane, interview, September 2006.

45 *Australian*, 6 May 2000.

46 Macfarlane, interview, September 2006.

47 Macfarlane, interview, September 2006.

48 Sid Marris, *Australian*, 18 May 2000.

49 Brian Toohey, *Australian Financial Review*, 20 May 2000.

50 Macfarlane, interview, September 2006.

51 Evans, interview, April 2008.

52 Macfarlane, interview, September 2006.

53 Budget Paper No. 1, 2000–01, 1-27-29.

54 Macfarlane, interview, September 2006.

55 Macfarlane, interview, September 2006.

56 Macfarlane, interview, September 2006.

57 *Australian*, 8 March 2001.

58 Costello, p. 152.

59 Sinodinos, interview, February 2009; Lynton Crosby, interview with the author, April 2009.

60 Sinodinos, interview, February 2009.

61 Geoff Walsh, National Press Club speech, 3 December, 2001.

62 Macfarlane, interview, September 2006.

63 Macfarlane, interview, September 2006.

64 Macfarlane, interview, September 2006.

65 Ian Macfarlane, speech, 6 December 2001.

66 Ian Macfarlane, speech, 4 April 2002.

38 Tampa: The Ultimate Portrait

1   This chapter draws on the best account of the *Tampa* crisis: David Marr and Marian Wilkinson's *Dark Victory*, Allen & Unwin, Sydney, 2003.

2   Arne Rinnan, interview with Sally Loane, ABC Radio 702, 27 August 2001.

3   Australian official, background interview, March 2009.

4   John Howard, interview with the author, February 2009.

5   Max Moore-Wilton, interview with the author, June 2008.

6   Paul Keating, interview with the author, May 2008.

7   Philip Ruddock, interview with the author, May 2008.

8   Ruddock, interview with the author, May 2008.

9   Chris Conybeare, interview with the author, June 2008.

10 Frank Brennan, *Tampering with Asylum*, University of Queensland Press, St Lucia, 2007, pp. 254–6.

11 Ruddock, interview with the author, May 2008.

12 John McMillan, 'The Courts v The People: Have the Judges Gone too Far?' Judicial Conference of Australia, 27 April 2002, p. 14.

13 Mary Crock, 'Refugees in Australia: Of Lore, Legends and the Judicial Process', research paper presented at the Seventh Colloquium of the Judicial Conference of Australia, 2003.

14 Marcus Einfeld, 'Detention, Justice and Compassion', in Mary Crock (ed.) *Protection or Punishment?*, Federation Press, Sydney, 1993.

15 *Brennan J, AG (NSW) v Quin* (1990) 170 CLR 1, pp. 35–8.

16 John McMillan, 'Immigration Law and the Courts', address to Sir Samuel Griffith Society, 15 June 2002.

17 Dr Margaret Kelly, submission to Senate Legal and Constitutional Affairs Committee, 29 July 2005.

18 McMillan, 'The Courts v The People: Have the Judges Gone too Far?'; McMillan, 'Immigration Law and the Courts'.

19 Moore-Wilton, interview, June 2008.

20 Moore-Wilton, interview, June 2008.

21 Marr and Wilkinson, p. 40.

22 Chris Barrie, interview with the author, December 2008.

23 Ruddock, interview, May 2008.

24 John Howard, media interview, 30 August 2001.

25 Marr and Wilkinson, p. 46.

26 John Howard, interview with the author, February 2009.

27 Paul McClintock, interview with the author, July 2008.

28 Moore-Wilton, interview, June 2008.

29 Sally Loane, ABC Radio 702, 27 August 2001.

30 Moore-Wilton, interview, June 2008.

31 Moore-Wilton, interview, June 2008.

32 Howard, interview, February 2009.

33 Peter Costello with Peter Coleman, *The Costello Memoirs*, Melbourne University Press, Melbourne, 2008, p. 162.

34 Michael Wooldridge, interview with the author, February 2009.

35 Ruddock, interview with the author, May 2008.

36 Arthur Sinodinos, interview with the author, February 2009.

37 McClintock, interview, July 2008.

38 Howard, interview, February 2009.

39 Sinodinos, interview, February 2008.

40 McClintock, interview, July 2008.

41 Peter Shergold, interview with the author, May 2008.

42 Federal Court of Australia, *Victorian Council for Civil Liberties v Minister for Immigration and Multicultural Affairs*, 2001.

43 John Howard and Philip Ruddock press conference, 27 August 2001.

44 Paul Kelly, *Australian*, 1 September 2001.

45 John Howard, *A Current Affair*, Nine Network, 28 August 2001.

46 Marr and Wilkinson, chapter 5.

47 John Howard, House of Representatives, *Hansard*, 29 August 2001.

48 Marr and Wilkinson, pp. 80–2.

49 Howard, *Hansard*, 29 August 2001.

50 Kim Beazley, House of Representatives, *Hansard*, 29 August 2001.

51 Kim Beazley, interview with the author, April 2009.

52 Michael Costello, interview with the author, March 2009.

53 Beazley, *Hansard*, 29 August 2001.

54 Marr and Wilkinson, p. 99.

55 Marr and Wilkinson, pp. 103–6.

56 Ruddock, interview, May 2008; John Howard and Philip Ruddock, press conference, 1 September 2001.

57 John Howard, interview with Charles Woolley, *60 Minutes*, Nine Network, 2 September 2001; John Howard, press conference, 1 September 2001.

58 Howard, press conference, 1 September 2001.

59 Barrie, interview, December 2008.

60 Howard, *60 Minutes*, Nine Network, 2 September 2001.

61 Howard, interview, February 2009.

62 Barrie, interview, December 2008.

63 Howard, press conference, 1 September 2001.

64 Brennan, chapter 6.

65 Ruddock, interview, May 2008.

66 Moore-Wilton, interview, June 2008.

67 House of Representatives, *Hansard*, 19 February 2002, p. 439.

68 Peter Reith, interview with the author, January 2009.

69 Matthew J Gibney, *The Ethics and Politics of Asylum*, Cambridge University Press, Cambridge, 2004, p. 1.

70 Michael Costello, interview with the author, March 2009.

71 See Matthew J Gibney, 'The State of Asylum', Working Paper No. 50, *New Issues in Refugee Research*, Refugee Studies Centre, University of Oxford, October 2001.

72 Go to www.unhcr.ch

73 'The Problem with the 1951 Refugee Convention,' Research Paper No. 5, 2000–01, Parliamentary Library, Parliament House, Canberra.

74 Refer Astri Suhrke & Kathleen Newland, 'UNHCR: Uphill into the Future', *International Migration Review*, Spring 2001.

75 Monica Duffy Toft, 'Repatriation of Refugees: A Failing Policy?' unpublished research paper, p. 6.

76 Adrienne Millbank, 'Australia and the 1951 Refugee Convention', *People and Place*, vol. 9, no. 2, 2001.

77 William Maley, 'A Global Refugee Crisis?', in *Refugees and the Myth of the Borderless World*, Keynotes, no. 2, Department of International Relations, ANU, Canberra, 2002.

78 Erika Feller, *The Georgetown Journal of International Affairs*, winter/spring 2002, refer www.unhcr.ch

79 John Howard, CNN interview, 31 August 2001.

80 See Thuy Do, 'Statistics: Refugees and Australia's Contribution', in *Refugees and the Myth of the Borderless World*, Keynotes, no. 2, Department of International Relations, ANU, Canberra, 2002.

81 Brennan, p. 262.

82 Ruddock, interview, May 2008.

83 Moore-Wilton, interview, June 2008.

84 Ruddock, interview, May 2008.

85 Figures provided by Immigration Minister's office, June 2008. There were fourteen people who were resettled non-refugees.

86 Kim Beazley, interview with the author, April 2009.

87 Paul Kelly and Dennis Shanahan, *Australian*, 23 November 2007.

88 Brennan, p. 246.

39 The Seduction of Bush

1   Alexander Downer, interview with the author, January 2006.

2   Downer, interview, January 2006.

3   Greg Hunt, interview with the author, January 2006.

4   Downer, interview, January 2006.

5   John Howard, interview with the author, May 2006.

6   Richard Armitage, interview with the author, November 2008.

7   John Howard, interview with the author, February 2009.

8   John Howard, Lowy Lecture, 31 March 2005.

9   Philip Flood, interview with the author, February 2009.

10 Howard, interview, May 2006.

11 Hugh White, interview with the author, April 2009.

12 Michael Thawley, interview with the author, March 2006.

13 The author, at an adjacent table, observed these personal dynamics for an extended period.

14 White, interview, April 2009.

15 Downer, interview, January 2006.

16 Hugh White, interview with the author, March 2006.

17 Philip Flood, interview with the author, March 2009.

18 Flood, interview, February 2006.

19 *Australian*, 5–6 July 1997.

20 Thawley, interview, March 2006.

21 Interview with the author, Australian official, July 2008.

22 Thawley, interview, March 2006.
23 Howard, interview, May 2006.
24 Howard, interview, May 2006.
25 Ashton Calvert, interview with the author, April 2005.
26 Paul Kelly, *Australian*, 8 December 1999
27 Downer, interview, January 2006.
28 Howard, interview, May 2006.
29 Paul Kelly, 'Eyes East', *Weekend Australian*, 11 November 2000.
30 Michael Thawley, discussion with the author, November 2006.
31 Thawley, interview, March 2006.
32 Thawley, interview, March 2006.
33 Interview with Paul Kelly, *Australian*, 15 July 2000.
34 Thawley, interview, March 2006.
35 Downer, interview, January 2006.
36 Greg Hunt, interview with the author, December 2005.
37 Downer, interview, January 2006.
38 Alexander Downer, speech, The Australian APEC Studies Centre Conference, 29 August 2002.
39 Thawley, interview, March 2006.
40 Michael Thawley speech, Australia and the United States in the New Century, Chicago, 30 May 2003.
41 This approach is documented in Ross Garnaut, 'An Australia–United States free trade agreement', *Australian Journal of International Affairs*, vol. 56, no 1, 2002.
42 Garnaut, 'An Australia–United States free trade agreement'.
43 Thawley, interview, March 2006.
44 Paul Kelly, *Australian*, 9 December 2000.
45 Thawley, interview, March 2006.
46 Thawley, interview, March 2006.
47 Joint press conference, US Department of State, 22 March 2001.
48 Armitage, interview, November 2008.
49 Downer, interview, January 2006.
50 Thawley, interview, March 2006.
51 Tom Schieffer, interview with the author, January 2005.
52 Peter Hartcher, *Sydney Morning Herald*, 11 September 2001.
53 Thawley, interview, March 2006.
54 Howard, interview, May 2006.
55 Howard, interview, May 2006.
56 Thawley, interview, March 2006.
57 Howard, interview, May 2006.
58 Armitage, interview, November 2008.
59 Don Russell, discussion with the author, June 2005.
60 Downer, interview, January 2006.

40 Brothers-in-Arms

1 John Howard, *AM*, ABC Radio, 19 September 2001.
2 Ashton Calvert, interview with the author, April 2005.

3 Tom Schieffer, interview with the author, January 2005.

4 Schieffer, interview, January 2005.

5 Max Moore-Wilton, interview with the author, June 2008.

6 Schieffer, interview, January 2005.

7 *The 9/11 Commission Report*, WW Norton and Company Ltd, New York, 2004.

8 Donald A DeBats, Tim McDonald, Margaret-Ann Williams, 'Mr Howard Goes to Washington', *Australian Journal of Political Science*, vol. 42, no. 2, June, pp. 231–51.

9 John Howard, press conference, Australian Embassy, 11 September 2001.

10 DeBats, McDonald, Williams, 'Mr Howard Goes to Washington'.

11 DeBats, McDonald, Williams, 'Mr Howard Goes to Washington'.

12 John Howard, interview with the author, May 2006.

13 Michael Thawley, interview with the author, March 2006.

14 DeBats, McDonald, Williams, 'Mr Howard Goes to Washington'.

15 DeBats, McDonald, Williams, 'Mr Howard Goes to Washington'.

16 Thawley, interview, March 2006.

17 Howard, interview, May 2006.

18 John Howard, press conference, Ambassador's residence, 12 September 2001.

19 Howard, press conference.

20 Interview with John Laws, 12 September 2001.

21 John Howard, speech at the opening of the Magna Carta Monument, 26 September 2001.

22 Interview with John Laws, 12 September 2001; interview with Mike Munro, *A Current Affair*, Nine Network, 12 September 2001.

23 Howard, interview, May 2006.

24 Howard, interview, May 2006.

25 Howard, interview, May 2006.

26 Dennis Shanahan, *Australian*, 14 September 2001.

27 John Howard, *60 Minutes*, Nine Network, 16 September 2001.

28 Thawley, interview, March 2006.

29 Schieffer, interview, January 2005.

30 Thawley, interview, March 2006.

31 Howard, interview, May 2006; March 2009.

32 Alexander Downer, interview with the author, January 2006.

33 Richard Armitage, interview with the author, November 2008.

34 John Howard, press conference, 14 September 2001.

35 Howard, press conference, 14 September 2001.

36 Richard N Hass, 'The US–Australia Alliance in an East Asian Context', in Henry Albinski and Rawdon Dalrymple (eds), *The United States–Australian Alliance in an East Asian Context*, conference proceedings, University of Sydney, 29–30 June 2001.

37 *The 9/11 Commission Report*, p. 51.

38 *The 9/11 Commission Report*, pp. 333–4.

39 *The 9/11 Commission Report*, p. 335; Bob Woodward, *Plan of Attack*, Simon & Schuster, New York, 2004, p. 26.

40 Bob Woodward, *Bush at War*, Simon & Schuster, New York, 2002, p. 52.

41 John Howard, press conference, 4 October 2001.

42 John Howard, press conference, 17 October 2001.

43 Howard, press conference, 4 October 2001; Alexander Downer, press conference, 4 October 2001.

44 John Howard, farewell to the SAS, 22 October 2001.

45 Hugh White, interview with the author, April 2009.

46 Downer, interview, January 2006.

47 White, interview, April 2009.

41 Integrity Overboard

1 Lynton Crosby, interview with the author, April 2009.

2 Senate Report, Select Committee on a Certain Maritime Incident, October 2002, p. 30. This chapter draws heavily on this report as well as the Bryant Report, an internal assessment of the 'children overboard' issue commissioned by Max Moore-Wilton and conducted by an officer from his department.

3 Senate Report, Select Committee on a Certain Maritime Incident, pp. 31–5.

4 Senate Report, Select Committee on a Certain Maritime Incident, p. 53.

5 Senate Report, Select Committee on a Certain Maritime Incident, p. 53.

6 Philip Ruddock, interview with the author, May 2008.

7 John Howard, interview, Radio 2UE, 8 October 2001.

8 John Howard, interview with the author, February 2009.

9 Bryant Report, p. 8.

10 Max Moore-Wilton, interview with the author, June 2008.

11 Chris Barrie, interview with the author, December 2008.

12 Barrie, interview, December 2008.

13 Moore-Wilton, interview, June 2008.

14 Senate Report, Select Committee on a Certain Maritime Incident, p. 66–76.

15 Bryant Report, p. 23.

16 Senate Report, Select Committee on a Certain Maritime Incident, p. 111.

17 Barrie, interview, December 2008.

18 Peter Reith, interview with the author, January 2009.

19 Barrie, interview, December 2008; Transcript of Evidence, A Certain Maritime Incident, p. 783.

20 Transcript of Evidence, A Certain Maritime Incident, pp. 784–5.

21 Mike Scrafton, interview with the author, January 2009.

22 Senate Report, Select Committee on a Certain Maritime Incident, p. 116.

23 Scrafton, interview, January 2009.

24 Senate Report, Select Committee on a Certain Maritime Incident, pp. 115–17.

25 Scrafton, interview, January 2009.

26 Peter Reith, *Sunday Sunrise*, 14 October 2001.

27 Senate Report, Select Committee on a Certain Maritime Incident, pp. 58–61.

28 Senate Report, Select Committee on a Certain Maritime Incident, pp. 58–66.

29 Senate Report, Select Committee on a Certain Maritime Incident, pp. 84–5.

30 Barrie, interview, December 2008.

31 Senate Report, Select Committee on a Certain Maritime Incident, pp. 84–6.

32 Reith, interview, January 2009.

33 Peter Cosgrove, interview with the author, February 2009.

34　Senate Report, Select Committee on a Certain Maritime Incident, p. 127.

35　Barrie, interview, December 2008.

36　Peter Shergold, interview with the author, May 2008.

37　Scrafton, interview, January 2009.

38　Senate Report, Select Committee on a Certain Maritime Incident, pp. 129–32.

39　Barrie, interview, December 2008.

40　Scrafton, interview, January 2009.

41　Barrie, interview, December 2008.

42　Scrafton, interview, January 2009.

43　Senate Report, Select Committee on a Certain Maritime Incident, pp. 142–5.

44　Scrafton, interview, January 2009.

45　Senate Select Committee on Scrafton, Scrafton Evidence, 1 September 2004.

46　Senate Report, Select Committee on a Certain Maritime Incident, p. 88.

47　Reith, interview, January 2009.

48　Arthur Sinodinos, interview with the author, February 2009.

49　Transcript of Evidence, A Certain Maritime Incident, pp. 345–6 & 361.

50　Transcript of Evidence, A Certain Maritime Incident, p. 19.

51　Moore-Wilton, interview, June 2008 and May 2009 (three times).

52　The interviews were in June 2008 and on three occasions in May 2009.

53　John Howard, interview with the author, May 2009.

54　Moore-Wilton, interview, May 2009. There is, however, a discrepancy with Moore-Wilton's recall that he told Houston to advise Reith on the issue while the evidence suggests that their phone call occurred on the day after Houston had advised his minister.

55　Arthur Sinodinos, interview with the author, May 2009.

56　Max Moore-Wilton, interview with the author, July 2009.

57　Howard, interview, February 2009.

58　Senate Report, Select Committee on a Certain Maritime Incident, p. 123.

59　Paul McClintock, interview with the author, May 2009.

60　Senate Select Committee on Scrafton Evidence, 1 September 2004, pp. 40–1.

61　John Howard, press statement, 16 August 2004.

62　John Howard, *PM*, ABC Radio, 27 August 2004.

63　Howard, interview, February 2009.

64　Sinodinos, interview, February 2009.

65　Senate Selection Committee on Scrafton Evidence, 1 September 2004, pp. 42–3.

66　John Howard, ABC Radio National interview, 9 November 2001.

67　Howard, interview, February 2009.

68　House of Representatives, *Hansard*, 19 February 2002, p. 440.

69　Senate Estimates, Finance and Public Administration Committee, 18 February 2002, pp. 54, 72, 87, 95.

70　Senate Estimates, Finance and Public Administration Committee, 18 February 2002, p. 87.

71　Senate Estimates, Finance and Public Administration Committee, 18 February 2002, p. 72.

72　Howard, interview, May 2009.

73　Paul Kelly, *Australian*, 28 August, 2004.

74 John Howard, media release and attachments, 27 August 2004.

75 Transcript of Evidence, A Certain Maritime Incident, p. 58.

76 Howard, interview, February 2009.

77 Barrie, interview, December 2008.

78 Howard, interview, May 2009.

79 Transcript of Evidence, A Certain Maritime Incident, p. 9.

80 Transcript of Evidence, A Certain Maritime Incident, pp. 7–8.

81 Transcript of Evidence, A Certain Maritime Incident, p. 4.

82 Senate Report, Select Committee on a Certain Maritime Incident, pp. 152–3.

83 Scrafton, interview, January 2009.

84 Barrie, interview, December 2008.

85 Scrafton, interview, January 2009.

42 Election 2001: The Howard Consolidation

1 John Howard, interview with the author, February 2009.

2 Kim Beazley, interview with the author, April 2009.

3 Michael Costello, interview with the author, March 2009.

4 Lynton Crosby, interview with the author, April 2009.

5 Beazley, interview, April 2009.

6 Crosby, interview, April 2009

7 Lynton Crosby, 'The Liberal Party', in John Warhurst and Marian Simms (eds), *2001: The Centenary Election*, University of Queensland Press, St Lucia, 2002.

8 Ian McAllister, 'Border Protection, the 2001 Australian Election and the Coalition Victory', *Australian Journal of Political Science*, vol. 38, no. 3, November 2003.

9 Peter Reith, interview, Radio 3AK, 13 September 2001.

10 Commonwealth Election 2001, Research Paper No. 11, 2001–02, Department of the Parliamentary Library.

11 Beazley, interview, April 2009.

12 Howard, interview, February 2009.

13 Geoff Walsh, National Press Club speech, 3 December 2001.

14 *Sydney Morning Herald*, 9 November 2001; Commonwealth Election 2001, Research Paper No. 11, 2001–02, Department of the Parliamentary Library.

15 Walsh, National Press Club speech, 3 December 2001.

16 McAllister, 'Border Protection, the 2001 Australian Election and the Coalition Victory'.

17 Rodney Cavalier, 'Reflections', in John Warhurst and Marian Simms (eds), *2001: The Centenary Election*, University of Queensland Press, St Lucia, 2002.

18 Kim Beazley, discussion with the author, May 2001.

19 Crosby, 'The Liberal Party'.

20 Paul Kelly, 'When Johnny Comes Marching Home', *Australian*, 27 October 2001.

21 Bob Hogg, *Australian Financial Review*, 1 November 2001.

22 Walsh, National Press Club speech, 3 December 2001.

23 Bob Hogg, *Australian Financial Review*, 8 October 2001.

24 Kelly, 'When Johnny Comes Marching Home', *Australian*, 27 October 2001.

25 Brian Loughnane, interview with the author, February 2009.

26 Beazley, interview, April 2009.

27 Paul Keating, 'Labor Pains Produced the Enduring Growth', *Sydney Morning Herald*, 8 November 2001.

28 Keating, 'Labor Pains Produced the Enduring Growth'.

29 Phillip Clark, interview with the author, January 2008.

30 Howard, interview, February 2008.

31 Kelly, 'When Johnny Comes Marching Home', *Australian*, 27 October 2001.

32 Howard, interview, February 2009.

33 Bob Hogg, *Australian Financial Review*, 1 November 2001.

34 Kelly, 'When Johnny Comes Marching Home', *Australian*, 27 October 2001.

35 Paul Keating, 'Dark Future Indeed for a Nation Absorbed by its Fears', *Sydney Morning Herald*, 25 October 2001.

36 Les Carlyon, *Bulletin*, 4 December 2001, p. 28.

37 Peter Costello with Peter Coleman, *The Costello Memoirs*, Melbourne University Press, Melbourne, 2008, p. 229.

38 Howard, interview, February 2008.

39 Howard, interview, February 2008.

40 Costello, p. 229.

41 Howard, interview, February 2009.

INDEX